AF668605

THE WISDOM OF VASIṢṬHA

A Study on 'Laghu Yoga Vāsiṣṭha'
From a Seeker's Point of View

Other books by the same Author :

- A Silent Journey: In Search of Oneself
- Insights into Existence: Essays on the Upanisads
- Tapestry: A Collection of Short Stories
- Encounters: A Collection of Stories
- Humanscapes: Stories on Human Nature
- Splendour of Isolation: Thoughts in Verse

"*The Wisdom of Vasistha*" was released by H.E. Late Dr. A.P. J. Abdul Kalam the Hon'ble President of India at Rashtrapati Bhavan on October 18, 2004.

THE WISDOM OF VASIṢṬHA

A Study on 'Laghu Yoga Vāsiṣṭha'
From a Seeker's Point of View

RAGHUNANDAN

MOTILAL BANARSIDASS PUBLISHERS
PRIVATE LIMITED • DELHI

Second Revised Edition: Delhi, 2018
First Edition : Delhi, 2004

ISBN : 978-81-208-2043-2

Also available at
MOTILAL BANARSIDASS
41 U.A. Bungalow Road, Jawahar Nagar, Delhi 110 007
1 B, Jyoti Studio Compound, Kennedy Bridge, Nana Chowk, Mumbai 400 007
203 Royapettah High Road, Mylapore, Chennai 600 004
236, 9th Main III Block, Jayanagar, Bengaluru 560 011
8 Camac Street, Kolkata 700 017
Ashok Rajpath, Patna 800 004
Chowk, Varanasi 221 001

MLBD Cataloging-in-Publication Data
The Wisdom of Vāsiṣṭha :
A Study on 'Laghu Yoga Vāsiṣṭha'
From a Seeker's Point of View by Raghunandan
Includes Appendices and Index
ISBN : 978-81-208-2043-2
I. Hinduism II. Philosophy III. Spiritualism
IV. Yoga Vāsiṣṭha V. Raghunandan

Printed in India

by RP Jain at NAB Printing Unit,
A-44, Naraina Industrial Area, Phase I, New Delhi–110028
and published by JP Jain for Motilal Banarsidass Publishers (P) Ltd,
41 U.A. Bungalow Road, Jawahar Nagar, Delhi-110007

निष्फलं निष्क्रियं शान्तं निरवद्यं निरंजनम् ।
अमृतस्य परं सेतुं दग्धेन्धनमिवानलम् ।।

I seek refuge in One Who has transcended time, Who is beyond all activity, attributes and mind, Who is the Supreme Bridge to Immortal Principle, and Who is like a bright lamp without any smoke as all its fuel (of worldliness and desire) has burnt out.

—Śvetaśvtaropaniṣad 6.19—

Dedicated at the Lotus Feet of

Sage Vasiṣṭha
Gautama, the Buddha
Ācārya Śrī Śaṅkara Bhagavatpāda
Paramahansa Shri Ramakrishna
Maharshi Shri Ramana

TABLE OF CONTENTS

PREFACE

A quiet beach with golden sand. The sun showers its fusion energy on the billions of grains of sand and the sand in turn reflects it back. The same solar energy has a different effect on the ocean that absorbs it through its perpetual movement to supply heat and energy to the myriad of creatures in its body. A child, oblivious of the heat is absorbed in a strange play : It is building a home with moist sand in its own capacity and skill. It appears that the child has provided place for everything, including its pet dog! Just as the child stands back to appreciate its own creation, a strong wave comes and washes it off. The child just claps its hand in glee, undisturbed. The reaction may not be the same every time. It may even cry in sadness and disappointment.

This is the story of man, he builds the castles of relationships and possessions, until the wave called time changes it all, and even if there is no change, the wave called death makes him withdraw from it all. And like the child, he is ready again for one more game of building, the game called life. There are some of us who have lost the zest or the enthusiasm, as we have realised the uselessness of all effort, as it has become repetitive. On top of it all, there is a strange kind of discontentment. In spite of achieving the so-called success, there is a feeling of incompleteness. Such persons start looking back in retrospection, and searching in their own mind for the cause of this phenomenon. These tend to move towards spirituality.

To such persons *Vedānta* has much to offer, though even this interest in spirituality in general and *Vedānta* in particular may take a scholastic turn. The interest may remain at the level of mere discussions. *Vedānta* can bring about a transformation in a seeker when it is studied with the principal aim of practising. *Yoga Vāsiṣṭha* is one such reference book that offers guidance at each and every step to all seekers. The following essays were written by the author during his study of the text. They are the peeps into his contemplations, or the line sketches of the flashes he had. The original Sanskrit text is an infinite mine of Truth and the sole purpose of this book is to create an interest to take up the study of the original.

Laghu Yoga Vāsiṣṭha was introduced to the author by late Prof. Satyanarayana Shastry. He is very grateful to him for creating the sustained interest in *Vedānta* in general and *Vāsiṣṭha* in particular. He gratefully acknowledges the help he received from all friends in understanding himself. Shri Lakshmi Niwasji Jhunjhunwala, Chairman, Ramarpan Educational Society, for his paternal encouragement, for getting this book published by Motilal Banarsidass, the famous Indological Publishers and for getting it released by H. E. Dr. A. P. J. Abdul Kalam, Honourable President of India at Rashtrapati Bhavan; to Vasantha, the author's companion in his life's journey, for her unflinching support and encouragement at all the trying periods of his life. This flower is offered at the feet of Sage Vasiṣṭha, who is one of the seven *Ṛṣis* of this age.

INTRODUCTION

Waves hit the rocks with a mysterious rhythm, creating snow-white froth. As billions of bubbles in the froth break simultaneously, they produce the effervescence. Freshness is created in the person sitting on the beach who is observing all this. The air is moist and salty, adding to the feeling of elation and joy in the person. As the waves recede, new ones start approaching the beach to continue the perpetual movement. The gulls in groups fly overhead, their shrill voices communicating with one another, their attention deeper into the sea, where a few catamarans ply, carried by their sails fluttering in the winds, while the fishermen try their luck with the catch. Perhaps the gulls are transmitting to the onlooker, some innate truth, at once simple and profound.

As though they have succeeded, the onlooker notices that the activity becomes more intense nearer the beach, while it starts decreasing as the depth increases. When the attention settles on the horizon, it is noticed that deeper in the ocean there is total calmness. The froth with the billions of bubbles, waves small and large, the movement and everything is nothing but water. Similarly, *everything* is Reality, Truth, God or whatever the name referred to 'It'. One does not see the background, as one is too involved with the superficial. If one is too obsessed by the waves and the froth, one is bound to take all these as different. And for the activity to take place, there has to be the background of something which is totally quiescent. Behind all the change taking place, there has to be something that is changeless. And that there is nothing like horizon—the meeting of the land and the sky—and in a way, every place is essentially a horizon.... These are not just thoughts but are the experiential *peeps.*

Each one of us has some similar experience, perhaps at different locations and occasions, depending on our innate taste and nature. And almost every one of us pauses to ponder about the why and wherefore of life. Though, not everyone pursues the thoughts, either due to more pressing needs and the priorities, or we are simply *afraid* to think about them. This much is certain, that some time or the other we do take them up. Such persons who dare to take up the fundamental questions, to dissect and analyse them, become the pioneers in leading the humanity, by ushering a meaning to life in particular and existence in general.

The search for Truth and Meaning to life has been in two directions. The first—and perhaps the obvious, is the external that has come to be known as science. Using the method of curiosity-observation-experiment-inference, it tries to explain the phenomena or External Nature. The present conclusion is that, the age of our Solar system is approximately five billion years;[1] it was a great cosmic coincidence, that the compounds of Carbon, Hydrogen, Nitrogen and other elements evolved into Homo-sapiens—human beings—through millions of intermediate species consisting of plants, insects, reptiles, birds and animals. That our solar system is only one among billions of stars in our galaxy which again is one among infinite galaxies, estimated to be more than all the grains of sand of all beaches on earth!

This understanding has come through thousands of years of struggle, sacrifice and devotion of many persons. Such persons dared to think differently, and to live for more than just survival. Though these are but small steps in unlocking the infinite mysteries of the infinite Universe, they have

1 10 followed by nine zeros, that is, 10,000,000,000 = 10^9

definitely helped us in knowing our place in the Universe. The scientific method has prepared the mankind in combating the natural challenges and to increase the comfort level, which subsequently, has given more leisure. Whether man is using the leisure constructively or not, is another question.

Aristotelian logic, the foundation of science, had its advantages. It channelised the random thinking to more creative aspirations. It helped man to pose and answer questions, beginning with 'what', 'why' and 'how'. It helped in the elimination of the avoidable fanaticism. We are presently in an age, when every theory is put on the anvil of reason and experiment, to be scrutinised to the extent that only 'probability' has become certain! The present *information explosion* only suggests that the knowledge is infinite.

This conclusion has forced the scientists to re-think about their mode of approach. The high energy physicists are beginning to realise that there is nothing like 'objective observation' as it is difficult, if not impossible, to ignore the role of the 'observer' in the process of observation. To put it simply, the scientists have started thinking of the importance of the 'subject'.

To come to this conclusion, they took thousands of years, while it had become very obvious to the *Ṛṣis* or the sages, that the more one gets involved with the external, the more complicated it gets. That was why, they tried to find the source of this grand universe, instead of dwelling on the details. Not unlike the onlooker giving more importance to 'water' principle and giving less importance to waves and froth in the sea. They tried to find solutions to the riddle that is life, by seeking the Ultimate Cause. And so, the search took the second direction : the inner dimension. We will not be wrong in saying that the inner search appears to be older. It was initiated by some unknown persons in the east, who discovered, that the mystery only deepens as one tries to know the world outside, which is accepted by the modern physicists; that the knowledge is limitless; and that all the knowledge, whenever it unfolds, only makes us more and more aware of our ignorance! A distant echo of this realisation can be heard in the words of Socrates who said:

> 'I know only one thing, that I know nothing'!

Probably, it was with these realisations that they discovered the other direction of search: the inner. *Kaṭhopaniṣad* says:

> 'The Self-existent Reality has made the windows of senses, which open only outside, that is why we can perceive only the outside and not the inner Self. A patient man of sharpened intellect, with an intention of achieving immortality, turned his gaze inward'.[2]

This verse almost succeeds in explaining spirituality. The scientific observations require the help of senses. Scientists extend their limited[3] senses through extensions like microscope, telescope and other instruments. And as such, the senses can perceive only what is outside. That is, the eyes can only see what is outside or separate from the body, and so it is with the other senses. This is what is hinted at by the above *Mantra,* when it says, the windows of senses, which open only outside. But to experience the subjectivity one does not need any senses and one can do it anywhere and in any condition. Only is *patience* required, which is referred as *Dhīratā* in the *Mantra.* The word, *Swayaṁbhūḥ*—self-evident, or self-existent, is used to suggest this thought. So the process

---

2 पराञ्चि खानि व्यतृणत्स्वयंभूस्तस्मात्पराङ्पश्यति नान्तरात्मन् ।
कश्चिद्धीरः प्रत्यगात्मानमैक्षदावृत्तचक्षुरमृतत्वमिच्छन् ॥ 2.1.1 ॥

3 The ears are sensitive only to a narrow band of sound called the 'audio frequency'; eyes, to a band of electromagnetic radiation called the 'visible light'; and so on.

of *looking within* is spirituality. In fact, it *starts* with the process of introspection.

However, this search for the *Pratyagātma,* the Self or Subjectivity is possible—at least in the beginning, under certain conditions, more or less like the scientific experiments, which are to be carried out under controlled conditions. Just as an immature child cannot either understand the ways of science or perform the experiments, an indolent, restless and indulgent mind cannot possibly do introspection and the self-analysis, for which, certain amount of poise and subtlety are mandatory.

Normally, most of us are easily excitable and are basically restless and we try to keep ourselves away from spirituality. Lack of knowledge of the theories of science has not stopped us from reaping the benefits of science for increasing our comfort level. Similarly, the conclusions of the spiritual scientists—if one may call them—have helped mankind in preserving its sanity and spiritual well-being. There has been an unbroken line of Masters and seekers who have preserved this tradition, over thousands of years. The observations, conclusions and recommendations have come to us through the dialogues which had taken place in the secluded hermitages in deep forests, or on mountains. These dialogues form the *Upaniṣads,* which are the foundations of our Culture.

Some of us are of the opinion—and it is a justified opinion—that, because of this love for seclusion, our national psyche has leaned towards escapism and a fatalistic approach towards life. But why was seclusion necessary? It had a specific purpose. The mind as such is very restless connected as it is with the senses. So the places chosen for the work had to have a calming effect on the mind instead of excitement. And forests, mountain tops or any such places which abound in beauty of nature make an ideal setting. The nature of their search was such that they could not afford any excitement or indulgence. And the social obligations keep the mind extroverted most of the time. This is true even of a scientist who keeps himself to his laboratory or library and opts to be in seclusion during his research.

But not everyone is a hermit or a scientist, and a troubled or a tense man might take to seclusion as a means of escape from his problems or responsibilities. For such behaviour we cannot blame the seclusion. And the fact is, that an unsuccessful person running away, is neither happy in his own life, nor is he able to contribute for the growth of the society. On the contrary, he takes his whole world of fears and desires with him to forest or to the Himalaya!

The *Upaniṣads* are very mystical. They are necessarily so, as they are utterances of the *Ṛṣis* in non-ordinary states of consciousness achieved during the meditative moods. Like the Zen *Koans,* helping the monks to have *Satori,* the first spiritual *glimpse,* through an element of surprise, or a shock for the intellect and reason, the mystical utterances help the sensitive seeker to get glimpses into those very states which the *Ṛṣis* experienced. It is obvious that the *Upaniṣads,* can be used by only the recluses and seekers having the eligibility, with a certain amount of growth like mental calmness and introversion.

To cater to the common masses, who too have the right to inherit the Truth enshrined in the *Upaniṣads,* some sages developed the *Purāṇas, Itihāsas* or mythology, which indirectly hint the great truths of the *Upaniṣads.* This literature got so popular, it would not be an exaggeration if one said, that *every* Indian knows the mythological characters very well. The mythology helped bringing moral and ethical discipline to the society, but failed to create a genuine interest to study the life transforming *Upaniṣads.* Instead, the *Purāṇas* only strengthened the imaginative faculty and fantasies of the mind.

A scripture, giving the truths of the *Upaniṣads,* at the same time using a common man's language with illustrative stories, helps a beginner as well as an advanced seeker. This is where *'Yoga Vāsiṣṭha'* becomes relevant, which enunciates a doctrine, then elucidates it with stories, and at the end once again, gives the summery of the mystical truth.

Yoga Vāsiṣṭha—the name of the scripture— indicates that it emanated from Sage Vasiṣṭha, and comprises of thirty-two thousand verses. Its authorship is attributed to Sage Vālmīki. An abridged version of six thousand verses has been called as *'Laghu-Yoga-Vāsiṣṭha'*.[4]

His other work the *'Rāmāyaṇa'* is called an *Itihāsa,* and is very much on the mind and lips of common folk. But *Yoga Vāsiṣṭha* has not been known by many for obscure reasons. When one takes up the study of this great work, one not only gets inspired to go in for the Divine adventure, but discovers practical hints and guidelines at all stages of *Sādhanā.* One is almost tempted to believe that there may have been a deliberate attempt on the part of the self-appointed custodians of our culture—the pundits, to keep the society in darkness, and for exploiting it through its desires and fears. The *Upaniṣads* were mostly beyond the reach of common man, and the *Purāṇas* were too indirect and abstract in their approach, so all that has remained are some distorted stories.

However, books like the *Yoga Vāsiṣṭha* definitely act as the light on the path to seekers. They point out that the stories have deeper significance even to a casual reader. Unfortunately, *Vasiṣṭha* did not become popular. But then, it has continued to be a kind of guide-book for many a seeker throughout and continually. The lay-out of the great text is such that it gives almost all the details required for all stages of *Sādhanā*. It has six *Prakaraṇas* or sections, like the *Rāmāyaṇa,* which has six *Kāṇḍas*.[5] It is believed by some that the

---

4 This work seems to have been undertaken by one Abhinanda, a great Sanskrit luminary from Kashmir.

5 The Six *Kāṇḍas* are: *Bāla, Ayodhya, Araṇya, Kiṣkindhā, Sundara, Yuddha* and *Uttara.*

Rāmāyaṇa was written by Sage Vālmīki for the purification of mind and to create a mood of seeking in the society. It is well known, that the story of Śrī Rāma, gives an exemplary ethical and moral behaviour in an individual, and a glimpse into the ideal culture, through the description of Ayodhyā. For only on a strong ethical and moral foundation can one hope to build the super-structure of spirituality.

What happens to a person who has experienced fully all aspects of *survival* characterised by the desires and fears and has come to a stage when she or he starts wondering about the real meaning of *life?* What are his observations and conclusions? What is his mood? The first section entitled *Vairāgya Prakaraṇa*—the episode on disinterest in the life of indulgence— tries to clear these initial doubts of a seeker. In the very second *Śloka* of this *Prakaraṇa,* it says that only a person who has realised that the life characterised by only acts of survival is limited and meaningless, and who aspires for something permanent which brings freedom, is eligible to take this scripture for study.

The second section, *Mumukṣu Prakaraṇa,* gives the basic qualifications of a *Mumukṣu* or an aspirant seeker after liberation. Most of our gross desires have an element of speed in them, in the sense that we are in a hurry to fulfill them. The first quality of the mind involved in the inner search is *Śama* or the sweet patience, achieved through quietening of senses. The basis of science is the basic discontentment in what we *have* and contentment in what we *are.* While in spirituality this is reversed, through *Saṁtoṣa.* With *Śama* and *Saṁtoṣa* the mind and senses quieten when the seeker acquires an ability to penetrate into deeper questions.

The seeker then becomes capable of such observation that she or he is in a position to observe the mind and its activity. This process is known in *Vedānta* as *Vicāra. Vicāra* brings the awareness in the life of a seeker. In spite of sincere efforts, it so happens sometimes, that the doubts linger on, causing impediment in progress. Not so, when one is fortunate to get the company of the enlightened and experienced wise, referred to as *Sādhusaṅga* in this scripture, which assures progress. Sage Vasiṣṭha calls these four noble steps *Śama, Saṁtoṣa, Vicāra* and *Sādhusaṅga* that provide the required milieu to the seeker for the *Sādhanā,* as the four sentinels of the palace of *Mukti* or Liberation.

Normally, it has been noticed by most seekers that in spite of controlling the senses and the lower mind, the intellect and reason—so necessary for the development of Science, keep delaying the seeker from going deeper within. Not only to help in breaking through the shield of reason, but also to stop the intellect from raising its hood again, it is necessary to *satisfy* it with some reasonable *food.* Śrī Ādi Śaṅkarācārya gives the simile of using a thorn to remove a thorn from a part of the body.

There have been many schools which advocate directing the attention inside straight away. But *Vedānta* has always believed in recognising every faculty of the human being. It either takes Epistemology—that division of Philosophy which investigates the origin and mechanics of knowledge, or takes the origin of the Universe. Like the *Upaniṣads, Vāsiṣṭha* takes both simultaneously. It advocates the view, that the origin of knowledge as well as the Universe is same, that is, the 'I'-principle. This is called as the *Dṛṣṭi-Sṛṣṭi-Vāda* or the view that 'the world exists, as long as the perceiver exists'. To put it in common man's language, *Yoga Vāsiṣṭha* takes all the problems at the subjective level.

The marked difference between the Western and the Eastern thought is that the West tried to solve the external problems using external means and the East tried to find the subjective solutions to those problems. The Sages were convinced that the so-called external problems were only *symptoms* of the internal disease. The third episode, *Utpatti Prakaraṇa* deals with the origin of 'I' principle. There are nine stories which illustrate that fear, ignorance and bondage, are all linked with the 'I'. Unlike some *Śāstras* which directly or indirectly discourage women from taking to this search, *Vāsiṣṭha* tells us through its stories that not only are women eligible for life spiritual, but they are capable of doing very well, so well that they even free their men-folk from the self-created bondage. Story of Līlā in this *Prakaraṇa* illustrates this aspect and also has some practical hints for the seeker so as to make him aware of his own level of perception, understanding and being.

Movies have been a source of recreation of the present times. In spite of the fact that we all are very much aware of the fact that it is but a play of light and shadow over the screen (big or small) most of the times we get involved with it and even identified with the characters. Something very similar happens to us when we start forgetting that the actor, the perceiver as well as the knower or the 'I', is very much a part of our own creation. And by identifying with the action, the perceived and the known, we get totally bound.

The fourth section called *Sthiti Prakaraṇa* has five stories to illustrate such behaviour. It describes the effect of crystallisation of the 'I', due to repeated births. The crystallised ego takes many births for emancipation. If we carefully study the text we discover that most of us have to pass through the stages of flowering, fruition, ripening and emancipation of the ego. It appears that *Sthiti* or preservation of 'I' is an important if not a mandatory stage of growth, as it is during this time that an individual learns through experiences, bringing in the three aspects of Existence. Firstly, when there is the identification with the physical body; secondly, the identification with the psyche; and thirdly, when there is identification with the whole Cosmos.

It is very difficult to convince a man that he is asleep, and it can be only done by awakening him. A man, who is involved with his ego and its manifestations, is in a kind of sleep. What we are individually is the result of our involvement of many births. Longer a man is in such involvement, deeper is his lack of awareness. Some of the sages rightly comment that the experience of the pairs of opposites is like the calls or the shocks given by Providence to wake the man up. When one notices that life as such, is full of pain with intermittent pleasure and that it is impermanent, there is a shock which forces one to enquire into the why and the what-for of life. By such repeated musings, one gets motivated to take up the quest.

When one really starts the quest, the problems of a different dimension commence. At this time he realises the difficulty in sincerely persevering the chosen path, as the tendencies start creating obstacles in progress. *Upaśānti* or *Upaśama Prakaraṇa,* the fifth section has nine stories giving some very valuable hints about quietening the mind, for annihilation of the ego or 'I'-ness, the root cause and also the creator of the binding tendencies. In the stories, each character is a representative of a particular aptitude with typical problems and doubts. In fact, this book specialises in throwing very valuable hints on practical spirituality.

Perhaps the crest jewel of this sacred book is the last section called *Nirvāṇa Prakaraṇa.* Its fifteen stories, try to convey the deepest thoughts embellished with the finest narrative form. It would not be an exaggeration if one said that it almost achieves the impossible task of communicating the incommunicable. The occult details of *Prāṇa Vidyā,* the Science of *Prāṇa*; the esoteric significance of ritualistic worship; the secret of action; the relationship between the *Guru* and the *Śiṣya;* true renunciation; methodology of *Ātmavicāra;* the deeper aspect of *Citta-Śuddhi*—the purity of mind; the seven stages a seeker has to pass through, as he progresses towards *Mukti;* and the total freedom, are some of the topics discussed in this section.

One of the most difficult problems a seeker faces on his meditation seat is the obstinacy of time. Either he gets carried away by the regrets of the past, or swept off his feet by the anxiety for the future, or anchored to the excitements of the present. This text helps us in overcoming this problem, by suggesting, that time as such is a myth and a mental creation, like everything else.

When we study this scripture we find that many thoughts are repeated, which is quite typical in such texts. This is done with a specific purpose of helping the seeker to make the ideas a part of her or his being, unlike the other treatises which may be for scholarly pursuits or entertainment or for evoking emotions. The *Vedāntic* texts are mainly meant for transformation of life through *Swādhyāya* or self-study, which not only consists of careful study, but deep contemplation on the truth enshrined therein. During such moments, a seeker tries to observe his own behaviour and nature, and understand it.

As is the case with most of our spiritual and religious literature, there is disagreement regarding the authorship of this scripture, time and other details. But then, the authors of such scriptures never bothered to claim any authorship, for they were totally un-identified with the puny body-mind complex and felt that it was an insult to the Universal Spirit with which they had identified and were convinced that they were only Its instruments.

And also, these pursuits of authorship and the period interest only the academicians and not the sincere seekers who are interested only in making most of the available time. Paramahansa Shri Ramakrishna, the great visionary of nineteenth century, used to tell of two persons entering a mango grove. One man goes on finding out the varieties of fruits, the number of trees, branches and leaves, while the other happily plucks the mangoes, and eats heartily for nourishing his body! He did not be-little anyone, but only differentiated their priorities. There cannot be two opinions about the nourishment this scripture has for all seekers, at all the stages of their *Sādhanā.*

In the following essays, an attempt has been made to present some of the truths discovered while studying the text. They are some of the thoughts during *Swādhyāya* of this great scripture—a peep into author's meditations. No claim of any mastery, either in Sanskrit or in the power of understanding of the mystical language used in the text or the power of expression in English is being made. The book has been of great help to the author in his life-journey. The essays aim to encourage the friends who are interested and yet unable to approach such texts owing to the lack of knowledge in Sanskrit, and to convince them that it is not all that difficult to take up the study of the original, which has a mine of Wisdom.

Like the glimpses of Existence or Truth we get, when we are on a beach through the waves and bubbles and the vastness of the sea itself, there are many suggestions in *Yoga Vāsiṣṭha,* some very kind, some others not so, yet others positively shocking! Gold needs to go through the fire and face the hammer-head before it gets converted into an ornament of exquisite beauty, to be finally handled lovingly by the wearer. In a similar way, one has to go through the fire of austerity, face the hammer-head of discipline to become an ornament adorning the Existence. And the beauty is that, one becomes what one already is!

THE DIVINE DISINTEREST

Vairāgya Prakaraṇa

1

The Origin of Disinterest

The bus negotiates a stiff gradient, almost with a complaining tone! The Coniferous Pines, called locally by the names *Cheed* and *Deodar* abound the hill slopes surrounding the winding, serpentine road. One is satiated to the brim with the different shades of green intermingled with other colours scattered by the flora of the Pir Panjal Range. In this joyous mood, one notices that the bus enters the famous Jawahar tunnel. The outer light very gradually gives way to darkness. Through the window, there comes the smell of moisture and smoke from the exhaust of the bus; and the sound of tires plying on the moist asphalt road. The cold dampness creates a tingle all over the body. It is as though with the ineffectiveness of the sense of vision, all the other senses have opened up. It is good that the driver forgets to switch on the artificial lights in the bus. For the darkness has an entirely different quality, congenial for introspection. After a while, once again the soothing darkness gives way to equally soothing light. As the bus emerges out, one suddenly beholds the Great Himalayas, snow-peaked, pure —almost untouched by human beings, imposing with their gigantic size. And one is totally lost, enveloped by both beauty and sheer awesomeness.

Vastness of Existence evident in Nature humbles us. The mountains for instance, not only make us aware of our puniness but also of our impermanence. The size, the element of timelessness and the myriad of life they support, have something to do with the effect they have over those who are sensitive. When we have something to learn, the most important pre-requisite is, the mood of humility and receptivity. To create the mood of humility and receptivity, prayer plays a very important role. All the scriptures begin with such prayers which not only help the preceptor and the disciple to come in tune with each other, but also to give certain valuable hints on the subject under study and on the life itself in general.

> 'Salutations to that Supreme Principle, manifesting through three planes of heaven, earth and space, shining within and without (through body, senses, mind, intellect, and ego), both manifest as well as unmanifest as there is nothing beyond this Principle, which is present as *Ātman* of all beings. Persons qualified to study this *Śāstra* should neither be *Ajñānis* (those indulged *only* in mundane thoughts and actions), nor those who have known That Principle, but only those who have realised the limitations of their existence and firmly resolved to free themselves'.[6]

These two opening *Ślokas* of *'Laghu Yoga Vāsiṣṭha'*[7] throw light on the Goal as well as the Path. Our so-called normal understanding of the world with all its beings is characterised by multiplicity. Everything looks unconnected and separate, due to our superficial outlook. We forget when we see or meet a person that it is not only the physical shape and appearance

---

6 दिविभूमौ तथाकाशे बहिरन्तश्च मे विभुः ।
यो विभात्यवभासात्मा तस्मै सर्वात्मने नमः॥ 1.1.1 ॥
अहं बद्धो विमुक्तःस्यामिति यस्यास्ति निश्चयः ।
नात्यन्तमज्ञो नो तज्ञः सोऽस्मिन्शास्त्रेऽधिकारवान् ॥ 1.1.2 ॥

7 All the verses quoted here are from the book bearing the same title, Published by Nirnayasagar Press, 26/27 Coalbhat Street, Bombay.

but there are many things like emotions, thoughts, likes-dislikes, etc., which are deeper, and which are beyond the purview of the senses as well as the mind.

The first verse confirms that beyond multiplicity and distortion, there is Unity and Harmony. This *Śāstra* helps us to take steps towards such understanding. However, can anyone take-up this scripture for study? And by taking it up, will she or he derive benefit? Like any knowledge, the science of *Adhyātma* too has certain eligibility norms, which are given in the second verse. It explicitly tells us that it is not meant for *Ajñānīs,* who are said to be such persons, indulged *only* in the act of survival. It is not that such persons are in any way *banned,* but their very nature and priorities they keep for themselves, will not allow them to appreciate any other dimension of life.

Even if such persons take up the study of this scripture, it can be at the most for scholarly pursuits. Paramahansa Shri Ramakrishna used to give an analogy: The mother frees herself from the child to do other house-hold chores, by providing it with toys. As long as the child is busy and happy with the toys, it forgets the mother. But soon as it remembers its mother and realises, that so far it was only engaged with the toys, and feels the necessity of its mother, it starts crying! The mother is left with no other alternative, but to stop all her work and press the child to her bosom.

The second verse only means that those involved with the *toys* in the form of family, material wealth, or name and fame, may not even realise that there are many more dimensions to life. While the persons who have freed themselves from this limited life do not need such book, just as the person having reached his destination does not need any route map! The gist of the eligibility as given in the second verse can be understood through another example: A man in deep slumber cannot possibly get the thought of waking up. And the Person, who is awakened, does not need any such thought. But a person who is becoming aware of the misery and other limitations of sleep in the *dream* requires some *dream motivation* to wake up. Scriptures like the *Upaniṣads* and *Yoga Vāsiṣṭha* give ample motivation for such persons.

Learning invariably involves the process of 'listening', which is qualitatively different from 'hearing'. While hearing is only a sense activity, listening is a deeper process, which has not only the act of gathering the sound through an instrument called the ear, but also some intricate intellectual processes like co-relation and comprehension. Listening has a much deeper significance as and when one becomes capable of silencing the mind. Consequently, not everyone can listen, though hearing is done by everyone.

The scriptures like the *Upaṇiṣads* and *Vāsiṣṭha* are mostly in the form of dialogues between the *Guru*—the preceptor and *Śiṣya*—the disciple. It is not a dialogue in the ordinary sense, but a kind of intimate communion. Three things govern such communion, *Deśa*—place, *Kāla*—time, and *Pātra*—eligibility or aptitude. For a perfect transfer of the wisdom, all the three should be ideal. *Vāsiṣṭha* is a dialogue *and* also communion between the Master Vālmīki and the disciple Bharadwāja.

The eligibility of a seeker is called as *Sādhana Catuṣṭya.* In his immortal work *Vivekacūḍāmaṇi,* Ācārya Śaṅkara mentions about it:

> 'First *Nityānityavastuvivekaḥ,* the ability to discriminate between the Real and the unreal; next comes *Ihāmutraphalabhôgavirāgah*—the spirit of detachment from the enjoyment of the fruits of actions here and hereafter; after that is, *Śamādiṣaṭkasampattiḥ*—the six essential treasures like *Śama, Dama, Uparati, Titīkṣa, Samādhāna,* and *Śraddhā;* the last is *Mumukṣatvaṃ*—the burning aspiration for liberation'.[8]

---

8 आदौ नित्यानित्यवस्तुविवेकः परिगण्यते इहामुत्रफलभोगविरागस्तदनन्तरम् ।
शमदमादिषट्कसम्पत्तिर्मुमुक्षत्वमिति स्फुटम् ॥ विवेकचूडामणि 19 ॥

Each of the four qualities is mandatory and forms a step towards the Life Divine. *Viveka* which can be roughly translated as discrimination, dawns on a person when she or he starts realising that everything which can be perceived is temporal. Whatever he wants to possess, eludes him. Material things he wants to acquire and the relationships through which he wants to transact, are all impermanent. And even if they are permanent, he has to part with them at the time of his death. The questions start forming in his mind, is there anything which survives time and death? With these questions, a special attitude sets in, the receptivity and sensitivity to observe. Such a person has put the first step necessary for a seeker.

Through keen observation and discrimination the seeker discovers that almost all the actions are being motivated by the desire for the fruit. This desire for fruit sets a vicious circle of expectation, attachment infatuation, anger and depression. Even the so-called righteous acts like charity and pilgrimage are motivated by the desire for name and fame or a life in heaven after death. For a person whose discrimination has developed fully, it is easy to see that enjoyment at any plane cannot be permanent. And one has to totally give-up all craving for the temporal if one has to achieve the Permanent. And this is the second step: *Ihāmutraphalabhogavirāgaḥ*.

How can one stop the mind from either dwelling on or craving for the impermanent? This is through the third step *Śamādiṣaṭkasampattiḥ* —the six essentials, which are *Śama* —patience of mind, *Dama* —self-control, *Uparati*—self-withdrawal, *Titīkṣā*—capacity to endure all sorrows and suffering, *Śraddhā*—power to understand the exact import of all scriptures and the words of Guru, and *Samādhāna*—tranquility attained by constant contemplation of the truths learnt from scriptures or Guru. When these three steps are taken by the seeker, she or he becomes a *Mumukṣu*—one who has the burning aspiration for liberation from this limited and impermanent life. He has total dedication and devotion for achieving the goal. These are the qualities of the disciple, while the Master has to necessarily be in a much higher state of 'Being' and should be able to come down to the disciple's level, and guide him towards freedom.

This life is a great paradox, a homogeneous co-existence of the opposites—like pleasure and pain, life and death, joy and misery, right and wrong, and the like. Many a time, we find it very difficult to accept them as they are and experience a conflict leading us to misery. The conversation opens with a query from Bharadwāja to Vālmīki on this phenomenon. Bharadwāja requests Vālmīki to tell him about the path traversed by Rāma to transcend this world of duality.

In his epic *Rāmāyaṇa,* sage Vālmīki has described the value based living, through Śrī Rāma's life. A doubt creeps into the mind of a serious reader of this work: 'Why should one lead a value based life?' As it is seen, Rāma's life is not at all a bed of roses. On the contrary, it is full of trials and tribulations. Even after his 'almost flawless' life, characterised by sacrifice and justice, most of the time he gets only pain in return, whether he was miserable or otherwise is a different question. Vālmīki's second work *'Yoga Vāśiṣtha'* answers this question explicitly, that righteous life is not an end in itself, but only a preparation for something higher. It takes the help of questions that arise in Rāma's mind, his quest, and his ultimate triumph, with the help of Sage Vaśiṣṭha, in great detail. A seeker finds this work very useful in all stages of his journey towards the Truth.

Sage Vālmīki begins his exposition by saying that pain and paradoxes exist only in ignorance. Ignorance is the inability to understand that there is a great difference between the appearance and Reality. The sky *appears* blue, but in reality it is colourless. Ignorance lies in the act of remembering and getting involved with, the *Draśyaṃ*—the seen, which is impermanent and fleeting. While the wisdom lies in seeing the Principle behind the fleeting, and attaining quiescence.

Unless one attains this vision of discrimination, the *Śāstra* only becomes a burden and a source of further pain. Though the *Śāstra* is meant for alleviating the ignorance, it only helps in mere scholarship. And scholarship can never be of any help. The vision of discrimination is the capacity to look behind the gross, and this can be developed through *Antarmukhatā,* or introversion of mind. This introvertishness should not be confused with brooding. It has a different quality altogether. While brooding is characterised by *involvement, Antarmukhatā* is non-involved awareness.

Antarmukhatā cannot be achieved till one has the *Vāsanās,* the fragrance or impressions. A *Vāsanā* is an affinity or attraction for something. There are two types of *Vāsanās* : the impure and the pure. Impure *Vāsanās* are the attraction for the impermanent, which intensify the *Ahaṁkāra* or the 'I-ness' and are therefore binding. While the pure *Vāsanās* dilute the affinity or attraction for the impermanent, bringing about the sublimation of *Ahaṁkāra. Vāsanās* are the memories of either enjoyment or pain that one has experienced. And this memory or impression binds us to the objects of senses, through our *Rāga*—likes or attractions and *Dweṣa*—dislikes or aversions. Most of us are under the impression that by fulfilling the desires we get satiated. While the fact is, we get more strongly bound to the sense objects instead of freeing ourselves from them. A verse from *Śrīmadbhāgavataṃ* puts it very beautifully:

> 'The desires for sense objects cannot be eliminated through the enjoyment of senses; just as, the fire cannot be put off by pouring ghee into it, which only makes it more intense'.[9]

The sage classifies the *Vāsanās* as pure and impure, only to impress upon the seeker the two directions of the mind.

---

9 न जातु कामः कामानामुपभोगेन शाम्यति ।
हविषा कृष्णवर्त्मेव भूय एवाभिवर्तते ॥ 9.19.14 ॥

By impure *Vāsanās* he only means, such impressions which increase the extrovertishness and the urges or hungers like food, sleep, fear and procreation, or the pride, sense of possession, jealousy, and other feelings. While pure *Vāsanās* are those which make us fluid, non-involved and free. A beginner should develop pure *Vāsanās* for eliminating the impure ones, just as a thorn is to be removed from the body with the help of a needle, which is only another thorn! With this introduction Sage Vālmīki starts narrating the journey of Rāma, the prince among men.

Rāma had finished learning various branches of knowledge which were demanded of a Crown Prince and was spending his youth in a happy and sportive way. At that time an innocent wish of visiting the places of pilgrimage, natural beauty and hermitages arose in him. He approached king Daśaratha with a request to fulfill the wish, who readily agreed. And so, Rāma along with his three brothers, friends and attendants had a very happy pilgrimage. When Rāma stepped into sixteenth year of his life, the attendants noticed a great change coming over the prince. Loss of interest in performing his daily ablutions like bath, a distaste for food, lack of sleep, and engaging in the act of brooding for hours. The servants, unable to bring him back to what they considered normalcy, reported this matter to king Daśaratha. The father in the king, who was very much attached to the son, called Rāma and inquired affectionately. But Rāma said that it was nothing and avoided the matter altogether.

About this time Viśwāmitra, the great sage visited the court of Daśaratha. And according to the habit and tradition of his illustirous Raghu dynasty, Daśaratha promised to fulfill the wish of the sage. The enlightened sage stated that he was unable to perform a great sacrifice due to the atrocities of the *Rākṣasas* (demons) and made a request to send Rāma with him, as only Rāma could bring the culprits to book. On hearing this wish from Viśwāmitra, Daśaratha became pale, as he could not possibly bear the separation from his dear son. He sought an excuse of young age and inexperience. But this polite refusal could not be tolerated by the Muni, who with annoyance, wished the family of Daśaratha well and started for his hermitage.

Sage Vasiṣṭha, the *Guru* of the Solar dynasty, silent so far, intervened and pacified the *Muni,* and urged Daśaratha to send Rāma. For this would not only save the name of his dynasty but also be of very great benefit to Rāma. Thereby, to Daśaratha prove that Rāma was in no condition to shoulder the responsibility, summoned the servants and asked them to describe the condition of their Master.

On hearing from the attendants the condition of Rāma, Viśwāmitra declared that this was due to the disinterest in the temporal life and was not due to any failure or disappointment. This state was really the setting in, of a receptive mood of a person to change the course of his life. Rāma entered the court and sat on the floor, after duly taking the dust of the feet of all elders. Then sages Vasiṣṭha and Viśwāmitra motivated Rāma to describe the cause for his present state of mind.

Normally, a man approaches religion, either due to some failure to acquire or enjoy a material object, or the loss of a near and dear one. There are the others who approach the religion or scriptures for appeasing their thirst for knowledge. But persons like Rāma and Siddhārtha Gautama, turn towards spirituality due to a conviction of the temporal nature of life and the world. Such persons lack nothing and are totally satiated. They are also highly successful as far as the life's achievements are concerned. Many a time, especially in our country, we find persons taking to spiritual life because they are not successful in their worldly life. This episode seems to point out that the most ideal state for taking up spirituality is the state when one has observed existence and has understood its temporal nature.

One feels totally fulfilled on observing and becoming one with the nature. Most of us tend to get enamoured by the external beauty and get carried away by it. After enjoying the scenic beauty on way to Kashmir, the drive *into* the Jawahar tunnel helps us come out of the other side of the tunnel, and to experience the grander vision of the existence. In a similar manner, if one is able to go *inside* and observe the inner world, we learn many things and in turn, become eligible for something infinitely grander and a more fulfilling experience than what we usually call pleasure or happiness. This is the real purpose of life. But perhaps, each one of us has to wait patiently for the *turning point* which sets in when our eyes turn away from the life characterised by *only* survival.

2

The Limitations of the World

One is enveloped by peace in the expansiveness of the desert. An occasional howl of the wind accompanied by the shifting dunes, reminds one of the eternal change. The silhouette of a caravan of camels and persons, with the backdrop of the red, gigantic, setting sun, brings in an aspiration for reaching home early. The heat of the desert forces us to appreciate the power of the sun and earth's response. Though being in a desert can be quite uncomfortable, especially on a clear day! Not only the pleasant experience is remembered, but an unpleasant or a painful one is also remembered, perhaps a little more vividly. Every one of us nurtures the memory of an experience that has been enjoyed in a place be it a desert, a valley or a mountain. While the pleasant experiences bring in a mood of nostalgia, the unpleasant and painful ones may bring in regret, bitterness or depression. Each experience thus exercises an influence over one's consciousness depending on the priorities one keeps, the likes and dislikes one nurtures or the expectations one nourishes and other innumerable factors. We share these experiences with our friends and unfortunately with that, the utility of the experience itself is over.

The evolved persons however, utilise their memory not only to avoid the mistakes or blunders once committed, but also to intensify their progressive evolution. Gautama the

Buddha, it is believed, remembered all his past births. In his discourses, he used to explain the difficult concepts through his own experiences from past births. This legacy has come to us in the form of *'Jātaka Tales'*. Over two and a half millennia stand between us and the Buddha, and it is quite natural for us to doubt the validity of the claim made by his devotees, on the power of his memory. This much is certain about persons like the Buddha: they have the most useful memory. The memory which stops them from repeating the same mistake differentiates them from the common lot. Most of us know the temporal nature of all material things including the body. But all our actions are contrary to this knowledge, and we act as though we are going to live forever! This is what makes us the sheep, while persons like the Buddha and the Christ, the Shepherds who tend and lead the flock to safety and freedom.

Our rich cultural heritage is enshrined in the scriptures, which run in three streams: *Śruti*—that which is heard, like the *Upaniṣads; Smṛti*—that which is remembered like *Manusmṛti* and *Dharmaśāstras;* and *Purāṇas*—mythology, using symbology and allegory. While the *Upaniṣads* are mostly in the form of dialogues, some of the *Smṛtis* have been preserved through millennia in the form of *Sūtras,* or aphorisms. The *Sūtras* are the briefest possible statements, almost like the mathematical formulae. The language adopted being Sanskrit, which by its very nature is suggestive, each *Sūtra* can have a voluminous explanation.

The *Sūtra* treatises begin typically with either word *'Atha'*[1] —meaning 'and now' or *'Athāto'*—'and now therefore'. Without the proper background, one is tempted to conclude that perhaps the initial portions of the texts are missing. But actually, the texts are more than complete!

This one word *'Atha'* hints at the pre-requisites to be fulfilled by the aspirant before taking up the practice. For example, in the *Sūtras* dealing with methods of Self-realisation, the word expects the aspirant to be aware of subtleties of life and death; that she or he must have developed sufficient disinterest towards the objects of senses and the relationships in and with the world in general. Not because the objects are difficult to get, but because *the interest for the permanent has been evoked;* not because there is a kind of *repulsion* towards the objects, as their contact gives birth to anxiety, tension, worry and excitement or pain, but because the genuine *attraction* towards a way of life, different from the ordinary. The aspirant is ready to stake his everything for this new life, as she or he is not aware of what is in store for future. And thus, is more than prepared to embark on a Divine adventure.

This psychological condition is reached by some of us when we experience a kind of emptiness at the end of the so-called successful life, even after fulfilling all the desires and ambitions. What are the thoughts and convictions of such an aspirant? How does the person look at the world? These and other pertinent questions are answered in this *Sarga.* It tries to describe the necessary conditions for the onset of spirituality in the life of an individual. In short, it explains the full significance of the word *'Atha'*.

A person reaches this state when she or he is able to discriminate between the success and the failure of human birth. She or he has to go through certain experiences, very much like the ripening of fruit after journeying through the earlier stages. Though, it is not mandatory that one should pass through all the stages in one life, for the journey of the soul to find and realise itself, is eternal. And a lifetime is like a moment in eternity. In the royal assembly of the court of Daśaratha, Rāma discoursed on the cause and effect of the condition he was in, at that time.

From the discourse it appears that he was in a highly ripened state, so as to have a very clear understanding of life with all its intricacies. The first thing that strikes us, even to the point of disturbance is the relentless law of change. Everything, from a galaxy to a grain of dust, is in a state of flux, though the change as such is very slow, so slow that we are not conscious of it. The unconsciousness is due to our involvement and indulgence with the life. People and objects around us appear so real due to our identification. But then, a time comes when one is able recognise the change. There are these changes taking place at the physical level through the childhood, youth, middle-age and old-age. A once handsome man or a beautiful lady gets withered with time.

Perhaps one of the strongest goads for the *Viveka* is death. Everyone of us experiences the loss of a near and a dear one, sometime or the other in life. Though most of us take these changes for granted, the persons with a developed discrimination see through this, and it is at this time that one experiences a strange and a fearful disturbance. The very ground from under one's feet seems to have been taken away. But this mental churning which accompanies this initial fear helps in giving a clearer picture of everything around. What are the things that stop us from developing *Viveka?* It is our indulgences and involvements. Rāma proceeds to describe them in a very methodic manner.

Our identification with the world of objects is through the senses. We have a firm conviction that we feel happy only when we possess all the objects of senses. For that, acquisition of wealth is the first step. Wealth, the other name of which is greed, is a potential source of worry, tension and misery. A rich man *is likely* to become a victim of pride and greed which motivate wrong or evil action. Another weakness that can afflict the rich is the fondness for flattery, which in turn make them sacrifice the objectivity. Flattery, which can be defined as the *'empty spoon feeding'*, has with it a string of favours attached. One does not rest content only with the acquisition of wealth, one continues to seek power. In the words of Rāma, there is a hint of what was to come, for we see now the moneyed class playing, *'hand in glove'* with the politicians and bureaucrats, to make the lives of the ordinary more and more miserable with each new day.

We see a poor man, miserable *because he does not have;* a rich man, miserable *because he has and does not want to lose it!* Then there is the class—which constitutes the majority of mankind—which is miserable, *because it is neither* and is unable to accept its position in between! We have the cases of couples being miserable because they do not have children, while there are others, who have, *but the children may not be affectionate and obedient or it may be they are abnormal!* In a way, misery appears to be the common factor for all human beings.

Rāma seemed to have been fully aware of this aspect of life, as he negated the wealth and power, in spite of the fact, that he did not have any dearth of it and was the darling of the whole kingdom. But he had observed that acquisition of wealth is followed by greed for power. Greed assumes different forms, by only changing its objectives. Shri Ramakrishna used to warn the seekers of the two enemies *'woman and gold'*, which stood for *'lust and greed'!*

Rāma started talking about 'life' as it is usually interpreted or understood. To most of us, life is only *means to enjoy the sense objects obtained through greed.* This results in misery. Life is temporal, like a droplet of water on a leaf, which can fall off any moment. We are totally unaware and act as though we are going to live forever, through our favourite occupation of sense indulgence and acquisition of objects. Such persons are worse than the ordinary animals and birds which at least lead a life in tune with nature.

Rāma made a wonderful statement that learning is a burden to persons without discrimination; knowledge is a burden to persons leading a life of indulgence; mind is a burden for the mentally disturbed; and for the person who keeps searching for happiness outside due to wrong orientation and has not experienced the joy within, health, handsome body, mind, intellect, ego, and action, why, even life itself is burdensome. It is like the load on the head of the load carrier. The emptiness and misery experienced in life, in spite of all the material possessions and physical comforts is due to the forgetfulness or lack of awareness of the purpose for which life is meant. This forgetfulness is due to *indulgence and involvement*[10] with the external.

Rāma gave a glimpse into his logical understanding, and the extent of his objective observation, as he took up the subtler aspects. By peeping into one's own behaviour superficially, one discovers that without any apparent reason there is infatuation, fear and such other feelings which are associated with the indulgence and involvement. In fact, we are able to gauge the intensity of indulgence or involvement through such upheavals.

On careful and impersonal observation we can see that *Ahaṁkāra* or the 'I-entity' is really behind all these and is the real culprit. This 'I- ness' is the gate through which all kinds of negative feelings like desires, discontent, pride and misery enter. That is why this *Ahaṁkāra* or the 'I-am-ness' is considered to be the primary delusion and which manifests itself into other grosser faculties, among which, mind and body are the grossest.

It is like a hand which tries to grab at the objects of senses. The main activity of *Manas* is that of seesawing between *Rāgas,*[11] the attractions and *Dweṣas,*[12] the repulsions. Consequently, *Manas* is characterised by the randomness of thought, which stops us from containing any joy within as we move about restlessly.

Like the inability of *Karaṇḍaka* or a wicker-basket, to hold water, *Manas* drains the energy on useless things, and life itself becomes meaningless. And we suffer from one of the most dreadful of diseases : discontentment. The discord of

---

10 Indulgence is of the senses and involvement is of the mind.

11 '*Rāga* is the craving for happiness' Patañjali Yoga Sūtras : 2-7.

12 '*Dweṣa* is avoidance of unhappiness' Patañjali Yoga Sūtras: 2-8.

discontent is struck by desires, the primary contents of *Manas*. Rāma continued his discourse by explaining about desires.

During the moon-less night in the sky of consciousness, that is, during the unaware moments filled with desires, a pack of owls called passions and anger play. All good actions aspired earlier get destroyed due to desires, as they destroy the discrimination—between right and wrong, virtuous and vicious, and other pairs of opposites. Fear enters the minds of even the bold, and hearts of the wise, through desires. Under the influence of desires even great persons have experienced the fals.[13]

It is the desire which goads them to grope at things beyond their reach; and even if they are successful in fulfilling the desires, there is no lasting fulfillment, as the desires keep changing. It is just like the useless effort to seek the horizon! This peculiar behaviour is due to the involvement with the senses. By their very nature, senses seek their objects and the *Manas* married to them gives birth to desires. The body composed of the five elements, subject to change, illness and death, is tenanted by *Ahaṁkāra,* the householder with ten mischievous cows (the ten organs of knowledge and action[14]), and servant *Manas,* beget *Saṁkalpa*—ambition, with desire its partner.

The ocean of *Saṁsāra,*[15] is characterised by change, and the body, which is only a part of this *Saṁsāra,* also undergoes a constant change. Rāma starts describing these changes which constitute the growth of the body. Childhood is one which has only misery to offer as it is characterised by

13 Viśwāmitra had succumbed to lust during his quest.

14 *Jnānendriyas* (organs of knowledge or senses): eyes, ears, tongue, skin, and nose.

Karmendriyas (organs of action): tongue, hands, legs, excretion, and procreation.

15 *Saṁsāra* means that which is repetitive, cyclic, circular, etc.

weakness, inability to express one's feelings and thoughts, ignorance and other types of helplessness. In this weak body there is a weaker mind owing to its constant fluctuations. The most predominant emotion of childhood is *fear.* A child is afraid of teachers, mother, father, people, why even the elder children! Another aspect of this difficult stage of life is its total dependency on others for its very existence.

Having somehow crossed over the period of ignorance and fear, one steps into youth, that period dominated by excitement and arrogance. The excitement is due to the sense attractions, and the arrogance is due to the intoxication of pride. Excitement robs one of the discrimination, while arrogance robs of the receptivity as well as sensitivity, leaving only exhaustion and regret. The sexual attraction, which predominates youth has been a part of our consciousness through billions of years of evolution. As it was through this attraction that the species have been preserved. And there is nothing wrong with it, but a *helpless and animalistic involvement* in this act is definitely not in keeping with *humanness* which is considered to be the acme of evolution.

There was a tone of despicableness when Rāma spoke on the youth. But a seeker has to be very harsh to himself. Whatever causes diversion from his chosen path has to be negated. Rāma's tone only confirms his burning aspiration and an impatience to rise above the normal cravings and hunger. Childhood characterised by helplessness, is replaced by youth that is dominated by excitement, dreams and ambition, which in turn is devoured by the old age.

Dotage is accompanied by disease and pain, which in turn cause delusion, forgetfulness and even certain obsessions like suspicion. The inability to fulfill one's desires—may either be due to physical ailment or failure—brings in cynicism. The talks always begin with: 'In our days, it was not so bad. Those were the days when we had some values governing our action!' Such *'looking down'* upon others is one of the ways in which the old bring out their inner *poison*—a method of catharsis.

It is said that when a copper plate in the ancient Mesopotamian Civilization was decoded, it was found to contain some critical depreciation of the youth of that time! To prove one's utilitarian usefulness, he or she will give the opinion or advice unasked, and in turn invite the irritation and anger of the youth. All this results in the intolerance and wrath among different generations.

The younger generation ignores such 'perpetual advisors', which evokes irritation and anger in the old. Thus the old age can create the vicious circle of, helplessness, cynicism, opinion or advice, irritation or neglect and finally misery. Rāma analysed the reason for such a vicious circle.

He said, that the desires and impossible dreams, that are unfulfilled, remain like the owls resting in the tree hollows, which come out in the form of imaginary fears and suspicion during nights. Attraction for material possessions increases in old age, while the body and senses do not permit any enjoyment, causing irritation and misery.

These stages in life are possible only with the background of *Kāla* or time, the cause for the change. *Kāla* is change as well as death, because change means, the old giving way for new, which is possible only with the death of the old. Nothing can survive this change, and there is no discrimination whatsoever! For there is no difference between the good and the bad, between the rich and the poor, between the young and the old, between the wise and the ignorant. Everything that is born must die and decay.

Time is the greatest healer and simultaneously greatest disease. The suffering or pain heals as the time elapses, and for everyone without exception, it brings old age and death! In our ignorance, when we resort to certain action or entertainment we say, 'we are passing or killing time.' But the truth is otherwise, *the time is killing us!* The destructive force or the energy which helps *Kāla* perform his work has been called by Rāma as *Caṅḍī*—the destructive *Śakti.* Rāma gave the description with all her attributes and insignia. She is described as having the three *Guṇas* as the lotuses, blue *(Tamas)*, red *(Rajas)*, and white *(Sattwa)* on her breast.

We cannot conceive of fire without its power to burn; the water without its power to wet; or a snake without its wriggling motion. Similarly, *Kāla* and his destructive power are described by Rāma only to gives a graphic description, while the only thing which matters is that the ultimate culprit is the mind which in turn is a manifestation of *Ahaṁkāra*. It is *Ahaṁkāra* which breeds selfishness that stops us from having the 'eye' to recognise the noble men, having the capacity to guide us towards enlightenment. Further, *Ahaṁkāra* creates the feeling of jealousy in us, that nurtures the inability to consider others' happiness or pain as our own, thus making us insensitive. Cowardice is one of its main companions.

Most of the men we come across, including ourselves, have this nature, while it is very difficult to find the truly illumined. If one is able to give up the company of this ghost called *Ahaṁkāra,* then and only then, shall we be able to see through the illusion, that is, this *Saṁsāra.* Many of us are blissfully unaware that we are enveloped by this illusion, some of us who understand these things intellectually, are unable to restrain ourselves from getting involved with the temporal world made still smaller by our selfishness and limited vision of immediate needs.

Rāma was tortured by these thoughts, and he longed neither for life, nor death; neither pleasure, nor the company of relations and friends. These doubts had made him disinterested in performing the normal actions. He finally appealed to the great Munis to help him remove the confusion by unlocking the mysteries of *Ātman*. He became silent, eager to receive instructions from the enlightened Sages Viśwāmitra and Vasiṣṭha. Sage Vālmīki concludes this *Sarga* by comparing Rāma with a peacock standing in silent expectation, facing the dark thunder clouds of monsoon.

Sage Patañjali in his *Yoga Darśanaṃ,* has very crisply condensed the thoughts and feelings of Rāma in a single *Sūtra.*

> 'To the persons who have developed discrimination, all is misery on account of the pains resulting from *Pariṇāma*—change, *Tāpa*—anxiety, *Saṁskāra*—tendencies, as also due to *Guṇa-Vṛtti-Virodha*—the conflict between the functioning of the *Guṇas*—nature and *Vṛttis*—tendencies'.[16]

It is a common understanding that virtue and vice beget pleasurable and painful experiences respectively. We see in this *Sarga,* that Rāma was suffering in spite of his nobility. In spite of the availability of all material comforts he was not at all comfortable. Though he is learned in all the scriptural and secular knowledge, he was disturbed. The above *Sūtra* clarifies our doubt. In general, it means that all experiences are either actively or potentially full of misery to the wise person whose spiritual perception has awakened. Such a person observes that change, anxiety, habituation and conflicts between one's nature, and one's thoughts and desires are inherent in life. If we ponder over the four causes for misery given in the *Sūtra,* it becomes very clear.

The first affliction is the constant change which is referred to as *Pariṇāma.* Everything in this world is subject to change. Lord Buddha used to say, that one can never step into the same river twice because, the water is flowing incessantly. The Science has come to a conclusion that *everything* is changing. So actually, neither the river, nor the person remains the same. The phenomenon which stops us from recognising this eternal change has been called as *Māyā.*

The second affliction inherent to human life is the anxiety. All pleasures, indulgences and the so-called happiness are associated with anxiety directly or indirectly. For we are

---

16 परिणामतापसंस्कारदुःखैर्गुणवृत्तिविरोधाच्च दुःखमेव सर्वं विवेकिनः ॥ 2.15 ॥

either interested in avoiding what is painful or are involved with the acquisition or retention of happiness bringing objects. Most of us have such fears and anxieties gnawing our vitals constantly, though we may not acknowledge or be conscious of the fact. *Saṁskāra* means tendencies or habituation. Every experience we pass through produces an impression on our mind. If the experience gets repeated then the impression becomes deeper, resulting in our acquiring the habits of various kinds which make us get used to particular kind of environment, modes of living and pleasures.

The law of change however, is at work simultaneously, which is constantly changing our outer environment, circumstances and people. The result of this simultaneous action of two natural forces is that we are constantly acquiring new habits, getting used to new circumstances and also being forced out of them! This continuous necessity for adjustment in life is a source of constant discomfort and pain to every individual.

Guṇa-Vṛtti-Virodha is the opposition or conflict between the natural tendencies caused by the preponderance of one of the *Guṇas* and the states of mind which are constantly changing. For example, there is a lazy man who is predominantly *Tāmasic* by nature. He hates activity and is unfortunately placed in circumstances where he has to exert himself for his living. So he desires constantly a peaceful and inactive life and the result of this strong desire entertained persistently is that in his next birth he is placed in an environment where he is forced to be inactive. But in that life he may have the preponderance of *Rajas* in his nature and he therefore wants activity!

Nobody seems to be satisfied with his lot or circumstances. Everybody wants what he has not got! Our desires cannot by very nature of things find immediate fulfillment and there necessarily is a certain time lag in their realization. During this intervening period, our nature, temperament and the desires may undergo considerable change and when we face the fulfillment of our own desire, we may hardly believe that we ourselves desired what has now come to us.

The four types of afflictions inherent in life produce such conditions, that anybody who has developed *Viveka* or discrimination cannot possibly consider the so-called happiness of ordinary life as real happiness. While it is true that a man immersed in temporal pursuits of pleasures and power, life may appear to consist of a mixture of pleasures and pain, joys and sorrows.

A wise man whose spiritual faculties have awakened however, *all* life must appear full of misery and its temporary happiness merely a sugar-coated pill containing pain and suffering inside. This is the condition Rāma was in—the *'Atha'* position, when an intense aspiration to free oneself from life and its limitations, *Vairāgya* or a disinterest towards life of indulgence and involvement, had dawned.

The lengthening shadows cast by the caravan of camels and men with the background of giant red sun create a desire to reach home at the earliest. Similarly, when the scorching sun of endless desires sets, it makes way for the cool moon of *Vairāgya* or the disinterest creating an aspiration to seek the eternal *home* of the Self, for it is this *Vairāgya* or the *divine disinterest,* which sees through the mirages of oases in the form of little pleasures, that ordinary life has to offer.

3

The Story of Śuka

Near the hillocks and away from the villages, there are groves. The villagers call these *Nāgara-Vanas* or the snake groves. The canopy of foliage is so thick there, that hardly any light seeps through. The trees in various stages of development support the creepers embracing them, seemingly in a mood of mutual affection and attraction. Some of the trees after living a full life fall to become food for many a microbial and insect life, reflecting the perpetuation of life. One can see the birds extremely busy in every kind of activity. The squirrels, chameleons, lizards and monkeys, everyone *at home* with the grove. There is a pleasant smell of dampness of earth, wild flowers, fruits, fungi growing on the tree trunks, and of the flora in general. Though every experience mentioned, is an integral part of *survival* it is so mingled with everything else that one is enveloped in a state of timelessness and the taste of eternity is just around the corner. A tangible mood of interdependence can be perceived. It may be because, for hundreds of years neither a single tree in the grove has been touched, nor any creature has been killed by the villagers, owing to the feeling of awe and wonder.

There is a conceptual plan of building up so-called the 'Bio-reserves' by enclosing some forest areas for protecting plant and animal life. Long before this was even conceived, in India there existed this tradition of *Sacred Groves.* As with other aspects of our national character, these groves had a religiosity attached to them, not without certain ethical norms and codes. Precisely for this reason, the biologists find these *Nāgara or Sarpa Vanas* store houses of rich biological information. This information in turn, gives us glimpses into the probable story of evolution.

Theories of evolution have come to us through different mythological stories as for example, the concept of *'Daśāvatāra'*—Ten Incarnations[17] and also from the long painstaking contemplations and research of the scientists. The research in this direction still continues, making way for new and sometimes startling discoveries. The Sciences like Biology, Anthropology and Cosmology try to pierce through the mystery of the life-form and the physical universe.

Presently, the psychologists have begun to recognise the evolution of the mind. The mythology tries to go deeper through its symbology, recognising not only the mental evolution but the evolution of the *being* as a whole. The *'Matsya'* or the fish represents the organic life in the sea, and Kṛṣṇa the perfect *Avatāra* or the Incarnation. Through such stories, spirituality was introduced to common man for giving a purpose and a meaning to life. The biological evolution as such, slows down, if not stops with humankind, but the other deeper and subtler evolution begins with it.

This subtler evolution has two dimensions. The most obvious one, understood and appreciated by most of us, is the 'ability to survive', and survive successfully; to increase the level of efficiency in the field of activity one is in; the quantity of material acquisition like money and comforts, and the social achievements like status name and fame. It may be because of this fact that most of us are able to perceive only

---

17 *Matsya* : Fish; *Kūrma* : Tortoise; *Varāha* : Boar; *Narasiṁha* : Man lion; *Vāmana* : Man Dwarf; *Paraśurāma* : Rājasik man; *Rāma* : Sāttwik man; and *Kṛṣṇa* : The complete man.

the material aspect of existence; this popular dimension has been called the *'Preyas'*, the pleasant.

In some very rare cases it dawns on some, to seek for the other and deeper aspects. This dimensional mode of life has been called '*Śreyas*', the good. One may turn to this dimension due to different reasons depending on the nature and aptitude of the person, like misery and failure; desire for material objects; thirst for knowledge; or due to the conviction that the life as usually understood, is *incomplete* without the deeper dimension.

Rāma and the Buddha belonged to the category of persons with the conviction about the temporality of life with all its experiences.[18] They had the experiential understanding of life which creates a mental turmoil. All that is required by such a person is encouragement and a little push.

This *Sarga* is devoted to impress upon the seeker that Rāma was in an ideal condition to pursue the quest. On listening to the arguments presented by Rāma, about his disturbed state, Sage Viśwāmitra encouraged him through words of appreciation and endearment and compared the state he was in with that of Sage Śuka, that of ideal receptivity, for receiving the seeds of spirituality. Like a hungry man seeing food everywhere, Rāma was very eager to gather a hint here or a suggestion there to alleviate his painful disturbance. The moment he heard the name of Sage Śuka, he wanted to know more of him, his struggle and the ultimate triumph. Sage Viśwāmitra told him the story of Śuka.

Śuka, the son of Sage Vyāsa, had developed the proper understanding of life through self-effort. Even with all the

---

18 'Oh Arjuna! Four types of persons of good deeds worship me. The distressed, the seeker of knowledge, the seeker of means, and the man of knowledge, Oh descendent of Bharata!' —*The Bhagavadgītā*: 7-16.

scriptural as well as experiential knowledge, he had basic doubts about the origin of the universe and the *Māyā,* the illusive power which binds us to the material existence. He approached his father Vyāsa to seek clarification. When suitable explanation was given, Śuka remarked that the same explanation was given in the scriptures. Vyāsa understood that the father-son relationship was coming in between the proper communion. So, he directed Śuka to the enlightened King Janaka for removing his doubts.

In spite of the fact that King Janaka had been informed about the arrival of the sage, Śuka was made to wait for seven days outside the palace gates. Then for seven days he was made to wait inside the palace garden, and for the same period in the inner chambers of the palace where beautiful maidens attending on him with choicest food and other forms of luxury. Whether he was placed in insulting situations or otherwise, Śuka never lost his equipoise. Noting that the sage had fulfilled the required conditions of patience and equanimity, Janaka met the sage and asked the purpose of his visit.

Śuka repeated the question he had asked his father. The philosopher king gave the very same reply as was given by his father pointing to the Non-Dual state. Śuka observed that these very explanations were given in the scriptures and also by his revered father. He said that he was unable to understand why at all, *Māyā* originates in the Lofty state of Reality.

Royal sage Janaka said that Śuka had already experienced the state, hence, had not come under the influence of pairs of opposites. The only thing that remained to be done was to transcend the delusion of *Māyā* altogether. And this was possible only by uninterrupted experience of Brahman, the One without the second. Enlightened Janaka then initiated Śuka into the mysteries of *Ātman* through direct experience. Having thus dissolved the vibration of 'I-ness', stainless Śuka attained quiescence and was freed from the pangs of birth, and the agonies of death. Concluding the story, Sage Viśwāmitra asked Rāma to follow the path that would be taught by Vasiṣṭha.

A free mind is that which is *non-identified* with enjoyments and sufferings. The natural inclination of the mind towards the objects of senses strengthens the bondage. Viśwāmitra made a wonderful statement:

> 'Wise say that the thinning of *Vāsanās* alone leads to freedom; The strengthening of *Vāsanās* towards sense-objects is bondage'.[9]

A *Jīvanamukta* is one who is effortlessly indifferent to sense enjoyments. The fact, Rāma had been able to analyse the intricacies of life, itself showed that the light of *Viveka* had dawned on him, and the doubts afflicting the mind could be eliminated by the enlightened Sage Vasiṣṭha, who was aware of the mystery of time, being the Preceptor of the world in this *Mahāyuga.* He then requested Sage Vasiṣṭha to initiate Rāma into the mysteries of *Ātman* through *Jñāna* stories.

The natural biological evolution has taken billions of years, from the simple to more and more complex organisms, until it has reached human beings, the most complex and evolved of all the species. After man, the evolution becomes deliberate. Because, among all the species, only human beings have the total freedom to choose or *not to choose* the evolution.

And very rarely do some persons choose to continue their subtler evolution. Just as the force of gravitation pulls us towards the earth, the force of attraction in the form of sense indulgence and mental involvement retards our progress. We should realise that indulgence and involvement keep the mind turned outward. And as far as human beings are concerned, the only direction of evolution is the inward. This

---

19 वासना तानवं राम मोक्ष इत्युच्यते बुधैः ।
पदार्थ वासनादार्ढ्यं बन्ध इत्यभिधीयते ।। 1.3.57 ।।

view, does not be-little the external indulgence but only makes a statement of fact for making us aware of the different dimensions of human search.

There have been two types of persons who have sought Enlightenment, which happens to be the culmination of all evolution. The first type is that which has experienced the world in all its phases, to the point of satiation. It is believed that the twenty-four Buddhas as well as the same number of Jain *Tīrthaṅkaras* were from the Royal lineage. And all of them had left their kingdoms and given up the life of luxury and preferred to embrace the life of mendicants. It may or may not be a historical fact, but it is definitely indicative of the fact that they belonged to a class of persons who chose the inner dimension after getting fully convinced about the temporality of the grosser facet of existence. Coincidentally, persons like Rāma and Kṛṣṇa, who are considered as the incarnations by the Hindu pantheon, had a royal background. It could be that if one has totally seen through the incompleteness of *only* the 'survival' aspect of life, through meaninglessness of sense indulgence, and of the other obsessive mental involvements like possessiveness and greed for power, based on one's own experience, the quest for the permanent becomes sincere and intense.

The second type of persons has been what may be called the 'intelligent'. They may not have the first-hand experience—at least in that very life, but their power of observation is so remarkable, that they do not waste their precious time or energy on the superficial. Persons like Kabirdās—a weaver, Raidās—a cobbler, Gorā Kumbhār—a potter, Sadanā—a barber and others like them were from the common lot, who neither abandoned their trades, nor found it necessary to do so. They had 'seen-through' the shallowness of all aspects of survival through the experience of others. Though most of them were unlettered as far as formal education is concerned, what they have said through their songs is enough to give us an insight into the level of their understanding. Whatever be the background, the fact remains that a seeker should have the proper understanding of life.

Existence may be compared to a pyramid with a broad base and a tapering vertex. The base constitutes the least evolved of the species, while the peak, the Enlightenment. Beauty of our culture is that it accepts all the phases of evolution as necessary. When one climbs a pyramid or a mountain, one starts going *away* from the ground. As and when one starts climbing the ladder of evolution, one starts giving less and less importance to basic urges and hunger. And as one starts becoming more attentive to the goal, the attraction for the lower drops off totally on its own because one gets possessed by the devotion to Enlightenment, the summit. The main difference between humankind and other species is that the evolution for other species is a matter of course, while for human beings it is a matter of choice.

We are all related very intricately through our interdependence, and are the important members—each one of us, of the 'Sacred Grove', that is this Web of existence. A *Sādhaka* or seeker tries to recognise his own place in the grove and to stretch to the capacity, even beyond his limits, for making himself eligible for the union with the Most Sacred—One without the second. His total being concentrated on the ideal he is ready to sacrifice everything for achieving his end. And such a person comes to be called as a *Mumukṣu.*

THE DIVINE LONGING

Mumukṣu Prakaraṇa

1

Conduct of a Seeker

The Himalayas, the youngest mountains of planet earth, are perhaps the most magnificent, not only because of their size, but due to the richness of flora and fauna. Rarest of flowers, animals and an infinite species of birds dwell there. The crystal clear, emerald green-blue lakes make perfect haven for a variety of aquatic life. One look is quite sufficient for a sensitive person to see through the industriousness involved in Nature. The pains which the birds take to build their nests; the labour which bees and ants put in gathering food; or the exertion of the migratory birds to move thousands of miles to protect and preserve their species from polar winters. The whole universe—from an atom to a galaxy, is eternally active, to the point of restlessness. Polar bears, snakes, frogs and many other living beings hibernate during long winters and hostile weather, when the food becomes scarce. The simple rule of existence appears to be *no activity means, no food!*

This is also the case with human beings. We not only observe this in individuals but even in nations. The developed nations have always been very industrious, while the developing or the under-developed nations have been less so. This is not only true from the materialistic or survival point of view, but more relevant, from the point of the inner growth of life. It is believed by majority of the Indian masses that the effort is not very essential for a person to grow spiritually.

Some of the philosophers have gone to the extent of saying that the Ultimate State is characterized by effortlessness. And so, how is it possible to achieve effortlessness through effort, they ask. The argument sounds very logical.

Then the Bhakti or path of devotion advocates total reliance on the God or the Chosen Deity, an attitude of total 'let go', because unless and until the individual 'I' gets eliminated one cannot possibly have union with Truth. And they ask, 'who' is there to make the effort as, everything is done by 'Him'? Then there is this common understanding of our masses that man's actions are governed by Providence, one may call it God, or Truth or Reality. These streams of thought are very 'lofty' in themselves. But unfortunately, they become very convenient 'philosophies' for a man with lethargic disposition.

Such thoughts have gone so deep into our national psyche that, we are what we are—incorrigibly lazy. The result is that we can be totally exploited by the politicians, or the bureaucrats or the businessmen for decades, without disturbing our pseudo-poise in the least! All these limitations of our society have convinced some of us that all spiritual practices tend to make us lazier, and force us to take an escapist attitude towards life. Mostly this observation is true, but in no way it means that, spirituality encourages lethargy.

Contrary to common belief, *Pauruṣa* or human effort has always been lauded in Indian cultural heritage. *Upaniṣads* and other *Vedāntic* texts have wonderful statements that evoke fearlessness, the will to pursue the highest ideal, as well as the confidence for generating infinite energy already within. However, these great scriptures have been beyond common man's reach, and only that which is *convenient* has seeped through. It has always been so, that if the ideal is beyond our reach, then we tend to bring it down, within our reach, through the approach of convenience!

While *Upaniṣads* goad us to give less importance to the external, they also recommend extreme watchfulness and care while treading the inner path for freeing us from the dependency on the sense-objects. Such texts are called the *Ucchāstras*. There are the other scriptures which give us the external facets of life, dealing with those efforts which increase our material and creature comforts, thus encouraging the dependency on the world of objects. These are included in the secular literature.

Our society always respects such persons, who prefer the inner quest and growth to the outer life of day-to-day subsistence, unconsciously realising that it requires greater effort and grit. The ideal pre-requisites of a person who takes up such life, the problems she or he faces, and the recommended suggestions to not only solve the problems, but to continue the journey with the same initial enthusiasm, form the subject of this episode, entitled *Mumukṣu-Vyavahāra-Prakaraṇa*.

One learns, the process of understanding life through personal experience, as well as the purpose and other possibilities or options available in life, through the *Ucchāstras* or scriptures dealing with the spiritual. The study of such scriptures is fulfilling as it is absorbing both intellectually and emotionally. Asking questions about existence gives a peculiar satisfaction. The first problem one faces is the lack of grit to overcome the attraction for intellectual dialogue and to commence the *quest*. Most of us remain as *collectors of information*. It is very tempting and easy to stagnate in the joys of philosophical discussions because, all that is required is a little common sense and a flair for words.

The act of plunging headlong into a life of seeking is very demanding. The moment of decision to embark on such mysterious journey into oneself, can be called as the *turning point*, which has to happen to every person sooner or later. The factors which hasten this turning point, have been called by Vasiṣṭha as *Śuddha,* the pure *Vāsanās* or tendencies and which delay this moment, as *Malīna,* the impure *Vāsanās.* Pure *Vāsanās* are those tendencies which help the aspirant by creating a proper milieu. While the impure *Vāsanās* tie the aspirant to a life of stagnation. All our actions are governed by the self-made tendencies formed by *repeated* action. That is why, the Sage recommended the enhancement of *Śubha Vāsanās* which help in development of right effort (or *Samma-Vāyāma* of Lord Buddha).

Sage Vālmīki, the author introduces the story of Sage Vasiṣṭha. This is to remember in all gratefulness and humility, the source of wisdom that is being shared. The feeling in turn absolves him from the fear of the ego or pride—'I' am the teacher, which is the most dangerous of the impediments in spiritual life. The one who is sharing the wisdom with the aspirant becomes like a hollow flute through which the Divine can flow. In spite of the fact that Vasiṣṭha happens to be the foremost of the *Brahmarṣis,* he talks of his own discipleship. This also makes the receiver of wisdom more receptive, as he gets a conviction that it is possible to achieve the objective. Another reason is to bring home the point that the present *Guru* was also a disciple with similar if not the same problems and doubts in the mind. All this creates confidence in the disciple, that if the person teaching him presently can overcome the obstacles and reach the Ultimate Goal, he too can.

Vasiṣṭha began his teaching by stressing the importance of the mutual recognition between *Śiṣya,* the disciple and *Guru,* the preceptor. The most eligible disciple is one who can differentiate between an enlightened Master and an ordinary teacher. The real *Guru* never wastes his time and energy on an aspirant still under the influence of his lower mind and senses. By this it is meant, that unless one has transcended lower hungers, one cannot possibly recognise the *Guru* even if he is in front of his eyes!

Four sentinels guarding the gates of *Mukti* or Liberation are: *Śama*—patience, *Vicāra*—self-analysis, *Saṁtoṣa*—contentment and *Sādhu Saṅga*—association of the wise. The greatest of the deterrents on this journey is impatience, which is more so in contemporary times. We are always complaining about the non-availability of time and the avoidable impatience is on the rise. This is very much there in all the fields and facets of life. Consequently, speed dominates our life and in this spirituality is not an exception. One of the most common complaints of those who take to any practice—*Āsanas,* or *Prāṇāyāma* or meditation—is that in spite of practising it sincerely for *six months* (the period of time is stressed!) no appreciable progress is observed. This 'hurry to achieve' is to be totally avoided through the golden quality of *Śama*—sweet patience.

Every one of us has the capacity to observe, and many times we do ask fundamental questions. For instance, we observe a person suffering, perhaps, even to fulfill the basic needs of his family; he is known for his uprightness, honesty and integrity. We also see another person leading a very lavish, easy and comfortable life. But he is notorious as a very corrupt man. Our conclusion is: it is foolish and suicidal to be honest, and wise and pragmatic to be otherwise. However, we ignore the fearlessness of the first man, and the hypocrisy or the sycophancy of the second man. We observe, but tend to draw hasty conclusions. This is all right for material success, but for taking up the quest it is totally different, because such cleverness is very dangerous for a seeker. A seeker questions the normal conclusions which are ordinarily taken for granted. He questions his own experiences, life and death, and draws his own conclusions based on self-observation. *Vicāra* is taken as self-analysis, and this scripture suggests some practical methods leading to deeper meditative practices.

Saṁtoṣa—contentment is the third noble quality to be developed by a seeker. Discontent and expectation are the principal causes of impatience. We become impatient with the situation we are in, due to discontent and with other persons, due to our expectations. But *Saṁtoṣa* should not be taken as a *consolation,* which is only like a soother in a crying baby's mouth! The mood of contentment dawns, only when one has the *conviction* that going after the objects of senses, power and position is very much like chasing shadows or horizons, as there is nothing like a shadow or a horizon! And another thing is that he or she will have a feeling of satiation, either from the experiences of present or past lives. The *Saṁtoṣa* achieved through *Śama* and *Vicāra* brings in equipoise in conflicting and trying situations. However, we must not think that the person becomes cold and does not respond. On the contrary, she or he becomes more sensitive and large hearted to look at things more objectively as there is *no involvement.*

Initially, when this 'madness'—as it is normally called—starts in an aspirant seeker, others create all possible hurdles and also subtle atmosphere of hostility. It is not that they do not understand the nobility in the act, but only that, it is abnormal. Used, that most of us are to tread the beaten track, we would never like our near and dear one to adopt a dangerous way of life! Many if not most of the time such family or social hurdles cannot be crossed, and the aspiration gets aborted, at the stage of seedling itself. At such times, the aspirant needs the company of someone who has passed through the similar situation. If this happens, it is likely, that the aspiration becomes a quest.

Even the dawn of quest may be possible with a little determination and courage of the aspirant. But when the quest has started, *Sādhusaṅga*—association of the wise and experienced, comes as a real boon for facing the internal problems which are more difficult and stubborn. Praising this fourth sentinel of *Mukti*, Vasiṣṭha said that it is like the holy *Gaṅgā,* purifying everyone who approaches her. But there is a problem: it is difficult if not impossible, to find such Enlightened persons! It is not because such persons are not available in this age of *Kali*! Such persons have always been existing though in a microscopic minority to offer their guidance. But to recognise such persons, one needs certain pre-requisites or special eyes. When there is this burning thirst, and longing, one can receive the grace of company of *Sādhus*.

Paramahansa Shri Ramakrishna gave a beautiful simile to seekers: every seeker has a lamp, cotton and oil. As soon as the aspirant finishes cleaning, preparing the wick and oiling it, the *Guru* who has the matches, will appear and light it! And if the lamp is not ready, neither will he recognise the *Guru*, nor will the *Guru* be able to do anything. We can take the lamp to be *Śama,* cotton to be *Saṁtoṣa,* oil to be *Vicāra.* When these are ready, we are bound to get *Sādhusaṅga.* But till such time we can always take the help and guidance from the books depicting the conversations of the realised saints and other spiritual lore, which help in developing the three qualities.

These four sentinels on the gates of *Mukti* can give us freedom from the misery born out of our involvement with the world. Sage Vasiṣṭha urged Rāma to listen carefully, to what he had to say, which would have a mellowing effect on the limitations like infatuation and greed, and the mind would become like a wave-less lake in the autumn; that the stories which would be narrated by him would relieve the pining mind of its delusion. One must be careful however, to probe into the underlying significance, without just caring for the surface attributes or word meanings. Keeping these in mind if one listens to the stories, all the paradoxes such as attraction and aversion will vanish. Persons who have acquired such wisdom will never again be deluded.

The persons treading the path of *Ātmavicāra* never get afflicted by the all powerful *Māyā* and can maintain the equipoise. Such noble persons never waste their time, energy or talent on anything which directly or indirectly distracts them from the chosen path. In the absence of the company of the wise one must perform only such actions which create *Śubhavāsanās,* and seek the company of such *Śāstras* which help one in persevering the journey. Having totally devoted every moment for *Vicāra* the state of *Jīvanamukti* dawns. For such a *Jīvanamukta,* or who is an enlightened person, nothing is ordinary, as everything is Divine, and nothing is extra-ordinary as the essence of everything is known.

Though one is in such a lofty state, he moves about in the world like any other men, because he does not have anything to *show* as he is totally free from the desires and cravings, as he does not have even an iota of 'I-ness'. Having attained this state, the repeated vacillation from womb to tomb stops. But he continues the *Ātmavicāra* till the quiescent state of *Turīya*—the fourth, dawns on him. Though this state cannot be described in words we can know, that a person has attained this state from his behaviour, attitude and bliss he permeates to others. At this stage, this scripture gives us some very useful hints about the right method of *Ātmavicāra.* One should have the openness of mind so as to be able to listen even to a child, if they are consistent with the *Śāstras,* the words of the *Guru* and the self-experience. If they are not consistent with these touch-stones, they are to be rejected even if they are coming from the lips of the Creator Himself.

To convey that One Principle, beyond thought and description, and to create the mood of *Jñāna* in us, analogies are given. Though many persons negate these analogies with the argument that *Brahmajñāna* is beyond analogies, they are useful for a sincere seeker. Moreover, such persons who busy themselves in argument, tend to stagnate in mere verbal jugglery, and can be called ignorant. At the same time, Sage Vasiṣṭha warned that we should also not get stuck to the stories and analogies, as they only serve as fingers to point the moon. And getting involved with them would be as foolish, as taking the pointing fingers to be the moon! So one should neither be *against* the stories and analogies, nor *for* them, but be *open-minded* to make use of them to reach the Ultimate Goal. The restless activity seen in all creatures brings in tangible results and fruits to them. But it also makes them tired forcing them to sleep, characterized by lack of awareness. Moreover, such activity is in itself somnambulistic. For a seeker the activity has a different significance. It is *without rest,* which brings him peace, alertness and awareness till he unites with the One without the second. His path which starts with difficulties, leads him towards the enlightenment. But yes, his achievement may not be perceived by others, which is why the so-called normal, avoid the path chosen by him. They take it to be a tunnel leading one into darkness, without realising that the beaten track chosen by them does not have anything except repetitive births and deaths. This entire *Prakaraṇa* deals with the code of conduct of an aspirant.

THE ORIGIN

Utpatti Prakaraṇa

1

The Story of Ākāśaja

It is difficult to imagine that the same spot was covered totally with spotless snow a few weeks before; that the plant or animal life was practically non-perceptible; that the hills of snow would ever support any life except the coniferous trees which stand, bearing witness to all that happens here. But presently, the once desolate and cold ground has received the warmth from the bright sun, allowing life processes to start. The thick-soft-alive carpet of lemon yellow flowers on the ground is a proof to this. The other trees which were bald and leafless in winter are laden with flowers. Apple trees are dressed in light pink blossoms, the cherry and the pears with white ones. There is a very pleasant smell in the atmosphere as if Mother Nature is dressed up for the divine celebration. The hibernating life is slowly waking up, nay, stretching! The whole valley is reverberating with the sound of birds which have returned. The exhilaration in their tone is suggestive, that they may be exchanging stories of their adventure during the migratory period. The spring is here. Very few places in our great Country exhibit such distinct change of seasons. The place is the Valley of Kashmir.

Nature has many lessons to teach for a receptive learner, through the phenomenon of regularity in planetary movement, or the social behaviour of animals. But the readiness and receptivity stand as the great sentinels guarding the palace of understanding. Only a very few persons are able to befriend these sentinels and to seek entry into the palace. Carlos Castaneda, a graduate student of Anthropology from the University of California, Los Angeles, met an old Yaqui Indian, whom he calls Don Juan, and spent many years of apprenticeship under him. He learnt many deeper aspects of life. He has documented the meetings in a series of books. The meetings mostly took place in some breath-taking scenic spots, and the teachings are based on the observation of natural phenomena. When Carlos presented the first copy of the book to the Master, a very interesting conversation followed.

Carlos said that he had been receiving letters from many persons voicing their opinion that it is wrong to write on the apprenticeship. And that perhaps he was revealing things he should not. Don Juan said that it does not matter what one reveals or what one keeps to oneself. And that everything we do, everything we are, depends on our *personal power.* That if we have enough of it, one word uttered to us might change the course of our lives. But if we do not have enough *personal power,* the most magnificent piece of wisdom may be revealed to us but, that revelation will not make the least difference. He then lowered his voice as if he was disclosing a confidential matter to Carlos :

> 'I'm going to utter perhaps the greatest piece of knowledge anyone can voice. Let me see what you can do with it.
>
> 'Do you know that at this very moment you are surrounded by eternity? And do you know that you can use that eternity, if you so desire?... Do you know that you can extend yourself forever in any of the directions? Do you know that one moment can be eternity? This isn't a riddle; it's a fact, but only if you mount that moment and use it to take the totality of yourself forever in any direction.'

Staring at Carlos, Don Juan continued, smiling,

> 'You didn't have this knowledge before, now you do, I have revealed it to you, but it doesn't make a bit of difference, because you don't have enough personal power to utilize my revelation'.[20]

The understanding eludes most of us, while very few amongst us succeed in learning from the book of existence. This is because we waste our precious energy over the trivia of life by taking them seriously, and taking those issues lightly, on which the very purpose of life rests. We are more than satisfied by engaging ourselves in the toys—as called by Shri Ramakrishna—be it struggle for 'survival' or even the search for possessions, or craving for name and fame, or the madness for power over others. After *growing up* and discovering the other dimensions of life, one starts observing life in all its intricacies. Only when one becomes a *Mumukṣu* by adopting the way of life characterized by *Śama, Saṁtoṣa,* and *Vicāra,* can one benefit from the truths and hints laid down in this scripture. Because, wisdom can dawn on only such a person, though a scholar may understand *intellectually* and offer opinions or at the most interpretations. The capacity to transform one's life through such scriptures like *Yoga Vāsiṣṭha* is what is meant by don Juan when he says one should have *personal power.*

The feeling of frustration, depression, misery, laughter and joy are peculiar to human beings. No doubt, the other animals too feel the discomfort or otherwise. But they are not *obsessed* by these very feelings. These very feelings—the negative as well as the positive—can become instrumental in giving birth to some of the most nagging questions arising in the human mind: 'What is the purpose of this universe and life?'; 'What is its origin?'; "Where does it all originate?'

---

20 *Tales of Power* by Carlos Castaneda, Penguin Books, 1974, pp. 14-15.

Having stressed the necessity of preparation sufficiently in the two earlier *Prakaraṇas,* Sage Vālmīki proceeds to enter into the detailed teachings of Muni Vasiṣṭha through this episode entitled *Utpatti Prakaraṇa* or the Origin. Mostly, we attribute our happiness and misery to the world outside. It is quite natural that we either get *positively involved* with it, through our attraction when we are happy, by trying to possess it; or we get *negatively involved* with it, through our aversion for it when we become unhappy, as we try to escape from it. The extreme involvement and the resultant misery becomes the starting point for the fundamental questions.

The human attempt to seek answers to these questions has formed the Science of Philosophy. We have also known that most of the explanations offered are less than satisfactory as each view is either partial and may even be a fantasy of the mind. We find innumerable explanations on the origin of the Universe each more confusing than the other! Science has been the most influential development of the human mind. It says that if we ask the right question in a right way, the question itself opens the doors to the truth. If we go through our ancient literature, we find that this conclusion is only an echo of the depth of understanding of our sages. Some of them asked : '*who* perceives the universe?' The answer is obviously 'I', as behind every possible experience or action, it is there ('I' see, 'I' feel, 'I' think etc.).

This century has given many a shock to some of the basic conclusions of Science which were so far taken for granted. 'Objective observation' had been the founding principle of science. Theory of Relativity, Quantum Physics, has conclusively proved through a series of experiments and observations, that there is nothing like *objective* observation. A simple illustration is that of a rainbow. Each one of us *perceives the rainbow in her or his own way.* In other words the rainbow is unique and personal to each one of us, though we all may be seeing it at the same time! This only means that the rainbow is there for one as long as one perceives it.

We may stretch this conclusion a little further—as our sages did. The cause of the *perception,* we call the world, is 'I' or the subject. So the question takes a more fundamental form : 'How does this "I" originate?' and 'What is this "I"?' *Yoga Vāsiṣṭha* advocates *'Dṛṣṭi-Sṛṣṭi-Vāda'* which holds that the world exists only so long as *it is perceived* : *'Manodṛśyam Idaṃ Sarvaṃ'* (this whole world is the object perceived by the mind). In other words, whatever is experienced or the world of objects is nothing but a creation of the mind. A standard example is given in *Vedānta,* as it tries to suggest at this conclusion. Like the vast ocean comprising of waves, froth etc., is only water, this world of objects is nothing but "I" the perceiver. It should be remembered that all explanations are limited and never exhaustive. They all have only one practical use, which help our inner growth. If we extend the explanations or similes, we have the danger of getting involved with mere verbal jugglery.

In an interesting game called 'communication' the participants sit in a circle. One person begins by whispering a message to his neighbour which in turn is conveyed to his neighbour, until the message *returns* to the person who started it. Most of the time the message is totally distorted! Something very similar happens when there is the perception of the external world. The senses receive the external stimuli—sound, light, touch, taste and smell, and pass them on to the *Manas. Manas* interprets according to its likes and dislikes and either passes it on to *Buddhiḥ* or rejects them if it is not important in *its* view! *Buddhiḥ* again understands the stimuli with the help of memory. Such sense perception happens to be the basis of scientific experiments and thus the knowledge in general.

According to *Vedānta,* such experience is still *Parokṣa* or indirect, because it needs the mediation of at least four entities: *Manas* or mind *buddhiḥ* or intellect, *Citta* or memory, and *Ahaṁkāra* or the 'I-ness'. All the interpretations by mediators are governed by the likes and dislikes of the mind, notions and obsessions of the intellect, and, pride and prejudice of the ego, which have been termed as *Saṁkalpa* and *Vikalpa* by sage Vasiṣṭha. Yet almost all of us give so much importance to our sense perceptions that we get ourselves miserably involved with them. This is due to the fact, that by very nature these instruments (senses, *Manas* and *Buddhiḥ)* are necessarily extrovertish. Because, their very function depends on *seeking their corresponding objects.* All such objects have been included in the word '*Dṛśya'* or *the seen* in this *Sarga.* And the experiencer has been referred to as *'Draṣṭā'* or *the seer.*

Like all *Vedāntic* texts, *Vāśiṣṭha* also advocates that *Jīva* and its grosser companions (I-ness, *Citta, Buddhiḥ, Manas,* senses and body) are nothing but the manifestations of the Non-Dual Principle. It is only that, the *Jīva* gets so involved with grosser companions that it totally forgets about its own root in The Principle. Shri Ramakrishna used to give an example from *Purāṇas,* to illustrate the power of *Māyā* which creates this forgetfulness:

> 'Viṣṇu incarnated himself as a sow in order to kill the demon Hiraṇyākṣa. After killing the demon, the sow remained quite happy with her young ones. Forgetting her real nature, she was suckling them very contentedly. The gods in heaven could not persuade Viṣṇu to relinquish His sow's body and return to the celestial regions. He was absorbed in the happiness of His beast form. After consulting among themselves, the gods sent Śiva to the sow, who asked the sow, 'Why have you forgotten yourself'?
>
> Viṣṇu replied through the sow's body, 'Why. I am quite happy here'. Thereupon with a stroke of his trident Śiva destroyed the sow's body and Viṣṇu went back to heaven'.[21]

---

21 *Gospel of Shri Ramakrishna* by M, Vol. I, IXth impression, p. 226, Shri Ramakrishna Math, Mylapore, Madras.

It is like our day-to-day experience of the dream. As long as the dream exists, we never realise that it is unreal. When we are awake, we cannot possibly imagine that there can be any truth in it! And yet, all the characters, scene and everything else is nothing but the *dreamer's creation.* Similarly, this universe with all its multiplicity is only a manifestation of the Supreme Principle.

But the mechanism of this manifestation is however, very mysterious. Once this happens, *Jīva* gets manifested itself into *Saṁkalpa*—conception, which then becomes a *Vikalpa*—false notion, and finally, into the world of multiplicity. The word 'ornament' signifies nothing but the material with which it is made. Similarly, the word 'universe' means Brahman. The entire process of *Saṁkalpa-Vikalpa-multiplicity* has been named as the *Saṁsāra*—that which is repetitive like a circle, vicious or virtuous, depending entirely on the approach. That is why, it has been called the *Saṁsāra Cakra*—the wheel of *Saṁsāra.* This must be very obvious from the monotonous nature of our ordinary life dominated by almost accidental birth, the struggle for survival and finally death.

Sage Vasiṣṭha then proceeded to tell about *Saṁsāra* and the nature of bondage. The involvement of *Draṣṭā* (seer) with *Dṛśya* (seen) is bondage, and the lack of it is liberation. The seen, which is the *Jagat,* is the conception of multiplicity of 'I' and 'you', the prime *Saṁkalpa,* the root cause of bondage. The moment all multiplicity merges into the 'seer' without any re-manifestation, the Liberation is attained. But the seed of *'Dṛśya'* is dormant in the seer himself in the form of *Saṁskāras* and *Vāsanās.* The venerable sage then began his detailed teaching with the story of Ākāśaja—the son of Ākāśa.

Once upon a time, in the lineage of Brahman, Ākāśaja was born, with *Jñānākāśa* as his cause. He enjoyed uninterrupted *Samādhi* and Oneness with all creatures. Having seen him for a long period of time, Kāla the conditioned time, wondered how he was unable to devour Ākāśaja until then, while nothing in the universe is beyond his affliction. With an intention of destroying Ākāśaja, Kāla approached the twice-born's[22] habitat, and was dazzled by the spiritual aura. Undaunted, Kāla pierced through and unsuccessfully tried to seize him, as Ākāśaja was immovable like the Divine Will.

Kāla approached Yama—the God of Death for counsel relating his difficulty. Yama said that this universe has arisen through activity, and activity alone can destroy it. That the weapon of destruction in this universe is the impression of past actions. And asked Kāla to look for the past *Karmas* (actions). When again Ākāśaja was approached for the purpose, Kāla did not find any. When Yama was informed of this he observed after much deliberation, that Ākāśaja was born out of pure *Ākāśa* and was none other than imperishable *Jñānākāśa,* which does not have any cause, either instrumental or material.[23] That was why, he was not affected by any action and there was no impression on him. Having heard Yama, Kāla returned to his own realm in great awe.

Listening to this story, Rāma observed that the son of *Jñānākāśa* was none other than Brahman, self-created, Non-Dual and of the nature of *Vijñāna* (that which transcends knowledge). Sage Vasiṣṭha replied that the story clarified it further and continued: At the end of the *Manvantara,* the confident Kāla who had always swallowed the universe at such times, again tried unsuccessfully to swallow Ākāśaja. Yama said to Kāla that it was impossible to destroy *Jñānākāśa* which transcends all elements and thus beyond his grasp. Only on manifestation it becomes *Cidākāśa*—the psychic plane, and then *Bhūtākāśa*—the elemental plane comprising of space, air, fire, water and earth and then only, into the senses and

---

22 Twice born refers to the enlightened person who is born to his parents bodily, and to his Guru spiritually.

23 Instrumental cause, is the intelligent cause, and Material cause is the gross cause, like the potter and the clay respectively for pot.

finally, the body having dimensions. Yet mysteriously, *Jñānākāśa* remains unaffected and beyond form.

Rāma raised a genuine doubt: while all souls possess two types of bodies, the lasting *Ātivāhika* and the temporary *Ādibhautika,*[24] how is it that Brahmā possesses only *Ātivāhika?* The Sage replied that all *Jīvas* have two causes: Brahman, the instrumental cause, and the universe, the elemental and material cause, due to which they have the two bodies corresponding to each cause. But Brahmā has *Brahman* as the only cause. This universe is nothing but a self-evolved modification of the mind and at the same time has the nature of pure consciousness. Rāma further sought clarification for this paradoxical statement. The *Ṛṣi* replied smilingly.

Non-Dual *Brahman* is causeless, all pervading, and eternal. This can manifest itself sportively into *Brahmākāśa,* the realm of Brahmā, the Creator who also has similar nature. But when there is *Saṁkalpa*—the tendency for multiplicity and to notionalize—it becomes *Cidākāśa,* the realm of thought, which is all pervading but has a cause and is *not* eternal. In *Cidākāśa,* the mental activity has come to a point where the *Vikalpa*—the conception of fancy—the mythical 'I', 'you', and 'others', commences.

With this, there arises the need for other mental functions and *Bhūtākāśa,* the realm of gross elements. Like a dream generating other dreams, the mind generates the differentiation and multiplicity. Through such affinity for multiplicity it has a fluctuating nature such as confusion, excitement, intoxication of pride and moroseness of depression. During the *Mahāpralaya* or the great deluge, *Ākāśas* get absorbed in their subtlest essence and the solitary silence. This state of Quiescence though beyond words, has been named variously by the experienced persons.

---

24 *Ātivāhika* is the subtle body with which the Jîva lives, separated from the *Ādibhautika* the gross physical body.

At this juncture, Rāma observed that it must be extremely difficult if not impossible to achieve this State. With an encouragement in his tone the Sage said, it does seem difficult but it is perfectly possible. For if it was impossible, then there would be none who are experienced. Only one requires patient perseverance, as also the company of the wise. The effort should be to annihilate *Aśubha Vāsanās* which force the consciousness *outside,* that is, towards the grosser manifestations. This can be done by developing *Śubha Vāsanās* and be-friending the four sentinels of the gates of *Mukti.*

This *Sarga* introduces the seeker to the graded manifestations from the Causeless and Limitless Brahman to the gross physical body, through the concept of *Jñānākāśa, Cidākāśa* and *Bhūtākāśa.* The first vibration of manifestation has been called *Saṁkalpa,* which takes the form of *Jīva.* It is like a stone kept on top of a mountain starting to roll and gain momentum. As this manifested state becomes habitual, it is taken to be a natural state. Shri Ramakrishna Paramahansa used to say that there are three types of men: those bound by fetters of the world, the seekers after liberation, and the liberated or the ever-free. This was illustrated through the example of fish:

> 'Suppose a net has been cast into a lake to catch fish. Some fish are so clever that they are never caught in the net. They are like the ever-free. But most of the fish are entangled in the net. Some of them try to free themselves from it, and they are like those who seek liberation. But not all the fish that struggle succeed. A very few do jump out of the net, making a big splash in the water. Then the fishermen shout "Look! There goes a big one!" But most of the fish caught in the net cannot escape, nor do they make any effort to get out. On the contrary, they burrow into the mud with the net in their mouth and lie there quietly, thinking, "We need not fear anymore; we are quite safe here!" But the poor

things do not know that the fishermen will drag them out with the net. These are like the men bound to the world'.[25]

Limitedness gives us a feeling of security and safety. This feeling of contraction caused by *Saṁkalpa,* ends in the state of 'I am the body' feeling. This has been crisply given in Theory of *Kleśas* by Sage Patañjali in his *Yoga Darśanaṃ.* He classifies the *Kleśas* into five:

> '*Avidyā*—the lack of awareness of Reality, *Asmitā*—the sense of "I-am-ness", *Rāga*— attractions (likes), *Dweṣa*— aversions (dislikes) towards objects and *Abhiniveśa*— clinging to life, are the great afflictions or causes of miseries in life'.[26]

Kleśa is normally taken as misery, but Sage Patañjali takes it as the cause for misery. The *Kleśas* enumerated in *Yoga Darśanaṃ* at the individual level help us to understand the deeper aspects in *Yoga Vāsiṣṭha* which takes a much broader perspective and deals *Avidyā* on a cosmic level. If we try to represent the *Kleśas* diagrammatically :

A		
V		
	A	RĀGA
I	S	
	M	
D	I	ABHINIVEŚA
	T	
Y	Ā	DWEṢA
Ā		

---

25 *The Gospel of Shri Ramakrishna* by M, Vol. I, IXth impression, 1988, pp. 86-87, Shri Ramakrishna Math, Madras.

26 अविद्यास्मितारागद्वेषाभिनिवेशाः क्लेशाः ॥ 2.3 ॥

Combining the concepts presented by *Yoga Vāsiṣṭha* and *Yoga Darśanaṃ,* a clearer picture emerges which is very helpful to a seeker. At the *Jīva* (individual) level the theory of *Kleśas* is very useful. *Avidyā* is the fundamental cause of other *Kleśas* according to the *Sūtra*:

> '*Avidyā* is the breeding ground for all that follow *(Asmitā, Rāga, Dweṣa* and *Abhiniveśa)* whether they are dormant, attenuated, overpowered or expanded'.[27]

From the All-expansive State the tendency to shrink and contract starts for no apparent reason. This tendency called *Avidyā,* has been called by *Vāsiṣṭha* as *Saṁkalpa,* when the *Jñānākāśa* shrinks to *Cidākāśa.* Only, the *Saṁkalpa* is at the cosmic level. All these are only hints to a *Sādhaka,* giving the mechanism of involution of consciousness from the Ultimate State. If the *Sādhaka* is in an advanced stage of growth, such hints are more than enough for him to retrieve back to *That State.* Such a person is able to utilise consciousness itself as he is spiritually highly developed and all that is needed in unfolding the highest states of consciousness is a little stimulation from below.

Many of the books on spirituality and *Vedānta* begin with teachings for persons at such highly evolved stage. The teachings of *Bhagavadgītā* are totally condensed in the second Chapter. They are only suggestive and for the sake of those who are not so advanced, the *Gītā* continues, to come down to their own level, in the following sixteen chapters. Similarly, this story of Ākāśaja is more than enough for persons like Rāma, who have the personal power to not only understand the teachings but to transform their way of life. But our sages who were all compassion to their fellow beings took great

---

27 अविद्या क्षेत्रमुत्तरेषां प्रसुप्ततनुविच्छिन्नोदाराणाम् ।। 2.4 ।।

pains to encourage even such persons who may have begun to get interested in taking the first steps in the direction.

A very natural question that arises in the minds of *Jijñāsus* (seekers of knowledge) is, 'Why does the perfect Non-Dual state *fall* into the rut of multiplicity, to experience misery?' This question does not have a satisfying answer on the mental and verbal planes. But then, one can always have some plausible explanations, to quieten the mind, and to continue the quest.

Shri Aurobindo gives a very beautiful explanation:

> 'What is the purpose and origin of this disharmony—why came this division and ego, this world of painful evolution? Why must evil and sorrow enter into the divine Good, Bliss and peace? It is hard to answer to the human intelligence on its own level, for the consciousness to which the origin of this phenomenon belongs...is cosmic and not an individualised human intelligence. ... To the human mind one might answer that while in itself the Infinite might be free from those perturbations, yet once manifestation began, infinite possibility also began.
>
> ...For once it appears that it acquires, for the Soul descending into evolutionary manifestation, an irresistible attraction—*an attraction which in human terms on the terrestrial level might be interpreted as the call of the unknown, the joy of danger and difficulty and adventure, the will to attempt the impossible, to work out the incalculable, the will to create the new and the uncreated with one's own self and life as the material, the fascination of contradictories and their difficult harmonisation—these things translated into another supraphysical, superhuman consciousness, higher and wider than the mental, were the temptations that led to the fall*'.[28]

28 *'Letters on Yoga' by Shri Aurobindo,* Volume 22, Shri Aurobindo Centenary Library, Deluxe Edition, 1970, pp. 28-29.

If it was the spirit of adventure that was the fundamental *Saṁkalpa,* then it must be very much possible for us to reverse the process. By leaving the beaten track of ordinary life, and venturing to walk the unknown trails and to embrace even death, if necessary. That is how a seeker feels when the quest starts, a Divine Adventure into one's own Consciousness.

Many have lost their lives in the expeditions for exploring the unknown terrains, like the Mount Everest, the Poles or the wild untamed jungles in Africa and Amazon. Those who have returned after putting the summits and acmes they had set for themselves under their feet have declared their achievement through their radiant smiles. And those who did not return and had died in the attempt, must have had the satisfaction of making a sincere attempt, and for having the courage to sacrifice their everything for what they believed to be the mission of their life.

It is true, that the Divine Adventure asks much of a seeker. It demands the so-called normal life, the accompanying likes and dislikes, pleasure and pain, and a much greater effort. But what he gets in the process, is not just a radiant smile, but radiance; not just name and fame but That which transcends name and fame; not just a sense of achievement but that fulfillment which the human mind cannot even imagine, which the "One" gets after successfully returning from the abysmal depths of matter to the heights of Pure Consciousness. Compared to what the seeker gets, his sacrifice is paltry or even petty!

2

The Story of Līlā

A cloud of mist enveloped the region in an intimate embrace. Visibility got reduced to just a couple of feet. Though the eyes were helpless in bringing the sights from world without, the other senses were too eager to exhibit their talent. There was the olfaction, which brought in the smell of the mist itself; the humid earth; the fungi growing on the trees; the pungent smell of red ants and the humus of fallen leaves. The audition seemed to have improved remarkably. One could hear the sound of droplets of water falling from the wet leaves from tree tops to the fallen ones on the ground as though in remembrance of the relationship that was ended by the act of nature; the chirping of a variety of birds in the act of waking up; and in the background of all sound, there was the soft murmur of the river flowing as a monotone for the terrestrial music. It appeared as though, even the tactility had improved. The sounds heard so far seemed to touch the experiencer, while the mist settled as millions of droplets on the hair and the fibres of the woolen shawl, and created goose pimples.

The absence of vision had helped enlivening the other senses, which are otherwise taken for granted. At the same time, along with the senses the mind too had taken to the flights of imagination. There were foot-steps on the dry leaves; the weird sounds of some of the birds gave an impression of someone whispering an unknowable secret; an old forgotten rustic tune was heard. Just a little observation was sufficient to understand, that the foot-steps were one's own, the whisper and the tune were one's own creations. If there is fear, reason is definitely helpful. But if the mood is one of awe and wonder and in some way touching the deeper layer of one's being, reason becomes a spoil-sport and an avoidable burden!

The same conclusion is drawn from other common experiences. We may see a destitute or an invalid who can be our beneficiary. The resultant compassion may goad us towards some acts of service or charity. But reason and intellect intervene, and start forwarding all sorts of *valid* arguments against the noble act. As the explanation, that the beggars and other parasites on society are being encouraged through such acts! And reason happens to be so powerful a weapon that it is very difficult to cut.

Our culture recognises intellect and reasonable thought as instruments for understanding the Existence, having the capacity to take us to higher faculties like intuition. But unfortunately, the intellect has presently become so powerful that it seems that we have become its instruments! We want sense proofs and reasonable explanations, without which, we do not accept anything as knowledge. Consequently, it becomes all the more difficult for us to understand the suggestive implications of our scriptures and make use of them. The scriptures employ different means in their attempt to convey that which transcends communication. The *Purāṇas* through their symbology in the stories and the *Upaniṣads* and other *Vedāntic* works through both reasonable and paradoxical statements. While works like the *Yoga Vāsiṣṭha* succeed in giving us glimpses by combining both these techniques.

The most stubborn of the obstacles one has to face while embarking on a spiritual voyage is the mental rigidity, and a kind of resistance to free ourselves from the grip of senses, and in turn the dependence on the intellect. It is obvious, that most of our understanding of the world is based on the information supplied by the senses, *chosen* by the mind, coloured by its likes and dislikes. On such sense information the intellect *interprets,* refracted by its own limitations! What remains is only a distorted, vague or confused description! And yet, we are very confident of the efficiency of our senses, of our reason and intellect. Unless one loosens this grip, the instruments have, over him or her, one cannot begin one's quest. To free himself of all obsessions one has to become fluid and open. The teacher of Carlos Castaneda, Don Juan puts it eloquently:

> 'The first act of a teacher is to introduce the idea that the world we think we see is only a view, a description of the world. Every effort of a teacher is geared to prove this point to his apprentice. But accepting it seems to be one of the hardest things one can do; we are complacently caught in our particular view of the world, which compels us to feel and act as if we knew everything about the world. A teacher, from the very act he performs, aims at stopping this view.... It is the single most important technique that an apprentice can learn'.[29]

Moreover, the man unseen is much more than the man seen—only the tip of an iceberg. Our view *about* the world, *limits* the world to the description given by our limited senses, mind and intellect. We laugh at a person who takes the world, seen through the frame of a window to be the *whole world.* And yet, this is exactly what we do when we give so much importance to the sense data. Spirituality recognises the complete man, accepting him with all his facets and the levels of existence. The story of Līlā, gives us further glimpses into the levels of existence. Though the *Vāsiṣṭha* names them as the three *Ākāśas,* a seeker has to remember that the names are only symbolic, used to suggest the levels of manifestation of the Reality.

---

29 *Tales of Power* by Carlos Castaneda, Penguin Books, p. 229.

There was a pious and just king named Padma. His wife Līlā was like a shadow and mind to him. Being very attached to the king, Līlā thought of finding out means of achieving the immortality for her Lord and for maintaining his youth perpetually. Fear is natural, which protects life and is necessary for self-preservation and perpetuation of species. But *Abhiniveśa* or clinging to life is predominantly found in us human beings. We have different institutions for justifying *Abhiniveśa.* Marriage, family, society, and nation being some of them. We make use of different means for fulfilling this clinging : cleverness, greed or infatuation. Sometimes, the most subtle and lofty of all emotions, Love is also misused. This aspect has been depicted through the desire of Līlā.

She consulted some men of authority in the field of *Mantras* and rituals. They said that all practices could only help her acquire occult powers and could not possibly arrest death in the world. Giving a thought over it, she decided to propitiate Saraswatī—the goddess of learning, to keep the *Jīva* of her beloved husband in the palace itself in case he dies before her, so that she could be in his sweet company till her own death. Without the knowledge of King Padma—her husband, she started performing arduous penance consisting of prolonged fasts, chanting and worship, as advised by the wise men.

Full of appreciation for Līlā's sincere efforts, goddess Saraswatī manifested on the perceivable plane and asked Līlā to seek boons. After offering the goddess respectful worship, Līlā sought two boons. The first boon was to allow her lord's *Jīva* to remain in the palace even after his death. And the second was an appeal to the goddess to make herself visible whenever she was called. These boons were conferred on Līlā by Saraswatī.

Years later, King Padma died. Goddess Saraswatī hovering in the same plane appeared before Līlā, and advised Līlā to cover the body of the diseased husband with flowers for keeping the body fresh, and observed that only the flowers would wither with time. Following the advice Līlā spent a few days in the company of the lifeless body. But after all, how can one be happy with a corpse? Every time she looked at the body, the pleasant memories of his company came to her mind, increasing her misery. Meditating on Saraswatī, she entreated the goddess to take her to wherever her husband was.

The goddess explained Līlā that the three planes of existence are named *Cidākāśa* also called *Jñānākāśa*—the spiritual plane; *Cittākāśa*—the mental plane; and *Bhūtākāśa*—the elemental plane. Out of the three planes *Cittākāśa* is the intermediate plane which is characterised by restlessness as the consciousness jumps from one object to another in the *Bhūtākāśa*. The restlessness in the two lower *Ākāśas* is due to the host of *Saṁskāras*. By eliminating the *Saṁskāras*, the light of *Cit* or the Pure Being, manifests Itself. When the understanding dawned on Līlā, she could become receptive to Saraswatī's Grace, and experience the state of *Nirvikalpa Samādhi*.

Līlā was able to escape from the imprisonment of the physical body. In a quiescent state, Līlā beheld the capital city of an empire, and later the emperor himself, who was young, handsome and powerful. Līlā was surprised to recognise her beloved husband Padma in that emperor. After visiting the other parts of the empire, she returned to her own palace. After duly meditating upon the goddess Saraswatī, she sought a clarification, as to how her husband could condition himself to a state which was equally illusive and capable of producing bondage, as the one he had already experienced in the Padma-creation.

Saraswatī replied that it was due the act of *differentiation* that had begun in the *Jñānākāśa*, which *descended* onto the *Cittākāśa*, as a *Saṁkalpa* or desire, for kingship, that in turn manifested as Padma-creation onto *Bhūtākāśa*, the elemental realm. As the desire remained unfulfilled even after the Padma-creation, he *willed* the second birth as emperor Vidūratha.

The Padma-creation itself was a part of a *Saṁkalpa* of a Brahmin named Vasiṣṭha who lived in Girigrāma or mountain village, along with his devoted wife Arundhatī.

Though they were not *the* Vasiṣṭha and Arundhatī[30] as far as either knowledge or experience was concerned, they were very devoted to each other. There came a retinue of a king with all his regalia near the village. On seeing it, there arose a *Saṁkalpa* in the mind of Vasiṣṭha, and accordingly he performed all his duties sincerely keeping it in his heart. But he died, without fulfilling it.

Arundhatī, unaware of the desire in her husband's mind had sought boons similar to Līlā's, from Saraswatī. And when the pious Brahmin expired, his *Jīva* kept hovering in the hut. But unable to bear the separation from the husband for more than eight days, she had joined his subtle body to become Līlā. For Līlā this explanation seemed too fantastic to be true. She raised a genuine doubt as to how could it be possible for the Brahmin couple living in a hut, in which the *Jīva* of Vasiṣṭha hovered, to be the Padma-creation which had a large kingdom. And how could such a kingdom be contained in a small hut?

Saraswatī smilingly replied that beings like her, who *flowed* with the Divine Will, never found it necessary to transgress the truth. The Brahmin's *Jīva* definitely hovered invisibly in the hut. The kingdom or regality *did not have any material reality,* but was only an ideation, born when the Brahmin had seen the retinue of the king. The goddess added that the Vasiṣṭha-Arundhatī creation was causal to Padma-Līlā creation, which in turn, was causal to Vidūratha creation. Saraswatī continued

30 Sage Vasiṣṭha who is teaching Rāma, and his wife Arundhatī.

that only due to the difference in subtlety Līlā *felt* that the creations were different.

Reality is all inclusive and contains every conceivable universe. Space and time are modifications of mind and are illusive. Even the present conclusions of Science agree with this view, when it says that *space and time are relative.* The involvement with the body and senses stops one from remembering the former life and experiences. This identification with the present life and experiences has to be overcome for the recollection, which paves way for the transcendence of the process of birth and death. This can be illustrated with experiences from everyday life.

When one sleeps, the body as such is limited to the space occupied by it. But in the dreams seen by the person, which are *created* by the mind due to incomplete desires, there are things, scenes, nature and people, who are all the part of the ideation. In the wakeful consciousness, when one is walking on a hot day, the image of water, the reflection of the trees or other objects in it are all part of the optical illusion called *mirage.* However, *during* the process of dreaming or being under the influence of the mirage, whatever is seen or experienced is *real,* though on waking up, or on seeing through the mirage, one can easily laugh over it. A *habitual dreamer* keeps believing in the events and things in the dream, and goes on *creating* newer or more complicated dreams until it becomes an obstinate habit.

This happens to be the case with most of us. Not only do we enjoy the self-created illusions, but have made the dreams a major part of our entertainment through the motion pictures. So much so, that the people connected with the film industry have been rightly called as the *Dream Merchants!* We dream not only while we are asleep but even while awake, as there is an undercurrent of dreams. This is because we have the habit of being in a perpetual dream! Goddess Saraswatī was suggesting Līlā that Vasiṣṭha-Arundhatī creation itself was a dream, in which Padma-Līlā creation was a dream-within-a-dream, and the Vidūratha creation was a dream-within-a-dream-within-a-dream! And to understand the unreality of these dreams, she had to wake up to the state of *Cidākāśa or Jñānākāśa.*

On hearing these facts, a natural curiosity took birth in Līlā's mind to witness the Vasiṣṭha-Arundhatī creation. Saraswatī said that the *Saṁkalpa* had become so intense for Līlā that her dream had acquired a grossness. Consequently, she had to withdraw into herself, till she became quiescent *Jñānākāśa,* which alone would give her the ability to enter or leave the various creations at will. Looking at Līlā compassionately, the goddess commented that she was not yet free from desires, which enhance the formation of the subtle mental body called *Ātivāhika.* This mental body, in turn generates a gross body. Like the melting of snow in the sun, the gross body changes permanently into the subtle body, on attainment of *Jñāna* through the abandonment of *Vāsanās.* This particular state has been called the *Jīvanamukti.*

On being asked by Līlā as to what efforts should be made by her to realise the end, the goddess replied that the higher states can be cognised by developing the capacity for *Śravaṇa* (listening), *Manana* (contemplation) and *Nididhyāsana* (meditation by *living* the truths discovered during the *Manana*). *Śravaṇa* is possible only for the mind which is free from all distraction causing desires. This is possible only through constant *Vicāra* that this world with all its objects is only a *notion.* The process of *Vicāra* consists of engaging oneself in finding the root of the *Ahaṁkāra,* the 'I-notion'. When one becomes aware that the 'I' is only a non-existent shadow without any substance, the delicate relationship between the *Draṣṭā* (seer) and the *Dṛśya* (seen) snaps, and the certainty that binds the *Citta* to the seen or the world, evaporates, leaving only a quiescent condition of freedom and *infinite possibilities,* when one can achieve *total control* and *mastery.*

Līlā experienced the *Nirvikalpa Samādhi* through the grace of goddess Saraswatī. She became free from the trammels of gross body and could remain motionless. In this state, Saraswatī and Līlā rose in *Jñānākāśa* in their *Ātivāhika* bodies, and observed many strange things. They manifested themselves on the plane of Girigrāma, and found the children immersed in pain due to death of their parents. The two visitors were invisible to the people in that plane. Līlā, who had attained a *mastery over her desires* and was of *Satsaṁkalpa* (Pure Being), willed that they both should become visible. The people, taking them to be the Divine Beings worshipped them. Then the eldest son entreated them to relieve them from the load of grief due to the death of their parents. Līlā by just touching their fore-heads gave them relief.

When Saraswatī, the goddess of learning asked her devotee to express her further aspirations, Līlā wanted a clarification. How was it that the persons in the Vasiṣṭha-Arundhatī creation were able to see her, while the people in the royal assembly of Vidūratha were not? With great patience, Saraswatī replied that Līlā had developed pure *Jñāna* when they visited the Girigrāma. But she had many unfulfilled desires and attachments while in the plane of Vidūratha. She had experienced the Vidūratha creation without any voluntary control, but only due to Divine grace. Even at Girigrāma Līlā had been invisible till she had *created* the conception of 'I' through pure *Saṁkalpa.*

Overjoyed after the *experiential* knowledge, Līlā said that she had known her previous eight hundred births and had understood that all these births *and the worlds* had been created only by the *Māyā-Vikalpa* (the modifications of *Māyā).* Presently she was standing on the shores of *Mukti* (Liberation). They both first manifested in the plane where the body of king Padma lay. And then in the plane of emperor Vidūratha. They found that the invincible king of Sindhu had waged war against him and his army had been reduced to one-eighth of its original size. He had been resting at the end of a tiring day. When he saw these two ladies with spiritual radiance, he saluted them. With the grace of Saraswatī he recollected his former births and the gloom of *Māyā* cleared off enabling him to recognise himself as the same Padma, and Līlā to be his devout consort.

Vidūratha wanted to know how it had been possible for him to remember all the events that had transpired during the long period. Saraswatī replied that the trance called death is always accompanied by a great delusion of rebirths, which in turn are accompanied by innumerable deaths. The conception of time was only due to the *delusion of actions* performed while alive, under the influence of *Māyā*. All these—birth, death, action, etc.—are in space and time which in turn, are nothing but mental conceptions. Even the waking state *appears* to be long due to the day-dreams called *Vikalpas*. In reality there is nothing like life and death, but only Pure *Jñāna*.

The process of interaction between *Draṣṭā* and *Dṛśya* (the seer and seen), *creates* this illusion of material reality to the universe consisting of beings and things. The universe itself arises out of *Ahaṁkāra* and the other related multiplicity like 'mine', 'you', 'he', etc. Saraswatī said that Vidūratha had become recipient to this knowledge through the love of Līlā. The king wanted to know from the goddess, when he could resume the body of Padma. To which the compassionate goddess replied that a situation had been created for the destruction of this body through the attack of the king of Sindhu.

Just then the enemy army walking through the defense of Vidūratha's fortress. In panic his queen was seen to enter the chamber. To the pleasant surprise of Līlā, the queen looked her own mirror image. She was told by the goddess that due to the love towards her she had become part of the king's *Saṁkalpa*. Leaving his queen to the care of trusted servants the king went to defend the palace. The queen's eyes beheld goddess Saraswatī whom she had always worshipped. After duly paying her respects the queen sought a boon from the goddess to allow her to join her husband, *with* her body, wherever he would be. The goddess assured the queen that her wish would be fulfilled. Līlā wanted to know why *she* had been unable to retain her gross body while experiencing the Vasiṣṭha-Arundhatī creation.

Saraswatī replied that one gets *whatever one wishes.* Since Līlā had wished to acquire *Jñāna* before, and longed for the Divine vision, the goddess had bestowed it on her. While the queen of Vidūratha was being driven by excess desire had sought the boon accordingly. And their lord Vidūratha (also Padma and Vasiṣṭha!) had longed for higher spiritual stage and had to experience the Non-Dual Principle, he had to experience the death, while the king of Sindhu had sought the sovereignty which had also been granted. Thus everyone had got what one wanted!

Meanwhile, king Vidūratha was killed. With the blessings of Saraswatī, Līlā raised herself in *Ākāśa* preceding Padma and his *Saṁkalpa* consort, to wait for them in the palace where his body lay. But she discovered that her body in the state of *Nirvikalpa Samādhi* had been cremated by the ministers taking it to be lifeless. Saraswatī asked Līlā to abandon the *idea of gross body* and to remain free in her *Ātivāhika* body. The *Jīva* of Vidūratha was allowed to enter the body of Padma and all the three of them were blessed by the goddess, so that they could achieve *Videha Mukti.*

This story seems to be too fantastic to be true, and too complicated to comprehend! But it helps the seekers in abandoning the rigid view of the world. When the definiteness of the world view is lost, the *obsession* and *involvement* with it also reduces. Then the mystery of the Being opens-up. This story is not so fantastic when we go through some of the strange contemporary discoveries of the modern scientists.

The world view of the Physicists has changed radically, from the mechanistic view postulated by Rene Descartes and Sir Isaac Newton. The idea of space-time continuum, the new vision of the electromagnetic radiation postulated by Albert Einstein and the subsequent theories, have more than succeeded, in shattering the view of the world as entertained by most of us. The scientists have become so open and fluid that they are convinced that *no description is complete* and can be at the most *only a view from a particular angle.* Geoffrey Chew, a scientist, has tried to put it beautifully in his 'Boot-Strap' theory, that nature can never be understood in its *entirety,* and whatever little understanding one can obtain, can only be partial.

With such large strides in human understanding about its own nature, it is quite easy to appreciate the purpose of the story. Goddess Saraswatī symbolises the faculty responsible for the power of discrimination, analysis, and synthesis. She helps the seeker to come out of the obsessions and attachments with *Dṛśya,* the world. Unless this is done it is impossible to quieten the mental activity which keeps *creating* deeper and deeper dreams. After quietening the mental activity which is possible only by *complete* elimination of the *Vāsanās,* one can experience one's Being, Which is beyond mind and its conceptions like space and time. The story also suggests that even birth and death are mental modifications. More than anything else, it gives a technique to quieten the mind by *tracing the 'I-ness',* which also does not have any *real* existence but which is only a shadow of the Non-Dual, Eternal and Infinite Self. The Eternal Self has been called as *Jñānākāśa* suggesting expansiveness.

There is an episode from the life of Chuang Tzu, the Taoist (Chinese) Master, which questions the sense of importance we give to the waking state. It is said, that one morning he was found to be in a depressed mood by his disciples. When they asked him the reason for his being in such a state, he told them sadly, that he had dreamt that he had become a butterfly. Unable to understand the reason for depression for such a simple dream, they asked him why it had caused depression. The Master said that presently he was not sure *whether he had dreamt that he had become a butterfly, or it was the butterfly which was dreaming that it had become Chuang Tzu!* The great hint he gave through this practical lesson is, that just as the dream with all its details is the creation of the dreamer, it is very likely that this so-called everyday world of which we are so certain, is also a creation of the experiencer who has been called as *Draṣṭā* by our *Vedāntic* texts, the compassionate poetic outbursts of our *Ṛṣis* in their lofty spiritual flights.

There are many things which are beyond the reach of human intellect and reasonable or logical explanation. But it should not be *presumed* that they do not or cannot exist. Carl Sagan, a distinguished Cornell University (U S A) astronomer writes in his book *Cosmos:*

> 'There is an idea—strange, haunting, evocative—one of the most exquisite conjectures in science or religion. It is entirely undemonstrated; it may never be proved. But it stirs the blood. There is, we are told, an infinite hierarchy of universes, so that an elementary particle, such as an electron, in our universe would, if penetrated, reveal itself to be an entire closed universe. Within it, organised into the local equivalent of galaxies and smaller structures are an immense number of other, much tinier elementary particles, which are themselves universes at the next level, and so on forever—an infinite downward egression, universes within universes, endlessly. And upward as well. Our familiar universe of galaxies and stars, planets and people, would be a single elementary particle in the next universe up, the first step of another infinite regress.

> 'This is the only religious idea I know that surpasses the endless number of infinitely old cycling universes in Hindu cosmology'.[31]

Whenever we tread an unknown ground in quest of knowledge, we have to start from either what has been told by the earlier scientists, or make certain assumptions. Similarly, a seeker has to have some faith in the words of our ancient sages, who were totally unselfish, so as not even to claim the authorship of the greatest heirloom of mankind, the *Upaniṣads.* Their only concern or interest was to help the fellow beings achieve what they had achieved. So the least we can do, is to be open to their words. It is very much like having trust in the capacity of the coach, and also water, before jumping into water for learning the art of swimming.

31 *Cosmos* by Carl Sagan, Random House, New York, pp. 265, 267.

3

The Story of Karkaṭī

A large valley formed by sand dunes all around. The eyes ache for a change in the environment, to behold something alive, perhaps an oasis. The sun shines continuously and mercilessly. It is believed, that every minute it produces enough energy to suffice an year's energy needs of the earth. In a depression created by the dunes however, there is a semblance of some plant life almost matching the colour of the hot sands. They have an appearance of the stubble of growth on an old and weathered chin! The only shades in green are available through large cacti. Even they, are due to the angle of the sun, and not their foliage. As the eyes pine for shade and the lips and throat for a little wetness, the hands reach for the water canteen. The heat is so much that even the 'once-cold-water' has become warm and insipid! The effect of the water nevertheless, is helpful to alleviate the oppressive heat. All of a sudden, there is a whiff of cool breeze, giving respite from discomfort. The eyes turn in the direction, and the heart gladdens to behold the rain bearing clouds, which *may* sprinkle a little water on the harsh landscape. As the water canteen is lowered, a drop of water from it falls on a seemingly dead plant.

There is a sudden explosion, as though a small cracker going off, and a pod breaks, scattering the seeds far and wide from the mother plant. A seemingly insignificant plant in the harsh desert terrain, becomes a source of hectic activity, not only without, but more so within the mind of the onlooker, as a chain of questions. If an accidental drop of water has the capacity to initiate such wonderful *hope*—for it is only a hope, as the seed may or may not germinate, the sapling may or may not grow into a plant, ...—in the plant, what would happen with a small shower, a life-cycle? The Botanists give us to understand, that it is always so, in harsh terrains. The life cycle of plants is very fast in the deserts. Every drop of water fallen on the sands is made use of by the plants. And as the harshness returns to the landscape, the plants again *wait* patiently for the meager shower.

Our life too is somewhat like the desert plant. A small whiff of breeze in the form of an insignificant shock of happiness is enough to start a life cycle of dreams in our mind. And we hold on to such moment not unlike the desert plants holding on to the precious life giving liquid. Life is a great paradox. Every one of us desperately wants to be happy most of the time. But most of our actions generate the opposite effect, that is, misery! We want peace and life without any disturbance. But our very effort to achieve it leads us to anxiety, tension and other avoidable feelings! All we are left with is, some moments, free from tension or anxiety, which we call happiness.

If we do some retrospection, during the moments of misery or for that matter, our so-called happiness, we are surprised to discover—most of the time, if not all—that sometime or the other we have sown the seed which is being harvested *only at that moment.* How does it happen? A Sufi story suggests an answer to this question.

There was an old lady—who was also a *Sufi Faqīr,* in a small village. She was quite happy and content in her tattered clothes, her lamp-less hut, and her half empty stomach! Many people were interested in knowing the secret of her happiness. In spite of her best efforts, she was unable to make them understand the simple yet invaluable secret, as their *interest was only academic!* But determined that she was, she thought of a practical method of teaching them.

One late evening, during the twilight, she started repairing her torn clothing sitting in her lamp-less hut. When the darkness enveloped, the needle accidentally slipped away from her fingers. Obviously, that was the only needle she had. She desperately started searching for it on her mud floor. But the darkness and her failing eye-sight did not allow her.

Just as she was wondering her next course of action, her eyes fell on the street lamp just outside her dwelling. Enthusiastically, she came under the lamp, and started searching for the lost needle. A youth, who used to respect her, was passing by. Finding the old lady in search of something, he asked affectionately as to what she was searching. When she told him about the lost needle, he too joined her in the search. Gradually, a crowd gathered and joined her in the search. Nearly an hour later, after the back-breaking search, a youth asked the old lady to tell him the exact spot on which she had dropped the needle.

Intentionally waiting for the whole crowd to become attentive, she said at last, that she had lost it *in the hut!* They laughed at her stupidity and asked her how she could possibly get the needle under the street lamp, if she had dropped it in her hut. Without ruffling her feathers in the least, she said that the hut was dark, while there was light *outside!* The crowd laughed once more. Someone commented amidst the peels of laughter, that she had to illuminate her hut, instead of looking for the lost needle under the street lamp.

Calmly she said that, what had happened was not all that funny and this is what the whole world is doing all the time. There is happiness *within,* but all search for it *outside,* in the objects, in name and fame or in the struggle for power over others. Just because we feel the darkness within ourselves and experience the difficulty to see, we direct our search *outside* because there is light and everything can be perceived clearly.

She concluded that, she may have a lamp-less hut but *she was well lit inside,* and that the *aim of the Religion is to teach us to light the lamp within.*

Having somehow developed certain notions, we have also started believing them to be true. Two events take place. As far as the chronology is concerned, one follows the other. Just because of the chronology, we *think* that they are related or connected. A particular incident takes place, and there is either a spurt of happiness or misery. We are almost certain that there is a cause-effect relationship in this. But it is not necessarily so. It may be only a *reaction.* The two events do take place, but they need not be related. If observed very carefully, one finds that there is a gap between them. It surprises such an observer, when it is discovered that *at the psychological level, the action-reaction is only a force of habit.*

This phenomenon has been called by Carl Gustav Jung, a very competent colleague of Sigmund Freud, as *synchronicity.* The force of habit or synchronicity depends on the milieu one has grown-up in since childhood. *Vedānta* calls this as *Saṁskāra* or the impression. This is obvious from the difference in reactions for the similar if not the same incident by different persons. What may be very disturbing for some may not be so for others, and it is likely that for some others it may even be positively pleasurable! Some of us who are sensitive, may be very upset or even angry when we see something wrong, like the prevalent corruption in the society. They go to any length of pointing it out, even at the risk of personal safety. Most of us are not really bothered about it. It may be either due to our involvement with our own day-to-day problems or due to *lack of courage.* While many may appreciate these acts!

If we begin with a wrong note, we cannot possibly hope to achieve the right music. Our premise itself is wrong, due to which we *have to* suffer the consequences. The result is more and more misery, while intermittently, there are infinitesimally small gaps of misery-free or tension-free moments. We call them our pleasurable or happy or even blissful moments! But even this suffering is only an attitude or approach to life. An episode from the life of Lao Tzu, the great sage of Tao illustrates this point.

Once, Lao Tzu was on his walk with his disciples. In the market, a man approached him and without any warning, started scolding the sage. He alleged that Lao Tzu was misguiding the youth. The sage patiently allowed the man to finish his act and then asked whether he had anything else to say. The man, who was obviously shaken by the stoical behaviour of Lao Tzu, went away. The disciples were stunned, at the same time, did not understand how their master could remain unruffled. The very next day, the same man approached Lao Tzu in a mood of repentance, and sought forgiveness. The sage only smiled and said that his act did not require anyone's forgiveness, since he had not committed anything which could be called objectionable. Asked to explain how this was possible, the sage replied by a counter-question.

If one is standing under a tree to avoid the storm and rain, and a branch of the tree breaks injuring the person standing under the tree, would he blame the tree, or would he get angry with the storm? Obviously not. In a similar way, the sage continued, that a storm raging in the man's mind had caused an out-burst of harsh words. And he *only happened* to be near the victim!

This nearness or synchronicity with *Dṛśya* (the seen) gives us an impression that it is *the cause* for our misery or happiness. The impression has become so strong, that it has almost become our nature to get totally *indulged* in it. The intensity of the *reaction* depends upon the intensity of *indulgence.* More intense the indulgence, more violent is the reaction.

As a helpless tiny seed, the *tendency for involvement* always looks innocent in the beginning, but Himalayan when it becomes an indulgence. The starting point is the initial *Saṁkalpa,* which *creates Ahaṁkāra.* And this *Ahaṁkāra* becomes the root cause for myriad of grosser manifestations like *Citta, Buddhiḥ, Manas, Prakṛti,* etc., which get superimposed on the *Jīva.* The story of Karkaṭī brings home this point.

A *Rākṣasī* (a female demon) named Karkaṭī, lived on the Northern slopes of the Himalayas. Being a demoness, she had a huge body and tried to satisfy her almost insatiable appetite, by attacking the innocent people chancing to cross her ways. But she remained hungry most of the time! With an intention of appeasing her hunger, she performed intense *Tapas* by standing on one leg to propitiate Brahmā the Creator. Pleased with her perseverance, Brahmā made himself visible to her and offered a boon. She made a request to Brahmā to allow her to become a *Jīva-sūcikā* or a living needle thereby, she could appease her hunger by entering into the bodies of every living creature.

Brahmā observed that she would become a *Sūcikā* with a pre-fix *'Vi'* and be called *'Visūcikā',* a micro-organism causing the epidemic Cholera. She would afflict those ignorant persons living in unsanitary places, feeding themselves on unwholesome, stale and dirty food. He also gave a method to bring relief to the afflicted persons. The gigantic Karkaṭī then reduced herself to a tiny *Sūcikā* and entered the minds and bodies of the ferocious and the timid and started appeasing her hunger. With time however, she became abhorrent of her own actions, and noticed that she had become more and more agitated and despondent, by her never ending desires.

She started wondering about her own cruelty and became repentant. With the repentance, she gave up her evil actions and thus eliminated the fluctuations of the mind. This gave way to calmness, poise and peace in her being. She was purified of all effects of her past actions. Since there was absolutely no motivation behind her penance, Brahmā appeared, this time voluntarily and announced that she had achieved *Jīvanamukti* state and had attained pure *Jñāna.* Thus Karkaṭī remained in the actionless state of *Nirvikalpa Samādhi* for a very long time, enjoying Bliss, beyond all duality. But as soon as she returned to the normal state with the conception of 'I', which brought her in contact with the mind and identification with the body, hunger and pain revived which is the nature of body and mind. Her old *Saṁskāra* of the taste for flesh raised its hood. She roamed around the jungles on the Himalayan slopes, consuming the bodies of the ignorant and the vile as she had been directed by Brahmā. On a very dark and fearful night, the King of the hunters, to whom the forest belonged, came to the forest along with his minister to scare away the cruel creatures infesting the country. Karkaṭī could not help appreciating the courage of both these men. She tested their fearlessness with her scary and wild voice and appearance. But it failed to have the desired effect on them. Understanding, that the two had unlimited power she wanted to test their *Jñāna.* She asked them ten questions, with a condition that she would make them her meal if they failed to answer.

Rākṣasī Karkaṭī asked: What is that atom which is the cause of the origin, the preservation and the destruction of infinite heterogeneous universes springing up like bubbles on the surface of the ocean? What is that which is *Ākāśa* and yet is not? What is that which though is unlimited, has a limit? What is that which though moving, moves not? What is that which though is, yet is not? What is that which manifests itself as *Cit* (consciousness) is yet inert? What is that which portrays picture in the *Ākāśa*? What is that atom in which are latent all the micro cosmos, like a tree in a seed? From where do all things originate like undulations in water, being not different from the cause, like foam in the ocean? And in what will these two (undulations and water) become merged as One?

The minister replied that all her questions point towards the same Non-dual Brahman, beyond the reach of the intellect, mind, and five senses. It is endless, absolute *Jñāna,* more subtle than *Ākāśa,* and is the *Paramāṇu,* the Supreme Atom of the atoms. All mundane eggs arise out of It, and into which they are absorbed. No attribute can be given to Brahman, neither external nor internal, and hence It can be compared with *Ākāśa* and yet, It is not the elemental *Ākāśa,* as It is pure *Jñāna* itself. No abode can contain the limitless Brahman, yet it abides in all as *Sat.* Through its intimate relationship It moves, it is devoid of any movement as there is *no space outside of Itself.* It cannot be known by pointing to it as 'this' or 'that', as It *exists* not as objects, but as *existence Itself.*

Overjoyed to listen to the replies of the able minister, Karkaṭī then directed the questions to the King, for fathoming the depth of his understanding. Without really replying the individual questions, the king straight away started explaining the method of experiencing the Non-dual Reality. He said, that Brahman can be attained by abandoning all the *Saṁkalpas* and *Vikalpas;* that the origin and dissolution of the universe is nothing but the birth and death of *Saṁkalpas* of the mind, for the universe is nothing but a mode of consciousness; that the quintessence of the *Vedas* is to quieten the modifications of the mind; that the Non-dual Reality *transcends* all words and thoughts, which are limited, and It represents a State beyond existence and non-existence; and that all questions asked by Karkaṭī referred to Brahman or the Ultimate Reality.

The explanation given by the king increased the calmness and quiescence of Karkaṭī. Offering her salutations to both of them, she awaited their further command. The king asked Karkaṭī to desist from the massacre of the innocent. As she nodded assent, the kind hearted king asked her as to how she would appease her hunger. The *Rākṣasī* replied that she would resort to the state of *Nirvikalpa Samādhi.* She gave her word of honour to both of them that she would never hurt any creature thereafter. The king however, offered an alternative. He said that there were, in their kingdom such heinous criminals, awaiting execution. And if she so desired, she could accompany them to their kingdom and live on the flesh of such people. Karkaṭī accompanied them and did as she was told. After a while, she proceeded to the Himalayas and spent the rest of her days in meditation on the Non-dual Brahman to achieve *Videha Mukti.*

This story as others like it, illustrates certain very deep truths. The foremost one being, that *everyone, virtuous or otherwise* is eligible for Truth. All that is required is the will to achieve and the perseverance. If one has the *Śubha-Vāsanās* then one proceeds straight away towards enlightenment; if not, then one succeeds in satisfying the temporal needs, as shown symbolically by Karkaṭī's wish to become a *Jīva-sūcikā* for satiating her gross urge. We have the examples of many women and men who succeed in achieving their desires, before our very eyes. However, a time does come when such successful persons experience an intense emptiness in spite of their success, as a realisation dawns on them that the desires are insatiable. At such times, they start re-directing their will-power and perseverance towards the subtler needs of life.

Since they have the power, the grit and the will to achieve, and added to this they also have the *conviction in the uselessness of the desires,* they become one pointed. The second truth is that a genuine repentance for the past actions and a determination *never to repeat them* purifies their minds. We have the example of robber Ratnākar transforming himself into the Ādi Kavi Vālmīki who incidentally is the author of this great work. There is also the case of Ahalyā, the wife of Sage Gautama—narrated by Vālmīki in the *Rāmāyaṇa*—becoming a stone due to her interest in the king of Gods Iṅdra, and getting absolved by the touch of Rāma's feet. And she is counted among the five *chastest women!*

These stories should not be taken literally. In the case of Ratnākar, he *understands* his folly, repents and performs arduous penance to the extent that the termite-ant-hill grows over his body. That is why he is being called *Vālmīki,* the one who is of *Valmīka* (the ant hill). Similarly, Ahalyā's turning into a stone is an allegory to indicate her intense *Tapas*. There is a beautiful *Śloka* in the *Bhagavadgītā*:

'Even if you are the worst among the sinners,
You will cross over the ocean of sins,
Through the boat of *Jñāna*'[32]

Going a step further, *Yoga Vāsiṣṭha* says, that both virtue and vice are part of the great dream which is *created* by the *Saṁkalpa*. The scripture keeps repeating the statement, that nothing is impossible with sincere effort and perseverance. The only hassle in this adventure is one's own mind, its lack of purpose and determination. Another great hint it has for the seeker is that one should not be hasty in becoming judgmental about others.

Shri Aurobindo, known as the 'Prophet of Indian Nationalism' due to his contribution towards the spirit of Nationalism, has made more positive contribution towards the Freedom of Spirit. One of the grandest and radical spiritual truths he has presented is that of the *overall* development of the being. Our normal notion of development is restricted to the *higher and upward* growth. Which is from Animal-man to Man-man, to the Divine-man and so on? But Shri Aurobindo said that the growth does not mean *only* the higher *at the cost of the lower;* Growth encompasses both *lower and higher;* that the full growth of a being means, 'It' experiences, the inertness of the rock, the helpless wakefulness of the plant, the restlessness of birds and animals, the pleasures and pains of man, and the other higher transcendental states of consciousness *simultaneously*.

32 अपिचेदसि पापेभ्य: सर्वेभ्य: पापकृत्तम: ।
सर्वं ज्ञान प्लवेनैव वृजिनं संतरिष्यसि ।। 4.36 ।।

This story of Karkaṭī seems to voice a message of hope for all of us, that no matter which state we are in presently, if we make sincere efforts to transform ourselves, the change *will* happen. It does not matter where one is placed, whether the milieu is conducive or otherwise. For the Ultimate Reality, there is nothing like the external or internal, low or high. For these pairs of opposites are only part of the limited mind which is an infinitesimal manifestation of the Reality. An episode from the life of Ādi Śaṅkarācārya is worth recalling at this point.

The great patriarch of the *Adwaita* School of *Vedānta* was at Vārāṇasī. One day he was going for a bath in the river *Gaṅgā* and descending the steps of one of the innumerable *Ghāts,* when he saw, a *pariah*[33] climbing up the stairs. There were some dogs accompanying the low-caste man. Śaṅkara asked the *pariah* to move and to give way to him, a high caste Brahmin! It is said, that the man asked him as to what, he was supposed to move. If it was the body, then the bodies of both of them were made out of the *same five elements,* and so, they both were essentially the same; if it was the mind, then both their minds were only infinitesimal parts of the *same universal mind;* while the *Ātman* was already united as It is One and indivisible!

The devotees and followers of Śaṅkarācārya claim that it was the Lord Śiva himself, who had come to teach the Ācārya. But it is better to accept him as an enlightened out-caste. There is an instance of the enlightened butcher *Dhrama-vyādha,* in the *Mahābhārata.* We have numerous instances of enlightened saints continuing their family trades.

Most of all, it stresses that the world as we understand it, is only a view or a *mental description,* and has only an apparent reality. It is a source of excitement, anxiety as well as misery.

---

33 A low-caste man of unhygienic habits and one is supposed to eat stale flesh.

Thereby it depicts the play of consciousness after the initial *Saṁkalpa*. This initial *Saṁkalpa* limits the infinite consciousness to the limited 'I' and consequently other grosser manifestations. This limiting process has been called *Māyā,* and has the binding influence.

The dialogue of Karkaṭī with the king and his minister, in the form of questions and answers introduces us to the practical spirituality. The journey begins with questions and the search for the answers. But finding their *intellectual solutions* is only a beginning. The real *quest* begins only when one starts getting the conviction that the real thing is to seek the *Origin* through *Antarmukhatā*. And the real reaching is in tracing the 'I' pı inciple by retracing the steps from the grosser manifestations and negotiating the initial *Saṁkalpa.*

Life is similar to the desert plant. It can *wait* through the scorching heat of the sun in the form of desires and the consequent anxiety, worry, excitement, depression and misery, for the small droplet of the life-giving liquid. The droplet may be in the form of an incident, an encounter or an experience, to explode the seeds and begin a life cycle of growth. The growth however, may take *any* direction, the higher or the lower. If the growth is higher, which is the inner, then there may be the initial difficulty, but slowly the path of growth broadens to give the right direction. If it takes the lower—which is the outer, initially the path is *convenient* and seems broad, but becomes narrow as it solidifies the *Ahaṁkāra* and takes one towards ambition, search for power and repetitive pain, which may force us to change our view and mode of life. But ultimately, it does succeed in re-collecting its own Real Nature containing *everything,* which melts the pairs of opposites and fuses with the *Adwaita, the Non-dual,* when even the difference between the inner or the outer evaporates.

In a terrestrial desert, spring blooms only for a short period, while in the subtler plane of Consciousness there is *eternal spring* as one transcends space and time.

4

The Story of Aiṅdavas

It was the hour of twilight. The birds were retreating into nests for the night instinctively, after a typically hectic day. The sun had already set and the darker hues of red in the western horizon had changed to violet. The pioneers in the form of the first stars had made their appearance. Then the cosmic canopy assumed a dark velvety bluish hue, in preparation for the multitude of twinkling miracles. We call them stars. It was a moonless dusk or perhaps, the moon was yet to appear on the scene! Then the eyes beheld the Orion, the great constellation. It agreed with the shape of the Hunter. But then in our nomenclature, it is named *Mṛgaśirā* or the deer's head. When this was remembered, the constellation *appeared* to be the head of a deer! Then the eyes fell on Great Bear or the *Saptarṣi* (the seven sages), in the northern heavens. As the twilight stretched itself into the night, the great constellation rotated around Pole-star, tiny and almost hidden in the twinkling multitude!

The Cosmos has always evoked a feeling of expansiveness in the human beings. At the same time it has also given a sense of belonging to the universe in the human heart. 'It is a gut feeling', as some say, that we are intricately related to *everything,* the seen and the unseen; that the twinkling of the distant stars is very deeply dependent to the light which illuminates our thinking process, in some mysterious way. Every one of us is filled with wonder and awe at the breath-taking phenomena. The experience *depends on one's nature and background.*

A man beset with problems, finds solace, when he looks at the star filled sky. May be when he compares himself with the cosmos, or cosmic events, his problems appear insignificant, even petty; a poet or a painter beholds beauty, may be due to the arrangement at a superficial level, and real order at a deeper level; a scientist finds a wonderful opportunity, for observation and learning, as he is able to peep not only into space but also time, as the distances involved are so large that they are measured in terms of light years.[34] The stars or galaxies we see today, existed *years back,* as the light left the sources years back!

Like the great constellation *Saptarṣi,* which is apparently controlled by a seemingly insignificant point in the sky, known as the Pole-star, *everything* in the universe controlled by some unknown and unknowable Principle. Unknowable because, all knowledge comes under the purview of the activity of the senses and mind, which are but *Its* grosser manifestations. While the cause *transcends* every manifestation. The wise persons called this Principle variously, depending on what they wanted to convey. However, they repeatedly warned, that *no name can contain It, and no description, can describe It!*

Yet, paradoxically our planet is *literally flooded(!),* with such literature which is speculative, hypothetical and either loftily or sometimes, grossly imaginative, *about* the elusive Principle! This branch of knowledge has been of vital interest to man since the dawn of human History. Perhaps, the loftiest in the flights of human thought has been the legacy of the *Upaniṣads* which has come to us in the form of dialogues between the preceptors and the disciples. The same methodology was used by the Greek philosopher Socrates, which is preserved in the

34 The distance travelled by light in one year, 9.4607x 10^{12} Kilometres.

writings of Plato, his most famous disciple, entitled *The Dialogues.*

In our country the dialogue form of transfer of knowledge has had a very long tradition. Not only the *Upaniṣads,* but almost all the later scriptures have been in the similar form. From *Śrīmadbhāgavatam* and *Bhagavadgītā,* cherished by the spiritual aspirants, to even the children's stories like *Hitopadeśa,* and *Pañcatantra,* have come to us in this form. Almost every kind of hagiographic[35] literature of any faith or religion consists of mainly two portions, of the biographic sketch of the saint who guided the people, and the conversations and dialogues he had with his followers and disciples. The life sketch gives inspiration to those who have not had the privilege of being with the saint. While the conversations and dialogues clarify the doubts of the aspirants.

A seeker will do well to remember, that these scriptures were *dialogues,* very different from *discussions or arguments.* In a dialogue there is a communion between persons, in which there is a genuine *transfer* of not only theoretical knowledge, but more so, the experience at a deeper level of consciousness. A discussion or an argument is only at the intellectual level, which *may be* accompanied by comparison and the spirit of competition. Moreover, when these dialogues are *remembered* by the persons involved in them, or by the seekers who take them up the book for *Swādhyāya* at a future date, they are of a very great help.

The Gospel of Shri Ramakrishna, recorded by Mahendra Nath Gupta, who humbly called himself 'M', has guided many an aspirant during all the phases of the spiritual journey. The book started only in the form of a diary meant exclusively for the author's individual reference and need. 'M' was a teacher and could visit Shri Ramakrishna only on Saturdays, Sundays or holidays. He used to *re-live* those precious moments with

---

35 Late Latin from Greek, 'hagio' : sacred, 'graphia' : writings.

the Master by going through the entries in the diary. From the biographical details available, we understand that while blessing the listeners with his rich learning and experience under the master, 'M' would get transported to the very presence of the Master and re-live the experiences, transcending space and time. Till date, if one reads the book, one *can experience,* something more elevating than the common, day-to-day, mundane happiness. And if one follows and makes the teachings a part of one's life, then one starts feeling the Divine even in the mundane life.

The *Swādhyāya* of a scripture like *Yoga Vāsiṣṭha* can really benefit only such a person who goes beyond the limited words and word-wars, and tries to *feel* the suggestive hints therein. For, the words *only try to clothe the experiences, which transcend expression.* There is an unrecorded incident on the greatness of Shri Aurobindo's epic poem, *'Savitri'.*

A professor, who had been considered as an authority on Shri Aurobindo's literature, was visited by a man, seemingly very ordinary in his appearance. When the professor inquired into the purpose of the visit, the man expressed his inability to *read* the epic.

Fond of listening to one's own voice as professors usually are(!), he did not allow the man to continue. Instead, he started describing the terseness of the saint's language. After a while, again the man said, that was *not* the case, but *he had difficulty in reading* it. Once again the professor said that he was not at all surprised, as *everyone could not have access to Shri Aurobindo's* writings.

But again the man said in an appealing tone, that he was unable to read *as he could not see the words any more. Instead, a very quiescent blue light emanated from the book, ushering in a feeling of calmness and peace.* It is said, that the professor was humbled and he fell at the feet of the visitor. The professor said respectfully, that the Saint had mentioned that each word represents and has been filled with Supra-Consciousness, that can be experienced only by the pure and the innocent!

The necessity of innocence is being repeated, as the contemporary system of education mostly stresses the *intellectual* development at *the cost of other higher faculties* like sensitivity and *intuition.* Perhaps, this has been one of the main reasons why the deeper teachings were lost in the mire of hair splitting arguments of the pundits which incidentally, are beyond the reach of a common man or even a sincere seeker.

Typically, there are two tendencies in human beings. The first has been called as *'Pravṛtti'*, the tendency for *involvement.* The second has been referred to as *'Nivṛtti'* the tendency for *freedom. Pravṛtti* takes us towards involvement with the *external* (the world) through identification with *Ahaṁkāra, Buddhiḥ, Manas,* senses and body. Such an involvement and identification gives us the *conviction* in the permanence and reality of the world. Most of us are governed by this tendency. Almost every one of us acts as though the life is eternal. Our sense of belonging with the gross possessions or relationships proves that we all have *conveniently* forgotten the most obvious and most certain truth. An interesting episode from the *Mahābhārata,* illustrates this point.

The Pāṇḍu princes were in exile in a forest. They felt very thirsty. Sahadeva, the youngest of the five brothers was sent to fetch water. The direction of the pond was given by Nakula from a tree. Sahadeva reached the pond and was about to drink the water, when he heard a voice forbidding him, and to drink only after answering the questions posed by it. Thirsty that he was, Sahadeva not paying any heed to the words drank the water and collapsed. He was followed by Nakula, Arjuna and Bhīma, who too fell due to their impatience. Worried about the younger brothers, the eldest of the Pāṇḍu princes, Yudhiṣṭhira, approached the pond and was shocked to find his brothers dead.

However, unable to bear the thirst he too touched the water, only to be stopped by the voice. Instead of continuing to drink, Yudhiṣṭhira stopped and requested the voice to ask the questions. A very interesting conversation followed between the two. One of the questions was : "What is the most surprising phenomenon in the world?" Yudhiṣṭhira's reply was: 'Man sees death every moment, and yet he acts as though he is immortal!'

Man clings to everything, from body and sensations to *Ahaṁkāra,* the 'I-ness', which happens to be the subtlest of the manifestations. This *tendency to cling* has been called as *Pravṛtti Lakṣaṇa.* Most of us fall into this category. There is another tendency which is opposed to this: the *Nivṛtti Lakṣaṇa. Nivṛtti Lakṣaṇa* dawns on those fortunate few, who have seen through the temporal nature of the world, as most of us understand the world. The three stories in the episode under discussion, the *Utpatti Prakaraṇa,* hint at the fact, that the world as we perceive it through the senses and the mind is only a manifestation of the Ultimate Reality, which *transcends all Its manifestations.*

The Transcendental Reality cannot be perceived by the senses, or conceived by the mind. Sage Vasiṣṭha suggests through this story of Aindavas or the sons of Indu, the moon that the world is made to appear as eternal and real through the *desire.* One gets liberated when one frees oneself from the snares of the *multiplicity creating desires.* And that the process of *creation* of multiplicity, is so subtle, that it is not known, even to the creator!

Once, Lord Brahmā (the Creator) rose at the dawn of *his* day. Refreshed by the sleep during *his* night, during which all creation merges into One Fountainhead, he surveyed the *Ākāśa,* before taking up the act of creation. The *Ākāśa* started pervading everywhere, through his mind. Simultaneously, it began to fill with all kinds of creations. Unable to restrain his awe at the mystery of creation, Brahmā summoned one of the innumerable suns in the Cosmos, wanting to know the author of the creation. The sun was surprised at the ignorance of the Creator and said that he could explain it only through a story.

In a place called Suvarṇatala in the island of Jambu, near Mount Kailāśa, there lived a descendent of Sage Kaśyapa, a noble Brahmin named Indu. He, along with his wife resorted to propitiate Paramaśiva, for they did not have any off-spring. Both performed arduous penance tasting only water and *remaining motionless most of the time.* Pleased with their devotion, Mahādeva (the Great God) appeared and offered them a boon. They were blessed with ten sons and were freed from all pain. In course of time, the parents died.

The thought of performing penance crossed the mind of the ten sons and they retired to Mount Kailāśa. They also, pondered what they hoped to achieve through the penance. At first they thought of becoming *leaders of men,* but realised that it was too insignificant. Even the thought of becoming emperors seemed too paltry. So finally, they decided to become Brahmās, the Creators. They engaged themselves in deep meditation, and *willed* themselves into becoming what they intended. That was how, the ten *Lokas*[36] were created, and the ten kinds of creations were generated by these ten personages in *their psychic Ākāśas.* The sun submitted to Brahmā, that out of the ten suns, he was one. Having said this, the sun disappeared from the sight.

The story illustrates certain subtle processes symbolically. The creative faculty in us, responsible for the outward manifestation is One and all-pervading consciousness, which is being referred to as Brahmā, the Creator. Every process in the perceptible universe is cyclic in its nature. That is, day and night; seasons; rest and activity; and so on. One of the deepest fears troubling us is the *fear of being lonely,* which is

---

36 Refers to the ten planes of consciousness.

very obvious from our own experience. All our activity is to dispel the loneliness from our mind. But after this fear and the consequent struggle, we discover that amidst the company we have sought so desperately, we would like to be alone! It is an altogether different thing, that we have mastered the art of *wearing masks!* This conflict however, throws some light on this phenomenon.

Most if not all of us, have a mistaken notion that *life is synonymous with activity, and death with non-activity.* Paradoxically, we are aware that rest and activity are only obverse and reverse of the coin we call life. One without the other, is not only unhealthy, but even unimaginable. If we are obsessed with either activity or rest, we can definitely say, that there is something seriously wrong. Seeking company is synonymous with activity and wanting to be alone is like needing rest. But our wrong notion of life and death makes us afraid of loneliness. None of us is scared to sleep, though it is *temporary death!* This story hints that even the Cosmic creation and dissolution is cyclic like activity and rest.

The next reason and perhaps a stronger one, is that while we are alone, our inner weaknesses, desires, and obsessions do not allow us to rest. The most common ailment of our time is insomnia. Psyche, which is the huge factory of desires, suspicions, anxiety and worry, is running round the clock! And the most unfortunate thing is that it is totally automatic and it seems there is no one to control it! Consequently, we use tranquilisers, alcohol in our desperation, which can offer only temporary relief, while there are others who resort to work as a means of escape. Such persons have been called *workaholics!* In seeking such shallow and myopic alternatives we only succeed in getting diversions from our inner problems. If only we peep within, we are bound to find that we are goaded towards activity by this mood of avoidance, may it be our learning, occupation, recreation, or even the so-called service to our fellow beings.

The second hint this story offers us is, that unless the mind is *totally* quietened, the thoughts are very much there even during the period of rest. They exist in seed form, to sprout into fully grown trees immediately on waking up. This is very obvious from our daily experience. Brahmā not being aware of his own creation signifies this fact. The greatest tragedy in our life is that most of our problems are *self-created.* But we have forgotten that we are the authors of our own life-histories, due to which we suffer, and suffer needlessly.

Iṅdu, the moon, the name of the Brahmin in the story, has been associated with the mind in our mythology. He did not have any progeny, and propitiated Paramaśiva, the supremely benign, the God responsible for death and destruction of evil. He is also associated with renunciation and *Yoga.* If we remember Him who is synonymous with death, during all actions, He or the memory of death, gives purity to actions. Another very important practical hint given here is that the couple did the *Tapas* by remaining *motionless most of the time.* This means, that the mind has to become *totally silent* which is *its* motionlessness, to have the experience of Paramaśiva.

The ten sons, so obtained, are capable and noble. The ten sons may also refer to the ten instruments: five *Jñānendriyas* (the organs of knowledge : ears, skin, eyes, nose, and tongue) and five *Karmendriyas* (the organs of action : speech, hands, legs, the organs of excretion and generation). Ācārya Śaṅkara enumerates them in his *Vivekacūḍāmaṇi* :

> 'The ears, skin, eyes, nose and tongue are organs of knowledge, for they help us gain knowledge of objects, *Viṣayas* or stimuli. The organ of speech, hands, legs, the anus and the genital organ are the organs of action since they have the tendency for work'.[37]

---

37 बुद्धीन्द्रियाणि श्रवणं त्वगक्षि घ्राणंच जिह्वाविषयाव बोधानात् ।
वाग्पाणिपादा गुदमप्युपस्थः कर्मेन्द्रियाणि प्रवणेन कर्मसु ॥ 92 ॥

If the instruments are *blessed* by the memory of Paramaśiva, they become auspicious and they remain *our instruments instead of our being their instruments!* Then they have *Tapas*—penance, or the *right effort* as the guiding principle, which alone helps them negate all the temporal goals and seek the Eternal.

Developing that awareness, which makes it clear that whatever is perceived or experienced is only a creation of the mind, and seeking the origin of the mind ('I') is a necessary step towards the *real evolution,* is another important lesson we learn from the present story. Paramahansa Shri Ramakrishna used to say that we should get acquainted with the Creator before getting enamoured by the creation, because, the creation is so captivating that we invariably forget the Creator. Maharishi Shri Ramana, used to give the master key for solving *all* problems of life, by suggesting that before one gets disturbed by any situation or problem, one must ask *'who'* is it that is getting disturbed.

There is a wonderful prayer expressed in a *Mantra* of *Iśa Upaniṣad*:

> 'The face of the Truth is covered with a golden orb;
> Oh Nourisher, and the Guardian of travelers!
> Uncover the orb for me, so that I, an aspirant of Truth,
> May behold the Truth'![38]

The creation is so blinding that almost all of us are unable to behold the Creator. We have involved ourselves in the self-hypnosis through the *notion, that it is difficult,* and that we cannot possibly experience the Truth. The only course open to us is to develop a strong faith in ourselves that if others could do it *we too can!* We should also remind ourselves *constantly* that whatever is perceived through the senses and

---

38 हिरण्मयेन पात्रेण सत्यस्यापिहितं मुखम् ।
तत्वं पूषन्नपावृणु सत्यधर्माय दृष्टये ।। ईशावास्योपनिषद् 16 ।।

mind *need not be the absolute truth.* As and when this dependency on our senses, and the *conviction on the reality* of the world experienced by the senses or conceived by the mind, reduces, the golden orb or the glamour starts waning and the Non-dual Reality starts waxing.

The star filled sky has always been an object of fascination for the mankind. It has consolation for the man afflicted with worry, tension and misery. It has inspiration for the poet and artist. It has an inexhaustible source of information for the scientist. It has mystery and awe for a deeply sensitive person. There is a relationship, an imperceptible and definite bond, which links the experiencer with the universe.

This truth dawns on him when he looks at the stars and the star systems. He can realise that he is not only an integral part of it, but that he too has a definite role—no matter how insignificant, to play in it. Only he has to *look beyond* the obvious. He has to discover the vibration of the universe and *vibrate* with it. He *can* do this, with perseverance, sincere effort and a little help from the wise in person or in the form of books like the *Vāsiṣṭha.* Everyone of us has the capacity to look beyond our sense perception and the *creations of the mind,* to behold the Truth which is always there at our beck and call, though it depends on the intensity of our call and of course, our aspiration.

5

The Story of Indra

The apples, cherries and pears were in blossom. Strange as it may seem, but there was not even a single leaf on any of these plants. All of them were dressed like the brides in white or in pale pink! Even while some of the plants were in the process of blossoming, bees, the winged guests started arriving. Though the apiary was nearly three kilometers away from the orchard, they had come all the way there. The constant and monotonous hum was an indication that they were participating in the creative process of fertilizing the blossoms. And for the work, they were being rewarded with a droplet of honey by each blossom. The blossoms had attracted the bees with their colour and fragrance. Though this grand exchange is meant only for the self-preservation, it has a great lesson in the natural harmony and mutual co-existence.

Bees are one of the most organised of the insect species. Their behaviour has been observed and the scientists have recorded certain surprising, if not startling, facts. They have what are called the *scouts* in each beehive, which are on the look-out for the flowers. When they locate the food in the form of blossoming or blossomed flowers, the scouts return and are said to execute what has been referred to as the *'bee-dance'*. The bee-dance gives the other bees all information, such as the direction and distance! And the worker bees negotiate large distances, sometimes up to sixteen kilometers towards the flowers and return to their hives to deposit the droplets of honey!

Shri Ramakrishna, who was not only a great teacher but, also an eternal learner, has spoken on these creatures from the insect world. In a simile, he has compared the bees with the common house-flies. He says that a fly sits with pleasure on a sweet and enjoys it. It also sits on filth with equal, if not more pleasure. While the bee sits only on flowers. An ordinary and uncontrolled mind is like a fly. It dwells on good as well as bad or vicious thoughts. Unless and until we transform the mind to become like a bee, we cannot experience the Divine.

It is true that in the ultimate analysis, thoughts, the virtuous or the vicious, are different not in kind but only in degree. However, for a beginner it is very important to guard his mind from indulging in *wasteful and energy dissipating* thoughts and occupations. The saint of Dakshineswar Shri Ramakrishna used to say, that a young plant is to be protected from cattle, by fencing it with a protective hedge around it. But once it grows into a tree, even an elephant can be tied to it.

Indra is a very paradoxical *Deva* (God). He is the king of Gods, and is known for his prowess. So much so, that he is supposed to be the presiding deity of the arms. The depiction in numerous stories in the *Purāṇas* is not very commendable to his character. Indra is shown as an extremely jealous and cunning person. Whenever a person performs penance, he feels threatened and tries to disturb the person, in all possible ways, including the seduction through the heavenly nymphs. Viśwāmitra, is one such person, who experienced a fall due to Menakā. Indra is not only cunning, but also easily excitable and very sensual. For him seducing even Ahalyā, the chaste wife of *Ṛṣi* Gautama,[39] is not only imaginable but possible. For achieving this he can even resort to impersonation!

39 As narrated in Canto 48, of *Bālakāṇḍa* of Vālmīki Rāmāyaṇa.

Such exploits in our mythology sometimes makes us feel embarrassed to openly discuss them with people from other thought streams. A question arises as to why such stories were included in our scriptures. Mostly, we waive them off by explaining that they are just a bunch of some stupid stories written for some vicarious purpose by some perverts, and add that only the *Upaniṣads* represent our culture, while the *Purāṇas* are only the later additions. By doing so, we not only become closed to a very rich store of useful hints, but also negate our grand spiritual heritage. On the contrary, if we have enough patience to examine the deeper aspects we can derive immense benefit from them.

We have to remember, that our Culture *never believed in any division* of life, into the two opposing fragments called *the spiritual* and *the mundane.* Life for us has always been an organic whole. Everything has a place in it, and which is recognised as an integral part. Thus lust is not a taboo, but has a very important function in life. So also jealousy, anger, greed and the other so-called negative manifestations of the mind. They all are of great help in propagation and preservation. But *definitely, they are not the ends in themselves.*

Indra represents the mind in all its functions. At the gross level, it is associated with the senses and is responsible for gathering the information from the sense stimuli. Necessarily, at this level, it is restless and excitable. This is called in *Vedānta* as *Manas.* At a slightly deeper level, it has been called as *Buddhiḥ,* and is responsible for analysis and decision making. But then, it can also be cunning and scheming! Then comes *Citta* or the function of remembering. Not only the good things are remembered, but the unpleasant as well and perhaps, a little more intensely! The *Ahaṁkāra* ('I-ness'), which is the subtlest of the gross manifestations, governs all other functions, and controls them. It can however, generate jealousy, pride, egoism, egotism and other undesirable qualities.

With this background, we can not only understand Indra's nature, but can begin to have appreciation for it. For, he is all-powerful and anything is within his reach. While he can cause our fall, he can become instrumental in our *real evolution.* While he can excite us into indulgence, he can also make us sensitive and open to existence, so as to become one with it. While he can make us the victims of greed, we can become eligible for the emperorship by *experiencing expansiveness and large heartedness* through his grace. This knowledge can be of great help to a seeker in developing the will, a mandatory pre-requisite for the Divine adventure.

It is our common experience, that although, we are surrounded by many desires which are nourished by us, hardly a few get fulfilled. This is so, due to the fact, that they are mostly *passing thoughts,* without any strength of their own. However, if they are strengthened by the *will,* we find that we can even make the impossible dreams come true. The will is weak due to diversion, excitement and our *Rāga* (likes) and *Dweṣa* (dislikes). Consequently, the desires remain at the level of *wishful thinking.* We understand this, if we just study the lives of not only the *top achievers,* in every field, but also persons like Genghis Khan, Adolf Hitler, Benito Mussolini and other enemies of existence.

It is said that persons like Hiraṇyakaśipu and Rāvaṇa were so powerful as to have control over even the elemental forces. But for a seeker the control or mastery has only *one* aspect: *control or mastery over oneself through the control over one's mind, emotions and thoughts!* Two of the innumerable ways in which one can have such control are, by the power of strong determination, generally referred to as the *will;* and through the power of proper understanding. *Yoga Vāsiṣṭha* recommends the second path. This is the reason why it dwells so much on the mechanism of the process of creation of the *Ahaṁkāra* ('I-ness'), the principle behind every conceivable activity in the manifested world.

The most persistent hassle and hurdle, which stops us from experiencing the Non-dual Reality, is the *obstinate conviction in the reality of the world of objects.* The first *Sarga* in this *Utpatti Prakaraṇa,* the story of Ākāśaja, shows that it is possible to be in the world, yet out of it—like a boat floating on water without allowing the *water to be in it.*

The story of Līlā illustrates, that even a person involved with the world *can* come out of its clutches. For, what binds us to the world is *our own attachment to it.* Shri Ramakrishna, used to say that one must rub one's hands with oil before breaking open the jack-fruit, else the hands will be smeared with its sticky milk. He advised the seekers to first secure the oil of divine love, and then only to set the hands to the duties of the world.[40] By oil of divine love, the great Master meant, the discrimination born out of understanding, which alone lightens the burden of the seeker. Through the third story of Karkaṭī, the author tries to stress that everyone, no matter of what background, can break the strong bonds binding us to the world. In the fourth story of Aiṅdavas, sage Vālmīki tries to show us that the creation is only of and in the mind; and that it is of equal importance as our dreams. The story of Iṅdra, which is under discussion, declares that it is the mind which strengthens the conviction of the reality of the world.

The country of Magadha was ruled by king Indradyumna (having the aura of Iṅdra). Queen Ahalyā was very dear to him, even dearer than life. As if a former episode of Ahalyā—wife of sage Gautama—and Indra was being re-enacted, the queen had a secret love affair with one Indra. The two lovers passed their days in pleasure. But as always, truth and untruth, or virtue and vice, cannot be hidden for long and it shows itself. Some persons having respect and admiration for the king reported the matter. The shock and dejection came out

---

40 *The Gospel of Shri Ramakrishna* by M, IXth impression, Shri Ramakrishna Math, Madras, p. 82.

in the form of wrath. The king ordered the straying couple to be sunk in deep water. But this did not affect the couple in the least. Determined to punish them, he subjected them to many ordeals like trampling under rutting elephants, throwing them to flames, etc. In spite of such tortures, the couple remained unaffected. Instead, they merely smiled, regarding each other with firm minds as they sat opposite to each other.

Bewildered at the foiled attempts to inflict pain, the king asked them about the secret of their being proof against torture. The pair said, that as they enjoyed peace and bliss in each other's company, they were totally oblivious to the body and nothing could affect them. And that all bodies (past, present as well as the distant future), are just manifestations of the mind. They continued that just like the forest thriving on water, the body exists only due to mind. Consequently, even if the body gets destroyed, the mind can assume new bodies, to its liking.

If the mind is quelled, then the body has no intelligence. Hearing these words, sage Bharata, who was sitting close to the king, observed, that though the couple was involved in sinful activity, they spoke the words of wisdom. Therefore, they were banished from the kingdom so that they might enjoy each other's company in foreign lands.

There are similar stories in our mythology. It is said, that a great Brahmin pleased with the king Bhartṛhari, gave a divine fruit to prolong his youth and life. Being very much in love with queen Padmākṣī, his wife, he gave it to her. But the queen had a secret lover to whom the fruit was offered! The lover in turn, gave it to a prostitute, *whom he loved!* The prostitute, thinking deeply offered it to Bhartṛhari, whom *she secretly admired and loved!* She thought that if the king partook of the fruit, the country and the people would be highly benefited. Greatly surprised, by the return of the same fruit, Bhartṛhari traced it to the queen and her secret lover. He exclaimed :

'The woman of whom I keep thinking all the time, is not at all interested in me and is in turn love with another man. She does not interest him at all, but is infatuated to another woman. But that woman does not have any feeling for him but is enamoured of me. Fie on the woman I love, the man she loves, the woman he is infatuated, the God of Love, and me'![41]

This insulting situation was too much for the queen who committed suicide. The king developed a great dispassion and became a disciple of Gorakhanātha and later a great *Yogi* himself. He has authored the *Śaṭakatrayaṃ* or three hundred *Ślokas,* a hundred each on *Śriṅgāra* (Love), *Nīti* (ethics) and *Vairāgya* (disinterest).

We have many other stories dwelling on the infidelity of a spouse. And surprisingly, we find that for a similar, if not the same situation, there are different reactions depending on the spiritual growth. However, the main point in this story of Iṅdra is, not about the reaction, but the strong control of the mind over the body.

Vedānta always recognises the intimate relationship between the mind and the body, in the sense, that the mind is subtle body, and the body is gross mind. Due to this inter-relationship the body can be easily controlled by the mind, while the mind can be controlled by the body with an effort. For it is easier to control the gross with the subtle. When the mind is absorbed in some action—sport, recreation or the intellectual pursuit—we hardly notice any discomfort of body. It is a very common experience, that there is no consciousness of any injury *during* the play, though we do experience the pain later.

There is sufficient proof of body becoming resistant to painful stimuli under hypnotic conditions. Basically, pain is

---

41 यां चिन्तयामि सततं मयि सा विरक्ता साऽप्यन्यमिच्छति जनं स जनोऽन्यसक्तः ।
अस्मात्कृते च परिशुष्यति काचिदन्या धिक्तां च तं च मदनं च इमां च मां ॥

a nerve stimulus felt by the senses, meant for self-preservation. The senses keep collecting the external stimuli like sight, sound, smell, taste and touch, as well as the bodily stimuli of either discomfort like hunger and pain or of comfort and pleasure. But unless the mind *recognises* them, it is not possible to experience them. That is why, we *feel* only a few of the thousands of stimuli collected by the senses. The collection and rejection of sense data, is one of the functions of the mental activity. When this activity is involved with any other function, it does not register the sense stimulus.

While one is reading an interesting book, or is involved in some absorbing thoughts like worry(!), he cannot hear someone calling his name, or someone greeting him. As and when the mind gets involved with deeper functions like the act of remembering, one is farther away from the body and the senses. In this story, we see that the lovers were totally oblivious to all the discomfort. Not only that, but they were confident of *creating* new bodies, being aware that the body is only a grosser manifestation of the mind. We have the popular story of Prahlāda being tortured by his own father Hiraṇyakaśipu, remaining unaffected due to his total absorption with the divine name and the meditation on the divine form.

One is tempted to conclude, that these stories are exaggerated. But we have some cases—though rare—of persons undergoing surgical operations without any anesthesia, and experiencing no pain. Swami Trigunatitananda (a direct disciple of Shri Ramakrishna) and Maharishi Ramana of Tiruvannamalai, are two such persons. When asked how it was possible, they had identified with the Non-dual Reality, and were in control of *everything*, body, mind and being. There is an episode from the life of Shri Aurobindo, the great sage of Pondicherry which illustrates the control one is capable of having, not only on one's body *but even the nature around.*

There was a cyclone in the sea one late evening. The Mother, a disciple of Shri Aurobindo, was going around the *Āśrama* and arranging to close all the windows. But when she personally entered Shri Aurobindo's room, she was pleasantly surprised to see, that there was not even a sign of the cyclone there, and the loose sheets on which the sage had written were lying scattered, undisturbed. And *all the windows were wide open!* It was as though the cyclone had not dared to disturb the room in which the sage stayed! He was so totally in control of the internal nature, that even the external nature had been *forced* to become calm and peaceful. However, for most of us, the bodily pain is a reality, and that persons like Shri Aurobindo are rare indeed. But this is because *we believe the pain to be real!*

Through this story sage Vālmīki tries to suggest the seeker, that if he wants to, he can overcome all the hurdles, physical, mental as well as the social, to march towards the Non-dual Reality. If the Indra-Ahalyā pair could achieve such non-identified state for even an immoral purpose, then is it not possible for a seeker who has the lofty ideal of Self-realisation as the beacon?

One of the first hurdles the seeker has to cross, is the bodily discomfort or its needs and hungers. The wisdom spelt out by this story is, that the gross physical body and its subtler companions are only the manifestations of the Ultimate Reality. If we keep our attention of 'That', which is the abode of *everything* then every obstacle only becomes a stepping stone towards the destination. To climb a step, one has to exert and put in effort. But then, the effort or the exertion is necessary for any endeavour, be it material or spiritual.

These so-called hurdles can be crossed over with the help of the impeccable intent, the single pointed devotion to the chosen ideal. Speaking of Narendranath (the future Swami Vivekananda) Shri Ramakrishna used to give the example of the Homā bird :

> 'The *Vedas* speak of the *Homā* bird. It lives high up in the sky and there it lays its eggs. As soon as the egg is laid, it begins to fall; but it is so high up that it continues to fall for many days. As it falls it hatches, and the chick falls. As the chick falls, its eyes open; it grows wings. As soon as its eyes open, it realises that it is falling and will be dashed to pieces on touching the earth. Then it at once shoots up toward the mother bird high in the sky'.[42]

About the ordinary who posed themselves as great pundits, he would say that they are like the kites, though high up in the sky, their eyes are on the dead animals!

It is said, that the bees prefer to die than to sit on filth. There is another example of *Cātaka* bird which waits for the droplets of rain when the star *Swāti* is in ascendance. A seeker will do well to be choosy about his thoughts which are nothing but the *guests of the mind.* If she or he *entertains them* they are bound to visit us regularly! And the strongest thoughts are usually of possession and indulgence. In the words of Guru Nānak, this world is nothing but a *Dharmaśālā* or *Sarāi,* the way side rest house for the pilgrims. Many of us have made it our home, and have forgotten to proceed to our destination. That is why, man *can never be satisfied* with all the material achievements which belong to the *Sarāi.*

The memory of our decision to embark on this pilgrimage however, is very much there deep within, in spite of the layers of distracting desires which are but temporary. Once this memory is refreshed, in the company of the wise or the wisdom from the books like *Vāsiṣṭha,* the bee or the homā nature does manifest. The human birth becomes a meaningful, purposeful and fulfilling journey within. Where, one does not travel in either space or time, but transcends all the manifestations to *be* in the control room of existence.

---

42 *The Gospel of Shri Ramakrishna* by M, Shri Ramakrishna Math, Madras, IXth Impression, p. 88.

6

The Story of Manas

After crossing many small and large hills through the winding road that passes through lush green and thick forests, one reaches the valley, surrounded by the *Sahyādri* mountains. A river, having its origin somewhere in the mountains, flows. The river is not very deep, but a dip in the water is very soothing, relieving the fatigue of night's journey on a vehicle for the pilgrim. The advent of a new day is announced by the reddish hue of dawn on top of the mountains. With it, the eyes and the other senses open up and become receptive to the grandeur of nature. One can behold the clouds moving along the mountain peaks high above; the tropical jungle peopled by the ancient trees with their imposing sizes, convince man of his puniness. They stand witness to time and act as sentinels guarding the sanctity of the place; it is the home of many a beautiful birds and a rich wild-life. Man is only a visitor. Perhaps to discourage unwanted elements, the mandatory rigorous self-discipline is imposed on the pilgrims.

It attracts thousands of devotees every year, in spite of the fact that one has to observe a very strict self-disciplinary period of forty days. The season of this pilgrimage is during the winter months of December and January. Especially, on the day of *Makara Sankrānti,* lakhs of persons reach there. One gets the transport only up to *Pamba,* from where one has to trek to the temple of Ayyappa on the mountain top of

Sabarimala. The Deity is supposed to be the outcome of the union of two great Gods, Viṣṇu and Śiva. Just near the temple, there is a shrine of a Muslim Saint Vāvar. Sabarimala is a haven of the devout and many have a very firm belief that if one is sincere all the desires will be fulfilled. In the past one and a half decades, it has become all the more popular as the devotees from all over the country reach there.

If one is interested in not only having a quiet *Darśana,* but also the glimpses of real nature, and wilderness, then the best time is, during the first five days of every Malayalam month, when the temple is open. The river Pamba, having its source on a mountain top, flows incessantly. Presently, the trekking route has been laid. One can imagine how it would have been, when the devotees had to walk bare foot, that is one of the conditions laid down for the devotees, on the wild forest trails. Even to this day, the forest on the mountain slopes is truly breath-taking. The girth of many of the trees is over thirty feet, and the height reaches over two hundred feet. This indicates that man's 'look of greed' has not yet touched the forest slopes.

Consequently, the wild life too has been protected, for whatever reason, religion or inaccessibility. There are elephants, leopards, bears, hyenas and a host of other animals. One cannot have the *Darśana* of these fellow-creatures, if one visits the shrine during the pilgrim season. They all must be fighting shy of the multitude of pilgrims, who come there to seek peace. In the process however, the pilgrims take away the peace of the jungle!

When we visit the places like Sabarimala abounding in the forest and wildlife wealth, we notice remarkable differences between the human beings and the so-called wild animals. While the wild beasts hunt for their *food,* the human beings do it for *sport!* We derive *pleasure out of violence.* The animals also struggle for existence, and try their level best to save themselves from becoming food to the carnivorous animals.

But they accept the death quite gracefully when it comes to them. The human beings on the other hand fret and fume for every little incident, and there is a *mood of complaint* in almost everything that happens to us! And death is perhaps the most frightening event for us.

Paradoxically, that is the grandeur of human birth. It appears selfish, greedy, mean, violent and cunning. Even then, it has been accepted by our *Ṛṣis* as a higher link in the chain of evolution. The cow may never utter a lie, a tree may never steal, but they will remain as they are born, a cow and a tree. But man is different. He may murder, he may take the help of lies to achieve his ends. But he can also become a sage in his own right! He may exploit the fellow-beings, but he can also become so large hearted, as to give-up his *everything* for their sake. He can and does deplete the natural resources and plunder nature, but it is the man who becomes aware of the follies and awakens himself and tries to awaken the fellow-men.

The fact remains, that there is exploitation and other not-so-laudable qualities, which are bringing the humanity to the brink of disaster and it seems, an imminent catastrophe. The most common and abundant commodity seems to be *the misery!* To this extent the Lord calls such existence as *Dukkhālayaṁ Aśāśvataṃ* (temporal house of misery), in the *Bhagavadgītā.*[43]

Many a time, we find that in spite of our best intentions, we are confronted by misery. And we—especially in our country—are tempted to conclude, that life as such is a miserable struggle for existence with intermittent glimpses of happiness; that there is no other way to live than of meek acceptance. Why does the life become a house of misery and how can a qualitative transformation of the life, as most of lead can be achieved, forms the main purpose of *Adhyātma Vidyā.*

---

43 Chapter 8, verse 15.

There are *Vedāntic* suggestions, scattered in the *Upaniṣads* and other texts, to indicate that *almost every event, good or otherwise, is there because we wanted it to be there.* We identify with our problems so much that we are convinced that the events *should have a disturbing effect* over us. There are many enlightening episodes from the life of Gautama, the Buddha, not only inspiring us to transform our way of life, but also show us the path towards a life of freedom and bliss.

As his wont to beg his food from people, Tathāgata stood in front of a house for the purpose. The master of the house was sitting on the verandah. Looking at the handsome and a very healthy constitution of the beggar, he started scolding him. The master observed that in spite of such strong constitution, he had resorted to begging; that irresponsible people like him were responsible for the sorry state of affairs afflicting the country....And observing no change in the mendicant he got more annoyed and started using abusive language. Hearing the angry voice of her husband, the lady of the house, peeped out through the window. When she discovered that the victim of her husband's wrath to be no other than Tathāgata himself, of whom she had heard so much, she called her husband inside and revealed the mendicant's identity.

Embarrassed, he came out and fell at the Lord's feet, sought pardon for his behaviour, and offered him food with all respect and devotion. The Buddha partook of the meal without any hesitation whatsoever. When Śākyamuni was about to take his leave, the house-holder asked as to how it had been possible for the Lord not to be angry or feel insulted by his harsh and impertinent words or remarks. The Buddha smilingly replied by asking a counter-question:

> 'What would happen to the food you offered, if I refused to eat? Where would it be?'

The man replied with hesitation:

'It would remain with me.'

Tathāgata explained smilingly :

'Similarly, the harsh words were refused by me!'

If we just observe ourselves and our companions, it becomes obvious, that for a similar situation there are different reactions by the different persons. This is logically explained by the Transactional Analysis, a recent development in the field of Psychiatry. The psychiatrists explain the peculiar human behaviour through a concept of '*Life-Scripts*'.

It is based on the hypothesis that each one of us acts a role in this great drama of life, in strict accordance to a script written in the formative period of our life, which is between one and five years. During this formative period, the *'blue-print'* of our life is finalised. This no doubt depends on many factors including heredity, environment and milieu. The notions about specific stimuli-reaction, right or wrong, that have been going on for a very long time in the society or family, continue to influence the impressionable mind during the formative stage of life. And that is how, if one may say so, that we become like computers with key-boards. Press a key, and we *'Run'* the pre-recorded programme! And the beauty is that our keys are so very sensitive, it is not even necessary to touch!

As has been already pointed out, that one of the most wonderful aspects of our grand culture is the acceptance of *everything* as a part of the Divine. There is no division of existence into the two opposites like, Sacred and Profane or Divine and Satanic. *Taittirīyopaniṣad* brings home this point in the *Ānanda Mīmāṁsa* portion of the chapter called *Brahmānanda-Valli.*

Science has made many positive contributions for the human welfare, of which the concept of measurement is one. While Science has succeeded in quantifying only the gross material things, this *Upaniṣad* has tried to quantify *Ānanda* or *Bliss!* As in any scientific treatise, at the very outset it defines a unit of bliss as: a youth who is noble, energetic and healthy both physically and mentally. He is full of desires, at the same time; he has the whole world—peaceful and plentiful—at his disposal. The amount of bliss enjoyed by such a youth is defined as one unit *Mānuṣa Ānanda,* the maximum possible bliss that can be enjoyed by a human being. Then the *Upaniṣad* starts naming intermediate species of beings having higher and higher capacity for enjoyment.

Each of these species has a hundred times more capacity than the preceding one. Thus it names, *Manuṣya Gandharva, Deva Gandharva, Pitṛ, Ajānajāna, Karmadeva, Deva, Indra, Bṛhaspati* and *Brahmā* (the Creator). In this way, the Brahmā's *Ānanda* is 10^{18} times more than the human being's *Ānanda!* It may be asked, as to how this analysis is useful to us. It not only gives us the hierarchy of beings in the different planes of existence, but more importantly, it tells us that *qualitatively the Ānanda is the same while only the quantity increases.* It means that all beings *are essentially the same as far as the quality of bliss is concerned.* The only difference being, that the *dependency on the object of enjoyment decreases progressively in the higher beings.*

There is one more very important point made by the *Upaniṣad.* All along the analysis, it keeps repeating one sentence, every time it defines the *Ānanda* of a being :

> 'This is also achieved by *Śrotriya,* one who is living the spirit of the *Śrutis,* and has become *Akāmahatasya,* or *desire less*'.[44]

A little introspection will make us understand that *every thought is a potential desire.* And our entire struggle is to fulfill or quieten these thoughts. This means, that if one is able to quieten the mind, one can achieve the status of higher beings in this very body-mind complex. We have some persons who are more happy and content than others, or those who are more dissatisfied with their lot and life. The Science and Technology has definitely made more objects of enjoyment

---

44 श्रोत्रियस्य च अकामहतस्य ॥ 2.8 ॥

available. But unless we take the help of *Vedānta,* to *increase the capacity to enjoy,* it will only increase our restlessness and discontent, which is our present experience!

Sage Vasiṣṭha told Rāma, that we have two bodies, a subtle one which is connected to the mind, and a gross one, the elemental. The subtle mental body is characterised by tremendous speed which is the nature of mental activity and fluctuations. Though the gross body is inert, it is a manifestation of *Saṁkalpa* of the mind. On this, Rāma sought a clarification about the nature of the inert body, which is only a manifestation of mind. The sage replied that the form is assumed through the *Saṁkalpa* made at the subtlest level of *Ātman.* All conceptions associated with the activity arising out of *That,* are all forms of mind, *Ahaṁvṛtti*—the I-ness being the subtlest and physical body, the grossest. Thus everything, misery or bliss, is *self-created.*

The sage assured Rāma, that it does not matter how the mind proceeds or whatever form it manifests in, as long as it is made to tread the path leading to its origin, that is *Ātman.* This process alone is conducive to progress. To illustrate this point, the sage narrated the following story to the prince.

In a dense frightening forest lived a person, having countless arms, and eyes. His mind, having an extended form of *Ākāśa,* moved everywhere with great speed. This person was involved in a very strange action: he was inflicting injury to himself with sticks. And unable to bear the pain, he cried and yelled piteously! Sometimes he would dash himself against objects, jump into a deep well and make himself more and more miserable. Then he would raise himself out of the well and indulge in masochistic actions. He would run away from the self-created misery and go to a fruit garden so as to plunge into the diametrically opposite emotions of elation and excitement.

This plight of existence continued. Seeing the miserable life, Brahmā, the Creator, taking pity on the person, appeared before him to ask who he was and why he was indulged in self-infliction and subsequent suffering. The person replied, that he was unable to find any suitable action to engage himself, and that for him, the greatest pain was the heterogeneous differentiation set up by the Creator, who was his real enemy. Only due to Brahmā had he identified himself with pain and pleasure, the cause of suffering.

Having said so, he surveyed his own body, and started melting. This freed him from the many bodies he had assumed himself in many births. Then the person laughed aloud and became extremely calm and composed. Many similar persons appeared on earth, who were needlessly causing themselves injury and some followed the advice of Brahmā while the others continued to suffer needlessly. Even now there are many such persons in the world. However, there are some wise men, who in spite of living in the great forests with thorns, continue to rejoice and remain totally undisturbed by external situations.

On Rāma's request to explain the esoteric significance of the story, Sage Vasiṣṭha explained that the interminable forest in the story is this *Saṁsāra* which is without beginning, middle or end, and is associated with the dreadful *Māyā*. The person residing in the forest of the world, filled with fury and wrath stands for the mind, whirling in pain. The person approaching the mind is *Viveka,* the discrimination. Through discrimination, the mind attained to the quiescent state of *Para Brahman.* When the mind turns away from *Parābrahman,* it gets entangled itself in *Vāsanās* of sense objects. The well into which egos sink after torturing their bodies is *Naraka,* the hell. The fruit garden refers to *Swargaloka,* the heaven, full of enjoyments. The forest of trees abounding with thorns is *Bhūloka,* the earth with the two sexes full of passion. The person falling in and rising from the well refers to man or woman, experiencing the fruits of *unconscious* (wrong) actions in hell and rising from it again to take birth.

The words 'Creator is the real enemy' and 'It is only due to him that there is the identification with pain and pleasure' are the outbursts of the mind in its last gasp of death through discrimination. The mind half developed in *Jñāna* trying to annihilate the desires, gives out such a cry for aid as a last bid to survive. The final calm joy and the consequent laugh is the bliss arising out of the mind merging into pure *Jñāna.* The real bliss arises only when the mind destroys even its subtle form. The pain experienced by dashing against rocks and lashing oneself, refer to the pain due to involvement and indulgence with the world of objects. Concluding this story, sage Vasiṣṭha said that the *Saṁkalpas* and *Vāsanās* the self creations of man, enmesh him as in a net and in bondage, not unlike the silk worm in its cocoon. He advised Rāma to delve into the workings of the mind, by tracing the subjectivity, the 'I-ness' and to develop non-involvement.

The esoteric meaning of this story has been revealed by the sage himself. A doubt crosses our minds, as to who would be interested in inflicting pain on oneself? We all feel that it is not at all so, and on the contrary, we seek happiness. The persons who inflict self-injury are considered to be mentally ill by the society, and the illness is called masochism. Apparently, the conclusion drawn by the sage appears to be extremistic!

The observations of 'Transactional Analysis' clarify this point. It says that every one of us tries to seek 'attention' from others, and our mental health depends on the attention which is called as a *stroke* and this need is being called as *stroke hunger.* The attention in the form of *appreciation* is called as a *positive stroke,* and *depreciation* as a *negative stroke.* And if a person does not get any positive strokes, he or she will try to do something even if it is a wrong action to attract attention, and to invite wrath of the companions. There is a repetitive pattern of this process involving a particular behaviour. It might be that someone employs anger, someone else acts in a foolish manner, other may use other unpleasant means. This *'self-indulgence in feelings of guilt, inadequacy, hurt, fear and resentment is called racket'*.[45] And this repetitive behaviour which always concludes in unhappiness or misery has been called as a *game.*

In this sense most of us play *games to make ourselves and others miserable.* Since the positive happiness is difficult, we invite misery through our own thoughts and actions. This has been symbolically illustrated in the story. The 'I-ness' and other manifestations ending with the gross physical body, are the progressive stages into *Saṁsāra,* plunging us into attachment, anxiety, worry, anger, misery and depression. The stories in this *Prakaraṇa* try to convince us that as and when the manifestation becomes grosser, the misery also increases. The only solution to this problem is, through *Antarmukhatā* for tracing the *origin of the 'I-ness'.*

It is true that as compared to animal existence, human life appears to be beset with problems and full of struggle. It appears to be out of tune and almost *anti-existence.* But the beauty is that through all such trial and tribulations man *does* realise the purpose of his existence one time or the other which is to rise from his sub-human level to supra-human levels; to lend a helping hand to the fellow beings, and to become a source of great bliss not only to himself but to others who come in his contact. Perhaps, at that time he will be in a position to declare as Swami Vivekananda did :

> 'We should look upon man in the most charitable light. What are you but machines until you are free? Should you be proud because you are good? Certainly not. You are good because you cannot help it. Another is bad because he cannot help it. If you are in his position, who knows what you would have been? The woman in street, or the thief in jail, is the Christ that is being sacrificed that you may be a good man. Such is the law of balance. All the thieves and the murderers, all the

45 *Principles of Group Treatment,* Eric Berne, p. 308.

> unjust, the weakest, the wickedest, the devils, they are my Christ! I owe the worship to the God Christ and to the demon Christ! That is my doctrine, I cannot help it. My salutation goes to the feet of the good, the saintly, and to the feet of the wicked and the devilish! They are all my teachers, all are my spiritual fathers, all are my Saviours. I may curse one and yet benefit by his failings; I may bless another and benefit by his good deeds. This is as true as that I stand here. I have to sneer at the woman walking in the street, because the society wants it! She, my Saviour, she, whose street-walking is the cause of the chastity of other women! Think of that. Think, men and women, of this question in your mind.......Whom shall I blame? Whom shall I praise? *Both sides of the shield must be seen*'.[46]

The pilgrimage of Sabarimala, which demands not only the physical rigours but also the moral and ethical code of conduct—at least for a period of forty days, opens the mind and hearts of the devotees. Though most of them may embark on it only to fulfill or on fulfillment of some desires, the place and the period spent in the serene and sylvan surroundings has a calming effect on the mind of the most, if not all the devotees. Every pilgrim is, bare-footed, bare-chested, bearded, and wearing a black *Muṇḍu (Dhotī),* not only *looks* an equal to every other pilgrim, but even *feels* the comradeship with the others and the fellow- beings in the region.

Most of the pilgrim spots in our magnificent country are on scenic spots amidst sylvan surroundings abounding in nature, to remind us of the oneness of existence, to convince us that life is worth all the problems and struggle. And to make us understand, that there is nothing like the problems or struggle, but *there is only the effort towards fulfillment.*

---

46 *The Complete Works of Swami Vivekananda,* Vol-II, Adwaita Ashrama, Calcutta-14, XIIIth edition 1976, p. 34.

7

The Story of a Lad

The moonlight splashed over dancing ripples of vibrating water surface, giving an appearance of a lake of molten silver. The thick and dark foliage, adorning the trees on the embankment of the lake, the carpet of grass, and the earth as a whole, was bathed in the moonlight. Similar ripples, but of joy, were dancing in the heart of an onlooker beholding the scene. When the eyes turned to look into the details, it seemed as though the plants were no more ordinary plants but persons, giving a standing ovation to the grand scene. Each of these *plant-persons* had a distinct and a singular form, plucking at the strings of imagination of the onlooker. Their height, shape, and their *posture* enhanced the awe and wonder in the heart.

It is our common knowledge that, any situation or circumstance evokes a different reaction in different persons depending upon the attitude and aptitude of the person. For thousands of years, it is believed that, the moon is directly or indirectly connected to the mind.[47] For some the moon evokes fear, for others love, some others depression and yet others an innate joy, and perhaps even enlightenment as it was in the case of Siddhartha Gautama who became the Buddha on the *Vaiśākha Pūrṇimā,* the full moon night in the

---

47 चन्द्रमा मे मनसि स्थितः ।। रुद्रप्रश्नो लघुन्यासः ।।

summer month. What is the reason behind this difference in mental reactions?

From time immemorial, the question has often repeated itself in the human psychic stream : What is the purpose of this creation? This question no doubt has assumed different forms ("What is the goal of life?; What is the end point of all this?" etc.), but the spirit of which continues to remain and haunt the human thought. Explanations and counter explanations have been forwarded. Unfortunately, nothing seems to have had any satisfying effect. But the effort has been really grand and is paving way for the evolution of human thought. Some theories were only hypothetical and impractical and some were immature. However, many of them were interesting and thus instrumental in the spiritual evolution and growth.

Two of these theories are not only interesting, but have proved very efficacious to the seekers. However, these theories should not be taken *only* for quenching the intellectual thirst, but for *making use of the hints we get therefrom.*

The first of these theories suggests, that the creation is devoid of any substantial reality of its own, *without the perceiver or the experiencer.* Ācārya Śaṅkara the propagator of *Adwaita Vedānta,* declared

'Brahman is Truth. The world is unreal'.[48]

This statement however, led to a whole lot of misinterpretation and confusion. The objection was definitely very valid : How can the world which is experienced through the senses and *hence material* be unreal? Some of the great thinkers who have made positive contributions to the World thought and culture have vehemently opposed this view and have observed that this is a very negative and escapist explanation leading to lethargy and complacency. And they

48 ब्रह्म सत्यं जगन्मिथ्या...

are right! But unfortunately, we all—including the great men—tend to forget that all explanations are only *convenient* and are *only different points of view!* Due to this very reason, they are necessarily *incomplete.*

These explanations are convenient as they help the mind in doubt, not unlike a supporting stick to a weak man. But if he expects the stick to do the walking for him he is sadly mistaken! Some persons, who have struggled and suffered due to the evils of the caste system, have interpreted Hinduism as nothing but *Cāturvarṇaṃ,* the four-fold division of *Brāhmaṇa, Kṣatriya, Vaiśya* and *Śūdra.* Many western scholars have confirmed that it is difficult if not impossible to find the fifth type of human being, and that our sages had a perfect understanding of human nature. The understanding and knowledge is not responsible for its misinterpretation and misuse, but *we are.* Just as the knowledge of the inter-convertibility of matter and energy or Albert Einstein is not responsible for the genocidal weapons but the *human greed for power.*

Similarly, when some of us even hear the name of Ācārya Śaṅkara, we remember only the *Māyāvāda,* without bothering to look into the details. He wanted his *point of view* to be made use of in helping the animal-man to become a human-being, then to a Divine-being and finally to Divinity Itself. Śaṅkarācārya, who *walked three times* around this wide Country, organising the Sanyāsins, into the *Daśanāmi* or the order of ten names;[49] who revived the decaying Hinduism; who introduced the present form of the ritualistic worship *(Ṣoḍaṣopacāra Pūjā)* by synthesising *Tantra* and *Yoga;* and an almost flawless Commentary on the *Upaniṣads, Gītā* and the *Brahmasūtras.* And all this was accomplished within the short

---

49 *Araṇya, Āśrama, Bhāratī, Giri, Parvata, Puri, Saraswatī, Sāgara, Tīrtha* and *Vana.*

span of only three decades. How could such a person preach escapism or be blamed of being an escapist?

It only shows that we have misunderstood his view of the Reality. By the statement, he seems to have implied that the world is an illusion in *our interpretation of the world of multiplicity.* He gave the famous simile of mistaking the rope for a snake, in a dim light. Actually, there is no snake, only a rope. It is a snake *till we make sure that it is only a rope!* This misunderstanding of the world of multiplicity was called as *Māyā* by him, and which happens due to *wrong identification.* Moreover, even the oft-quoted statement is incomplete, for he had said:

> 'Brahman is Truth. The world is unreal. *The Jīva is Brahman alone and not different*'.[50]

The above statement, brings about a transformation in our outlook towards life. Because, by understanding the *spirit* of the statement, the life characterised by differentiation through the puny wells called 'I', 'you', 'he', 'she', 'it' or 'they' merges into the Oceanic life of Unity and Oneness. This in turn brings about fearlessness, love and harmony. From his life, it is very obvious that Śaṅkarācārya had realised the state of Adwaita. Not only that, he helped many others to achieve the state.

The second theory is *Bhedābheda* ("Identity and difference"), which is an important branch of *Vedānta.* Encyclopaedia Britannica mentions :

> 'Its principal author was Bhāskara, probably a younger contemporary of the great Śaṅkarācārya. The mainstay of Bhāskara's philosophy was the conviction that the world and Brahman are not mutually exclusive, but rather, mutually reinforcing.

---

50 ब्रह्मसत्यं जगन्मिथ्या जीवो ब्रह्मैव नापरः ।। शंकराचार्य कृत बह्मज्ञानावली 18 ।।

> Since the world constitutes *action* and the Brahman is the essence of *wisdom,* he held that both action and wisdom are necessary for a purposeful life. Śaṅkara held that *ultimately* only total resignation and withdrawal from the action is necessary to attain *Mukti* or total freedom. Against this, Bhāskara upheld the doctrine of *Jñāna-Karma-Samuccaya*—cumulative effects of action and wisdom, and declared that a person should withdraw only after an active life in which he fulfilled his obligations. On the important issue of the relationship between Brahman (the Absolute) and the world (the relative), Bhāskara taught that the two are identical; if, he said, Brahman is the substantial cause of the world, then the world itself is real'.[51]

This theory appears to point at the hypothesis that the world is only a manifestation of the Absolute, into a mentally comprehensible plane, that is perceptible by senses, and as much real as the Absolute. The view of Bhāskara and many others, should make the society more responsible because it is more comprehensive.

If both these theories are examined superficially, they seem diametrically opposite to each other. This apparent contradiction has been the cause for many a word-battle, obviously without any positive result. Shri Ramakrishna Paramahansa, one of the greatest unifiers, solved the paradox effectively. He said that Brahman and Its power of manifestation (creation, preservation and destruction) are not different. Both are inseparable as the fire and its power to burn, the water and its wetness, the snake and its wriggling motion, and so on. Similarly, Brahman and the world are not different, but only the two different aspects of the same Reality. However, he said that, we experience only the world without realising the Principle behind it.

---

51 *Encyclopaedia Britannica,* Vol 2, XVth edition, p. 187.

Shri Ramakrishna would give another simile: For climbing the terrace of the house, one has to climb the stairs. And while climbing the steps, one actually *negates* each step by saying to oneself: 'This is not the end', and continues climbing. But once on the top one realises that the steps as well as the terrace are made out of the same bricks, mortar and lime! It is necessary to 'negate the steps' initially, for getting rid of the complacence, and to achieve the totality of experience. For realising the underlying Principle, and to overcome the *attraction* for the world and its objects, one has to '*negate*' it. He would say, that mind is milk and the world is water, if one mixes them both, then one can never get pure milk again. But if one curdles the milk and churns it to get butter, then it *floats on water.*

Viveka (discrimination) helps us develop *Asaṅga,* non-involvement with the world. One is never over-careful with the mind, a past-master in giving *convenient justifications!* It says, that the act of withdrawing the senses from their objects is *escapism.* The fact is, that whenever one is trying to achieve anything, one cannot help being selective. For instance, if a student is preparing for an examination, he has to avoid diversions; a scientist involved in research cannot help restricting most of his life to his laboratory or library. Similarly, a man seeking his own origin or roots, cannot help being introvertish. If such a person is being called an escapist, then we have to call the student as well as the scientist escapists! This is also true, that the mind has the tendency to escape from problems and unfortunately, in our country, spirituality has been one of the main *escape routes!* But then, we are not referring to such straying cases.

The present *Sarga* helps us develop the discrimination, through this story. It illustrates the way in which the involved and the indulgent mistake this world to be real and taking the physical life to be *the be all and the end all of existence.* This mistaken notion of taking the impermanent to be permanent, arises out of the *Saṁkalpa*. For example, we see children getting up from their sleep, crying for the toys they had *seen in their dream.* Or for that matter, the adults shedding tears while watching a movie! For an onlooker, both the child as well as the adult suffer needlessly due to the lack of awareness.

Sage Vasiṣṭha narrated the following story :

A certain immature child requested its mother to tell a story for diversion. She related an entirely mythical story, as if it were true!

Once upon a time, three princes of boundless courage and good qualities lived in a city called *Void.* Of these three, two were *never born* and the third had *never entered any womb!* These three, desirous of acquiring everything, started on their quest, and rested in a forest of *Ākāśa,* full of countless fruits, and fed themselves with them to appease the hunger. Continuing their journey thereafter, they came across three rivers with dashing waves, winding their way on the outskirts of the forest. Of these three rivers of fast currents, two had no water, while in the third, the white sand of the river bed was fully visible. They bathed and drank the waters of the third river.

At sunset, they retired to a town *yet to be created* and built three houses! Of these three houses, two did not exist at all, and the third neither had the supporting walls nor the superstructure! The three princes went to reside in the three *non-existent* houses. They found three golden vases near them, of these two were shattered to pieces, and the third one was in a pulverised state! In the pulverised vessel there was a quantity of rice equivalent to six measures *minus* ten measures and cooked it. After so doing, they distributed it to innumerable *mouth less* Brahmins. And then, the three princes partook the remaining meal. Delighting themselves thus, in hunting and other pursuits, they spent their time joyfully. When the mother concluded the story, her innocent child rested in the profound conviction of the genuineness of the mother's tale. Sage Vasiṣṭha concluded, that the ignorant conceive and observe this world to be a reality.

This story, again symbolically illustrates the three planes of manifestation as different from the unmanifest State. The three *unborn* princes refer to the *Saṁkalpa* in three *Ākāśas* manifested as the *Kāraṇa* (the Causal), the *Sūkṣma* (the Subtle) and the *Sthūla* (the physical) bodies. They are *unborn* as they do not have any independent or separate existence, other than the Reality. All other things described in the story are the *Vikalpas* or fancies that bind us to the world. They do so because, they rob us of our *fluidity* as the *all-pervasiveness gets distorted to finiteness.* It is very much like the stick *appearing* bent when immersed in water; or like the white light getting refracted through a prism, to form a spectrum of seven colours.

In the case of the manifestation in three planes, however, the water or the prism, responsible for the distortion is the *Saṁkalpa,* and the spectrum has infinite names and forms. This story implies that for achieving the *Antarmukhatā,* one has to get rid of the indulgence and also involvement with the world of multiplicity. This is possible only when one keeps reminding oneself of the temporality of the world, *as it is perceived through the limited mind and senses.* Though we can see the sky through a window, we cannot perceive it totally, as by very nature the window is very much finite.

The Cosmologists say that it is impossible to *see* all the stars and the star systems adorning the Universe, because of the limitations of the senses, natural or their extensions like the telescopes. While the cosmologist is aware of the limitations in the process of observation, most of us are unaware, and many of us have forgotten the limitations of the mind and intellect. Which is very obvious from the argument and word wars that are being perpetuated through our so-called intellectual achievement especially in the field of Philosophy! This avoidable confusion is due to the fact, that the *perception of the senses and the interpretations of the mind are taken to be the Gospel Truth!* And presently, the Science has almost come to a conclusion that *seeing need not be believing!*

Whether it is *Adwaita* or *Viśiṣṭādwaita* or *Bhedābheda,* everything is only *an* interpretation, *an* explanation or *a* view. Not unlike that of a blind man *about* his understanding of the elephant. Because all explanations use language. And language by its very nature is limited. But yes, these very explanations *can become bridges* between the manifest (comprehensible) and the unmanifest (incomprehensible), if one is careful in avoiding the involvement with the words!

Unfortunately, History stands evidence to man's attempt for the *misuse* of these views; to indulge in verbal wars; and in justification of his limitations. The religions of Hindu origin based their explanations on the theory of Transmigration of the Soul and on the eternal Life, with a noble intention that man must *seek* the Eternal. Instead, he became lethargic and adopted a life of procrastination. Perhaps, seeing through this, the religions of Jewish origin, hypothesised that there is only one life, which is to be utilised for going nearer to the Divine. Instead, man concluded, if there is only one life, it should not be *wasted* on some vague idea of Divinity, and should be used for eating, drinking and being merry! It has been noticed, that invariably, one who indulges in the philosophical arguments does so, only for *postponing* the journey towards oneself; for *avoiding* the peace existing already in the heart.

The full moon of Vaiśākha—the second month in the Indian Calendar—has very special significance in the life of The Buddha. It is said that he was born, got enlightenment and left his body, on the same day. One of the biographers records the great event of enlightenment. After many years of arduous spiritual practices including fasting, Siddhartha Gautama reached the outskirts of Gaya, and rested under a Peepal tree. A lady who had come to worship the tree offered him milk pudding. That day Siddhartha started evaluating his journey, and discovered that he was attached to the *effort.* Soon after this realisation, he had a very restful and dreamless sleep, in which every attachment was washed off. It was early morning, and he could see a single star, bright and shining, slowly and steadily disappearing. As it disappeared completely, to give way to the bright blue, expansive sky, Siddhartha was awakened and the ordinary Peepal tree became the *'Bodhi Vṛkṣa'*, the tree of enlightenment.

The full-moon lights up the entire world with its soothing light. A child may imagine a ghost standing, instead of a banana plant. A disturbed mind may get more excited. A thief or a murderer may plan a crime. A poet or a painter may draw inspiration for his creativity. And a mystic may go nearer to his Goal. Amidst all these, the moon lights up the night world in its *borrowed light.* In a very similar way, all the theories are there to light up the path which has to be traversed by each one of us. Whether we make use of it or misuse it to *justify* our limitations or to *postpone* our journey, is entirely up to us.

8

The Story of a Siddha

The passengers get down from the bus, that has to be taken on to a ferry for crossing the river *Gaṅgolli.* It is monsoon and the river is carrying cascades of water in all her majesty. Though the water is muddy, it has tremendous life force in it. As the passengers start boarding the ferry, some of them are visibly scared at the prospect of falling over-board, while others are excited about the boat ride. For the rest, it is only a daily routine and probably, all they are interested in, is in crossing over to the other side of the river and get on with their business of earning livelihood.

The ferry leaves the northern bank, and begins its slow journey like a hesitant and shy bride entering her new home. The wavelets hit the base of the ferry, while the boatmen dip their tall bamboos into the water. A pleasant rhythmic sound of wood coming in contact with water, brings in a mood of peace and well being. Suddenly, a gruff male voice, intensely musical, starts singing a Marāṭhī devotional song of Saint Tukārām.

The river, the setting and the mood created thereof are so ideal and poignant, that a few travelers are visibly moved. And all that fatigue resulting from hours of continuous travelling by bus on bumpy roads gets totally eliminated and they are refreshed. It will not be a mis-statement if it is said, that no matter how great is the strain or pain, it gets eliminated with time or such experiences. As time *is nothing but a flow of experiences both pleasant and unpleasant.* Rightly has it been said, that time is the greatest healer. No wound, whatever be its intensity, can last permanently. Either the intensity of the pain wears off with time, or the time erases the painful memory of the experience, by offering alternate and more pleasant experiences.

In this sense, time has been a very great blessing on the human kind, for it is not known—so far, whether other beings have any concept of time or not. Paradoxically, human kind suffers due to this very conception of time! Our mind is always obsessed with time. All along it keeps nurturing, the memories and regrets of the past; brooding of what has to come (or what should or should not come!), of the future; or seeped in the excitement of the present.

For people leading an ordinary life, this is not a problem at all. On the contrary, it is very helpful. For example, let us take a father who has to face the problem of arranging for a huge sum for his daughter's marriage, or son's education. He is no doubt troubled by the worry, but only for a short time. As it gets eliminated either by a future hope, 'everything will be all right', or by confidence through his past experience— 'last time I had solved the problem successfully'. That is, by changing the mental scale of time, past, present and future, we avoid the unpleasantness and pain, not unlike a musician, changing notes in his music. However for a seeker, time happens to be a very obstinate motivation for mental activity he struggles to quieten.

'But what is this time? And how do we perceive it?' These particular questions have tickled the human thought since the dawn of human reason. We have been trying to reasonably understand time and *can only deduce* some of the aspects of this great mystery. There cannot be any doubt, that every one of us perceives time.

Encyclopaedia Britannica makes an interesting observation:

> 'Time is basically a dimension of change and time perception then, is the capacity to interpret changes in sensory and bodily stimuli with respect to their temporal relations'.[52]

If it is an interpretation of sensory and bodily changes, it follows, that the length of this duration becomes shorter or longer, depending upon the effect of the change. It is a common experience known to almost everyone of us that certain instances seem longer to us than the others. For example, if we are waiting for a friend, time seems to be longer, evident from the action of looking at the watch every few seconds, than when we are with the friend enjoying say, a movie. In other words, the length is governed by the unpleasantness or the pleasantness of the experience.

Though we have been experiencing this for a very long time, it was given to Dr. Albert Einstein, at the turn of this great twentieth century, not only to explain scientifically the relativity of time and space, but also prove the interdependence of time and space. He coined a new phrase 'space-time-continuum'. He called time, the *fourth dimension* and made a very bold conclusion that:

> '...there is no absolute time—the events that are simultaneous in one frame of reference may not be so in another...'[53]

It is not necessary for a seeker to know the scientific or technical details of time. But from these scientific conclusions an important fact becomes obvious : time like space, is also a mental concept and is relative, as senses, the grosser manifestations of mind, are mandatory for noting the change. And what is of primary importance for a seeker is *how it*

---

52 *The New Encyclopaedia Britannica,* 15th Edition, Volume 11, p. 779.

53 Ibid., , Volume 25, p. 843.

binds her or him to the world through involvement and indulgence. The crux of the problem is that like the erroneous conviction of the reality of matter and hence, the space, a similar notion of the reality of time increases the involvement and indulgence with the world. So the most important step a seeker can take in the direction of growth is, developing the conviction that space and time are only mental concepts.

This however, is easier said than done, as the habit of taking them to be real has gone into our marrow. The story of Siddha illustrates this fallacy of time and space, and the habit of forcing realty on them which are temporal.

At the end of the previous story, Sage Vasiṣṭha blessed Rāma to be *Nirvikalpa* after removing all *Vikalpas. Vikalpa* is a wrong notion or misunderstanding having its roots in the two mental concepts of space and time or in Einstein's word 'space-time-continuum'. In the stories so far narrated, the enlightened sage tried to convince seekers that the world with its multifarious forms is temporal and does not have any independent existence of its own. In this *Sarga,* he extends it to time.

It is evident from our ancient spiritual literature, that relativity of time was known to our sages. The knowledge may not have been technical, but was definitely *practical,* as far as the seeker is concerned.

A beautiful simile is given by *Vedānta* to describe the state the common men are in. There is a pond of clear water through which one can see the bottom. If a man gets into the pond and disturbs or agitates the water, the dirt at the bottom gets mixed with water making it muddy. If one wants to see the clear transparent water again, one has to patiently *allow* the dirt to settle at the bottom. The *Saṁkalpas and Vikalpas* are nothing but the agitative mental activity and have to be allowed to become quiescent. This is being hinted by the sage through a word *Manaḥ-praśamana* in the following verse:

'Oh Rāma! With the quietening of the mind, what remains is only liberation'.[54]

Sage Vasiṣṭha said that the ignorant suffer due to self-created *Saṁkalpas* but not the *Puṇḍits,* who are sharp-witted, and are constantly involved in *Vicāra,* due to which they are ever free. He urged Rāma to accept the permanent and reject the impermanent. Rāma was reminded that it is only due to a wrong notion that one is bound, because how can the ever free and infinite be bound? Mind alone is responsible for this false notion of bondage. By quietening the mental activity one rediscovers the freedom which is ever ours. Through the play of mind in objects, proximity appears to be a great distance, and vice versa.

The moment we hear the word *Puṇḍit,* we normally take it to mean, a 'scholar'. But the word actually has a much deeper meaning :

'Those whose minds always dwell in the *Ātman* are *Puṇḍits*'.[55]

With this interpretation, it becomes clear as to why the word '*puṇḍit*' is used by the sage. A *puṇḍit* knows clearly and perfectly the meaning and purpose of life and how to chart his course through it. He does not *create any more agitations* through *Saṁkalpas,* but starts quietening the mind. It is our common experience that fear increases if one thinks more about that which creates the fear; if one is *worried about the worry,* the worry increases! That is why the sage urges the seeker, through Rāma, not to think himself bound, because that is the primary bondage. *Brahmabindūpaniṣad* declares :

'Mind alone is the cause for bondage and freedom, in the human beings'.[56]

---

54 मनःप्रशमने राम मोक्ष एवावशिष्यते ।। 3.8.4 ।।

55 पण्डा आत्मविषया बुद्धिः येषां ते पण्डिताः ।

56 मन एव मनुष्याणां कारणं बन्धमोक्षयोः ।। 2 ।।

Vasiṣṭha started telling the story : A king who traced his lineage to Hariścandra ruled over the country of Uttara Pāṇḍava. He was prosperous, wise and extremely brave. This king, who was known by the name Lavaṇa was once seated on his throne in his court when a man, well versed in the art of magical tricks walked in. After paying due respect to the king and the courtiers, he entreated the king to allow him to demonstrate his feats. The king agreed, and the magician waved the bunch of peacock feathers and mesmerised the king, who saw the following events pass before his eyes :

A messenger sent by the king of Sindhu entered the court with a magnificent horse and said that it was a gift from his master to king Lavaṇa. The Siddha (magician) asked the king to mount the steed. But as far as the courtiers were concerned, the king was staring blankly as if in sleep. Lavaṇa under the influence of magician's spell stared like a statue for a period of five *Muhūrtas*.[57] Then his body lost its rigidity and relaxed, to fall in front of the throne, and his ministers propped him up. When the king recovered gradually, he started narrating his experience.

When the Siddha waved the peacock feathers in front of his eyes, the king became giddy and noticed a horse, which was mounted and ridden speedily for a long distance. Like the ignorant wallowing in their wealth due to non-discriminative mind, he entered a thick forest. His mind and senses became totally uncontrollable when he saw plants full of delicious fruits and heard the reverberating divine music. While riding this way, a creeper high up in a tree twined around his neck, and the horse bolted out of sight like sins from a bather in the Gaṅgā. He was left dangling in mid air, and the cool winds blowing made his body numb, which continued for the whole night. As the dawn broke he got

---

57 *Muhūrta* is a unit of time used in ancient India to denote 48 minutes.

released, but was unable to find any human being around. Exhausted and hungry, he spent some time, when he saw an outcaste girl. The girl had some food in her hand. He literally begged for the food, and consequently had to pay a penalty. The girl refused as she did not want the king to eat from the hands of an outcaste and took to heels.

Finally, he found her out after a long chase, when the girl agreed to give him the food only on the condition that he made a promise to marry her in her own place in presence of her parents and to live with her. Reluctantly—due to extreme hunger, the king made that promise and appeased his hunger, and got entangled with her. The couple led a normal life of involvement and ignorance, and had children. After living in such a way for many years, when the king had grown old and weak, the region was afflicted by famine, with no water and food. They abandoned the country with their children. But on way, the wife and two of his children died due to extreme hunger, weakness and exhaustion. The youngest child climbed his lap and cried piteously to feed him. In sheer frustration the king wanted to put an end to his miserable life by falling into the great forest fire.

When the king was about to plunge into the flames, he found himself falling from the throne, and saw his courtiers lifting him up and heard the musical instruments. Only then was he relieved to find that he was not the down-trodden man but king Lavaṇa, the descendent of Hariścandra! The king said that it was because of the fascinating power of the Siddha that he lost his senses. He concluded that he had learnt that ego of man experiences different states. Just as he finished saying this and wanted to know who this Siddha was, Śambarīka the Siddha disappeared from the view in the twinkling of the eye. Sage Vasiṣṭha concluded by saying that the Siddha was no other than the Divine *Māyā,* sent to prove the fact that the Universe is the mind itself. The wise say that the light of *Parabrahman,* alone appears as mind and space-time and hence the universe.

In a masterly way, this symbolic story illustrates the subtle aspects of existence. King Lavaṇa, the descendent of Hariścandra denotes that an individual is always free, king-like, and totally devoted to Truth, —as Hariścandra personifies Truth and has been referred to as *Satya* Hariścandra. In the words of Sage Vasiṣṭha, Śaṁbarīka, the Siddha happens to be the Divine *Māyā*. *Māyā* is a special word, used to denote so many subtle processes involved in creation. That is why, this section of the scripture has been called *Utpatti Prakaraṇa*. *Māyā* has different meanings depending on the context. Normally, *Māyā* is interpreted as the illusion or that which is not. *Yoga Vāsiṣṭha* however, takes a very general interpretation as *Saṁkalpa,* which is the tendency for contraction of the infinite consciousness. This tendency precedes thought, and thought is a potential *Vikalpa* or wrong notion, this truth is clarified later on in the text.

The space-time-continuum is created under the influence of *Māyā*. With this idea of space-time the paraphernalia of *Vikalpas* and finally the paranoia, become part of life. While *Vedāntic* texts call this tendency *Māyā,* the *Yoga Sūtras* call this *Avidyā,* the first of the five *Kleśas,*[58] though the concept of *Māyā* is at the universal level while the *Avidyā* is more at an individual level.

All the stories in this *Prakaraṇa* aim at convincing the seeker that it is quite natural to take the world seriously. It is this seriousness that breeds the *Vikalpa* and its faithful companion, misery. During his training, Carlos Castaneda used to seek clarification by asking all sorts of questions to don Juan, his teacher. It had almost become an obsession for Carlos, to get explanation for *everything*. Once, don Juan reluctant to answer a question, left him for a while. Carlos suspected a little annoyance in his mood. An interesting conversation followed :

---

58 Refer *The Story of Ākāśaja,* for details on *Kleśas.*

'Are you angry at me, don Juan?'

I asked when he returned. He seemed surprised at my question.

> 'No! I'm never angry at anybody! No human being can do anything important enough for that. You get angry at people when you feel that their acts are important. I don't feel that any longer'.[59]

Not only anger, but any mental involvement or sense indulgence is possible only when the world becomes important. When the goad for the first evil, namely, importance, has been overcome, then one can slowly move inwards. These directions, outward and inward are only to indicate the movement towards the subtler planes of existence, that is, from body, through senses, mind, intellect, memory, to 'I-ness'. If *Antarmukhatā* is achieved, then one can say, that one has put the first and mandatory step in the direction of spirituality.

When we have the experience of poise, and a sense of oneness with nature, the mind drops the space-time, and we experience something that is transcendental. The river, the movement of the boat, the mild breeze which somehow invigorates our being, or for that matter *anything that has quietening effect* on us, invariably is a *beyond mind* experience. Whether to make use of these to go beyond the mind, or to misuse them by giving importance to the objects of senses, as we mostly do, or to abuse them by becoming addicted to only the sense-object contact, is left to the choice of the individual.

---

59 *Teachings of Don Juan* by Carlos Castaneda, Penguin Books, p. 73.

9

The Story of Lavaṇa-I

A Sufi saint who was a very hard task-master, had three disciples. All of them respected their Master but with an element of fear. Once he called his disciples and told them that he would clarify their doubts the following day. They were quite happy as they had so many doubts. Next day at the allotted time they sat in front of the Master, who looked at the first disciple. The disciple got up and asked him :

'Master, how can one free oneself, from the torturing thoughts of the past?'

The Master looked into the eyes of the disciple and ordered gravely :

'Ask a question *closer to home!*'

Meekly the disciple sat down without understanding the significance of the command. After a while, the second disciple got up and asked :

'Master, what will I get if I sincerely and diligently practise what I have learnt from you?'

Again the Master looked into his eyes and thundered :

'Ask a question *closer to home!*'

The third disciple was at a loss to know what to ask and was panicky! But he got up when the Master looked in his direction and asked humbly:

'Master, what do you mean by, asking a *question closer to home?*'

For the first time that day there was a smile on the face of the Master. He said affectionately :

'I thought you would never ask! By *question closer to home,* what I mean is, that question which is relevant, which affects you immediately, and that which can transform your life.'

Looking at the first disciple he observed :

'You are interested in asking about the past, which is gone and no longer relevant to you. Moreover, by dwelling on it, you only strengthen it. And you,'

He continued, looking at the second disciple :

'Are interested in things yet to come, which only helps in intensifying your fantasy and the tendency to move away from the Reality that is already slipping from you!'

Then looking at everyone with affection he said :

'What I meant was to ask such questions which have bearing on life *at present.* How is my mind behaving *at the moment?* Is my body tensed or relaxed *at the moment?* What is happening to me when fear grips—for I have to ask a question closer to home!—*at the moment?* Such questions have always, definite answers. Remember, *to see far, one has to see what is near.*'

The difference between the Western Philosophy and our cultural thought is that the Western Philosophy has *mainly* contributed to speculative thought and hence may be called as the arm-chair Philosophy. While the Eastern thought in general, and Indian culture in particular has been more practical, connected as it is with day-to-day life. This does not in any way mean, that the Western Philosophy was of no use to human growth. Through Philosophy,[60] man has learnt to

---

60 From Greek, 'philosophos' which means 'love for wisdom'.

ask questions, to doubt and to seek answers to his questions. These form the essential steps to knowledge, to improve the human lot, and more importantly, to make the ordinary man into a thinking human being. Every branch of knowledge or its application has had its origin in Philosophy. And interestingly, with the introduction of experimentation, the sciences started parting from Philosophy.

If one were to classify the questions into types, one finds that there are only two : the 'why-s' and the 'how-s'. The why-s led to speculations. Why is this Universe created? Or the purpose; why is there so much variety in the creation?; why do we die? etc. The list of such questions is endless. A myriad of answers got generated in the human thought according to the milieu—geographical or cultural. This stream of questions gave way to the man's observation of the surroundings or the *outside.* The questions beginning with 'how', became more interesting as they directly affected our day-to-day life. For example, these questions become basis of the human power of invention which has given us Technology.

Even from the point of view of abstract thought, the answers discovered are of use to us in our day-to-day life, as explained by the story on 'questions *closer to home.*' More stress is given on the questions beginning with 'how' in the eastern thought. For example, how does one become angry? How does one die or how *can* one die? This led to a revolution in the direction of human thought, when the human being started observing *himself.* It led man to the inner search, the science of spirituality.

The search *outside* became an *Objective* search and the search *inside,* the *Subjective* search. We should in no way take the western quest to be purely materialistic, and the eastern as purely spiritual. Because it is quite obvious from our deplorable condition at present, that we are poor materially and more so, spiritually. Our incorrigible lethargy is the main cause for our downfall. Material progress demands hard work, while the spirituality demands harder effort, sharper wit and stronger awareness. Nation as a whole, we resorted to consolatory philosophy that helped in the *justification* of our laziness. By quoting scriptures we chose escapism, while conveniently neglecting *Pauruṣa* or the effort.

The scriptures like *Upaniṣads* and *Yoga Vāsiṣtha* keep stressing that the human effort is of primary importance without which *nothing* can ever be achieved. If we just take a cursory glance at places like Varanasi, or Haridwar and Rishikesh, we find innumerable people in ochre robes of *Sannyāsī*. Among them there might be only a very few—who can be counted on finger tips, who are genuine seekers. The rest are only in quest of their daily bread and shelter. However, we should not blame spirituality or renunciation for this sorry plight, as even a devil can quote scriptures to justify its acts!

A seeker has to become aware of one of the most important facts of spirituality, which is not to have *blind faith.* Fortunately the present times are such, that it is very difficult to have any blind faith, as *everything* is shrouded in doubt! But this is an apparent fact for most of us, as the present trend seems to point out. For example, in spite of the fact that we doubt everything, we believe many things if they are presented to us through our *blind spots.* There is a wonderful episode from the life of Shri Ramakrishna and Swami Vivekananda.

Once in presence of Shri Ramakrishna, a man started praising the *Bhagavadgītā* to the skies. This would not have been surprising had any other man done it, but the man was known for his critical attitude towards anything that was Indian. So Vivekananda—who was then, Narendranath, was a little surprised at the change of heart. When he left, the disciple commented on the change of heart in the gentleman. Shri Ramakrishna smiled and observed that, it was not surprising at all. He said that probably, the man had come across a copy of the *Bhagavadgītā* translated by an Englishman.

But Narendranath was not a person to take *anything* for granted. So he followed the gentleman, and found that he was carrying a book, which was a copy of the translation by Charles Wilkins with a foreword by Warren Hastings, the first Governor General of Bengal and the founder of British rule in India!

This particular episode, gives an insight into how the great Master had felt the pulse of the intellectuals of this country. Subsequently Swami Vivekananda decided to go to West for addressing the so-called educated Indians from the western platform! Even today, we are not very far off from that situation. For many of us the news published in Newspapers is very *authentic,* although they may be misrepresenting, exaggerating or even scandalising the truth! Similarly, we have certain *scientific superstitions!* That is, *whatever is explained in the name of science!* So a seeker has to guard herself or himself against taking anything for granted. But at the same time, the questions asked should not be only for gathering information which becomes, only a spiritual gossip! All along the questions should be only for silencing the mental activity. Questions like these lead us to a fruitful quest.

One such Person who asked a fundamental question that transformed his life was, Bhagawan Shri Ramana Maharishi of Tiruvannamalai, South India. He has described it in his own words :

> 'It was about six weeks before I left Madurai for good that the great change in my life took place. It was quite sudden. I was sitting alone in a room on the first floor of my uncle's house. I seldom had any sickness, and on that day there was nothing wrong with my health, but a sudden violent fear of death overtook me. There was nothing in my state of health to account for it, and I did not try to account for it or to find out whether there was any reason for the fear. I just felt "I am going to die" and began thinking what tc do about it. It did not occur to me to consult a doctor, or my elders or friends;

I felt that I had to solve the problem myself, there and then.

'The shock of the fear of death drove my mind inwards and I said to myself mentally, without actually framing the words : "Now death has come; what does it mean? What is it that is dying? The body dies." And I at once dramatised the occurrence of death. I lay with my limbs stretched out stiff as though *Rigor mortis* had set in and imitated a corpse so as to give greater reality to the enquiry. I held my breath and closed my lips tightly so that no sound could escape, so that neither the word "I" nor any other word could be uttered. "Well then" I said to myself, "this body is dead. It will be carried stiff to the burning ground and there, burnt and reduced to ashes. But with the death of this body am I dead? Is the body I? It is silent and inert but I feel the full force of my personality and even the voice of "I" within me, apart from it. So I am the Spirit transcending the body. The body dies but the Spirit that transcends it cannot be touched by death. That means I am the deathless Spirit." All this was not dull thought; it flashed through me vividly as living truth which I perceived directly, almost without thought process. "I" was something very real, the only real thing about my present state, and all the conscious activity connected with my body was centered on that "I". From that moment onwards the "I" or "Self" focused attention on itself by a powerful fascination. Fear of death had vanished once and for all. Absorption in the Self continued unbroken from that time on'.[61]

But such questions and the subsequent mood of quest happen only to a microscopic minority, while the rest of us overlook our own capacity to seek, due to our indulgence

---

61 *Ramana Maharishi and the Path of Self Realisation* by Arther Osborne, Published by Rider & Co., London, p. 17.

and involvement. Some of the most common questions asked by us are : Why this creation? or When did this creation come about? But the same questions can be used for starting a quest, by replacing why with how : How is this creation brought about? Because this very question gives birth to another and more relevant question : *How do I perceive this universe?* This forces the seeker to examine himself, his own mode of observation and the experience of the universe.

Utpatti Prakaraṇa answers this question very minutely. We experience the external world through our senses housed in a body. Information so collected by the senses is accepted or rejected, analysed, understood and remembered or forgotten by different functions of the mind. But all this is possible only with the entity called 'I' which is the governing faculty of all functions. And in a way, there is no creation without this *Ahaṁkāra* or 'I'. Which brings us to a logical conclusion that the creation of the universe *for the individual* is the creation of 'I'. The obstinate habit of getting involved with the gross and superficial world as experienced through the senses is due to the loss of awareness of the Reality, which happens to be the very basis of existence. This has been illustrated through the stories in this *Prakaraṇa* so far. The present *Sarga* or the chapter, which is the conclusion of this episode, sheds further light on the finer aspects.

In this *Prakaraṇa* so far, sage Vālmīki has tried to hint at the fact that *Dwaita* or the *otherness* stops us from experiencing the Reality. This *Dwaita* is the outcome of the manifestation of 'I-ness' and its progenies which give the *outward* direction to the consciousness. For making the consciousness flow *inward,* it is necessary to eliminate the *Vṛttis.* This can be possible only with a mind which is free from all fluctuations. The tree of *Māyā* flourishes out of the seeds of *Citta-Vṛttis* or modifications of the mind. And these modifications or fluctuations are at various levels: body, senses, *Manas, Buddhiḥ, Citta,* and *Ahaṁkāra,* which are to be tackled at the respective levels for achieving quiescence. The methods to eliminate the modifications are followed by different schools of *Yoga,* which have long tradition of transfer of knowledge through a line of preceptors and disciples.

Yoga Vāsiṣṭha however, gives a broad and general outline which is applicable to any school. It says that *panacea* prescribed by the wise for the removal of the diseases of the mind can be found very easily by the mind alone. Those who are freed from the longing for objects, are able to avoid them easily can be called human beings. While the others who are still under the influence of the basic hunger for the sense objects are at best worms in human garb. If the mind is divested from the *Saṁkalpa* of 'I', and directed to the *Ātman,* it can be turned back. Like one iron shaping the other iron as hammer and anvil, pure mind of a person should mould his impure mind. In a *Mumukṣu* the pure aspiration strengthens his effort, and helps him abandon the restless activity of the mind. Gradually, when the activity becomes quiescent, *Brahman* the ever shining Principle is experienced.

The general guideline, has four aspects : *Śama*—sweet patience, *Vicāra* or contemplative analysis, *Saṁtōṣa* or contentment, and *Sādhusaṅga,* the association of experienced wise. These are the necessary aspects common to *all* the methods used to quieten the mental activity. Already an elaborate discussion on this, is made in the *Mumukṣu Prakaraṇa.* But when these four aspects are taken care of in the practice adopted by the seeker, the problems get eliminated. These four aids also come in the realm of the mind, which are referred to by this scripture as the *pure Vāsanās,* and the crocodiles that infest the ocean of life like desire, anger, greed, infatuation, pride and jealousy are called here as the *impure Vāsanās.* Along with pure *Vāsanās, Pauruṣa,* or the courage to face any eventuality, and *Prayatna* or the persevering effort, take care of the rest. That is how, a seeker doing *Swādhyāya* of this sacred text will find an often repeated suggestion : 'Overcome the impure with the pure', whether it is mind or the *Vāsanās.*

The significance of this suggestion is not only philosophical, but very practical, affecting our day-to-day life. Whenever an action is undertaken, it is observed that there are two opinions given by the mind : *Preyas*—the pleasant and *Śreyas*—the good. Even if it is a reply to an insignificant question. One reply to it may be a lie, but which is convenient and has no consequent problem or effort. For example, there is a road accident, and one is a witness to it. It is very easy to tell that one has not seen anything, which sets the person free. The other is the truth. If one proceeds to volunteer as a witness, then there can be no end to his visits to the police station or court—for no fault of his!

We stand at a fork, as it were, and have to decide the course before undertaking the action. *Kaṭhopaniṣad* states :

> 'The good is different, and so is the pleasant, both of them have different uses having the binding effect; Between the two, the person who chooses the good, gets the auspicious, and the person choosing the pleasant falls'.[62]

For a seeker it is mandatory to learn to discriminate between *Śreyas* and *Preyas.* This discriminative faculty is present in everyone of us. Even a thief or a murderer hears an inner voice, guiding him in whispers. It is an altogether a different matter if some of us choose to ignore it! We are aware, that it is very difficult to find *the Guru* these days, not because such great Persons are unavailable, but we have not developed the proper eyes to recognise them! The capacity to listen to the inner or the silent voice within is of great help. It is true that it calls for a sacrifice of our convenience and comfort, which

---

62 अन्यच्छ्रेयोऽन्यदुतैव प्रेयस्ते उभे नानार्थे पुरुषँ सिनीतः ।
तयोः श्रेय आददानस्य साधुर्भवति हीयतेऽर्थाद्य उ प्रेयो वृणीते ॥ 1.2.1॥

is not very easy. This is why, Sage Vasiṣṭha repeats the words *Pauruṣa* and *Prayatna.*

This inability to listen to the inner voice is caused by two *Vāsanās* : *Bhogavāsanā*—the tendency to experience;[63] and *Bhedavāsanā*—the tendency to differentiate. *Bhogavāsanā* is that tendency to experience the external world through the windows of the senses. This is gross as compared to *Bhedavāsanā.* This gross tendency leads us, towards indulgence. That is how *Vairāgya* or disinterest towards the objects of senses is the first step in spirituality. When this *Bhogavāsanā,* becomes thin, one becomes aware of the *Bhedavāsanā,* which is very subtle, which *limits* the Non-dual Reality into 'I', 'you', 'he', 'she', etc. It is this differentiation which gives an apparent reality to the world, although it cannot exist on its own. This tendency takes us towards involvement in the form of identification with the persons or the objects as '*mine*' or '*not mine*'. And involvement and indulgence happen to be the most obstinate of all the habits.

Every one of us is very much aware that death is the only certain thing in our life, which separates us from the things or persons from us. But paradoxically, we continue to act as though we are eternal! Almost all the saints have directly or indirectly suggested that we remember the death at least once in a while, to bring in some sanity into our restless and mad lives. A doubt crosses our mind : if one remembers the death all the time, will such person not lose all interest in life? It is possible, but not necessary. It is possible, when the attitude is unhealthy, for example if one is deeply attached to objects and people. But a seeker is supposed to have developed dispassion and disinterest. For him, it is mandatory to *befriend* death, if such an expression could be used. *Vāsiṣṭha* has some practical guidelines.

---

63 Though normally *Bhoga* is taken to be desire in a more general sense, it is to be taken as *experience.*

In recent years, the modern industry, or for that matter, even recreation like sports and games have come to recognise the attitude one should have to achieve one's goals. The word 'training' is found to be associated with the industry and the sports arena. Long hours are spent on counselling and on boosting the morale. The general method is to fill the persons with a 'You can do it and Win!' message, which is nothing but the positive attitude. Most of us get attracted to listen to spiritual discourses, where all these lofty thoughts are discussed. In India at least, it will not be an exaggeration if one were to say, that most of us have had an opportunity to listen to such discourse at least once, and be convinced if not inspired by it. But unfortunately, it does not have any effect on our subsequent behaviour, as we continue to be our old selves! Why is it so? We get the answer to this question if we just listen to the persons coming out of such discourses. Invariably many of them, if not the most, say that 'the discourse was very good, *but* how can *we* follow it in our life? This is possible only for the extraordinary persons, not ordinary mortals like us!'

Swami Vivekananda used to say, that the greatest lesson our culture has for mankind is fearlessness and self-confidence:

> 'One idea comes out of all this—the condemnation of all weakness. This is a particular idea in all our teachings which I like, either in philosophy, or in religion, or in work. If you read the Vedas, you will find this word always repeated—fearlessness—fear nothing. Fear is a sign of weakness'.[64]

Addressing the people of his own country, India, he said:

> 'The only cause is that you are weak, weak, weak; your body is weak, your mind is weak, you have no faith in

---

64 *Complete Works of Swami Vivekananda*, Adwaita Ashrama, Vol. 1, p. 47.

yourselves! Centuries and centuries, a thousand years of crushing tyranny of castes and kings and foreigners and your own people have taken out all your strength, my brethren. Your backbone is broken, you are like downtrodden worms. Who will give you strength? Let me tell you, strength, strength is what you want. And the first step in getting strength is to uphold the *Upaniṣads*, and believe— "I am the Soul". "Me the sword cannot cut, nor the weapons pierce; Me the fire cannot burn; Me the air cannot dry; I am omnipotent, I am the Omniscient." So repeat these blessed words. Do not say we are weak; we can do anything and everything. What can we not do? Everything can be done by us; we all have the same glorious Soul, let us believe in it. Have faith, as Naciketā; aye, I wish that faith would come to each one of you; and every one of you would stand up a giant, a world mover with a gigantic intellect—an infinite God in every respect. This is what I want you to become. This is the strength that you get from the *Upaniṣads*, this is the faith that you get from there'.

Like the home crowd cheering a sports team to boost its morale, an unknown sage in an *Upaniṣad* addresses the humanity :

'Listen! Oh sons of immortality, You have the capacity to have control over the divine world! I have experienced this Infinite Person. Only on experiencing Him a man crosses over the death'.[65]

The *Vāsiṣtha* says that 'I am not Brahman', 'I am weak', 'I am bound' and such other thoughts have a binding effect. While the thought 'Everything is Brahman, or all pervading', leads to freedom. It is well known, that half of the responsibility of getting well lies in the determination and

65 शृण्वन्तु विश्वे अमृतस्य पुत्रा आये धामानि दिव्यानि चक्षुः ॥ 2.5 ॥
वेदाहमेतं पुरुषं महान्तं आदित्यवर्णं तमसः परस्तात् ॥ 3.8 श्वेताश्वतरोपनिषद्॥

'the will to get well' of the patient, while the other half with effort of the doctor. Many a time, we see that a very serious accident victim with even a brain injury recovers, while a person without the will to survive, may die in spite of the best efforts from the doctor. To this statement of sage Vasiṣṭha, Rāma sought a clarification : What is this *Brahman* or *Ātman*? To which the sage replied.

'That' which is beyond the trammels of sense indulgence, 'That' which is beyond the speed of desires and That which is there in everything. 'That' which empowers the *Jñānendriyas* the instruments of perception and *Karmendriyas* the instruments of action, but which cannot be perceived by them, 'That' which is beyond the scope of comprehension of the instruments of understanding is called Brahman. What really happens when one experiences Brahman is *Pratyabhijñā* or 'recognition'. How can we recognise It, if it were not within our own experience? One is not aware of it because one has forgotten It, due to involvements and identification with the grosser manifestations. This incorrect identification and becoming its slaves is what is called *Māyā*.

Instead, if we achieve mastery over the grosser manifestations, all of them will obey like the ministers obeying the king. Initially, we identify with our own ego, then gradually we identify with the objects, and persons. This is naturally preceded by the differentiation between 'I-mine', 'you-yours' and other paraphernalia of the world of multiplicity. So the first and foremost thing one has to do is to achieve the non-attachment with the objects by developing the basic conviction that in spite of the multiplicity, essentially all is One. This has to be accompanied by *Ātma-Vicāra* by questioning the *reality* of the body, senses, and mind. The methods which can be adopted to achieve such non-identification are spread throughout this scripture.

However, we almost never doubt the reality of the world, of our relationship with it and the gains and pains we derive out of such relationship. Every seeker gets this doubt and wants to know the reason for this misunderstanding. Rāma, the seekers' representative asks the sage. In reply to the question from Rāma, Vasiṣṭha reverts back to the story of Lavaṇa who became a Cāṇḍāla, under the magical influence of Śāṁbarika, the Siddha, as narrated in the previous *Sarga.*

Lavaṇa the descendent of Hariścandra, one day while alone in the royal garden, thought of performing *Rājasūya Yajña* mentally, which his ancestor had performed with his physical body. Through his *Saṁkalpa,* he willed all the necessities of the *Yajña,* including the *Munis, Tapasvins* and Brahmins, whom he worshipped. The *Yajña* came to a grand conclusion with the distribution of all his wealth. When he woke up from his reverie, it was late evening. As a rule, all persons performing *Rājasūya Yajña* have to undergo intense suffering for a period of twelve years. While persons like Hariścandra, and Yudiṣṭira had to suffer physically[66], for Lavaṇa the suffering was mental as his *Yajña* was mental. And that was why the celestial messenger assumed the guise of a *Siddha* and meted out the suffering to the king.

Suffering is always an outcome of either involvement or indulgence caused by *Avidyā. Avidyā* by nature is the lack of awareness, and flourishes under non-awareness. *Vāsiṣṭha Caṅdrikā,* the gloss on *Laghu Yoga Vāsiṣṭha,* says while introducing the seven states of *Ajñāna:*

> '*Avidyā* arises and flourishes in lack of *Prajñā*—inner awareness;
> How can it possibly arise when there is *Prajñā*' ?[67]

---

66 Both Hariścandra and Yuḍhiṣṭhira had to suffer untold trials and pain before or after the *Yajña.*

67 अविद्या विद्यमानैव नष्टप्रज्ञेषु विद्यते ।
नाम्नैवाङ्गीकृताकारा सम्यक्प्रज्ञस्य सा कुतः ॥ 3.9.89 ॥

The awareness as well as the lack of awareness is said to be septenary in nature, and have been called *Jñāna-sapta-bhūmikās* and *Ajñāna-sapta-bhūmikās.* They are mutually interdependent. There may be innumerable subdivisions overlapping one another in the septenary division of both these states, like the infinite colours and shades arising out of the three basic colours. But broadly, the state which takes us towards the Unity from multiplicity is the *Jñāna* state, while that which takes us towards multiplicity, involvement and indulgence is the *Ajñāna* state. Understanding this basic mode of division, it becomes obvious that there have to be infinite levels of '*being*'.

The nomenclature of the septenary division of *Ajñāna* states is: *Bindujāgrata, Jāgrata, Mahājāgrata, Jāgrataswapna, Swapna, Swapnajāgrat* and *Suṣuptī.* The state in which the cognition of 'I' is in seed form, or in which there is *tendency* to differentiate is called *Bindujāgrata.* In this state, the *Jīva* has manifested but, the clear differentiation has not yet arisen. In *Jāgrata,* the feeble conception of 'I and he' and 'mine and yours' has arisen, and this is the second state. The differentiation *materialises,* that is, I, you, etc., start having a binding influence on the *Jīva,* due to the repetition of many births, in the third state of *Ajñāna,* which is *Mahājāgrata.*

Jāgrataswapna is that state in which the mind holds undisputed sovereignty over the things of the world through previous effects and experiences. The *Jīva* is overpowered by the seen or unseen objects and dwells on them constantly. The fourth state of *Jāgrataswapna* is experienced in the *Jāgrata* state and is of various kinds, through various delusions like water in mirage, silver in mother of pearl, blueness in the sky, etc. Pure *Swapna* state is that in which a review is made of the innumerable events which one passes through in a moment, as if in a dream or reverie. The sixth state of *Swapnajāgrata,* is that normal waking state where one recollects the things or events of the past but *thinks* that it is present, not as a vision but as if real. The last and the seventh state of

Suṣupti, is characterised by the intelligence that is beset with pain and misery, when one is totally ensnared in *Māyā.*

One might wonder as to why so much of effort and so many words are being used to describe the states of *Ajñāna.* It is like the milestones crossed when one is on a journey. The details of topography help the traveller to locate himself. The journey of the *Jīva* is infinitely long and arduous. As some teachers say, that we have come a long way from 'Home'. Although the question 'How long from Home?' is very difficult to answer, classification of these *Ajñāna* states gives us an inkling into the present level we are in.

A seeker, who has stopped questioning and has started the quest, will definitely get an idea of his present position. In finding out one's own position, one does self-introspection. Sometimes, when one discovers that one is way down in these seven *Ajñāna* states, it is likely that one gets discouraged. That is why, one has to avoid negativity and the depression accompanying it. The introspection should help one understand the difficulties for overcoming them. Just as, an examination is meant to evaluate the extent to which one has understood the subject, and not for creating a fright!

Many of us do get some fundamental doubts about the life we are leading presently, and about the life we *ought* to live. The robopathic, and mechanical lives characterised by our search for the basic necessities, do get us on our nerves. Most of us find diversions in the objects of senses and a life of indulgence to *avoid* such feeling. And many of us find Philosophy or Metaphysics a very good diversion or even a source of entertainment with an 'ego trip'. But for only a few of us, these doubts become the turning point in our life for transforming it.

Yoga Vāsiṣṭha is of great help to such persons who have experienced the life transforming turning point in their life, as it not only clarifies those doubts, but gives clear cut instructions to commence the quest for the spiritual evolution.

10

The Story of Lavaṇa-II

The sun is at the concluding lap of his westward journey. The Peer Panjal mountain ridge forms a formidable wall, a curtain, where the sun withdraws, as he finishes his act. After a hectic activity of the day, so necessary for the survival, all beings are moving for a much needed period of rest. As if to help them, slowly a soothing blanket of darkness gets covered over the existence from the eastern horizon. Though the blanket has in it the tiny twinkling wonders to give pretense of light, the valley starts merging in the darkness. The mind, so far busy in absorbing the beauty all around, starts losing the motivation to seek *outside,* stops for a while and begins its *inward* movement. One can learn and experience many subtle things by just being attuned to the nature. This harmonic relationship of nature with everything else has been called *'Ṛtam'*. The word 'rhythm' in English is from the same root.

The capacity to flow in *both* outward and inward directions is what differentiates human beings from other beings. Extrovertishness is natural and constitutes most of our actions, while introvertish ness is not. This turning of one's attention from the outside to oneself is the main feature of spirituality. Spirituality has been called as *Adhyātma Vidyā*—the science of *one's own Self.* Unfortunately, most of us are aware only of the outer and are ignorant, sometimes totally, of this inner direction. So religion and spirituality for most of us, is a means for leading a moral and ethical life, and at the most, we take it to be a means for the improvement of the life after death.

Generally, it is believed that the right time to start thinking of religion and spirituality is the old age, after fulfilling all the responsibilities one has either acquired coincidentally, or has forced upon oneself. We are of the impression that when one has retired from the *active life,* a very sophisticated way of naming involvement and indulgence, one can *easily* direct the mind to things spiritual! While the fact is mostly otherwise. For if we do not *train* our mind to come out of the beaten track of fight for survival and also propagation of species, at an early stage, the mind refuses to leave the track.

Shri Ramakrishna makes the following observation about such people :

> 'The bound souls are tied to the world by the fetters of "woman and gold". They are bound hand and foot. Thinking that "woman and gold" will make them happy and give them security, they do not realise that it will lead them to annihilation. When a man thus bound to the world is about to die, his wife asks, "You are about to go; but what have you done for me?" Again, such is his attachment to the things of the world that, when he sees the lamp burning brightly, he says : "Dim the light. Too much oil is being used." And he is on his death bed!'
>
> 'The bound souls never think of God. If they get any leisure they indulge in idle gossip and foolish talk, or engage in fruitless work. If you ask them the reason, he answers, "Oh, I cannot keep still; so I am making a hedge." When time hangs heavy on their hands they perhaps start playing cards'.[68]

---

68 *The Gospel of Shri Ramakrishna* by M, IXth Impression, Vol. I, p. 87.

Unless one is aware of the direction of one's life, it becomes only an involvement in trivia. Ādi Śaṅkarācārya opines in his *Vivekacūḍāmaṇi* :

> 'Three things are rare indeed, Human birth, burning desire for liberation and the capacity to surrender to a man of wisdom, and wherever they are found, are due to the Lord's Grace'.[69]

If we take it to be only a struggle for survival and propagation of species, there is no difference between man and other creatures. It is possible, that the other creatures are better, for at least they do not disturb the ecological balance. Man has become extremely cruel, selfish and so greedy that he has brought the world to the brink of self destruction. Howard Lovecraft, an American author observes:

> 'This earth of ours is ailing, and the disease is *mankind*!'

But in spite of the prevailing situation or the population explosion, human birth is very rare! A short story which had appeared in *Candāmāmā,* a magazine for children young and old (!), illustrates this point.

There lived a giant in a forest. But he was the only surviving giant inhabiting the earth. Not having any company, he was fed up of life and wanted to commit suicide. He tried jumping off the cliff, only to crush the ground beneath! No amount of poison worked on him. The water could not drown him. Nothing worked. Unable to know the next course of his action, he started roaming about aimlessly. In a forest he saw a sage sitting under a tree, and was attracted towards him. Soon as he came near, he experienced a peculiar peace. Sitting near, he waited for the venerable man to come out of the meditation. When the sage opened his eyes, he beheld a strange creature sitting in front of him.

---

69 दुर्लभं त्रयमेवैतद्देवानुग्रह हेतुकम् ।
मनुष्यत्वं मुमुक्षुत्वं महापुरुषसंश्रयः ॥ 3 ॥

Noticing the sadness on the giant's face, he enquired the cause for the sadness. When the giant explained, the *Ṛṣi* smilingly said that he would try to solve the problem. Whispering a *Mantra* in the giant's ear, he said that with the help of the *Mantra* he could adopt any form. Then he whispered another *Mantra* which would bring him back to his original form. The *Ṛṣi* asked him to try assuming different forms for a month, and take a final decision about the form, which would be permanent.

The giant took a human form and started roaming about. In a village, he found a huge crowd listening to a man boasting about his adventures. Having finished the entertainment the crowd dispersed after a while. The giant, who was in a normal form, asked the man whether he had come across any giants. The man replied in the affirmative and boasted again about it. But when the giant took his real form, the man started shivering and begged for mercy! The giant only remarked that the man's courage was only verbal and not at all real.

When he entered another town, he heard that a rich man was in search of an eligible young man for his daughter. The giant took the form of a handsome youth and approached the rich man. The man made enquiries and said that he loved his daughter more than his own life. To which the giant assumed his real form, and threatened the man that if he did not give the daughter to him, he would... The rich man did not even allow him to finish, as he readily agreed so long as *he* was spared! Again the giant only pitied the man and remarked sarcastically that his love was limited to his own life, and left.

Finally, he came across a house in which a large group of devotees were engaged in singing devotional songs. Whole night it went on, and the giant came to know that it was organised by the holy man in ochre clothes, sitting on a deer skin in a corner, totally lost in ecstasy. Early next morning, when all the devotees had left, he approached the holy man.

He asked the man, as to why he was always in prayer. The man said that God was his very life, without whom he could not possibly live. When the giant asked him, what would be his reaction if a giant attacked him. With all the poise he could *exhibit,* the man said that he was not worried as God would surely look after him. As usual, when the giant took his infamous form, the man forgot all devotion, surrender and his poise, and started shivering and appealing for mercy! The giant commented that even the devotion was only at the superficial level in man.

Almost in disgust, the giant returned to the sage, who was as usual in deep meditation. The very sight of him made the giant forget all the bitterness towards human beings. He calmly waited for the *Muni* to come out of his meditation. When he came to, the *Muni* enquired about his experiences. As the giant narrated all his disappointing experiences, the *Ṛṣi* wanted to know whether he had decided about the form he would like to take permanently. Unhesitatingly, the giant said that he wanted to become a human being! When asked as to why he chose it although he had bitter experiences, the giant said that in spite of the unpleasant encounters with men whose nature seemed to be mostly hypocritical, mean and selfish, he felt that they *have the capacity* to raise themselves to *Ṛṣi-hood.* And he wanted to become a *Ṛṣi!*

Human birth is rare and invaluable due of the total *freedom* to make use or misuse of or abuse the opportunity to evolve. The other creatures have no choice but to evolve in a definite manner. And the main difference between the human beings and the other creatures is the awareness and the lack of it. Man in the initial stages is very near to the animals because he mostly acts at the instinctive level, goaded by the basic urges and hungers. At this level there is practically no difference between him and the other animals. But with the development of intellect and subsequently intuition he starts evolving into a human being and to grow towards superhuman hood.

In this *Sarga, Vāsiṣṭha* describes this evolution through stages, or the *Jñānabhūmikas* which are also in septenary classification. *Śubhecchā* or a feeling of discontent in ordinary life and an attraction for finding out the esoteric meaning to life, is the first stage. *Vicāraṇa*—the enquiry into it, through discussion and contemplation is the second. The third stage is *Tanumānasī*—the melting of the extrovertishness of the mind. *Sattvāpatti* is the fourth when the mind gets the ability to enter within.

Asaṁsakti is that fifth stage when the *Saṁkalpas* have become thin. From the practice of these five steps the thought on inner as well as the outer objects ceases, and one starts deriving delight in one's own self. This is when one enters *Padārthabhāvanā*—the sixth stage. And the seventh stage is *Turya* when one merges with the Reality. Only the first five stages are within realm of effort of the seeker, while the other two are really the stages that she or he enters without any effort after stabilsing in the earlier stages.

Tattvajñāna is a release from the fluctuations and resulting upheavals of mind. Such a release alone leads one to *Mokṣa.* Before this, one has to understand the nature of one's mental involvement and the sense of indulgence. One starts getting involved with the world positively by *Rāga* or the sense of attraction towards objects; and negatively by *Dweṣa* or aversion. Both *Rāga* and *Dweṣa* originate in the *Bhedavāsanā* or the tendency for differentiation and multiplicity. The indulgence with the objects starts with the *Bhogavāsanā*—the tendency for experience. With this understanding, not only intellectual but experiential, the connection between the self and the world becomes fluid and one is able to recognise and appreciate the freedom that already exists.

In other words, one is able to have mastery over one's mind and senses which are really our slaves, but due to our dependency over them *we have become their slaves!* Though this dependency is an obstinate habit, we can be weaned away from it with effort and perseverance. That is why the scriptures like *Vāsiṣṭha* declare that the *Avidyā* or ignorance which is nothing but the involvement and indulgence with the world as unreal, because, it is only a *temporary habit of involvement with the temporal world!* Dreaming is temporary, and one need not continue to dream eternally. Though most of us require a nightmare to wake up!

It must be remembered that it is not mandatory for everyone to realise one's folly and come out of it. Man is perfectly free *not* to and to continue to get afflicted by the ups and downs of life! Our notions originate in the *Granthi* or the causal knot of *Saṁkalpa,* or the conception of thought, with 'I-ness', and culminate in the identification with the world and its objects. But when one finally realises that there is some other dimension to life than mere survival, one commences his pilgrimage. The march of the individual from the deluded state, to the enlightenment consists of the above mentioned stages of *Jñāna.*

The journey necessarily begins with the gross and proceeds to the subtler and culminates in the subtlest. When one starts experiencing discomfort with the fluctuations of the mind, one is in search of the method to calm these fluctuations. *Yoga Vāsiṣṭha* gives a very comprehensive definition of *Yoga* :

> 'The technique of calming down the mind is called *Yoga*'.[70]

Continuing, sage Vasiṣṭha gave the cause for the continual affliction of the human beings to be the wonderful *Māyā.* And to make it more interesting he reverted to the story of king Lavaṇa. After waking up from the hypnotic state induced by *Siddha* Śaṁbarīka, he remembered the places he had experienced in the state. To test the validity of his experience,

70 मन: प्रशमनोपायो योग इत्यभिधीयते ।। 3.8.132 ।।

Lavaṇa wanted to see whether such places really existed. With his retinue, he started going around the kingdom and covered the three directions. Finally in the North, the fourth direction, he came across the forest he had passed and suffered. And then he reached the town where he had lived as an outcaste. To his surprise the king came across all those things and people associated with that life. The old mother of his late wife, and the other people who had survived the great famine were still there.

The lamenting old woman narrated the story of her daughter who had chosen a king for her husband, and borne him children. The king instructed his minister to relieve the poor people of their distress and conduct them to his kingdom. Reflecting over the situation again and again he requested his preceptor to initiate him into the mysteries of the *Ātman*, and attained quiescence through sincere effort. Rāma, who represents all seekers, asked a question. 'How was it that the things felt in the regions of the perturbed mind, objectified themselves in the physical plane?'

With infinite patience the great sage replied, that it would become clear when he would narrate the story of Gādhi (in *Upaśama Prakaraṇa)*. For the present it was enough to understand that the powerful *Māyā* is capable of creating heterogeneous objects. And also that it is only a very great coincidence whereon, the *Vāsanās* of the mind coincide with the world of objects. King Lavaṇa took the illusion created by Śambarīka to be true. The Caṇḍālas living on the slopes of the Vindhyās mistook this illusion in the mind of Lavaṇa to be real through their own mind. That which dawned on the mind of Lavaṇa as *Jāgrataswapna* was reflected on the Caṇḍālas as *Jāgrata,* and vice versa.

This is because, the individual mind-stuff as such is a part of the universal mind. Hence, every mind is connected with every other mind. And through a great and inexplicable coincidence, they get connected to one another. The play of

Māyā is such that it is beyond all imagination and its prowess can be overcome only by *Jñāna.* All these things can be comprehended only when the mental activity ceases so as to give us the separateness with the activity, be it the 'I-ness' or memory or intellect or *Manas.*

This brings us to the conclusion of *Utpatti Prakaraṇa,* which stresses mainly one point repeatedly. That the world of objects is the manifestation of the initial *Saṁkalpa,* the conception of thought, giving way to the *Vikalpa,* or the intensification of thought, through the manifestation of the mental activity. The three planes of manifestation—*Jñānākāśa, Cidākāśa* and *Bhūtākāśa* are being described to help the seeker to understand the order of subtlety. *Jñānākāśa* is the pre-*Saṁkalpa* state, and in this state, one is in total control of activity as well as quiescence; In *Cidākāśa,* the activity has already started with 'I-ness' and there is every likelihood of involvement with the mental manifestations. Therefore the quiescence at this state, requires a little effort; and in *Bhūtākāśa* the manifestation has become gross and the involvement as well as the indulgence has started and demands *Pauruṣa* or will and *Prayatna,* or sustained effort.

The external and the internal have a very strong connection. That is why a seeker unable to discount the external milieu, tries to search such places where she or he will have least disturbance. In this sense, many a time it seems that the seekers are trying to escape from their responsibilities. Many succeed in getting such milieu. But most have to be content with whatever comes to their lot circumstantially. At such times Mother Nature comes to their rescue. The dusk and dawn experienced every day help one to achieve the *Antarmukhatā,* a mandatory pre-requisite for understanding oneself. That was why, these periods of the day are being called as the *Sandhyās*—the juncture especially the night and day at dawn, and day and night at dusk or twilight—were considered to be very helpful for contemplation. The practice called

Saṅdhyāvandanaṃ or prayers at twilight, is performed at these times of the day.

With the *Antarmukhatā* one begins to recognise the inner mechanism of the being, as described in the stories of this scripture, giving very valuable hints for all sincere seekers.

THE SUSTENANCE

Sthiti Prakaraṇa

1

The Story of Śukra

After covering nearly eight kilometers on the asphalt road with lush paddy fields on both the sides, the bus stops at the foot of the hill for allowing some of the passengers to get down, and continues its onward journey to Kanyakumari, the land's end. The hill or rather hillock, is named *'Marutamalai'*—the medicinal hill, after the mountain carried by Hanumān with *Sañjīvanī,* to revive Lakṣmaṇa, who had been fatally injured by Indrajīt, the son of Rāvaṇa. It is claimed by the local people that a portion of the mountain had fallen! For persons unused to trekking and mountainous tracks, it is quite a strenuous climb. The hillock which is otherwise quite bald, has bushy growth consisting of thorny plants, and some of these plants, it is claimed, do have some medicinal qualities.

For about four hundred feet, there is a cobbled path leading to a small temple. From there on, there is no regular path, and one has to follow one's own instincts to reach the top through gorges, thorny footpaths and rugged terrain. Many a time, those from the plains, not used to climbing the hills, find it very difficult to continue and tend to give up the effort. But on reaching the peak of the hill which is about a thousand feet high, everyone finds the effort worthwhile.

One is suddenly exposed to the infinitude of the ocean in the three directions of South, East and West, for an angle of 270 degrees. On the Northern side, one can see the other hills. After this initial shock of exposure to something which is infinite, when one goes into the details one can very clearly make out the corner of this great country, as one sees on a map. Two seas, the Arabian Sea and the Bay of Bengal, and the Indian Ocean can be made out quite distinctly through the different colours. The wind blowing incessantly soothes the tired body, bringing the coastal fragrance, which also may be the reason for its name.[71]

There are only one or two caves on top of this hill which are occupied by some wandering seekers on a temporary basis. Sometimes, they are empty. There is no physical comfort or convenience on the hill. Unless one wants to stay on top for the spiritual practice, there are no other attractions. Invariably, whoever goes on top, finds it very easy to come down the hill. This experience is also quite common on a much subtler level for the seekers. Life of Sage Viśwāmitra serves as a very good example to explain this.

Many stories are available on him in the *Purāṇas,* and the glimpses of his achievements can be found in the *Vedic Mantras.* He has been called as the *Mantra-draṣṭā* of the famous '*Gāyatrī*'. But unfortunately, most of us know only the infamous episodes of his life: his greed for the Divine cow *Nandinī* and his subsequent hostility towards Sage Vasiṣṭha; his fall for the heavenly nymph Menakā; his unreasonable attitude towards king Hariścandra; or his extremely volatile temper! These incidents are very strong warnings for the seekers, to illustrate that the path of spirituality is very slippery. One can fall *any moment* if one is not careful. In fact, one can *never* be *over-careful!*

Once on a street of the temple town of Madurai, Tamil Nadu, an aged Sannyāsin was walking. A shop keeper touched his feet in reverence, and asked him a funny question. A donkey was standing nearby. Pointing to it he asked the

---

71 Marut is one of the names of God of wind.

Sannyāsin to tell him which of the two—the beard and the tuft of the donkey's tail—was superior. The old monk looked at his own beard, the tuft of the donkey's tail, and said that it is difficult to reply the question, and walked away! After many years, a youthful monk came to the shop keeper, and urged him to accompany him, as his master lying on his death bed, wanted to meet him. When both of them reached a hut, they saw recognition in the eyes of the old monk who said that only then he had been able to reply the question.

The shop keeper had almost forgotten. Reminding him of the question, the monk said that his beard was definitely superior to the tuft of the donkey's tail! The surprised shop keeper commented that the reply could have been given even at the time when the question was asked. The old monk said earnestly, that it was many years back, and he *could have fallen from the path he had chosen,* had it been so, then the tuft of the donkey's tail would have been superior. But now, there was no time for him to slip, as he had come to the last few breaths of his life. Saying this the monk left his body! Thus the example of Viśwāmitra serves as a warning.

But we should also remember the power of determination and perseverance of sage Viśwāmitra, which made him give up his kingdom and royal comforts to choose the life of an ascetic and *stick to it;* the grit and enterprise making it possible for him to create a new *Swarga*—heaven for king Triśaṅku; his infinite love and compassion making him choose the name Viśwāmitra, which means friend of the universe;[72] and his contribution of the sacred *Gāyatrī Mantra* having the power to transform *anyone* into a *Brāhmaṇa*—one who is treading the path of *Brahman.*

Normally, we are unable to appreciate the positive qualities and exaggerate only the negativities, because mind

72 His earlier name was Kauśika.

as such, thrives only on that *which is not,* instead of dwelling on that which is. When the habit of dwelling on and the subsequent brooding and worrying about things not available continues and becomes stubborn, we tend to become negative and cynical in our approach to life. One very important thing which a seeker has to remember, is such cynicism invariably becomes a hurdle in spirituality.

There is a great classic in Kannada language, entitled *'Mahābrāhmaṇa'*,[73] written by *'Devuḍu'*, giving a very positive side of the great sage Viśwāmitra. This sage is one among the *Sapta Ṛṣis*[74]—the seven sages of this *Manvantara*—the day of Brahmā, the creator. In the classic the author narrates the way in which greed for Nandinī, the divine cow gets transformed into an aspiration; the anger on sage Vasiṣṭha who has the cow and who refuses to part from it, gets transformed into a quiet determination to emulate him and to become a *Brahmarṣi*. But most of all the explanation of the Menakā episode given in the book can form a good introduction for this episode entitled *'Sthiti Prakaraṇa'*.

Śrī Devuḍu, the author, writes that for achieving one's goal, one requires the will-power. Greater the goal, greater the will-power. Viśwāmitra had not only to achieve *Brahmatva* for himself. But had to become instrumental in helping others to achieve it. This will-power is directly proportional to the *Ahaṁkāra*. Śrī Devuḍu says, that the 'I-ness' crystallises with *'Bhoga'* or experience in general and sense indulgence in particular. At that time Viśwāmitra had to increase his will-power, or the crystallised 'I' very fast. And that was possible only with the indulgence in some heavenly pleasure. That was why, the episode of Menakā the heavenly nymph was necessary. In this sense, it was not really a *fall*.

---

73 Published by D V K Murthy, Mysore, IIIrd Edition, 1976.

74 The seven sages are: Viśwāmitra, Jamadagni, Bhardwāja, Gautama, Atri, Vasiṣṭha, Kaśyapa.

It is not necessary that everyone has to agree with the opinion of the author. But, one cannot possibly ignore certain facts. For example, a person does not have anything, he has neither material wealth, nor any other achievements. He cannot *renounce* anything! What can a pauper give up? A rich man can give up his riches, a king his kingdom or a famous man his name and fame. And if a poor man claims that he is giving up, mostly what is given up is the *effort,* and to move towards lethargy(!), unless, he is fully aware of the *uselessness* of material things including name and fame. A seeker has to totally avoid moving towards *Tamas*—ignorance and lethargy.

It has been pointed out in the last episode, that the origin of duality and hence the multiplicity, and the universe is the *Ahaṁkāra.* So all the paths either directly or indirectly recommend the annihilation of this ego. Broadly, this can be achieved in two ways : the first one is to directly annihilate it; the second is to make it so powerful, that the power itself helps the process of its own annihilation. Shri Ramakrishna used to give a very beautiful simile clarifying this point.

The fish entrapped in the net of the fisherman can escape in two ways : One, by reducing itself to the extent, that even the mesh of the net is big enough for it to escape. And the second, by increasing its size to such an extent, that the net is no longer sufficient to contain the fish. The first path is the path of *Bhakti,* and the second, is the path of *Jñāna.*

Since *Yoga Vāsiṣṭha* is a *Jñāna Śāstra,* it recommends the second method. Moreover, once having involved with the *Ahaṁkāra* and its other grosser manifestations, if we allow them to grow, ripen and fall on their own, not unlike the harvesting of fruits, the transformation is total and irreversible. If one starts *negating* the ego and its manifestations without allowing them to ripen, a re-manifestation is likely. Present episode entitled *Sthiti Prakaraṇa* gives us the nature of sustenance of the mental manifestations. It proves beyond any doubt that the *Universe as such is created by the Reality; having been created, is preserved in the Reality; and having been preserved, it once again merges in the Reality.*[75] And while explaining so, gives valuable hints to seekers for buffering the effects of involvement and indulgence. In all there are five stories in this *Prakaraṇa,* each with a practical hint or two.

One of the most enigmatic questions that keeps pestering our minds is, that why in spite of one's being good, one has to suffer? In other words, why does one suffer without any apparent reason? *Vedānta* says that *none else, but the victim is responsible* for the experience he or she is undergoing. Many, if not most of the times, we are tempted to make *others* responsible for our present condition, if it is miserable. And paradoxically, we take the credit for our success stories! That is, '*I* succeed due to *my* effort, while I fail due to *others*' faults!' The most important point which a seeker does well to remember is that he must learn to take *all responsibility for all her or his actions.* There is a beautiful thought which sums up all this :

> Every person
> all the events of your life
> are there because you have
> drawn them there.
> What you choose
> to do with them is
> up to you.[76]

This way, the tendency to blame others, or to complain and grumble about the events, or being in a mood of helplessness, gets eliminated, which happens to be the most obstinate of the hurdles in even ordinary life, not to mention the life divine, wherein, every step and every thought is important. This means, that when one takes to the life of

---

75 यतो वा इमानि भूतानि जायन्ते । येन जातानि जीवन्ति ।
यत्प्रयन्त्यभिसंविशन्ति ।। तैत्तिरीयोपनिषद् 3.1 ।।

76 *Illusions* by Richard Bach, published by Pan Books, 1979.

seeking, one has to transform the somnambulistic life into an enlightened life characterised by total awareness of all actions including thinking. That is why, the act of accepting the events and persons as they are, is the fundamental and mandatory step towards the quest divine.

This *Prakaraṇa* begins with a statement from Vasiṣṭha, which says that the picture of the universe appears first as a reflection on the stainless screen of *Cidākāśa,* very much like the objects seen by a dreamer on his mental screen. When one is able to attain the attitude of *Sākṣī*—Witness, to this manifestation, one attains the state of *Ātmajñāna,* full, immaculate and all pervading. It is like a mirror which remains unaffected while reflecting the image of any object. The difference between the mirror and the *Brahman* is that while the object reflected by the mirror is separate from the mirror, *everything,* the object as well as the image are parts of the same *Brahman.* There is nothing which is essentially other than *Brahman.*

The present *Sarga* illustrates this fact through the story of Śukra. Once Muni Bhṛgu was engaged in *Tapas* on the slopes of lofty Mandāra Mountain. His son Śukra was intelligent and had an aura of spirituality. Śukra being a constant companion to his father was in the intermediate and neutral state between *Cit* (consciousness), and *Acit* (matter), like king Triśaṅku who was in the middle plane between the earth and the heaven.[77] Śukra thus was neither able to go higher nor come lower down to the material plane. Sage Bhṛgu on the contrary, was in the state of *Nirvikalpa Samādhi.*

---

77 King Triśaṅku desired to go to heaven *with his gross body,* and sought help from sage Viśwāmitra. But when he reached the portals of heaven, he was refused entry. Enraged, Viśwāmitra created a new heaven for him which was in between the earth and the heaven. This was called as *Triśaṅku swarga.* Even today this phrase is used in India which means '*neither here nor there*' in common parlance!

Son Śukra sitting by the side of his father, looked up through the pure *Ākāśa* and beheld a *Deva* lady there. He got sensually attracted to her form and became enamoured. Closing his eyelids he travelled in the vast regions of the mind to know about the level of her existence. Through his overpowering desire for her he discovered that she belonged to *Devaloka.* The moment he resolved to go there, he reached the plane, and came face to face with *Devendra,* the king of gods. While living the life of luxury there, Śukra saw the lady in a group of damsels and then through his *Saṁkalpa* he created darkness and spent a long time in the company and sensual enjoyment with the lady.

Śukra then descended to *Bhūloka* (the earth) from the *Devaloka,* fearing that the fruits of his noble actions had been wasted. And during the descent, he forgot all about the Reality. His *Jīva* got mingled with the moon-beams and then into dew, which descended on a paddy field and got converted to paddy. The rice in the fertile stalks was cooked and eaten by a Brahmin of Daśārṇa country and was converted to the seminal fluid. Śukra thus in the form of sperm ultimately emerged as the son through the womb of Brahmin's spouse. Associating with other seekers he performed austere *Tapas* over a long period.

In this forest he once again became a victim of *Ajñāna,* and had a human offspring through a deer, and getting attached to it, he fell from the state he had achieved and got involved with the material world. Passing through many incarnations by subjecting himself to a series of births and deaths generated by the *Vāsanās,* he finally incarnated in the body of a *Tapaswin* and a son of a *Muni* on the bank of the holy Gangā.

After narrating the journey of Śukra's *Jīva,* sage Vasiṣṭha started telling about the body of the son of sage Bhṛgu, which was lying by the side of his father, and the life had departed from it. The rays of the sun, aided by the wind had reduced it to a mere skeleton. Having spent many years in the state of *Nirvikalpa Samādhi,* sage Bhṛgu opened his eyes to behold the shriveled body of his son. The father in the *Muni,* got disturbed at the sorry plight of his son, and began cursing Yama, the god of death, who he thought, was responsible for this condition. Yama appeared before him.

Yama suggested the sage not to misuse the power of his Tapas over anger as nothing could destroy him since he was only doing what was required of him by the laws of nature. The Lord of death said, that the son alone was responsible for his sorry condition and went on to explain what really had happened including the details of numerous births. Yama continued that in the present birth, Śukra had attained mastery over his senses and mind, and was engaged in intense *Tapas.*

The Lord of death added that it is the *Ātman* alone that is mind, and the acts of the mind, and not the bodily acts, are alone true acts. Through its life in the world, *Ātman* is called *Jīva;* it is called *Buddhiḥ* through its certainty of knowledge; it is called *Ahaṁkāra* when the conceptions of 'I' and 'mine' assert themselves, with the signs of anger, greed, lust, etc. Yama concluded, by saying that if the *Muni* wished to know more about the series of his son's lives in dream, all he had to do was to use the divine vision. When sage Bhṛgu was convinced of the facts, he apologised for his irrational anger towards Yama.

The God of death then led the sage to the bank of the Gangā, and saw his son in the state of *Samādhi,* passing under the name Vāsudeva. Coming out of his *Samādhi,* Vāsudeva beheld both these persons and sought their blessings. Sage Bhṛgu blessed him to attain *Ātmajñāna.* And Vāsudeva saw all his past births through *Jñāna-vision* and was freed of future births. After understanding what had happened, he remarked in wonder that the strange delusion called *Prakṛti* had transformed into the universe in his own mind. Having seen all that is to be seen, and knowing all that is to be known, he had been released from the pain incidental to re-births.

After this the three reached the Maṅdāra hills and saw the body of Bhārgava. Kāla, the Lord of death asked Vāsudeva to enter the body like a king in his city and then administer the duties of the Guru of Asuras or the demons. When Vāsudeva did so, Bhṛgu his father nourished and purified the body through his power. Concluding this story, sage Vasiṣṭha said that this was how, both son and the father annihilated the impure mind which is the real enemy to pass their days in the state of *Jīvanamukti*.

If one is not careful, it is quite likely that the above story may get reduced to a mere fantasy. That is why, one has to analyse the small hints given intermittently. Comparison of Śukra's state to that of Triśaṅku—his inability to *go higher up or come lower down* is only symbolic. A seeker passes through a neutral state which is in between two consecutive states. At such times there is a possibility of stagnation. And invariably such a state causes unrest and fluctuations. Normally, the fluctuations which we come across our day-to-day life are distracting and disturbing. But the fluctuations experienced during the periods of stagnation are *helpful* for going to subtler planes.

An illustration may prove helpful. When a space-ship has to negotiate the inter-planetary distances, it has to overcome the gravity exerted by the planets, which keeps the space-ship in their gravity-belts. The space scientists have devised an ingenious way to overcome this problem. When the space-craft is to be launched it requires a very large thrust or force, to escape from the atmosphere and the gravity of the earth. At the same time the weight of the space-craft is to be minimal, restricting their choice of the rocket engines. They achieve this feat by the principle called the *slingshot effect.* The space-ship is launched and allowed to escape the atmosphere by the firing of powerful jet engines. Then the space-craft is made to revolve around the earth twice or thrice so that it gains sufficient momentum (force due to the mass and velocity). A slight change in the angle of the trajectory helps the space-craft to escape the earth's gravity. That is, the space-ship makes use of the gravity itself to escape from the clutches of the planet's gravity! Through Śukra sage Vasiṣṭha tries to give an indirect hint, that during the moments of stagnation, the fluctuations can be used to go to deeper levels. But one has to have infinite caution, else it is quite likely that the seeker may go to the grosser levels. Like a small mistake in the angle may make the space-ship into a satellite of the planet!

Involvement in *Cittākāśa* (the mental plane) is the primary fluctuation that has been called as *Saṁkalpa* which can help the seeker to ascend to *Jñānākāśa* as a spring board. But if one is not careful and loses the awareness, then one descends to the gross material plane which has been called in this scripture as *Bhūtākāśa.* In the description of Śukra's descent given in this Sarga, the author mentions the moon-beams, dew, paddy and other things. These are all symbols which represent the various stages of the descent.

Each birth creates new *Vāsanās* or tendencies which can become causal to the subsequent births. In spite of the intensification of *Vāsanās,* through repeated births, *Pratyagātma*—the Inner Being, keeps remembering its Ideal state characterised by total freedom and absolute bliss. This is why, on obtaining sufficient experiences, an aspiration starts steadily taking over the lower *Vāsanās.* One of the surest signs of this process is the feeling of general discontent in man in spite of fulfilling the goals set by him, and the nagging question that follows after each achievement: "Is this all?" The aspiration to get back to the original state is like the persistence and perseverance of the sprout in the seed, which manages to break the ground open to bloom into a sapling. How this sapling of aspiration is nurtured depends on the individual.

According to this scripture, the most important step a seeker takes in the right direction is, by assuming the responsibility for all the events in his life and all his actions. With this the mood of complaining about life ceases. When Carlos Castaneda was in a complaining mood, don Juan, his teacher gave him a wonderful analysis of the habit of complaining, with the following words:

> 'When a man decides to do something he must go all the way.' he said, 'But he must take responsibility for what he does. No matter what he does, he must know first what he is doing, and then he must proceed with his actions without having any doubts or remorse about them.'
>
> I protested that it was an impossibility, because there was no way to avoid doubts and remorse.
>
> 'Of course there is a way,' he replied with conviction. 'I have no doubts or remorse. Everything I do is my decision and responsibility. The simplest thing I do..may well mean my death. Death is stalking me. Therefore, I have no room for doubts and remorse..You, on the other hand, feel that you are immortal, and the decisions of an immortal man can be cancelled or regretted or doubted. In a world where death is the hunter, my friend, there is no time for regrets or doubts. There is only time for decisions.
>
> 'You are complaining,' he said softly, 'You have been complaining all your life because you don't assume responsibility for your decisions. If you would have assumed responsibility, you would not have any complaint. To assume responsibility for one's decisions means that one is ready to die for them.
>
> 'It does not matter what the decision is,' he said, 'Nothing could be more or less serious than anything else. Don't you see? In a world where death is the hunter, there are no small or big decisions. There are

only decisions that we take in the face of inevitable death'.[78]

While Don Juan is quite plain and direct in his use of words, as he takes the help of death, *Yoga Vāsiṣṭha* is indirect in its approach in giving the same advice. *Manas, Buddhi* and *Ahaṁkāra* are also transient, and the fall and the consequent suffering is the outcome of one's own *Saṁkalpa*. This scripture assures every seeker that it is very much within one's power to retrace the steps and be with oneself.

Another important point this *Sarga* stresses is that one gets easily attached to one's own creation or manifestation. This is illustrated by the outburst of anger in sage Bhṛgu on seeing his son's lifeless body. This is noticed in every one of us. We get attached to our children, be they be the human or mental children in the form of things of creativity!

It is the experience of those who love to climb mountains that it is quite strenuous to climb but not so much to come down. Climbing small hills like *Marutamalai* may not demand so much effort. But it is the experience of almost everyone, that while coming down there is absolutely no effort, and the path seems to be so familiar while doing so! Similarly, if not in a more intense sense, treading the path of spirituality demands all the sincerity and perseverance. And invariably, the fall comes due to involvement at the psychic level, and indulgence at the sense and body level. *Kaṭhopaniṣad* says:

> 'The experienced wise say that the path of spirituality is as tough and dangerous as walking on the razor's edge'.[79]

---

78 *Journey to Ixtlan* by Carlos Castaneda, Penguin Books 1979, pp.-59-60.

79 क्षुरस्य धारा निशिता दुरत्यया ।
दुर्गं पथस्तत्कवयो वदन्ति ।। कठोपनिषद् 1.3.14 ।।

Perhaps it is only due to this inherent danger and challenge, a seeker loves to tread this path, not unlike the adventurers responding to the challenges nature has for them on the mountain peaks or in the depths of the ocean or even in the infinity of space.

2

The Story of Dāma, Vyāla and Kaṭa

'The earth was the colour of the sky; the hills, the green ripening rice fields, the trees and the dry sandy river bed, were the colour of the sky; every rock on the hills, the big boulders, were the clouds and they were the rocks. Heaven was the earth and the earth heaven; the setting sun had transformed everything. The sky was a blazing fire, bursting in every streak of cloud, in every stone, in every blade of grass, in every grain of sand. The sky was ablaze with green, purple, violet, indigo, with the fury of flame. Over that hill it was a vast sweep of purple and gold; over the southern hills a burning delicate green and fading blue; to the east there was a counter sunset as splendid in cardinal red and burnt ochre, magenta and fading violet. The counter sunset was exploding in splendour as in the west; a few clouds had gathered themselves around the setting sun and they were pure, smokeless fire which would never die. The vastness of this fire and its intensity penetrated everything and entered the earth. The earth was the heavens and the heavens the earth. And everything was alive and bursting with colour and the colour was god, not the god of man. The hills were transparent, every rock and boulder was without weight, floating in colour and the distant hills were blue, the blue of all the seas and the sky of every clime. The ripening rice fields were intense pink and green, a stretch of immediate

> attention. And the road that crossed the valley was purple and white, so alive that it was one of the rays that raced across the sky. You were that light, burning, furious, exploding without shadow, without root and word. And as the sun went further down, every colour became more violet, more intense and you were completely lost, past all recalling. It was an evening that had no memory'.[80]

So wrote J. Krishnamurti after watching the sunset at Rishi Valley, with the children studying in the school guided by his *Being* and teachings. Krishnamurti, was called by some as the Reluctant Messiah. He was of the conviction that instead of *feeding on information* through books and media, one learns more intensely through nature. Life which is also a part of nature has the capacity to teach *everything* to man. Without the feeling for nature, he used to say time and again, all our so-called achievements are of no avail and even petty.

> 'We are losing the feeling for trees and so we are losing love for man. When we can't love nature, we can't love man. Our Gods have become so small and petty and so is our love. In mediocrity we have our being, but there are the trees, the open heavens, and the inexhaustible riches of the earth'.[81]

A doubt crosses our mind, as to what is it that stops us from being sensitive to nature. Whether it is resistance to the good, or an inclination towards bad, the culprit is always the same: the 'I' and its shadow, the 'mine'. There is always a *partition* of this 'I' and 'mine' between the experience and the Reality, as every experience is *interpreted* and consequently coloured by the partition. Whenever we say that we appreciate

---

80 *Krishnamurti's Notebook* by J. Krishnamurti, Krishnamurti Foundation India, 1991, pp. 188-189.

81 *J. Krishnamurti: A Biography by Pupul Jayakar*, Penguin Books, 1986, pp. 263.

something, it is not the thing *as it is* but the *image* of the thing which is carried by the 'I' and 'mine'. In the paragraph quoted above, Krishnamurti attempts to describe his experience with the nature at sunset, which is totally *innocent* and untarnished by the *experiencer!*

Those of us who are totally involved with the world *created* by our puny 'I'-s, and its images, the above state is very difficult to comprehend, not to speak of experiencing that state. At the most, we may appreciate the beauty of the language used to describe the indescribable. But then, persons like Krishnamurti or for that matter, scriptures like *Yoga Vāsiṣṭha,* do not want us to be only the mute *appreciators,* but practical treaders of the path. Their gestures in the form of words, have tremendous power to transform us, *if we so wish!*

This *Sarga* begins with a clarification from sage Vasiṣṭha about ripe renunciation. The ripe renunciation, can be achieved by one, who has resorted to *Ātma-Vicāra* or self-contemplation by calming the disturbing modifications of the mind, by abandoning the *Saṁkalpa* or tendency to think, through the elimination of the effects of the *'seen'* as well as the *'mentally conceivable'*. This can happen only by identification with the *'seer'*, that is possible by the development of *Jāgarūkatā*—constant awareness. The ripe renunciation makes it possible for the one who has it, to be watchful of the infatuation towards the *repetitive sense objects or Saṁsāra,* which in turn helps the seeker in transcending the *taste* amidst the taste inducing objects.

This *Pakva-vairāgya* or the ripe renunciation in turn cuts the *Hṛdayagraṅthi*—the binding knot of *Saṁsāra,* very much like the mice cutting asunder the knots of the net around the legs of the entrapped birds.[82] After destroying the snares of both good and evil *Vāsanās,* one is freed from bondage. It

82 The story of Citragrīva (pegion king) and Hiraṇyākṣa (mouse king) from Pañcatantra by Viṣṇu Śarmā.

is like the *Kaṭakabīja*—the clearing nut, clarifying the dirty water through sedimentation. Only when the mind is divested of all desires, and is indifferent to pleasure and pain, can it be considered to be pure and free from the grip of *Māyā,* very much like the bird freed from the cage, flying in the open limitless sky. Such a person has the capacity to not only aid but to *bless* the *Trimūrtis*—the three principal deities, *Brahmā, Viṣṇu,* and *Maheśwara.*

The Supreme Principle should be attained through ceaseless *Ātma-Vicāra,* the self-enquiry. Delusion of re-birth envelops like mist, so long as there is no serious enquiry about the nature of the universe and the 'I'. Only when a person cognises the *Tattva* or Reality, when he perceives objectively that the countless universes and the egos are no other than the rays of the light of imperishable *Ātman* or the Self. Only he can be called as the cogniser of the *Tattva,* who experiences objectively that it is the Infinite *Ātma-Jñāna* alone which manifests Itself as various potencies, and is the cause of all possible ideation, yet remaining Non-dual. Only such a person can be called as the cogniser of the *Tattva* who perceives that *Ātman* alone IS, which transcends being and non-being and yet nothing is apart from *'It'*.

Continuing, sage Vasiṣṭha said that like a travelling wayfarer seeing things in different quarters without any longing for them, the knowers of *Brahman* are never affected by the sense objects in spite of being amidst them. The experienced wise remain as unaffected as a traveller coming across men in a marriage party. The only vessel for crossing the ocean of rebirth is the mastery over the mind. Only such persons can attain *Mokṣa* who have controlled the serpent mind, full of the *venom of activity. Muni* Vasiṣṭha urged Rāma to achieve the quiescence of mind, through the destruction of *Vāsanās* or the tendencies.

It is not that the mind is to be treated as an enemy, as the mind devoid of *Aśubha-Vāsanās* or the tendencies which involve it, can act as an able minister or a diplomat, helping the seeker recognises the Self through discrimination. It can also act as an invincible general capable of controlling the wild and rebellious senses and taming them to unquestionable obedience. Such mind can also be compared with a nourishing and caring father and an intimate friend as it alone can have nourishing concern and give true counsel. The virtuous mind ascertains that one always treads a virtuous path and frees one from the binding effect of the world.

This jewel called the pure mind gets stuck in the mire of weak *Vāsanās,* and goes beyond control. But if it is washed of its impurities in the waters of *Jñāna* or wisdom, *Mokṣa* or the Liberation discloses itself. That is why one must cease to differentiate 'I', 'you', 'he', etc. Having given up the differentiation one can attain Reality in spite of engaging in activity. The mind which has an attraction for the temporary sense objects is false because it is also temporary. To warn Rāma of the dangers in the path of spirituality, the sage narrated the following story of the three *Asuras* Dāma, Vyāla and Kaṭa.

There was a powerful *Asura* by name Śaṁbara, an adept in the art of *Māyā* or illusive magic. Once he insulted Devendra by defeating him with his powerful army. The hide and seek and the cunning battles continued without any conclusive result. Śaṁbara deciding to put a punctuation to the war-games, created three *Asuras* Dāma, Vyāla and Kaṭa through the power of his *Māyā.* They all had Atlantean shoulders *without any idea of life or death.* Since they *did not have any desires or Vāsanās,* they knew neither victory nor defeat, neither pleasure nor pain, or any other pairs of opposites. This made them invincible, and the Devas were put in jeopardy. With no option the Devas resorted to consult Brahmā, the Creator. Brahmā assured them that Deveṅdra would eliminate the *Asuras* after a millennium. Until then, he advised them to challenge the *Asuras,* but to withdraw at the nick of time. If this is done, the God said, the three *Asuras* would develop *Ahaṁkāra,* which in turn would create the fears and desires, the definite invitation for Yama the God of death!

The Devas did as they were told and gradually the three Asuras Dāma, Vyāla and Kaṭa, started developing the notion of 'I', along with it the other *Vāsanās* like fear, desires, sense of enjoyment and pain. When the *Abhiniveśa* or the mortal fear of death crystallised in them, Deveṅdra challenged them. By that time however, he did not even have to fight as the three *Asuras* succumbed to *fear!* Sage Vasiṣṭha explained concluding the story, that the repeated thinking of the world confirms the binding effect on the soul.

Seemingly an ordinary grand-mother's tale! But it is packed with one of the subtlest hints for seekers. The three *Asuras* Dāma, Vyāla and Kaṭa are to be taken together. Dāma means a rope, Vyāla means mischievous or wicked and Kaṭa means to divide. Together it means the mischievous rope of division or multiplicity. The divine and the demonic forces existing in the consciousness are always at loggerheads as explicit from our conflicts. And as compared to the divine, the demonic forces *seem* very strong and have an *initial* upper hand.

In this story, Śaṁbara, the cunning chieftain of the demons creates the three *Asuras* who have *no desires or Vāsanās or even the sense of the pairs of opposites.* The author of this scripture introduces a catch for the seekers through this point. Even when it is an evil force, if it does not have the immediate desires to divert its energy, it becomes almost invincible. Take for instance, the contemporary problem of militancy and terrorism. The militants *seem* invincible because, all their energy gets converged on the violent activity, so much so, that they appear to be totally *unafraid* of death. They are prepared to face any eventuality or discomfort and hence they are apparently beyond the pairs of opposites. But then, the fear is not *absent* but only *dormant.* Moreover, it is only due to the preoccupation with the energy dissipating actions, that one is able to *overlook* the pairs of opposites. The surest test whether the fearlessness and going beyond the pairs of opposites is the outcome of such actions, and the motivation behind the action. Since the motivation is vicious, there can be only misery in store for both the victims and the persecutors.

The second point the author makes through this story is, the detrimental effect of the habit of dwelling on repetitive thought, which alone gives the intensity to the illusive reality to the world and the accompanying manias and phobias. An example from everyday life will clarify. If one has misunderstood a gesture or action of an acquaintance or a friend, one can go on building opinions and views about the person to this extent that one may even stop seeing the person as the acquaintance or the friend! If two friends are talking and laughing, a third friend who sees them laugh, especially, if the friends happen to see *him* while laughing, he starts thinking that perhaps, they are laughing *at him!* Similarly, one goes on thinking about the words uttered unintentionally or inadvertently by the other, not because what was uttered was wrong, but, because the ego was hurt. Obviously, misery has to be the result!

J. Krishnamurti used to say, that we seldom meet the real person, instead meet only the *image we have made about him.* The image created by our opinions, likes and dislikes, or even utility! Our public and social life is totally influenced by these images. A seeker has to take care not to dwell on such thoughts stressing on the 'I' and 'mine'. Such repetitive thought alone is responsible for our *Saṁsāra.*[83] The *Bhagavadgītā* calls this kind of repeated thinking as *Dhyāna* or dwelling and the outcome is *Sangaḥ* or association. A crisp analysis of misery is given by it in just two *Ślokas* :

---

83 *Saṁsāra* means that which is repetitive.

'By dwelling on the objects, man gets associated with them; through association and attachment, desire is evoked, resulting in anger when the desire remains unfulfilled. Anger results in infatuation, resulting thereby in forgetfulness; forgetfulness robs him off his reason; and the absence of reason results in absolute doom'.[84]

Don Juan, the teacher of Carlos Castaneda, says that the world as we know it is only a description of the world, which has been *repeated* to us innumerable times by our elders and surroundings. This *solidity* of the world—through repetition—binds us to that very description or the view. This view or image in turn gives *us the solidity.* And it is mandatory for a seeker to be fluid and light. Castaneda writes about the fantastic statement of Don Juan:

'He looked at me with squinting eyes and pointed all around us with a sweeping gesture of his arm'.

"The secret of all this is one's attention". he said.

"What do you mean, don Juan"?

"All of this exists only because of our attention. This rock where we're sitting is rock because we have been forced to give our attention to it as a rock".'[85]

This agrees with the statement of *Vasiṣṭha,* which says that the world exists and also gets the solidity because of the mind. Even at the material level we have the example of crystallisation. When a super saturated liquid cools down, a

84 ध्यायतो विषयान्पुंसः सङ्गस्तेषूपजायते ।
सङ्गात्संजायते कामः कामात्क्रोधोभिजायते ॥ 2.62 ॥
क्रोधाद्भवति सम्मोहः सम्मोहात्स्मृतिविभ्रमः ।
स्मृतिभ्रंशाद्बुद्धिनाशो बुद्धिनाशात्प्रणष्यति ॥ 2.63 ॥

85 *Tales of Power* by Carlos Castaneda, Penguin Books, 1979, p. 232.

crystal starts forming around a small *centre.* Our crystallisation happens in the saturation of repeated thought around the small centre of 'I'!

A seeker can *never* be a fanatic. He can neither be a world fanatic—who has the conviction of the world and *only* world. Nor can he be a spirit fanatic—who believes that there can only be the spirit. This fluidity and openness of the mind was referred to by Shri Ramakrishna as the freedom of a master of the multi-storied building, who has the access to all floors, unlike the servant who has many limitations due to bondage. But what is the cause of this bondage tying us to the world derived out of our own attention? This question has been replied by the *Vasiṣṭha* in this *Prakaraṇa.* In the present story of the three *Asuras,* it tries to hint at the thought through repeated false challenges!

The repeated challenges by the Devas, and the withdrawal at the spur of the moment, first of all brought in a sense of importance in them, which gradually made way for the attachment to the body, and eventually resulted in the mortal fear of death. Again, the explanation of Don Juan to Castaneda is very practical and relevant here:

> 'My sense of annoyance grew, until I had to make supreme effort to even take notes.
>
> "You take yourself too seriously", he said slowly. "You are too damn important in your mind. That must be changed! You are so goddamn important that you feel justified to be annoyed with everything. You are so damn important that you can afford to leave if things don't go your way. I suppose you think that shows character".
>
> "That's nonsense! You're weak, and conceited"!
>
> "I tried to stage a protest but he did not budge. He pointed out that in course of my life I had not ever finished anything because of that sense of importance that I attached to myself".

"Death is our eternal companion.... How can anyone feel so important when we know that death is stalking us? The thing to do when you're impatient is to turn to death and ask advice from it. An immense amount of pettiness is dropped if your death makes a gesture to you, or if you catch a glimpse of it, or if you just have the feeling that your companion is there watching you".

"I argued that it could be meaningless for me to dwell upon my death since such a thought would only bring discomfort and fear".

"You're full of crap!" he exclaimed. "Death is the only wise advisor that we have. Whenever you feel, as you always do, that everything is going wrong and you're about to be annihilated, turn to your death and ask if it is so. Your death will tell you that you're wrong; that nothing really matters outside its touch. Your death will tell you, "I haven't touched you yet".'[86]

This conversation appears very dramatic. But on deeper contemplation, or through a little *Vicāra,* one is bound to get convinced, that when one remembers death of others, one will either get totally scared and be in the state of *Abhiniveśa,* the extreme fear of death, or will drop all pettiness, as he or she realises that practically there is no time for such pettiness at all! And the reality is that we do not have time *even to get scared!* With a little eligibility on one's part, it is seen that it is always the pettiness that loses the ground. Pettiness includes pride, lust, greed, selfishness, and the like.

Scriptures like *Vāsiṣṭha* prove that the root cause of pettiness is the *Ahaṁkāra* –'I-ness'. Once this is handled and is kept at bay everything gets controlled. This story points out, that as long as one does not have the sense of 'I', one does not know fear, involvement and indulgence. But if one

---

86 *Journey to Ixtlan* by Carlos Castaneda, Penguin Books, 1979, p. 38, and pp. 50-51.

is repeatedly struck with any ego creating vibration, it gets crystallised and becomes so overwhelming that it can cause total destruction. In other words, the 'I-ness' is the centre around which the periphery of the worldliness is sustained.

The world as such is very beautiful. It is the worldliness that stops us from *being a part of the beauty*. The senses as such are nothing but the windows through which the Reality can flood in. It is sensuality that bars the windows to allow only the description or images of the world to reach our consciousness. There are no boundary walls to distinguish one country from the other; there exist no differences among the beings of the world as the present day Genetic Scientists declare. The worldliness, the sensuality, the description, the images, the boundaries and other differences are all creations of the initial *splitting vibration* called 'I'. And the seeker tries to transcend this 'I' through sustained and sincere effort.

3

The Story of Bhīma, Bhāsa and Dṛḍha

The sky turned dark with the clouds of dust and it appeared that the sun as well as the light had taken to flight! The climate had changed suddenly, as the place was invaded by the dust. The breeze, so far quite comfortable and pleasing, made way to a wind that was gathering strength every moment. The people rushed to seek shelters for avoiding the dust storm, and also the inevitable rain. It looked as though the water, the wind and the dust had decided to make their presence felt to mankind, which always has a needlessly high opinion about itself! Nearly six hours later, the trio left a trail of destruction in the area with the damaged buildings, twisted electric and telecommunication poles, and uprooted trees.

However, when the storm passed, a surprising thing could be noticed that, while the tallest buildings were the most affected, the humble dwellings were the least! The huge trees had been uprooted, and the smaller ones and the bushes were not! And the grass, could *smile happily* as it always does, at the hesitant sun, because *nothing* had happened to it!

Most of us have the *notion* that the big, the massive and perhaps the famous, is beyond the reach of destruction. If this were true, then the earth would be still ruled by the dinosaurs! *Eco-friendly* technology is making us aware of the role of mega industries in the quick depletion of the natural resources, and the pollution which is both on physical and also the psychological level. Physically our land, rivers and oceans are being spoilt. And psychologically, our inner peace is being eroded by the introduction of *needless* desires through the *Consumerism,* which makes us buy things we neither need nor can afford!

Late nineteen sixties saw a youth rebellion in the west. They rebelled against Technology, against hypocrisy and against the established value system based on the material possessions. There were two streams. One was an escape through the minor and major psychedelic drugs. This became more popular. Even the music they liked or produced had the shades of their likes and dislikes. This first stream—known as the *Flower-children,* almost succeeded in ruining itself. There was another, a smaller group of people who started searching for an alternative way of life. The second stream turned to the eastern philosophy and spirituality. Many of these persons discovered the purpose of life.

Such *defense mechanism* of the humanity has been noticed from time to time in the History of mankind. It is like a man walking on tight-rope, he balances himself by bending his body to the left and right alternatively to reach the other end of the rope. Only in the case of human behaviour, probably, it has to reach the extremes to withdraw itself to the other side! On one side is the inclination towards material growth, which *seems* to negate spirit totally; on the other side is spirituality which *seems* to negate the material.

Actually, these inclinations do not negate each other, as each cannot exist without the other. Matter without consciousness is dead; and consciousness cannot manifest itself without matter. They necessarily co-exist with each other. But it is only due to the total attention on one, the other becomes *less important* and goes into the background.

There are certain drawings or sketches depicting an old lady. When one looks at it from a particular perspective, the figure depicts the old lady. But from another perspective it resembles a young girl or a woman. The beauty of the sketch lies in the fact that one can see *only one at a time!* The human perspective appears to be somewhat similar. And the key lies in utilising both the matter and the spirit for *transcending duality*.

This has been very logically explained by the *Vedānta* through two key words: *Draṣṭā*—the seer or the perceiver, and *Dṛśyaṃ*—the seen or the objective world perceivable by the senses. *Yoga Vāsiṣṭha* observes that *Dṛśyaṃ* has only a relative existence depending on the *Draṣṭā* the seer, *assumes* screens of *Rāga*—likes and *Dweṣa*—dislikes, through *Saṁkalpa* or the primary vibration which is a *potential* desire. *Rāga* and *Dweṣa* give birth to the grosser manifestations like fear, anger and jealousy.

We observe that these manifestations are absent in an infant, as *Ahaṁkāra* or 'I-ness' has not yet developed in it. Consequently, the perception of the world is very clear and strong. But over the years, it learns—through either the milieu or the gathered information—to include the *description of the world* in its perception, and gradually overlook the perception entirely and to stick to the *description!* But the infant's bliss is through its ignorance *(Ignorance is bliss!)*. While the aspired state is qualitatively different, as different as being childish and *childlike*.

Normally, an infant is not enlightened. Its innocence is out of its ignorance, purity an outcome of inexperience, and awe or sense of mystery is due to the lack of maturity. An enlightened person is definitely *like an infant,* pure and guileless. But at the same time, there is total understanding, innocence is because of the innate *trust,* and purity owing to the complete detachment to the *Dṛśyaṃ* the world of objects. In such a person, the 'I' has dropped, and there is no one to *interpret* or *opine* or *colour* the experience. While in a child the 'I' is in a *potential or seed form,* as it only awaits the congenial condition for manifestation and growth.

Ahaṁkāra, the 'I-am-ness' is at various levels, the grossest being, 'I am this body', and the subtlest is the feeling of *Being.* And according to its level of manifestation, it is either helpful or otherwise to the seeker. The *Ahaṁkāra* gets ripened through the *Vicāra* or the meditative contemplation on the suggestions of the scriptures, the company of the holy, as well as the experiences life has for us. It ultimately falls off on its own, like a ripe fruit or a dried leaf. The present *Sarga* is a continuation of the previous one, intended for stressing the value of the spiritual literature and the need to understand the differentiation of the three *Ahaṁkāra-s* or the egos at the three planes of consciousness.

Warning against the tendency of the mind for *involvement* and *indulgence* the venerable Sage Vasiṣṭha said that one reaps only pain through the identification with the worldly possessions like sons and other relationships. While the surest way of elimination of the worldly malady is the large heartedness. Such persons, who have become one with *Brahman,* have nothing to fear as they are ever protected, just as the universes are protected. Only such ones who have elevated themselves with true love, and are ever engaged in the ceaseless *Vicāra* can be called as 'men'. The rest of the mankind is mere brutes.

In spite of being afflicted with life's problems, and whatever the consequence, one should not perform such actions which result in either involvement or indulgence. An action is good or otherwise, depending on its result of reducing the activity of mind. Even a noble action having a wrong or vicious motivation has adverse and harmful effects, like Rāhu[87] who had to suffer in spite of drinking the *Amṛtaṃ* or the elixir of immortality. The men of stable mind never

87 After the *Amṛta Maṅthan* —churning of ocean for the elixir, Rāhu had to suffer by having his head cut off for partaking, the *Amṛtaṃ* through unfair means.

get carried away by the lower temptations and hungers, as they have reached higher states through the mastery over the senses and mind. If the readers of *Ātmajñāna* works, meditate regularly on the truths enshrined therein, the mind gets ripened by degrees to ultimately achieve the infinite *Ātman.*

The sage then advised Rāma to be careful of egoism or fear or laziness, and to tread the path as laid down in the spiritual scriptures, and to take shelter under the benign feet of the Enlightened Wise for crossing over the ocean of *Saṁsāra.* The Enlightened Persons help those who approach them in annihilating the *Ahaṁkāra,* clouding the being. This sprout called *Ahaṁkāra* has its branches of 'I' and 'mine', everywhere. Thc 'I' can be destroyed completely, only by the fire of *Jñāna* or the wisdom.

Rāma enquired from the *Ṛṣi* about the nature of *Ahaṁkāra,* about the ways of mastering it, the results of such mastery, and whether a person associated with the *Vāsanās* of the body can achieve it.

Vasiṣṭha replied that there are three levels of *Ahaṁkāra,* according to three *Ākāśas,* or the planes of consciousness. Of these, two are always beneficial, and the third is to be always shunned. The awareness achieved through *Vicāra,* and *Viveka* or discrimination, which enables one to know that the multiple worlds and the Supreme Principle are part of the Self, is the *Supreme Ahaṁkāra.* The awareness that the Self is eternal and subtler than the exterior universe which is perceivable by the mind and senses and transcends the universe is the second *Ahaṁkāra. Jīvanamukta-s* or the liberated, usually dwell on these two levels, and help seekers to cross over the *Saṁsāra.*

The consciousness which identifies with the limited mind-senses-body is the third and the grossest *Ahaṁkāra.* Most of us are the slaves of the *Ahaṁkāra* at this third level. All suffering is a consequence of this *Ahaṁkāra* and is the root cause of re-birth. This puny *Ahaṁkāra* is to be eliminated at whatever cost. And sooner one annihilates this, by elevating oneself to the two higher *Ahaṁkāra-s,* the earlier one becomes recipient to the *Brāhmic* Bliss. And to illustrate the characteristics of three *Ahaṁkāra-s,* the sage narrated the following story which was only a continuation of the story told in the previous *Sarga.*

After the destruction of the *Asura-s* Dāma and others Śaṁbarāsura became greatly incensed against the *Deva-s.* Analysing his mistakes in the earlier venture, he discovered that the *Asura-s* could be forced to be the victims of *Ahaṁkāra* and hence fear etc., as they lacked *Ātmajñāna.* This time he created three more *Asuras* Bhīma, Bhāsa and Dṛḍha, who were stainless without any influence of the mind. They were enlightened without a trace of either doubt or desire. They fought with the *Devas* relentlessly for countless years.

Whenever the idea of 'I' and 'mine' entered their mind, they probed within to seek the origin of 'I' through subtle *Vicāra.* And the 'I' and 'mine' vanished like wealth from the non-charitable person. And such persons who have freed themselves from *Ahaṁkāra* through *Ātmavicāra* are never touched by fear and are content with whatever they have or get. They have the equipoise to guard them under all circumstances. That was how, Bhīma, Bhāsa, and Dṛḍha were able to defeat the *Deva-s* repeatedly.

The *Deva-s* approached Viṣṇu and sought asylum and help. Having assured them of his help, he reached the battlefield and flung his weapon *Sudarśana,* the discus. The three *Asura-s* were burnt and were carried at once to Vaikuṇṭha, the abode of Viṣṇu. Thus *Vāsanā-s* cause bondage; and with their disappearance, one attains to freedom. Concluding the story, Vasiṣṭha urged Rāma to develop *Viveka* through constant *Ātmavicāra.*

As the previous *Sarga,* which suggests the three qualities to go away from the divine, this story gives three qualities necessary for experiencing the divine. Bhīma means formidable or tremendous; Bhāsa is to be taken as light, lustre or brightness; and Dṛḍha indicates stability and firmness. By introducing the three levels of *Ahaṁkāra* the sage clarifies it. The three qualities suggested by the names of the Asuras appear to be the three methods of freeing oneself from the bonds of *Ahaṁkāra.*

This becomes very clear, if we try to peep into the characteristics of the three *Ahaṁkāra-s.* The grossest *Ahaṁkāra* identifies itself with the body-senses-mind complex. And the characteristic feature of this complex is the instability. By nature mind is restless, the senses are wayward, and the body totally unstable. One can control all of them with *Dṛḍhatwa*—firmness.

The intermediate *Ahaṁkāra* is that which separates itself from the manifested world. In other words, it *differentiates* itself from the world and overcomes the misery generated by the involvement and indulgence (as evident from the so-called normal life!). But even then there is the feeling of *Dwaita*—the otherness. This otherness can be combated through *Bhāsa*—the light of awareness.

And the supreme *Ahaṁkāra* is that which makes one aware, that the world and all *experiences* are part of the One which is Whole. This releases us from most of our limitations, because there is total negation with the dual nature and identification with the Whole. But even then, it is not complete, as there is still the trace of *identification.* That is where the third *Asura,* Bhīma or the Bigness becomes helpful, through the identification with the infinite. The two *Ahaṁkāra-s* that is, awareness and identification with the infinite, no doubt have no *binding* effect. On the contrary, they are helpful in transcending the limitations of the mind-sense-material world. But just as one need not retain the needle after removing the thorn from the body, one does not need this *Ahaṁkāra-s* after the enlightenment.

That is how in the story, these three helpers are referred to as the *Asura-s,* and Viṣṇu—the Sustenance Function of the

Reality, himself *eliminated* them with his discus. This aspect has been very beautifully explained by Shri Ramakrishna through a parable :

> 'Once a rich man was passing through a forest, when three robbers surrounded him and robbed him of all his wealth. After snatching all his possessions from him, one of the robbers said: "What's the good in keeping the man alive? Kill him." Saying this he was about to strike their victim with his sword, when the second robber interrupted and said: "There's no use in killing him. Let us bind him fast and leave him here. Then he won't be able to tell the police." Accordingly the robbers tied him with a rope, left him, and went away. After a while the third robber returned to the rich man and said: "Ah! You're badly hurt, aren't you? Come, I'm going to release you." The third robber set him free and led him out of the forest. When they came near the highway, the robber said: "Follow this road and you will reach home easily." "But you must come with me too", said the man. "You have done so much for me. We shall all be happy to see you at home." "No" said the robber, "it is not possible for me to go there. The police will arrest me." So saying, he left the rich man after pointing out his way.
>
> 'Now the first robber, who said: "What's good of keeping the man alive? Kill him", is *Tamas*. It destroys. The second robber is *Rajas,* which binds the man to the world and entangles him in a variety of activities. *Rajas* makes him forget God. *Sattwa* alone shows the way to God. It produces virtues like compassion, righteousness and devotion. Again *Sattwa* is like the last step of the stairs. Next to it is the roof. The supreme Brahman is man's own abode. One cannot attain the Knowledge of Brahman unless one transcends the three guṇas.'[88]

---

88 *The Gospel of Shri Ramakrishna*, by M, IXth impression, Shri Ramakrishna Math, Mylapore, Madras, pp. 218-19.

The lowest *Ahaṁkāra* which identifies itself with the mind-sense-body complex is *Tāmasic* and *Rājasik,* destructive and binding as the *Asura-s* Dāma, Vyāla and Kaṭa. While the *Sāttwic Ahaṁkāra* is like the *Asura-s* of the present *Sarga* or the subtler *Ahaṁkāra* is *Asuric* or demoniac! The 'I-am-ness' happens to be the root cause of all the ills of existence. At the grossest level, it gets indulged with the world of sense objects, and at the subtler levels, it identifies with the mind and ideas to make us victims of pride and egoism or egotism. The two stories illustrate the evils of *Ahaṁkāra* and give us the means to annihilate it.

Whether it is a dust-storm, or a tornado, having the destructive power, it can and does destroy the life and property. But the blades of grass remain untouched by it. The blade of grass is too insignificant for the tornado to touch. Not only that the blade allows the cyclonic wind to pass over it without *any resistance,* but retains its original strength. Life is full of trials and tribulations for those who have identified and have sustained the *Ahaṁkāra.* But those who try to become *nothing,* just flow with the existence, never even leave their foot-prints on the sands of time. But yes, they leave behind a *fragrance that has a soothing effect on the existence!*

4

The Story of Dāśūra

The rough metalled road packed with red soil meandered through small hillocks. At some places the rocks had been cut to create the space for the road. On both of its sides there was a multitude of trees of all species and shapes. But the principal among them were the cashews and the tamarind, which spread their mildly pungent fragrance. The road took a course that led into the deeper woods. As one continued, the road became rather steep and the woods thicker. The trees were populated by *Langoors,* the black faced long tailed monkeys, who curiously watched the pilgrims or nature lovers as they walked by. Amidst all the chirpings of birds and other sounds, one could distinctly listen to the water falling from a height. The descent started and one was led to a cup like formation and the two waterfalls, one larger than the other. The larger one was called the *Rāmatīrtha,* while the smaller one was called *Lakṣmaṇatīrtha.* This place was a few kilometers from the sleepy little town of Honnavar in what is now called as the *Uttara Kannada* district of Northern Karnataka.

The twin-water fall, named after the two royal brothers from the epic *Rāmāyaṇa,* was claimed to have curative powers by the local people. It was said that even mad persons were brought back to sane life, if they were made to stand under the water fall. As is very common in every part of our country where everything gets a religious tinge, the twin water fall had been considered to be a place of pilgrimage. Even at the peak of summer, the fall did not dry. And one more interesting thing about this was that no one knew the origin of the water. And some of the orthodox people even said that it was irreligious to seek the origin! Perhaps to defy this denial, many a youth tried to find out the origin.

One does not know whether anyone succeeded or not, but they all must have had their share of adventure. And at least a few stories for their children and grand-children! Something similar happens when one starts thinking deeply about the world around us, the order, the rhythm, the beauty, and the inter-dependence. The question, 'What is the origin of this creation?' is natural to most of us. We do not know whether there is really an answer to this question, but definitely this appears to be one of the *primary* questions that may have given birth to Philosophy! It appears that the various theories of Creation are the interesting stories of adventure from those who ventured to pursue this question in the wonderful world of thought!

Scriptures like *Yoga Vāsiṣṭha* advocating the *Adwaita*—the Non-duality, keep repeating that multiplicity or the world is only a manifestation of the Ultimate Reality. Invariably, this statement of fact gives birth to the question, 'How does the Non-dual, ever-perfect *Brahman* manifest itself into the imperfect world with its multiplicity'? in the mind of a seeker.

The experienced wise say that this question does not have any answer at the intellectual level. And when one transcends mental activity, the problem is not solved, but it gets *dissolved.* An episode from the life of Gautama, the Buddha illustrates this point. Buddha, as it is well known, always discouraged philosophical discussions and stressed on the experimentation and experience.

It is said that once a wise old philosopher came for a discussion with the Buddha. As his wont, the enlightened one was sitting under a tree. The visitor was about to start the discussion, but the Lord said that he could discuss only when the man of knowledge stayed with the *Saṅgha* for a year and observed all the discipline and followed the spiritual practices. The Buddha promised that he would have the discussion with the philosopher at the end of the year.

A man sitting under a nearby tree started laughing and said that if at all one wants to have a talk with Tathāgata, it has to be at the very beginning. Because, after an year with Tathāgata, one's life will be totally transformed and there could be no discussion as one would transcend all thought! The philosopher looked helplessly at the enlightened one, who only smiled and said for the discussion to take place his condition had to be followed! Thirsty that the philosopher was for knowledge, he stayed on and followed every little rule and diligently practised meditation.

At the end of the year, Tathāgata called the man and made him sit in front of him and asked him to begin the discussion. The man who had experienced the deep states of his Being, and had transcended the mind, just touched the feet of the Lord and said that all his questions, and even the desire for discussion had dissolved!

But not everyone is expected to be at such a lofty level so as to start the quest right away. And with most of us the mind with all its activity is so strong, that unless some food is given in the form of explanations to its questions for appeasing it at least *temporarily,* it cannot start the quest. Here comes the role of the different theories of the origin. And there are so many of them that one is bound to get confused. But one need not get confused with such diversity, as each theory is only a *point of view* of the intellect. The present *Sarga* devotes a small portion for *one such view.*

At this juncture, we have to face a real paradox in spirituality. All along we are told, that the Truth transcends all language and description; and that we should not get attached to the words. Logic, of which we are all so proud, says immediately, then why use words at all? If *IT* is beyond language, then how can one possibly *talk* about it? The question is very logical. But we must remember that logic as such has only two openings : either 'yes' or 'no'. But life has not only these two, but *both,* as it transcends mind. And language and logic are both children of the mind! However, logic and language can definitely be *pointers* to *indicate* the Truth. The human weakness for words makes us hold on to the words instead of using them to understand and experience that which they indicate.

That is why, we must remember that the purpose of these view-points is only to quieten the intellect and its questions. Perhaps for this reason, sage Vasiṣṭha starts this story with a sound advice for the seeker to develop disinterest in the world and to totally eschew sense indulgence and mental involvement of any kind. One may ask, what a theory of creation or the origin of the universe has got anything to do with involvement and indulgence? Actually, any mental activity is a potential desire—taking the comprehensive view of the desire to be, the continuance of mental activity. Involvement and indulgence act as fertilizers for the perpetuation of this activity!

Vasiṣṭha said that the seeker has to transcend all mental activity and experience. For this, he continued, one has to use the mind itself just as one makes use of a thorn to remove the thorn from the body. The sacred *Śāstras* play the role of the needle in removing the thorn of ignorance. And if one gets stuck with the words used in the *Śāstras,* then the very purpose of the scriptures is defeated. But the *Jñānins,* who have given us these scriptures out of their compassion for us, are neither governed by the mental activity nor do they find any need for it, as they transact in this world from an entirely different level. And they *make proper use* of the words, for transcending the words themselves.

Vasiṣṭha warns us through Rāma, that one has to consciously remember to slowly but surely *loosen the grip* of the attachment to the objects of senses as well as the mind. Without this primary understanding, whatever one does or thinks, takes one only towards bondage.

It was at this point, that Rāma asked as to how possibly could the heterogeneity that is experienced by the senses and conceived by the mind be *One* without the second? To this question, Vasiṣṭha replied that it is almost like the one *Ākāśa* though permeating all objects, being inseparable from them is also distinct from them. And though it manifests as *Ahaṁkāra* and its illusion inducing progeny, it remains totally unaffected by them. But the ignorant identify themselves with these manifestations subjecting themselves to pain inducing rebirths. And the beauty is, that even the so-called ignorance and suffering is possible only because of the imperishable and one Reality which is behind *all experiences.*

A few examples may help us to understand the seemingly confusing statement. The air *carries* the vibrations of sound without itself getting affected; it *carries* the molecules which create a sense of fragrance or oppressive smell. Thus without the *carrier* air the smell or the sound is not possible. Similarly, the same water assumes the multiplicity of waves and froth, and without water, they cannot exist. However, the examples as always are incomplete.

There is the case of a person who acted as Abraham Lincoln. The drama group would travel all over the country to present the life of one of the greatest Presidents of America. The actor in the man playing Abe Lincoln got better of the man as there was total identification with the role. So much so, that even outside the theatre he continued to be Abe Lincoln, as it was no more a character for him, but a reality! Something similar happens to us when we wrongly identify with the manifested world instead of identifying ourselves with the Non-dual Reality, and suffer needless misery.

This Oneness with the Whole should be taught to only such persons who have developed sufficient dispassion, and are not likely to misuse the knowledge. This is not only because the theoretical knowledge helps only in the justification of even our limitations, but it may give a wrong impression in the person's mind, that only the intellectual explanation is *everything*.

Concept of *Adhikāra* or eligibility has been of very great importance in our culture. The attitude and the aptitude were very carefully considered before any knowledge was imparted in our *Gurukuls*. Even the modern psychologists agree with this, when they observe that the knowledge tends to become useless if the aptitude is absent, and it is likely to be misused if the attitude is wrong. Shri Ramakrishna would stop talking of spirituality if the worldly minded people came to visit him. Instead he would ask them to visit the temples of Kālī, Śiva and Rādhā-Kānta! Though the concept of *Adhikāra* or eligibility is lofty in itself, even this has been one of the causes for some great sciences to have a natural death. Because, even the knowledge became a *property* of certain Pundits, who refused to impart it even to the genuine persons.

Rāma wished to know the order of manifestation of the Non-dual Reality. The sage said that the Non-dual Reality sportively conceives the space and time, and then through its own power assumes a Universal body which further goes into a succession of individual souls. At the Non-dual level an initial *Saṁkalpa* manifests from the subtle plane to the grosser planes. To indicate this Sage told Rāma, that the *Saṁkalpa*, for sound creates *Ākāśa* or ether; for touch, *Vāyu* or air; for sight, *Tejas* or fire; for taste, *Āpah* or water; and for smell, creates *Pṛthiwi* or the earth.

In spite of telling Rāma about the order of manifestation, Vasiṣṭha suggested, that instead of getting involved with the mode of creation, one should be more concerned about the means of transcending this multiplicity of creation. He said that the world is like an intensely long dream, and only waking up from sleep, can break it! The reference to dreamlike nature of the world characterised by multiplicity, suggests that even the explanation of the order of the creation is also a *dream explanation!* Just as the dream does not have any regularity, the creation too does not have any certainty about it. That is why, the sage said one should not pay more attention to pain and gain and to remain unstained as a lotus leaf by the water. To explain the illusory nature of the world he narrated the story of Dāśūra.

In the country of Magadha, there lived a *Ṛṣi* named Saraloma, with his son Dāśūra. After leading a long life of *Tapas* Saraloma attained *Videha Mukti,* liberation from the body. Being very much attached to his father Dāśūra wept bitterly over his father's death and forgot to perform even his daily actions. Observing the pitiable condition of Dāśūra, who had a great capacity, a goddess appeared to him as an invisible voice, and said that only the ignorant dragged themselves to the condition he was in, and that he should put his effort in liberating himself from the limitations of *Saṁsāra.*

The divine voice had a transforming effect on him, and Dāśūra shook off his sorrow, and started performing *Tapas* strictly according to the Vedic injunctions. But he was not satisfied with the purity of any place. With an intention of finding a pure and congenial spot for his *Tapas,* he performed arduous penance by offering parts of his own body in fire. Lord *Agni* appeared before the *Muni* and asked about intention of the sacrifice.

When Dāśūra told him that he had been unable to find a pure place and that he wanted to sit on a tendril on top of a tree. *Agni* granted the boon and Muni Dāśūra found a *Kadamba* tree in the forest and sat on a tendril at its top. Unable to attain the *Brahma Jñāna* directly, he performed the rituals like *Gomedha*—the sacrifice of cow; *Aśwamedha,* that of horse; and *Naramedha*—that of man, according to the Vedic injunctions to develop a steady and clear mind. At once, the priceless *Jñāna* took possession of him and pervaded his being. Thus Dāśūra became free from the cycle of birth and death by eradicating the *Vāsanās* and continued to live on the tendril of the *Kadamba* tree.

One day, a Goddess appeared and he asked her identity. The Goddess replied that she was aware that he had attained to the limitless *Jñāna,* and that she was the Goddess presiding over the forest. But she did not have any son while all other divine beings enjoyed the parenthood. And troubled that she was, she had approached him to bless her with a son, else she would enter the fire out of grief. The *Muni* handed her a flower with all compassion and said that she would become a mother soon. However, as she had threatened to enter the fire in case her wish was not granted, the son would attain *Jñāna* only after facing many hard trials.

After some time a son was born to the Goddess, who trained him in all the branches of secular knowledge. Then, brought him to Sage Dāśūra and requested him to instruct him so that he could attain to *Ātmajñāna* or Self-realisation. The sage asked her to leave her son with him. The son of the Goddess was initiated by the *Muni* through spiritual stories, deeper aspects of *Vedānta* and methods of contemplative meditation. It was during one such communion that sage Vasiṣṭha heard a conversation between the preceptor and the disciple, as he passed by the *Kadamba* tree.

The *Muni* was telling his disciple the symbolic story of *Saṁkalpa Puruṣa* or the person created by *Saṁkalpa* or the tendency to think, for convincing him of the unreality of the world with all its multiplicity and to bring in the quiescence of mind. He was telling that the initial *Saṁkalpa* has potency to create countless thoughts, which are potential desires with a possibility of ultimately becoming *Vāsanās* having a binding effect. He was advising the disciple to perform such actions which present themselves spontaneously without any *Saṁkalpa.* Because it is the *Saṁkalpa* which makes one choose between them, as choice takes one away from the state.

On hearing these words of Sage Dāśūra, the disciple wanted to know more about the *Saṁkalpa.* To which the Sage replied that *Saṁkalpa* is nothing but the manifestation of the Supreme Principle as visible things. It has a very humble beginning as the primeval seed. This seed becomes a sapling to gradually turn itself into a mighty tree, and to totally obscure the vision of *Paramātman,* the Ultimate. The growth of this *Saṁkalpa* tree leads to one's fall. One should never pay any attention to *Saṁkalpa* and on doing so, one only nurtures it and makes it invincible. At the same time, it is not all that difficult to do away with the *Saṁkalpa.* In fact, all that is required is the control over one's thoughts. One has to annihilate the external *Saṁkalpa* with the internal one. Having destroyed the impure mind with the pure mind, one can rest firmly in one's *Ātmajñāna.* With these words he encouraged the disciple to attain to *Ātmajñāna* by taking refuge in *Pauruṣa* and *Prayatna.*

In this story Sage Vālmīki, the author of *Yoga Vāsiṣṭha,* tries to impress upon the seeker the importance of *Saṁkalpa* which alone is responsible for the manifestation of multiplicity—the primal cause of misery. As other stories in this scripture, this one also is likely to be misinterpreted, if one reads it superficially. It is very symbolic and has a wealth of hints for the seeker.

Attachment to anything or anyone has a binding effect. And Dāśūra who is attached to his father is no exception. He is reminded of his duties by an invisible voice. The formless voice always comes from within when one is afflicted with some misery. And death of a near and dear one is perhaps the most ideal time, as one is in a receptive state. At the commencement of the spiritual journey, many persons get the feeling of lack of purity in the surroundings, and they usually start searching for *ideal* or *congenial* places. This is when one starts getting distaste for the society and the milieu. And for the introspection to start many persons have to stop socialising, though all need not do it.

Dāśūra offering his parts of his own body to the fire does not mean that he was a masochist! Spiritual practices have been called as *Tapas,* in our culture, which means 'to heat' or 'to burn'. So, Dāśūra was dissociating with his body through *Tapas.* Incidentally, Dāśūra means one who can 'give up courageously'.[89] His seeking the boon to sit on a tendril of a tree for his penance is also symbolic. If one has to sit on a tendril, one has to be very light. But the lightness here is more at the psychological level than at the physical.

The psychic lightness can be achieved only by eliminating the desires, by the burdens of past and future and by transcending time. Secondly, the tendril remains a tendril only for a short while. Consequently, to sit on a tendril one has to remain ever fresh and young! This is also symbolic suggestion to the seeker that he can remain ever young only when he transcends time. *Kadamba* is a type of tree, the buds of which blossom when there is thunder and lightning.[90] Dāśūra sitting on the tendril of *Kadamba* means that he sits with the lightness of the mind which transcends time and in turn, blossoms with the flashes of truth.

Further, Vālmīki the author gives the means of enlightenment. Dāśūra he says, was unable to get the *Brahmajñāna* directly, and had to resort to *Gomedha, Aśwamedha,* and *Naramedha* to achieve the steadiness of mind! It is difficult, if not impossible to perform these sacrifices at present time, which follows that the path chosen by Dāśūra is

---

89 'Dā' means to give. Karṇa was called as *Dānaśūra*–a man of great charity as *Dāna* means charity.

90 कतिपयकुसुमोद्गमः कदम्बः ।

not available to us. If one takes these as the rituals involving the sacrifice of cow, horse and a human being, then not only the path is closed, but the path will be *criminal!*

But then, even these sacrifices are symbolic. *Go* not only means a cow, but it refers to speech. *Aśwa* means a horse, but it also means the senses, as they are very fast in seeking their sense objects. *Kaṭhopaniṣad* says :

> 'The sense organs they say are the horses, and the roads for them are the sense objects'.[91]

While *Nara* definitely means a man, it can also be interpreted as the *Ahaṁkāra.* Taking this meaning, we get an entirely new interpretation. Speech is a bridge between thought and action; the external action can be controlled through control of speech. The senses are to be controlled for controlling our desires, and if the *Ahaṁkāra* or 'I' is under control then everything else is in control! A very beautiful *Mantra* from *Kaṭhopaniṣad* says :

> 'Let the wise man merge speech in the *Manas,* and *Manas* in the *Buddhiḥ;* let him merge the *Buddhiḥ* in *Mahat,* the great self, and again in the self of peace'.[92]

No matter where a flower blossoms, it has to spread its fragrance. In spite of the fact that Dāśūra got enlightened in a forest, a seeker sought him out to inherit his enlightenment. The advice of the preceptor to his disciple was to remain in *choiceless awareness,* that is, to accept things as they come without any preference on his own. This is one of the surest ways of transcending time. This incidentally, was his own approach to the Reality. For one can only guide the others only on the path one has trodden oneself.

---

91 इन्द्रियाणि हयानाहुर्विषयांस्तेषुगोचरन् ॥ 1.3.4 ॥

92 यच्छेद्वांमनसि प्राज्ञस्तद्यच्छेज्ज्ञान आत्मनि ।
ज्ञानमात्मनि महति नियच्छेत्तद्यच्छेच्छान्त आत्मनि ॥ 1.3.13 ॥

The fact that sage Vasiṣṭha told an order of manifestation to Rāma and concluded this *Sarga* with the dialogue between Dāśūra and his disciple, wherein, the role of *Saṁkalpa* and the importance of its elimination has been stressed shows, that the order of creation was told only to temporarily appease the intellectual hunger of Rāma. And sooner the seeker realises the importance of saving his time and energy by abstaining from intellectual and word jugglery the better it is for him. However, the intellectual discussion has a tremendous fancy for the intellect which continues to fall for it!

The scenic spots like Rāmatīrtha create a milieu of appreciation for the nature. If one is an intellectual adventurer, then it may urge him or her to *question* about the origin and seek *intellectual explanations*. But if one is a pure adventurer, it may make him *seek* the source. There is no doubt that this creation or the manifestation has a powerful influence on the mind, senses and body. But if one chooses to seek the *creator* or the *source* of manifestation, then he reaches the *Ahaṁkāra,* and in turn discovers that it is the *Saṁkalpa* which is the source of *everything*. Reaching that, one finds that one was always there, and that only due to wrong identification it had been what it was : a problem!

This story inspires every seeker to be a real Dāśūra who can sacrifice his everything : body, senses, mind, intellect and the ego. And through such sacrifice gain *whatever* we seek through the things that are given up!

5

The Song of Kaca

The air carries a pleasant smell of moist earth mixed with that of the leaves of different plants, some of whom are known to have the medicinal qualities. The deer, the bison, and a variety of other animals abound this place. And the place is known as *Pākhāl,* named after a crystal clear lake. A wildlife sanctuary is attached to it. The lake and the sanctuary are in the Telangana region of Andhra Pradesh, about 70 kilometers from a town known as Warangal. Like such places that are protected from the exploitation of human beings(!), it has an ethereal beauty. One feels as though one is on a different planet. The thick forest cover, the crystal clear lake, the wildlife and a variety of feathered friends abounding it, make it an ideal place for a retreat. In that sylvan area of several square kilometers, there are only two buildings separated by at least five hundred meters, and are maintained by the Departments of Public Works and the Forests.

The approach to this scenic place is delightful as the crowded and stifling civilization gives way, gradually, to the wild nature as one leaves the towns to pass through villages and hamlets. The road is lined with thick shady trees, the green paddy fields, and the rural innocence on both of its sides. As one enters this reserved forest, one feels protected and safe. It can also be called a *sacred grove,* as there is a wide variety of botanical species which have become extinct elsewhere. Because the people have abstained from cutting any tree or killing any animal, there is an atmosphere of fearlessness created by the flora and the fauna.

In forests one is always vulnerable to many dangers, but much less than one, who is used to the civilized ways, can ever imagine! There is the rough terrain with all its thorns, insects, snakes and animals that definitely follow the rules of their own, of which we may not be aware. And one of the most dangerous things is the mire of the quick-sand. The caretakers of the inspection bungalows warn the visitors not to venture too near the lake as there are some dangerous spots where many lives have been lost. They tell the visitors that even if one were to accidentally venture into the quick-sand, the first thing that should be avoided is *panic.* For it is the panic that makes us restless and forces us to make unnecessary effort which only takes us *deeper into the mire.* If the victim keeps still, then the others can make efforts to bring him out.

Something similar happens to the one in the *Saṁsāra,* but with a basic difference. That is, most of us are unaware of the *mire of involvement* that entangles us to the world. Consequently, we are totally oblivious to the dangers. And the one, who has realised that he or she has been enveloped by the mire and that happiness is only the reverse of misery, panic is the first thing to be avoided. By panic, what is meant is the *'hurry to transcend the mire of involvement'*. This hurry or speed to *achieve* the freedom takes us towards intense mental activity. Because, this hurry happens to be yet another desire! The more we nurture any desire, the deeper do we get into the mire!

It must be accepted that the contemporary trend governing humanity is the *goal orientation.* Everything—our education, entertainment as well as our social system, is governed by *goals.* The main role of education seems to be to infect us with ambition. Everything else is secondary. This is necessary or may be even mandatory for survival in the world. And without any goal one tends to stagnate at the *Tāmasic* level, as it has happened in our country. Most of us are incorrigibly lethargic, and others are yet to overcome the slavish mentality, which is dominated by jealousy. Due to this avoidable emotion, most of us are involved in leg pulling politics even in the scientific field. And we are still lagging behind in the field of Science and Technology in spite of our talent.

Goals have a very important role of enthusing us towards action from lethargy, from complacency to efficient proficiency. Goal is a bridge which takes us from animalistic existence, to the human level, making us aware of a life which is more than mere survival. For instance, let us consider the case of one who wants to build a house or a huge bank balance. For him, the house or the bank balance has become the goal. Consequently, the ego starts *'missing'* the goal, and does not rest till the goal is fulfilled. It thus creates restlessness. To achieve them, one strengthens one's will, and plans all the methods of acquiring them. In other words, the ego and the path are created by the goal. This is how the bridge of goal works to enthuse us to activity at the level of survival.

Even at the psychological level the goal of knowledge helps in the better understanding of life, when one discovers a deeper dimension to life than mere survival. Certain values, like inner or self discipline enter our life. The search for a meaning and purpose of life enter the consciousness. With this enquiry, necessarily one develops distaste and a disinterest towards the basic urges like hunger and procreation. One becomes a seeker of truth. Up to a certain stage of this inner journey, the goad of goal is useful. It gives a direction to the wayward life, brings in trust and devotion.

However, goal is only a *bridge,* and if we make it our *home,* misery is inevitable. We definitely have to *make use of it* at the grosser levels, but should not continue to hang on to it at the subtler levels. And if the goal becomes powerful, the *ego too becomes equally powerful,* if not more powerful. That is how, fear and greed have been *used* by the organised religions to control the society. They have made even *God* into a *goal.* It is very obvious, that every goal only nurtures the ego while creating the path for its achievement. By its very nature, goal is subordinate to ego, as goal is *achieved* by the ego. And if God is made into a goal then achiever is superior to God, which can never be!

In the path of devotion, it is said that the devotee can *never* meet the Divine. Because, the devotee's presence itself proves that the 'ego' is still present. The moment ego melts into nothingness only then, God becomes a Reality! Ego is the only barrier, hindering the God experience. That is why at this level, the goal happens to be the greatest hurdle. This is precisely the reason why, certain spiritual traditions like Zen, insist on calling their path as the *Goal-less Path,* or the *Gate-less Gate.*

There is another dimension to this. The thought 'I am', gets nurtured with every activity. Greater the achievement, more vehement and strong is this declaration. And with this declaration, there is a pseudo satisfaction of 'being somebody'. Paradoxically, with every brick added to this mansion of 'I-am', a *storey* is being added to the multi-storied building of *fear.* Because, one sees death everywhere and at every step. It is observed that, whether it is a great man or an ordinary man, he has to part with this world someday. With this observation, the man of achievement—who is necessarily more observant and intelligent, gets a parallel thought that 'I may not be'! And to combat this fear, he further gets involved in the activity to bloat his ego! Thus he gets involved in a vicious circle of, ego followed by fear, which in turn is accompanied by ego. As one succeeds in dropping the ego, the fear automatically vanishes.

This point is being repeatedly stressed because, along with the idea of goal, the concept of time enters. With time, are born desire, speed, anxiety, worry and all other manifestations of the heightened activity of the mind. This *Sarga* starts with a suggestion to Rāma by sage Vasiṣṭha that one should be devoid of any desire or volition. That one should be like beautiful gems emitting a dazzling radiance without any volition on their part. If the gem is kept on a red cloth it becomes red, on a green cloth, green and so on. In absence of desire or volition, there can be no idea of the *Kartṛtva* or doership. Another way is to identify oneself with the universe and to see that the universe as the *Kartṛ* or doer. And the third way is not to identify with either the universe or the individual but with that Reality which is transcendent. These are the three ways in which one can vanquish the ever growing mind. One should try to choose any one of these three methods and transcend the limitations of the mind.

To understand these three methods one requires a little background. The activity of mind exists through the relationship between the individual and the world of objects—taking the comprehensive interpretation of an object to be, anything that is *held* by the mind for continuing its activity. This relationship is effected through what has been called by the *Vedānta* as *Tripuṭī,* the joining triplex or the three joiners. The object, the experiencing, and the subject; the seen, the seeing and the seer; the knowledge, the process of knowing and the knower; or the content, the act of cognising and the consciousness.

For most of us, these three joiners are all intermingled and are in a state of a kind of homogeneity where there is no distinction. This is because of the speed of mind due to desires. Only when the mind is slow can one differentiate between the object and the subject, the seer and the seen. But the process of the joining is still not discernible as it is the subtlest. Some Vedāntins call this as *Guptam* or the *hidden,* just as the river Saraswatī is hidden in the *Triveṇī-Saṅgam* or confluence of the three rivers of Gaṅgā, Yamunā and Saraswatī. The cognition or the relationship with the world or the activity called the mind is *not possible,* even if any one of these is absent.

The spiritual paths for transcending the activity of mind try to handle any one of the *Tripuṭī* or the three joiners. The first method recommends that one should eschew the *Kartṛtva* or the 'doership' while performing the actions. This suggests the changing of content by the consciousness without any involvement or indulgence with the consciousness. For instance, if one sees a man suffering, one tries to alleviate his suffering *without any expectation in return.* This has been called as the *Niṣkāma Karma,* the action without any desire or any consideration for any gain. A question arises as to how is it possible to perform such action. As most of our actions are result oriented, and that too such results which are beneficial to us.

Even in such action there *is* a motivation. Only the motivation is not material, but the poise of the consciousness. Reverting back to the same example, the suffering man creates a painful vibration in the consciousness, and by the outward action of lending a helping hand, one is brought back to a condition of poise. That is, the outward situation is changed for changing the reactions in the consciousness. Through this method one is freed from the binding effect of all actions. Here action or volition is used to transcend action. This method has been known as *Karma Yoga,* where Freedom is the goal. In this, the attraction for the material result of action is given up.

The second method suggested by the sage is, that which involves the change of consciousness and not the content. One does not change the content—the world of objects, but *sees* it *as it is.* One acquires the *clarity of vision* to behold the Truth through this method. While observing the world, the consciousness *reacts* positively or negatively. One just *observes* these reactions in the consciousness. J. Krishnamurti, used to say that one has to *'Listen to the desire as you listen to the wind amongst the trees'*.[93] In this method one makes use of the content, that is, the world and the reactions of the mind, to attain the clarity of the consciousness. Here knowledge or understanding is made use of to transcend the mind. This is known as *Jñāna Yoga,* which has Truth as the goal, where the identification with the content is totally given up.

And the third method is that which allows the consciousness and the content to change each other. The basic premise is that by their very nature the consciousness and the content influence each other and we need not try to influence them or exercise any control over them. So this method suggests a 'letting-go' and to allow the Reality to take over the activity. The Reality is usually the personal God whom one loves. This is known as the path of *Bhakti* where Love is the goal. Here feeling for God, who is the sole doer, is the means to transcend the mind, with Love as the goal. With Love, surrender and sacrifice are so spontaneous that one transcends all mental activity.

There is another way, which neither allows the consciousness to change the content, nor the content to change the consciousness, nor is there the mutual change. There is transcendence through the understanding that seeker is the sought, that thinker is the product of thinking. The seeker takes a quantum leap to transcend mind. Everything is allowed to be 'as it is'. One has to only see 'what is', as J. Krishnamurti used to say. He has put it very eloquently:

> 'A river receives everything—the sewer, the corpses, the filth of the cities it passes, and yet it cleanses itself within a few miles. It receives everything and remains itself,

---

93 *J Krishnamurti : A Biography* by Pupul Jayakar, Penguin Books 1986, p. 206.

> neither caring nor knowing the pure from the impure. It's only the ponds, the little puddles that are soon contaminated, for they are not living, flowing, as the wide, sweet-smelling flowing rivers.
>
> 'Our minds are small puddles, soon made impure. It's the little pond, called mind, that judges, weighs, analyses, and yet remains the little pool of responsibility'.[94]

To see 'what is', the first and the foremost thing one has to learn is to *transcend time* because time is mind. To quote J. Krishnamurti again:

> 'Life is a vast flowing river. The mind holds in its net the things of the river, discarding and holding. There should be no net. The net is of time and space, it is the net that creates here and there; happiness and unhappiness'.[95]

In this fourth way, the transcendence happens when there is a total non-identification with the content as well as the consciousness, and one just flows by being in choice-less awareness. Obviously, this requires a greater alertness than the other three paths. Whichever path one chooses to tread depending upon one's aptitude, or predisposition, one transcends the mental activity. To illustrate such transcendence, the sage narrates the state Kaca was in. Once, a song burst forth from Kaca the son of Bṛhaspati, when he returned from the state of *Nirvikalpa Samādhi* or the *Samādhi* without any vibration, in an exhilarated joy:

> 'There is nothing I have to do; there is nowhere for me to go; there is nothing for me to accept and nothing to abstain. Whether I am in the body or out of it, in the *Ākāśa* or on the earth, *He* alone pervades. *He* alone shines in every being'.

94 Ibid., p. 262.

95 Ibid., p. 206.

Such experience is obviously beyond mind, transcending all description. But even then, the experienced wise in all compassion have tried to share their experiences. Their poetic expression has the power to not only point out the state, but even trigger a similar mood in a sensitive seeker. *Upaniṣads* and other Vedāntic scriptures are filled with such verses, excelling in their poetic expression. Language does not matter much, though Sanskrit used to be the language at that time, which had almost perfected in poetic expression. There is an immortal work in Kannada by Shri D. V. Gundappa, entitled '*Mankuthimmana Kagga*'. Two of its translated verses express the mood Kaca was in:

> 'Seeking *Brahman* in world transactions,
> Seeking *Brahman* in all *Jīva* forms,
> Feeling *Brahman* in body and sense experiences,
> This is the secret of salvation–MANKUTHIMMA. 753
>
> Once in garden and then in friends' company,
> Once in music and then in philosophy,
> Once with family and then in silence,
> Experience *Brahman*—MANKUTHIMMA. 754'[96]

Whatever the path one chooses the most important thing she or he has to avoid is the indulgence at the material level, and involvement at the psychological level. By being always alert and aware the seeker can succeed in transcendence. It is said of Kaca, that he was so unshakable in his resolve that *nothing* could distract him from his chosen path. Devayānī (the daughter of Śukrācārya[97]—the preceptor of the *Asuras* as well as Kaca), could not succeed in wooing him. He only looked upon himself as her elder brother, and extended all his sympathy and help in the later years.

---

96 *Thus Sang Mankuthimma* by A Narasimha Bhat, Asheervad Publications, Kasargod, p. 95. This is an English translation of the work.

97 Śukrācārya is the same enlightened sage described in the first sarga of this *Prakaraṇa*.

All the efforts *with involvement* like fear, only add to the misery when one accidentally gets into the mire of quick-sand. The only course open is to be still and unmoving. Similarly, having known that we are *involved* in the mire of the repetitive world of existence, if one learns to distinguish between the content and consciousness and understands the path suitable to one's growth, one has more than succeeded in making the journey called life into a joyous celebration.

6

Conclusion of Sthiti Prakaraṇa

The mighty Himalayan foot-hills surround the valley from all sides and the serpentine road passing through most of the hills, is like a thread joining them. From a mountain top one can see the terraced emerald paddy fields cultivated by the hill farmers. The paddy stalks dance in the pleasant mountain breeze, to send the fragrance of the ripened paddy in all directions. The rustic songs of the farmers, the jingle of bells around the goats grazing the rich pastures with their intermittent bleats, greet the ears.

For a tourist, this may bring in a kind of 'once in a lifetime' thrill of joy. It is likely that he may even feel that his life is worth living *because* of this experience! All these experiences may become a part of his permanent memory. And he may keep narrating them—may be adding his own embellishment!—throughout his remaining life. If he is creatively inspired, he may even paint pictures in words or colours, to be repeatedly enjoyed or interpreted, or even scorned by the posterity! But if one talks to the farmer or the shepherd who has lived there throughout, one may or may not find such a mood. The farmer and the shepherd may be singing only for warding off the worry pestering his mind; he may even be doing it just mechanically without any feeling whatsoever, as it has become a habit! And maybe, the tourist vehicles are evoking, a feeling of being useless or even initiating a mood of frustration.

The drastic difference in their moods is due to the fact that while the tourist is *only a visitor,* without any burden to tie him to the ground, the farmer *owns the land* and is tied to the place by his desires, dreams and the consequent anxiety and worry! And if one considers the whole life to be only a journey and oneself to be a traveller, then one learns to be in the eternal present. J. Krishnamurti used to say:

> 'The trick lies in living lightly as a guest in one's house, or in one's body. To be a guest is to have no sense of attachment; to step lightly on earth'.[98]

There is a mythological story appearing in *Mārkaṇḍeya Purāṇa,* in which there is a portion called *Durgā Saptaśatī,* or the seven hundred verses on Durgā, wherein, the stories on the Mother are related. A demon propitiates Lord Śiva to seek a boon that with every drop of his blood fallen on the ground an equally strong and powerful demon should rise. He becomes invincible and the gods find it almost impossible to vanquish him. This is why, he comes to be known as *Raktabīja,* the 'blood-seeded'.[99] With the help of Mother Kālī who by extending her tongue and not allowing even a drop to fall on the ground, kills him. But Raktabīja only symbolises 'ego'. Almost anything or even *nothing* helps it to grow!

Most of us feel elevated if our actions are appreciated and praised, and we try to perform such actions which are praiseworthy. But such actions change with changing times. For instance if knowledge is considered valuable at one time, money may be so, at some other time. All our actions are for nurturing our 'worthiness' or in simple words 'ego'! Obviously with every positive adjective attributed, the ego gets strengthened. Then we have the sense of possession or the 'I have' or 'my and mine' attitude. One tries to prove his worth through the *association.* Something or someone becomes great

98 *J. Krishnamurti: A Biography* by Pupul Jayakar, Penguin 1986, pp. 466.

99 *Durgā Saptaśatī,* VIIIth Chapter.

not by itself or oneself, but because '*I* possess it' or '*I* know him or her'. These are the most common nourishments for the ego! Then there is another type of ego gratification. When a person fails to get appreciation which is nothing but an attention from others, he tries to perform rebellious actions, and may even become a criminal. A criminal gets a vicarious or even sadistic pleasure of creating fear and terror in others, and derives a satisfaction when his name appears in the news paper! Even this is forgivable, as it is done in ignorant unconsciousness. But there are very subtle and dangerous props that remain hidden under the garb of religiosity. One spurns wealth and position, one's family ties, comfort, and may deliberately choose to live a life of penury. Through such acts one puts on the mask of 'holier than thou' attitude and hence egoistic. In short, any and every act only strengthens the ego!

All the examples only go to prove that the ego requires only the *attention.* In this sense, *Raktabīja* is the *Ahaṁkāra* which goes on multiplying itself on the ground of attention. And all actions, including thought, supply this ground. Mother Kāli is that power, which has total mastery over the time as it transcends mind. She stops the blood from falling on the ground of attention. But if one takes the story literally, one may even develop an aversion for mythology!

The first *Sarga* of this *Prakaraṇa,* the story of Śukra, illustrates the power of attention to create innumerable births. Initially, it starts with a seemingly harmless involvement, which gradually becomes such a powerful attention that it ties one to the world of objects. However, attention is not all negative and has its positive aspect of overcoming stagnation at the lower levels. In other words, at the unconscious level which is characteristic of the lower or animalistic existence, attention helps one to rise to the *human* level. A muscle works when it is contracted, and relaxes back on its own when its work is over. But if one consciously stretches it, and allows it to relax, then the muscle is more relaxed. Here the contraction and the stretching *appear* to be similar, but their effect is diametrically opposite.

The story of Dāma, Vyāla and Kaṭa, illustrates the innate and inseparable relationship between ego and fear. Any action, be it physical or psychological, only nurtures the ego. And with the ego or the 'I-am-ness' a subtle feeling of 'I may not be' also starts to accumulate. Consequently, as and when the ego increases, the fear too increases in the same if not in greater proportion.

The story of Bhīma, Bhāsa and Dṛḍha, brings home the point that *everything,* including the ego, is only a means to transcend all mental activity, and one should take care to see that one does not get bound to the means. The fourth story of Dāśūra illustrates the glory of sacrifice and renunciation. It is not that one exerts any strain to give up the attachment, but by attaching oneself to the highest ideal of transcendence, the hold over the lower *eases.* When such dropping *happens,* one achieves the *total non-identification.* This has been very aptly described by the song of Kaca. Sage Vaśiṣṭha suggests Rāma the methods by which one can achieve the transcendence.

This *Prakaraṇa* helps us understand the *modus operandi* of the *Ahaṁkāra* or the 'I-ness'. The factors that sustain it and nurture it are given broadly. The initial *Saṁkalpa,* which is the *contracting tendency of the Infinite consciousness,* manifests as the involvement. This involvement further descends from the *Jñānākāśa,* the absolute plane, to the *Cittākāśa,* the psychic plane and finally to the *Bhūtākāśa,* the elemental plane, in the increasing order of grossness.

Each one of us is unique and singular in this great existence, entirely differing from others. Accordingly, we exist at different levels. Those of us at the grossest level of *Bhūtākāśa* can understand only that which is immediately connected with our body, for we have taken ourselves to be nothing but bodies. Perhaps, such of us have to cover a long way even to have any attraction for the subtle, let alone understand the truth therein. But when we are repeatedly ambushed by pain and misery, we are forced to re-think about the validity of our presumption that body with its urges and hunger is *everything*. This is how; the pain contributes positively towards our growth.

Then comes the role of our actions to fulfill the hungers and desires. Every effort in that direction strengthens the ego, and every success or even failure, only exaggerates our multiplying desires in the form of goals. But since we cannot help seeing death and impermanence all around us, slowly and steadily the fear, that we may have to part with our possessions or achievements, and fear that *we may not be able to fulfill our self-set goals,* keeps increasing. The fear, if it is not properly handled may become *Abhiniveśa* or the mortal fear. But if one tries to understand it, one will be able to see through the vicarious role of the ego behind the fear, and with that very vision, the fear drops, because ultimately, fear and ego are the obverse and the reverse of the same coin. This happened to Maharshi Ramana of Tiruvannamalai. He was led to *Ātmavicāra* through the fear of death.[100]

When one is able to understand, that *Dṛśyam* or the seen, has its existence only due to *Draṣṭā* or the seer, one develops the capacity for *Ātmavicāra.* The process of *Vicāra* helps in loosening our hold on the *Saṁsāra,* and everything becomes more and more fluid. With this capacity for *Ātmavicāra* one is able to see that *everything*—the body, the senses, the desires, the anxiety, the worry, the anger, the fear as well as the ego—is only a means to transcend the limited body-mind complex. Although, one may look upon these things as obstacles during the period of suffering!

This *Prakaraṇa* stresses mainly on sustenance of *Ahaṁkāra,* the factors which are contributory to its growth and its *modus*

---

100 This has been narrated in The Story of Lavaṇa-I.

operandi. If the seeker studies this episode carefully, she or he is bound to find various practical hints giving insights into the inner ways and workings of the ego and hence the mind. If the seeker uses these hints for *Vicāra* or meditative contemplation, then only this lofty *Śāstra* becomes a bridge to cross over the limitations of life. But if the book remains *just another book,* which is used *only* as a source of information, then it will be like a person boasting of visiting a country by just studying the map or literature of that country!

Map is a practical guide, but one has to necessarily travel through, go through the hardship, meet the people and breathe its air to understand and experience the country. Similarly, the scriptures are maps which give outline details of the inner. Yes, they are the outbursts of those who had experienced the truths. But their outbursts cannot possibly become the truths of the reader; it can at the most be an imitative intellectual understanding! However, a seeker can definitely take the scripture to be an invitation for the Divine Adventure. A beckoning for a Divine Celebration!

The serpentine road that connects all the hills is the *Ahaṁkāra,* the 'I-ness'. An onlooker sitting on top of a hill is unaffected by the road, the rough terrain, the thorns or the pains and gains of the farmer in the terraced fields or the shepherd in the emerald plateau. By being a *watcher on the hill,* one remains totally pure, and yet, blissfully aware, enjoying the beauty abounding the place. *Ahaṁkāra* is a great paradox, without it one is totally unconscious, even with it most of us are totally unconscious and miserable! But if we have to make the life into a divine harmony, then we have to make use of *Ahaṁkāra,* as a musician using his voice or the instrument for producing music. In the wrong hands, the instrument becomes only a painful noise, as the *Ahaṁkāra* has become to most of us. Learning to have a balanced view through the map of this *Prakaraṇa,* one can learn to sing in tune with the existence. Nay, one can *allow the existence to sing through her or him!*

THE QUIESCENCE

Upaśama Prakaraṇa

1

The Story of King Janaka

Amidst thousands of kilometers of coast line of this great country, a sandy beach. It can be any place and situated in any of the states in our Indian sub-continent. The sea representing the state of cosmos in all its aspects is turbulent on surface with its waves, lashing out at the rocks strewn on the beach, which are seemingly holding tightly to the ground in fear of being dragged in! The sun is a golden shining disk, the birds, the gulls, wag-tails and crows are in symphony with the movement. One can also see that the breeze is particularly violent, and the fishermen are taking advantage of its strength to venture deep in search of their catch. Amidst this grand activity, within, the sea itself is silently deep, or deeply silent, totally unconcerned about the intensity of the activity on the surface.

The sea calls the beach-stroller perpetually towards itself, with its waves gesturing the welcome. And everyone enjoys wading into the foamy water; if the stroller is also a swimmer, she or he will take the invitation little more seriously to go in to enjoy the swim and the tingling salinity; and if one is further more adventurous, one may even venture to explore its unknown mysteries. In fact, not only is the sea representative of the whole cosmos, but *everything* is! Only the example of the sea illustrates the idea rather well.

Most of us wade through the vast sea called life, perhaps wetting our toes, or at the most our ankles. This is when we take the life with all its immensity to be just a survival. We just keep doing what others are involved in: earning our livelihood, propagating the family and may be fulfilling certain social obligations by following some norms. There are certain rare persons who venture to swim in to enjoy its movement, when they start realising that life has some more dimensions to it than just survival and start asking deeper questions. This is when they start experiencing the *salinity* of life through myriad and paradoxical experiences. Rarer still are those who having deeper priorities in life, choose to plunge into the ocean, and are prepared to face any hardships or even to give up their very lives.

Among such innumerable persons who dare to dedicate their lives for seeking the meaning of existence and in turn, understand themselves, a very few succeed in their effort. The *Bhagavadgītā* puts it beautifully:

> 'Among thousands of men, rarely does one strive for perfection; even among those successful strivers, only rarely does one understands and experiences Me in essence'.[101]

Out of such persons who succeed in experiencing the Reality, only very few are able to retain their compassion for the suffering people, and try to lend a helping hand. Because the experience as such is so overwhelming, that the person is totally lost in it. Shri Ramakrishna used to tell a parable to explain this phenomenon.

> 'Once four friends, in the course of a walk, saw a place enclosed by a wall. The wall was very high. They all became eager to know what was inside. One of them climbed to the top of the wall. What he saw on looking

---

101 मनुष्याणां सहस्रेषु कश्चिद्यतति सिद्धये ।
यततामपि सिद्धानां कश्चिन्मां वेत्ति तत्त्वत: ।। 7.3 ।।

> inside made him speechless with wonder. He only cried, "Ah! Ah!", and dropped in. He could not give any information about what he saw. The others, too, climbed the wall, uttered the same cry, "Ah! Ah!", and jumped in. Now who could tell what was inside'?[102]

The concept of *Bodhisattva* in the Buddha's teaching is noteworthy: the compassion to save others. That is why, Shri Ramakrishna used to say :

> 'According to some people, Śukadeva only saw and touched the Ocean of Brahman; he did not dive into It. That is why he could return to the world and impart religious instruction. According to others, he returned to the world of name and form, after attaining the Knowledge of Brahman, for the purpose of teaching others. He had to recite the *Bhāgavatam* to King Parīkṣit and had to teach people in various ways; therefore God did not destroy his "I" altogether. God kept in him the "ego of Knowledge".'[103]

Only such persons who have been able to retain the 'I', be it out of compassion for the suffering humanity or out of wisdom, can become bridges between the Infinite and the finite. Only such persons come to be known as the *'Gurus'*, having their *Being* in the Reality, yet their feet very much on the ground. The language becomes their servant, not otherwise, as in the case of the most of us. Whatever they say is in tune with the *Vedas* or any sacred scriptures. Or rather whatever they utter becomes *Vedic* or Sacred! Because, all the sacred scriptures have come to us through the utterances of such persons in the sacred states of Realisation.

The teachings of such persons have always been very simple, though they have been presented in the complicated terms by the intellectual followers and *Puṇḍits*. The Buddha

---

102 *The Gospel of Sri Ramakrishna* by M, IXth impression 1988, p. 268.

103 Ibid., p. 268.

taught, through what has come to be known as the *Jātaka,* the stories of his previous lives; so did the Christ, who taught in simple parables and stories; so did every enlightened person including Shri Ramakrishna in modern times, who illustrated their teaching through day-to-day examples. This is because, by its very nature the Truth is simple, obvious and plain. And we *escape* from the grip of the Truth through our *complicated mind,* with its projections like the desires and justifications!

Being receptive to the compassion of the great persons like The Buddha, the Christ and others like them, is being simple. Simplicity and innocence can, not only help us in understanding what they are hinting at, but may even trigger off the very experiences of these great men. This episode which has been aptly named as *Upaśama Prakaraṇa* has very useful hints for all the seekers who have the *Abhīpsā* or the burning aspiration to quieten the mental activity. *Upaśama* means quiescence.

A phenomenon which initiates the quest in human beings is the mystery of death. It is true, that most of us *avoid* it consciously or unconsciously, because we take the death to be the *culmination* of life. Surprisingly, death is very much an integral part of life itself, as it is not really a culmination of life, but a *change.* And only when we see something change do we recognise life in it! For example, movement is inevitable for something that is alive. What happens in movement is the change of position in space; time is nothing but the movement between two events; and so on. In this sense, death happens to us every moment, as there is a constant change at all levels of existence. This way, a death called change is happening every moment, and the death as it is commonly understood is only the *crescendo* of the symphony called life!

Something that has gone up has to come down, like a wave merging in the sea or like a sound vibration merging into silence. The Buddha made a wonderful observation about life. He said that everything is subject to change, and that one cannot step into the same river twice. Even the modern High Energy Physicists claim that the whole of matter is nothing but the play of energy which is in a state of perpetual flux. And what we normally experience as the *solidity* is only apparent!

The contemporary discoveries seem to be only the echoes of the age old understanding of our sages. Lord Buddha had said:

> 'The entire *Lokas* are in flames,
> The entire *Lokas* are going up in smoke;
> The entire *Lokas* are burning,
> The entire *Lokas* are *vibrating.*
>
> But that which does not vibrate or burn,
> Which is experienced by the noble ones?
> Where death has no entry—
> In that my mind delights'.[104]

Through this seemingly short statement, the Lord has not only uttered a very great truth but has also given a wonderful hint to all seekers for achieving the quiescence. *Lokas* means a plane of consciousness. It is the very nature of all vibrations, that as they come up, so do they go down. The modern science tells us that all phenomena—which are experienced by the senses, are vibratory in nature; that there is a kind of restless flux and *everything,* including the *observer* is changing! This discovery is very much in tune with our *Upaniṣadic* declarations which indicate that the mind, the intellect and the *Ahaṁkāra* are *vibratory* in nature and are constantly changing.

Unless there is something changeless or that which transcends all change, the change cannot be even detected! So if one tries to identify oneself with the changeless, the

---

104 *The Discourse Summaries* by S. N. Goenka, Vipassana Vishodhan Vinyas, 1990.

change ceases to have any effect. When this happens, one succeeds in attaining the *Sākṣī-Bhāva* or the witness attitude, which has been called by some, as one being a *watcher on the hill.* Lord Buddha gave this theoretical background only to clarify the practical method to be adopted by the seeker. He called the technique as *Vipaśyanā,* which may be roughly translated as the special way of seeing, consists of non-involved witnessing, as one sees a traffic on the road, or the flow of water in a river.

Yoga Vāsiṣṭha gives innumerable hints to achieve the quiescence from all mental activity. In the *Utpatti Prakaraṇa,* it gives the origin of the *Ahaṁkāra*—'I-ness' and in *Sthiti Prakaraṇa,* its sustenance. The stories therein, illustrate very clearly that the root of this world is, the *Ahaṁkāra,* and that they have the same root in the Ultimate Reality, which transcends all movement and change. But the *Ahaṁkāra,* and subsequently the world of objects are only *Its* manifestations, and are like waves on the ocean. Having their origin, they get nurtured to grow and due to this very fact, they necessarily decay and finally die. The episode under discussion has ten *Sargas,* which directly or indirectly give practical hints for quietening the mental activity.

It is said of a Sufi Master Salih, that he used to keep repeating to his disciples that whoever keeps knocking continually, the door shall be opened to him. One day Rabiya, another extraordinary woman Sufi Master was passing by. She observed that the Master cannot keep telling his disciples that *the door shall be opened,* because the door *was never closed!* The story does not say anything about the reply of Master Salih. Evidently he did not say anything. Superficially, the story appears to be suggesting that Master Salih was wrong, and Master Rabiya corrected him. But we should remember that Master Salih was an enlightened Master and had awakened many disciples, and had led them towards enlightenment. Actually, this story clarifies a great paradox in spirituality.

There have been two main streams of approach in spirituality. One has always stressed that the seeker has to put a lot of effort to achieve the goal of enlightenment; that the effort must be without any break; and that the effort is never wasted and even if one dies without achieving what one strived for, she or he will be taking up the search in the next birth(s), to ultimately triumph. This has been the approach of most of the schools of *Yoga* and *Vedānta.* The seeker has to make all kinds of preparations *for experiencing the Truth.* The second just asks the seeker *to drop the Ego!* Obviously, the second stream is meant for only the select few who have come to a very ripe state wherein, the ego is about to fall off on its own.

After the experience, the seeker invariably feels that *It* had been always there, within the reach but only in his ignorance he felt otherwise. A person who has 'That' experience feels, that *why and how can anyone possibly miss It!* Such persons normally do not and perhaps, cannot be of much help to the struggling seekers, because they have transcended the turmoil of all mental activity and may not be able to come down to the so-called ordinary plane of consciousness. While some of the Enlightened Persons, in their compassion for the struggling humanity, can and do come down to the level of the seekers, to become a bridge between the mind and the Reality which transcends all mind. In this sense, in the story under discussion, Rabiya represents the state of an enlightened person who wonders how the obvious Truth is not *known* by others; and Salih, that of a compassionate master who has come down to the level of his disciples, to lead them by hand, and to spread the *infection of Enlightenment!*

In the strictest sense, there is nothing like a Royal road to Enlightenment. There cannot possibly be, as each seeker is really unique and singular. Even then, there are very broad guidelines to achieve the quiescence from all activity. This *Sarga,* starts with a useful hint from Sage Vasiṣṭha. He said that the infatuation towards *Saṁsāra* is prolonged by the two *Guṇas: Rajas and Tamas,* just as a building is supported by the firm pillars. And the courageous endowed by the *Sattwa Guṇa* drop the attraction like a snake moulting its skin, as a realisation dawns on them that everything verily is only a manifestation of the Reality, the illusion of separateness gets dissolved.

One of the most wonderful contributions of Indian *Darśanas*[105] and culture to spirituality is the concept of the three *Guṇas.* The term *Guṇa* can be taken as rope, characteristic, quality, or mental state, by which one gets tied down to the inert and the insentient. Or the three *Guṇas* can be also taken as three different influences under which every human mind plays such an endless variety of roles at different moments in its changing environments. The concept has been clarified by many of our scriptures. The *Bhagavadgītā* even devotes a complete chapter for it.

In the present context, *Sattwa* can be taken in as *non-activity*—a complete mastery over activity, light of wisdom and balance; *Rajas* as *activity*—helpless activity, involvement, and restlessness; and *Tamas* as *inactivity,* inertia, ignorance and covering. These *Guṇas* are born with the manifestation and are part of Nature. They generate a feeling of attachment, and successfully create the delusion. In other words, these *Guṇas* are part of the *dream* called the *Saṁsāra,* which gets manifested with the initial *Saṁkalpa,* the tendency to think.

To wake up from this dream, one has to first realise that one is under the influence of a dream. This is where the experience of pain, misery, and death as well as the knowledge of impermanence of *everything* comes to our rescue. After being repeatedly afflicted by the turmoil of the opposites which constitute life, one starts thinking seriously about the

---

105 *Darśana* means vision, evidently practical, as opposed to Philosophy, mostly speculative in nature.

meaning and goal of all life. As the dispassion dawns and a disinterest in the mundane existence gets nourished, one is ready to make efforts to wake up from the dream. This is done by retracing the steps of manifestation by making use of *Sattwa,* the least powerful of the three *Guṇas.* That is why, throughout this scripture the sage keeps repeating that one should overcome the *Aśubha-Vāsanās* characterised by *Rājasik* and *Tāmasic* tendencies, with the help of *Śubha-Vāsanās,* which are mainly *Sāttwik* tendencies.

The sage then proceeded to suggest Rāma to adopt the attitude that this whole universe is only a manifestation of the Ultimate Reality and is not separate from It. This view helps in elimination of the separateness resulting from 'I' and 'mine'. With the elimination of separateness, there will be neither misery nor infatuation, neither birth nor the one who is born, and one will be able to see everything *as it is.* One will transcend the pair of opposites, ever *Sāttwik,* unconcerned about retaining one's possessions, and also about avoiding the problems. One will be equanimous, happy in and with oneself, stable minded, peaceful, silent within and without, pure like a crystal. Whatever comes to one's lot is accepted totally without any expectation from anyone or any action. These qualities will help the seeker to be the *Vijwaraḥ–Vigatatāpatrayaḥ,* one who has transcended the difficulties on three different planes of body, mind and *Ahaṁkāra.*

A person, who has the above qualities, is in his last birth, and the *Ātmajñāna* dawns easily to him. Such persons are called the *Ārya-s* who are compassionate and full of love, who accept everything *as it is* and are filled with wisdom. Such persons attract all people like the melody of a flute attracting the attention of even the cows. Broadly, there are two types of paths leading towards *Mokṣa.* In the first type, one follows the instructions given by the *Guru,* to whom one surrenders everything, and one is enveloped by the Truth and *Jñāna* in the very birth, failing which, the seeker continues in the future births what had been learnt in the previous birth, and ultimately receives the Benediction.

In the other path, a person being endowed with a stainless mind becomes recipient of spontaneous *Jñāna,* like a fruit falling unexpectedly from above. Shri Ramakrishna used to tell a beautiful parable to illustrate the spontaneous enlightenment:

A *Tāntrik* practised in a deep forest. He was almost at the end of his *Sādhanā,* all that required was that he should sit and meditate by sitting on a consecrated corpse. A traveller on his way home, came to the spot and was curious to see the *Tantric* busy in his spiritual practice. The *Tāntrik* had finished preparing his meditation seat by worshipping the corpse, when the wayfarer heard a tiger's roar. Immediately, he climbed a tree to protect himself. But the *Tāntrik,* unaware and busy in his practice, was attacked by the tiger and was dragged away.

Seeing that there was no danger, the pilgrim got down, and just out of curiosity, sat on the consecrated corpse. Immediately, Mother Kālī appeared and offered him a boon! The man was surprised and asked the Goddess, that while the person who had really worked for the Mother's vision had become the tiger's meal, he who had been totally ignorant of the spiritual ways, had the privilege of Her vision. The Goddess smilingly replied that it was destined that the *Tāntrik* should become the tiger's meal, while the traveller had to only sit on the corpse, as he had the necessary purity of mind!

This story just goes to suggest that there is no beaten track, no hard and fast rule in spirituality. In fact, we have to always remember that each one of us is unique, and has a unique and singular approach to the enlightenment. Consequently, each one of us has to discover the method, for herself or himself. After the discovery, one starts treading the path and if she or he is unable to achieve the transcendence in that very life, one may get it in the next birth, though it may appear to be unexpected. The revered sage Vasiṣṭha then proceeded to narrate the story of one such person, who became such a recipient of *Ātmajñāna.*

King Janaka ruled over a region called Videha, known for his wealth, liberality, fearlessness and the sense of justice. One day in spring, he was strolling in the royal garden and was feeling attuned to the nature around. Then he heard some ethereal voices of the *Siddhas* who had withdrawn themselves from the visible world. Through their songs they were giving some wonderful hints for *Vicāra,* the meditative contemplation. One was singing that, the *Ātma-Jñāna* arises as one succeeds in merging the knower and the known. Another sang, that one should meditate on the Reality, after eradicating the *Vāsanās* for the sense objects, to experience the 'eagle vision'. The third *Siddha* intoned, that after becoming all-expansive by identifying with the neutral centre between *Sat,* the existence and *Asat,* the non-existence one should be with the *Ātman,* the light which lights up all lights. Still another declared that, one should contemplate on the effulgent *Ātman* which is the 'I' in all *Jīvas* or beings.

Another *Siddha* joining in, said, that searching for the God without and neglecting the God within, is like abandoning the precious *Kaustubha*[106] and going after the ordinary shells on the beach. And that unless one completely overcomes the lesser desires, *Ātman* can never be attained. And those who continue their involvement and indulgence with the gross, in spite of their knowledge should be called as the donkeys which can only carry the burden without ever knowing what they are carrying. Through the rod of discrimination the sense-serpents are to be disciplined at the level of the mind itself. *Mokṣa* is attained when the mind has been totally quietened.

---

106 The gem adorning the neck of Lord Viṣṇu.

Having heard the songs of *Siddhas*, Janaka was panic-stricken like the serpent being stunned by the sight of an angry eagle. Leaving the cool and fragrant royal garden he went into his mansion to contemplate on the truths he had heard from the *Siddhas*. His own life, and of others, came in front of his eyes. All the actions emanate from the helpless restlessness. As his mind became introvertish, it became obvious to him that compared to the eternity of time, the human life was but a moment, and the human size was but a speck in infinite space. And with the realisation, came a surprise as to how could he possibly squander away the invaluable life on things which are gross, impermanent, and energy dissipating.

Antarmukhatā, the inward flow of the mind, brought in the realisation that the main culprit and the root cause of all disturbance, misery and the cycle of birth and death, is mind. With this very vision, king Janaka dropped it, and transcended the activity and the turmoil called mind. After a long time, when he came down to the so-called normal plane of consciousness, the understanding continued and he decided to continue his responsibilities, as the head of the country, and to devote his life towards spontaneous actions without any trace of the *Kartṛtva*—the doer-ship, and came to be known to the posterity as the enlightened King, and an adept of *Karma-Yoga* so much so, that even Lord Kṛṣṇa takes his example in the *Bhagavadgītā.*[107]

Concluding the story, sage Vasiṣṭha told Rāma, that Janaka attained *Ātmajñāna* through the grace of the *Siddhas* whom he considered as his Gurus; that the precious most jewel of *Ātmajñāna* is very much in every heart though it is covered by the *Vāsanās* like desire and hatred; and if one attains to the *Jñāna,* nothing will afflict such a person, just as

107 मनुष्याणां सहस्रेषु कश्चिद्यतति सिद्धये ।
यततामपि सिद्धानां कश्चिन्मां वेत्ति तत्त्वतः ।। 7.3 ।।

the person wearing a diamond armour is not at all affected by the poisonous arrows. And the person aspiring for the Brāhmic state should be free of all desires.

Many stories have been attributed to King Janaka and this is only one of them. Janaka's name has been mentioned not only in *Rāmāyaṇa,* but in other *Vedāntic* scriptures like the *Bṛhadāraṇyaka Upaniṣad* and *Aṣṭāvakra Gītā.* Efforts have been made by the scholars to find out whether it is the same Janaka or different persons having the same name. However, more pragmatic persons have totally avoided the involvement in the eternal debate of historical dates of our saints and sages, and have derived benefit out of the teachings and hints found in the various scriptures.

In this scripture the name appears to be symbolic rather than Historical. Janaka means the progenitor or father. He is said to be ruling over the kingdom of *Videha*—that which transcends the body. The present context seems to suggest that, it is the *Ahaṁkāra,* which has transcended the body consciousness. At this level, one is bound to experience the poise and there is no disturbance from the desires and their companions. And this very poise helps one to be more receptive to the Truth that always surrounds us. It has been accepted in field of spirituality that whoever makes any effort whatsoever towards understanding oneself, the help appears. In fact, it is not that it appears, but the help is already there, only that one becomes open and receptive to it.

The greatest impediment for receptivity is the wall of activity, called the mind. Normally what happens is, that we see or hear only that which is conditioned by our mind. The conditioning is of the likes and the dislikes, and the impressions based on the limited self as well as the selfishness. If one succeeds in crossing over the barricade, as in the case of King Janaka in this story, one gets the vital hints for the methodology of *Vicāra,* unasked. The fact that one is in a state of receptivity shows that the activity of the mind has reduced to a very great extent. And for one who is in the state where the activity of mind has been quietened, it is not very difficult to trace the origin of *Ahaṁkāra.*

When one succeeds to achieve this Janaka state—where the *Ahaṁbhāva* the feeling of 'I', is free of any other manifestation, one is able to separate oneself from the *Draṣṭā, Dṛśya* and *Darśana,* and in that very vision, the involvement gets dropped on its own. Similarly, all such hints only trigger off the quiescence. In fact, anything and everything helps one to achieve the quiescence. After enlightenment, one spends the remaining time in one's body blissfully, depending upon one's nature and aptitude, either performing spontaneous actions as Janaka and others like him did or by just remaining silent, spreading the fragrance of enlightenment.

The ocean seems invincible and destructive with its tall waves reaching out to the sky. But deep within it, everything is calm and silent, so much so, nothing happens to it when even the rivers in spate come rushing and merge in it! The waves, no matter how high and destructive, do come down to become the limitless and calm ocean. Similarly, all activity is only superficial and temporary. This is more so, as far as our inner life is concerned. Identifying ourselves with the material world, senses, desires and depressions, we are invariably tossed and turned in the world. A glimpse of the silent depth convinces that the activity has relevance to it only with reference to this depth. And such a glimpse is possible only when one completely transcends the superficial activity at the periphery; when one is able to move towards the centre of *Ahaṃ-Vṛtti*—the vibration called 'I', which is the *Janaka,* ruling over *Videha*—the region transcending the gross manifestations like the body, senses, and mind!

2

The Story of Puṇya and Pāvana

The Chinars have turned flaming red, while the apples, cherries, pears, walnuts and chestnuts have started dropping their leaves. It is fall in Kashmir. The precursor for winter has its own charm and beauty. If one looks at the gradual change of colour from myriad greens to the innumerable shades in red and orange, the early morning frost on the grass, the multi-pitched cries of the birds in the process of migration, or for that matter a *physical* silence which envelops the valley during the nights, one is bound to admire the wonderful changes in nature. The regularity with which the seasons change and the change itself is not as evident in other parts of our country, as in Kashmir.

However, if one looks at the baldness of the trees, and a peculiar dryness in the air, then one is likely to get discouraged. Fall is the *season of dusk* ushering in the end of the year, and an end does bring in the depression. It has been observed by many that invariably the patients in asylums, the prisoners in their cells experience bouts of depression during dusk and twilight. May be it evokes a thought of impermanence and inevitability of death in their mind. And why do we experience uneasiness, if not fear at the thought of death? May be most of us see that the death punctuates the activity of the person who dies; we do not see the person transacting with the world anymore; that in spite of the wish to remain in the world, she or he is forced to leave his *hold on the possessions.* We see many persons leaving their dreams or desires unfulfilled, when overtaken by the death.

Desires unfortunately, are never-ending. It is like a person in search of the horizon, the nearer he goes to it, the farther it recedes from him! It is said, that Alexander the Great, met an astrologer while in India, who told the conqueror that he *may* conquer this whole world, but then, *there was only one world to conquer!* This thought had depressed the great Macedonian emperor, making him re-think about his conquests. On his death bed, he had instructed the attendants that his empty hands should be seen by everyone during the funeral, so the world could know that even he had to die empty-handed! What we really are afraid is not the death, but the prospect of leaving the things we have come to call our own *through identification!* Because, we have not yet had the experience of death, or rather, we *do not* remember the experience.

Socrates, one of the greatest of thinkers humankind has ever produced, was being given the hemlock. His disciples were crying at the prospect of losing the company of their Master. It is said, that Socrates asked his disciples to cry *after* his death and not when he was still alive! As he felt that a great thing—his death—was happening. They asked him how was it that he was not afraid of death. He said :

> 'Why should I be afraid? I have lived my life, I loved it, and it was beautiful. I have known it, but there is no need to go on repeating it forever! Now something new—death is at hand. I am enchanted at the prospect of taking on this great adventure. Now I would like to see what death is'.
>
> One of the disciples, Crito said :
>
> 'But Master, everyone is afraid of death'.
>
> Socrates said :
>
> 'I do not know. I do not understand why people are

afraid of death. If atheists are right that one dies totally and nothing is left, then there is nothing to be feared—Socrates will not be there, so why be afraid? I was not there before I was born and I do not feel any fear about it. I will be disappearing if the atheists are right. So, what is there to fear'?

'Or may be the theists are right. They claim that even after the physical death, one continues to be there. If I am going to be there then why should I be afraid? The fact is I am thrilled at the prospect of finding out the truth of death myself, which is going to be a new field of knowledge'!

This episode from a great life illustrates that the reason for fear at the prospect of death is our identification. And this identification is a characteristic feature of *Ahaṁkāra,* evoking the fear of death. The *Sarga* under discussion tries to impress upon the seeker that death happens only to the *Ahaṁkāra.* Such a death is voluntary—the puny 'I' melting into the infinite Existence. When this happens, paradoxically, one is born into the life eternal. This has been very crisply expressed by the following *Śloka:*

'When the constrictive conception of "he". "I", etc., is gradually destroyed, the expansive *Jñāna,* which is all this universe will arise'.[108]

The constrictive function of 'I' has been very beautifully put in a very short treatise on Vedānta entitled *Pratyabhijñā Hṛdayaṃ* by Kṣemarāja :

'The *Ātman* or the individual Monad is merely a contracted centralised form of universal consciousness, which is obscured by *the mental world of the individual* which fills it.'

---

108 अयमेवाहमित्सस्मिन्संकोचे विलयं गते ।
समस्त भुवनव्यापि विस्तार उपजायते ॥ 5.2.4 ॥

'It is nothing but the ultimate reality which, descending from the stage of pure consciousness, becomes the individual mind, by becoming *contracted to* and assimilated with the images of objects present in the field of consciousness'.[109]

The identification with the world of objects always begins innocently enough, with the variety of *Rāga* or attraction and *Dweṣa* or aversion, but it gets crystallised with the sense of differentiation through 'I', 'mine', 'he', etc., which becomes the cause for bondage. That is why, the sage urged Rāma to transcend attachment and aversion or hatred towards objects in the field of consciousness. He said that such transcendence becomes easy for such persons who are endowed with qualities like the freedom from *any* longing, even for *Mukti* or aversion for *Bandhaḥ,* or bondage, who are devoid of delusion, confusion, deception and violence. That is why, sage Vasiṣṭha continued, one should try to understand the mechanism of attachment through which, the attachment itself *drops*.

Rāma observed that it is easier to drop the body than the *Ahaṁkāra*. He felt that with the annihilation of *Ahaṁkāra,* the body will perish like a tree felled at its root. Sage Vasiṣṭha then answered with all patience, that it is not only possible to annihilate the conception of 'I', but mandatory for enlightenment. There are two paths to destroy the *Ahaṁkāra*.

Normally, we think with certainty that we live for objects and the objects are meant for our utility, and in the absence of objects, 'I' cannot exist and vice versa. In the first path, through *Vicāra* one should differentiate oneself from the objects. But the *Vicāra* is possible only for one whose mental activity has slowed down. For slowing down the activity it is necessary to reduce the sense indulgence and also mental involvement. That is why one should start with abandoning

---

109 चितिसंकोचात्मा चेतनोऽपि संकुचितविश्वमयः ॥ 4 ॥
चितिरेव चेतनपदादवरूढा चेत्यसंकोचिनी चित्तम् ॥ 5 ॥

the craving for the fruits of actions and performance of all action *as if* in sport. This is called *Dhyeya-tyāga* or the renunciation of the object which can be imagined. Having destroyed all *Vāsanās* and developed equipoise if one is able to abandon the burden of body, it leads one to what has been called as *Jñeya-tyāga* or renunciation of the known, the second path.

Both these paths lead the pilgrim towards *Jīvanamukti*. The sage then went on to describe the qualities of *Jīvanamuktas*. Those whose minds are not afflicted in this life by exultation, fear, anger, poverty, sin or pain which arise in them through the past actions in this or previous lives are the *Jīvanamuktas*. Those who are ever in a state of transcendence with their mind quiescent, even while performing actions, and whose company is sought by the wise are the *Jīvanamuktas*.

Continuing, sage Vasiṣṭha hinted that even as the attraction for the external objects ceases, the internal thirst or *craving* remains, which is called *Tṛṣṇā*. *Tṛṣṇā* is the mental attraction and longing for *anything*. And when even this internal craving ceases completely, one reaches the state of *Mukta-tṛṣṇā*. The *Bhagavadgītā* puts it in a *Śloka:*

> 'Though the sense objects recede for him who negates them externally, the *taste* for them lingers on; but for the one who has experienced the Self even this disappears'.[110]

A *Kagga* (quatrain) by Shri D. V. Gundappa says :

> 'Best of feasts is the essence of the Supreme Brahman,
> Nothing to beg when you have tasted it.
> Vanishes then the distinction of the renouncer,
> renunciation and the renounced

---

110 विषया विनिवर्तन्ते निराहारस्य देहिनः ।
रसवर्जं रसोऽप्यस्य परं दृष्ट्वा निवर्तते ॥ 2.51 ॥

And you become the monarch of the universe—
MANKUTHIMMA'. 752[111]

The sage blessed Rāma to become a *Mukta-tṛṣṇā* and immovable like an ocean without waves or foam. Then he told about the four stages of certitude or convictions. The first kind is in which the 'I' identifies itself with this body, and thinks that it is *the be all and the end all* of existence.

As this idea is too limited it leads one to painful bondage. The second type of certitude arises when the 'I' learns to disengage from the gross objects, including the thoughts, and considers itself *separate* from them. This certitude leads one to *Mokṣa* and arises in the wise.

The direct cognition within that even the universes are but the modes of 'I' and that the 'I' is indestructible is the third type of certitude. This is the state of *Mokṣa* and is full. The fourth type of certitude arises when the known and the knower are cognised as unreal and that the 'I' is One without the second which pervades everywhere. This fourth is the incomparable and the supreme *Mokṣa.* Of these four the first is associated with bondage and is responsible for creating *Tṛṣṇā.* While the other three are to be found only in the *Jīvanamuktas.*

The first kind of conviction, involving the identification of the 'I' with the body is perhaps common to most, if not to all of us. And that is the root-cause of all our misery. It does not however mean that one has to *negate the body,* for the body is also a manifestation of the same Ultimate Reality. It only means that by *limiting* our vision to only the gross and impermanent manifestation, the misery is imminent. For one seeks permanence in the temporal. The sage is suggesting the seeker to broaden one's outlook. With such broadened outlook, one sees the world outside non-seriously. Carlos Castaneda observes such an attitude in his teacher don Juan.

111 *Thus Sang Mankuthimma* by A Narasimha Bhat, p. 95.

Once when Don Juan explains Carlos that not all questions can be answered verbally, Carlos is very adamant to repeat his questions. He observes that Don Juan leaves the place totally avoiding any reply, and he suspects that his questions have annoyed Don Juan. An interesting conversation follows which has been quoted in an earlier chapter.[112]

The *Bhaktas* adopt this non-seriousness towards the world by taking it to be a *Līlā* or sport of the Lord. If one becomes serious by giving more importance than absolutely necessary, one is bound to become miserable. The *Yogis* treading the path of psychic control try to make use of their will power for controlling the senses and mind. While the persons adopting the path of *Karma Yoga* give up their attachment to the fruits of their action. The method recommended by *Vāsiṣṭha* is the path of *Jñāna,* in which one develops these certitudes or *the mental postures.* The progressive certitudes help the seeker in *climbing the hill,* which help her or him to loosen the grip of attachment over the world of objects.

Sage Vasiṣṭha urged Rāma to be in the world and yet not *allow the world to be in him!* It is like the boat which can float only when the water is not in it. He indirectly hinted this, by saying that it can be done by slowly turning the attention from the world outside to world within. He said that one must become the Master of action and not its slave. When one turns the attention within, one discovers that the senses and the mind needlessly grip the world of objects. When one has realised this, one learns the attitude of an actor on the stage. Shri Ramakrishna used to say that one should live like a maid servant in her master's house. Though she calls the master's son as 'my Hari', she knows very well he is *not hers.* Her children are in her own hut. Or like a mother tortoise, which in spite of swimming in the ocean, has her mind on the eggs on the shore. There is another *Kagga* by D. V. Gundappa :

---

112 *The Story of Siddha.*

'Build two separate rooms in mind's abode,
Play as a common human being in the outer room,
And rest alone in peace in the silent inner room,
This is the supreme yogic principle—MANKUTHIMMA 701'.[113]

This attitude of non-involvement alone helps in mellowing the *Ahaṁkāra,* and can be developed by gradually eliminating the differentiating thoughts like 'I' or 'you', birth or death, pleasure or pain, etc. The more one dwells on such thoughts the more does one entangle with the world, not unlike the silk worm, which weaves a means for its own death through the cocoon. Though the process is meant for its metamorphosis, the cocoon is put in boiled water for drawing the silk thread out of it. To illustrate this point the sage narrated an ancient story.

On the banks of the Gaṅgā, there lived the two sons of a *Ṛṣi* named Dīrghatapas which means long continual penance. Their names were Puṇya or Virtue and Pāvana or Purity and lived near Mahendra Mountains. They were performing *Tapas* along with their father and virtuous Puṇya attained *Jñāna* in course of time through the performance of actions without being attached to the fruits thereof. But his brother Pāvana had a fluctuating mind as his *Jñāna* was only partial. The father after eliminating all desires and becoming indifferent to mundane existence gave up his body that had formed a nest for the birds of *Ahaṁkāric* action. On account of absence of desire the *Ṛṣi* attained Brāhmic bliss.

As soon as the body of the *Sāttwic Muni* expired, his consort breathed her last like a bee deserting a lotus flower. The elder son Puṇya, finding his parents dead made preparations for their last rites. But the younger brother Pāvana began to drown himself in the ocean of sorrow. He roamed in the forest in agitation, and could not shake away

---

113 *Thus Sang Makuthimma* by A. Narasimha Bhat, p. 88.

his grief even in the presence of his calm brother. And Puṇya performed the funeral rites without any disturbance as he was convinced that death is inevitable to life. After the rites Puṇya talked to his brother Pāvana who was full of sorrow.

He lovingly reminded Pāvana that it does not behove a *Tapasvin* to get entangled in sorrow; that both the parents had attained to a supremely quiescent state; that Pāvana has had innumerable parents who have died and he at that moment was aware of only the parents of his present life and not the myriad of lives he had lived in different countries. The impressions like good or bad, friend or foe are created by the subjective pleasantness or the unpleasantness as experienced by the *Ahaṁkāra*. Thus Puṇya helped Pāvana to revive his own capacity to come out of the situation he had put himself in. The sage said that the two brothers lived in Brāhmic Bliss and ultimately attained the *Videha-Mukti* or total liberation even from the body.

Concluding the story the sage said, that Rāma must eliminate the root cause of all differentiation by achieving the quiescence of mind. And compared to this state of quiescence, everything else is as insignificant as a blade of grass, the *Kṣīrasāgara*—the ocean of milk, is not so infinite, the full moon so bright. Nay, even Lakṣmī the goddess of wealth residing in the fragrant lotus bestow such a boon. And the ghost of desire spoils the lustre of the pure mind like a cloud enveloping the moon. *Mokṣa* is nothing but the destruction of the impurities of the mind in the form of desires.

This story tries to forewarn the seeker of one of the impediments in her or his journey. With much effort one finally succeeds in overcoming the temptation of intellectual discussion, and plunges into the quest. That is what is meant by *Dīrghatapas* having two sons called *Puṇya* and *Pāvana*. *Puṇya* represents virtue or the goodness which has *manifested as action*. That is, the goodness is no more a concept in mind or a verbal expression —as is the case with most of us who involve in the critical discussions on the problems in the society—but has come to the level of practice. While *Pāvana* means purity which is purely a subjective concept! Both of them exist within. In fact, the seeker tries to take guidance from the concept to plunge into sincere practice. If only the concept predominates, as it happens in the case of mere scholarship, then one succeeds only in nurturing and expanding the ego.

The main reason for this is that a concept is always at the level of thought which is but a grosser manifestation. And however lofty be the thought, it is impermanent and changes all the time. Precisely for this reason, it hardly has the desired effect on our life. Even when one starts the practice, one is not out of the danger of a fall, for one is exposed to the danger of the *'holier than thou'* attitude which is nothing but the *Ahaṁkāra* that has entered through the back door! The seeker tries to give up such actions which enhance the sensual and other involvement, but in turn gets *involved* with the *Ahaṁkāra!*

In the story, we take the two brothers as the two postures of the seeker who is involved in performing continual penance *(Dīrghatapas)*. *Puṇya* represents the practical side, while *Pāvana* the theoretical side. That was why, persons like Swami Vivekananda said, that 'an ounce of practice is much better that tonnes of theory'. Scriptural study forms an integral part of spiritual practice which has been called as *Swādhyāya.* But actually, the scriptural study is necessary only for understanding the *modus operandi* of *Sādhanā.* When one begins the practice, one is expected to slowly give up the dependence on the books and to transform it to the *study of the Self* which is the real meaning of *Swādhyāya.* There is another aspect to this story. One of the most stubborn obsessions of the mind is the attachment to the past or the concern for the future. The seeker gets disturbed if not shaken when these pester him. The story implies that through practice one has to overcome this obstinate mental problem.

The *shadow* called 'I' is responsible for all the problems that man creates for himself and to suffer needlessly. The panacea for this avoidable misery is to turn one's face away from this shadow and to face the sun of *Ātman*. The fall, the death or in other words, any pain is supposed to give us a glimpse into something beyond death, change or pain. It is like a person walking with his back to the sun, who should realise that the shadow in front of him is there *only because of the sun behind him*. But usually, it so happens that he sees only the dark shadow and exaggerates it!

Khalil Gibran puts it beautifully:

> 'How unjust to themselves are those who turn their backs to the sun, and see naught except shadows of their physical selves upon the earth'.[114]

The fall is only an indicator of the inevitable change. The dusk is only an intimation of the dawn. And the death is only an invitation to something beyond change, which is deathless. If one takes pain to be, only as a messenger who informs us that there is something wrong with our health,—like the stomach ache or fever, one starts taking steps towards freedom from pain like approaching a doctor or changing the life style.

The fall in Kashmir is mandatory for the plants who prepare themselves for the snow-fall, an opportunity for them to *draw in* their sap, a kind of introversion, the look within. Similarly, pain and death are mandatory for us to re-examine our understanding of life.

---

114 *Secret of the Heart* by Khalil Gibran, p. 150.

3

The Story of Bali the Great

The clouds rumbled, the wind lashed at the trees which were followed by a heavy downpour. The lightning struck, lighting up the heaven and earth. It was as if Indra the god of rain was eager to make up for the lost time! The river had turned earthen in colour, carrying the mud from the mountains. She had gathered so much momentum as to uproot smaller trees who had unsuccessfully tried to resist her flow. As and when the rain's intensity increased her force increased and she wore a terrible look to frighten the people dwelling on her banks. This had happened with almost all the rivers on earth. And the suffering taught man to harness the power in water to his advantage. It is true that even today we have the phenomenon of floods in some of the rivers, but it has taught man that it is possible to harness *any* power, macro as well as micro.

Ironically, as and when he is seemingly getting control over the *external* forces, like water, wind and nuclei of atoms, it appears he is losing control over his own *inner forces* like thought, emotions and desires! In spite of the claims he is making over the newer modes of education, it appears that all he has been able to do is to confuse himself with the load of increasing bulk of information, instead of gaining more clarity. The science and technology, his proud creations have become like the Frankenstein monster who tried to kill its own creator, as they have made man, at the most into a civilized barbarian! For all he seems to be interested in is the sophistication of war-fare, which he had managed with stones and other crude weapons in his cave man days! J. Krishnamurti said:

> 'The scientific mind is precise and clear in its investigation. But it is not a compassionate mind, for it has not understood itself. The religious mind is capable of thinking precisely, not in terms of the negative and positive; therefore that mind can hold within it the scientific mind. But the scientific mind does not contain the religious mind because it is based on time, on knowledge; it is rooted in success and achievement. The religious mind is the real revolutionary mind. It is not a reaction to what has been. The religious mind is the only mind that can respond totally to the present challenge and to all challenges at all times'.[115]

One has to be careful not to confuse the *religious mind* mentioned by Krishnamurti to be that mind which is rooted in beliefs and rituals. He has very crisply clarified it as *the mind that goes into itself.* That is, the mind which is capable of observing its own activities; there is so much objectivity that one is able to *observe even the observer.* This has been called the *Antarmukhatā* by *Vedānta.* Krishnamurti predicted that only these two, scientific and religious, minds could survive in future. But unless the scientific mind becomes an all inclusive mind it can and does create only Frankenstein-s to bring about an imminent destruction and catastrophe to this earth. And the religious mind is an all inclusive mind. He was hinting that for the good of mankind it is very necessary, if not mandatory, to develop and nurture the religious mind.

An incident from the life of a saint illustrates the readiness of the religious mind to respond to challenge. He was an old

---

115 *J. Krishnamurti: A Biography* by Pupul Jayakar, Penguin India, p. 241.

Sannyāsin visiting Jaipur, and was being seen off at the Railway station by his devotees. Just when the train started moving, one of the devotee pressed a small bag into his hand. When the train picked up speed, the old *Sannyāsin* opened the bag to find it filled with currency notes! Being of childlike nature, he started counting them! It was a first class compartment with only another passenger, a young British lady. No one knows how the greed got better of her, but she said that if he did not hand over the bag, she would shout that he had tried to molest her. The Swamiji just looked at her blankly and made a sign that he was hard of hearing and that she better put it in writing. The lady did just that. Taking the note in his hand, the Swami smilingly addressed the lady:

'Now you can shout'!

Analysing our actions, we find that most of them are only *reactions* to our own impressions, opinions and obsessions about the situations or people and seldom *responses* to the real situations and people. This is because the mind is governed by the judgment and prejudices forgetting that each situation and person is unique and is never a repetition. And the mind is necessarily so, as it can function only as a receptor of external information, as an analyser governed, as well as coloured by the memories of past experiences under the supervision of 'I'. In this sense, most of us transact only with the *image* of the person and seldom to the person directly, as observed by J. Krishnamurti.

How does one become a victim to such wrong notions? In his most popular and monumental *Prakaraṇa Grantha,* the explanatory scripture, entitled *Vivekacūḍāmaṇi,* Ācārya Śaṅkara points out *Māyā* or the nescience to be:

> '*Māyā* is also called the "unmanifest", and is the power of the Lord. It is without beginning, comprising of the three *Guṇas* and is superior to its effects. It is to be inferred only by one who has a clear intellect, from the

> effects it produces. It is this *Avidyā* which projects the entire universe'.[116]

One of the powers of the Ultimate Reality is the power to *delude* Itself! This has been called *Māyā,* and is of the nature of deep sleep where one is in a state of 'I do not know'. Which falls under the influence of the three *Guṇas—Tamas, Rajas* and *Sattwa.* The Ācārya then goes on to describe the nature and effects of the three *Guṇas.* He describes *Tamas* as :

> '*Āvṛti,* the veiling power, is the power of *Tamas,* which makes things appear to be other than what they really are. It causes man's repeated births, initiating the action of *Vikṣepa*—the projecting power'.[117]

> 'Absence of correct judgment, or contrary judgment, lack of definite belief and doubt, these certainly never leave one who is under the influence of *Āvṛti.* This along with the *Vikṣepa* gives endless trouble'.[118]

Āvaraṇa—the veil, appears to be the causal problem which in turn gives way to *Vikṣepa.* The nature of *Tamas* is bondage through ignorance. Man gets totally bound due to *Rajas.* When the Ācārya takes up the *Rajoguṇa* he writes :

> '*Rajas* has *Vikṣepaśakti,* the projecting power. Activity is its very nature. From it the initial flow of activity has originated and also the mental modifications such as, attachment and grief are continuously produced'.[119]

---

116 अव्यक्तनाम्नी परमेशशक्तिरनाद्यविद्या त्रिगुणात्मिका परा ।
कार्यानुमेया सुधियैव माया यया जगत्सर्वमिदं प्रसूयते ॥ 108 ॥

117 एषावृतिर्नाम तमोगुणस्य शक्तिर्यया वस्त्ववभासतेऽन्यथा ।
सैषा निदानं पुरुषस्य संसृतेर्विक्षेपशक्तेः प्रवणस्य हेतुः ॥ 113 ॥

118 अभावना वा विपरीतभावनाऽसंभावना विप्रतिपत्तिरस्याः ।
संसर्गयुक्तं न विमुंचति ध्रुवं विक्षेपशक्तिःक्षेपयत्यजस्रम् ॥ 115 ॥

119 विक्षेपशक्ति रजसः क्रियात्मिका यतःप्रवृत्तिः प्रसृतापुराणि ।
रागादयोऽस्याः प्रभवन्ति नित्यं दुःखादयो ये मनसो विकाराः ॥ 111 ॥

'Desire, anger, greed, hypocrisy, arrogance, jealousy, egoism, envy, etc. are the dreadful attributes of *Rajas* from which the worldly tendencies of man are produced. *Rajas* is therefore the cause for bondage in life'.[120]

Since the nature of *Rajas* is bondage through activity, it drives man under its influence to the tiresome activity characterised by egoism as well as egotism. A *Śloka* from the *Bhagavadgītā* says:

'The action, motivated by desire and again accompanied by ego is tiresome, has been understood to be the *Rājasik* action'.[121]

While in the same work the third *Guṇa, Sattwa* has been described by the Ācārya as:

'Pure *Sattwa* is like clear water, yet in combination with *Rajas* and *Tamas,* it provides for the transmigration. But when the light of Self gets reflected in *Sattwa* alone, then like the sun, It lights up the entire world of matter'.[122]

Manifestation of *Ahaṁkāra* happens only under the influence of the three *Guṇas.* So it has all the characteristics mentioned by the Ācārya. But *Āvṛti* and *Vikṣepa* are really noteworthy, in the sense that understanding them will help the seeker in learning to observe the mechanism of involvement well. The first activity of the mind or rather, the activity which creates the mind is the act of constriction or the act of *focusing.* This is more or less, in all activities of the

120 कामःक्रोधोलोभदंभाद्यसूयाऽहंकारेर्ष्यामत्सराद्यास्तु घोराः ।
धर्माएते राजसाः पुम्प्रवृत्तिर्यस्मादेषा तद्रजो बन्धहेतुः ॥ 112 ॥

121 यत्तु कामेप्सुना कर्म साऽहंकारेण वा पुनः ।
क्रियते बहुलायासं तद्राजसमुदाहृतम् ॥ 18.24 ॥

122 सत्तवं विशुद्धं जलवत्तथापि ताभ्यां मिलित्वा सरणाय कल्पते ।
यत्तात्मबिम्बः प्रतिबिम्बतःसन्प्रकाशयत्यर्क इवाखिलं जडम् ॥ 117 ॥

mind. This constriction in turn, limits the scope of understanding, not unlike the horse with blinkers on, is capable of seeing only the front.

The explanation of Ādi Śaṅkara no doubt is very clear and exhaustive. But no one has explained the nature of the three *Gunas* so simply as Shri Ramakrishna had through his parable of three robbers.[123] *Sattwa* no doubt, has the capacity to point out the Truth, still it is a thief! The seeker has to overcome the influence of *Rajas* and *Tamas* taking the help of *Sattwa,* as Vasiṣṭha asks the seeker to eliminate the *impure Vāsanās* with *pure Vāsanās.* And Ācārya Śaṅkara seems to suggest that one has to overcome the *Vikṣepa* and make the mind calm and then one is able to allow the wisdom to dawn in her or his consciousness.

Sage Vasiṣṭha told Rāma that one has to eliminate all impurities of the mind like desires and fear to become a recipient of *Mokṣa.* He said, that if it is not possible to control the desires, etc. directly, one can attain *Jñāna* through the path followed by Bali the great, through his intelligence. He continued when Rāma asked the sage to be enlightened about the nature of that course. There once lived a matchless *Asura* king by name Bali reigning in *Pātāla* like an emperor. He made the whole world tremble with his prowess and was able to humiliate even the Gods. Being the son of noble Virocana he ruled for many years.

One day he ascended to the topmost storey of his luxurious palace, and reflected with disgust for the material pleasures of Saṁsāra. With all his so-called material achievements, the pleasure he had been deriving, were not only momentary but repetitive. He wondered as to why even the intelligent persons do not get disgusted with them or are not ashamed to seek such enjoyments again and again and

---

123 Refer to the Story of Bhīma, Bhāsa and Dṛḍha.

to waste years and lives. With all the comforts of living, the quality of his life had not improved. He discovered that he was under the influence of restless action. Contemplating thus, he tried to seek *'That'*, which is permanent and free from all illusion and activity.

He was overwhelmed with joy as he remembered the conversation he had with his respected father Virocana at that very spot. On his request to remove his doubts, omniscient Virocana the father, had replied by telling him a story:

There is a beautiful country which is unlimited, all-pervading and without any precincts. That is the source from which everything has arisen, and into which everything gets absorbed. In this country there exist neither the five elements, nor hills, nor forests, nor holy places, nor *Devas*, nor any other ancient souls. The name of the king is Mahādyuti—the Great effulgence, who is omniscient, all-pervading, the cause of all and perfectly quiescent and full. He is silence itself, and the actions *happen* around through the minister appointed by him. The moment minister thinks of a thing though non-existent it appears instantaneously; though existent it disappears mysteriously. This minister does not have the power to enjoy anything on his own, nor does he know anything by himself. Though he acts in presence of the king, the king is always alone.

On listening to the story, son Bali enquired the nature of the resplendent country without any mental disease and boundary and the means of attaining it. He also wanted to know more about the king as well as the minister, and the method of conquering the minister. Father Virocana replied happily that the minister is almost invincible to any outside force and could only be controlled through the king. In order to dispel the doubts, Virocana proceeded to explain what the king, the minister and the country symbolise:

The country stands for incomparable and eternal *Mokṣa.* The king is the *Ātmic* Reality inseparable from *Mokṣa.* His creation, the minister typifies the mind. The mind can only be controlled skillfully through the development of complete *Vairāgya,* the divine disinterest, and *Asaṅga,* the non-attachment. Persons without any idea of the wisdom that is contained in the true *Jñāna* books maintain that out of four parts into which they divide the actions of the mind or time, two parts are to be devoted to sensual objects, a quarter to a study of *Jñāna* books and the remaining quarter to the worship of the blessed Ācārya. But the partial knowers maintain that two quarters are to be devoted to the contemplation and worship of Ācārya, a quarter to meditation upon the truth contained in *Jñāna* books and the remaining to the actions of organs. Both these classes affirm that *Jñāna* wili prevail on such persons treading as they suggest. While the third class who are of full *Jñāna* affirm that *Mokṣa* is easily attained by those who devote the four parts to the four purposes of study of *Jñāna* books, of *Akāmatā,* or desire-less-ness, of self-cognition and the path of worship of Ācāryas.

Saying thus, Virocana blessed his son Bali that he may attain *Mokṣa,* through intelligent subjugation of desires through *Ātmavicāra,* as through subjugation of senses with *Vairāgya, Ātmavicāra* is induced, while the *Ātmavicāra* brings about the renunciation of desires. They are mutually dependent like the full ocean and the clouds. Having earned wealth in proper ways, for looking after oneself and others without violating laws and observations of the country, one should through that wealth resort to the wise of rare *Sattvaguṇa* and there attain *Vairāgya,* and thereby develop *Ātmic* inquiry.

Bali was extremely happy to recollect the conversation he had with his respected father long time back. So he decided to act according to the advice of his father. Meditating upon himself he started cogitating on the questions like 'Who am

I'? and 'What is my real nature'? He reflected for awhile, and decided to invoke his *Guru* Śukrācārya who had cognised the Reality, and inquire to act accordingly. Having closed his eyes he meditated upon his Guru in true affection. Then Śukrācārya, whose form was true *Saccidānanda Ākāśa,* appeared before Bali. The king saluted and having worshipped him he lay bare his doubts.

Śukrācārya explained the king that all manifestations that we perceive, without *any* exception are *Jñāna* only; all that is beyond our perception is again *Jñāna* only; that which is conditioned and that which is not, is again *Jñāna;* the one who was asking the doubt (king Bali) and the one who was clarifying the doubt (Śukrācārya) are *Jñāna;* the whole universe is nothing but *Jñāna.* This Truth can be cognised, when the mind is without any modifications. After initiating Bali thus, the Ācārya withdrew.

Listening to the potent advice of the Ācārya, Bali fell into a state of deep *Vicāra.* With the mind directed inward, it transcended the body, mind, and intellect, to behold the Reality within. With that vision when he looked outside, he experienced that everything there is only a manifestation of the same Reality. And then, he really understood the words of Śukrācārya. Remaining in that state for a while he passed into *Nirvikalpa Samādhi.*

While Bali was in this state his courtiers in search of their king, reached the topmost storey of the palace. Finding him in *Nirvikalpa Samādhi,* they waited a long time for him to come to the normal state. When Bali finally did, he started performing his duty without any egoism or egotism. Having that pure vision, he was never disturbed in any adverse situation, or amidst pleasure or pain. In spite of the unlimited armies of good and bad thoughts crossing his mind, he was established totally at the Centre, the Primal Cause of all. Concluding the story, the sage urged Rāma to be established in Reality and thus control the seemingly rebellious mind.

Most of us are familiar with the story of charitable king Bali's largeheartedness. His readiness to give *everything* in charity; of Lord Viṣṇu appearing in the form of Vāmana—the dwarf, and seeking three steps; of Vāmana covering the entire earth with his first step, and the entire heaven with his second step; of Bali's taking the Lord's third step on his own head; and ultimately, his going down to Pātāla or the nether region. Vāmana has been considered to be an *Avatāra,* the manifestation of the Reality for saving the good and fighting the evil.

Bali means sacrifice, as he is represented in the story. And sacrifice, can generate a lot of power as evident through his invincibility and control over even the gods. But when even this sacrifice or charity is done only for the sake of nurturing the ego, it does have adverse effects like arrogance, pride and indulgence. This story only symbolises that the ego is ever ready to raise its hood with any or every act! Someone becomes a victim to pride because he is powerful, someone else to anger, other to austerity and may be some other person for righteousness or even *humility!* This is because the ego gets strengthened by any activity which has the *doership* behind it.

But then there are times when everyone of us, without exception, has to face the basic questions, when one is forced to accept that there is this repetitiveness in the world of objects, experience, thoughts and feelings. At such times, one remembers one's father. In Bali's case it was *Virocana,* which means the sun, the moon as well as the Agni, or in general the light principle, which helps one to see, and in the case of a seeker it is *Antarmukhatā.* It helps the seeker in gaining the ability to do *Vicāra.* While Śukrācārya is the *Guru* principle in each one of us. He is considered to be the preceptor of *Asuras,* the demonic forces, able to guide and control the evil forces. The greatest evil is *Avidyā,* the ignorance, *Āvṛti,* the covering. Through *Vicāra* the mind changes its direction. The *Guru* principle helps in knowing the all-pervasiveness of wisdom and to ultimately be in the state of *Adwaita—the No-otherness,* which alone eliminates fear and all other evils.

Even in the popular story, Bali's offering the earth and heaven to Vāmana represents his transcending the gross body, and subtle body respectively. While offering his head for the Lord to keep his foot symbolises his transcending the ego for the achievement of quiescence. The three steps demanded by Vāmana from Bali, represent *Śravaṇa* (listening), *Smaraṇa* (remembrance), and *Ācaraṇa* (practice). Sage Vasiṣṭha thus gives an indirect alternative for eliminating the desires and other fluctuations in the mind through this story. Here the seeker is urged to observe the mind from the subtler level. The *Bhagavadgītā* describes the order of subtlety in the following *Śloka:*

> 'The senses are subtler than the body, *Manas* is subtler than the senses; *Buddhiḥ* is subtler than the *Manas,* He (*Ātman*) is subtler than the *Buddhiḥ*'.[124]

Consequently, we find that the senses can be controlled by the *Manas,* which in turn can be controlled by the *Buddhiḥ,* which can be controlled by the *Ahaṁkāra,* which again can be controlled by the Self or *Ātman.* But one thing to be remembered is, that one is able to go to the next subtler level *only when the activity has slowed down at the grosser level, at least comparatively.* Which brings us back to the importance of developing *Vairāgya.*

Floods in the rivers bring in destruction and spells havoc to the beings who come under its force. They inundate the villages in its waters. They erode the soil and carry away the top soil. But they also bring fresher soil from the mountains or from upstream. And floods are a great sight to the one

124 इन्द्रियाणि पराण्याहुरिन्द्रियेभ्यः परं मनः ।
मनसस्तु परा बुद्धेर्योबुद्धेः परसस्तु सः ॥ 3.42 ॥

who is on the hills watching. Similarly, the flood of desires, of lower appetites, of pride, of hurt, and the other manifestations of ego, sweeps away the common man under their influence. But for one who has constructed the dam of "Self-control" they become a source of power. And for the one who has transcended them by being in a subtlest level of *Adwaita* they are natural spectacles like the lightning, or the dark clouds carrying tonnes and tonnes of pure water, or of birds in graceful flight, which only evoke pure bliss and joy.

4

The Story of Prahlāda

It was a pitch dark night, and one could hardly see the road. The sound of crickets, toads, and owls filled the atmosphere. A weary traveller was walking on that lonely path, and had miles to go before resting his complaining feet. His parched throat was demanding water, and his hungry stomach, food. But knowing that he could get them only on reaching the next village, he tried diverting his attention. Suddenly, he heard some foot-steps following him. He turned around, there was no one there! As he continued, again those foot-steps could be heard. He tried increasing his pace, and the sound of the steps behind him also seemed to increase! He stopped, and so did the steps. It dawned on him, that someone was following him. Perhaps, it was a friend, having a practical joke at his expense!

But it struck him that in that particular area he had no friends. Cold sweat started forming on his brow as a question appeared : 'Could it be the robbers'? Out came an answer: 'But how could there be only one'? And as the mind started racing, a very dangerous prospect became evident that it must be an evil spirit!! With that thought, his got transfixed to the place. And spontaneously, he remembered the monkey God Hanumān, for he had heard that when one takes the name of that great God, no evil spirit can ever come near! As he started chanting *'Mahāvīr'* loudly he discovered that his fear started reducing, and he continued the journey. A little later, he discovered that it was only the echo of his own foot-steps and laughed!

Though there is some humour in it, this happens to most, if not all of us! There are times when we become victims of fear, anger, greed and the like, and we *project* these very emotions on the external world. The only difference between the traveller of the above story and the rest of us is, that we seldom realise that they are echoes of our own in the form of desires, inner irritations or obsessions. And we keep on blaming the world for our failures and problems.

To run away from one's own desires, one starts condemning the world outside. And this critical attitude evokes jealousy, which in turn gives birth to a sense of guilt. When there is this sense of guilt, it is *projected* as anger outside, and one starts feeling that *people* are angry on him! All we have to do is to observe a person when he joins a group or an institution. He finds everything about it, congenial to him because, either it is necessary for him or he does not have any other alternative. The same person, when about to leave because he has an alternative, finds everything about it bad, even evil and hostile!

The mind is like a film projector *projecting* its own *images* on the screen called the world. Irving Stone has written a biography of Vincent Van Gogh, the Dutch painter.[125] The author writes that when the young Vincent, in his teens, falls in love for the first time, he learns to see the bountiful colour of the nature around him. It is unfortunately a one way affair as he is not all tnat handsome; he is rejected by the girl. When this happens, the same world appears totally grey and insipid for him!

As a young man, when Vincent is working as a preacher in a coal mining town, he is overpowered by a sense of comradeship with the sturdy miners. He discovers the sense

---

125 *Lust for Life* by Irwing Stone.

of movement and arrangement, and starts sketching, and goes on to pour his life blood into the paintings. If we analyse his life, the world as such did not change for him at those occasions and neither has it changed after the death of the great painter. However, this phenomenon of change is according to the *inner moods,* which again depend upon the *Ahaṁkāra.* This observation made our sages conclude that the world as we experience it is only a *projection* of *Ahaṁkāra.*

The second thing to be considered is the natural tendency of the human being to look for some principle beyond change and death, whenever he or she is facing the fear of change or death. Perhaps this is how the religions were born. Human being recognises that he is limited by circumstances beyond his control. Plagued by changes right from birth to death, he feels intuitively that there must be some power not conditioned by changes and calls that power God. Even when one does not apparently believe in God, one has faith in something which he thinks is greater than himself. He may not call it God but may do so by different names, such as 'moral sense', 'conscience', etc. Even a total wretch, about to commit suicide, may hear a voice from within, asking him to desist from such extreme action.

Normally, when we transact with the world, we have a tendency for egotism, which keeps repeating '*I* did this' and '*I* did that'. And most of our problems are the creations of the ego. When the problems go beyond the bearable limit one takes refuge in the principle called God. And when one takes refuge in such principle, which is greater than oneself, the ego melts into that principle, dissolving with it; its own creations may be for a very short time. Shri Ramana Maharshi puts it very eloquently in his *'Uḻḻadu Nārpadu'* or The Truth in Forty Verses:

> 'In those who due to fear of death, take refuge in God who is beyond death and birth, the ego disintegrates before their physical death; thereafter, how can the

thought of death occur again in those who are by nature immortal'?[126]

Man tolerates the problems—of course, created by himself!—up to a point, but then he needs something to release him from his own cocoon. He finds refuge in something which is stronger and greater than him. And God, who is beyond all change and death, is an ideal refuge. The moment he *genuinely* gives up his efforts, he gets released from pain or other *diseases*! It is like a person who is caught in a whirlpool, struggling and fighting with water, suddenly realises the futility of the struggle, and gives it up. The whirl definitely takes him down, but as and when he starts going down *willingly*, he discovers that the diameter of the whirl starts reducing, until he is thrown out from a point. And he saves himself by giving up the struggle. But most of the time people die as they never give up the struggle, in turn creating panic in their mind. And panic is a sure killer!

Animals do not experience any anxiety over the death, as their life is governed by instinct, at the *totally* unconscious level. They accept death as readily as life. While the awakened persons like the Buddha, also accept death as readily as life, because they are at the *totally* conscious level. Thus both have no problem as they act from their totality. And only the whole has the potentiality to act. While man as such, is in between. He is partly conscious but mostly unconscious. For example, the conscious part understands that anger is bad and *decides* to give it up. But a situation arises which provokes an angry reaction. This reaction comes from the unconscious part, which is larger, and one gets angry. Again the conscious part starts regretting and repenting. But since it is only a small part it is impotent and cannot *do* anything!

126 मृत्युंजयं मृत्युभिया श्रितानामहंमतिर्मृत्युमुपैति पूर्वम् ।
अथ स्वभावादमृतेषु तेषु कथं पुनर्मृत्युधियावकाशः ।। 2 ।।

Man is a bridge between the *totally unconscious,* or the animals and the *totally conscious,* or the awakened. He is only a becoming. Man is only a *process* and that is his misery. His unconscious part will not allow him to rise higher, while the conscious part will keep urging him to! In the process, there is an endless conflict and anguish. There are only two possibilities for coming out of this dilemma: either animal-hood or Buddha-hood. Rising towards Buddha-hood is really an arduous enterprise demanding sincere effort, and there is no guarantee that one *will* achieve it! So invariably, he chooses an easier alternative: falling to the animal-hood, that is, unconsciousness, with the help of sense indulgence or intoxication. During the moments of indulgence or intoxication, he falls into the unconsciousness. This way, he tries to become a whole, though it is only the unconscious whole. Life is characterised by movement. So he has to move forward or backward. Moreover, since man cannot remain in the state of conflict continuously, he seeks means of escape.

There comes an occasion in everyone's life, when one discovers that all the occupations to come out of the conflict are only sedatives making one more and more unconscious; that they are only repetitive, temporary and energy dissipative; and that *after* the experience, one is again in the same conflict. This is the turning point when the mind starts seeking a permanent solution, which lies in making the life more and more conscious.

One of the preliminary steps man takes is to search for an anchor of permanence. He may call it by any name, God, Reality, Providence, etc. As and when he sincerely *remembers* it, his puny ego melts into that refuge. And this experience, he discovers, does not in any way *take him towards unconscious.* In fact, there is a qualitative difference between this and the sense indulgence or intoxication. This experience makes man move towards total consciousness. However, there is a great problem in this : Initially, when he takes the refuge, it is quite effective but gradually, it wears off.

Such a person has to take one precaution : he has to do this anchoring, *with awareness and not mechanically*. Else, it is bound to degenerate into the religion, as it is generally understood and practised and that is, to seek more objects of indulgence through demands to a Personal God! This is so, because again the unconscious part is much larger than the conscious part which drags him down! But when it is done with as much of awareness as one is capable, more and more actions become conscious and one develops the capacity for *Aṁtarmukhatā* and *Vicāra*. The present *Sarga* tries to bring out this point through the story of Prahlāda.

Sage Vasiṣṭha asked Rāma to be attentive to the story of another *Asura* king Prahlāda who attained to true *Jñāna* through his intelligence. After the death of Hiraṇyakaśipu, the sad son Prahlāda grieving over his father's death started thinking that there have been countless *Asuras*. And they all had very strong bodies and the matching minds with invincible power over the external nature. But all of them have fallen victims to the power of Viṣṇu. This itself shows that their so-called power was much inferior to Viṣṇu's power. And so it is better to take refuge in Him. With these thoughts he started doing *Tapas*. Seeing their king engaged in such noble activity, the *Asuras* too started spending more and more time in contemplation of Hari, which is one of the names of Viṣṇu, to start shedding their *Āsuric* tendencies to become more and more *Sāttwic* and devout. Iṁdra and other *Devas* marveled with fear at this unprecedented event and were skeptical about the sincerity of these once vicious persons having a change of heart. Approaching Viṣṇu, they expressed their concern about the genuinity of the intentions of *Asuras*. And that they may have an ulterior motive behind. Lord Viṣṇu, smilingly assured them that the *Tapas* of the *Asuras* was genuine enough, as Prahlāda was their king who had been known for his *Viṣṇu-Bhakti*—devotion to Viṣṇu. He continued that if good persons incline their minds towards vice, then manifold evils ensue; but if the vicious incline towards the virtuous path, then immense good will result. On hearing these words of Viṣṇu the *Devas* left and started forgetting the animosity with their former antagonists, the *Asuras.*

Prahlāda, did the *Upāsanā* of Viṣṇu with the *Aṣṭākṣarī-mantra.*[127] *Auṁ Namo Nārāyaṇāya.* He resorted to the ritualistic worship of the great God. Gradually, he started spending more and more time over it, and to reap benefits like calmness, compassion, etc. Which in turn increased the love in his heart. He was relieved of the sadness he had been experiencing over his father's death. Prahlāda started employing all the sense organs in the worship thus increasing his sense of oneness with the existence. But the mind continued its persistent attraction for the sensual objects.

Seeing that Prahlāda's mind was seesawing between the partial spiritual experience and sensual enjoyment, Viṣṇu, the Lord of the three worlds, manifested Himself in the heart of Prahlāda, His devotee. Enraptured by the presence of his chosen Deity, Prahlāda mentally worshipped Him and offered prayers. Pleased with this, Viṣṇu offered him a boon. Prahlāda sought eternal bliss which transcends all pain. Viṣṇu blessed Prahlāda that the final *Ātmic inquiry* will arise in him for the ultimate quiescence to dawn upon him. With that Viṣṇu retired from his devotee's heart.

Gratefully remembering the Lord's words, Prahlāda began the *Ātma-Vicāra* with the fundamental question 'Who am I?' His mind being very calm and in a state of *Samatva*—equipoise, he was able achieve *Antarmukhatā.* The leading questions like 'What was I before?, What is the nature of this 'I', which identifies itself with the world?', started arising along with the *Bhāvanā* or the feeling. And gradually, he came to a conviction through experience, that he is not the body—which is limited by its grossness and which gets its activity only through the *Prāṇa;* he could not be the inanimate sound

---

127 The eight-syllabled mantra.

which is experienced through the organ of the ear and which decays into silence; he was not the sense of touch which too is not conscious, and attainable by the skin that perishes and can be experienced through *Cittam;* he was not the form which too is unconscious on its own as it is propelled only by the seer; neither was he the inanimate taste which is obtained by the tongue that is insignificant due to its temporal nature and which depends on the substance; he was not the smell, that is detected by the unconscious nose, depending on something subtler; he realised that he was free from all *Bhoktṛtva* or the experiencer-ship and was only pure consciousness, luminous, all pervasive, and eternal.

Though he had started the *Vicāra* by turning his mind inward, he discovered that the same Reality pervades within as well as without; that it envelops the lowest being to the highest *Loka* or the plane of existence; that there is nothing else but *That;* that It is the movement in the moving and stillness in the stable and stationary; that though It transcends all its manifestations, the manifestations *cannot* exist without It. In joyous ecstasy Prahlāda exclaimed that he had discovered 'That' principle sought by every being through every action big and small; and which is at the sub-stratum of all and gives them the power to function, and yet remains untouched by them. And in his ecstatic mood he started singing praises and the glories of That Principle called by various names: *Kūṭastha, Brahman,* and *Saccidānanda.* Prahlāda knew that this *Jñāna* was possible only through *Manonāśa,* or the quiescence of mind through *Viveka,* discrimination. He felt convinced, that all speech and thought failed to describe his experience.

The noble son of Hiraṇyakaśipu remained in this state of *Nirvikalpa Samādhi* for a very long time. And in his benign presence, the *Asuras* too forgot their real nature characterised by cruelty and other negative qualities. Viṣṇu, the protector of all worlds and their laws started contemplating the well being of the creation. He felt that without the *Āsuric* power, the *Devas* were being deprived of war without which the creation would cease to exist, because even the *Devas* would become quiescent. Without the *Devas* the *Yajña* and other noble actions will be lost. If the creation ceases before its allotted time, the *Dharma* will also cease. That is why the *Asuras* should prosper!

Musing thus Viṣṇu left his serpent coach and approached Prahlāda in Pātāla which had been transformed into *Satyaloka,* the plane of Truth. He sounded Pāñcajanya, the great conch, creating vibrations in all the three planes and to awaken Prahlāda from his *Nirvikalpa Samādhi,* from the subtlest plane through the activation of *Nāḍis,* to the gross physical plane, where he started perceiving the material objects of the senses, only after they were seen by him as a reflection on the glass of his inner *Prāṇa.* Prahlāda recovered the consciousness gradually, and beheld the great Lord Viṣṇu and experienced an incomparable joy and fullness.

Blessing Prahlāda, his devotee, Viṣṇu urged him to look after his wealth which was coveted by even Indra, the king of *Devas;* and that he need not abandon the body prematurely; and that as long as the mind is not haunted by attraction and aversion towards the sense objects it hardly matters whether the body exists or not. This Jīv*anamukti* state of Prahlāda will help in the smooth running, and fulfill the purpose of the creation. Moreover, only by keeping the body alive till the end of the *Kalpa,* the Brahmā's day, would Prahlāda play his role in this creation. Convincing Prahlāda to preserve his body, Viṣṇu performed the coronation of Prahlāda, who ruled Pātāla—the nether world, wisely.

On listening to this wonderful story, Rāma asked Vasiṣṭha as to how Prahlāda the king of *Asuras,* could return to the normal state *after* attaining to *Jñāna?* To which the sage replied, that in *Jīvanamuktas* the *Vāsanās* are like burnt seeds, and they never return after the deep experiences, as had by Prahlāda. But in some cases these *Vāsanās* no matter how pure, or *Sāttwik,* are very difficult to erase, and continue to remain like the ordinary *Vāsanās* during *Suṣupti.* Through these pure *Vāsanās* the *Jivanamuktas* are awakened to the world of objects.

This story is a store of wisdom for seekers as it not only hints at the subtle truths through allusions, but gives a practical method for doing *Vicāra.* The story of Hiraṇyakaśipu and Hiraṇyākṣa is well known. These *Asura* brothers had become invincible, so much so, it is said that like Bali in the previous story, they had control over the five elements. They had performed arduous penance to obtain a boon from the Creator Brahmā, that they should neither be killed by man, nor animal; neither during the night nor day; neither inside the house nor outside; and neither in water nor out of it. During the period of their penance, it is said that the *Devas* attacked *Pātāla,* and defeated the dis-organised *Asuras.* Iṅdra was taking away the chaste wife of Hiraṇyakaśipu, and she was expecting. Nārada, a great devotee of Viṣṇu intervened, and gave shelter to the lady in his *Āśrama.* The growing child in her womb heard the glories of the great Lord Viṣṇu and was naturally attracted to Him.

Hirṇyāksa took *Pṛthiwi,* the earth, to *Pātāla* and Viṣṇu had to assume the body of *Varāha* the great boar, to kill him and to revive the earth. The *Varāha* is considered to be an *Avatāra,* an incarnation of Viṣṇu. While Hiraṇyakaśipu started noticing that his son Prahlāda was getting attracted to Viṣṇu—his arch enemy, he started dissuading him mildly. But finding that Prahlāda continued his pursuits, he started torturing him in all possible ways. But Prahlāda was never troubled, instead he started appealing to his father to take refuge in the all pervasive principle called Viṣṇu.[128] Wild with anger, Hiraṇyakaśipu asked his son whether his Viṣṇu could be found in the pillar. Getting a positive reply, the *Asura* broke it and

128 Viṣṇu means 'All Pervasive' and also 'worker'.

from it manifested Viṣṇu as Narasiṁha, half man and half lion, and killed the *Asura*. It is said that, only Prahlāda could pacify the anger of Narasiṁha.

Hiraṇyakaśipu means one who has the golden seat or cushion. Gold has always been associated with greed. Shri Ramakrishna used to advise his disciples to always be alert about 'woman and gold' meaning, lust and greed. In this way, Hiraṇyakaśipu symbolises one who is established in greed. To overcome greed one has to take refuge in Narasiṁha, the man lion, that is, one has to adopt a fearless attitude because, greed is the outcome of fear, which can be confronted at twilight zones. And the mental twilight zone, is the moment when the mind is neither directed inside, nor outside; and neither active nor passive.

While Prahlāda means extreme happiness, who derives joy by taking refuge in the all pervasive principle Viṣṇu. When one starts broadening one's consciousness one is bound to derive happiness. The present story is meant to bring home the point that a person starting his spiritual journey with surrender to a personal deity, *need not* end it there. Of course, if the surrender is total, when one entirely eliminates the *Ahaṁkāra*, then the journey ends with it. But normally, the *Ahaṁkāra* is so powerful and cunning that it bounces back in unrecognisable forms!

Prahlāda started with *Upāsanā* of Viṣṇu through *Arcanā*, the ritualistic worship, which is a stepwise method to learn the art of melting the ego into the Chosen Deity. The devotee starts with preparing his mind for the *Upāsanā* through the acts like cleaning the place of worship, collecting the articles for worship like the flowers, and preparation of food offering etc. He tries to employ all his senses for the worship of the deity. This procedure purifies the senses as they are directed to the deity, when the eyes are engaged in decorating the deity and beholding its form, nose is involved in smelling the auspicious incense, and so on. The devotee tries to do

Āvāhanaṃ or invoke the deity first outside then in himself. But there are two dangers in this: the mind may remain extrovertish, and it may continue in its sense involvement, as it happened with Prahlāda.

At such times, the devotee's earnestness helps him to observe that his sense experiences bring in expansiveness (Viṣṇu), which makes him start the *Vicāra*. The enquiry leads him towards the realisation of the temporality of the sense experience, and takes him to the cause of *Bhokta* or the experiencer. The method of enquiry has been very nicely dealt when Prahlāda examines his sense experiences, senses and ultimately the *Draṣṭā* or the 'seer', which can be felt only when the grosser activity of the body, senses, and *Antahkaraṇa* ceases, which has been called by Prahlāda as the *Aṁanana,* where the mind has stopped thinking, *Nirmama,* where *Ahaṁkāra* has stopped, as the feeling of *'mine'* has ceased as a consequence of which, *Kalakālanvārjita,* where one goes beyond the resultant conflicts.

This helps the seeker in realising that whatever he had so far accepted or rejected based on his trivial experiences of happiness and sadness are there only as long as there is the separateness, the *Dwaita-Bhāva.* With the oneness there is the experience of the ever existing balance. It is as if he *wakes up* from his sleep of the ignorance characterised by his preoccupation with his senses, desires and mental fantasies. There is a very beautiful story by Jorge Luis Borges of Argentina, one of the greatest writers on metaphysical fantasy, to illustrate this:

> 'So many years on the run, expectant, and now the enemy stood at my door. From the window I saw him working his way up the hill. Labouring along the steep road, he leaned on a staff, a clumsy staff which in his hands was no more than an old man's cane, not a weapon. Although I was waiting for it, his knock was so weak, I barely made it out. At the door I fumbled with

the key to let the man in. I feared he was going to collapse all at once, but he took a few faltering steps and stumbled, utterly worn out, on my bed.

I bent over him so that he could hear me:

"One believes that the years pass by for one." I said to him, "but they pass for everyone else too. Here we meet, at last, face to face and what happened before has no meaning now".

While I spoke he unbuttoned his overcoat. His right hand was in the pocket of his suit coat; something there was aimed at me, and I knew it was a revolver. Then he told me, in an unwavering voice:

"To get myself into your house I fell back on your pity. Now I have you at my mercy, and I am unforgiving".

I tried to get out some words; I am not a strong man and only words could save me. I managed to utter:

"It is true that long ago I ill-treated a certain boy, but you are no longer that boy, and I am no longer that callous brute. Besides, revenge is no less vain and ridiculous than forgiving".

"That is just it." He replied, "Because I am no longer that boy, I am about to kill you. This has nothing to do with revenge. This is an act of justice. Your arguments, Borges, are stratagems of your terror designed to keep me from my mission. There is nothing you can do now."

"There is one thing I can do." I said.
"What is it?" He asked.
"Wake up." I said

And I did'.[129]

---

129 'Episode of the Enemy' from *Ficciones—The Book of Imaginary Beings* by Jorge Luis Borges.

Absence of light accompanied by the instinctive fear can create many a mental aberration, in turn increasing the already evoked fear. The best solution at such time is the light which helps in dispelling not only the darkness but also the aberrations. Similarly, the desires, fears and conflicts are the denizens of unconsciousness or sleep. Sometimes, they create pleasant dreams bringing in *relief from misery,* and at other times they usher in nightmares. While most of us have taken them to be real and needlessly suffer in the process, some of us have realised that our life is dominated by the unconsciousness and aspire to come out of it. A very few of us wake up from our sleep to find the existence as it has always been—in blissful celebration!

5

The Story of Gādhi

Azure Blue sky. Not even a cloudlet to malign its purity. It is like an infinite dome over the equally majestic Himalayas, which are aspiring to touch it. The clear white peaks, result of glaciations of snow over millions of years, stand as a bridge between the earth and the heaven. The peaks have been acting as the benign sentinels and as the uninvolved witnesses to the History of mankind. They have discouraged innumerable invaders; helped genuine travelers with a thirst for knowledge; smiled benignly at those adventurers who were prepared to risk their lives to stand on their peaks, not only with an intention of *conquering* the peaks, but may be, to borrow the *vision of the peak,* though only for a short time; or given shelter to many a seeker plunging into another kind of adventure, with an aspiration to achieve the *non-involved witness-hood.* The sky and these magnificent mountains have infinite secrets that are beyond man's comprehension.

Having an humble beginning at a lonely cave in the Himalayas, she starts her long journey towards the ocean. At the source, she is just a trickle, gathering strength very gradually, flowing through broad gorges, falling into great depths, imbibing the fragrance from the mountain herbs, earth and wild flowers. Her sister meets her downstream, and they strengthen each other till their combination becomes a gusty torrent. This phenomenon gets repeated at many other places: *Rudra Prayāga, Karṇa Prayāga, Deva Prayāga,* and

Prayāga or Allahabad. At *Gaṅgā Sāgara*, she merges with the ocean. If one sees her humble beginning in that trickle inside the almost unapproachable cave, one can never imagine that she affects so many, and has become a cradle for such a wonderful culture as ours. One may even have misgivings about her benevolence, after experiencing her violent upheavals, doom's day floods and cruel droughts!

Something similar happens with another phenomenon called mind. While the river—the flow of water, is at least predictable, the mind—the flow of thoughts, is not. This is necessarily so, because the water is governed by the physical laws as it is gross. It can move only in one direction—towards the ocean. While the thought has the freedom, to move both ways towards the world of objects, as well as its own source. Even the movement of water depends on the terrain. Thinking, on the other hand, has the freedom which is truly *mind boggling!* And this very freedom can become a gate *as well as* a wall. For a person *using* the freedom to find out the source of thought and experience it, freedom becomes a gate for liberation, while a person misusing the freedom to *involve and indulge* with the sense objects, desire for power or control over others, and other facets of *Ahaṁkāra,* the very freedom becomes an impregnable wall of a high security prison!

There is another similarity between the mind and the river from another point of view. The *Gaṅgā* at *Gomukh* is already one with the ocean. Because, the source and the merging place are the points at two extremities of the same river. Similarly, the individual mind is already a part of the cosmic mind, and has the power of that universal mind at its disposal. That is why, each and every enlightened Person, declared directly or indirectly, that every being is already united with the Reality, only in his ignorance does he think otherwise. This ignorance has been called as the *Māyā*. *Māyā*[130]

---

130 या मा सा माया ।

itself means: 'that which is not', which is only apparent. And *Sādhanā* consists of shattering the nightmare of multiplicity and *remembering* or waking up to the Oneness of existence.

There is an interesting story of a rich *Sheikh* in search of wisdom. He came to know that there are wise men in his sheikdom who can share their wisdom with him. Out of all such wise men, there was one *Sufi* mystic living in a small town, who was really extraordinary. But he refused to come to the court in spite of many attempts by the officials. The people told them that only sincere persons could meet him and that too under a tree where he presently stayed. It is said, that the *Sheikh* took the best diamonds and precious stones in a velvet bag to exchange them with the wisdom. Reaching the town, he searched for the *Faqir.* Finally, the *Sheikh* saw a very ordinary looking man in torn clothes and hungry looks. But accompanying man confirmed that this was the man. Hesitantly, the *Sheikh* asked the man as to where he could find happiness.

Suddenly, the *Faqir* grabbed the bag containing the precious gems and started running, with the panicky *Sheikh* at his heels. But the *Faqir* knew of all the lanes and by-lanes of the town and was soon lost in the maze. Dejected and tired the *Sheikh* retraced his steps to the tree where he had initially found the *Faqir.* And to his surprise, found the old man in the same spot with a smile. When he approached the tree, the *Faqir* returned the unopened bag. And the *Sheikh* was extremely happy. Looking at the beaming face of the rich man, the Faqir asked what had made him so happy. The *Sheikh* answered honestly, that the lost bag of gems had made him unhappy and now that it was back with him, he was happy! The *Sufi* mystic commented that he had come to him with a question on the whereabouts of happiness. His snatching the jewel bag and running was the answer.

The happiness is all the time with every one of us but, we apparently lose it in our forgetfulness. We imagine that it is lost or stolen in the maze of our involvement and indulgence. There are various examples in *Vedānta,* like *Daśamonaṣṭaḥ*[131]—the lost tenth man, or the person searching for the ornament which is around his own neck all the time(!), bringing out the purport of the above story. As and when a seeker starts treading the path she or he has chosen for himself, there are times when the mind starts asking about the nature of *Māyā* —the ignorance or forgetfulness.

In spite of the fact that a seeker comes across many explanations on *Māyā* in different scriptures, she or he does not get a clear picture of the same, unless it becomes a part of her or his own understanding. The present story is of one such seeker who was interested in gaining the first hand experience. Of course, it is *not mandatory* that *every* seeker should have such experience, because there is nothing like should and must or mandatory on the mental and spiritual plane. But this is also true, that invariably there comes a time, when a seeker recognises this veil of ignorance. And sage Vasiṣṭha continued, saying that the greatest obstacle on the path is this world bewitching *Māyā,* which is the prime cause of the cycle of repeated births and deaths. This can be destroyed only through mastery over the mind. To illustrate this, he started telling Rāma the story of Gādhi.

In the country of Kośala, there lived a Brahmin named Gādhi. For reason best known to himself, he abandoned his family and retreated into a forest for intense Tapas consisting of standing in neck deep water for long hours. Lord Viṣṇu manifested before him. Gādhi was extremely happy and came

---

131 Ten men on their journey were crossing a small stream. On reaching the other bank, they wanted to ascertain that all were safe. But when each one of them counted they could find only nine, and *the tenth man was lost*! A wayfarer, saw their plight and made them aware that while each of them had counted his companions, he had forgotten to include *himself* in the counting!

out of water and fell prostrate on the bank of the river. He worshipped and praised the Lord, thus identifying himself with those very qualities. When the Lord offered a boon, Gādhi sought to know the true nature of *Māyā*. Viṣṇu acceded to the request and said that the Brahmin would have the experience in due course.

A few days later, he remembered the boon of Lord Viṣṇu on way to a tank filled with lotuses. Dipping his head in water, he forgot to chant the Vedic *Mantras*, as was his habit. And he found himself dead in his own village amidst his relatives. His wife, mother and all others were weeping bitterly over his death. His lifeless body was consigned to the flames and was reduced to ashes. Thus Gādhi saw himself dead and burnt, while he was in the water of the tank thus getting himself involved in illusory visions that were imagined by him!

The life of Gādhi being over, he found himself reincarnating in the womb of a low-caste woman of dark complexion. With great difficulty she brought him up with all the love and care. He too grew up into manhood with body, dark as charcoal by the name of Kaṭañja. He was strong and had none to equal him in his valour. He married a girl of the same caste and lived happily, with children born out of this union. As time elapsed dotage and grayness set upon him. Constructing a house of leaves at a distance, he started living as *Tapasvin*. The children too advanced in age and became old. Death seized them all, except Katañja.

Being tired of incessant loneliness experienced in solitude, the survivor's mind became confused; he was sick with desire and began to wander in different lands. At last he reached a country called Kīra. The king of the country had died without leaving any heir to the throne. The people had decked the state elephant with precious gems, and let it loose to go its way and select the king. The tusker in search of a person to rule found a *Nīca*, the low caste, akin to its own colour and raised him up on its neck with its long trunk. The subjects were overjoyed and the newly selected king was taken to the palace in grand procession. The old courtiers and the commander-in-chief began to obey his orders. The new king, assumed the name Gavala, befitting his position and power, he reigned over the land attended and loved by all.

One day after eight years, Gavala removed his ornaments and started roaming on the street outside the palace without any regality appearing as a true *Nīca.* A group of outcasts were moving towards him playing upon their *Vīṇā,* the stringed instrument. The oldest of the group, recognising the present king of Kīra, approached him in true love and addressed him with affection in his old familiar name Katañja, his dearest relative. And enquired his whereabouts and his presence in this distant land. Feeling ashamed with the familiarity shown by his past relative, he refused to recognise him and retreated to the palace.

The ladies of the inner palace however, had witnessed the scene which had passed between their king and the low-caste men. Surprised, they informed the minister. Unable to find anyway out of the situation, they were stunned and perplexed. But Gavala acted as if nothing had happened. And the ladies, the courtiers and others started avoiding him as if he were a corpse. Then the subjects held a solemn conclave and came to a conclusion that they all were contaminated by the association with the *Nīca*; that no amount of penance could purify them; and that the only course open to them was mass immolation in fire. With this resolution, they fell into a large pyre as the moths entering fire. The king too became afflicted in heart, by this act. Blaming himself for the death of his courtiers and the subjects he too entered the fire.

While the body of Katañja was being burnt, the body of

---

132 A unit of time measuring 24 minutes.

Gādhi which had taken a plunge into the water of the tank began to palpitate and quiver and in four *Ghaṭikās*,[132] covered by the veil of *Māyā*. Ruminating on the experience he rose from the water, and sitting on the bank he meditated upon the troubled *Jīvas* running about in the world with agitated minds, and was temporarily relieved at heart with some doubts still lingering. He spent some days in deep thought. A guest arrived in his hermitage. He was looked after by Gādhi in the best possible way. On performing their daily devotions during the *Sandhyā* after the sunset they engaged themselves in narrating *Ātma-Jñāna* stories to each other. Muni Gādhi noticing the extreme emaciation of the body of the guest inquired into its cause.

The guest replied that at the request of his relatives he spent a month in the famous and wealthy country of Kīra. While he was staying there, he came across a person who related the following anecdote. A king ruled that country wisely for eight years. But his true identity of being a *Nīca* was brought to light. With the discovery, all the subjects coming in his contact entered fire, and the king too followed. Hearing this, the guest fled from that country and went to Prayāga in order to absolve the sins by taking a dip in the confluence of three rivers, and also performed *Cāṅdrāyana Vṛata*[133] there. At these words of the guest, Muni Gādhi was surprised at the way in which the stranger had narrated his own history.

To verify the truth of events of his imaginary life as *Nīca*, he travelled to the country of Hūṇas, and saw his birthplace and other places he had dwelt. It was exactly as he had seen in the trance under water. He proceeded further north to the Kīra country and saw all those things related to his life as the king Gavala. He heard the events of his life told by the

---

133 An observance beginning with fifteen morsels of food on the full moon day, a person reduces them one by one till he reaches the new moon day when he increase it one by one daily.

people there. Then he reached the slopes of a great hill to become a great *Tapasvin.* After the elapse of an year, Lord Viṣṇu again appearing before him observed that Gādhi had seen the glory of *Māyā,* and asked him the reason for performing the *Tapas* at the hill-side.

Gādhi, the *Tapasvin* after paying due respects to the Lord, expressed a doubt as to how *his* mental experience of delusion could manifest itself as real. To which the dark blue cloud coloured Lord Viṣṇu replied that this earth and other things in the universe have their substratum in the mind and cannot exist apart from it. Almost all persons in the world in this universe of dreams, delusion and egoism, look upon it as real and enjoy or suffer it. The universe rests only in the *Citta,* and one need not be surprised if the *Citta* containing this whole universe objectifies the life of *Nīca,* which is only an infinitesimal part of the universe.

The *Ekāgratā* or single pointedness of the mind of Gādhi got reflected in the life of a *Nīca* woman in some inexplicable way, giving birth to a child in the Hūṇa country which in turn followed its own course as Katañja, Gavala and his immolation in fire, after his subjects. Coincidentally, the guest too became a part of this great illusion, and came to the hermitage and narrated the story of Gavala. Like *Kākatālīyayoga* or the analogy of a crow and palm fruits,[134] the ideation of *Nīca's* life reflected itself in the minds of all living in the Hūṇa and Kīra countries. This is how the ideation got more and more strengthened, assuming apparent reality.

The Lord continued, that the ignorant get impressed by the idea of differentiation like 'He, you, I, this that, mine, etc.' will continue to sink into the mire of pain. But those who have cognised earth and other things of the universe as

---

134 A palm fruit falls on the ground and the cause of it is attributed to a crow perching upon that tree at that time. The crow's sitting, may only be one out of many causes.

not different from the 'I', will never grieve. Those with a mind free from desires and firm *Buddhiḥ,* or the clarified intellect, never give any importance to desires. But since Gādhi was not yet free from these progeny of differentiation: the desires, he had got swept off his feet at the time of experience and forgot himself. Viṣṇu told Gādhi that in the wheel of delusion, mind is the axle. The *Māyā* does not affect such person who has quietened the mind through *Viveka.* The Lord blessed him saying that he will acquire true *Jñāna* after performing Tapas, or penance, for ten years in the cave of the hill. Gādhi thus freeing himself of all delusion through the advice and the grace of the Lord attained the state of *Jīvanamukti* on performing *Tapas* for ten years absolving himself of all attachment.

Like all the electrical appliances deriving power from the same source, minds of all beings are connected to the cosmic mind. That is why there is an undercurrent of unity and agreement amidst all the diversity. For a man who is being aware of *only* the diverse forms and behaviour, it is very difficult to even appreciate the thought of unity. Shri Ramakrishna, used to give the example of the dolls and shapes made out of sugar candy. For a child, they are all different, but for an adult it is very plain, that only their external forms are different while they all have the same taste of sugar.

Drawing power, as the individual minds do, from the common source, it is not surprising that once in a while some minds get linked and vibrate alike to have the same thoughts and feelings. Two people find themselves thinking the very same thought simultaneously, though one may succeed in voicing it before the other. Moreover, most of us share many experiences as is common in the world of objects. Of course, our impressions and interpretations are definitely according to our innate nature.

A startling statement is made by don Juan to Carlos

Castaneda when he returns to normal consciousness after an experience of a state of *parallel reality.* Castaneda describes the place and events that have been experienced, and wonders whether they were only part of his imagination or have any element of truth in them. Don Juan assures him that whatever is experienced in *any* state of mind is true and continues in that plane of existence, and that the science or the logic cannot explain it as there are many things which are unexplainable. He adds, that the events and the things and people seen in dreams *continue,* even after waking up and that most of us lack the power to *go back into* that world.[135]

Yoga Vāsiṣṭha makes an attempt to offer explanations through symbolic stories. In the story of Lavaṇa, at the end of *Utpatti Prakaraṇa,* and in this present story, the author *materialises* the psychological or inner experiences. In both the cases, the men under the influence of *Māyā* discover that their experiences are not only psychological, but real even at the physical level. Their individual minds are connected to one cosmic mind, although the bodies are different. And through some inexplicable reason two or more minds get connected and are able to feel and experience the feelings and experiences of one another. Explaining this experience to Gādhi, Lord Viṣṇu uses the word, *Pratibiṁba,* or reflection, hinting that though separated by large distances, the thoughts and feelings are *caught* by the mind, indicating that each mind is a receiver and a reflector. Another very important statement made by the Lord is that Gādhi was swept off his feet when he was not *aware,* indicated by his failure to chant the Vedic *Mantras.*

The story tries to convince the seeker of the illusive power of *Māyā.* Surprisingly, this power is initiated and nurtured by the individual mind itself. While the Cosmic mind is one, the individual mind connected to it, differs at the superficial level

---

135 *Journey to Ixtlan* by Carlos Castaneda, Penguin Books, 1979.

governed by the likes and dislikes. When exaggerated, desire becomes a mania, while the repulsion becomes a phobia. It is a common experience, that each mind perceives the world, and interprets it according to its own level and starts projecting its own mental modifications on to the world. It is like the coloured vision of a person wearing coloured glasses. And yet there are many things which are beyond normal, logical explanation.

Once, D. H. Lawrence, the famous British novelist was strolling in a lush green garden. A child came and tugged his coat tail and asked a strange question:

'Uncle, why is it that the trees are green?'

Lawrence paused for a moment, looked around at the trees, and looked at the innocent blue eyes of the child and said:

'Because the trees are green, just as your eyes are blue!'

And that satisfied the child! Material things, though bound by the physical laws are many times inexplicable. As and when we enter subtler planes of existence, explanation becomes more and more difficult. *Māyā,* the cause of manifestation of existence including *Ahaṁkāra,* is the subtlest, and necessarily transcends all logical explanation. One can only see through it and transcend it.

Up to man, the evolution is logical, as it follows certain physical rules and pattern. But the evolution as it is understood by us and as explained by our biologists stops with the human being. Because, man is endowed with the power of thought which gives him superiority over all other species, and to a very great extent, control over the external nature. But life means to move progressively ahead, till one gets more fulfilled than one is in the previous state. And man's fulfillment lies in the change of plane altogether from the physical to the spiritual. It is a quantum leap from the known into the unknown.

A man under the influence of a dream never realises that it is a dream. Whether it is a pleasant dream or a nightmare, he is influenced by it. The only course open to him is to wake up into an entirely different state of consciousness. And when he does, there is only a relief and a smile on his face, because he realises that the entire universe in his dream or the nightmare was *his own creation.* When one wakes up to a transcendental consciousness, which contains all the three states of wakeful, dream and deep-sleep states, one cannot help smiling at one's wrong identifications, and subsequent tears and laughter.

The *Gaṅgā* is already one with her Lord *Sāgara*—the Ocean, even as she hesitatingly trickles down in the cave of *Gomukh.* But the excitement of the journey through the sylvan Himalayan slopes, the adventure of jumping into the deep gorges, the pleasure of communicating with the flora and fauna, the fun and frolic of disturbing the landscape through floods, the satisfaction of appeasing the thirsty, and the peace of inspiring many a seeker is the privilege of mother *Gaṅgā,* and others like her.

The infinite Azure Blue sky remains untouched by the presence of threatening thunder clouds. The cirrus clouds try to beautify the sky by their fleeciness. But the sky remains undisturbed by them knowing its own self. Similarly, a seeker tries to drop his identification with the clouds of *Ahaṁkāra* and the subsequent delusion, and experiences the Union with the Reality. And the beauty is that she or he is already one with It! It is only a mistaken *notion* of helplessness, which has been appropriately called as *Māyā.* And even the *Māyā* has its role in initiating the seeker's own experience of scenes and acts, he has to play in the drama of existence.

6

The Story of Uddālaka

The sun was in its zenith flooding the earth with its abundant energy, while the earth was parched and cracked, thirsty for water. The trees appeared to be looking up towards the sky for clouds, the messengers of plenty. The foliage had lost its green colour, not only due to the sparse supply of sap, but also the guest in the form of a layer of fine dust, settled on the leaves due to winds and an occasional vehicle passing by or the dust carried by the hooves of the cattle going to and fro their grazing lands. The winding road of red mud was leading further into the thickening forest. About fifty paces from the road, there was a pond reflecting the trees on its bank, and an old stone temple where the villagers offered their devotion, shared their woe and joys. The pond was a spot where every inhabitant of the village had to visit at least once in a day. And that included the cattle. For it was the only source of water for the village.

That day, the heat was more oppressive than ever. The old men were resting under a huge banyan tree with a cool shadow, while the middle-aged were sitting around, speculating about the monsoons, and the youth as well as the children were absorbed in their dreams and play. The fields were tilled, the soil lumps broken and receptive, the thatches of the huts repaired and ready to face the monsoon. And now, their eyes were full of plans for the harvests and the resultant prosperity. Suddenly, an old man sat up, his eyes shining, and nose turned towards the South East. Everyone became alert, following the direction of his gaze. He did not have to say anything, for they all could get the smell of the damp earth. The youth climbed up a hillock nearby and noticed with satisfaction, the dark of clouds laden with the precious water.

Instinctively, all of them moved towards the ancient stone structure of the temple to offer their gratitude. And the very next day the monsoons hit the place. The thirst of the earth was quenched, the dust in the atmosphere re-entered the earth, and was washed off from the leaves. It was as if the rain had rejuvenated the entire earth. And in a matter of days, the earth was dressed in a lush green garment of grass. The new shoots from the sleeping seeds below the ground, and the tree branches above, saw the light of the day! It was not that anything new was *created,* but the care offered by the rain, *woke up* the system towards its full bloom.

Human beings are also like this. In a certain milieu, they *forget* the power within, to suffer needless misery. While in a proper milieu, they *remember* their own strength to move towards the destiny of fulfillment. Perhaps, that is how it has always been. Unless one has experienced the blinding darkness, one may not know the value of light; unless one has gone through the pangs of misery, joy is taken for granted; and unless one has known the turmoil of disturbance, one may not be able to appreciate the restful peace. Just as the dryness and the sweltering heat of the summer has the role of giving the taste of earth to the leaves, who are otherwise separated from it, the turmoil and the misery churns the consciousness, to whip out means and methods for overcoming them.

None of the creatures, except the human beings can recognise and *understand* the paradoxes of life, as only man is endowed with a *reasoning mind.* Mind has its advantages, as also the disadvantages. The *Manas* (sensing the world),

Buddhiḥ (reason) and *Cittam* (memory) are no doubt necessary and useful as they have been instrumental in ushering all the progress made by man. But the desires, greed, fear, suspicion, and the like have always created anxiety, worry, tension and violence. During such times, latter have been having stronger influence on the human destiny.

The mind gets its motivation for occupation and strength through non-existent things. For instance, man was always fascinated by the birds. This fascination made him realise that he did not have any wings needed to fly in the sky. The limitation goaded him in developing wings through his power of invention, and succeeds in covering large distances in small intervals of time through airplanes and jets. However, such inventive geniuses are necessarily few in number and many, if not most of us, are under the negative influence of the mind. The mind dwells on things *which are not,* and becomes a victim of desires, greed, and the like. The ambitions and the goals we set for ourselves are products of such thoughts, directed at the non-existent things. Since the mind exists only on the non-existent, the wise have said, that mind itself is non-existent! It is a negative phenomenon like darkness which is nothing but the *absence of light.* So also is the mind, which is an *absence.*

There are two ways of dwelling on non-existent things : the past with memories, nostalgia, or hurts, wounds and bitterness; and future with dreams, ambition or goals, fantasy, anxiety and worry. On a careful self-observation and analysis one is surprised to discover that the mind *never can remain in the present, or the here-now.* And this state of here-now, is always a state of poise that transcends the duality of paradoxes. Consequently, mind evaporates when *one is in the present,* and with the dissolution of mind, one transcends the duality—the prime cause of pain. This wonderful discovery made the spiritual scientists, devise various techniques and methods to wean the seeker out of this stubborn habit called mind or more appropriately, *minding!* And like all habits, mind is also an activity.

Since each one of us has a singular and unique nature, our individual mental occupation differs. Consequently, no two persons can have the *identical method* for quietening the mind. The sages no doubt have given suggestions for four broad categories of persons. They are, action oriented, reason oriented, emotion oriented and will oriented. This does not mean that such persons do *not* have the other faculties, but only that they are governed by one of them *predominantly*. We find in our sacred texts like the *Upaniṣads*, or the *Bhagavadgītā*, many techniques. In fact they are so diverse, as to be very confusing! So the first task of the seeker is to discover her or his own nature. Though this is very difficult, the thrill of seeking and the joy of discovery make the seeker's journey worthwhile and adventurous.

While giving several hints, this grand scripture also helps one in understanding one's own nature through the characteristic features of mind and *Ahaṁkāra*. In the last *Sarga* the phenomenon of *Māyā* was described through the story of Gādhi. *Māyā* starts affecting the mind, with lack of awareness or *forgetfulness*. The present *Sarga* gives practical hints on the mind quietening techniques through certain yogic practices.

Muni Vasiṣṭha continued that a careless mind attracts problems, and the only cure of this disease called *Saṁsāra* is through *Manonāśa* or the destruction of mind. The mind indulges in the present through external objects, and in the future and past through *Saṁkalpa*, *Āśā*, and *Anusaṁdhānaṃ*. Sage Vasiṣṭha urged Rāma to eliminate these which afflict the mind every moment. And by so doing, he assured, one can achieve virtue. *Vāsiṣṭha Caṅdrikā*, the gloss on the scripture, defines these three activities as:

> '"I will do such and such a thing", this mental action is *Saṁkalpa*.

"This should happen to me", such wishful thinking is *Āśā*.
Repeated recollection of the past is *Anusamdhānaṃ*'.[136]

Pure awareness, devoid of any such mental activity has been called as *Pratyakcetanāṃ,* a state of tranquility. When this tranquility becomes a part of one's nature, there is no room for any disturbance. This is adherence to the Truth, this is the auspicious, all knowing, quiescent and Ultimate state. The sage blessed Rāma to succeed in eliminating ignorance, through *Viveka,* diligent effort and also understanding the essence of spiritual books.

In the following *Ślokas,* Sage Vasiṣṭha gave some very valuable hints to Rāma for quietening the mental activity. Though engaged in normal activities like talking, giving up, accepting, opening or closing the eyelids, etc., one should be ever engaged in the contemplation of the Infinite and live the essence of the wisdom. Totally severing the *Bheda-Vāsanās* like 'this-I', 'that-he', etc., being ever established in the One, one should live the essence of the wisdom. Purging the mind of all impurities and destroying the bondage causing desire, live the essence of the wisdom. Through equanimous vision transcending the disease causing paradoxes like good-evil and auspicious-inauspicious, one must live the essence of the wisdom. Giving up even the differentiation of spiritual and mundane, one should live in the world by getting attached to the pillar of *Ātman* achieve the stability. The moment one gets this *change of view* one is totally freed from all conception of duality and its pain giving progeny.

The first of these *Ślokas* uses the very line as two of the loftiest of the *Ślokas* from the *Bhagavadgītā,* expressing the same idea:

---

136 एवमेव करिष्यामिति मानसं कर्म संकल्पः ।
इदं मे स्यादिति प्रार्थनमाशा । अतीतानुस्मरणमनुसन्धानम् ।। 5.6.5 ।।

> 'The experiencer of Self is convinced that He is totally free of any activity as He is not the doer, in spite of being in the process of seeing, hearing, touching, smelling, eating, going, sleeping, breathing, speaking, renouncing, accepting, closing and opening of eyelids, as all these activities are nothing but the senses coming in contact with their objects.'[137]

These grand *Ślokas* not only describe the state of the experienced wise, but analyse the reasons why others fail to achieve the state, thereby suggest methods to do so. The first suggestion is to avoid indulgence at the sense level, and instead try to witness *all* actions as if from a distance. Every one of us is familiar with such acts of witnessing in day-to-day life. The most common one is, when a friend experiences a personal loss. We approach him or her, and try to offer consolation. Every person approaching such a sufferer, especially in our country, gives a philosophical flavour to his speech made to console the sufferer! This is so because the *adviser* is not *involved* and it is happening to someone else. But it is altogether different, if the same thing happens to those very persons who *had* offered such consolation to *others!*

What these *Ślokas* suggest is to transcend the indulgence at the body and sense level, and involvement at the psychic level. Whenever there is an experience of happiness one touches this state of no-mind, though for an infinitesimal length of time. This truth slips out of our observation not only because of the tiny interval of time but due to wrong identification with the ephemeral things like the body, or those things related to the body, like objects of senses, family, etc., that are *nearby* during the experience. Their contact may

---

137 नैव किन्चित्करोमीति युक्तो मन्येत तत्ववित् ।
पश्यञ्शृण्वन्स्पृशञ्जि-त्रिघ्रन्नश्नन्गाच्छन्स्वपञ्श्वसन् ॥ 5.8 ॥
प्रलपन्विसृजन्गृह्णन्नुन्मिषन्निमिषन्नपि ।
इन्द्रियाणीन्द्रियार्थेषु वर्तन्त इति धारयन् ॥ 5.9 ॥

have resulted in the experience of pleasure or pain, but what actually happens is, the mind gets *enfeebled* and touches a silence.

The next culprit is the *Ahaṁkāra* which brings in 'I-mine', evoking attachment and infatuation. To overcome the problems he suggested the seeker to eliminate desires or *Bhoga-Vāsanās* having the binding effect and to totally eschew *Bheda-Vāsanā,* having the blinding effect that *differentiates* things, events, or ideas like good and evil. As both these *Vāsanās* nurture and enhance the mental activity. The mind becomes stronger with each birth, and consequently, the whole effort gets diverted towards gain and loss of objects in the world. And by quelling *Ahaṁkāra,* which happens to be the main root of the activity of mind, this duality vanishes. After giving this introduction, Sage Vaśiṣṭha proceeded to narrate the story of Muni Uddālaka.

Muni Uddālaka lived on the slopes of Gaṅdhamādana hills, thick with sylvan and fragrant forests. He was of sharp intellect and inquiring spirit, and had purged his mind of all impurities. And yet, he had not succeeded in making his mind quiescent. But due to his *Niṣkāma Tapas,* or penance without any longing for the fruit, and observance of *Yama* and *Niyama,*[138] clear discrimination dawned on him. He began to meditate thus:

> 'What is the state, beyond all pain, the imperishable state which transcends the pangs of rebirth? Should I not seek this, instead of falling victim to the *Saṁkalpa*? He put his efforts to concentrate his mind, but it jumped

138 अहिंसासत्यास्तेयब्रह्मचर्यापरिग्रहा यमाः ।। पातंजल योगसूत्र 2.30 ।।

Yama or vows of self-restraint comprise abstention from violence, falsehood, theft, incontinence, and acquisitiveness.

शौचसंतोषतपःस्वाध्यायेश्वरप्रणिधानानि नियमाः ।। पातंजल योगदर्शनम् 2.32 ।।

Purity, contentment, austerity, self-study and self-surrender constitute *Niyama* or observances.

> from one sense object to another or from one thought to another. The internal turmoil expressed itself on the physical plane through his restless wandering in the forest. At last Muni Uddālaka came across a cave where no creature lived which was totally secluded and hard to approach. There the Muni *entered alone.* Spreading the deer skin over a grass mat, he adopted the Lotus posture and started reflecting'.

The Lotus has always found a place in the poetry of the *Vedānta.* It grows healthily in stagnant muddy water. In spite of the fact that it is born in such water the Lotus remains untouched by it. Although it is nourished by the mud and dirty water, it does not inherit any of that dirtiness or stench. On the contrary, the Lotus has always stood for the symbol of beauty and purity. Rāma has been called as *Rājīvalocana*—the Lotus eyed, not only because of their beauty, but also because of their discriminative and discerning nature. More than anything else, the Lotus symbolises *Viveka* or discrimination, arising from paradoxical experiences one meets and greets at every stage of the journey called life.

Padmāsanaṃ[139] or the Lotus posture mentioned here is not just a physical posture but more a mental posture of *aloneness,* to be adopted by a seeker interested in *Vicāra.* The most important thing is to totally quieten all mental activity. Uddālaka adopted a technique of addressing his own mind. Mind is like a mischievous child and it can be brought under control in three different ways: the first, by cajoling; secondly by admonition; and thirdly by disinterested witnessing. In cajoling, there is an effort towards understanding, while in admonition there is this force of the will and in the disinterested witnessing there is an effort to dissociate from the activity.

---

139 वामोरूपरि दक्षिणं च चरणं संस्थाप्य वामं तथा दक्षोरूपरि पश्चिमेन विधिना धृत्वा कराभ्यां दृढम् ।। हठयोगप्रदीपिका 46 ।।

Uddālaka started addressing his own mind thus: 'Oh my ignorant mind! of what use is your illusory activity? Why do you choose the hot and poisonous desert instead of the garden of Kalpa trees? All your activity is useless, capable of producing intense pain. Why are you not able to fix yourself into a state of quiescence? Oh the ever expanding and foolish mind of mine do not die like the *Kuraṅga* deer that get attracted to the sound of music created by the hunter. Do not be like the tusker madly in search of its mate, in search of the sense object of touch. Or like a moth, which loses its life for the light or the sense object of sight. You should not associate with the taste and die like a fish caught in the bait. Oh mind, do not be after even the smell to die like a bee in quest of honey, to get trapped in a lotus. Each of these dies through sound, touch, sight, taste and odour. But you are afflicted with all the five combined together. In those persons who have become recipient of *Ātmānusaṅdhānaṃ,* or being in the Self, *Manas* or the lower mind has been transcended'.

> 'Without giving up the grosser activity, how can you possibly feel and understand the subtler activity? Though the five organs are without any *Vāsanās,* they still have an *attraction* for their respective objects. So it is mandatory, that your grosser activity be totally silenced, behold the culprit of "I", the root cause of all *Saṁkalpa.* Having done this, you will see, that all your limited feeling will vanish, and the experience of all expansiveness dawn'.

Many enlightened persons have adopted this method of addressing mind in this way, not only to achieve quiescence for them, but to guide the struggling seekers. Ācārya Śaṅkara in his *Upadeśa Sāhasrī* addresses the mind thus :

> 'Oh mind, indulging in vain ideas like *me* and mine, you are not treading the path towards true peace and happiness, but that of danger. You have no discrimination of the right and wrong. On the other hand, I am always content and blissful, as I do not

depend on anything in the outside world. The proper thing for you then, is to remain quiet'.

'As I am not different from the Supreme Reality, I am always content and without any desires. Being always content, I desire no welfare for myself. Since I wish your welfare, please take my advice and have *Śama,* that is, be quiet'.[140]

Saint Kabir addresses the mind in one of his many songs:

'Oh mind, why can't you be patient?
We sense the Presence that cares for the
Animals, birds, insects, and other creatures,
If It gave you radiance while you were in the womb,
Won't It care for you outside?
Oh mind, forgetting the beauty of *Sahib* within,
Why do you roam about aimlessly?
Ignoring the beloved you go after the other as you do,
There has to be failure in whatever you do'.[141]

Samartha Rāmadāsa, the spiritual preceptor of Chatrapati Śivājī has written, what have come to be known as *Manāce Śloka* in Marāṭhī. These 205 verses are addressed to the mind and have been of great help to seekers all these centuries.

In the process of addressing his own mind, Muni Uddālaka realised, that the real culprit is *Saṁkalpa,* which must be tackled instead of senses. And the *Saṁkalpa* arises

---

140 अहं ममेति त्वमनर्थमिच्छसि परार्थमिच्छन्ति तवान्यईहितम् ।
न तेऽर्थबोधो न हि मेऽस्तिचार्थिता ततश्च युक्तः शमएवते मनः ॥
यतो न चान्यः परमात्सनातनात्सदैव तृप्तोऽहमतो न मेऽर्थिता ।
सदैव तृप्तश्च न कामये हितं यतस्वचेतः प्रशमाय ते हितम् ॥

141 अरे मन धीरज काहे न धरे, पसु पंछी जीवकीट सबकी सुद्ध करे, गर्भ वास में खबर लेतु है बाहर क्यों बिसरे
मन तू हसन से साहिब के भटकत काहे फिरे, प्रीतम छॉड़ और को धारे कारज इक न सरे ॥ कबीर दास ॥

from the mistaken notion of separateness. In this way, he went on transcending the grosser to behold the subtler principles governing his mental activity.

Sage Vasiṣṭha continued his narration: As and when Muni Uddālaka became more and more quiet, his body too adopted an elegant posture depicting his inner state of stability. In such state the sound of *Praṇava* vibrated spontaneously from him. When he intoned the first sound *Akāra,* in the *Praṇava,* having three and a half *Mātrās, Prāṇa,* the cosmic energy entered his body making it shine with effulgence. Then the process of *Recaka,* or expiration took place as the *Prāṇa* left the body, to make it light and burden less. The *Jñānāgni* or the fire of wisdom pervaded his being and burnt up all the residual *Vāsanās.* This first stage of *Praṇava* was not through the *Haṭha Yoga,* for it has a tendency to create pain. In the second stage of *Ukāra,* the immovable *Kuṁbhaka* took place, characterised by equilibrium of the external and internal breath, to bring about a state of total awareness of the body. Then the *Makāra* or third quiescent stage of *Praṇava* called *Pūraka*—inspiration, was reached. With the last half *Mātrā* of *Makāra,* total fulfillment was attained.

Muni Uddālaka, reached a state of quiescence, beyond body, senses, and mind. With these disturbing activities gone, he overcame the darkness to behold the spiritual sun, eliminating *Moha* (delusion). Gradually, he passed into *Nirvikalpa Samādhi,* the state of total quiescence. Being in the state for long, he became *Cit* (consciousness) itself, and was totally freed from attraction and aversions. Noticing this great event, the *Siddhas, Devas,* and others started flocking around him offering him their respects and also *temptations!* But the Muni was too aware to succumb to such temptations. Transcending time, Uddālaka was ever engaged in *Nirvikalpa Samādhi* and merged in the *Cit-Sāmānya* (Universal Consciousness), and then into *Sattā-Sāmānya* (Universal Beness).

Rāma then requested the sage to throw more light on the state of *Sattā-Sāmānya.* To which Vaśiṣṭha replied: When the mind being denuded of all *Vikalpas* becomes the all pervasive *Cit-Sāmānya,* and ultimately, becomes totally devoid of all thoughts, then this *Cit-Sāmānya* is itself *Sattā-Sāmānya.* When all visible things cease to have any disturbing effect on one's consciousness, and when the knowledge of all mental modifications, or *Vṛtti-Jñāna,* gets merged into the consciousness of the Self, then this consciousness is itself *Sattā-Sāmānya.* When all internal and external objects get annihilated and the traces of mind exist as Consciousness itself, then this *Cit-Sāmānya* is *Sattā-Sāmānya.* Like a tortoise withdrawing itself into its shell, if one withdraws oneself into the Self, then this state is *Sattā-Sāmānya.* That supreme vision nurtured by *Jīvanamuktas* and *Videhamuktas,* is *Sattā-Sāmānya.*

This Divine vision arises in such persons who have either developed *Samādhi* through the wisdom of *Viveka,* or voluntarily, through memory of previous actions, but never in ignorant persons who are still under the influence of body, senses, mind or *Ahaṁkāra.* Such vision is inseparable from the wise, like wind and atmosphere, or earth and odour. After living in this state for a long period, for him there was no time as he had transcended time, Uddālaka became a *Videha-mukta.*

A man used to earn his livelihood by catching the colourful birds from the forest and selling them to people interested in having them as their pets. One day, he was waiting for a transport by the side of the road. His wire cages with the innocent prisoners were kept on the ground. The bird-catcher was brooding and did not notice that one of the cages had opened, and a bird had managed to come out. The free bird started exploring the surroundings. While the others, victims in other cages, started making noise. But the man was too involved with his thoughts to hear the sound. Surprisingly, the free bird did not take any advantage of its freedom. Instead, it *re-entered* its cage! Meanwhile, a pedestrian saw the open door of the cage and pointed it out to the bird-catcher, who promptly closed it! The fate of the bird was sealed! Something similar happens to the human beings. Every now and then, we do find openings for escape, but we are very concerned about the security, social norms and customs, and *our own love for bondage,* like the bird, and miss many opportunities.

Like an anchor grounding or at least restricting the movement of the ship, mind with its activity enslaves the consciousness. Keeping it at the levels of body, senses, mind, intellect and ego all the time. The greatest impediment a seeker faces, is this ever present activity of mind that keeps changing its *content,* by constantly changing the levels of being all the time. Added to this, it also has the movement in time, like the past and the future. The only way in which the mind ceases to exist is, in the *present.* All imaginable methods try to keep the consciousness on the present. Of course, each method tries to do this from a particular level. For example, *Āsanas* do this by developing awareness at the body level. But then, unless there is persistent effort it is rather difficult. Even in an experienced seeker who has enfeebled his *Vāsanās,* like Muni Uddālaka in this story, the mind keeps jumping from one object to another.

This story suggests some Yogic techniques leading the aspirant towards *Samādhi.* It mentions the words *Yama, Niyama, Āsanaṃ, Pūraka, Recaka* and *Kuṁbhaka,* the last three of which form steps of *Prāṇāyāma.* However, it should be taken as only a general suggestion, as it keeps repeating that it has nothing to do with the *Haṭha-Yoga.* An aspirant interested in curbing the mental activity, necessarily leads a disciplined life, which is done through *Yama, Niyama;* the body, which is only the gross manifestation of the mind has to be steadied through *Āsanaṃ;* breathing is connected very intimately with the mind, that is where the *Prāṇāyāma* comes in. Only after these stages, can one hope to handle the mental activity directly, through meditation.

Generally, a seeker commits three mistakes on the meditation seat. And the three mistakes are at three different levels. First and perhaps the most gross of the mistakes the seeker commits, is *the involvement with the thoughts.* One sits and tries to keep the attention on the chosen *Mantra,* or *Devatā,* or even on one's breath. Very soon, one gets carried away into the current of thoughts. Only after a while, does one realise that one is sitting for the meditation trying to calm the mind! Through constant practice one is able to retain the memory of the *effort* for longer intervals. When this happens, one succeeds in keeping oneself *apart* from the mental activity to an extent.

At this stage, one tends to commit the second mistake of *trying to stop the thoughts.* This enforcement does have a temporary quietening effect. But when one slackens the force, the activity starts with vengeance. It is like traffic congestion. With the red signal, the traffic is *forced* to stop, but as and when it gets changed to green, it continues, perhaps with more intensity! Many meditators, experience this. During the period of their sitting, the mind does behave itself, and they have an experience of calmness. But when they get up or cease their effort, the thoughts come in torrents. So once again, the best solution is to be a non-involved witness to these thoughts. This *apartness* helps the seeker in developing the *Sākṣī-Bhāva,* and though the activity may take time to cease it will definitely cease to have a disturbing effect.

The activity does not disturb the seeker anymore, and perhaps it has thinned down to a great extent. But then one notices that there are such thoughts which one may not get during the *normal* times, when one is not on the meditation seat! They may be on violence, greed, or lust. One may not get them even in dreams. This is when the seeker tends to commit the third mistake: *of changing the thoughts from bad to good.* This act of changing the thoughts seems only justifiable, because the thoughts produce *Rāga* or attraction, and *Dweṣa* or aversion. Paradoxically, by changing the thoughts one only increases the likes and dislikes, as it means that one still has the *preferences* and *choice!* At this stage of the journey, anything and everything, only helps in *continuing* the mental activity. And the whole process of meditation is really meant to reduce this activity! A question arises as to why such thoughts float in the consciousness during meditation and not other times when one is engaged in the worldly activity? Actually, this is only apparent. While one is engaged in the so-called worldly activity, the attention is on so many other things, that one does not take note of the thoughts—may be dreams or nightmares!—which form a steady undercurrent of the consciousness. But when there is no other activity, as is the case when one is on the meditation seat, the undercurrent becomes very prominent.

The second and perhaps the stronger reason for this phenomenon, is that in spite of the fact that the mind has been quietened, the activity as such has not been *totally* curbed. It is very much there in the deeper layers of consciousness. The *Vāsanās,* forming the prime cause of the activity, are to be totally eliminated which takes infinite patience of the seeker, and perhaps, time. The difference between the so-called good and bad thoughts is only one of intensity and not of quality. But, if one learns to adopt the posture of *Sākṣī-Bhāva,* then one just becomes a disinterested witness, observing without any involvement, the mischievous child called mind.

In the mind quietening technique suggested by the Lord Buddha, one starts by observing the incoming and outgoing breaths, and then the sensations in the body, and finally on to the subtler activity of the mind. But the key is non-involved awareness. One is asked *never,* to change the breathing pattern, to hate or love *any* sensation, thought or emotion.

When one succeeds in *accepting* these *as they are* then one transcends the activity and gets established in the centre. Consequently, even when there is a tornado on the circumference, one is not disturbed. This is the implication when this story tells that Muni Uddālaka *entered the cave alone.* He was totally non-involved and had become a pure witness, established at the centre of his consciousness.

The parched earth awaits the monsoon, while the dusty leaves await the cleansing shower to remove the layer of dust over them. But they depend totally on the whims of nature. We too have to wait till the disturbing mental activity with its sense cravings, journeys into time, and the ego trips thin out. And we are privileged, to have the freedom to get disturbed and miserable—as we mostly do, or to change the mental posture of involvement to that of a non-involved witness. This posture is not really very difficult, but the eons old habit of the mental activity makes it so.

Constant change is the rule of existence. Whether it is the drought or the flood, spring or winter, nothing is eternal. And this constant change is perceivable only due to something *changeless.* The eye of the storm remains peaceful while its arms spell disaster wherever they cross. If one is able to remain at the centre or the eye, then nothing disturbs. But at the same time, one has to be careful not to have *any preference,* because it is the *choice* which takes one *away* from the centre. Without a centre the circumference cannot exist, and without a circumference, the centre becomes a meaningless point. The solution for the problem called mind is non-involvement, either with the circumference or the centre which alone paves way for the real freedom.

7

The Story of Suraghu

Heavens sprinkled snowflakes gently on the earth, flooding it with an ethereal light. The snow covered road was lined on both sides, with pines, dressed in white, like a community of brides! There was a strong stinging breeze accompanying the snow-fall that penetrated even the thick and protective winter clothing. The steep road could be seen from the open window of the horse buggy which was the only mode of transport to the distant destination : a castle on top of a foothill of the Caucasus. The buggy was coming closer to the castle, and Ouspensky, was approaching the turning point of his life.

Peter D. Ouspensky, a Russian philosopher and occultist had already carved out a name for himself in the scholastic world of philosophy. He had published a book entitled *Tertium Organum—the Third Way or Method.* And yet, he did not feel fulfilled with all the recognition and fame. And so began his quest. When he heard of George Gurdjieff, he was fascinated and sought an interview with the mystic. It was a very remote place, away from the turmoil of civilization where Gurdjieff stayed. All the scholarship did nothing to stop a peculiar nervousness that was creeping in. Finally, he reached his destination.

It is said that the mystic was in his room with his disciples at that time. When Peter sent his card inside, a person with shaven head and scary mustache, peeped out of the door, and the blood shot eyes were appraising the well known author. After a while—which Ouspensky felt like ages!—the man ordered him to write down all he knew on paper and withdrew inside. For the first time, Ouspensky started *really* assessing and evaluating his so-called knowledge. To his utter surprise, he realised that all his knowledge was only a collection of words in the form of hypotheses and theories without any personal experience! That cold night in winter, cold sweat broke on the brow of Peter Ouspensky!

Nearly an hour later, the commanding eyes could be seen again through the crack of the open door, Ouspensky confessed that he had not yet finished. The man said he could take all the time... Nearly three hours later, Peter handed over the piece of paper, totally blank! The man smiled for the first time, and asked him to enter the room. The man was Gurdjieff himself. The great Master welcomed him and said that when one realised that one knew nothing, one was really ready to learn! And so started Ouspensky's journey into himself.

Gurdjieff's teaching was based on his observation, that all actions of man are somnambulistic. During most of our actions we are asleep *to the action.* Our sleep is metaphysical, and hence our eyes are open. But there is an undercurrent of incessant dreams, and the external action as such, is mechanical. Gurdjieff used to advocate the path, which he called *'Self Remembering'*. This was called by Saint Kabir as *'Surati'*. Gurdjieff used to make his disciples perform action with total awareness. Mind, used to as it is to tread the beaten track, soon forgets and resorts to its old ways of dreaming, desiring, planning, rehearsing, etc., *during* all action. It has to be brought back again and again to the moment of action, or it has to be *present* to the action.

One of the greatest problems a seeker faces is the forgetfulness that he or she is on the path. And it is so easy, that it appears that the forgetfulness appears to have become a part of our nature! The ochre or white cloth, tonsured head or matted locks, *Rudrākṣa* beads or water gourd or any other thing which marks out a monk or a recluse was perhaps more necessary for *the seeker himself* than others who came into his contact. Because, looking at these things and using them, reminds the seeker of *her or his chosen way of life, constantly.* It is an altogether a different matter if such persons use their clothes and decorations as *investments* for exploiting the society or more dangerously, for *self-agrandization* and nourishing one's own ego!

All the paths without exception lead us towards the *self-remembrance.* In the first two limbs of Patañjali's system of *Yoga, Yama* and *Niyama,* the social as well as personal behaviour is disciplined. In the next three limbs of *Āsanas* or posture, *Prāṇāyāma* or breath control, and *Pratyāhāra* or abstraction, one is introduced to awareness through body, vital force and senses respectively. In the last three limbs, viz., *Dhāraṇā* or focusing, *Dhyāna* or meditation, and *Samādhi* or trance, one handles the mental activity directly. This method was hinted in the preceding story of Uddālaka. Similarly, all other paths direct the seeker gradually towards self-awareness. Having got established at *the Centre,* one remains unperturbed amidst all turmoil of activity.

This *Sarga* begins with the enumeration of various means and methods for quietening the mental activity. Sage Vasiṣṭha said :

> 'The Supreme State can be attained, through *Vairāgya* and *Abhyāsa* (of) contemplation and constant remembrance of the essence of the *Śāstras,* guidance of *Guru* and practices like *Yama, Niyama,* etc., or through *Prajñā* alone'.[142]

---

142 वैराग्याभ्यासशास्त्रार्थप्रज्ञागुरुयमक्रमैः ।
पदमासाद्यते पुण्यं प्रज्ञयैवैकयाथवा ॥ 5.7.2 ॥

The two mandatory wings necessary for the seeker in his spiritual flights are *Vairāgya* or renunciation and *Abhyāsa* or continual practice. They have been mentioned by Sage Patañjali in his *Yogadarśanaṃ*. After explaining the five types of *Vṛttis* he draws an outline of the whole scripture in these two words:

> 'Their (*Vṛttis'*) elimination is brought about by *Abhyāsa* and *Vairāgya*'.[143]

The *Bhagavadgītā* also mentions these, when Arjuna expresses his doubts regarding the success of a seeker in controlling the mind :

> 'The mind is no doubt very difficult to control, oh mighty-armed!
> But it can be controlled through *Abhyāsa* and *Vairāgya,* oh son of Kuṅti'.[144]

Apparently, these two concepts appear simple to us, as they are the most common words in possibly every language of India. However, the truth is that they are as difficult as their simple appearance! It is likely that one may take a lifetime to even *begin* practising them. *Abhyāsa* has been defined by sage Patañjali as:

> 'Effort towards being firmly established in that state (of *Citta-Vṛtti-Nirōdhaḥ)* is *Abhyāsa*'.[145]

Whatever effort directed towards the attainment of that transcendental state, is *Abhyāsa*. However, this effort should be for a long time, without any interruptions, and there should be devotion and a spirit of reverence.[146] Consequently, all

---

143 अभ्यासवैराग्याभ्यां तन्निरोधः ।। 1.12 ।।

144 असंशयं महाबाहो मनो दुर्निग्रहं चलम् ।
अभ्यासेन तु कौन्तेय वैराग्येन च गृह्यते ।। 6.35 ।।

145 तत्र स्थितौ यत्नाभ्यासः ।। 1.13 ।।

146 स तु दीर्घकालनैरन्तर्यसत्कारसेवितो दृढ़भूमिः ।। 1.14 ।।

other things like *Swādhyāya,* or self-study, guidance from *Guru* and *Yama-Niyama,* or the abstinence and observance, mentioned in the above *Śloka* come under *Abhyāsa.* And *Vairāgya* has been defined as follows:

> 'The awareness of the perfect mastery of desires in one who has ceased craving for all objects, seen or unseen, is *Vairāgya*'.[147]

Vairāgya has already been dealt elaborately in the first episode entitled *Vairāgya Prakaraṇa,* through Rāma's behaviour and observations about life. In short, any effort to avoid distractions on one's path is *Vairāgya. Yoga Vāsiṣṭha* makes an additional statement: 'or through *Prajñā* alone'. *Prajñā* or the awareness is the key idea in this *Śloka. Any* practice or effort without this mandatory companion is totally useless, as only the awareness can help us avoid mechanicalness in our practice. This is evident from our common experience.

In our country, we have thousands of people practising the so-called religion, in the form of ritualistic worship, counting beads and chanting names. Many of us practise even *Āsanas, Prāṇāyāma* and *Dhāraṇā,* for long periods and *continually,* so much so, that some of us partake of the food only after performing our daily devotions! But unfortunately, all the years of practice does not bring about *any* change in our life-style and habits! For instance, while telling beads and chanting names, the fingers move while the lips do the chanting. But the mind *continues* it planning, scheming, or brooding! Or the practitioner *forgets* that he has to be *totally awake* during the practice! The forgetfulness makes the practice mechanical, reducing it to empty gestures, and meaningless rituals.

Prajñā is so all-encompassing, that it has the capacity to help the seeker in everything else, including *Abhyāsa* and

---

147 दृष्टानुश्रविकविषयवितृष्णस्य वशीकारसंज्ञा वैराग्यम् ।। 1.15 ।।

Vairāgya. That may be the reason why, George Gurdgieff stressed only on *self-remembrance.* After entering into the inner circle of disciples, Ouspensky was asked by Gurdgieff, whether he remembers *who he is,* all the time. Without any hesitation, Peter said that he does. But when he was made to sit with closed eyes and just repeat 'I am Ouspensky', Peter discovered that he could do so only three times after which the mind would get distracted! When Peter confessed it, he was told by the Master that he was not an exception, but a general rule! Gradually, he was made to perform every little action no matter how insignificant, with total awareness.

Nearly three months later, Gurdgieff took Ouspensky to a town nearby. Ouspensky discovered to his utter surprise, that almost everyone walked and performed action *as if* in deep sleep. It was as though everyone was suffering from somnambulism.

They were driving the vehicles, walking, talking, eating, and even laughing in sleep! He was frightened, and requested Gurdgieff to take him back immediately. Psychologists agree on this point that the long distance drivers of vehicles tend to spend most of their time *in fantasies* to avoid fatigue! While their eyes are on the road and their limbs handle the vehicles, mechanically!

At the above statement of Vasiṣṭha, Rāma posed a question. There are two classes of men, one class frees itself from all pain to attain the Non-dual *Jñāna* through *Samādhi,* by remaining in the world of action. While the other class, disengages itself totally, from all the worldly activity to retire into *Samādhi.* Rāma wanted to know, which of these two classes is superior.

Sage Vasiṣṭha replied that peace arises out of *Samādhi* in the hearts of such persons who have seen through the temporality of the world made of three *Guṇas.* Some of them remain in *Swarūpa-Samādhi* without involving themselves in any external activity, nor longing for any objects. While others go into *Samādhi* amidst all activity. There is no difference between them, *provided the mind remains calm.* Such calmness generates the merits of great *Tapas.* The person, who is in such state, transcends all pleasure and pain, in spite of being engaged in action. And if the mind is agitated while sitting motionless, it is no *Samādhi* at all. But if the mind is free of all *Vāsanās* even if the body is intensely active as when one is while dancing, such a state is *Samādhi.* There is no difference whatsoever between the *Jñānins* who retire into a forest and those who remain amidst the world of activity. With the elimination of all *Vāsanās* any action performed is *as if not done,* like the mind of a person deeply engaged within, does not hear the story told by the story teller. If there are innate *Vāsanās* inside, it performs actions in the dream state, even if the gross mind is quiet and the body paralysed.

Sage Vasiṣṭha continued that the two types of visions called *Dhyāna* and *non-Dhyāna* differ through the steadiness and the fluctuation of mind. Therefore one must destroy all *Vāsanās,* which generate thoughts. The Quiescence and *Kaivalya* pertain to the mind only. A mind devoid of all worry and desire rests into the state of *Nirvāṇa.* After freeing oneself from the snares of 'I' and its host of conceptions, it hardly matters where one lives, whether one lives in a house or the hills or any other place. The abode of householders of quiescent mind, not tainted by any *Ahaṁkāra* can well be a forest. Persons strolling through a market without any longing for things therein are like the persons who never go there. Similarly to persons full of spiritual beatitude, cities and woods do not make any difference.

The enlightened sage continued that whenever the mind is agitated, the universe too appears agitated. For the world *as one perceives it,* is only the manifestation of one's own mind. On the other hand, if one is calm within, the world too appears calm and beautiful. A person, who is continually directing his energy towards silencing the mind by eliminating all

Vāsanās, does not get involved with any wasteful activity. Vasiṣṭha Muni reminded Rāma, that the essence of what he had said so far, was to help the seeker understand that the prime goal is to quieten the mind, just like all the names are simplified into one *Praṇava,* or *AUM* to describe the *Brahman.*

The comparison between one who retreats from action, and the other remaining amidst action, as asked by Rāma, crosses our mind once in a while. This much is true, that perhaps to stop *questioning* and to commence the *quest,* one has to retreat from such disturbing environment which keeps the outward flow of the mind. Like the wonderful example of Shri Ramakrishna, in which he compares the mind with milk, and the world with water, to keep the milk pure, we have to keep it away from water!

But then, just physical retreat or stillness is not enough. If one sits still in a meditative posture—may be like a statue of the Buddha, but is unable to keep his mind from wandering it is of no use. On the contrary, there is the danger of the ego creeping in, which nurtures the complacency that if one is doing *spiritual practices,* one is superior to others, who are not! There is a beautiful *Śloka* in the *Bhagavadgītā* :

> 'A short-sighted man keeps *remembering* the objects of senses, having controlled *Karmendriyas*—the instruments of action, he is said to be engaged in the act of hypocrisy'.[148]

Vaslav Nijinsky is a legend in the field of dancing. The most wonderful aspect of his dance was the unbelievable jumps and drops he would take, during the ballet. The people who saw him dance felt that the gravitation had very little effect on him! It was as though he had become a feather in breeze! When people asked him as to how he achieved this next to impossible task, he replied that he too was as much

148 कर्मेन्द्रियाणि संयम्य य आस्ते मनसा स्मरन् ।
इन्द्रियार्थान्विमूढात्मा मिथ्याचारः स उच्यते ॥ 3.6 ॥

surprised as the audience! Because, he said frankly, when *he tried,* he never succeeded. But it always happened, when *he* lost *himself* in the dance. What he meant to say was that the *dancer* had totally merged with the *dance.* And that there was no *'dancer's ego'*. Unfortunately, his companions could not understand him nor did they try to, and thus help him. Consequently he was declared to be schizophrenic, which ultimately forced him to retire in 1919, at the age of twenty-nine. Had he come in contact with a person like Gurdgieff, things would have been altogether different!

The symbol of *Naṭarāja* or the Lord of Dancers, is based on this concept that, in spite of all the hectic activity of the *Tāṇḍava-dance* in which creation and destruction goes on simultaneously and continually, the dancer as such—Lord Śiva—remains unaffected and is totally merged with his dance. In other words, the dance has become totally spontaneous and effortless. Similarly, when the activity of the mind (including *Ahaṁkāra)* has been quietened, the external activity and state makes no difference. And such person's external condition, activity or withdrawal from it, depends on her or his nature. Another aspect of *Śiva* is: *Śāntaṃ-Śivaṃ-Adwaitaṃ*—totally peaceful, devoid of activity, auspicious and Non-dual. This again has an esoteric and hidden meaning, behind it. Existence cannot be, without its two wings of activity and rest. The dance represents the activity while the silence represents peace and rest. Both activity and rest co-exist from the lowest to the highest form of life. To illustrate that there is no difference between the two classes of persons, the great sage Vasiṣṭha narrated the story of Suraghu.

A class of hunters named Hemajaṭā lived in the Kailāśa hills in the Himalayan range. They were adepts in archery. Their king Suraghu, a matchless warrior reigned over the kingdom administering justice with an impartial spirit. Naturally he had to protect the virtuous and chastise the vicious. Sometimes his justice would bring pain and misery to those who did not lead a *Dhārmic* or righteous life. The following ideas crossed his mind. Being their king he had a position of power and strength. In fulfilling his responsibilities, some people were being afflicted by his justice. They may have committed the crimes due to some innate helplessness. Was not their misery his, who was their king? At the same time, it was his duty to mete out punishments according to the *Dharma Śāstras,* to protect the virtuous and the meek. Thus there was a conflict in his mind. At this time, Muni Māṇḍavya appeared, to whom he poured out his tale of woe of the conflict.

Muni Māṇḍavya consoled him by telling him that all the stains of the mind will be washed away through *Ātma-Vicāra,* like fog disappearing in the rays of the sun. He continued that one has to engage oneself in reflecting over the questions: 'Who am I? Whence came this universe? How came birth and death'? Such *Vicāra* takes one to a subtler state, when the mind becomes subservient to the will, freeing one from all conflict and the resultant pain. For a calm mind, that is free from all paradoxes, the worldly actions appear trivial, while the same paradoxes appear as the insurmountable obstacles to a disturbed mind.

The great sage Māṇḍavya observed that the farther one is from these snares of the universe, the nearer will one be to the *Brahman.* Unless one is totally free from the objects, the true Principle cannot be cognised. So the first thing one has to do is to eliminate the *longing* for the objects of senses. As and when the longing drops, one becomes available to pure *Jñāna.* If after dropping the gross *Vāsanās* one succeeds in eliminating the *Vāsanās* of even the body, the stainless, beneficent Principle will dawn on the person. The Muni returned to the abode of silence.

Suraghu, the king of hunters withdrew to a solitary place and began to inquire into the origin of 'I'. Examining his own body, he noticed that it is the most affected among things which are subject to change and it was childish to apply the epithet to body. Composed as it is of bones, flesh, etc. it is the grossest of all manifestations. Then he saw through the ten *Indriyas,* the instruments of knowledge and action are always referred to as 'my' *Indriyas.* The *Indriyas* are also only grosser manifestations. Thus, reflecting Suraghu achieved *Antarmukhatā,* and the mental activity turned its attention totally on the 'I', which melted into the cosmic Principle. Having establishing himself into the Infinite, the rush for the objects of senses and the mind vanished. His vision became equanimous, freeing him from the *bondage* of actions and hence from the paradoxes of duality.

Suraghu had a friend called Parigha in the race of Pārasīka, who too was a king. Finding that his subjects suffered greatly on account of drought which continued for ten long years in his kingdom, Parigha was heartbroken. That was why, he gave up all desire for food, and performed arduous *Tapas,* feeding himself upon dry leaves. This action of his, brought him the name Parṇāda.[149] In due course, Parṇāda attained *Ātmajñāna.* He appeared before Suraghu, who welcomed him with reciprocal affection. They exchanged their experiences. After making enquiry about the welfare of his friend, Parṇāda made a long speech on the qualities and characteristics of *Ātmajñānis.* While Suraghu listened to him in all joy. When Parṇāda concluded that Suraghu had attained the Brāhmic State and that his heart had been liberated, Suraghu smilingly added that one can attain the Highest when all longing for the fruit of action ceases and the mind remains quiescent. He said that such an enlightened man can never experience forgetfulness as there is the continual and constant current of *Prajñā* as the *Śruti* or the monotone which guides the music.

Activity of *any kind,* mostly originates with desire for fruit of that action. In fact, almost all our actions are motivated by the desire for their respective fruits. And desires are nothing

---

149 Parṇāda is derived from *Parṇa* meaning leaves.

but *peeps into future,* when we *stop accepting* the condition we are presently in. This great goad for action called desire is the one which contributes to most of the progress made by human beings. Not only that, but it gives us the will to survive and live. While for most of us desire is almost as mandatory as breath itself, for those of us who have got glimpses into the deeper dimensions and have realised that survival is *not the only* aspect of life, desire becomes a great barrier.

Moreover every action, no matter how insignificant, has a potential conflict in it. For a king like Suraghu, who is meting out his duties justly it is more so, as he has to be very objective to punish the wrong doers. But if he becomes sensitive to the pain of others, and is also very much conscious of his duties, as was the case with Suraghu, this duty consciousness becomes a great burden. It is at this time, that one needs spiritual guidance. When one arrives at a stage in which she or he is receptive to deeper truths, the help arrives on its own.

Maharshi Ramana was approached by people from all walks of life. In his presence everyone would experience a peace, of course, according to the eligibility of the one who approached him. The seekers who had managed to calm their gross mental activity would be invariably given one panacea for *all* their problems! For a person having a conflict he would ask: '*Who* is having this conflict?', and suggest her or him to trace out the *experiencer* of the conflict. Initially, it was always confusing as invariably the answer would pop up: '*I* am having the conflict, *Who* else?!' The Maharshi would then ask the person to trace this very entity whom she had called '*I*'.

But if the conflict was to the point disturbance then the person, would not be able to catch the mood of this wonderful question. And that was why, the great sage Ramana would recommend some easier methods to such people, so as to have their mental activity under control. And when the mental activity had reduced considerably, invariably, the suggestion would work wonders as it led the seeker towards *Antarmukhatā* the mandatory preliminary step in spirituality. Muni Māṇḍavya advised Suraghu to start the process of tracing the root of all experience, the 'I', which led him towards enlightenment.

While Suraghu does his spiritual practices while performing his duties, Parṇadā's life illustrates that one can also totally withdraw from active life to plunge into a life dedicated to *Sādhanā,* and to receive the same *Jñāna,* that was caught by Suraghu. One thought that gets repeated often in this *Śāstra,* is the *uniqueness* of the individual. There is no hard and fast rule with *should,* and *must.* Almost *anything* can trigger a disinterest and renunciation towards things which *were* held dear to heart, leading one towards the spirit of inquiry. This is evident from the lives of innumerable saints, including a robber, like Ratnākar who became the Vālmīki the great author of the present scripture, and a murderer, like Angulimāla who was transformed under the guidance of the Buddha. This repetition is done to warn the seeker that she or he should be careful *never to imitate.*

There are millions of species of living organisms, including those which are *in between* like the viruses! And there is perhaps more variety on the psychological plane, with its varieties of moods, emotions and thoughts, having a constant kaleidoscopic change. The creativity of the Reality or Truth is so infinite that it can go on for ages and yet remain inexhaustible! By imitating what we do is to undermine this wonderful fact and in turn underestimate ourselves.

Adventure sports are becoming more and more popular. Whether it is a thrilling ride on the rapids through the mountainous terrain, or scaling the heights of a snow peaked mountain, or skiing on the slopes of mountain glacier or skating on a crystal clear lake behind a speeding boat, or jumping from the mountain peaks for hand-gliding, or participating in car and motorcycle races and rallies, human beings are definitely seeking something more than just sensual pleasure.

Because in spite of the fact that sensuality is reckless as far as the health is concerned, it cannot be callous towards life. When some of these adventurers were asked as to why they involve in such dangerous sports, the answer was that they felt alive only when they faced the challenge of death. If we just analyse, we are pleasantly surprised to discover, that in those moments of danger, the adventurer is *forced* to be totally *alert.* And to the people for whom life has become mechanical and boring, a few moments of alertness act as elixir to renew their zest for life!

Each one of us has the capacity for achieving the Highest through the singular path, *meant* for each one of us. The act of searching for that very path, the trials and tribulations one faces during the search and the joy of its discovery are more than any adventure we embark on, in the physical plane. Because, what really is mandatory in spirituality is the *unbroken Prajñā* or the *awareness.* And even if there is an insignificant lapse on the part of the seeker, he can become a victim of a great fall into the abysm of unconsciousness animal-hood.

Aitareyopaniṣad declares:

> 'Existence has the eye of *Prajñānaṃ,* it exists in *Prajñānaṃ* and it rests in *Prajñānaṃ,* and that is why, *Prajñānaṃ* is the Highest *Brahman'.*[150]

When a seeker sows the seed, nurtures the seedling, looks after and protects the young plant and cares for the tree of awareness, the awareness in turn does the same to the seeker, only in a more benign way! And without this mandatory companion, no practice can do *anything* to the seeker, except perhaps, give an elusive satisfaction of reaching the horizon! The awareness gives the much needed patience, and in turn makes the seeker dance his way to enlightenment, lightly and gracefully without any anxiety or worry. Because, the awareness makes the seeker realise that every step is the horizon she or he had been seeking!

---

150 प्रज्ञाने प्रतिष्ठितं प्रज्ञानेत्रो लोकः प्रज्ञा प्रतिष्ठा **प्रज्ञानं ब्रह्म** ।। 3.1.3 ।।

8

The Story of the Dialogue Between Bhāsa and Vilāsa

A rivulet sang shyly, almost in a whisper, careful not to disturb the sleeping monk under the *Pipal* tree. The night birds like the bats and the owls were retreating to their nests, tired after their nocturnal activity for survival. The other birds were stretching their wings and slowly beginning the songs of adoration and welcome to a new dawn with fresh experiences. While the tree itself was slowly stirring to the gentle morning breeze. Stars—the guardians of the night, were slowly merging into the expansive sky that was turning from velvety blackness to a Prussian blue. The horizon became violet-red with the presence of dawn, which has been addressed as the sister of the sun in Vedic hymns.

The eyes of the monk opened very gracefully, like the petals of a lotus blossoming to the rays of the sun. They beheld the only shining object in the sky: planet Venus. He sat in the *Siddhāsanaṃ,* and continued to gaze at the planet which slowly started disappearing into the infinite blue expanse, his mind too disappeared and he finally woke up from his long sleep, to become the Buddha, the Enlightened one. The tree, the river, the birds and the whole surroundings became witness to one of the rarest events. It is said, trees have played a very important role in the life at the Buddha. He was born under a tree, he got enlightened under a tree, he invariably lived and taught sitting under trees, and he dropped his body under a tree. So much so, for more than two or three hundred years after his death, the Buddha was represented by a tree. It was much later that the statues of a figure in the yogic meditative posture were introduced to symbolise Him.

It is said when one of the two friends—an early riser, tried waking up his friend—a lover of sleep, saying that the latter did not know what he was missing : the freshness in the air, the bird-songs, the dawn and the wonderful sun-rise! The other just peeped through the folds of his blanket and observed with a yawn, that the early riser did not realise what *he was missing: the early morning sleep, the sweetest sleep!* And went back to sleep. Each one of us has his own or her own value system. A wish to share what is most enjoyable to us, with our dear ones is quite natural. But if they have never had the opportunity to taste it, they are resistant. Shri Ramakrishna used to tell a parable to illustrate this point:

> 'Once a fisherwoman was a guest in the house of a gardener who raised flowers. She came there with her empty basket, after selling fish in the market, and was asked to sleep in the room where flowers were kept. But because of the fragrance of the flowers, she could not get sleep for a long time. Her hostess saw her condition and said, "Hello! Why are you tossing from side to side so restlessly?" The fisherwoman said: "I don't know friend. Perhaps the smell of the flowers has been disturbing my sleep. Can you give me my fish basket? Perhaps that will put me to sleep." The basket was brought to her. She sprinkled water on it and set it near her nose, then she fell sound asleep and snored all night'.[151]

Sleep is not just physical, but in a more intense way metaphysical. While the physical sleep can be broken with little or

151 *The Gospel of Shri Ramakrishna* by M, Sri Ramakrishna Math, Madras, IXth Impression, 1988, pp. 433-34.

no difficulty, the meta-physical sleep is very very difficult to overcome. This is so because, it is an ancient sleep deeply connected with our sub-conscious or the unconscious, which helped us to evolve from inanimate to animate level *and to survive.* This collective mind is very much there, as a part of each brain and mind. Thus most of our activity is instinctive and unconscious. Like the incomplete carving of a slave in captivity by the famous sculptor and painter Michelangelo, man slowly struggles to come out of his unconscious existence. Man is only stirring in his unconscious sleep and is only partially conscious of his limitations. Precisely for this reason, man knows misery—as different from pain, and joy—as different from only sensual appeasement or the *absence* of misery. He becomes aware of his limitations and tries to come out of them to move towards more and more freedom. This movement is a long and arduous journey of the individual towards freedom. And understanding the dynamics of desire come a long way in one's inner journey.

Desires are either the modified pleasant experiences of the past, or the imagined pleasures at the mental level, which help the mind to intensify its activity. Every desire, big or small, makes the groove in which the mind moves. If we observe the desire closely we find that it is always an *improved* past experience! For example, if we have had a brief experience of happiness through a sense, we try to have a *prolonged* experience. That is how, the consumerism succeeds in tempting the consumer, by *promising* long lasting, or stronger pleasures. And we cannot possibly desire anything which is unknown. So much so, for most if not all of us, even God is a projection who fulfills our desires. Because for most of us God is unknown, while we approach him with some demand or the other! More radically, even the so-called God is our desire! We either approach him out of need or out of fear, evident from our demand for the fulfillment of a desire or for immortality, as we are afraid of death!

In this sense, desire is like an avenue which gives room to move for the mind and as the past is dead and no more, it is like a dead weight which gives *momentum* to the activity called mind, while the future is only a projection of past. And in this process of dwelling in either past or future, as both are almost identical, we sleep to the present, making our actions somnambulistic. In the strictest sense, time consists of only an eternal present, while the past and the future belong to mind! Psychological time characterised by the *becoming,* does not move but *we move,* giving a feeling that the time moves! Consequently, the act of desiring or in general the activity of mind does not require *any awareness* as it keeps moving on the beaten track, as all the acts become mechanical or robopathic. The awareness on the other hand, is always in the present where the desire or the past projected into future, can never exist.

The Buddha has given a very practical understanding of the desires, and given out means of transcending them. In the method of meditation suggested by him, which is called as the *Vipassana,* or a special way of seeing: One is required to start by observing the incoming and outgoing breath, and then gradually pass on to the bodily sensations, mind and on to subtler planes. Initially, the seeker cannot keep his attention on the breath even for a short while. But as and when one is able to do so, she or he is asked to start observing the bodily sensations *without any involvement.* Naturally, one finds that there are pleasant as well as unpleasant sensations. One is asked neither to *like* the pleasant nor to *hate* the unpleasant sensations.

The most important thing the seeker is asked to practise is to maintain the equanimity amidst the pleasant as well unpleasant sensations and thoughts and to abstain from all *reaction.* Tathāgata suggests that, the equanimity, alone leads us to *Samma-ditthi*—the right understanding, of the world *as it is,* and not as *it appears to be.* He assures that such understanding leads one to *Paññā (Prajñā)* or awareness. Normally, we understand or misunderstand a situation or person *coloured* by our desires which in turn are based on our *Rāgas*—attractions and *Dweṣas*—aversions. While the attractions are related to the pleasant, and the aversions to the unpleasant experiences of the past that get strengthened by the positive and negative involvement respectively. He gives out a very vivid analysis of the *Chain of Conditioned Arising* :

'With the base of ignorance, *reaction* arises;
with the base of *reaction,* consciousness arises;
with the base of consciousness, mind and body arise;
with the base of mind and body, the six senses arise;
with the base of six senses, contact arises;
with the base of contact, sensation arises;
with the base of sensation, craving and aversion arise;
with the base of craving and aversion, attachment arises;
with the base of attachment, the process of becoming arises;
with the base of the process of becoming, birth arises;
with the base of birth, aging and death arise, together with sorrow, lamentation, physical and mental sufferings and tribulations.
Thus arises this entire mass of suffering'.[152]

The best way, the Buddha suggests, is to refrain from any kind of reaction—positive by craving, or negative through avoidance or aversion. In other words, the mind as such is just a storage instrument like the hard disk drive in a computer. And it is not only the mind of an individual, but of the existence itself. It is the memory gathered during the millions of years of evolution. Each individual cell has a mind of its own, as far as its functions and reactions are concerned. It is said that if we gather all the information inherent in all

---

152 *The Discourse Summaries* by S. N. Goenka, Vipashyana Vishodhan Vinyas, Bombay, 1990, p. 91.

the systems in the body, including the brain, it cannot be contained even in the largest library! While describing the structure and functions of brain Carl Sagan says:

> 'Like all our organs, the brain has evolved, increasing in complexity and information content, over millions of years. Its structure reflects all the stages through which it has passed. The brain evolved from inside out. Deep inside is the oldest part, the brainstem, which conducts the basic biological functions, including the rhythm of life—heartbeat and respiration... Capping the brainstem is the R-complex, the seat of aggression, ritual, territoriality and sexual hierarchy, which evolved hundreds of millions of years ago in our reptilian ancestors. Deep inside the skull of every one of us there is something like a brain of a crocodile. Surrounding the R-complex is the limbic system or mammalian brain, which evolved tens of millions of years ago in our ancestors who were mammals but not yet primates. It is a major source of our moods and emotions, of our concern and care for the young.
>
> 'And finally, on the outside, living in uneasy truce with the more primitive brains beneath, is the cerebral cortex, which evolved millions of years ago in our primate ancestors. The cerebral cortex, where matter is transformed into consciousness, is the point of embarkation for all our cosmic voyages. Comprising more than two-thirds of the brain mass, it is the realm of both intuition and critical analysis. It is here that we have ideas and inspirations, here that we read and write, here that we do mathematics and compose music. The cortex regulates our conscious lives. It is the distinction of our species, the seat of our humanity. Civilization is a product of the cerebral cortex'.[153]

153 *Cosmos* by Carl Sagan, Random House, New York, 1983, pp. 275-77.

And so, our so-called mind is more an activity in the gross brain than the subtle. All our responses, hungers and desires are reptilian or at the most, part of cerebral cortex. Our arguments, show of superiority, and the arms race, is nothing but an aspect of territoriality; and our desires are nothing but *modified* or *altered* urges for survival! But then, the brain requires energy—electro-chemical, to function. Like a computer which cannot function on its own, without the energy supply, the activity of mind too cannot start without the individual's energy in the form of attention. And so, we *need not* be the helpless victims of either the desires or mind, because *we* only activate them with *our* energy. Unfortunately *we are* helpless for various reasons. One of them being the strongest memory of the instinctive reactions in the long history of evolution from the lowest life forms to human beings. The second and perhaps a stronger reason is, that we can continue to be unconscious and instinctive to tread the beaten track! Every spiritual practice consists of freeing oneself from the old habit of instinctive reaction and to become the master of one's instruments, instead of being their slaves. That is why, Swami Vivekananda used to say that the goal of life is a journey of the animal-man to Man-man and then towards the Divine-man. The present *Sarga* intends to show that life without *Samādhi* is just a dark and tragic story of pain and misery.

Sage Vasiṣṭha said, that after their dialogue, Suraghu and Parigha performed their activity according to their nature. The bull of *Jīva* or the being continues his slumber under the shadows of *Moha* or infatuation in the forest of *Saṁsāra*. He is only guided by basic instinct, and blind and mindless reactions. This is because he is bound by strong cords of desire. Wisdom lies in realising oneself to be separate from this lower activity. One can achieve this with the association of the wise and the experienced.

If the wise and experienced persons do not live in a place, a place which is like a beautiful oasis, becomes poisonous and vicious. As the beauty or the sense comforts only enhance the animal instincts which further deepen the groves of the mind. At such a place that is devoid of wisdom, wealth, friendship, *Śāstras,* even the charitable actions do not help one in attaining *Mokṣa,* as these only increase the ego. Only awareness helps in attaining freedom. If the mind is made receptive to the higher influence and thus commence the spiritual inquiry, one can reach a subtler life consisting of the ripe mind that creates no disturbance.

When the activity in the mind as such stops, one experiences *Turya*—the fourth stage, in which all objects cease to have their individual influence on one's being. Instead, one develops the unified vision over all of them, like the goldsmith seeing only gold in all the myriad of ornaments. This however, can never be described verbally as it is an experience beyond speech and mind. Only after this experience, that the *Vāsanās* for objects cease; that the light of the non-dual Principle dawns. Through equal vision the duality gets eliminated. This is the experience of all great souls. But without this man continues to go deeper into the mire of *Saṁsāra.* To illustrate this, the Sage said, that he would narrate a story.

Atri, the great sage had two sons who were *Munis.* They lived in his hermitage on the hills of Sahya. Their names were Bhāsa and Vilāsa, and loved each other so intensely that they seemed to be like the offshoots of one and the same trunk. On the death of their parents they went through the necessary obsequies and parted from each other sorrowfully. After spending a lot of time in the woods in penance, they denuded themselves of all desire. Then they met again.

It was Muni Vilāsa who spoke first, expressing his joy on meeting his beloved brother Bhāsa. He inquired whether the latter had mastered the mind and whether he was happy. To which Bhāsa happy on the reunion with his beloved brother said, that the mind still involved in the *Saṁsāra,* and still he was very far from the state of knowing. He was still under the influence of mind, and was subject to the wheel of birth and death. And so long as one was not open to the Non-dual state, one could neither be happy nor peaceful. In course of time, when they had sufficiently engaged themselves in *Ātma-Vicāra* and *Tapas,* both the brothers became receptive to the state of *Kaivalya* or the perfect state.

Man's effort to alleviate the discomfort in nature, and to exploit its resources with the hope of increasing the comforts in expectation of increasing the happiness, has resulted in the civilization. The two offshoots of this pursuit are Science and Technology. It is true, that they have more than succeeded in the first two objectives. But unfortunately, the happiness still eludes man. A poor man, who does not have enough to make both ends meet, is no doubt unhappy. Hunger may be gnawing at his vitals, there may not be enough cloth to hide the his and his family's nakedness. He may not have a roof over his head. But when one looks at the rich we see misery! There is no satisfaction even though he is surrounded by the plenty; no comfort in spite of comfort giving objects; although his coffers are filled to the brim there is no fulfillment.

This does not, in any way mean, that we have to deny this important external development. Science and Technology are to be used, to feed the hungry, to clothe the naked and to provide shelter for the shelter-less. However, *man should not be used by them!* They are our tools and instruments, but unfortunately, man has become their tool! Man is distinguished from other animals only because of his capacity to think, reason, and understand. The instruments which help him do these are the brain—which as we know is the most advanced computer!, and the mind, a storehouse of impressions and potential desires! Just like Science and

Technology, which are the products of these very instruments, but perhaps in a more intense way, brain and mind have become highly dominant discords in man's life, because he has become their slave.

When does any slavery stop? When the slave *realises* that he is a slave. And that is possible only when the slave is able to *stand apart, even from himself.* The repeated shocks in the form of pains, indicate that there is something wrong. A man who is too involved with either his sense indulgence or ambitions does not even realise the slavery in his actions. But one who gets repeated punches from existence, is bound to do so, sooner or later. At such times, he succeeds in learning about the limitations of his instruments. He may begin by observing others, but ultimately he has to come to himself, when *Vairāgya* or renunciation dawns on him. With this wonderful companion he is able to befriend others like *Abhyāsa,* which is an effort to *stand apart* from the brain and mind, and *Viveka* or intuitive discrimination, which in turn encourages *Vicāra* or the meditative contemplation.

Siddhartha Gautama, did not have any dearth of comforts. In fact, his father Śuddhodhana, had seen to it that his son is never exposed to any kind of discomfort. But the previous experiences and observations precipitated when he saw the old man, the dead body and the monk with a peaceful countenance. His withdrawal from the kingship was only a beginning which blossomed into a fruitful withdrawal into himself. And the enlightenment dawned on him when he succeeded in disconnecting himself totally from these instruments.

Tathāgata spent almost forty years helping those in misery, spreading the fragrance of the enlightenment, after that cosmic event under the *Bodhi* tree. He must have taken the help of the brain and the mind while guiding and speaking to his disciples for leading them towards enlightenment and also freeing others from misery. But he used them as a master employs his servants, to do his bidding. And yet, *He* did not say anything, because he had freed himself from the instruments. He must have walked hundreds of miles, from village to village in his ministry. Yet, *He* did not move at all, as he had become like a car, the engine of which has been put off, and is moving only due to the inherent momentum down the hill!

9

The Story of Vītahavya

As the twilight fades, one can barely make out the surrounding stark volcanic landscape. The crescent moon hangs over the distant horizon. While the silhouettes of half a dozen telescopes rise from the mountain like temples dedicated to the night sky. Nearly fourteen thousand feet below, the waves lash at the warm beaches of Hawaii's Big Island. It is the summit of Mauna Kea, where the temperature is near freezing. It holds *Keck Telescope,* collecting and focusing starlight from throughout the universe with a primary mirror of glass that measures ten meters across. Telescopes like these have become the eyes of the astronomers who peep into space and time.

An astronomer strains his eyes to look into the past—as the light from the stars and the star systems that he beholds presently had left its sources years back, some of them even millions of years! It is like having a review of the events that took place long back. As his eyes seek the celestial object—a distant galaxy in some constellation, he becomes totally oblivious to his surroundings. The freezing cold has hardly any effect over his body. The sandwich kept in a paper plate goes stale and coffee, cold; the disturbance caused by a letter from home, the problem of a slight misunderstanding with his friend,... just vanish from his consciousness. For him the telescope is not just an instrument, but his *own extended eyes!* The computer decoding thousands of signals, and directing the mirrors is no more an electronic device, but his own brain. He has totally identified with his instruments—telescope, computer, etc. The only thing principal in his attention is the object of his search, and a thirst to absorb as much information as possible.

Man's condition is almost similar to that of the astronomer. He too is lost in his ruminations on the past, or projections into future. His instruments are the senses and the mind. At the same time, there are some vital differences. Though the astronomer is lost while at work, he does return to the present, may be after a few hours, when the eastern horizon again starts blushing! Man is not only seeped in the mire of sense indulgence to become a slave to his senses, but has also become a helpless victim of his *Antaḥkaraṇa*—the inner instrument. So his sleep of self-forgetfulness is much deeper and chronic!

Most of us are so, because of the fact that we consider ourselves to be *only* body, senses or at the most, mind. Such indulgence and involvement is only natural, because millions of years of evolution and the struggle for survival demanded it. The bank of knowledge, preserved as it is in the brain, helps us to survive while facing day-to-day problems. This self-preservative instinct has been named by Sigmund Freud as *Eros*. All activity of all the creatures, whether it is fear, hunger, sleep, or procreation, comes under *Eros.*

It would have been of little consequence, if man too *remained* stuck to only survival. But man as we know, is a rational and thinking creature, and this fact creates complications. By his very nature man *cannot* be satisfied with mere survival. But since he is endowed with wonderful body, senses and an equally wonderful mind which by nature are turned outwards, all he can think and dream of, is bettering his external life by improving and increasing the sense objects that give him pleasures, although they are momentary. The other plane he involves himself is the mental plane. He wants to explain his surroundings as well as his own behaviour, and his search has brought about a revolution through the information he has gathered and is continuing to gather. He is moved by certain events and conditions, to the familiar emotions of fear, anger, disgust, wonder and love. Thus the mind and the intellect react to the *external* situation.

Consequently, he is obsessed only by the *outside* at the cost of the *inside* which is infinitely larger. The science—which is his own brain child, too recognises and pursues only the external objects that can be perceived only by the senses, including those *extensions* like the Telescope, Microscope, etc. So Science and, her all powerful daughter Technology, aim to make life more and more comfortable. Even man's attempts to explain his own behaviour is directed *outside,* because he tries to understand *himself* by looking at *others,* who are *outside.* That is how all his efforts tend to leave most of himself, from observation. Scientists around the world, are slowly realising that in their method they are considering only the tip of the iceberg leaving most of it, as only the tip is *perceivable* to the senses or the sensitive instruments which are only their extensions. However, all actions performed, are in some way or the other have satisfaction and happiness as their aim, which are the *inner* phenomena. But the search for them is unfortunately directed outside. Because of this, instead of being comfortable and leisurely, man is becoming more and more greedy, anxious, tense and miserable.

As the sense gratification is only temporary, he remains dissatisfied. His aspiration to better himself, and his perpetual state of discontent definitely help him to progress technologically but they also generate frustrations. Because by very nature, senses and the mind are limited in their capacity to enjoy. Moreover, the repeated sense indulgence further reduces their capacity. There is an episode in *Kaṭhopaniṣad.* Naciketā approaches Yama, the Lord of death for knowing the *Brahman.* Just to test the sincerity of the aspirant, Yama offers him celestial enjoyments in lieu of the sacred knowledge. Alert Naciketā observes:

> 'Oh Destroyer (Death), the enjoyments you have offered me are not permanent and keep reducing the capacity of the senses. And this life itself is very short, so let the vehicles, dances and songs remain with you'![154]

Sigmund Freud discovered that there is another complimentary instinct to *Eros,* it is *Thanatos,* the instinct for self-destruction or the *death wish,* leading man towards his death. Because of his extreme attachment to life, man gets more frustrated. Animals on the other hand, take death as naturally as life, because they do not suffer from attachment to life. Since man is extremely attached to life through his desires and dreams, he does get frustrated and can and does entertain a wish to end it all, when the desires and dreams do not get fulfilled.

In this sense, *Eros* and *Thanatos* together cover all desires necessary for survival, and form something like a bridge. Without them survival itself is not possible. They both are complimentary in the sense that they are just obverse and reverse of desire in general. However, life is not just survival. It is infinitely more. Our so-called ordinary life is governed by laughter, tears, feelings, compassion, love and much more, and transcends the limitations of desires for the objects of senses. We observe, that the hunger for the sense objects is only short lived. But then, subtler desires like the acquisition of power, knowledge and in short, those which are connected with 'I' and 'mine' are also external!

One should however, guard against making a very grave and yet avoidable blunder. One should never negate or look down upon or even *punish* the body and senses by either

---

154 श्वोभावा मर्तस्य यदन्तकैतत्सर्वेन्द्रियाणां जरयन्ति तेजः ।
अपि सर्वं जीवितमल्पमेव तवैव वाहास्तव नृत्यगीते ॥ 1.1.16 ॥

starving them or by other cruel methods, as glorified by the asceticism in some religions. It is said that in some monastic denomination of a religion, the monks *cut-off* their genitals to combat lust! In most of the religions, fasting, vigil and negating other senses is recommended. These no doubt are not so dangerous, but they may not have the expected effect.

There are some inherent dangers in such kind of attitude or practice. First danger is that the desires instead of getting eliminated, only get suppressed, further complicating the mind. When we starve a sense, or suppress a desire it comes out in some other form. A person practising celibacy *may* lean on gluttony to overcome suppression or *may* become extremely short tempered. Moreover, he or she may be under constant threat of the attack from those very things which are being avoided, in unguarded moments. Consequently, there is a *negative* attachment, as the person goes out of the way to avoid situations. He may be-little or talk *against* senses and their objects. In this sense, such persons tend to spend more time thinking—even if it is against—about those very objects!

There is a story to illustrate this: Two monks, a youth and an old man, were travelling. They were on their way to their Master's hermitage. On way they had to cross a small river. When they came near its bank, they saw a young woman lying unconscious. The youth approached in spite of the protests from his old colleague, and found that she was too weak to cross the river on her own and sought help. The youth spontaneously lifted her on his shoulder and took her across, and left her near her house on the opposite bank. The old man started scolding the youth for breaking the vow of monastic life, and for defiling himself by *touching* a woman. It continued till they finally reached their Master's hermitage. All along, the youth remained calm and refused to react in any way. When the old disciple, complained to the Master about the objectionable behaviour, the Master smilingly asked the old man, about the distance the youth had carried the woman. Innocently the old man replied that it was while crossing the breadth of the shallow river, which was about two hundred feet. The Master admonished the older monk, that while the youth had carried her for only that distance, and that too only physically, the old monk was still *carrying* her in his mind, which is a greater offense for a monk!

Second and perhaps a more fundamental problem with such an attitude is, that we tend to go on *dividing* existence into material and spiritual, body-senses and mind, profane and sacred, and so on. This division by its very nature, cannot take one towards the Ultimate Reality, which is *One and non-divisible.* The so-called gross, like the body-senses are nothing but *its* gross manifestations, while the mind, intellect and ego are the subtler ones. Moreover, these divisions are effected by the ego—which is nothing but the inconsequential *shadow* of the Reality, for its own survival! It is like a political leader who survives only by dividing the society! But a question may arise in our mind, that almost all the spiritual traditions do recommend the negation of body-senses and prove beyond doubt that we *cannot* possibly *experience* the Reality, because experience as such comes under activity—physical or psychological, as the Reality is *the Subtlest,* transcending all Its manifestations.

To make us aware of these problems, we find all the scriptures suggesting the seeker to *give up* the gross and to choose the subtle. By its very nature, the subtle *cannot* be perceived by the gross. To perceive it one has to go to subtler level, which requires that we have to shift our attention from the gross to subtle. Shri Ramakrishna used to give an example to explain this: A person interested in going on top of a terrace uses the stairs. Each time he climbs a stair, he has to *leave* the lower step to come to a higher stair. But once he is on the terrace, he realises that the terrace, the stairs and even the building itself is made out of the same bricks, mortar and lime! Shri Ramakrishna was so clear in his thinking and advice that there was no room for any conflict or confusion. This may have been due to the fact that he was not *corrupted* by the so-called education!

It is of primary importance for seeker never to have any antagonistic view towards body-senses, desires or material world in general. *Virakti* or the disinterest should be positive in the sense, that the gross has a *distracting* effect, making it very difficult, if not impossible to perceive the subtle. If one always keeps this in mind and studies the scriptures there is no danger of any negativity or division.

Sage Vasiṣṭha said that the best method of destroying the pain giving mind that is bound by the cord of desire is *Jñāna.* A stainless mind which is freed of all desire, even if engaged in worldly activity, is never bound. And the mind with *Rāga* or attractions and *Dweṣa* or aversions, though engaged in severe *Tapas,* will always be in bondage. A person without any internal craving, capable of performing action without any attachment, that is, attraction and aversion will alone, not have the characteristics of actor and enjoyer, whether he performs external actions or not. At this statement, Rāma asked as to what is meant by *Saṅga* or association, and what is it which leads to liberation. What is bondage? And how this bondage can be ended.

Vasiṣṭha replied that, by giving up the division between body and its occupant, from the mind one can become free. The conviction that one is *only* body-senses-mind is *Saṅga* or association and is the cause for bondage. The conviction that the Ultimate Reality is beyond the purview of space and time which leads towards equipoise is *Asaṅga* or non-association. Instead, the longing for the sense pleasures alone, causes bondage. Everything—seen and the unseen—is One and Only Reality. What can one possess or renounce, if one is of this conviction then she or he rises towards *Jīvanamukti.* The state of non-association of mind, when neither 'I' nor any other 'self' exists during the experience of pleasure or pain, is to be taken as a path leading towards *Mokṣa.* Such persons neither court action, nor inaction; as they are free from any desire for the fruits of action, they are not choosy of either action or inaction. The wise say that such persons are called *Asaṁsaktas.* Even the persons, who have renounced the fruits of action but not the action itself, are called as *Asaṁsaktas.* By such an attitude, the stains of never ending actions are effaced. It is through *Saṅga* alone that the long chain of births is undergone, which disappears at every stage like the bubbles on the surface of the ocean.

It will be appropriate to recollect the first verse of this scripture, which gives a few hints on the Ultimate Principle.

> 'Salutations to that Supreme Principle inherent in air, earth and sky, inside and outside, in whose luminance the Ātman shines'.[155]

From this lofty *Śloka,* we can safely infer that *division of any kind* is not advisable. And that if one does entertain, for pragmatic reasons like developing disinterest in the body, senses, mind, reason, and ego, it should be only for eliminating the gross distractions and for paying attention to the subtle. It has been observed, that almost all the astronauts when they behold the earth from space, forget every man-made division like boundaries, race, religion, country and continent. But then to do so, *they have to be in space, far away from earth!* The state of Asaṅga or the non-association refers to the act of distancing oneself from the gross and to *be* the Oneness of Existence.

Continuing, the respected sage said, that the attraction is of two types: *Vandhyā,* or fruitless and *Vandyā,* or respected. *Vandhyā* is found in the ignorant, and *Vandyā* is the ornament

155 दिवि भूमौ तथाकाशे बहिरन्तश्च मे विभुः ।
यो विभात्यवभासात्मा तस्मै सर्वात्मने नमः ॥ 1.1.1 ॥

of all the self-realised Persons. While *Vandyā* leads one towards *Ātma-Jñāna* and *Viveka* arresting the rebirths taking place in eons of time, *Vandhyā* traps one into the mire of attachment and continual rebirths. One should know the difference between the two types of attractions. Viṣṇu—the sustaining Power of this universe, acts without in the least attachment to the manifold action with *Vandyā* type of attraction. Similarly, *Siddhas,* or those who have achieved, and *Jñānins,* or those who have become wise, become the true protectors of this earth through this attraction. But mind as such, mistakes the bad things for good and gets more and more involved in them, inviting evil and creating hell through the *Vandhyā* attraction. Taking the help of *Vidyā* to remove *Avidyā* that goads the mind towards attractions, one who remains alert and awake all the while is a *Mukta.*

Upaniṣadic tradition has always insisted on gradual and if one may say *non-violent* method of quietening the mind. Total abstention or starving the senses from their objects, is always to be avoided. That is why; it is indirectly suggested here, to adopt a *higher* attraction *Vandyā,* so that the lower attractions *Vandhyā drop on their own.* What is this *Vandyā* attraction? It becomes very clear through the example of Viṣṇu, the Sustaining Power of the universe. Without this power, there can be no universe, and yet this power is totally hidden behind the myriad of activity that goes on in the universe. For example, the presence of electricity can be inferred only through its effects, as it always remains hidden to our eyes. In the earlier *Ślokas* the sage suggested that one to be detached from the fruits of action and to eliminate the doership. In this sense, one *uses* the attraction for freedom, to overcome the attraction for the objects having a binding effect!

Sage Vasiṣṭha then proceeded to describe the state of *Jīvanamukta,* who is in different *Avasthās* or states. Being in the minds of all creatures, he performs all actions, without any attachment to the actions, thoughts, objects, *Ākāśa* or space, ups and downs, quarters, enjoyments, five senses, internal *Prāṇas* or vital forces, head, face, five organs of action, body, the three states—waking, dream and deep sleep, colours or *Guṇas,* three conditions (beginning, middle and end), five *Tanmātras* (sensations),[156] or the five *Bhūtas* (elements).[157] Because of such non-involvement, such persons never associate themselves with the lower attractions.

Consequently, when such a person acts the action never binds her or him to either the world or the action. By transcending indulgence and involvement the mental activity becomes quiet. With such quietude of mind, one gets established in *Tūrya* (the fourth state), then transcends the realm of experience, to be *Ānandātīta, Jñānātīta* or transcending even bliss and wisdom.

The *Bṛhadāraṇyaka Upaniṣad* and other *Śrutis* dealing with the true path, suggest that the principle *inherent* in the gross and the subtle is the Supreme Principle. The author then gives three gems in the form of verses condensing positive attitude of the *Upaniṣads.*

> 'During the contact of the senses with their objects, the essence of happiness experienced without even a trace of separateness of the object and the experience, is said to be Supreme.
>
> 'When the seen and the sight merge into one another in the seer, the experience of happiness is unparalleled; hankering for the objects is bondage, freedom from this attraction is *Mukti.*
>
> 'That state of direct experience in which the seen and sight merge into one another is unattended by pain. Therefore, let the mind always have this state called as *Sauṣuptī* which serves as a beacon light'.[158]

---

156 *Tanmātras* are sensations : smell, taste, sight, touch and hearing.

157 *Bhūtas* are the elements: earth, water, light, air, and ether.

158 दृश्यदर्शनसंबन्धे यत्सुखं पारमार्थिकम् ।

Upaniṣads, on which our whole culture is founded, have always been life affirming. Life in all its shades was accepted. The normal life-span was divided into four portions—*Brahmacarya, Gṛhastha, Vānaprastha,* and *Sannyāsa,* which were to be lived totally. The first phase was devoted for learning, in which one had to spend the one fourth portion of one's life in the hermitages to taste non-involvement, meditation, etc., at the feet of realised sages. On return, one had to enter the second phase of marital life. In spite of hectic activity involving the married life, the training of meditation was helpful in non-involved action. The third phase of life consisted of gradual withdrawal from active life and moving towards retirement. Finally, there would be the total effort for spiritual practice. Naturally, there was no room for any negativity. The practice of initiation into *Sannyāsa* without the intermediate stages came much later after Mahāvīr Jain and the Buddha, to be followed by Ādi Śaṅkarācārya.

Moreover, the *Upaniṣadic* sages were very much aware, that negativity of *any kind* only increases the activity of the mind, leading a seeker towards suppression or even perversion. The tendency of the mind and senses is to flow towards their objects, which is only natural and healthy. If one starts, for whatever reason, to starve the senses with an attitude that *sense indulgence* is *bad,* then one can be certain that the mind would go more towards it. For instance, if one decides to go on a fast, there is every likelihood of one *seeing and imagining* the food in every situation! And perhaps that

---

अनुभूतिमयं तस्मात्सारं ब्रह्मेति कथ्यते ।। 4.9.42 ।।

दृश्यदर्शनसंबन्धे सुखसंविदनुत्तमा ।

दृश्यसंवलिता बन्धस्तन्मुक्ता मुक्तिरुच्यते ।। 4.9.43 ।।

दृश्यदर्शनसंबन्धे यानुभूतिरनामया ।

तामवष्टभ्य तिष्ठ त्वं सौषुप्तीं भजते स्थितिम् ।। 4.9.44 ।।

particular day, one may speak more about food, than on normal days! But, if one accepts everything as part of the Divine Existence, and *chooses* a particular way of life, rather than *rejecting* the other things as *bad,* she or he will have a better possibility of completing the journey.

Vasiṣṭha continued that the Reality is also *Turya* state. The *Ātman* is neither gross, nor subtle, neither perceptive nor non-perceptive, neither intelligent nor inert... as it transcends all states and is beyond all conditioning. The state called *Mokṣa* is neither *Devaloka* or the heaven nor *Pātāla* or nether world nor earth. *When all desires are destroyed, what remains is Mokṣa.* Even longing for *Mokṣa* can revive the desires in the mind, as it increases the *Manana* or the meditations to only increase the births and deaths. Therefore, the sage urged, one must destroy the mind and its thoughts, the root of all problems. Those who have worshipped the Ātmic Reality, which transcends body-mind, lose its consciousness though acting through it. Like a woman who performs her household duties, whilst her mind is engrossed in her distant paramour, a *Jñānī* always centres himself on the Brāhmic state. They neither long for things in future, nor ruminate upon things of the past, nor do they stagnate in the present. They appear as devotees amongst devotees; conduct themselves tactfully amongst the men of the world; as children amongst children; as old men amongst the old; as youths amongst the young. Knowing all things *as they are,* they are never attached. The world appears diversified only because of the fluctuations of the mind.

Shri Ramakrishna gives a few wonderful hints to the householders, through some day-to-day examples:

> 'Do all your duties, but keep your mind on God. Live with all—with wife and children, father and mother, and serve them. Treat them *as if* they were very dear to you, but know in your heart of hearts that they do not belong to you.

'A maid servant in the house of a rich man performs all the household duties but her thoughts are fixed on her own home in her native village. She brings up her master's children as if they were her own. She even speaks of them as "my Rāma" or "my Hari". But in her own mind she knows very well that they do not belong to her at all.

'The tortoise moves about in the water. But can you guess where her thoughts are? There on the bank, where her eggs are lying. Do all your duties in the world, but keep your mind on God'.[159]

One of the greatest hurdles for quietening the mental activity is the *incompleteness* of our transactions. Whenever there is an experience, the mind is *absent* to the experience as such. For example, there is a desire for eating something. When the eatable is brought in front, the mind remains on the object *it craved,* only for a moment, and then passes on to either past or the present. Consequently, the same mind tries to complete the transaction *mentally,* when the object is *not available!* This habit only increases its fluctuations. Whereas, if one totally lives the moment when the sense comes in touch with its object, the transaction gets completed, and there is no need for the mind to *recapitulate* the experience. Consequently the mind is ever fresh, and free from fluctuations.

Rāma, a prince among the seekers, sought a clarification: What cause the fluctuations of the mind? How can one eliminate these fluctuations? The great sage replied, that the fluctuations are not different from the mind, they both are as inseparable as the sesame seed and oil or the snow and whiteness. Mind exists because of the fluctuations. *Yoga* and *Jñāna* are the two methods of eliminating the mind; stopping

---

159 *The Gospel of Shri Ramakrishna* by M, Shri Ramakrishna Math, Madras, IXth impression, 1988, p. 81.

the modifications is *Yoga,* while *Jñāna* is *Samyagaveksaṇam,* or non-involved witnessing, from within. Persons well versed in the Vedic lore, claim that the mind is nothing but the fluctuations of *Prāṇa.* With the control of *Prāṇa,* the mind is also controlled. With the control of mind and its fluctuations, rebirth ceases like the daily actions ceasing at sunset.

Again Rāma interposed, to enquire about the means of arresting the motion of *Prāṇa* that vibrates ceaselessly. The sage replied with infinite patience: Having lived the life of *Vairāgya* and practised *Yoga* one must come out of the binding tendencies. By the single pointedness of a man intensely desirous of achieving something, one can control the *Prāṇa.* Through practice of *Pūraka-Kuṁbhaka-Recaka-Kuṁbhaka,* that is *Prāṇāyāma,* in a solitary place with a cheerful mind, one can bring the *Prāṇa* under control. The *Prāṇa* can be subjugated through the chanting of *Praṇava* or *Auṁkāra* in the stipulated manner. The vibrations of *Prāṇa* can be quelled through the practice of *Khecarī Mudrā.* One can gain control over *Prāṇa* by directing it from throat to the space between the eyebrows. The *Prāṇa* comes under the control of a person staying alone and practising *Mauna* or silence. Such hints and many more as transferred by various experienced wise through the traditions in different places and times are the ways in which the fluctuations of *Prāṇa* are brought under conscious control. Through constant and unbroken practice of any of these methods, the mind becomes quiescent and ready for *Nirvāṇa* or Transcendence.

In the above statement, the author tries to give some of the methods of controlling *Prāṇa* and hence the mind. Most if not all the practices are never to be practised without the guidance of an experienced teacher. Because, the practical aspects are seldom given in the books, and even if they do, they will be in symbolic language. This is so, as the most important hints are given only after the initiation in the secret schools. A novice should *never* do these practices by taking the help of books, as it can result in insanity or even death. However, it is quite interesting to note that most of these methods try to gain control over the gross manifestations like body posture or gesture, breath, sound, etc., to achieve the quiescence *indirectly*. The author continues to give the methods of *Jñāna*, which though taking longer, are quite safe.

After listening carefully about the methods of controlling *Prāṇa*, which help the mind to reach a state of equilibrium that help the mind from involving with the senses, Rāma appealed to the sage to narrate the methods of *Jñāna*. The *Muni* replied, that one should develop the conviction, that it is the *Brahman* alone which shines everywhere, which has no beginning, middle or end; that all *Śaktis* or powers are nothing but the manifestations of the *Ātman*, which are used in the worship of *Itself*. Such conviction eliminates all the problems created by duality.

Turning towards the Non-dual Principle, helps in eradicating the restlessness generated by the mind. When one enters into the Non-dual there is nothing to create the fluctuations of the mind. Such conviction makes one ready for turning inwards. Gradually, one starts seeing the Reality in all its manifestations, like one who is able to see *water* in waves, foam, bubbles, etc. At such state one cannot get agitated by the indulgences and involvements. To illustrate this, sage Vasiṣṭha narrated the story of Vītahavya.

A recluse named Vītahavya, lived on the slopes of the Vindhya Mountains. He had performed actions goaded by desires and was afflicted with mental and physical maladies, and was unable to get out of *Saṁsāra*. Wanting to escape from pain, he gave up the action and retreated to the forest. Erecting a hut of leaves, he seated himself in the Lotus posture on a deer skin. Slowly he succeeded in bringing back the mind from the objects and fixed it on the heart space. He noticed that though the mind was devoid of thoughts, there were *Prāṇic* fluctuations, which tended to re-activate the mind.

With this observation, Vītahavya began his *Vicāra,* wherein he started separating himself from the body, instruments of action, senses, mind, reason, and finally *Ahaṁkāra.* With this *Vicāra,* everything was brought under control. Like the flames get absorbed in themselves after having consumed the fuel, *Prāṇa* gradually merged into itself, and there was quiescence. After a long time, Vītahavya emerged to the wakeful state and found his body buried in a hillock of sand formed by the floods of water. The *Prāṇas* were unable to circulate freely. When he began to give attention to his mind, he began to perceive as if in a dream, that he had spent a hundred years as a *Tapasvin* on the slopes of mount Kailāśa; as a Vidyādhara for another hundred years; as Deveṅdra for five *Yugas;* then as Gaṇeśa. Thus, Vītahavya saw his former lives pass through his divine vision.

With the destruction of these bodies, he saw his present body which was buried deeply in sand. In order to lift the body out of sand, he approached the sun to seek the help of *Piṅgala.* With its help, the Muni recovered his gross body. Having spent a few days on the bank of the Narmada, the river flowing on the rocks of the Vindhyās, he realised that till then, he had been having conscious control over the organs and mind. He decided to merge into *Cinmātra* or the absolute consciousness alone, which remains after everything, merges into Reality. He felt convinced that with such awareness, he can remain unmoved and quiescent in spite of the continued lower activity. With practised ease he merged himself in the *Cinmātra,* and began to live as a *Jivana-mukta.*

All pleasure and pain, attachment and disgust, was eliminated and the *Muni* freed himself from rebirth and action. An innocent thought of reaching *Kaivalya* crossed his mind. For this purpose, Vītahavya the *Siddha* entered a cave one day. After adopting the Lotus posture again, he reflected : 'Oh soft Desire, please merge into non-desire, Oh Anger, be pleased to embrace the quiescence; I have enjoyed your company for a very long time; having amused myself with various tricks, Oh Enjoyments, my salutations to you; Oh Material Joy, you have nurtured me like a mother as to her own son, under your care I became oblivious to the pain-free *Mokṣa,* I offer you my parting farewell; Oh Pain, is it not due to you that I have been able to recognise the path towards *Ātma-Tattva,* the Supreme Principle? You have been the cause of my merging into the state of *Mokṣa.* Can I ever be ungrateful to you? Gratitude to you, my Saviour, Oh Body, my long standing friend, I take leave of you, for you have fulfilled the purpose of attaining *Jñāna.* My respectful greetings to you, Oh Lust, your insatiable hunger helped me to have a glimpse into your fault and the auspiciousness of the quietude of senses. Oh Good Deeds, you lured me towards you with the temptation of heaven, please accept my parting salutations. All of you, my respected friends, you have helped me in achieving Quiescence, I am ever grateful to you.'

Taking leave from them all, he dropped the activity called mind. Reaching the *Jñāna* state, he softly uttered *Praṇava* and gave up the *Saṁkalpa* completely. The Muni became 'That', the final aim of all *Śāstras.* Having dropped the fetters which are responsible for binding one to the *Saṁsāra,* Vītahavya was soon absorbed in the Non-dual State.

Vītahavya's journey into himself is illustrative of the problems of a seeker. His involvement with actions to fulfill his never ending desires represents of our own life. The feeling of frustration when our desires remain unfulfilled, or the '*empty-handedness*', each time we apparently succeed, do make us realise the pointlessness of desire. It also leaves us drained of the vital energy. This is when we start looking for other possibilities. The mind has to be brought under some control before one embarks on the path of *Vicāra.* The separateness of *'I'* from all the manifestations is always deep as is evident in case of Vītahavya. He transcended time and space to experience the Cosmic Oneness, that made him identify with the *Tapasvin, Vidyādhara,* Indra or for that matter, Gaṇeśa. It is like a wave suddenly realising its identity with the infinite ocean!

This story ends on an extremely positive note with Vītahavya's poetic leave-taking with the manifestations. This emphasises that *everything* in the universe, including the so-called negative, has a role to play in the journey.

Kātyāyanī, the wife of Sage Yājñavalkya is extremely happy, looking at the thousand milch cows, grazing on the mountain slope. She also has pride dancing in her bosom, as they have been won by her husband as a token of respect and appreciation for his wisdom, in the assembly of king Janaka. Looking at her, the sage smilingly asks her the reason for her happiness. She innocently replies that the sight of the cattle is very fulfilling. The sage, points out, that although she had seen such scenes earlier in her life, she had never been *so* happy! Then can she tell him why she was presently in such a happy state? Again Kātyāyanī replies innocently, that the cows she had seen earlier did not belong to her, while these cows belong to *her.* Yājñavalkya asks his dear wife to imagine the bliss of the person to whom this whole universe belongs. When he finds her quiet awe-struck by the possibility, he asks her to further imagine the bliss of the Person *who is this whole universe!*

Man finds the night sky tempting, as it evokes a sense of awe and wonder in him. While gazing, he finds all his worries and problems petty and insignificant. Compared to the vastness of space he, nay the earth, nay even the solar system dwindles into insignificance. Perhaps, this feeling of smallness compels him to melt into insignificance or in other words, identify himself with the vastness of space, like a wave dissolving into the ocean. While Astronomy initiates in him a spirit of inquiry and a voyage to understand his place in the universe, spirituality is a cordial invitation for him to *become* the universe and *more!* And both, are reliable ways to understand *himself.*

10

The Conclusion of Upaśama Prakaraṇa

The only settlement of a score of huts is also nearly two kilometers away. The lonely building having four or five rooms stands on a small hillock overlooking the vast expanse of vegetable gardens on one side, hills and wilderness on the others. There is absolutely no noise pollution as the silence reigns supreme. It no doubt makes an ideal haven for persons wanting to devote their time for contemplation or such other pursuits. For persons living in the cities with their crowds and rush and noise it is a very welcome change. The silence acts like a soothing balm for mind, pained as the mind is, with the competition, jealousy, anxiety, hurry and tensions.

But then, for those of us who have compromised with the life of speed and the accompanying tensions, even this soothing atmosphere becomes uncomfortable within a few days! There is a joke about a Bombay businessman going to *Matherān,* a hill station on the Western Ghats. On way, the driver stopped on the shoulder of a mountain for a while. The businessmen got out of the car with his family for a breath-taking view. But lo! he really lost his breath, fell unconscious on to the ground. There was pandemonium and someone rushed to get a glass of water, someone else tried to lift him... The wife however, was quite calm and she asked her son to bring him to the back of the car, and the driver, to start the car engine and to keep it idling. Soon as the exhaust fumes entered the lungs of the businessman, he opened his eyes! He wanted to know, the cause of this unexpected reaction on his part. The wife maintaining her composure said the cause was only the pure air, for her husband was used to pollution!

We may not be habituated to the pollution like the businessman, but we are addicted to our thoughts, desires, likes and dislikes, obsessions, and fears. Without them we feel empty, and the life appears devoid of any purpose. Many of us, if not most, feel that life without these tensions and worry is not worth living. This is because we see many around, who are leading a life without any of the tensions mentioned above, but they are just *vegetating,* seeped as they are in lethargy. And to an extent this observation *is* justified, at least in our country! Why and how this addiction does gets effected, makes a useful study.

A child is born with 'Self' but without any 'ego'. However, it is unconscious of that 'Self'. It is not related either to the 'Self' or to the outside world. The 'Self' is the centre, while the world is the periphery. Gradually, the child starts observing the mother who is related to it in an almost inseparable way. Through this and other contacts, the 'thou-I' relationship starts developing. That is, 'thou' comes first and then indirectly the 'I' follows, almost as a suggestion by the 'thou' consisting of parents, brother or sister. As these relations are able to see and recognise only the body initially they take the body to be the entity, and the conviction that 'I am the body' is the nurtured and strengthened.

In early childhood the 'I' or the 'ego' gets strengthened through other aspects like the reactions to stimuli or situations, and other habitual behaviour as *related* to the *outside* world. The experiences which strengthen the 'I' are *outside.* They get crystallised through tutoring in school, the do-s and don't-s and other norms framed by the society. As and when we grow up we reinforce the ego, through education, society, religion, culture and civilization. This is evident from the expressions: 'my knowledge', 'my community', 'my religion', 'my country', etc. That is, the 'I' belongs to something, or something belongs to 'me'. This 'I' definitely goads us towards activity, development and achievement. But it also generates the by-products like competition, worry, tension and jealousy, as the 'I' does not want to lose the things, or the 'I' does not want 'thou' to possess more things than the 'me'.

Thus from childhood to old age, we have never known the 'Self' but only the 'ego', nurtured by the periphery, may it be the society or the world in general. And we go on strengthening this 'I' or the ego through all our experiences and activity. While the physical body has been given by the parents, the 'ego' is a product of a long chain of experiences and impressions that collect as what is called as the mind, personality, and character. Consequently, the 'ego' is not a single entity but a collection of impressions of various sources of experiences: parents, teachers, society and the country. In other words the 'ego' is a *crowd,* which makes it very difficult, if not impossible to control! From our day-to-day experience, we see that after an outburst of anger, one vows *never* to get angry, but if and when a situation arises, one again loses control and becomes angry again! This is because, the entity becoming angry is entirely different from the one who takes a vow never to lose control!

George Gurdjieff used to say that man normally nurtures a *crowd* within, whom he calls the 'I'! Due to this crowd called 'I', he does not have any *will,* and only an individual can have it. So the human life is meant for becoming a *Self,* that is one and indivisible, by reducing the crowd. He would give another example : It is like a house, with the master of the house away or asleep and in his place, each servant assuming the responsibility of the master *by turns!* Unless the master awakens from his sleep or comes back, the situation remains chaotic.

This can be understood with another common experience: the inability to remain alone for a long time. Either one has to be with a friend or a relative, or in presence of artificial company, like the TV or a book or music. Even with these avenues gone, one is always with one's thoughts, dreams or fantasies! Because the layers of civilization and culture are so thick and we are so used to it, that it is almost impossible to accept the *aloneness,* because we have never known it. So man has a love-hate relationship with the 'ego' created by the society. The society needs the ego to create fear, obedience, and order in it. Thus man is literally helpless with this addiction! Without it, he cannot survive, and with it, he invites all misery! The ego *belongs* to the things, body, mind, society, etc. Ego can exist only through relationship. Our life and experiences are mostly at this peripheral level of ego. While the 'Self' remains untouched, as it is the centre.

All spiritual practices try to take one to the centre or rather, religion consists of moving towards the centre. To avoid the crowd, some seekers choose seclusion. For the ego is *related* to someone or something *outside* and cannot survive in seclusion or isolation. It is like a bridge which cannot exist without the two banks of a river. So with the avoidance of one, the bank of the outer relationships, the ego dissolves. But the dissolution depends on its strength. The more related one is to the outside world, the stronger is the ego and hence more difficult it is for one to shed the ego.

Moreover, the seeker must take care to see, that when he goes into seclusion, the ego does not *create* any more props like the experiences of light and sound and such other seemingly spiritual experiences! Because after all, the mind *is* creative in projecting the experiences heard from persons or read from the books. In doing so, the mind or the ego sustains itself, for its dissolution is its death! That is how, not all persons who take retreat into mountain caves or forests get enlightened. Only such a person succeeds in discovering his real *Self,* who totally drops all the props, in spite of the great problem of disorientation which follows the isolation.

The Vedāntic texts suggest milder methods by stressing on the reduction of involvement at the mental level and indulgence at the level of senses and body. The *Yoga Vāsiṣṭha* is one of them, suggesting either the indirect methods like the control of *Prāṇa* or the direct method of witnessing the mind. Control of *Prāṇa* or speech or any other action, helps one to slowly and steadily drop the façade called the *Ahaṁkāra.* While the *Samyagavekṣaṇaṃ* as it calls the art of non-involved witnessing which happens to be the aim of all methods of *Vicāra,* makes the *Vāsanās* or impressions, ineffective. Not only that, but almost all the methods—direct or indirect, take the seeker to this point of *Samyagavekṣaṇaṃ* or non-involved witnessing. Once reaching this point, this façade of ego and its companions fall off and one comes in contact with the *Self,* standing on Its own, without any need of the outside relationships. For the first time, such person starts *acting,* while most of us only *react* to the peripheral stimuli or situations.

It is said that once the Buddha was walking, and a group of angry people stopped him. They alleged, that he was misleading the people against the *Vedas* and the God Himself. They insulted him by using harsh words. The Buddha did not react at all. Instead, when they stopped, wondering why this person was not reacting at all, the Buddha observed with a smile, that if they had finished speaking, he would like to proceed as he had to reach the next village before the twilight! And if they had not, he would be passing by that place again, when they could have their say! Surprised, at such response, they asked him why he had not reacted to their insult. The Buddha said, that the insult affected only the periphery of body, mind and ego, while he was already established at the centre, and he could only *act* and not *react!* If they had been expecting any reaction from him, then he was sorry, for he had stopped all reactions since the day he realised! There is a beautiful *Śloka* :

'The *Prāṇas* move according to their nature,
The desires may even kill the mind,
Filled with the Bliss is the *Buddhiḥ,*
Nothing can ever happen to *Me*'![160]

The *Me* refers to the *Self,* or the Centre, from where the periphery is so distant, that It remains totally unaffected as the eye of the storm. Whatever happens, no matter how turbulent is the body, mind or the ego, the Self remains untouched. Moreover, the action initiated by the Self is total, in terms of energy and complete. So, only such a person lives totally, and in the here-now. Only such a one knows the joys of this creation, for he has the advantage of being at such a distance that all disturbance has transformed into *Līlā* or a play.

This *Upaśama Prakaraṇa,* suggests the means of loosening the grip of the *peripherals* like the body, senses, mind, reason and ego, and over limited understanding. It tries to give glimpses of truth, through contemplation of the characters in the stories narrated therein. This *Sarga* puts further light on the quiescence of mind, and on the methods of moving towards the centre.

Rāma sought a clarification for a doubt: How is it that such higher powers as walking in the sky, etc. are not found in a *Jīvanamukta.* To which sage Vasiṣṭha replied, that only those who have not attained to full *Jñāna* are afflicted by the desire of acquiring powers which are like any other binding thoughts. The *Siddhis* or powers can be acquired through medicines, *Mantras,* actions and time. And these *Siddhis* are of no interest to a true *Jñānī,* who has merged with the Reality, and transcended all desires. Because all the heterogeneous worldly objects come under the purview of *Māyā,* or temporality. But if an innocent thought arises in the

160 प्राणाश्चलन्तु तद्धर्मैः कामैर्वा हन्यतां मनः ।
आनन्द बुद्धिपूर्णश्च न मे किंचिद्भविष्यति ।।

consciousness of a *Jñānī* then he is more than capable of mastering the *Siddhis*. But the *Jñānins* have a conviction that the *Siddhis* lead one towards bondage.

It appears that Rāma did not catch the hint, for he continued, as to how *Yogis* live for very long periods of time. Sage Vasiṣṭha replied patiently: The *Yogis* move only through the motion of *Prāṇa,* else they are totally immovable. Those *Yogis* who have the *Prāṇa* under control live for long periods. If the activity of *Prāṇa* and hence the mind is quelled both externally as well as internally, then death and dotage do not afflict us. Only those can be said to have cognised Reality, who have totally eliminated the bonds of the mind. It appears, the sage had succeeded in convincing Rāma about the uselessness of the *Siddhis,* for he asked : What happens to the four qualities *Maitrī, Karuṇā, Muditā,* and *Upekṣā*?[161]

Vasiṣṭha replied that the quiescence of the activity of mind is at the two levels as the activity is composite in character. Its components are: *Rūpa* or with form and *Arūpa* or formless. The *Rūpa* component consists of the binding involvement and identification with objects, persons, etc. or the 'ego', which generates pain and bondage. This component should be destroyed as, it is this component which hinders us from cognising the Reality, as it ever forces us to hanker for pleasure or avoid pain. This component which has predominantly *Tamas* or inertia and *Rajas* or obsession for activity, gets quietened through *Jīvanamukti,* as only such a Person has the *Samadṛṣṭi* or equal vision, which helps her or him to transcend the duality of pleasure and pain, etc. After the *Rūpa* mind is destroyed, through quiescence, it transcends birth and death. But the four qualities of friendship, compassion, contentment and

161 Friendship, compassion, contentment and disinclination are the four noble qualities to be possessed by good persons.

disinclination blossom in the *Arūpa* mind of the *Jivanamukta*. They continue, till he attains *Videhamukti* or Disembodied-liberation.

Arūpa belongs to the *Sattwa*[162] and is still subject to change and a source of subtle bondage. A comparison is made between the *Guṇas* and chains. *Tamas* they say, is an iron chain, and *Rajas*, a silver chain, while *Sattwa*, a golden chain. So, even *Sattwa* has a binding effect on the individual, though the golden chain is quite decorative! The sage said that the Brāhmic State is that which transcends everything, and occupies a neutral centre between the pairs of opposites. Everyone must seek asylum into this State like the *Ākāśa* which contains the elements and yet remains unaffected by them.

Through the simile of the sky the author hints at the Brāhmic State as that state of total non-involvement. There might be thunder, lightning, heavy rain bearing clouds or the sunshine, but they do not have any effect on the sky which remains its crystal clear self. Yes, those under the *influence* of the elements are affected, but never the sky! In another sense the Brāhmic State is infinite, and all expansive, as explained by Ācārya Śaṅkara:

'Brahma refers to that which is the most expansive'.[163]

In spite of the fact that one is this all expansive, infinite Self, why and how does one gets afflicted by *Māyā*? Rāma asked this by asking the question as to what is the seed of *Māyā*?; and what is the seed of the seed? Sage Vasiṣṭha replied with all patience, that the gross body is the seed from which the sprouts of pleasure and pain are generated that enhance the ever-growing creeper of *Saṁsāra*. The cause of this seed of

---

162 Refer to the Story of Bhīma, Bhāsa and Dṛḍha, for Shri Ramakrishna's lucid explanation of the three *Guṇas*.

163 बृहत्तमत्वाद् ब्रह्म ॥ तैत्तिरीयोपनिषद् शंकरभाष्य: 2.1 ॥

this body is the mind which, following the track of desire is the cause for innumerable bodies. The tree of pain generating mind is encircled by the creepers of binding actions. This tree has two seeds: the motion of *Prāṇa,* and the *Vāsanās.*

The all expansive State of *Jñāna* gets conditioned through the vibration of *Prāṇa.* If the *Prāṇa* is prevented from spreading in all the directions, it tends to aid one's progress. When the *Prāṇa* gets directed towards the gross, the gross instruments like *Cittaṃ, Buddhiḥ, Manas* and senses along with the craving for their objects. If the *Buddhiḥ* becomes stable and unmoving towards other gross manifestations and objects, then one moves towards *Nirvāṇa.* Hence, it is advisable that one should control the fluctuations of *Prāṇa* and in turn, *Vāsanās.* The excessive movement of the *Prāṇa* towards the external objects is what constitutes the mind. And most of the persons live in this world with such mental turmoil. The sincere Yogis control the *Prāṇa* for controlling the mind. The wise say that the control of *Prāṇa* in turn controls the mind, bringing about *Samatva,* the equality of vision, and also generates happiness and deters sensual cravings.

Through the above discussion on *Prāṇa,* the author tries to suggest a method of mind control indirectly. It is appropriate to compare here the *Aṣṭāṅga-Yoga* of sage Patañjali. After devoting three *Sūtras* for *Prāṇāyāma,* the fourth limb, he gives the results of the practice in two more *Sutras*:

'From that is dissolved the covering of light.
'And the fitness of the mind for focusing'.[164]

The distractions which do not allow the mind to turn inward are basically those manifestations which have a natural flow *outward,* like the senses and *Manas,* which are referred to as the covering of light, mentioned in the above *Sutra* as

164 ततः क्षीयते प्रकाशावरणम् ॥ 2.52 ॥
धारणासु योग्यता मनसः ॥ 2.53 ॥

the external holds a great attraction for the mind. Once a person is able to gently remove the covering, the mind automatically becomes fit for focusing the attention on itself or ready for the inward journey. The other seed of the mind is *Vāsanā,* which supplies it with the tendency to move outward. The ego, subjecting itself to the clutches of *Vāsanās* so that, it completely *identifies* with the objects outside. These *Vāsanās* strengthen the covering of attraction on the mind. In other words, the mind is the process of identification of the 'I' with the changing phenomena. Through the mind, birth, dotage and death are caused. By eliminating the thoughts and the *Vāsanās,* through the act of non-involved witnessing with neither attraction nor aversion, the mind becomes quiescent.

A very great practical hint is given by the author to quieten the mental activity. The term *Vāsanā* can be translated as 'fragrance' or an impression, *which is always of the past.* The incomplete experience of the past, leaves its residue, as memory. And since an unsteady mind, never completes the experience, the impression keeps returning to the consciousness, which gets projected into *future* as the desire. With this fact, one can now consider the method suggested by the revered sage Vasiṣṭha. Non-involved witnessing consists of impartial witnessing of the thoughts arising in the mind, without choosing, or judgment. Two things are very easy for us, as they have become stubborn habits. First habit is on involvement in the thought, so that the whole body-mind is forced towards instinctive or unconscious action. The second habit is to pass a judgment on the thought either as *good* or as *bad.* This in turn forces us towards *reaction,* either positively, as seeking the good or negatively in avoiding or fighting the bad. Both these things generate and expend *Prāṇa* or the vital energy.

For this, the treatment suggested by sage Vasiṣṭha is *Samyagavekṣaṇam,* the non-involved witnessing. The energy created is to be *used* through the non-involved look, just *passively* observing the mental activity, whatever be its form: anger, lust, greed...or even the positive things like compassion, etc. When there is anger, instead of either expressing it *outside* on the cause of anger, or *judging* it as bad and directing it towards oneself, if one just observes it passively, then a transformation takes place. It is our common experience that anger releases a lot of energy in the system. This energy, gets dissipated, when we direct it outside or inside, at the *cause.* If same energy gets directed towards the search for the *source* of anger, in other words, if the energy can move only in one direction, the search for the source, it leads to energy conservation, as it does not get lost outside.

Many of us have a very high mental activity. Consequently, we are too involved even to realise the depth of our involvement. And the *Samyagavekṣaṇaṃ* becomes very difficult, if not impossible. For such of us, there are methods to develop this art. Two of these were evolved or discovered by the Buddha. The first, he called as the *Ānāpānasati,* the awareness of in-going and out-going breaths. Herein, one just pays attention to breathing. One discovers during the practice, that one can either be aware of the breath, or get swept away with the thoughts.

The second one is *mindful* action, that demands consciousness in every action, walking, eating, speaking, etc. By keeping the attention on things like breath and the gross activity, the internal dialogue stops. This is because the energy can move either outside for the gross activity, or inside as the non-judgmental, non-involved attention, or *Choiceless-awareness,* as referred to by J. Krishnamurti. What really happens is, that with the mental activity, time is born, time as past and future, which is responsible for all the mischief! And the awareness just does not allow any mental activity.

Sage Vasiṣṭha said that the mental activity stops, thus the *Vāsanās* too get eliminated, and such persons live an unattached life to work out the *Prārabdha*—the effect of past actions, like a potter's wheel continuing to revolve through the momentum given by the potter. They have pure *Vāsanās* goading them to selfless action, for the good of the world. Such persons become the Masters of their instruments like the mind and senses which are otherwise degrading. The two seeds of the mind are, fluctuations of *Prāṇa* and *Vāsanās*. If either of them ceases to exist, both perish. Through *Vāsanās, Prāṇa's* motion is caused; through *Prāṇa's* motion, *Vāsanās* ensue. And both these seeds have their roots in the *dependency on the external world.*

When one eliminates the *involvement* and *indulgence* with the sensations created by the objects, the fluctuations of *Prāṇa* and the *Vāsanās* get eradicated. For indulgence and involvement form the seed for visible things. With the destruction of this seed the sense objects cannot have any effect, like the sesame oil cannot exist in the absence of the sesame seed. So, *Saṁkalpa,* or the *recognition* itself is the cause of creation of the objective world. As in a dream, though one forgets oneself, one creates and sees all sorts of things through some inherent power within. The recognition and the subsequent creation of objects has been called as *Vṛttijñāna.* Those who have succeeded in eliminating the *Vṛttijñāna* with the help of *Viveka* are able to destroy the *Saṁsāra,* the repetitiveness of the perceived-perception-perceiver chain.

Rāma sought a clarification: how can the non-perception arise when there are no visible things? And how can the perceived vanish when there is no perception?

Sage Vasiṣṭha replied, that *Ātman,* the all-pervading one without any attraction or aversion, with neither the power of knowing nor not-knowing any inert object, does not have any consciousness for visible things. If one remains at this transcendental level one will be without the *Vṛttijñāna* though performing all actions. Only he who remains without allowing the objects to influence him is a *Jñānī, Jīvanamukta.* He is like a child in his consciousness. From such a state, one never falls and is steadfast in his *Samādhi,* though engaged in normal activities of life as he is dissociated with them without *Kartṛtwa* or the sense of doer-ship. The seed of this state of *Jñāna* is the lofty *Sattā-Mātra.* From this primeval *Sattā, Jñāna* rises as light from a flame.

This *Sattā* has two aspects. One is the heterogeneity and the other is homogeneity. The diverse objects though appearing diverse are yet one, as they are only the differentiations of one *Sat.* The heterogeneity is effected by *Kāla-Sattā* or time, *Kāla-Sattā* or division, and *Vastu-Sattā* or substance. Once these differentiations are understood, one transcends them and recognises the Non-dual *Sattā-Mātra.* Vasiṣṭha encouraged Rāma to meditate over these primeval causes so as to transcend them, and to discover *Sattā-Sāmānya,* the common thread behind *everything,* from the edge of which this universe arises, through *Saṁkalpas* of time, division and substance. This State is the cause of all; yet It is causeless. It is the essence of all; yet It is beyond any essence. That Great Mirror, reflects all the differentiated objects. It alone is ageless. It alone is *Ātmatattva,* attaining Which the mind becomes quiescent.

In an earlier *Sarga,*[165] the author introduced two *Vāsanās. Bhoga-Vāsanā*—the tendency to experience, and *Bheda-Vāsanā*—the tendency to differentiate. In these, *Bhoga-Vāsanā* is grosser and to eradicate it *Indriya-nigraha* or control of senses is necessary at the behavioural level, and *Vairāgya* or disinterest is necessary at the mental and intellectual level. The *Bheda-Vāsanā* is the cause for all differentiation or the *otherness,* and the three *Sattās* given above happen to be prime causes for *Bheda-Vāsanā.*

Rāma expressed his gratitude to the sage for explaining the seeds of involvement and indulgence. He appealed the

165 Refer to 'Story of Lavaṇa-I' in Utpatti Prakaraṇa.

sage to instruct him the ways and means of attaining the *Jñāna*. Vasiṣṭha replied that this can be done through properly directed efforts to understand the causes and in eradicating the *Vāsanās*. When one succeeds in doing this, the imperishable State of *Sattā-Sāmānya* dawns immediately. So the first step is to stop all indulgence and involvement with the visible things, and then with further strenuous effort the *Vāsanās* are overcome. As long as the mind is not destroyed, the *Vāsanās* are not destroyed; so long as the *Vāsanās* are not destroyed, the mind is not destroyed. They are like the seed and the sprout. In other words, so long as the mind and the *Vāsanās* are not destroyed *Tattva-Jñāna* is not attained. Further, they both cannot be destroyed till *Tattva-Jñāna* is not attained!

The *Vāsanās* clinging to us can be destroyed through either meditation or through the control of *Prāṇa,* or performance of action with neither attraction nor aversion. The four means for controlling the mind are: Cognition of One *Jñāna,* association of the wise, renunciation of *Vāsanās,* and control of *Prāṇa.* The subjugation of mind by these four means is like the settling of the dust when the rain showers on earth. Unless these four means are adopted or kept in mind by the seeker, all the so-called spiritual practices like *Tapas* or austerity, *Yajña* or sacrifice, pilgrimages to holy places or the rivers, worship of Gods, acts of charity, etc. are all waste of time and energy.

Cognition of One *Jñāna* is affected through the method of Self-inquiry, by a deep search for the entity 'I' which is behind every experience and thought. It is this inquiry alone that generates *Jñāna,* responsible for the equality of vision and stable-mindedness. These further help the bliss to blossom. *Saṅga* or the association and attractions of the mind, is responsible for the material objects, and which causes all other avoidable things like desires. This *Saṅga* can be overcome through the association of the wise and the renunciation of *Vāsanās*.

Rāma wanted to know more about *Saṅga*. The venerable sage replied that *Saṅga* is nothing but our attraction or aversion towards diverse objects of the world. In the case of the worldly, the impure *Vāsanās* imply *Saṅga*. While a *Jīvanamukta* takes the help of pure *Vāsanās* to transcend the duality by avoiding *reaction* to pleasure or pain. It can be said that one has overcome the *Saṅga* if one becomes indifferent to pleasure and pain, remains content in whatever one has, and performs action with total equanimity. The sage concluded that through these, one attains to Brāhmic Bliss.

Upaśama Prakaraṇa suggests hints to quieten the activity of the mind through the ten stories. Mind has been compared to a tree having two seeds of *Vāsanās* and *Prāṇa*. The whole *Prakaraṇa* gives details of tackling these two seeds from various angles. The most important being, through the development of awareness, and *Vicāra*. By becoming totally conscious of the gross actions, breath, *Prāṇa,* or even thoughts, and witnessing them *without any involvement or reaction,* the quiescence dawns. The *Vāsanās* get strengthened by involvement at the thought level, and indulgence at the body level. The other method is by trying to trace *Jñātā,* the knower, *Bhoktā,* the experiencer, and *Kartā,* the doer. In other words, the 'I-am' thought which precedes every act.

As far as the development of Science and Technology is concerned, the past hundred years have been very eventful. The standard of living has no doubt been raised, in the sense that the diseases considered to be beyond treatment have been controlled, if not eradicated; the common man has the capacity to purchase the appliances to reduce labour and has more time at his disposal; and his thirst for knowledge has led him to the point of embarking on journeys into microcosm as well as macrocosm. And necessarily so, for man had suffered in the past due to lack of proper facilities or opportunities for his creativity and drive to achieve.

Now is the time to shift his attention to understand *himself* who is the achiever, the creator and the knower. Because, without understanding himself, he is beginning to realise, that all the so-called development is only a move to increase the pain, suspicion, greed and jealousy. His strides into space are no doubt, attempts to seek for the Reality and Truth. The direction he has chosen involves more effort and time. The path is strewn with distractions and is a difficult maze to solve. This appears to be the most appropriate time for him to realise that there is another direction which is less lengthy. He has been endowed with leisure. It is only right that he learns to utilise the leisure for the purpose of peeping within; to discover the cause of human misery; and to usher in the age of peace and harmony.

Our inner problems peep like the cobras into our conscious minds and we avoid them—as we are afraid of them, by looking outside through the involvement or indulgence. Instead, if we look at them objectively with non-involved interest, we are bound to understand ourselves. By such understanding, we will learn to *accept ourselves as we are, and in turn accept the world with all its limitations as it is.*

The silence outside can initiate the silence inside if we learn to observe the play of inner functions. It is like allowing the dirt in the pond to settle down, so that the water retains its clarity to show what is within. But one must be patient enough to tolerate the eerie silence outside for a while, and also to bear the terrible noise that continues inside. It is easy to run away from such a place and to merge with the life of speed as it matches with the mind within. This can be compared to a person entering his room from bright sunlight. Finding it dark, he may come out. But if he waits, his eyes start adjusting and he slowly starts seeing the room with more and more clarity.

THE TRANSCENDENCE

Nirvāṇa Prakaraṇa

1

The Story of Bhuṣuṇḍa

Amidst the immovable infinitude called the Himalayas, a lonely cave on the shoulder of a mountain. The winds howl outside its gaping mouth. The soft drizzle makes way for the silent snow journeying slowly through the skies to settle on the ancient glaciers, adding to their thickness and strength. In welcoming this celestial guest everything becomes silent. It may also be in an expectation that is in the air for a great cosmic event. Unmoved by the chilling cold, undaunted by the wilderness of the high snows, a man sits inside the cave. It appears as though he is disconnected with his body. For it is hardly covered by any cloth, nor is there any *Dhuni,* the small warmth giving fire. His eyes gaze at the flame of a small earthen lamp. Though there is a parching thirst in those eyes, they are patient. So much so, they are ready to wait for an eternity if necessary.

Suddenly, the icy cold wind blowing outside, changes its direction. It seems as though it cannot contain its curiosity anymore to know what is happening inside the cave! Entering the cave, it blows off the flame of the lamp. And simultaneously, the long journey of the seeker in the cave comes to an end. He re-discovers his forgotten state. The other persons may call Him the awakened One, *Jñānī,* the Buddha or by any other name. Whether he chooses to leave that lonely mountain cave for sharing his wisdom, or remains where He is, and continues to spread the fragrance of his Enlightenment so as to effect a silent influence, is entirely up to his nature.

Though, the merger of the seeker and the wind blowing off the flame may only be the phenomenon of synchronicity as explained by Carl Jung, both the happenings are similar in nature. The light provided by the flame of the lamp illuminating the cave without, and the light of awareness, illuminating all the activity within, went off simultaneously. Whether the eyes of the seeker were open and gazing at the flame of the lamp, or closed and were gazing at the light within, made no difference. The blowing off however occurred almost together.

The turbulent activity called mind, is initially contained by eliminating the impure *Vāsanās* with the help of pure *Vāsanās*. This is achieved by leading a life congenial for seeking. Even the mellow *Sāttwik* activity like the renunciation, compassion, love, etc. is to be dropped ultimately for the quiescence, which is achieved by reducing the unconsciousness through awareness. Religion in general, directly or indirectly recommends *Sākṣī Bhāva* or the non-involved witness-hood. But it is like posting a person of authority, say a policeman, to keep the mischief of activity away! At this stage there is this presence of the policeman, which in the world of spirit may only be a light helping one to witness the inner activity with total awareness. This too is to be dropped. *Nirvāṇa*[166] refers to the blowing off this inner flame which is the *watcher,* or the *witness.*

But yes, this stage when one is ready for the *blown off* state is only the consummation, the fulfillment of all practice. Consequently, one cannot *do* anything to reach IT! One can practise *Yama, Niyama, Vicāra, Dhyāna,* etc. to develop *Prajñā* —the awareness. One can retain the continual awareness. But *the Entity Who is aware,* remains during any practice. The *seeker*

166 Nirvāṇa means 'like the blown off flame'.

remains, and continues to remain till there is a merger of the One who is aware with pure awareness, which has been called by different names: *Cit, Sattā-Mātra,* etc. This *Prakaraṇa* entitled *Nirvāṇa Prakaraṇa* tries to discuss the practices that take the seeker very near to the said stage, while giving broad hints about the State itself through suggestive language. It has in all fifteen stories packed with invaluable hints, in which the characters are representative of the seeker, as it also discusses the problems on way.

One of the greatest theories put forward by science is the relativity of time and space. Though the theory expounded by Albert Einstein is beyond the scope of understanding of laymen, this much is understood by everyone, that both time and space are eternally changing and are always relative to some hypothetical unchanging principle. While the fact is, *everything* changes, as the cosmos is in a state of dynamic balance. This *Sarga* begins with a statement from sage Vasiṣṭha, that there are nothing like the quarters, and time. And that the immutable and non-dual *Brahman* alone exists, because It *transcends* all change, beginning and end or destruction.

Vasiṣṭha said that one should constantly remember this fact to refrain from any identification with the changing phenomena. So long as there is even a trace of *Ajñāna,* the Ultimate State cannot be reached. So long as there is the desire to enjoy the world, the wrong notions will not wear off. All the changing phenomena are only an appearance, like the One vast ocean, ebbing and falling. As long as the 'I', identifying with the manifestations exists, so long do the illusions of *Citta* exist. As long as there is desire for the objects, with the idea of 'I' and 'mine', so long will the illusion exist.

The Reality envelops those who contemplate without any *Saṁkalpa,* on the all-pervading Self, the limitless *Jñāna.* They regard friends, even the assassins hired to kill them without any duplicity of mind, can be said to have truly worshipped the *Brahman.* Like a waterfall, or the rapids along the river washing the trees on the bank, those who have purged themselves of all impurities, who have not only understood but lived the Truth enshrined in the *Śāstras,* are like the Sun dispelling darkness. But those who in spite of the understanding the *Śāstras,* and even have practised incessantly, but have not cognised the Principle, will be tossed about by the *Vṛttis.* This is due to the fact, that for such people, it has only become intellectual knowledge.

Opening verses of the *Sarga* try to give a synopsis of the earlier *Prakaraṇas* in very bold strokes. The basic attitude of a *Jñāna* seeker has been given, so that the course of his voyage is set. The deepest hint is that even when one succeeds in curtailing the gross mental activity to a great extent through incessant practice, one can still wander aimlessly. This is mostly because the practice has just become a ritual or an empty gesture without any awareness. The author suggests keeping constant awareness as the beacon light, so that the aim of the practice is achieved.

Muni Vasiṣṭha went on describe the mechanism of *Avidyā* or the wrong notion. Out of *Sat-Cit-Ānanda,* the Existence-Wisdom-Bliss Absolute, the witness of all, intelligence arose. The intelligence which is subject to change created the three states, subtle, middle and gross, through the three *Guṇas: Sattwa, Rajas* and *Tamas.* These three kinds of *Avidyā* generate rebirth for all beings. The destruction of *Avidyā* constitutes the Ultimate State, and the involvement in *Avidyā, Saṁsāra.* The *Guṇas* are known as the *Prakṛti,* which has the hierarchy of beings from *Sattwa* through *Tamas,* from *Ṛṣis* who are totally conscious, to the inert trees.

On being questioned by Rāma as to how intelligence came to be embodied in trees and plants and trammels of excessive *Ajñāna,* Vasiṣṭha replied, that the intelligence in plants is that state when it is not without *Manas,* as in rocks, nor with *Manas* as an intermediate state between *Sat* and *Asat.* If they are without the duality inducing *Manas,* Rāma reasoned, why not consider the state of trees as the *Mokṣa?*

Vasiṣṭha replied lovingly, that the state of *Sattā* common to all can be achieved only after *Vicāra.* Only on complete experience and renunciation of all *Vāsanās* can one reach the State of *Sattā-Sāmānya.* The state of the trees is like that of seed or a sprout which has the latent tree in it, having *Vāsanās* in a dormant form. Both tree and an Enlightened Man have apparently same unity. But the unity is qualitatively different in both. Sage Vasiṣṭha said that one can achieve the *Mokṣa* only on completely experiencing and eliminating all *Vāsanās.* The experience helps one to understand the futility of *Vāsanās;* at the same time, one has to increase the consciousness, while making efforts towards their elimination.

The story of expulsion of Adam and Eve in the Genesis of the Bible can throw more light on this.

> '16. And the Lord God commanded the man, saying, 'Of every tree of the garden thou mayest freely eat'.
>
> 17. 'But of the tree of knowledge *of good and evil,* thou shalt not eat out of it; for the day that thou eatest thereof thou shalt surely die'. ...
>
> 19. 'And out of the ground the Lord God formed every beast of the field, and brought them unto Adam to see what he could call them; and whatsoever Adam called every living creature that was the name thereof'.[167]

It is a deeply symbolic story of what happens to *all human beings.* The instructions of Lord God *not to eat of the tree of knowledge* itself is an indirect invitation from God to do so! It is of everyday experience, that if we want to ensure that the children do something, all we have to do is to tell them *not to!* The second aspect is that the knowledge offered by the tree is that of *good and evil* or the faculty of judgment and reason. Further, even before allowing them to venture into eating,

---

167 *The Bible: Genesis-2* Authorized (King James) Version.

the God had taught them how to *differentiate* by asking him to *name* the different creatures. This is evidently a pointer that while all the creatures form the part of Eden, man alone has come out of it by becoming *partially aware,* through differentiation and judgment. Out of all creatures, man alone experiences a sense of shame.

It is not that God expelled Adam, but he *expelled* himself through judgment and differentiation. In the vegetable and animal kingdom, there is unity in unconsciousness. For example, they feel the hunger and appease it. They may either search or hunt for the food.

The predators kill their prey. But actually, it is only the force of hunger that is acting, there is no *killer* or *eater.* While in man it is totally different, there is the ego which differentiates *others* from *itself.* The ego is responsible for shame, hatred, and other feelings. That is why, we see that children before learning to differentiate the 'I' from the 'other', are as innocent as the animals. This 'I' is a distant echo of the stirrings of consciousness in the unconsciousness. The unity of unconsciousness has been divided, broken into two : ninety percent unconsciousness and ten percent awareness. The ego has started thinking of the right and the wrong, good and evil. It has also started looking down at anything *animalistic.*

Friedrich Nietzsche has said that man is only '*a becoming*'. He is in a state between the states of wholly unconscious, and wholly conscious. So there is no peace for him till he re-enters the Eden of Unity. But the gate through which he comes out of it, namely 'ego', is totally closed for him. He has to enter it through another gate, by increasing the consciousness to one hundred percent. And he tries to go back, by resorting to unconsciousness, through alcohol or drugs. But it can only be a temporary measure, for he does jump back to partial consciousness. It is like the fantasy of a sapling trying to go back to seed-hood, or a chick trying to re-enter the egg!

The sage continued by saying that the persons who have burnt *Ajñāna,* the seed of impure *Vāsanās* and have achieved the state of *Sattā-Sāmānya* never suffer from pain, whether they are embodied or disembodied. However, even a trace of impure *Vāsanās* like debts, disease, poison, anger and attachment is sufficient to afflict us all our life and to cause rebirth. For these *Vāsanās* are responsible for the conviction that the universe and the Supreme *Brahman* are separate, and this is the *Avidyā.* When requested by Rāma to throw more light on the state of the enlightened ones like Śaṅkara or Śiva and others.

The *Muni* replied that, for such persons, all manifested beings of the cosmos, whether great or small, are the stainless Brahman; *Jñāna* is Brahman; the world is Brahman; the five elements are Brahman; friends, kinsmen even enemies are Brahman. Just as this universe appears dark to the blind, and bright to those who have eyes, it appears blissful to *Jñānins* and painful to the *Ajñānis.* The sage added that whosoever perceives all as the part-less Brahman, such a person alone is Brahman; he alone achieves immortality. Though intellectually one is able to get an idea of what the sage is narrating, how can one achieve this state? Rāma voiced this doubt by appealing to sage Vasiṣṭha to explain fully the two paths of true *Jñāna* and control of *Prāṇa,* for eliminating all the *Vāsanās.*

To this query the sage responded with affection by saying, that the technique of crossing the ocean of *Saṁsāra* is called as *Yoga.* And there are two means of *Yoga* to avert the pain of existence. The two means of *Jñāna* and control of *Prāṇa* are to be classed under *Yoga;* yet ordinarily the control of *Prāṇa* in particular and elimination of fluctuations of the mind in general alone is called *Yoga.* To the temperament of some, *Yoga* is most desirable; to the temperament of others, *Jñāna* is most desirable. Vasiṣṭha observed that he had already explained *Jñāna,* and he presently would deal with the *Yoga.* As an illustration, he would narrate a wonderful story.

Once upon a time, Vasiṣṭha was amidst an august assembly of Devendra along with other enlightened sages. The stories of *Cirañjīvins* or the long lived came up and a *Muni* named Satatapah, told about such a *Cirañjīvin* living on the branch of the *Kalpa* tree on the north-eastern side of the mountain Mahāmeru. His name was Bhuṣuṇḍa, who was the longest lived *Yogin* capable of sitting in *Yoga* for any length of time and was totally desireless. He had the wealth of *Mokṣa,* greatest intelligence, and extreme quiescence with a capacity to clearly see the three periods of time of the Past, the present and the future.

Listening to this, Vasiṣṭha was filled with an intense aspiration of meeting this great person. Accordingly when Vasiṣṭha reached the *Kalpa* tree on top of Mount Meru filled with fragrant flowers, young swans which were chanting the *Sāma,* cuckoos, parrots, peacocks and other birds which were developing *Śiva-Jñāna* through Skanda. Bhuṣuṇḍa with an Atlantean form, full mind, observing inner silence, seeing the sage welcomed him, with the affection and necessary respect. He expressed his genuine joy in receiving the enlightened sage Vasiṣṭha. Bhuṣuṇḍa knew the purpose of his visit, and yet wanted to hear it from the sage himself.

Thereupon Vasiṣṭha requested the great *Yogin* to trace his lineage; the way in which he had attained *Tattva-Jñāna;* the duration of his present life; and how and from whom had the wisdom dawned on Bhuṣuṇḍa. The virtuous Bhuṣuṇḍa said that in the divine presence of supreme Śiva, myriads of *Gaṇas* or hosts, in peculiar faces and shapes live who are called as the *Bhūta-gaṇas* or the elementals around the Kailāśa Mountain the abode of Śiva. The *Śaktis* or potencies, having their abodes on top of mountains, earth, forests, cremation grounds and bodies, dance before him. These *Śaktis* are names Jayā, Vijayā, Jayantī, Aparājitā, Siddha, Raktā, Alaṁbuṣā and Utpalā, according to their degrees.

Alaṁbuṣā has a *Vāhana* or vehicle, by name Caṇḍa, a crow. Once, there was a festival where all the *Śaktis* had gathered in front of Śiva when they danced and laughed under excessive intoxication. Meanwhile in another part of *Ākāśa* their vehicles too were in a similar state. Caṇḍa sportingly united with the female swans which became pregnant. After the celebration the *Śaktis* retired to their respective places along with their vehicles. The swans narrated what had happened along with their present condition. The *Śaktis* accepted it as a Divine mandate, and gave the swans their freedom till delivering the offspring. The eggs were laid by the side of Mānasa lake. In due course the eggs hatched issuing twenty-one young ones, the progeny of Caṇḍa, and Bhuṣuṇḍa one among them.

The young crows prayed the Alaṁbuṣā, the *Brahma-Śakti,* who arising from her *Samādhi* graced them all with *Mokṣa.* In deep gratitude, they prayed the *Śakti* to guide them to choose a place for enjoying the bliss of *Nirvāṇa.* The *Śakti* guided them to the Kalpa tree. Vasiṣṭha, unable to restrict his thirst to know, enquired as to how the great crow, Bhuṣuṇḍa had attained such a long life. To which the great *Yogin* said that he and his twenty brothers had spent many *Kalpas* on that very tree, when at last his brothers discarded their bodies for *Mokṣa.*

Sage Vasiṣṭha asked further, as to how Bhuṣuṇḍa could survive the terrible *Pralayas* or deluges. Yogi Bhuṣuṇḍa replied that he left the nest and remaining in *Ākāśa* he performed the *Dhāraṇā* on the element contrary to the element of deluge so as to remain unaffected in the state of *Nirvikalpa Samādhi.* Explaining it further, he continued that during the *Pralaya* or dissolution brought about by the twelve Ādityas or Suns, he performed *Āpa-dhāraṇā,* the *Dhāraṇā* on water; for earth on *Agni,* the fire; for water on *Vāyu,* the air, etc. At the end of the Creator's night, he once again came back to the Kalpa tree. Drinking from these nectar like words, Vasiṣṭha was interested in knowing why the other *Yogis* do not continue to live in spite of their knowing the technique of *Dhāraṇā.*

Bhuṣuṇḍa of infinite patience replied that none can

possibly overstep the mandate of Parameśvara. It was His will that Bhuṣuṇḍa should act in such manner, and the *Yogis* in the manner which they do, as everything is preordained, following the universal law of nature. Then he went on to describe the multiple creations and deluges, of repeated incarnations of Viṣṇu, *Ṛṣis* Agastya, Nārada, Bharadwāja, Marīci, Pulastya, Ganeśa, Kārtikeya and others, *Samudra-manthana,* or the churning of the ocean to get the Ambrosia, the *Vedas* being saved by Viṣṇu, etc. He said that it is impossible to tell of every creation, as even for Vasiṣṭha to whom he was talking, this was the eighth time!

Bhuṣuṇḍa said all these are temporal things which are latent in One Reality, like foam in the ocean, and will revive and perish again and again. And that one can transcend death, by eliminating wrong action, desires, greed, anger, lust, and infatuation. One who establishes oneself in the Non-dual Reality is never afflicted by change and illusion. Bhuṣuṇḍa said that such a state was attained by him by engaging himself in meditation on *Prāṇa* and its control, due to which he ceased cognising the external things and arrested the death.

Death and impermanence have been the starting points of many an inquiry into spirituality. And India in particular has contributed positively in this direction. Observing impermanence and death all around a seeker starts thinking of the *possibility* of transcending death. So the discussion on those persons who are *Cirañjīvins* can be taken literally, or those persons who have known the Deathless Principle. And the latter position appears more practical from a seeker's point of view. The deathless crow Bhuṣuṇḍa symbolises: 'One who covers the whole universe in one's blissful flight'.[168] He has been described by the author as one who has transcended attraction-aversion, silently quiescent and full of poise.

---

168 भुवनेषु सर्वेष्वपि सुखं डयते विहरतीति भुषुण्ड इति प्रसिद्धः ।। वासिष्ठचन्द्रिका 6.1.66 ।।

Regarding the psychic powers, the great sage Patañjali in his *Yogadarśanaṃ* devotes a whole chapter giving all the techniques of achieving them. So it is not strange that Bhuṣuṇḍa had them. However, for an earnest seeker, they can only be a source of a great distraction. But we have to be open-minded so as to accept that such things exist. Another thing we will do well to keep in mind is, that the *Pralaya* and the creation are everyday happenings when we enter deep sleep and return to wakeful state.

Bhuṣuṇḍa the great Yogi then continued when Vasiṣṭha requested him to describe the control of *Prāṇa.* First he described the difference between *Prāṇa* and *Apāna,* as the vital forces having upward and downward movements respectively, and went on giving the eight courses of achieving control over *Prāṇa* and in turn *Mokṣa.* But he also added that one should take up *any* one of these eight courses without *any break in the practice,* for achieving the end. When the practice becomes a part of one's nature, then the course of the life is set. Another important thing was told, that Bhuṣuṇḍa had transcended time and so lived only in the present, without keeping any goal or aim, because the goal *projects* the mind into future. Having learnt about the mystic secrets, Vasiṣṭha returned to his abode reluctantly, for parting from *Jñānīns* can be very painful.

The mystic secrets have been intentionally avoided in this discussion as they can be learnt only under an experienced guide. One should never venture into the practice, through the theoretical knowledge on the length of *Pūraka*—inhalation, *Recaka*—exhalation, or *Kuṁbhaka*—holding of breath either inside or outside, obtained from the books. This can cause lot of complications. An experienced guide however, especially an enlightened Master, can bring about a speedy transformation, because an enlightened person guides the seeker according to his aptitude, level and capacity.

The purpose of *Prāṇāyāma* is mainly to increase the awareness and to reduce and ultimately eliminate unconsciousness. Here the breath is made use of for achieving the end. Breathing is such an act which is usually unconscious. However, it can also become a conscious action. By achieving control over breathing, one can slowly and steadily gain control over the unconscious. The method taught by the Buddha happens to be the safest. He called it as the *Ānāpānasati*—the awareness of the incoming and outgoing breath. One is asked to do *passive* observation, without any change in the speed or depth of breathing. At the same time, the seeker is suggested to increase the time period of this awareness without any violent force. When one tries to become attentive to breath, one cannot help but notice the stubbornness of the mind which strays again and again from the object of attention. It is to be brought back to breath repeatedly without any annoyance or impatience. The *Śloka* from the *Bhagavadgītā* puts it beautifully:

> 'As and when the vagrant and unstable mind gets distracted;
> There and then one should fix it on Self by taking it away from distraction'.[169]

Ānanda, the disciple and constant companion of the Buddha said one day to the Master, that in more than thirty years of his company, with the Buddha, he had *never* seen Him make *any* movement in his sleep. Nor had he seen Him make *any unnecessary* movement while awake. The Buddha is reported to have said that Ānanda had not practised the *Ānāpānasati* properly. The practice of *Ānāpānasati* eliminates unconsciousness. Even if the body is asleep, the mind is awake *all the time.* Breath is usually never taken seriously, for it is taken for granted. But if it is done consciously and with full awareness, it can become a door to *Nirvāṇa.* For that matter, *any act* can become a door, if it is lit by the light of awareness!

---

169 यतो यतो निश्चलति मनश्चंचलमस्थिरम् ।
ततस्ततो नियम्यैतदात्मन्येव वशं नयेत् ।। 6.26 ।।

2

The Story of Deva-Pūjā (Divine Worship)

The cloudless deep blue sky is reflected on the still surface of the lake. There is not even a whisper of breeze, and the lake surface appears like a flawless mirror. As one comes down the shoulder of a mountain, one starts observing the reflected images of the mountains and vegetation on the other the surface of the lake. For a moment the beholder of these images even loses himself in the images, forgetting the real objects! This happens every day to us. A photograph of a place or of a person is more attractive than the place or the person himself! This very phenomenon is used to their advantage by the people advertising and marketing the consumer products. An attractive image or a packing is enough to tempt a consumer into the vicious web of consumerism, which has been rightly said to be the art of selling goods to a consumer who neither needs them, nor can he afford!

A lie wrapped in sweet words or accompanied with flattery is more acceptable to us, than the truth which may be uttered rather harshly. We seldom note hypocrisy, accompanied as it is by false smiles or sweet words—that are nothing but the virtual images of thoughts, have become more important to us. The society in general has become so insensitive as to get carried away by sophistication and etiquette. But it does not in any way mean that this disease (dis-ease!) is incurable! The above observations prove that man as such, lives too much on the periphery without any concern or even memory of the centre. Once his attention starts withdrawing from the periphery and moves towards the centre, the transformation sets in.

All life starting from the botanical and animal life up to man is graded from simple to more and more complex form. And up to primates or the apes, the evolution is totally unconscious. The life *cannot help but evolve.* The scientists, whether they are biologists or anthropologists, agree totally on this point, that the evolution of the human body as such has stopped thousands of years back. This only goes to show that the horizontal evolution—if one may call this growth and mutation of the material body, has stopped for him. The dimension of evolution has shifted from material, to the spiritual plane or from the horizontal to the vertical plane for man. Because of this very reason, there is more freedom as any spiritual development by its very nature has to be conscious.

But then, mind with the help of the senses is *outgoing* as its function is to gather outside information. Man has depended on this instrument for his very survival during his days of *animal-hood.* As a result, they have become part of his trusted retinue. And in spite of leaving his cave and his movement towards civilization, science, technology, and other outward growth, man in general has not bothered to entertain any other thought in his mind, than mere survival.

Consequently, all his technology has only *improved* upon his already existing senses and brain. For example, TV, telescope and microscope are the extensions of his eye; computers are extensions of his brain; etc. It is almost like an airplane meant for flying is being used on the road! Unhappiness has become a common factor for all of us. Man is the only creature who is always in anguish. Because, he is not using himself for the purpose he is meant to fulfill. He is meant to evolve vertically, and not horizontally. The desires and craving for objects of senses are endless; thirst for knowledge is also endless.

This is where the observation of our *Ṛṣis* is extremely revolutionary. They said that the thirst for objects only increases with each effort to satisfy; that the mystery of the universe only deepens if we continue to search for it outside, before trying to seek *the experiencer, the knower.* Literally, this *was* a revolution. In evolution the senses are used to keep the attention outside, while man is meant for this *revolution* of turning his attention towards the origin of thoughts, experience, knowledge, and emotions, in short, towards *himself.*

It is true that unless he fulfills his minimum needs for survival, he may not even be aware of this inner dimension. However, it is not *mandatory* that man should and must turn his attention within. The change in the direction of attention or the turning point is totally dependent on the individual choice. We can choose to begin this revolution or completely ignore it and continue the animalistic life of struggle for survival. This freedom is peculiar only to mankind. But unfortunately, though man may choose to *remain at the level of survival,* life will not allow him! For life means movement and he is compelled to move in the horizontal direction and that is how he tends to *regress* into animal-hood. In fact, he becomes worse than an animal, which is obvious from the ecological mess he has created for himself in the name of progress!

The freedom involves a great responsibility. Man is what he is, only because of himself, and no one else is responsible. Jean-Paul Sartre, the French Existentialist philosopher has said, that *'Man is condemned to be free'*, because, all other animals have a pre-programmed and specific direction of growth. A dog lives and dies as a dog. But a man need not. He can die as an enlightened man or even as a great sinner worse than animals. The freedom to choose the vertical growth demands a great sense of discipline which is very obvious. For a person piloting an airplane has to comply certain rules and regulations connected with aviation. Perhaps there is an innate hesitation or even fear, due to which he tries to continue as nothing more than a social animal!

This *Sarga* gives the inner significance of the ritualistic worship of the chosen Deity. Sage Vasiṣṭha continued by saying that, the most of the humankind is conscious only of the body it identifies the 'I' with body composed of the five elements, and is governed by change and time. While the truth is that the five elements and time are temporary by nature. The sage gave the example of a person sleeping on a bed roams around in all directions in a dream body. This happens even in the wakeful state when one is in the act of day-dreaming, while all along the body remains on the same bed.

Saṁkalpa is the axle of the car of existence. Unless the axle is stopped totally through *Viveka* and *Vicāra* the chain of birth and death cannot be stopped. He added that unless one becomes conscious of this useless movement, no amount of scriptural study can be of any help to such a person. Instead, such a one will use even the *Śāstras* for only the material end, that is, to increase the involvement and indulgence. That is why, one must eliminate the lower mind which generates pain and fear. When one is under the influence of the lower mind, even an enlightened person may not be having any effect on such a person. The revered sage then went on to narrate the details of the meeting he had with Parameśvara.

Vasiṣṭha said that once he spent a long time on the Kailāśa Mountain worshipping Parameśvara, and performing *Tapas.* On the midnight of the eighth day of the first half of the lunar month of Simha, when it was pitch dark and everything was silent, he came back from the state of *Samādhi* he saw an incomparable light never seen before. In the splendour of light he beheld Parameśvara and Pārvatī. They were preceded by Nandī, the vehicle of Śiva. Vasiṣṭha along with his disciples worshipped them, and sought their blessings. The Great Lord in turn inquired about the *Muni's Tapas,* and the progress made thereby. The sage sought an esoteric explanation of *Deva-Pūjā.* To which Parameśvara replied:

Deva or God is neither Viṣṇu, nor Śiva, nor any other person having a body of five elements. Nor is it the mind. It is *Jñāna,* the Self without beginning or end. It is limitless and actionless, fit to be worshipped. And worship happens to be the best aid for the ignorant who are unable to rise to the lofty level. Just as travelers who are unable to walk large distances are told that their destination is only at a calling distance, so as not to let their spirits droop, the persons without *Jñāna* are told to worship diverse forms at first. But the wise declare that *Jñāna* cannot dawn in such a process. Their contention is that the worship of diverse forms does not help in transcending forms. It is beyond even the *Śāstras.* The God is the great *Sattā-Mātra* or Pure Being. Should this *Jñāna* subject itself to *Vikalpas,* it abandons its real nature and becomes individualised and separate. The One *Cit* (consciousness) contracts through contemplation, in regular succession into different states of *Avidyā.* Conditioned by space, time, and other powers it becomes the ignorant *Jīva,* fulfilling the functions of *Buddhiḥ, Ahaṁkāra* and *Manas.*

The Lord continued: *Ātmatattva* has all the *Śaktis* in It, which generate bondage and freedom. In *Ātman* there are *Śaktis* like *Icchā* (will), *Vyōman* (*Ākāśa* or space), *Kāla* (time), *Mahā* (might), *Jñāna* (wisdom), *Kriyā* (action), *Kartṛ* (agency of action), *Akartṛ* (non-agency), etc. The sportive *Śaktis* of *Ajñāna* generate birth and death. Non-identification of 'I' with the body is the supreme worship. One should always remember that the Supreme Principle is beyond all *Saṁkalpa* and hence all action which follows it. It includes everything and yet transcends everything. The external form of worship is only gross, it should be respected. For as long as there is the wisdom of *Viveka* within, so long shall the mind be in *Dhyāna,* even in this form of worship. One should be ever in *Jñāna* amidst all the actions, including the perception through senses. That is how, the contemplation on the *Ātmatattva* becomes possible, and all the sense objects become the articles for worship. The Great Lord assured Vasiṣṭha that even if the ignorant perform such *Dhyāna* and steadily increase the time of being in such state, she or he can merge in the Brāhmic Light.

Ritualistic worship has been performed by millions of Hindus for at least a thousand years. It is claimed that it was revived and reformed by the great Ācārya Śaṅkara during his life time. It has a few very important steps. First step is the preparation for worship. In this, after his own bath, the devotee collects the materials like flowers, cleans the place of worship, prepares sandal paste and the food offering. Then he lights the lamp in the temple, and purifies his mind through what has been called as the *Nyāsa,* which involves the invocation of various Deities in different parts of his body and mind. *Nyāsa* is meant to bring in the conviction of the existence of the Divinity within. This is followed by *Āvāhanaṃ* or the invocation of the *Iṣṭadevatā,* the Chosen Deity into the image to be worshipped. This is followed by bath, decoration, offering incense, light and food, *Stotras* or hymns of praise, and salutations and finally, leave-taking.

This practice of *Deva-Pūjā,* if performed with awareness, helps in purification of mind, preparing it for *Antarmukhatā.* In the preparation of the worship, like gathering the materials, unwanted thoughts are eliminated from the mind; in the practice of *Nyāsa* centering becomes possible; in the *Āvāhanaṃ,* the single-thought condition of mind becomes possible; and in the offering, all the senses are utilised for transformation, as it is not for oneself but for the *Iṣṭadevatā.* But then, human mind has the expertise of converting *anything* into a mechanical practice or an empty gesture! We have millions of persons performing the ritualistic worship, sometimes twice or thrice daily. We have lakhs of temples to offer our prayers. But unfortunately, we hardly see *any noticeable* change in either their attitude or way of life. On the contrary, we see such persons nurturing a false pride and a sense of superiority over the other so-called non-religious persons!

Mahādeva continued, by saying that He had dealt with external worship so far, and would deal with the internal worship. Instead of taking the help of an external image, one should resort to the internal Divine Presence, which pervades in all the centres, in *Manas, Saṁkalpa,* the *Prāṇa* and *Apāna.* The worshiper should continually contemplate on the inner Light which gives us the sense of *being,* and lights our mind and intellect, *Karmendriyas* and *Jñānendriyas,* and all the *Śaktis* or potencies. One should learn to become aware of all activity that takes place in the body and mind. With this awareness, one reaches the sanctum sanctorum or the innermost shrine, and comes face to face with the Self. Being identified with this Self or the Centre, the worshiper becomes capable of enjoying *anything* as the Non-dual Principle. Whatever be the experience one can never get either indulged or involved in it, from this level.

Even in the so-called gross *Deva-Pūjā,* while performing *Aṅga-Nyāsa* and *Kara-Nyāsa,* or the *Nyāsa* of parts of the body and hands, the *Mantras* chanted, distinctly place different Deities in different parts of the body and functions like speech, sight, hearing, touch, even physical strength, etc. When one chants them with awareness and *Bhāva* or mood, one can make even the ritualistic worship into a deeply esoteric practice.

Śiva said that just as the six different tastes—sour, pungent, bitter, astringent, sweet, and hot—are perceived only when the potency of taste is joined with the *Manas,* the internal significance of the worship can be felt only when there is quiescence of mind. With the quiescence, even the worldly objects become universal. But if it is done without quiescence, the spiritual entities like mind, intellect and *Ahaṁkāra* cannot be felt. One should be free of all desire and thought to reach the Centre called the Self. Like a washer-man removing the dirt from dirt, as the alkaline soil was used before the soap was invented, the impure *Vāsanās* are removed by pure *Vāsanās.*

Continuing the Great Lord said, that the practices like *Deva-Pūjā,* the company of an enlightened preceptor and his advice are all like the dirt removing soil. They help the aspirant to look for and succeed in discovering the Reality within. It is difficult to cross over this ocean of *Saṁsāra* without the help of *Guru, Śāstras* and disciple-ship. All the three are very important. An enlightened *Guru* alone can bring in the understanding of the essence of the *Śāstras.* And unless there is the real and earnest discipleship which has the virtues required for *Sādhanā*[170] he is not at all eligible for the initiation into secrets of spirituality. Those men who ignore the *inner call* in preference to the involvement and indulgence are sinners. The Lord blessed Vasiṣṭha that he be continually immersed in such esoteric worship of the *Jñāna,* and retreated to his abode with his divine consort, attendants and *Vāhana.*

Sage Vasiṣṭha said that ever since, he has been performing this *Jñāna-Pūjā,* and has totally gained control over the *Vāsanās,* and been enjoying the union with the *Jñānātman.* There on he blessed Rāma, that he too may attain the lofty state by performing all activity with an unattached mind. Rāma expressed his gratefulness and joy in not only learning the esoteric secrets, but in eliminating the desires to a great extent.

Unless man chooses to move in the direction he is meant to traverse, he is bound to regress in the direction of animal-

170 Refer to The Divine Disinterest and The Divine Longing.

hood. And always the choice is between awareness and instinct, or between consciousness and unconsciousness. And awareness *cannot* possibly be forced or even caused because awareness is always voluntary. Though, some outer situation or experience may become instrumental in helping one to look in a new direction. But it is not at all necessary that everyone should start changing from the materialistic to a spiritual way of life. Most of the time, when something goes wrong, we think of changing the outer circumstances like place or relationship, instead of making an effort to find out whether there is something wrong with us! For example, when we become angry, we invariably blame the person who caused this anger, instead of trying to find the source of anger. That is how, we keep changing our milieu, instead of transforming ourselves.

Deva-Pūjā as explained in this *Sarga* is really lofty and practical, in the sense, that it gives the inner processes that *should* take place with the outer rituals and gestures. In this awareness is the master key for the entry into the palace of the Spirit. This is true not only for the *Pūjā,* but *any* spiritual practice. In the external *Pūjā,* even the senses and their objects are purified as it were, giving an opportunity for the worshiper to transform his outlook. There is a very enlightening episode from the life of a Tamil saint who was a devotee of Viṣṇu in *Yoga-Nidrā* at a place called Shri Rangam.

The king of that place was a literally infatuated by the beauty of one of his wives. Once when the king was walking towards the temple with his retinue, the umbrella carrier did not position the umbrella properly as the harsh rays of the sun fell on his beloved wife's face. Losing his temper the king took the umbrella in his own hands to protect his wife! The saint seeing this approached the king and asked him why he had done it. The king said innocently that his wife who was the most beautiful of all the women, would suffer if he had not protected her from the sun. The saint told the king that he would show the king someone who was more beautiful, and took him into the sanctum sanctorum. Perhaps it was the presence of the saint, or may be the king too was ready, or it is likely that it was both, the king beheld the Lord in all His beauty and glory, and became an ardent devotee!

Shri Ramakrishna used to say, that the devotee gets an opportunity to sublimate all emotions by directing them towards the Divine. But there should be total awareness. Without awareness the practice becomes mechanical, empty and perhaps even harmful. In our country, what goes in the name of worship in the public or private temples is an opportunity to ask something from God! In other words, we have taken the worship to be a means for fulfilling the desires. One goes to the temple either to ask for something, or to lodge a complaint, or perhaps to honour the agreement decided by the devotee *in case his demand is fulfilled!* While the process is meant to *free* the worshiper from the activity called the mind.

When one beholds the beauty one gets enchanted and lost in it. One totally forgets oneself, the beholder, the experiencer. At other times when one experiences pain, one is obsessed by that which causes it, again forgetting the sufferer. Entrapped in the images, one forgets the real. The gift of spirituality dawns on such a person who tries to seek the *source* instead of the *cause* that may be outside; who tries to approach the Centre instead of the periphery that is this world; who starts the journey to the Fountainhead of all energy, all peace and all joy.

3

The Story of Bilva Fruit

The sun shines mercilessly. The asphalt road radiates the heat. Amidst this uncomfortable heat, thick, dark nimbus clouds can be seen in the horizon. The very sight creates relief and hope in the mind, that perhaps there is an end to the sweltering heat. From the direction of the clouds, a pleasant breeze ushers a physical relief. Slowly and steadily the clouds start moving and filling the whole sky, making the atmosphere cooler. At the same time the wind brings a lot of dust through the air. Suddenly, there is thunder and lightning followed by a cool shower of rain which quenches the parching thirst of the land and fauna. By dusk the rain stops as suddenly as it had started. The birds return to their nests to finally rest for the night, and everything becomes silent.

A new sound can be heard from the surroundings : the harsh croaks of the frogs. No one knows from where they come after the rain, and where they live during the drought-like condition. Scientists say that the frogs hibernate most of the time, and come out intermittently with the outbreak of regular monsoons or even a casual rain. This observation was perhaps behind the naming of a very profound *Upaniṣad* known as the *Māṇḍukya Upaniṣad.* In Sanskrit a frog is called *Maṇḍūkaḥ*[171] which means, that which manifests during rainy

---

171 मण्डयति वर्षा समये ---मण्ड् + ऊकण् ।

time. The process of hibernation may have been seen by the *Ṛṣi* as the process of *Tapas* and introspection. The rain has been attributed to involvement. So it is likely, that the croaks of the frogs are the declarations of the truth, though rather harsh, which warn the consequences of involvement!

If someone is told that his action or speech or thought is wrong, he may get annoyed with the person who points this out and may ask him to mind his own business! When a person is told that all his actions are unconscious, then the anger is more. For whenever a person wakes up a sleeping man, the sleeping man gets irritated for disturbing his sleep! And when the society is told that it suffers from somnambulism, its wrath can even exterminate the person or persons who bring in this awareness. That is how, a Socrates is poisoned, a Jesus is crucified, and a Mansoor is flayed and eliminated. It is an altogether different matter that after their death the same society organises religions in their names!

The society is tradition oriented. It is necessarily so, because otherwise it cannot have any control. Masses too are tradition bound because, it is convenient to travel on a beaten track. To traverse a new path, an unknown trail, requires alertness on the part of the traveller. Since it is a totally new path, the past experiences cannot be possibly helpful. One has only the present and absolutely no idea of the future or where it takes him. The journey may end favourably or otherwise; one may be lost and be left alone without any company. One can plunge into spirituality only when one is prepared to become a solitary bird and not before. Carlos Castaneda gives five conditions of a solitary bird as declared by San Juan de la Cruz:

'The conditions of a solitary bird are five:
The first, that it flies to the highest point;
the second, that it does not suffer for company, not even of its own kind;
the third, that it aims its beak to the skies;

the fourth, that it does not have a definite colour;
the fifth, that it sings very softly'.[172]

The preparedness for *any* eventuality can come only by conscious choice, and that is why, only an infinitesimal number of seekers, continues after taking to the path of spirituality. While for most, it becomes a passing or of casual interest, as it is only to get relief from the pressures of day-to-day problems due to involvement. For such persons even this interest becomes an involvement. Nature of mind, or rather *minding,*—because it is an activity, is to get itself *identified* with *anything.* One used to get identified with the sense objects, relationships, or ideas, before treading the path of spirituality, and now he or she gets identified with words like *Mukti, Dhyāna, Māyā,* etc.! Understanding this tendency of the mind, almost all religions directly or indirectly suggest the seeker to develop awareness.

If one does some retrospection on all the stories dealt in this great scripture so far, a very clear picture of the activity of the mind emerges: That the mind is only a peripheral phenomenon which is at the substratum of everything we call the world; that it has its origin in the *Ahaṁkāra,* the 'I-ness' which is nothing but an inconsequential shadow of the Self at the Centre; that more we get involved with the periphery, the more strong is the 'I-ness' and 'mine'; that more strong the *Ahaṁkāra,* more does one go away from the Centre; and that all spiritual effort is to leave the periphery and move towards the Centre. The Centre has been addressed by various names, each suggesting an aspect of the limitless Reality.

There are three levels of activity for the mind. First is the level of the sense objects, for example, sound. There is a sound

---

172 *Tales of Power* by Carlos Castaneda, Penguin Books, 1979. Compare with Shri Ramakrishna's 'Homa Bird' in *The Story of Indra.*

object, the process of perception and the perceiver. The object and the perception are on the periphery, while the perceiver is towards the Centre. At this level one tries to move away from the sense vibration, towards the perceiver and to become one with the perceiver. When dealing with the activity at this level, one tries to eliminate the impure *Vāsanās* with the help of pure *Vāsanās.* That is where *Indriya-nigraha* or control of sense organs, *Samtoṣa* or contentment, *Virakti* or developing distaste for the sense objects becomes relevant.

The second level is at the level of movement. While on the physical plane, we move in space, and at the mental plane the movement is in time. Either the mind gets projected into past, which is nothing but the memory of the experiences. The pleasant experiences are re-lived, and the unpleasant ones are shunned or remembered with bitterness. Future is nothing but a projection of the past as a desire to repeat the pleasant experiences and to avoid the unpleasant. For most of us, there is nothing like the present as we are either obsessed with the past or the future, and even if it is there, it is so only as a *bridge* between the past and the future! To arrest the movement, one is advised to be at the present. This is where *Śama* or sweet patience and *Viveka* or discrimination are of great help.

And the third aspect of the mind is *Ahaṁkāra* or the 'I-ness', which is behind every possible activity ('I' act, 'I' feel, or 'I' know) and is at the substratum. This 'I-ness' is the subtlest of the activity and is the primary activity, is the *primal fall,* if one may say so, the initial contraction from the all expansive State! Again this 'I-ness' has three levels. The first is, when one identifies with the periphery as 'my things' or 'my actions' or 'my thoughts and feelings'. The second one which is subtler, is that stage of the *tendency to get involved,* which has been named as the *Bhoga-Vāsanā* and *Bheda-Vāsanā.* And the last is the subtlest is *Asmitā* or the *Am-ness,* the beginning of duality or multiplicity. To curtail this activity *Vicāra* is recommended by the wise.

Yoga Vāsiṣṭha tries to tackle the activity at all these levels. It suggests the study of scriptures and company of the wise for gaining an understanding into one's own nature. Most of the time, we suffer not only because of the external circumstances, but more because of the lack of understanding *who the sufferer* is! Once this understanding dawns, then everything unfolds itself towards fulfillment.

Whenever anyone approached Shri Ramana Maharishi in suffering and painful state or for clarifying a doubt, he would always urge the person to find out *who* the *sufferer* or *doubter* was. Invariably, the person would be pushed into the state of *Antarmukhatā*. When one develops the capacity to look within, sooner or later, one is bound to discover, that there is nothing like the 'I-ness'. There are different shades of activity, physical as well as mental. And what we have come to believe as the 'I' is a non-entity, like humanity, forest or for that matter universe! There are individuals, persons or trees or stars. Factually however, humanity, forest and universe are only *conceptual groups!* So naturally one will not find the ego. Instead, one discovers the uninvolved witness or mute observer of all activity which transcends the activity.

Discovery of this gap between the Centre and the periphery is the essence of all that goes in the name of religion. Each experience has the potential to show us this gap, if one is sensitive. Unfortunately, the identification of the ego with the periphery robs us off our sensitivity. For example, when one says 'my house' there is no distance at all, because one *has become* the house! Similarly it is with everything else, viz. relationships, feelings, or thoughts! This gap increases when there is the sense of loss or failure or disappointment. And that is why, the ideal time for discovering this gap between the periphery and all activity, and the Centre or the actionless-ness, is when one has some kind of pain and suffering. It is the suffering that gives us depth, as it gives a shock to our identification and involvement.

This *Sarga* begins with a request from Rāma to sage Vasiṣṭha for continuing his sweet discourse. Vasiṣṭha said that, that which may have been pleasant at one time can have the very reverse effect at another. It only goes to show that if something is longed for, it becomes pleasant. But the same becomes bitter when an opposite feeling of aversion is experienced. That is why, one should transcend the likes and dislikes from the lower mind. The universe with all its multiplicity is only a creation of the mind. Therefore, the mind should be annihilated by destruction of *Vāsanās* or control of *Prāṇa.* The basic *Avidyā* has the property of contraction and expansion, through which the *Karmas* have their birth and death. That is why, one should annihilate the mind by the power of constant association with the *Guru* and the *Śāstras.*

The mind so destroyed by the control of *Prāṇa* or the arrest of the fluctuations of mind gives way to the Supreme State. Bliss arising when the visible things and vision are merged into the One seer is all-pervading Reality. Through such experience the mind is destroyed, generating infinite bliss. Such bliss does not have fluctuation, has no appearance or disappearance. The mind of such a *Jñānī* cannot be termed mind but only *Tattva* or Reality. That which becomes diverse is the mind. With the elimination of *Vāsanās* and fluctuations, through control of *Prāṇa,* it becomes immaculate like copper transmuting to gold. Then one has become the Non-dual, without distinction between Spirit and Matter. All the distinctions are of mind only. Since the mind itself is only a shadow of the Reality, the merger with the Reality is itself transcendence. Giving this background *Ṛṣi* Vasiṣṭha went on to narrate a brief anecdote.

A passing remark on the nature of *Avidyā* to be contraction and expansion is worth noting. The contraction referred to here can be taken as the process of involvement or identification, which creates an impression and a reaction, which is called as the *Karma*. And whenever, a desire is fulfilled through the gratification of senses, an expansion takes place—though, for a very short period of time. The expansion as such is the nature of Reality, and that is why the scripture calls it as *Paramārthika*, or Supreme. Unfortunately, *Vāsanās* do not allow one to remain in that expansive state for long, as there is the tendency for contraction, achieved through further desires!

The sage continued : There is a Bilva fruit of such huge dimensions that it cannot be possibly measured. It never decays even when the *Mahā-Kalpa* closes. Though it is the ancient of ancients, its glory is such that it is very soft and delightful. It remains unruffled even in the midst of the fierce storms and gales at the end of a *Kalpa*. It is the seed of Brahmā's egg. It is impossible to estimate the number of mundane eggs generated out of it, and absorbed in it. Though ever ripe, it never decays. It is the essence of all fruits. The fleshy part of the fruit is unlimited and represents all-pervading nature of *Jñāna*. The marrow of the fruit is the fluctuating *Cit-Śakti* which arising out of the fruit of Brahman produces heterogeneities of *Ākāśa*, the *Kalās* or parts, the imperishable *Dharma*, motion, etc. through the potency of its intelligence.

At this statement, Rāma commented, that this allegory had been understood by him. Bilva fruit is the supreme state of *Sat* or *Jñāna, Ahaṁkāra*, etc. are but the base aspects of *Jñāna*, which appears as one and the many, though it never has any basic difference. The marrow of the fruit of *Jñāna* is the extensive universe arising out of *Ahaṁkāra*.

The allegory of the Bilva fruit having immeasurable dimensions, and other impossible qualities appears far flung. It must be remembered by the seeker that the allegory must have been used with a specific reason of helping those on the path. As has been mentioned elsewhere in this rendering, that the symbology was used not only for giving literal beauty to the scripture, but for the seeker to associate the truth with life. Bilva is a fruit of a tree commonly called as the *Bel* or Aegle Mermelos. Its leaves are used for the worship of Śiva. The fruit which is spherical in shape has a strong flavour, and is very sweet when ripe. It is also used for medicinal purpose. The author might not have used it as an allegory solely for this reason.

Bilva has another implication. Bilva means a very small measurement of time. All of us are aware that the shortest moment is the *present.* Most of the time, if not all the time, we are either living in the past, or the future, so much so, for us time only means, either the past or the future! Present moment is only that very very narrow passage we use, to travel back and forth in time! Consequently, we are seldom aware of the present. Curiously there is nothing like the past or future, as past is only memories of experiences and future is projection of the desires in the mind! While the truth of the world and the experiences lies only in the present, in 'here-now'. This obstinate habit of being *elsewhere* in time and space is the root cause of all misery and discontent, which troubles the humankind.

Taking the example of a working man's daily routine will make it more clear. When he gets up he has already left for the office, with the result that he does all his work absent-mindedly. But since his mind was absent during the bath, breakfast, or his taking leave from the family, the mind tries to complete those actions by going back home, *after reaching the office!* His work in the office suffers, as his mind is not present there.... Thus almost all actions are somnambulistic. This is true even in our social behaviour which is full of hypocrisy. We are not happy to be with or to entertain someone, but cannot show our displeasure openly. So we put on a false smile and be with them only physically! Rarely, when there is some danger or an intense sense experience, we are available to the present. And we really live only during these brief moments.

Due to the incomplete actions, the mind tries to complete them through an internal dialogue. This inner noise does not allow us any rest or peace. Even our sleep is disturbed as the incomplete thoughts get completed through dreams! The life becomes a tiresome race to catch the horizon, a mad movement from one desire to another!

The Buddha in his eight fold path, has given a very significant dictum, called *Samma-Kammāṅta* or the right action. All actions are to be done with total awareness, by being there totally and not just physically! This not only helps us to complete the actions, so the mind is not burdened with the task of completion and hence it becomes more and more quiet, but the action itself becomes more and more efficient. Moreover, the mind cannot *be* in the present moment, and hence one transcends mind during the experience of here-now.

The Bilva fruit represents the Supreme state of *Sat* which is primary to everything in the universe; everything is born in the present, lives in the present and ultimately dies in the present. It is a homogeneous state, representing Non-duality, fragrant and sweet and delicious. That may be the reason why the sages chose to seek the Origin or the Centre of everything, as It alone can give the Unified Perspective. They were very much aware of the deepening mystery as one starts moving on the periphery. They recommended the seeker to seek this Origin or Centre before embarking on the journey outside. For this, one of the methods they suggested was to *be* in the mood of *here-now*. Such a person who has learnt to ride the present moment is bound to be ever young, as he does not have any burden of the past, since he has transcended the mind. To bring home this point, the author says that though the Fruit is ever ripe, it never decays.

Different persons have given different methods to suit the different times and individuals. J. Krishnamurti used to advise the seekers to complete each thought, so as to see and appreciate the gap of silence between two thoughts. But an ordinary man involved in the day-to-day struggle for survival as he is, it may be very difficult to observe the thoughts, as he is used to only the gross things. Perhaps Buddha's *Samma-Kammāṅta* is more practical for him. He has to only constantly remind himself of the *work at hand* till the gross actions become more conscious and aware, and lead him towards the higher dictum of *Samma-Sati* or right remembrance, or *Surati* as advocated by Saint Kabir.

The truth of our being somnambulistic is harsh, but to accept it even with a little whimper, is the first step in the direction of waking up. This acceptance makes us responsible for our present state, as we stop putting the blame on someone else. The right action, is the beginning of a wonderful journey towards realisation of sweet and fragrant Bilva fruit, Which is already within us or we are of IT!

4

The Story of Śīla

The bus slowly negotiates a steep gradient. It has left behind the concrete jungle of Coimbatore—an industrial city in south western Tamil Nadu, and has entered the lush green forest of the Western Ghats. A group of students from the local Government College along with the Head of the Department of Botany is in the bus. Peculiarly enough, there are only four Botany students and the other six students are either from the faculties of Arts or Commerce. Though the Botany students and their teacher are on a specimen collection trip, the others too are accompanying them as they not only respect the teacher who is like an elder brother to them, but are convinced that they too can learn more about life.

Professor Rajendran has been in the field of Life Sciences, with a few papers in International Journals to his credit. But he is more popular among the students for his innovating teaching methods, not only the life sciences like Botany and Zoology, but about *Life itself.* He is the Officer in-charge of the National Service Scheme of the college. The six boys belonging to the faculties of Arts and Commerce had been notorious and even dangerous because of their juvenile activities and considered to be having only nuisance value by other members on the Staff. But Rajendran has succeeded in bringing them around and hopes to utilise their extra energy for some constructive work through his love and patience.

As they get down from the bus almost in the deep mountain forest, one of the students wonders whether they have got down at the right place, for there is no sign of any civilization nearby, not even any huts. The teacher assures them that this is the spot, as he has come there more than twice. Leaving the rough road they start walking into the forest which gets thicker, every few steps. The group however, is in very high adventurous spirit and keeps progressing toward its destination.

Nearly half an hour and perhaps a kilometer later, the forest starts clearing and they hear the roaring sound of water. Taking the help of the sound, Rajendran leads the group. Suddenly, they come face to face with their destination of the day : a water fall. Everyone without exception is stunned by the breathtaking sight of the water falling from a height of nearly a hundred feet. The roar of the fall increases *as if* in welcome; the foam and the droplets reach them *as if* the fall is happy to have them! The trees have healthier foliage here. Gradually one begins to hear the other sounds, of variety of birds and insects dwelling in the region.

Climbing the rock overlooking the falls, the group sits in the shade of a boulder enjoying the nature around while relaxing. None of them has spoken, and yet, there is a perfect communication between them *through nature.* But the habit of language is obstinate and one by one, they start coming back to the verbal plane, and the last one to do so is the teacher and only because a question is asked by a student. Though he is hesitant, he starts talking, because of his love for the students. But he does not speak on the flora and the fauna, nor is it on the history of the locality or the fall. He speaks of nature and its beauty; on the influence of nature on life; and the wisdom it gives to the sensitive.

It is not that the students are able to understand him, but they have come to love this man so much, that they are able to *feel* what is implied rather than the words or thoughts.

The seeds are sown, and the farmer in Rajendran is not really bothered *when* they fructify, for he knows that the seed is a seed only because it has the infinite patience to wait for the opportune moment to die, only to become a sapling. All these outings have been undertaken not only for academic reasons, but more so for de-weeding and preparing the ground and for sowing the seeds of *humanness* in them! As a conclusion, he says:

> 'We will conduct a small experiment today. When you see *anything*, do not try to name it. Even if you know the name, just keep it aside, and look deeply without passing *any judgment*, like it is beautiful—ugly, good—bad,.... It is no doubt very difficult. But try it'.

And so starts their journey into the mystery of existence.

The suggestion is not all that mysterious as it apparently appears. This is how an innocent child sees the world, with all its senses fully open. There is no previous *knowledge* or in simple terms, label that comes in between the object and the observer. No names to block the senses! What happens when we name a thing? It loses the mystery enveloping it, as the name helps in recollecting the information we have about the thing, and the mind once again goes back to past or projects itself into future. The name *reduces* an unknowable thing, into a known label. For example, one sees a flower. It is facing the rising sun, has just blossomed. A few dew drops balance delicately on its petals reflecting the sunlight. The gentle breeze caresses the plant. A small spider, weaves a web very near to the flower, instinctively knowing that an insect will stray near attracted by the colour, fragrance and a droplet or two of honey.

The flower is connected with the earth through the roots of the plant. It is related to the sky, the sun, the air, insects, animals and man. Why, even the stars showering few quanta of light on it exercise an influence on it. It is related not only to the space, but time as well. But the moment we name the flower as the Rose it gets isolated and our experience becomes limited. Nay, the experience is blocked, as we go on *thinking* about the other roses, other places where roses are grown, the people who loved to decorate themselves with the rose (Jawaharlal Nehru!), ... while the rose in front of us goes unnoticed.

Most of our experiences—if not all of them, are really cerebral. Though we appear to be sensual, or materialistic, we are psychic as our experiences are only mental, though the thoughts may have their cause on the things outside! Religion is an art of being in the present, in the 'here-now' experience. That is where it differs from Philosophy, which is at the level of logic or reasonable thought. Many persons would approach the Buddha with different intentions. For clarification of their doubts, for testing *whether he was truly enlightened,* for having intellectual discussions or for seeking solutions to their problems or for eradication of their misery. He would discourage everyone except the last two types of persons. He would always give a simile of a blind man discussing the nature of light! No matter how deep were his discussions or intellectual knowledge, the Buddha would say, the blind will never be able to *know* light. He would add that he was a *Vaidya* or a Doctor, who can cure the disease of blindness, so that one could see and experience the light.

Man's spiritual blindness is of two types : He is really blind owing to his involvement and indulgence with the gross, so much so, that he is not even aware of his blindness. The second is, he knows *intellectually* that *man* is blind *(not he!)* and he knows all *about* the blindness and how to cure it *theoretically, and believes he can see!* Obviously, the second type is almost incurable! While the first type, can come to realise his follies and take steps for curing it. The Buddha never encouraged intellectual discussions, but stressed on the practical side of how to overcome the disease. It is unfortunate that his practical teachings were made into *Vāda-s* or arguments by his later followers.

This is mainly because of the nature of the mind to resort to thinking instead of *doing*. That was how Philosophy and Science parted ways. Philosophy starts and ends with logical thought, while Science no doubt begins with logical explanation but continues with experimentation that is based on the sense experience. However, the Science again limits itself to the sense experience as the senses provide data only *of the world outside* while completely ignoring the subject inside. This is where; religion differs from both Philosophy and Science. It begins with one's own behaviour and reactions to the outside world, and continues to travel within till the *Subjectivity* is encountered. But the temptation of involving oneself in intellectualisation is so great, that a seeker can fall an easy prey to it. For all methods are nothing but the tricks to quieten the activity of mind, or to bring about the death of the mind. And no one—especially the mind and ego, is interested in one's own death!

When the mind is free from the gross *Vāsanās* causing sense indulgence, one has to face the subtle *Vāsanās* that effect involvement. The gross have been called by this scripture as the *Bhoga-Vāsanās,* while the subtle ones as the *Bheda-Vāsanās.* One of the principle factors that take one away from oneself is the differentiating thought: "I and the world are different". In the previous *Sarga,* the great sage Vālmīki tries to give the hint of homogeneity of the awareness, by comparing It with the marrow of the Bilva fruit. The *Sat* or being aspect of the Reality, does not have either difference or no-difference, It is Non-dual. In this present *Sarga,* the author tries to touch upon the *Cit* or awareness aspect of the Reality.

Continuing his enlightening discourse, Vasiṣṭha started telling another wonderful story: There is a glorious, huge granite rock which is lovable, clear, soft to touch, indivisible, strong, having endless dimensions, dense and non-differentiable. Out of it innumerable lotuses have grown and bloomed. Some are visible while the others are not; some become the higher ones and some the lower. Some are firm in their own state. There are conch-shells beyond counting in the middle of these lotuses without roots. Discusses also grow in great number between the lotuses. Hearing this Rāma remarked that he observed one such rock of *Śāligrāma*[173] on which Lord Viṣṇu stood.

The *Muni* observed smilingly, that the granite he referred to was not ever seen by Rāma. He applied the word *Śīla* to the *Cit* in the heart, in which the different states of the world are. The *Śīla* is the *Jñāna* in the heart containing the worlds which are One yet many. In the Non-dual and strong *Jñāna* rock, there are hosts of universes. When even earth, space, air, mountains and the quarters are combined do not make an infinitesimal particle of the rock. In this *Śīla* the sacred marks of lotus, discuss and conch[174] are found. The *Śīla* is said to be in a deep sleep state. All the universes are but *Jñāna* itself, like the parts of the rock which are no other than the rock itself. The wise say, that the rock is beyond all change. Though as in the rock, heterogeneous universes with their various qualities are absorbed in the heart, the *Cit* is Non-dual without any difference.

The forest of lotuses appear to be immovable like a stone when seen from a distance, the universes without being differentiated in *Jñāna* are one *Cit.* Like the illustration of the marrow of the Bilva fruit, in which the innumerable mundane eggs merge with the *Sat,* the universes merge with the one *Cit.* Vasiṣṭha cautioned Rāma, that due to multiple universes, he should not conclude that there are many. He added that the *Cit* aspect of Brahman manifests as this motley of universe of forms just like the lotuses in a granite. One can reach the seat of *Ātman* through quiescence, equality of mind and *Jñāna.*

---

173 The sacred stone found in the river Gaṇḍaka, symbolizing Viṣṇu.

174 The symbols representing Viṣṇu.

At the very outset the author tries to give the non-ordinariness of the *Śīla* through various adjectives. *Snigdhā* or lovable, indicates that it creates a Oneness; *Spaṣṭā* meaning clear as it is self-luminous; *Mṛdusparśā* or soft to touch suggests that it has joy; *Mahāvistāraśālinī* means, of endless dimensions, indicating 'That' which is beyond space; *Nibiḍā* or dense, suggesting *only* 'That' and *nothing else; Nityanirandra* is non-differentiable. The granite stands for the *Cit* aspect of the Reality, which is One *without the second,* but at the same time nurtures the *tendency to differentiate* the cause for all imaginable things. It is deeply internal, when the process of thinking has not begun and yet, there is a *tendency to think.* Consequently, the lotuses symbolise the blossoming and withering nature of the phenomena; and the conch-shells, the vibratory nature as conch is associated with the sound.

These two *Sargas* are to be taken together. The Bilva Fruit refers to the *Sat* aspect or the *pure being,* while the *Śīla* to the *awareness.* Both these aspects have been dealt here with the view of helping the seeker to understand his own stage. There is another practical hint: the seeker can recognise his real nature through *awareness.* When one is in the state of *Prajñā* or awareness, there are two things, namely one who is aware, and the things of which one is aware. When one transcends the identification of things one is able to know the duality and hence the separation. When this non-identified state continues, one is pleasantly surprised to discover that the so-called external things exist only in the subject. Without the subject, there can be no creation. This is what is mentioned in the present *Sarga.* Whereas, the state of *Sat* even the subjectivity has dissolved to become one without the second.

Among all creatures only man is in a state of anguish. Surprisingly, the author of the story of his trials and tribulations is man himself! This is because among all the creatures, man alone has the capacity to be *aware.* However, the animal is still lurking in man, in the form of memory of all those stages of physical evolution he has undergone, as animal having unconscious or instinctive tendencies. At the same time, he has become aware perhaps vaguely, that he is no more an animal but something higher, and he has to rise above them. But the awareness is only an infinitesimal part of his total consciousness, the major portion (almost 99%) remains unconscious! This is the greatest agony of man. He attempts to overcome this agony in two ways : first and the easier, is to regress back into the unconscious through indulgence in basic urges; the second, which is arduous, is to go on increasing the conscious part till, *everything* becomes conscious. To avoid the unconsciousness, every religion without any exception, prohibits any type of intoxication, as it takes man towards the unconscious. All spiritual practices have the single aim of increasing the awareness by *conscious and deliberate* action.

Lao Tzu, the great sage of Tao, used to go for a morning walk every day. He used to be accompanied by his neighbour. They had a perfect understanding, that there would be total silence throughout the walk. Once, the neighbour had a guest, who too wanted to join the walk. The host warned him not to ever break the silence. They all walked silently and reached a spot from where the sun-rise was simply breath-taking. The guest exclaimed 'How beautiful'! They returned, and just as the neighbour and his guest were to part, Lao Tzu asked the neighbour never to bring the talkative guest for the walk! For the sensitive sage even the exclamation was an unnecessary noise!

Jesus, the Christ gives a wonderful suggestion through the words : 'Judge ye not'! Because with the judgment starts the avoidable mental activity, which in turn stops us from being in the 'here-now'. Most if not all of us, have the stubborn habit of constant mental chattering through the comparison with the past experiences or desires which are nothing but mental projections of the past into future. Instead, if we just flow with the existence by becoming more and more aware of the uselessness of the mental dialogue, we come to a point where we realise pleasantly, that we are part of this great organic existence.

In *Muṇḍakopaniṣad,* a simile of a spider is given. The Ultimate Reality is like a spider, which brings out the web from its own body and *lives* in it. Biologists observe that the spider knows about its prey getting entangled in its web through the vibrations created by the strands in the web. In the like manner the Reality and the existence in general, are more intimately connected with each other. *Vedānta* declares that both of them are *inseparable* like the dancer and his dance. The dance can exist only in presence of the dancer.

Most of us are familiar with the word 'Mother Earth'. As everything—animate as well as inanimate—is born to her, exists in her and finally merges in her, after death. The sages extended it much further and declared that it is 'Mother Existence' calling her *Prakṛti.* As they realised that everything is inter-connected. Nay, they went further and said that everything is *ONE* without the second: *Adwaita!* And needlessly the mind creates the walls of separation and in turn generates fear and its companions. But strange as it may seem, the creation of these walls and the resultant differentiation is a necessary part of growing up, from the unconscious state of matter to the fully conscious Buddha-hood!

5

The Story of Arjuna

In the stillness and quietude of the night, the only sound was that of the rustle of the thin curtain swaying in the gentle cool breeze. The stars could be seen adorning the dark and clear desert sky. The royal sentries had worn the soft shoes so as not create any sound as they walked to and fro while guarding the palace, for their master and king Ibrahim, was a very light sleeper. And necessarily so, for he was a just and kind king who was all the while interested in the welfare of his subjects.

It was past the midnight, and Ibrahim was in deep sleep. There was sound of footsteps on the terrace of the palace. Ibrahim was disturbed, and asked with a little annoyance:

'Who is there'?

'Do not get disturbed—my camel is lost, and I am searching for it'.

Ibrahim laughed and said:

'You madman! Get down! Camels are never lost on the roof of a palace. Go home'!

But then he could not sleep anymore. Contemplative that he was, Ibrahim started thinking that may be, the man was not mad after all; may be, he wanted to convey something symbolically. For the words, 'Do not get disturbed' had a soothing influence on him. Moreover, that search for the lost camel on the terrace of the palace appeared to have a message for him.

The next day, Ibrahim gave instructions to his officers to find the man as he wanted to know whether the man was really mad or the man of god. He described the voice—as he had only heard the voice. But they could not find him. By evening there was commotion at the gate. A *Faqir* or a beggar appeared near the gate and asked the sentry to allow him to stay in the *Sarai*—the inn, for a few days. The sentry was refusing him by telling him that it was not a *Sarai* but the palace of the king! The *Faqir* insisted that it was one, and travelers come and spend a few days there. When the sentry refused that it was the palace of the king, the *Faqir* said that he would talk to the king who appeared to be a foolish man!

When Ibrahim summoned the *Faqir* and heard what the beggar had to say, he was angry and asked him to clarify. The *Faqir* said:

> 'Listen! I had come here before. But then someone else was sitting on this throne. He too was a foolish man as you are, as he thought, that this was *his* residence. Now, you too are doing the same, by thinking it is *yours*'!
>
> 'Do not behave like an uncultured man, the person you met was my father, now he is dead'.
>
> The *Faqir* said smilingly:
>
> 'I tell you, I will come again and not find you here. Someone else will be here. He may be your son, who will claim this same place to be *his* residence! What kind of palace is this? People come and go—that is why I call this as a travelers' inn'!

Ibrahim recognised the voice. It was the same voice he had heard on the terrace the previous night. The king said:

> 'Then you are the madman looking for his camel on the roof'!

The *Faqir* said:

> 'Yes, I am the same madman. And you are not sane either! If you are looking for yourself in the riches, power, name and fame, then you too are looking for a camel on the roof'!

The king came down from the throne and said to the Faqir:

> 'You stay in this *Sarai,* I am leaving it now. All along I had the impression that this was my home. If it isn't my home, then I must go and search for my home before it's too late'.

Ibrahim became a mystic in his own right. Most of us are, all the while searching for our camels on the roof! We sow the seeds of thorny bushes and expect them to give us juicy and sweet fruits. And this impossible expectation can never be fulfilled. Man is in search of fulfillment, but his every possible effort leaves him more empty! We set goals to ourselves, and feel convinced that if we attain them, we will be fulfilled. No effort is spared. But when the goal is achieved, there is satisfaction only for a short while, till the mind sets another goal! If one does not succeed, the mind says that it is because of the *lack of sufficient effort!* The argument appears very logical. This continues till the end, till at last one is left completely empty.

Consider a rich man. Paradoxically, the more wealth he accumulates, the poorer he feels and so, he invests more effort and time to acquire more wealth! Same is the case with power and knowledge. And actually, the emptiness felt by man is *not outer but inner!* No matter how hard he tries, he cannot possibly fill it, because the outer or gross things by their very nature cannot fill the inner. Things—like objects of senses or wealth which is the means for obtaining the objects—pertain to the body; power is again outer, as it manifests in the society; and knowledge belongs to the brain which is also gross. While the inner emptiness can be filled *only by knowing the Self.* Until man understands this, he keeps searching for his camel on the roof! But the real trouble begins after the so-called understanding.

Self-knowledge is not at all easy because of the very deep fear. This is due to the fact that self-knowledge shatters the *image* one has created about oneself. With this shattering, the whole past crumbles as it is nothing but a nightmarish dream. But one has invested so much of time and energy in it, and presently one feels that it has been a great waste. And in showing *others* that one's life has been a great success, one deceives none but oneself! One has been thinking that one is unique, talented, good, and has been attributing all high sounding adjectives to oneself. But if only one peeps within oneself, one finds that it is only an image and not real. The castles built by the ego about oneself tumble down. Not interested in self destruction, the ego goes on creating more images. That is how everyone lives : creating dreams about oneself and of others. This is the fear.

A person who cannot look at oneself *'as one is'*, cannot look even at others. This is due to the fact that one gets reflected in others' eyes as the others are mirrors. Man is aspiring ease and happiness which is impossible with dreams sticking in his eyes. No matter how harsh the truth, only the truth can put him at ease. But the initial shock of exposure of the reality about oneself makes man *avoid* self-knowledge. And man has invented an ingenious method to avoid self-observation through myriad of occupations. When one is occupied with *something* one appears to be at ease. Modern psychologists claim that left without any occupation for long period, man becomes insane. Why should an unoccupied man become insane? Because of the fact, that man *is insane* and the occupation only helps him hide this fact.

Since it is difficult to observe oneself initially, if one observes the world outside, one finds that all activity is only an occupation to *avoid* self-observation. And if there is no occupation, then man may do something which is not needed at all. That is how, the proverb 'An idle mind is the devils workshop' has been coined. Actually the idle mind is, that mind which is avoiding the inner fact because, the mind or the ego *does not want to observe itself.* All religious thought insists on sitting without *doing* anything, for a few hours. If one succeeds in keeping oneself unoccupied for a few hours, soon one will get enlightened. *Mind in its unoccupied state is meditation; and in occupied state, the mind is the world or Saṁsāra.*

It does not matter which occupation—money, politics, knowledge or social service—it makes no difference, man's sanity is same: the sanity leaning towards insanity! Man wants to avoid himself through occupations. He is not happy with himself *as he is,* at the same time, expects *others to be happy with him!* How can that be possible? If one is such a person who cannot tolerate oneself, how can others tolerate him? But we do find that we tolerate one another for an entirely different reason. We tolerate others because *we get occupied with others.* And others tolerate us for the same reason. So the society as it is today is nothing but an *arrangement for mutual occupation!*

Unless one is able to look at oneself, one cannot have self-realisation. Though intellectually one is convinced of this fact, and consciously one is interested in knowing the Self, unconsciously—which is a much greater part of one's being—one does all one can to postpone this! In this conflict between the conscious and the unconscious, there is anguish. There is also another fact which is to be considered, that by nature we are unable to keep quiet as we are involved in incessant action, as there is an inherent restlessness due to the energy. How to make use of the energy to observe oneself, how to use gross action as a diving board for diving within, forms the subject matter of this *Sarga* entitled the 'Story of Arjuna'.

Overjoyed after listening to the enlightening discourse of Sage Vasiṣṭha, Rāma sought a clarification in order to fully experience the Bliss : How does the *Puryaṣṭaka* body create the universe over and over again like the image in the mirror. *Muni* Vasiṣṭha replied that *Brahman* having no beginning or end is the seed of the universe and becomes *Jīva* through differentiation. Subjecting itself to the idea of separateness, the *Jīva* becomes *Ahaṁkāra;* with contemplation it becomes *Manas;* with the certainty of intelligence, it becomes *Buddhiḥ;* through the five elements it becomes the sense-organs; with the thought of a container it becomes the body. The form having such a nature is called *Puryaṣṭaka* (*Puri* + *Aṣṭaka*) body which means, composed of the eight: *Ahaṁkāra, Manas, Buddhiḥ,* and five elements, by the wise.

Puryaṣṭaka is the transformed pure knower, or actor, or experiencer and witness into *Jīva* consciousness. Through this *Puryaṣṭaka* body, dreams upon dreams pile up and the universe appears real along with other illusions. Sage then suggested to Rāma that the path of *Asaṁsakti,* or non-attachment to be pointed out by Lord Kṛṣṇa to Arjuna, the son of Pāṇḍu would be ideal to live in this world of multiplicity. To this statement, Rāma wanted to know as to when Arjuna will be born, and what would be the path into which he will be initiated by Hari.

The sage said that Yama, the Death, performs *Tapas* to contemplate over the carnage of *Jīvas* perpetuated by him at the end of each *Mahāyuga.* The period of the *Tapas* varies from four to sixteen years. During this time the *Jīvas* greatly increase in number to burden the earth. At such times the Lord relieves the earth of its burden by withdrawing the manifestation. In the near future Yama will perform *Tapas* for twelve years, and the goddess of earth, unable to bear the load will seek asylum in Viṣṇu who will incarnate in two forms of Vāsudeva and Vijayā (Arjuna). The sons of Dhṛtarāṣṭra, Duryodhana and others along with their kin, will wage an unjust battle with the Pāṇḍu princes. In the battlefield, Arjuna will be overpowered by the mental conflict between compassion and sense of duty. Due to this *Dharma-Sūkṣma* or the inner conflict, Kṛṣṇa will initiate Arjuna into *Jñāna.* Vasiṣṭha reminded Rāma, that Kṛṣṇa is the *Śarīrin,* the spirit within the body, while Vijayā is the *Śarīra,* the body.

A question arises as to how sage Vasiṣṭha is able to predict the future course of events. It has to be remembered that time has its influence only on mind. In fact, *time is mind.* And the enlightened persons like Vasiṣṭha have transcended mind, and for them there is only here-now, which is eternal. And so they are able to see through what the ordinary men call the past and the future. As clarified by the sage himself, the indwelling spirit is Kṛṣṇa, while Arjuna is the body-mind-ego that has a tendency to suffer. Only on the realisation of the Spirit can the suffering be transcended.

The revered sage then proceeded to narrate the enlightening dialogue between Kṛṣṇa and Arjuna: The fluctuations of the mind must be fully eradicated as the Ātmic Reality cannot be known through the limited mind, full of defects. Once one identifies with the Reality one will be *Sat* only, which is beyond birth and death; no form to differentiate through terms 'I', 'you', etc. and no ego to identify with actions. Without the least longing for the fruits of actions and treading the path of *Brahmārpaṇa,* offering everything to *Brahman,* one will merge with *Brahman.* One can achieve *Mokṣa* by eliminating all *Saṁskāras* with *Tapas, Sannyāsa, Yoga* and *Jñāna.*

Thereby, Arjuna made an appeal to the Lord to explain what is meant by destruction of *Saṅga* (association, attraction, or identification), the offering of all things to *Brahman, Sannyāsa, Jñāna* and *Yoga.* Kṛṣṇa replied that the *Brāhmic* Principle is devoid of *Saṁkalpa,* pain or thoughts. The effort to attain to the Non-dual *Brahman* is said to be the *Jñāna* and *Yoga* by the wise. After true discrimination the cognition of the identity of the universe and the 'I' with *Brahman* is *Brahmārpaṇa.* The renunciation of the fruits of actions is *Sannyāsa.* The destruction of *Saṁkalpa* is the destruction of

Saṅga. Continuing Kṛṣṇa then initiated Arjuna into the means of worshipping Him. He said that the Ultimate Reality has two aspects: the first is the lower, with form and perishable, while the other is Non-dual and imperishable, without beginning or end. The second one is beyond the purview of mind and senses. So a beginner has to start with the worship of the aspect with form which gradually paves way for *Jñāna.* With that one can never be afflicted by the disease of existence called *Abhimāna* or identification with objects and instruments.

The wise say that those who are engaged in actions free of *Saṁkalpa* generating desires burn all bondage forming actions. The actions performed without even a trace of *Abhimāna* has the liberating effect. Such persons attain to *Jīvanamukti* and are washed away of all *Vāsanās.* Through this initiation into the path of *Asaṁsakti,* Arjuna was freed from all delusion and performed such actions that agreed with his own nature or *Swabhāva,* and was freed from bondage.

Activity is no doubt mandatory for survival. But then, it need not be obsessive as it is with most of us. Even thinking is included under activity by *Vedānta.* From the kaleidoscopic teachings of *Bhagavadgītā,* an important path recognised by many seekers is the path of *liberating action* known as the *Karma Yoga.* This path recommends the proper use of action to transcend action. The situation Arjuna is in, and also Rāma, at the outset of this scripture is similar though not identical. Both Rāma and Arjuna are trying to avoid action as both of them have recognised the binding effect of action. Vasiṣṭha and Kṛṣṇa help their disciples towards proper understanding, who help them get enlightened.

The one and only, and perhaps, the toughest barrier is the egotism or the sense of 'I perform the action'. This egotism begets indulgence at the level of body and senses and involvement at the mental level that happens to be the root cause of bondage. All other feelings like anxiety, jealousy, and the rest are but its progenies! Thus elimination of all indulgence and involvement becomes the principal method of *Karma Yoga.*

All our actions have their origin in some desire or the other. It will not be an exaggeration if it is said that without desire action is not possible. The desires in turn give birth to expectations, anxiety, and worry. And our so-called *normal* actions are tiresome and not efficient. So the first step is to make the action less tiresome and more efficient by not thinking of the fruits of the action, which initiate the action, *during the action.* This results in concentration of mind and *mindful action* as the Buddha calls it. With the thoughts of results or the fruit of action eliminated from the mind the anxiety and negativities disappear.

This attitude paves way to the ability of remaining in the *here-now,* and gradually towards unselfish action when one is able to come out of the narrow shell of 'I' and 'mine'. As one starts expanding the boundary of 'mine', the action starts becoming more and more effortless. With effortless action one starts moving towards spontaneity. With the grand virtue of spontaneity, the egotism starts melting until one arrives at the culminating point when there is only action devoid of the 'performer'.

An enlightened Zen Master was asked by someone what was the path *He* had taken. The Master simply answered that:

'*When I am hungry I eat, when I am sleepy, I sleep*'!

The reply appears very strange and funny. It is not. The sage is saying normally, our action is somnambulistic, in the sense that while we eat, we are doing so many other things besides eating. We may be worrying about the morrow; comparing the food with what we had eaten earlier; passing a judgment on the food; and also eating! The sage is saying that while eating *only* eating is taking place. Not even the 'eater' is there! And while sleeping only sleep is there without even the 'sleeper'. All actions have become just pure actions.

The essence of *Bhagavadgītā* is to transcend the egotism of all action. The egotism manifests at three levels. At the level of knowledge as the knower or *Jñātā;* at the level of action as the doer or *Kartā;* and at the level of experience as the experiencer or *Bhoktā*. It advocates a method by developing an attitude towards action. It calls such action as *Yajña,* in which the body, senses, and mind are totally sublimated and there is this identification with the Non-dual *Brahman,* which is said to be the state of *Brahmārpaṇa*. A *Śloka* describes it :

> 'That act of offering, in the *Yajña* is *Brahman*. The materials offered are *Brahman*. The fire is *Brahman*. The person who does the offering is again *Brahman*. Remaining in the state of *Brahman* has to necessarily reach *Brahman*'.[175]

Obviously, the above stage can be reached only with proper understanding of the secret of action and its practice at every moment. Spirituality has to be totally lived by making *every action meditative*. One has to constantly remember that one has chosen a particular way of life which does not have any place for indulgence and involvement. Such a way of life has been called as *Vairāgya* and *Abhyāsa*. That is why the Lord tells Arjuna of the two levels of worship. The first is the worship of the Reality with form, which is at the gross level of sense body and mind. It is mandatory that the worship should be performed through the gross actions. These actions are to be performed in the way described by the lord when the action helps in releasing one from the egotism.

The second stage is when one identifies with the Non-dual with the elimination of *Ahaṁkāra*. It is only then, when one is able to lead such a life, that every action becomes a spiritual practice, every thought a meditation and every word

---

175 ब्रह्मार्पणं ब्रह्म हविर्ब्रह्माग्नौ ब्रह्मणाहुतम् ।
ब्रह्मैव तेन गन्तव्यं ब्रह्मकर्म समाधिना ।। 4.24 ।।

a prayer. Ācārya Śaṅkara describes this stage in his *Śivamānasapūjā*:

> 'O Lord, You are my Self; Girijā, the Divine Mother is my mind; my *Prāṇas* are Your followers; and my body, Your Temple; all my sense experiences are the offerings made to You; and my sleep is a form of absorption in You. My wanderings are like the circumambulations and my speech is the prayer offered to You; whatever actions I perform may it all be the worship made unto You'.[176]

There is only one impediment for a seeker in achieving his goal: the *Ahaṁkāra* or the 'I-ness'. Peculiarly enough, this *Ahaṁkāra* exists only in human beings. The 'normal' mind is only partially (infinitely small) conscious, while most of it is unconscious. The small portion creates a shield called the 'I-ness' which not only offers a shield against the external world but also takes the mind back to 'total unconsciousness' or animal hood. This *Ahaṁkāra* grows with involved action. It is no doubt a necessary part of growth, but one need not continue to be dependent on it. As and when one starts growing, one has to drop it. Action happens to be a very, if not most important aspect of life. Lord Kṛṣṇa initiates us through Arjuna, a method of using action to transcend action.

Normally all our actions are just occupations to avoid Self-knowledge. Spirituality suggests that instead of avoiding or postponing the Self-knowledge, the inevitable destination of Existence, we should *use* action to know our Self. The path of *Jñāna* teaches us *Prajñā* or awareness; the path of *Yoga* suggests the elimination of thoughts; the *Bhakti* suggests the elimination of the ego through surrender; while the *Karma Yoga* offers a way of eliminating the *Kartā* or the *doership*

---

176 आत्मा त्वं गिरिजा मतिः सहचरा प्राणं शरीरं गृहं पूजा ते विषयोपभोगरचना निद्रा समाधिस्थितिः ।
सन्चारः पदयोः प्रदक्षिणविधिः स्तोत्राणि सर्वा गिरो यद्यत्कर्म करोमि तत्तदखिलं शम्भो तवाराधनम् ॥ 4 ॥

through the method of giving up the thought of the fruit of action, by increasing the *mindful action* or action with awareness. Every possible path either directly or indirectly takes one towards the elimination of the puny 'I' and subsequently, helps in the identification with the Cosmos.

A seeker comes across another obstacle. At any stage, he may begin to feel an aversion for activity, as in his opinion it is mundane! And *any* aversion is detrimental for quietening the mind. Moreover, one cannot avoid the actions which are necessary for maintaining the body. One more aversion that may crop up is towards the social obligations. But if one develops *Asaṁsakti,* as explained by the Lord, then one succeeds in rooting out aversion from the mind.

This *Sarga* gives out a broad outline of the secret of action as given out by Lord Kṛṣṇa in the *Bhagavadgītā*. Śrī Rāma too had become inactive at the end of his pilgrimage. After the initiation into spirituality by the great sage Vasiṣṭha, he not only performed what was according to his nature, but attained to the great quiescence and *Jñāna* or Wisdom. Normally we restrict our so-called religious practice to performance of worship or some practice like meditation for a period of an hour or two. While the rest of the day we act as though we are not at all religious, as our action is usually towards self-forgetfulness!

Zen tradition teaches 'meditative action' rather than meditation with closed eyes which is restricted to space and time. It suggests the seeker to transform all action into meditation by increasing the awareness. A Zen anecdote illustrates this:

> Somebody asked the master, Bokuju:
>
> We have to dress and eat everyday—how do we get out of all that?
> Bokuju answered:
> We dress, we eat.
> The listener said:

I don't understand.

Bokuju said: If you don't understand put on your clothes, and eat your food.

Boredom is experienced only by the ego, just as all other things. The Zen tradition teaches us to eliminate it and continue the action. For one who has succeeded in eliminating the *Ahaṁkāra,* every moment is fresh, like a dew drop sliding on a blade of grass, or the reflection of the rising sun on it. As the entity responsible for all comparison and judgment is not, time has made way to eternity, and she or he has identified with the infinite Existence, ... with *Brahman.*

No doubt, the journey is arduous for us, used as we are to such actions, which have an expectation of the fruits behind the actions. In fact, we tend towards inaction if we become disinterested in the fruits. But then, we have been performing such *self forgetful* action for ages, and our hands have always remained empty. Because all the fruits are mostly related to either the body like the material objects or brain, like the knowledge gathered through study or experience. Both the objects and the knowledge leave our company at the time of death. And awareness remains with the Self, as awareness only, is of the Self. *Spirituality teaches us how to increase the awareness.*

6

The Story of the Hundred Rudras

It was hot and humid and the bus, crowded. The occupants of the bus were in different moods, and each, in his or her own world. Some of them were travelling as a part of their routine, the others, out of compulsion, and yet others for sightseeing. Among the sight-seers, were two young men. Both of them were busy in a discussion. One—who was older than the other, was saying that not all things can be explained logically; and that in spite of all development there are many things which are beyond the scope of the intellect. The younger man did not agree. Each one of them was giving examples to explain his own point. In this involved occupation neither they experienced the discomfort of the crowded bus, nor did they notice the destination coming closer every moment.

As they got down from the bus, the shrieks of children selling flowers, vendors advertising their fare, conductors shouting the destinations of their buses greeted the ears. It was as usual, a busy, noisy, crowded area of the town. However, both these friends were too occupied in their discussion to take notice of the noise. At that time, the elder of the two, who had come there many times and presently acting as the guide, started telling about the history of the place to the younger one, who became all ears. As they came out of the bus station, the tower of the Bṛhadīśwara temple caught their eyes.

Though there was a heavy rush of people outside, the temple compound as such was quite empty, with very few people inside. Entering the temple, they approached the *sanctum sanctorum.* A priest was chanting some *Vedic Mantras* in his gruffly melodious voice, and another was distributing *Tīrtha,* the consecrated water and *Vibhūti,* the sacred ash. Failing to see the idol of Śiva, the newcomer asked the priest, who just pointed towards the *sanctum sanctorum.* But he asked once again, as he could not see it! The priest just pointed his right hand above.

There it was, a *Śivaliṅgaṃ* about eighteen feet high! The younger man, was totally unprepared to face this, and was lost in admiration. It was not only a feeling of admiration, but of awe as he was shocked into silence, making him oblivious to the external world. When he came back to the so-called normal consciousness, his friend just took him around the circumambient path around the shrine. When they came out of the temple, the elder friend asked the younger one to describe his experience. The latter confessed that it was not possible! He was however glad that he had made the trip. But as it always happens when the effect of the experience got worn off, there was analysis of the experience and then even the memory of the experience itself, was lost in the maze of thoughts and arguments!

This story is common to all of us. It will not be an exaggeration, if one said that almost every day, opportunities cross our way. The beauty of nature or perhaps a sense experience brings in a kind of fulfillment or a feeling of satiety, though, it may be only temporary. We just do not allow the experience to prolong, as either there is comparison, or new desires, or intellectual analysis of the experience itself. Even the seekers are no exception to such *reaction* to experiences. If we look into the 'why' of such behaviour, it can be of great help.

In case of the so-called day-to-day pleasurable experiences, the mind is extrovertish and the attention is naturally on the object. And there is this conviction that the object *alone* is responsible for the pleasure. This conviction continues even when one starts on a divine adventure! Yes, the seeker overcomes the hunger for objects through the practice of *Yama-Niyama*. But then, he starts longing for *spiritual experiences!* In this way, spiritual experiences become *in a way,* the objects of senses and mind, leading one towards *spiritual materialism!* It is at this time that a seeker faces the danger of developing the 'holier than thou' attitude. He may start looking down on all actions, other than the formal spiritual practices, taking them to be *materialistic or mundane,* while continuing to *expect* and *long for* the spiritual experiences.

The expectation of and longing for *anything* is mundane. As both these are associated with desire. And desire happens to be the food for thinking. Moreover, experience as such is at the level of multiplicity, because three things are mandatory for any experience : *Viṣaya* or *Bhojyaṃ,* the object; *Bhoga,* the experience; and *Bhoktā,* the experiencer, this group of three is called as *Tripuṭi.* This does not in any way imply that the spiritual experiences are to be *avoided!* The experiences are like the milestones indicating the progress of the seeker. The seeker should not *long* for them as basically he is trying to completely stop the activity of thinking. So the best way is to avoid such things which strengthen the *Ahaṁkāra.*

To eliminate the *Ahaṁkāra,* the path of *Jñāna* suggests the seeker to go on increasing the awareness. Through awareness, one goes on increasing the consciousness and decreasing that which is unconscious. Ego happens to be the most dominant part of the unconsciousness. *Prāṇa Vidyā, Deva Pūjā, Yoga,* and non-attached action help in increasing the awareness. With the increased awareness the *Tripuṭi* gets eliminated and one achieves the non-dual. In the path of

Bhakti, the concept of grace is introduced. It is said that the encounter with God cannot be *demanded,* because it can only be a gift. And gift, by its very nature cannot be claimed. The only hindrance for the encounter with God is the 'I'. That is why, the devotees say that the encounter of the devotee with God as such, is impossible. As long as the devotee, that is, the ego claiming itself as devotee, is there, God cannot come, and at that very instant when the ego melts, there is *nothing else but God!*

Without keeping this fact in mind all the time, a seeker tends to give importance to the experiences, ultimately causing delay in his progress. Of course, the seeker does realise the folly sometime or the other, to resume his march towards Non-dual Reality. This appears to be the theme of the *Sarga* under discussion. Sage Vasiṣṭha narrated the following story to Rāma.

An ascetic and a man of wisdom had an ability to get into the state of *Samādhi* at will. Through the repeated practice he had reached a stage of materializing all mental impressions into real images. The scriptures claim that every thought has its own reflected image. One day having returned from *Samādhi,* a thought arose in his mind that he should engage himself playfully in ordinary actions. With this thought, that he should become another, he at once transformed into another. Then the thought of re-becoming the ascetic did not arise. As if in a strange coincidence he became another person named Jīvaṭa. The mind of Jīvaṭa roamed on the streets of a certain town produced by a similar fantasy and dwelt there. In that town he drank alcohol and slept in that intoxicated state. In that sleep he dreamt as being a Brahmin who in turn dreamt of being an emperor of earth, who in turn dreamt as being an erudite Brahmin. The dreaming continued and he became a celestial lady, a deer, a creeper, a goddess, a beetle, a tusker, and finally a swan. The swan while flying in the sky saw a Rudra, and thus attained the form of Rudra.

The Rudra with his *Jñāna* attained to the highest state. At this stage the Rudra started to retrospect all his past lives and realised the power of *Māyā* in deluding those under its influence. Having complete control he dived into each life and traced his way to the former ascetic and awakened him from his trance. Thereupon the ascetic woke up to free himself from reminiscences of the illusory life. Again the Rudra contemplated on Jīvaṭa and reached a certain part of *Jñānākāśa* along with the ascetic. Thus Jīvaṭa attained the conscious state to accompany them. All the three—Rudra, the ascetic and Jīvaṭa, were full of *Jñāna* and realised the Non-dual Principle, in spite of having three separate bodies. They then visited all the incarnations. Being free from all stains, they discovered that the Divine *Brahman* alone incarnated in so many bodies and as so many resplendent Rudras. All the Rudras attained to *Jñāna* and returned to their respective abode on being asked by the principal Rudra. They lived their respective lives and quit their bodies, at the appointed time to merge into *Brahman.*

Rāma, who had been listening intently, remarked about the wonderful nature of the story and wanted to know the cause of the marvel of the *Saṁkalpa* of the ascetic to generate the living forms of Jīvaṭa and others which became real. Vasiṣṭha replied that everything is in *Cit* and comes out of *Cit* only. *Cit* being all, it becomes whatever it contemplates upon. That which is seen in dreams, and that which arises out of *Saṁkalpa,* will always manifest in the contemplated form.

An ordinary mind cannot bring this about, as its power is scattered. But through the practice of *Yoga,* the mind becomes one-pointed. If such persons long for objects or power through their *Saṁkalpa,* they attain them. The mind which has a taste for the objects is ignorant in spite of its power of concentrated thought. This taste is a great impediment to the pilgrim's progress. If such powerful mind turns its concentration on itself, it attains to *Jñāna.*

A clarification is not out of place at this juncture: Life and desire or wish, are intimately connected. An individual life is nothing but a representation of that individual's desires. And *desires never go unfulfilled,* though they may not get fulfilled immediately and may even take lifetimes. So the present life is a fulfillment of the desires of some past life. They take time to get fulfilled because the mind is restless and hence weak. The mind is like a genie, ready to fulfill any wish, provided it is under the control of the master! The problem with most of us is that *we are under its control!* And that is why, our wishes are like beggars' horses which cannot be ridden! However, a person who has his mind under perfect control—as it was with the ascetic who could willfully enter *Samādhi*—then he can objectify his thoughts.

But then, the desires as such drag the mind towards involvement. Even a *Yogi* who has his mind under control gets dragged into involvement, if there is any desire. This has been illustrated in the story when the ascetic starts *becoming* the persons or objects in his thought. However, the *Yogi* has an advantage over an ordinary person who does not have any control over the mind, in the sense, that he can retrace his steps to recollect the original state.

Rudra is another name for the *Ahaṁkāra* which is free from any identification or involvement. Rudra is also the name of Śiva in his destructive aspect. He is the destroyer of all evils. Since it is used in a scripture like *Yoga Vāsiṣṭha,* it has a special significance. The one and only evil in a seeker is the mind in its identified and involved state. Rudra helps in transcending the mind.

As we shall see in the coming stories, both time and space are the manifestations of the mind. Normally, when one is under the influence of mind, there is this horizontal movement, from the past to the present and on to the future; from one condition of the body, to another. There is another dimension to growth, and that is vertical growth where there is neither space nor time.

Almost everything in the material world, has to be achieved through effort—more or less, depending on the thing desired. One has to desire and the desire needs time or future : 'I *will* achieve it'. It requires time as well as effort. The time for 'becoming'. J. Krishnamurti says:

> 'There is a chronological time and the time of the mind. The time which is mind itself. There is confusion between the two. The psychological time is the process of becoming. This time as becoming, the "I will be", was born of the illusion and was a manifestation of the 'I', both self sustaining, maintaining and supporting itself through its own ignorance and by this process, its own potential energy as consciousness'.[177]

Desire or 'the process of becoming' is a state of discontentment in the prevailing situation and wants to become something else which will *seemingly* bring happiness. For instance, a man is uneducated and *thinks* that he will be happy if he gets a University degree; a man not having any money, *thinks* that he *will* be happy if he increases his bank balance; or a man not having any power *thinks* that he *will* be happy if he becomes a minister. In the process of desiring we forget that we keep moving into future. And future does not really exist, because of which we miss the precious present. The more we desire, the more we crystallise the habit of moving away from the reality of the present. If the physical or material possessions were causal in bringing about happiness, then it was *mandatory* that all those persons having money or power would have been happy. We know that if at all there is anything in common in the humankind, it is unhappiness and misery!

Everything in the world is achieved in time, and with effort. But the bliss which every one of us is seeking can be

---

177 *J. Krishnamurti: A Biography* by Pupul Jayakar, Penguin Books, p. 116.

achieved *right now!* Nay, it is already there, and mind is the only hindrance. All spiritual practices emphasise only on waking up from the sleep of desiring and becoming. As the desiring or becoming, always brings one into the realm of mind which is nothing but the time and space. The meditation is the state transcending the activity called mind. With a little awareness, one can realise that one exists at different levels both gross and subtle. If one is able to become aware at the subtler level, one can easily become a *Sākṣī* or *witness* to the gross level. So the *Manas* can learn to witness the body and the senses, *Buddhiḥ* can witness the *Manas, Ahaṁkāra* can witness the *Buddhiḥ,* and so on. We have this power in us and use it in day-to-day life.

When one is seeing a movie, one mostly gets identified with it. It is evident from our reactions during the experience, We are moved to tears, or carried over by the excitement. But if one remembers that it is only a moving picture, one laughs at the reactions. The movie is only an illusion created by the movement of the film at a particular speed! Tensions or worries visit us often. Sometimes they are so strong that we are unable to sleep. Most of the time, a defense mechanism in the form of a thought that 'everything *will* become alright', saves us from the problem. If we just observe ourselves we find that at the time of surfacing of the thought, we are *standing apart* from the problem.

This mood or posture of standing apart has been called as becoming a Rudra in the present *Sarga.* When this *Rudratva* or Rudra-hood dawns on a person, every event or situation becomes like an image on a water surface. Since the Rudra has achieved the state of non-involvement, he is able to go and awaken all the previous manifestations and help them to achieve the *Rudratva.* The key to life Divine is the *Sākṣībhāva* or the witness-hood.

Vedānta gives a beautiful example to illustrate the achievement of witness-hood. There is a small pond with crystal clear water. One can clearly see the bottom. If the water surface gets disturbed either due to wind or a person's entering the pond, there is turbulence and one cannot see the bottom anymore and the mud at the bottom gets mixed with water. No activity or effort can make the water transparent again. On the contrary, any activity will only help in worsening the situation! Instead if we *allow* the turbulence of water to reduce, and allow the mud to settle down, then and then alone the original state can be revived. But in the revival, only one thing is to be done: *not to do anything and to wait patiently.* Even in waiting there should not be any restlessness. There should be readiness to wait till eternity if necessary!

It is a full moon night. There is not even a single cloud in the sky. The river however, is in disturbance as the waves lash at the boulders in it and on its banks. The water appears like molten silver, and one cannot see any moon on its surface. Unless the winds subside the image of the moon cannot be formed. But as and when the winds calm down, a moving image of the moon appears on its surface. And when the winds totally stop the image becomes steady. The moon of reality on the surface of our consciousness cannot appear amidst the hurricane winds of desires. There are only two ways to overcome the problem. Either stop the wind through *Yoga* or learn to stand apart from it all, through what *Vāsiṣṭha* calls, as *Samyagavekṣaṇam* or art of internalised seeing.

This *Sarga* gives a few hints on *Samyagavekṣaṇam,* the art of inner observation.

7

The Story of Vetāla

The Quarter Guard had rung the bell thrice to give the time on that early morning. The sound of the bell had also alerted the sentries in the process, because generally, it is at this time when body tends to fall asleep! The sound of boots on the cobbled pathways, crickets and owls was the only disturbance in that silent hour. The sentries were specially instructed to be careful of any new persons in that area. It was just after the *Sepoy Mutiny* in 1857, and the place was the cantonment in a city in northern India. The British officers suspicious of every Indian were concerned about the new rebellious spirit showing in India.

A new sound was heard by a sentry, the sound of *Khaḍāvu*—the wooden footwear worn by the ascetics. The sentry—a young Tommy, challenged the new intruder:

'Friend or Foe?'

There was no reply. Instead, the man continued to approach the challenger. With annoyance the sentry challenged again. Light from the street lamp fell on a tall and lean mendicant walking slowly and confidently towards him. How dare he ignore the challenge, this beggar, thought the *Tommy* as the British soldiers were being called, and again challenged with anger. But the ascetic continued to be silent, and walk as if he had not heard the challenge. It was too much for the soldier, and he charged and pierced the bayonet into the stomach of the mendicant. A cry came out of the victim:

'*Tat-twam-asi* (That-thou-art)'.

Instead of pain there was the joy of recognition in that utterance. It was as though the monk had found what he had been searching all his life! As though the monk was not deceived by the uniform or bayonet or even the anger in those eyes. He had been once again convinced of the Truth he had already discovered, that everything material and conscious being is only One Truth in different forms! The soldier was confused, because he had attacked the monk fatally, and the man was dying, and the victim was all love for him. There was a commotion in the whole area and the Officer on duty rushed to the spot. A young monk too had joined the group. He had tears in his eyes. The old monk looking at all of them including his disciple, again uttered softly with a smile on his face and a strange light in his eyes: '*Tat-twam-asi*' and breathed his last.

The younger monk, told them that his *Guru* had been observing silence of speech for the past thirty-five years, and the Upaniṣadic statement '*Tat-twam-asi*'[178] had been the only speech he had ever uttered during that period; that he had realised the Truth and the State of Oneness with Existence; that his parting statement had only proved the fact; and that he had seen the Truth even in one who had made the fatal attack on him. Many others joined the swelling crowd of people. Most of them had *felt* that something strange had happened. It *was* a unique event in the sense that only one in millions attains to this state, and when such person drops the body—whatever be the reason, sickness, old age or even assassination, she or he is totally liberated from the prison of existence.

---

178 स य एषोऽणिमैतदात्म्यमिदँूसर्वं तत्सत्यूँस आत्मा **तत्वमसि** श्वेतकेतो ॥
छान्दोग्योपनिषद् 6.8.7 ॥

Such incidents have been recorded in many great lives. In this very century, when Gandhiji was shot at, from a point blank range, the only utterance that escaped his lips was *'He Rām'!* These great persons have one thing in common that they all have totally accepted the existence in all forms—friend, foe, animate and inanimate, even events including death, as their own. And they all have reached this state of Non-dual-ness, through different chosen paths, according to their nature and aptitude. And such persons have only love for the existence.

Every level of human existence is influenced by the mind. The influence is so strong that it is noticeable. Posture, gait, look as well as the speech, show the mental attitude of the person. Many a time we hear a person saying something, while the body tells an entirely different story! Psychologists observe that the body too communicates and this is called as the 'Body Language'. Moreover, even the physical health depends on the mental posture. It has been accepted by psychologists that the psycho-somatic diseases like Asthma, Acidity, Diabetes, and some skin infections are very deeply connected with the subconscious fears, phobias, obsessions and attitudes. They claim that there are different types of 'reactors' like: Nose reactors, Stomach reactors, and Skin reactors!

Another important thing is, that thought as such is verbal. If one observes carefully one finds that every thought creates a vibration in the vocal chords. And with every thought the body also moves, may be too insignificant to be noticed. The vow of silence has been recommended as an important mind quietening method. The silence is practised according to the level of the seeker. The four levels are body, senses, speech and mind. While practising bodily silence, the person keeps the body away from all activity as in the case of *Haṭha-Yogis.* At the level of speech, one eschews totally from speech. This has been called by Tathāgata as the *Arya-Mauna.*

Only *avoiding* the activity or speech however, does not help in quietening the mind. We are familiar with persons observing silence, having a dialogue through sign language or by exchanging notes of paper! This does in no way mean that the practice is ineffective. When one starts observing the silence of gross speech sincerely one becomes aware of, the speed with which the thoughts appear on the screen of consciousness, and the difficulty in controlling those thoughts. This way, one enters spirituality in the real sense through *Antarmukhatā*. As normally the mind is moving outward and with such practices one discovers another direction of movement.

In *Vipassana* the method developed by the Buddha, initially one is asked to observe total verbal silence. Then the seeker is asked to do the observation of breath 'as it is', without changing it. Through this practice one becomes capable of retaining the attention on a single thing. Then one is asked to observe the sensation all over the body. At the same time, one is advised never to get identified with the sensations or react to them either positively, or negatively. This posture of non-involvement helps the practitioner develop *Sākṣī-Bhāva*. In every method a particular facet is used to take the practitioner towards meditation, and through meditation, towards *Sākṣī-Bhāva*. Whatever the method, *Sākṣī-Bhāva* happens to be the ultimate goal.

Man has basically four facets of existence: Action, Thought, Will and Feeling. Normally he gets carried away by all these. He acts, but his action is unconscious; he thinks, but he is obsessed by the very thought; he wills but his will continues to be only a wishful thinking; he feels, but his emotions sweep him away. Action becomes *Karma Yoga* when one acts *meditatively* and with total *awareness*. Thought becomes *Jñāna Yoga* when one thinks *meditatively* and goes on increasing his *awareness*. Will becomes *Yoga,* when it is used *meditatively,* to control the mind or *Prāṇa*. Feelings become

Bhakti Yoga when one loves and feels *meditatively* and moves towards *Oneness.* Use of any faculty *with meditation* becomes a path to *Sākṣī-Bhāva.*

There are three ways of being: *Dṛśya,* the seen; *Darśaka,* the onlooker; and *Draṣṭā,* the witness. Man mostly sees or understands himself through the *others'* eyes that mirror him. Someone says he is handsome, he starts feeling so; someone says that he is wise and he gets easily convinced. To see these images in others' eyes he starts *creating an impression.* But unfortunately, he does not make any efforts to really become wise!

In other words, he becomes the scene or seen! He always expects others to notice him, and to appreciate him. He feels lost if this does not happen. It is said that when Elvis Presley—The King of Rock and Roll, when asked as to what was the most important necessity of his life, he was reported to have said 'ovation' and autograph hunters! Without them he confessed, he would die! The actors and actresses, politicians, singers, public figures, writers, poets, and such other persons live on applause and public opinion. If they do not see their names in the News Papers, they create scandals, so as to remain as centres of attraction!

One, who has become a *Dṛśya,* has completely forgotten himself and is all the while looking *outside.* But to be a *Dṛśya,* one has to put in a lot of effort. One has to be an achiever in some field or the other. Naturally it is not everyone's cup of tea! So most of us, resort to take an easier alternative: to become a *Darśaka,* an onlooker. Without *Darśakas,* those who become *Dṛśya* will have no audience, no one to appreciate them or take notice of them. The *Darśaka* involves himself with the *Dṛśya.* Due to this involvement, he undergoes the same amount of emotional and other disturbances. Because, his consciousness is turned outward and he is oblivious of the *One who is looking* that is himself.

Negligible number of persons are able to achieve the state of *Draṣṭā*. *Draṣṭā* is one who is totally aware of *himself,* or the one who is experiencing. At the same time he is aware of what is being experienced. In *Dṛśya* and *Darśaka,* the consciousness is like an arrow pointed outward, the target being the object. While in *Draṣṭā,* it is like an arrow having edges on both ends. Consequently, *Draṣṭā* is never excited with or depressed without the *Dṛśya*. A stage where the equipoise is retained in all situations. *Muṇḍakopaniṣad* describes the state of *Draṣṭā* eloquently:

> 'Two birds that are ever associated and have similar names, cling to the same tree. Of these, the one eats the fruit of divergent tastes and the other looks on without eating. On the same tree, the individual soul remains drowned as it were, and so it moans, being worried by its impotence. When it sees thus the other, the adored Lord and His glory, then it transcends all sorrow'.[179]

This *Saga* discusses some practical methods of attaining the quiescence, and ultimately the *Sākṣī-Bhāva*. Rāma requested Vasiṣṭha to explain the three *Maunas,* of *Vāk* (speech), *Karaṇa* (senses, mind), and *Kāṣṭha* (body).

The sage replied that there are two type of *Munis,* ordinary and supreme. The ordinary are called the *Kāṣṭha* or bodily *Tapasvins,* and the supreme are the *Jīvanamuktas.* The former category of persons develops firm will, through *Prāṇāyāma,* control of sense organs through *Haṭha-Yoga.* But those who having known the true nature of the universe, contemplate on the *Ātman* within and are quiescent, though

---

179 द्वा सुपर्णा सयुजा सखाया समानं वृक्षं परिषस्वजाते ।
तयोरन्यः पिप्पलं स्वाद्वत्त्यनश्नन्नन्यो अभिचाकशीति ॥ 3.1.1 ॥
समाने वृक्षे पुरुषो निमग्नोऽनीराया शोचति मुह्यमानः ।
जुष्टं यदा पश्यत्यन्यमीशमस्य महिमानमिति वीतशोकः ॥ 3.1.2 ॥

acting in the world are the real *Jīvanamuktas.* The true *Mauna* is that exalted state of rest. The control of speech is *Vāk-Mauna,* the subjugation of sense organs is *Karaṇa-Mauna.* And the cessation of physical action is *Kāṣṭha-Mauna.* With these three types of *Mauna* the mind is not totally silenced. And these three types of *Mauna* are practised by the first category of ordinary ascetics.

The wise say that the Brāhmic Bliss without beginning or end is the *Suṣupti-Mauna.* The mind free of all doubts after the realising the illusory character of this world with all the three *Guṇas* is the *Suṣupti-Mauna.* The realisation that the universe is no other than the ever full, auspicious *Jñāna* is termed by the wise as *Suṣupti-Mauna.* Equality of vision over all and the quiescent mind amidst all paradoxes is stated to be the *Suṣupti-Mauna.*

Suṣupti-Mauna has two subdivisions: *Sāṁkhya* and *Yoga.* Those who cogniser everything to be Brahman through *Samyak-Jñāna* or experiential wisdom, of the *Samādhi* of Brahman, the One without the second, and always in restful mind are the *Sāṁkhya-Yogins.* Those who attain the supreme through control of *Prāṇa,* and other activities quieten them are known as the *Yoga-Yogins.* The Ultimate State is same for the both. The venerable sage gave a wonderful hint about the State:

> 'The State in which the activity of *Prāṇa* and mind is completely annihilated and is freed from the trap of *Vāsanās* one attains the Supreme State'.[180]

Continuing, Vasiṣṭha said that without *Vicāra,* the mind appears to be real; but with *Vicāra,* it disappears like one's own death in a dream on waking up. Establishing oneself firmly in the single-pointedness upon the Non-dual Principle,

---

180 यत्र प्राणोमनोवृत्तिरत्यन्तं नोपलभ्यते ।
वासनावागुराक्रान्ता तद्विद्धि परमं पदम् ॥ 6.7.17 ॥

control of *Prāṇa,* and the subjugation of the mind are the three paths to cognise the meaning of *Mokṣa.* Out of these three if anyone should be mastered the others are also achieved.

> 'In all beings the *Prāṇa* and mind are inseparable like the flower and fragrance, or sesame and oil. They are like the supporter and the supported. If either of them is annihilated the other gets eliminated. The destruction of both will confer *Mokṣa* on all'.[181]

So long as thoughts are not thoroughly destroyed by regular practice, one should concentrate the mind on one truth at a time. Through such constant practice one-pointedness will dawn and the ghost-like thoughts vanish.

Not only does this scripture gives the details of the *Mauna* but it also gives valuable hints to achieve it. The intimate relationship between *Prāṇa* and the mind has been emphasised. Normally, *Prāṇa* is taken as the breath. But it is due to *Prāṇa* that the breathing takes place as both are related to one another as the cause and effect. Moreover, breathing is both involuntary and voluntary. By making it voluntary, we are able to become aware of the involuntary. That is why, we can make use of breathing to *perceive Prāṇa,* as in *Prāṇāyāma,* where the breathing is slowed down to achieve the *Antarmukhatā.* The Buddha in his *Ānāpānasati* or becoming aware of the inward and outward breath suggests only *remembering* the breathing *without ever changing the breathing pattern.* Besides these, there are infinite methods depending on the nature and aptitude of the seeker.

---

181 आविनाभाविनी नित्यं जन्तूनां प्राणचेतसी ।
कुसुमामोदवन्मिश्रे तिलतैल इव स्थिते ।। 6.7.21 ।।
आधाराधेयवच्चैव एकभावे विनश्यतः ।
कुरुतश्च स्वनाशेन कार्यं मोक्षाख्यमुत्तमम् ।। 6.7.22 ।।

Vasiṣṭha proceeded to narrate the story of Vetāla or the goblin. A Vetāla living in the Vindhya forests woke up in the *Turya* state after its long dream of births and deaths. Pressed by hunger it went about searching for prey. It had an enormous appetite. In spite of suffering from extreme hunger it never made prey of any human being without sufficient reasons. It left the forest for a country to find the worldly human beings. One night, it saw the ruler of the country patrolling his country. It thundered aloud, that it would eat him. Undisturbed, the king said that without *Jñāna,* the Vetāla's head would get splintered into thousand pieces.

The Vetāla replied that it had never killed any man without sufficient reasons; that a doubt was harrowing in its mind, and it wished that the king would relieve it. It asked the following questions:

> 'Of which sun are all the eggs the scattered units? Through what *Vāyu* does the endless *Ākāśa* shine? What is that Atom which when penetrated exhibits the same nature, like a plantain-stalk which is made up of layers? What is that non-differentiated primal Atom which expands itself into the infinite, small atoms of mundane eggs, *Ākāśa,* the numberless egos, the sun, Meru and other objects? Compared to that great mountain, the original formless Atom, these universes resemble a stone'?

The king replied that in the ever dawning sun of *Jñāna,* that all the universes shine. Compared to the rays of this sun, all the universes are only so many atoms. By this sun's light alone the universes shine. It is the power of *Brahman* which reduces *Kāla, Ākāśa, Cit,* fluctuation, and other existences to dust, and makes them shine in their true state. The *Brahman* shines in its own nature eternally in total quiescence, though dreams upon dreams arise in this prolonged dream of the universe. The *Brahman* alone shines within the infinite series of universes arising deeper and deeper in the recesses of space, like the plantain tree. It is this *Brahman* alone who is the supreme atom. It is endless and is the cause of Meru and other objects. In its vast expanse everything appears like an atom. This supreme *Ātman,* though having diverse forms is yet without form and is the nature of true *Jñāna.*

Hearing the above words from the king, the Vetāla cognised Reality and became quiescent in mind. Retiring to a solitary place, he entirely transcended his hunger and remained in pure *Samādhi* devoid of any fluctuation.

This story appears to be the repetition of the story of Karkaṭī in the *Utpatti Prakaraṇa.* Though the questions asked by Karkaṭī and the Vetāla have similarities, the context is different. In this *Sarga* all the answers are meant to push the listener into *Sākṣī-Bhāva.* Comparison of the *Ātman* with the ever dawning sun is quite symbolic. The sun lights up all the objects equally. The mist evaporates in its light. Similarly all the notions, identifications and involvements get transcended in its realisation. While everything else comes under activity, and hence temporal, the *Ātman,* or the *Draṣṭā,* alone transcends activity and is eternal. This is only *like* a sun, because all the suns derive their power and inspiration from *Ātman. Taittirīyopaniṣad* puts it beautifully to illustrate this:

> 'Out of His fear the Wind blows. Out of His fear the Sun rises. Out of His fear the Fire, Iṅdra and Death, the fifth, run'.[182]

This statement appears quite strange. It is true that all our actions are motivated by fear of death. But fear of *Ātman* appears too far stretched, as we are given to understand that *Ātman* is our own Self. How can one be afraid of herself or himself? But with the above background, it becomes clear. All the manifestations like the elements, body and mind,

---

182 भीषाऽस्माद्वातः पवते । भीषोदेति सूर्यः ।

भीषाऽस्मादग्निश्चेन्द्रश्च । मृत्युर्धावति पञ्चम इति ।। तैत्तिरीयोपनिषद् 2.8.1 ।।

function and exist only in and through activity. And if the activity stops it is death to them! If they identify with the *Ātman* the activity ceases.

While it does begin with the efforts to control the activity of the mind and *Prāṇa,* this *Sarga* finally suggests transcendence of activity, and not just its stoppage. That is why, it says that the *Brahman* reduces the fluctuations to dust, and allows them to function in their true state. The mind, senses and body lose their existence as *separate* entities and start functioning as the instruments of and under the light of *Brahman.*

It was very crowded near the temple. There was incessant activity and noise. No doubt, the temple with the pilgrims, the shops, and all that pandemonium was quite attractive, even pleasing for some time. But after a while it was getting on one's nerves. One walked out and behind the temple slowly and steadily leaving everything behind. The path led one to the foot of the hill *Aruṇāchala.* Gradually, he started climbing and the gap between the noise and the activity started increasing. Reaching the shoulder of *Aruṇāchala* one looked back and down. The temple could be seen, but it was more majestic from this distance; the noise too was there but it was not at all disturbing; and one could hardly perceive the activity, as one had become distant to activity. Similarly, if one develops a distance between oneself and the body-mind, one becomes what one already is: the *Draṣṭā.*

8

The Story of Bhagīratha

The air was cool and pleasant. Broad avenues lined with huge shady trees on both sides. Clean smooth road with not even a speck of dust on it. Each house, a dream fulfilled, with a lawn of its own and a white wooden fence. Everything seemed just perfect. No inquisitive neighbours, no unnecessary noise. He had left India, in search of a bright career, and he had achieved what he had always wanted. He was a recognised scientist in a leading University and had been contributing in the field of Genetic Engineering. He remembered the struggles he had to face, back home in India—no, he corrected himself *that* was no more his home, *this* was his home! He was glad he had taken this decision to respond to the offer from the University.

It was evening and the twilight was slowly giving way to a velvety black night sky. The University campus was ideal in every sense there was no pollution, plenty of free space and most of all, no concrete jungle! As he leaned back in the rocking chair his eyes fell on the violet horizon and his thoughts went back to the time when he had taken the difficult decision of leaving *his* country. His colleague had commented that he too was contributing to the *Brain-drain.* While he had argued that all he wanted to do was to work. And all he had asked was the research facility with a laboratory. What had he got in return to his ten years of hard work? *His* papers had been *pirated* by his boss to publish them in *his* name; there was unending back-biting and internal as well as external politics; and there were too many to stop him from doing *his own work!* He was glad, satisfied that he had made this country, the United States of America, the haven of the great, the powerful and the talented, his home. He was happy indeed...

Now why was he giving so many auto-suggestions? He asked himself. A person, who is really happy, does not remind himself of his happiness. Suddenly, the reason struck him. That very evening, he had gone to the department store. He had been addressed insultingly by the clerk, and most of those he had known and with whom he worked, had only smiled. Only one outsider, who was incidentally an Indian, had come to him and had said in Hindi:

> 'Bharat is our Bharat. Even if you are not recognised, at least none will insult you for the colour of your skin! But never mind you must get used to this aspect of the United States'!

These words and the light pat on his back had made him relax. They had gone out and had coffee together. He also gave a disturbing piece of news about a computer engineer meeting with a strange accident on his way to the presentation of his paper in front of a committee. Many Asians were being manhandled these days...

He had become nostalgic, remembering his small native town, the dancing paddy fields, and the innocent yet curious farmers with affection in their eyes, his own brother and sister, and most of all, his parents who kept asking him over the telephone as to when he would come back. He could not tell them that now he had become an American citizen, and that now it was impossible. Yes, he could go for a short visit. And he would go soon... With these thoughts he had become restless, even disturbed by the prospect of remaining in this alien country *forever.*

To avoid these thoughts he had started counting the blessings of the alien land! And that Indian brother *had been right,* India is after all his own India!

One does not know, whether he returned to his home land or accepted the alien land as his home. But the experience of insult and the subsequent encounter with one from *home* triggered off a longing to go home. This is what the enlightened masters do: to bring the message from *the Home* and to create a longing to return there. But only a few persons are fortunate enough to meet such masters, not because such Persons are not there, but because not all have the capacity to recognise them. That is when the scriptures come to our help. The scriptures are the compassionate and ecstatic outbursts of those who had returned *Home* and wanted the suffering people to transcend all suffering and be ever blissful. These outbursts give *peeps* into the experiences, the details of the paths they themselves had traversed and also the difficulties on way.

But not everyone has that type of interest, mandatory to take up the study of these scriptures. In our so-called normal life we experience pleasure and pain intermittently. We avoid the pain and seek pleasure. And many times we are unable to even trace the cause for the pain. This is when the pain does its part in suggesting that something is wrong. It is like a person who experiences pain if he wears the shoes which are undersized! Repeated pain or in general, any kind of discomfort—tension, anxiety, boredom and the like make us wonder as to whether the life we are leading or the life as we have understood it, is right. This is how we start looking for solutions for our painful problems elsewhere. The pain as such, plays the role of creating disinterest in the life of indulgence or involvement.

Pain is not the only reason for turning the attention inwards, boredom is another. While pain is experienced by everyone, boredom is felt by only those who have the ability to look at their own life objectively. They note that there is a kind of mindless repetition of action day-in and day-out. A bored person necessarily has to be an intelligent person who has a certain level of awareness or *mindfulness* in the words of the Buddha. The Buddha himself turned inwards due to boredom as well as his sensitivity to pain of others.

Another very important cause is the intense involvement and indulgence. When a person is totally seeped in either activity or enjoyment, that very indulgence gives him such a great shock, that he is forced to come out of it. The expectations precede involvements, whether in activity or sense indulgence. The conviction, that the satisfaction or happiness is *outside* is behind such expectations. Man interested in gathering sense objects, or who is after power, name and fame is bound to get a shock sometime or the other. Tulasidāsa, who was so madly in love with his wife that he rode a corpse to cross a flooding river, or Kanakadāsa who was so greedy that he lost all human-ness are the examples of men turning towards God and achieving Enlightenment.

Whatever the reason, man longs to change such a predominantly humdrum and robopathic life. This is when the enlightened persons and the scriptures play their role of extending an invitation to another possibility of life. Adventurous that human beings are, many take up this challenge. The Vedāntic texts like *Yoga Vāsiṣṭha* stress on continual effort to transcend the obstinate hurdles called the mind and the *Vāsanās*. For, it is easy to take up the quest, and rather difficult to continue with the same enthusiasm. *Śama* or the patience to wait for eternity if necessary, and to continue the effort, even in absence of any results is mandatory. To stress this point, the story of Bhagīratha was narrated by venerable Vasiṣṭha to Rāma.

Bhagīratha has become a synonym with effort, in fact, they are both taken together: *Bhagīratha-Prayatna*. He is said to have performed intense penance to bring down the divine

Gaṅgā from heaven. He bore tremendous hardships and hurdles, but never gave up the effort till he succeeded in his mission.[183] He remained undaunted in spite of continuous obstacles from all corners and brought down the *Gaṅgā*. The present *Sarga* appears to hint that if one transcends the mind one has achieved *everything*, or rather everything else becomes trivial.

Sage Vasiṣṭha told Rāma that an illumined mind is clear as *Ākāśa,* which can be achieved through non-fluctuating *Pratyagātman* or the Inner *Ātman.* The mind should be drawn away from the objects of senses and all actions should be performed without attachment. Mind devoid of desires or of despondency due to unfulfilled desires becomes peaceful. After achieving such a state, one becomes capable of performing his duties in spite of obstacles. Rāma requested the sage to narrate the power of Bhagīratha. Sage Vasiṣṭha started narrating the story.

There lived a king by name Bhagīratha who had cognised the non-dual Principle. He was just, charitable and sensitive to the needs of his subjects. He redeemed his ancestors from the nether world by bringing the divine *Gaṅgā* on to the earth. Even in his infancy the king was observant of ways of the world. It was quite strange for a child to get introduced to *Vicāra.* Retiring into solitude he realised, the nature of this universe to be discordant; that it lacked in newness; that it is temporal; that the entanglement increases with normal repetitive actions; and that the only true action is that, by performing which, enables one to attain the stainless One.

---

183 King Sāgara wanted to perform *Aśwamedha,* but Iṅdra stole the sacrificial horse and took it to the nether world. Sāgara's numerous sons found the horse near Sage Kapila, who reduced them to ashes due to their insolent behaviour. Āṅśumān succeeded in bringing back the horse.. Bhagīratha, Āṅśumān's grandson finally succeeded in bringing down the *Gaṅgā* to free his grand uncles from sage's curse.

Having understood the true nature of worldly objects, Bhagīratha was seized by aversion for them. He went in search of the *Guru* who could help him achieve the Oneness. Having found him whose name was Tritula, sought his guidance to achieve freedom from delusion. The Master said that if one could cognise the stainless *Jñānātman,* one could alleviate all pain and end the age old bondage, all doubts would clear and the traces of *Karma* would get destroyed. Then one would become the *Cinmātra* or absolute consciousness, that is the birth right of every being. The disciple asked of his *Guru* as to how one could get established in this consciousness.

Muni Tritula said that the mind would attain to *Swarūpaniṣṭha* or Establishment in self, through its own all pervasive intelligence. The wise who have achieved *Jñāna,* define it as the total *Asaṅga* or non-attraction, for objects, relationships, and indifference to pleasure and pain and equipoise, a ceaseless *Vicāra* and the direct cognition of the Reality. The annihilation of the *identification of the 'I' with the body* is the only medicine for the disease of repeated births and deaths. Again the sincere disciple Bhagīratha asked as to how the idea of 'I' which is firmly grounded in the body-mind be removed.

Tritula answered that the only solution is to withdraw the mind from the objects of pleasure through *Pauruṣa* or will and *Prayatna* or effort, and to rest the mind in the all pervading *Sat,* which eliminates *Ahaṁkāra.* If after transcending desire one remains in that *Śānta* or non-fluctuating state, the 'I' ceases to be, and what remains is the state of Non-dual Brahman. Having given up shame and other *contracting* differentiations totally, the *Ahamkṛti*—'I-do-ness' gets dissolved. Having assumed poverty without an iota of any of the three kinds of desire: for wife, progeny and wealth, having relinquished wealth in favour of one's enemies, free from *Ahaṁkāra,* if one lives without any load on the mind one becomes *Brahman,* the Supreme of the Supreme.

Vāsiṣṭha Caṅdrikā, the gloss on this scripture dilates on the *contracting differentiations* as follows:

> 'Shame and others refers to improper acts which *contract* the mind. The word *Ādi,* or others, means birth, pride of family and other destructive traits. It is said—"contempt, suspicion, desire or longing, shame, disgust, the five, family, discipline and caste are known as the eight bonds".'[184]

It obviously means that we should totally avoid the *Bheda-Vāsanā* of any kind, and should instead, identify with the all expansive *Brahman.* Actually, when one starts moving away from *Ahaṁkāra* the enemies cannot possibly exist nor does the pride or any of the eight bonds. It is like darkness which cannot exist in presence of light. Actually the darkness is nothing but the *absence* of light! Similarly, the constrictive eight bonds are the *absence* of expansiveness. Whatever has the constrictive effect, leads to unhappiness if not misery, which incidentally happens to be the highest common factor in human beings!

Continuing sage Vasiṣṭha said, that having heard the powerful advice from the enlightened Master Tritula, Bhagīratha performed diverse actions to control his mind. After some time, he performed a noble *Yajña* called *Agniṣṭoma;* after inquiry into the deserving and the non-deserving, all his justly accumulated wealth was spent amongst the poor. In three days he was left with nothing but a single cloth. He left his beloved country in favour of his enemy and full of the good qualities that behove a *Muni,* he wandered alone in the forests, towns, hills where he was not known. Shortly he

---

184 लज्जादि अनुचिते कर्मणि चेतसः संकोचो लज्जा ।
आदिशब्दाज्जातिकुलाभिमानादिग्रहणम् । तदुक्तम्–'घृणा शंका स्पृहा लज्जा जुगुप्सा चेति पञ्चमी । कुलं शीलं तथा जातिरष्टौ पाशाः प्रकार्तिता' ।। वासिष्ठचन्द्रिका 6.8.28 ।।

dispelled all desires from his consciousness, resulting in his merger with the *Ātman.*

Having wandered the whole earth, one day he entered the kingdom he had left in favour of his earlier enemy—for he had transcended all differentiation. He started begging alms at the gates of his former ministers and aids. Persons recognised him and shed tears at his approach. Even when the king at that time came to offer him back his own kingdom, desireless that he was he did not accept it, instead went away to everybody's disappointment.

Filled with bliss through true quiescence of mind, like his *Guru,* he remained in continual *Ātmic* vision. Enjoying equal vision and tranquil mind and supporting the body as if in sport, he was indifferent to the pairs of opposites like pleasure and pain, happiness and unhappiness, etc, as well as the eight *Siddhis,* the mystical powers. The king of the country in which Bhagīratha was at that time had died leaving no successor. When the mendicant Bhagīratha appeared he was chosen as the successor. Choiceless that he had become at that time, Bhagīratha wielded the sceptre. This news reached his former kingdom from where the courtiers approached him with an appeal to accept the responsibility rule that kingdom also as the king had died without a successor.

As it is not proper to spurn the wealth which comes unsought he acceded to their request. Maintaining perfect silence or control over the senses, quiescence of mind, equal vision over all, without any desire and ever steadfast in his mental state, he ruled over his empire. Then performing faultless *Tapas* for many years, he established sacredness by bringing down the divine Gangā on to the earth. The Gangā not only purified his ancestors but continues to do so even now.

The Buddha had helped hundreds of persons in achieving transcendence. In front of his very eyes, Ānanda—

the closest disciple who had stayed perhaps longest as Tathāgata's shadow—he had seen this happen. But unfortunately, Ānanda had not yet seen the light. He recorded each and every incident as well as conversation that the Buddha had had. The devoted disciple asked Tathāgata the reason for this delay. The Buddha smilingly replied that Ānanda had taken for granted, that being with the Enlightened One was enough to have *Nirvāṇa.* It was not at all so. He had added *'Appō Dīpō Bhava!'* or 'Be a light unto yourself!' and that he could only show the way. And each one of his disciples had to travel himself.

The Enlightened Masters or the scriptures give us an invitation to explore that which lies beyond the body-mind. Unless we take this invitation seriously and plunge into the divine adventure, they remain only as the neglected signboards or at the most as sources to increase our scholastic or egotistic arguments.

9

The Story of Cūḍālā

Winter had set in. The morning was particularly beautiful with, the smoke of the village hearths moving up lazily towards the heavens; the mist in the air blending with the smoke as if in courtship; the feathered songsters with their feathers filled with air appeared fat; and the rising sun got involved with smog and mist in a playful wrestle which ended in the surrender of the mist, to the inexhaustible source of energy. The animals too were calling their masters to release them so that they can go to the waiting pastures with honey like dew on them. The shepherds and the cowherds were preparing to leave and were releasing their animals from the sheds. The farmers were getting ready to go to their fields, to guard the birds and animals from doing any harm to their ripening wheat crops.

In an atmosphere filled with mist, a mystic sat under a tree. Nearby, there was a well out of which the rising water vapour could be seen. It was as though, the earth was offering the incense to the infinite sky. But for the ordinary, the water vapour showed the intensity of cold. This biting cold had very little effect on the mystic. Two of his companions also sat playing on the musical instruments accompanying him in his ethereal voice, singing the glory of the art of *listening*. The warmth spreading from his song made the companions oblivious to cold.

> 'Through listening alone the *Siddhas, Peers, Devas,* and *Iṅdra* exist;
> Through listening alone the earth and the sky stand;
> Through listening alone the islands, planes and the nethers move;
> Through listening alone the death does no harm;
> *Nānak* says—the devotee always remains blissful; and
> Through listening alone the misery and sin get destroyed'.[185]

The Person was Guru Nānak Dev.

A *Faqir* was seen approaching this threesome. His clothes were dusty, his hair and beard disheveled and his face wore a tired look. Obviously, he had travelled all night to reach the place. But most significant aspect of his personality was his eyes, aflame with an unknown thirst that appeared to have bothered him for lives. Looking into the serene face, and the eyes of Nānak Dev which were full of love, he said with an urgent voice:

> 'I have heard that if you want, you can reduce me to ash in a moment and recreate me in a moment. You have power over creation as well as destruction. This is a miracle. I do not believe it. But I want to see if it's true'!

When those pools of compassion looked into the eyes of the *Faqir,* they saw that the man was sincere, and he had not at all come there to test. It was not an idle curiosity either. The man was a seeker, with a great thirst for Godliness. He saw the fire of a gambler in those eyes, ready to gamble *everything* just to learn. Nānak Dev, asked him to come near him and sit.

185 सुणिऐ सिध पीर सुरिनाथ । सुणिऐ धरति धवल आकास ।
सुणिऐ दीप लोअ पाताल । सुणिऐ पोहि न सकै कालु ।
नानक भगता सदा विकासु । सुणिऐ दूख पाप का नासु ।। जपु जी : 7 ।।

Then he said:

'Close your eyes and sit quietly. I will demonstrate what you aspire so much'.

The sun rays were slowly dispelling the mist and spreading warmth. The two companions of Nānak Dev were also surprised, for he had never ever demonstrated any miracle. They were aghast, and were totally alert. The *Faqir* was not afraid, there was a childlike simplicity and trust in his posture. He became totally empty from within. It is said, that everything in the surrounding region was charged, as though in expectation of a great event. Nānak Dev too closed his eyes and kept his hand on the head of the *Faqir.*

Nānak Dev uttered the sacred sound of *'AUM'*. The story goes that the *Faqir* was reduced to ash. The saint uttered one more *'AUM'*, and the *Faqir* was created again! If we go by the story, we miss a great truth. Though it is apparent that the physical body remained, the process must have taken place *inside.* The man in his innocence and complete trust had made himself really quiet. And the saint's sound created within, a mood of *Pralaya* or dissolution, and he achieved *Śūnyatā* or *nothingness.* In other words, there was *nobody* inside and only *listening* was there. The *Faqir,* his aspiration, dreams, and the internal dialogue was reduced to ash. When Nānak Dev uttered the *'AUM'* in this state of nothingness, The *Faqir* came back to his senses, but it was no more the same man, a new man, a totally transformed man was there! It no doubt was a great miracle : the transformation of man.

Most, if not all the time, the art of *listening* eludes us, because there is a perpetual internal dialogue going on in our head. When something is said immediately the mind starts comparing with the store of knowledge within. In fact, it is not only with the ears but with all the senses. So, when Nānak Dev uses the word *'Suniyai'*, he means listening to the world *as it is* and *not as you* ***wants*** *it!* If and only if, we are able to keep aside all the preconceived notions when we come in contact with the world, we succeed in listening. Mahāvīr Jain, the twenty-fourth *Tīrthaṅkara* has suggested that such listening is one of the methods for achieving *Kaivalya.* He used to say, that one has only to become a *Śrāvaka* or one who has learnt the art of *listening.* There is a beautiful mythological story:

The seven musical notes *Sā, Re, Ga, Ma, Pa, Dha,* and *Nī,* wanted to meet and listen to a perfect singer. They went around three planes the nether world, the earth and the heaven. But since they knew the intricacies of music, they found some limitations or the other in each and every singer or musician. Frustrated, it is said that they approached Brahmā, the Creator. He said that Mahādeva was the perfect singer. Gladly they went to Kailāśa the abode of Śiva. The great God said that he would sing willingly, but he could do so only in front of a *perfect listener!* The notes were in a fix, as then they had to search for a perfect *listener!* When they appealed to the Great God, he smilingly took the name of Viṣṇu.

They approached Lord Viṣṇu and appealed him to come with them to Kailāśa, for listening to the music of Śiva. The Lord happily went with them. Two seats were arranged, one in front of the other for the great Gods. The notes sat on both sides *watching* the concert. Śiva started the *Ālāpa*—the introduction to the *Rāga.* It was observed that Viṣṇu was in rapt attention, so much so, that his eyes had got fixed and body had become like a statue. As the *Rāga* got developed,

Viṣṇu's eyes started watering as that *Rāga* had a mood of compassion. When the tempo[186] was increased, Viṣṇu started *melting.* And at the climax, there was neither Viṣṇu, the listener, nor Śiva, the singer, but there only pure music! The

186 Hindustani classical music has three *Layas* or tempos, *Vilaṁbit,* or delayed, *Madhya,*or middle and *Drut*–fast. *Madhya* is twice as fast as *Vilaṁbit,* and *Druta* is twice as fast as *Madhya.*

singer as well as the listener had merged into sound. Or rather, *they had become the sound!*

This is what happens between *Guru* the preceptor and *Śiṣya* the disciple. The Buddha has pointed out that, *the flame* ***only jumps*** *on its own, from a burning lamp, to a lamp ready to burn without any effort of either lamp.* In this process, there is absolutely no change in the host lamp, but yes, there is transformation in the guest lamp! Similarly, the Enlightened *Guru* does not *do anything,* and the disciple only waits patiently remaining totally receptive, till he *catches* the infection of Enlightenment. In this sense, the work of the disciple is to empty himself, of all *Vāsanās.*

The story under discussion is one of the most beautiful and important stories, if not *the* most important! Wherein, this scripture transcends the barrier of gender, which continues to plague the field of spirituality especially in our country: that only man is eligible for spirituality and it is the woman's duty to look after his needs while he strives for *Mukti!;* and that ***her*** *Mukti lies in her husband's Mukti!* This erroneous notion is shattered by this story. Of course, this lofty story is not required for a thinking mind which is mandatory to take up the study of this scripture, which helps in transcending mind itself. And gender is only a differentiation at the level of body. It has much more to offer for a seeker.

Sage Vasiṣtha continued his teaching when he blessed Rāma to be like the great Śikhidhvaja who had annihilated his mind. The disciple in Rāma appealed to the sage to throw more light on the life of King Śikhidhvaja who was absorbed in ever expanding bliss. The Muni obliged. King Śikhidhvaja was born in *Dvāpara Yuga,* in the seventh *Manvaṅtara.*[187] He

---

187 Four *Yugas, Sat-Yuga, Tretā, Dwāpara* and *Kali* constitute one *Mahāyuga.* A *Manvaṅtara* is one day of *Manu* and comprises of 71 *Mahāyugas.* The present *Manvaṅtara* is of seventh *Manu,* by name Vaivasvata.

was a just, pious, and charitable king. His wife was Cūḍālā, a pious and devoted queen who was a fit companion to the king. They lived in perfect happiness, peace and harmony. Having mastered all branches of knowledge, they spent their youth in performing all duties in perfect unison and that showed in their mental and physical health.

As the years glided past, so did their youth like water from a broken pot and the middle age fell upon them like the snow-flakes on lotuses of a pond. The desires, which they nurtured in their youth, began to decrease like waters in the autumn. In unison they began to contemplate that the body, senses, and mind are ever changing; that one has to reach such a state which is unchanging and expansive; and that such state cannot be achieved by those who are plunged in mundane existence. Therefore, they concluded, that *Adhyātma-Jñāna* alone is the cure for the disease of rebirth. With this conclusion, they started living a life of meditation and practical spirituality. They would associate themselves with the wise to learn the essence of the *Śāstras.* The *Śravaṇa* or listening was obviously followed by *Manana* or contemplation.

There are three stages in *Jñāna Sādhanā,* the method of *Jñāna. Śravaṇa, Manana* and *Nididhyāsana.* The first two steps are taken with enthusiasm and energy. A truth either heard, or read revolves in our mind for a while. We discuss it and convince ourselves intellectually and perhaps, are even able to convincingly express it, either through lectures or ink and paper! But then, it is only an intellectual pursuit and at the most a good hobby or pastime! It does not take us anywhere. On the contrary, it may even do harm as one may develop an air of superiority over those who are not as articulate. While the truth is, that one is at the same level with only a little more *information!* This can easily be known because when other things come in front of us, especially if the interest is only intellectual, the truth heard and discussed leaves us like the effervescence in an open bottle of soda!

This happened with Śikhidhvaja as he got involved with his kingship. But in the case of Cūḍālā, the interest was really deep. So, instead of keeping the wisdom learnt from the wise at only intellectual level, Cūḍālā started doing *Nididhyāsana* or meditative reflection, of the truths they both had heard and discussed with the wise. Muni Vasiṣṭha now entered into the methodology of *Nididhyāsana,* in just nine *Ślokas,* as he continued the narration:

By keeping her mind away from all other occupations, and allowing it *only* to do *Samyagavekṣaṇaṃ,*[188] or internal observation, Cūḍālā resolved, that she was going to understand herself, by analysing who *She* was in reality without seeking any outside help all by herself; that she would trace out *who it was that was having the delusion that 'I am the psycho-physical entity consisting of the body, mind and intellect.'* The first and the obvious question was 'Am I the body?'

Because, most of the time and most of us, take ourselves to be the body having a particular shape and form. With the question, she started observing the impermanence of the body through its ever changing condition, and its total dependence on *Karmendriyas,* the instruments of action for its very existence. But the *Karmendriyas* too are gross as they too are parts of the body. They definitely move, but are not *apart* from the body.

She then observed that the *Jñānendriyas,* the instruments of knowledge, are subtler than both body and *Karmendriyas.* But then, she discovered that they are totally dependent on *Manas,* like the road rolling stone, moving only because of the controlling rod and the power of men rolling it. Day-in and day-out, our senses come in contact with the outside world through the five senses. Thousands of stimuli hit them,

---

188 Observation of all the inner *Vyāpāras* or transactions without any involvement.

but only a few get registered in our mind, while the rest are just ignored. Then going behind the *Manas,* responsible for gathering the sense data, she discovered that *Manas* also depends totally on *Niścayātmika Buddhiḥ* the instrument responsible for decision making, and analysis, like a stone appearing to move the string and the finger while rotating. In other words, only those stimuli which are acceptable to *Buddhiḥ* enter our consciousness and remain as knowledge.

Cūḍālā reaching the level of *Buddhiḥ,* realised that even the *Buddhiḥ* is dependent on the *Ahaṁkāra* for its determinative power. And the *Ahaṁkāra* which empowers the *Buddhiḥ,* like the dam, which is responsible for the water to flow into canals. So, in comparison to the *Buddhiḥ,* Cūḍālā realised that her truer person is *Ahaṁkāra.*

A little discussion will not be out of place at this stage. In *Vedānta, Antahkaraṇa* or the inner-instrument means the mind stuff in general. *Manas* is that *function* of the mind, responsible for collection of sense data; *Buddhiḥ,* the function of analysis and decision; *Cittaṃ,* the activity of remembrance of past impressions. They are not in any way separate entities, but just functions of the same faculty of the mind stuff. But the functions are very distinct. Over and above or subtler than all these functions there is *Ahaṁkāra* or the 'I-do'-ness! For example, 'I sense', 'I analyse or decide' or 'I remember'. Most if not all of us are familiar to these facets of the body-mind complex. But yes, we are not *aware* of them as Cūḍālā was, in a non-involved way.

Transcending the *Buddhiḥ,* Cūḍālā realised that even *Ahaṁkāra* is without any essence and gross like a corpse, as it is derived from *Jīva.* In fact, it is only a *shadow* of *Jīva,* without any original consciousness of its own, and is a created illusion, like that of a ghost in the mind of a child who looks at a shadow on the wall. This is the penultimate stage in the *Ātmavicāra.* When one transcends *Ahaṁkāra* one meets face to face as it were with the *Jīva* which is a ray of the *Pure*

Consciousness, coming from *That Reality.* This *Jīva* alone manifests Itself as various functions of *Ahaṁkāra, Buddhiḥ, Manas, Jñānendriyas, Karmendriyas,* and body. Only in ignorance, do we take these manifestations to be separate and independent.

Cūḍālā took the final plunge, as she transcended even the *Jīva,* to discover that even the *Jīva* is only *an activity,* of manifestation and withdrawal. Like a child not regulated by rules and regulations, it creates and destroys, projects, withdraws or conceives the whole world of multiplicity. Even *Jīva* is like a reflection in a mirror. Being an *activity* and a *Prāṇa,* it rests in the consciousness. It is again activated by the Pure Consciousness, to cognise, perceive or experience the three states of consciousness, and to manifest itself as different functions of thinking.

The moment she realised this, the *Jīva* too melted into the Pure Consciousness, and she exclaimed ecstatically "Oh Indeed I have found out! I have discovered the great Truth! The *Jīva* lives because of the Supreme Force behind it—which is the ever permanent, all-pervading Pure Consciousness, the Self, the *Ātman*!"

From the level of *Ātman* she could see very clearly, that in spite of the activity of thinking and its subsequent delusion through the identification with the objects, and the resulting happiness or misery, the *Jīva* lives only through the power of Consciousness; that even by choosing the grosser manifestation and assuming the grosser body, the Consciousness remains aloof, as fire from water; that the self-created activity of mind through this process of manifestation or *Cetyōnmukhatā,* gets enlightened through the Consciousness; that the Reality is without any attributes; and that IT transcends all names and forms. There was this feeling of familiarity with this wisdom, as though, she knew it all along and it was only forgotten in the involvement and now *remembered.*

Vasiṣṭha continued by saying, that queen Cūḍālā through such continual *Antarmukhatā*, the internalisation of the mind, enjoyed the Reality and remaining in that state, went on expanding her Consciousness. Her actions were meticulous, without any longing for their fruits. She was unaffected by the pairs of opposites, and was untouched by desire and hatred. She thus became a receptacle of bliss, and her continual *Vicāra* or meditative contemplation and the resultant solidification of the *Ātmic* experience brought about the radiance of her being even at the physical level, and she became like a soft creeper with fresh flowers.

King Śikhidhvaja, noticing the glorious radiance that waxed day after day around the form of his wife Cūḍālā inquired as to how she had started reclaiming her youth and beauty, and how her mind had been blessed with tranquility, devoid of desire for enjoyment. Cūḍālā replied that she had abandoned this universe with *Rūpa* or form, and *Arūpa* or without form, that is within the perception of the senses as well as that which is beyond the senses, she had attained to the mighty and the incomparable One which survives destruction of all things; that she had cognised the substratum of all; that she had transcended all kinds of involvement, and had come to enjoy the radiance and beauty.

At this reply from Cūḍālā, her husband sarcastically smiled at her and said that such words do not behove her who was like a slender plant. For it appeared as though she was claiming herself to have been enlightened, and enlightenment is not possible for one who is surrounded by luxury and affluence. And even the greatest of men have achieved the state only after giving up everything and prolonged penance. He told her that she was deluded like some people who having not the courage to plunge headlong into a life of seclusion and effort, only *imagining* that lofty state! Laughing loudly, the king departed.

Cūḍālā only smiled compassionately at the king who was still drowned in ignorance, characterised by duality and involvement with the visible universe. She only hoped that he too would come to understand himself and reach the state she had achieved. Yet, the couple continued to live together harmoniously and happily as before. Preserving her equilibrium of mind, the wife gained complete mastery over her desires. But there arose in her, through her own volition, an innocent and playful desire to be a 'walker of the sky'. For this purpose, seating herself in a meditative posture she retired to a solitary spot. After mastering the posture, she started the practice of taking the *Prāṇa* upwards.

At this point Rāma asked Vasiṣṭha to enlighten him as to how the *Siddhis* or psychic powers like *Ākāśagamana,* or the art of walking in the sky, etc. might be developed after a long and arduous practice. The sage replied that though Rāma had interrupted him in the middle of the story of Cūḍālā to know the details of some yogic practices, he would gladly tell him. First and fundamental step is to divest oneself of all affinity for objects, except those on which the mind intends to concentrate upon. This is followed by proper diet, an easy posture, purity of body and mind, knowledge of the essence of *Yoga Śāstras,* and uninterrupted practice under the guidance of a *Guru.* One should completely rid oneself of anger, greed, attachment to objects, and hatred for others. If he observes the nature of the *Prāṇas* and masters them, as a master his servants, their nature will enable him to rule the universe, to attain *Mokṣa* as well as develop *Siddhis.*

Thereafter, sage Vasiṣṭha proceeded to explain the finer aspects of the practice of *Prāṇāyāma, Bandhas* or neuro-muscular locks, *Mūlabandha, Udyānabandha* and *Jālandarabandha,* taming of the *Kuṇḍalinī Śakti* through which one can not only develop all the *Siddhis,* but also keep away the diseases from affecting us. To which again, Rāma wanted to know more about the origin and destruction of diseases. What followed was an excellent analysis of disease.

The enlightened sage Vasiṣṭha said that the pain that afflicts the body is called the *Vyādhi* or secondary disease, while the *Vāsanās* afflicting the mind is termed as *Ādhi* or primary disease. The present afflicted state is reached through the absence of transcendental *Jñāna,* want of control over the sense-organs and the perpetual desire and egoism in the mind. The delusion gets intensified through the forgetfulness through the causes just mentioned. With the growth of such delusion the mental disease also grows like snow in winter. When the intense desires of the person begin to manifest themselves externally and the ignorance dominates, he performs unhealthy actions and these in turn breed bodily diseases. The body is subject to disease through such actions as eating of unwholesome food, living in unhealthy areas, doing things at unreasonable times, inflicting injury to oneself and others, association with the wicked, longing for improper things, evil desires, bad thoughts, the swelling and contraction of the orifices of the *Nāḍīs* in the joints, etc. and the interrupted flow of the beneficial *Prāṇa-s* throughout the body. These internal causes flourish as diseases in the body. The body attracts effects to itself according to the nature of its countless affinities, good and bad, whether in the previous births or the present one.

Continuing, Vasiṣṭha narrated the manner in which *Vyādhi* originate and are eliminated. The wise say that *Ādhi* has two sub-divisions: *Sāmānya* or ordinary, and *Sāra* or essential. The *Sāmānya* include those which are incidental to the body, and *Sāra* is the rebirth to which men are subject. If the primal causes that is, the bad thoughts are destroyed, all diseases afflicting the body also vanish. But *Sāra* will never end except with *Ātmajñāna,* like the misapprehension of a serpent in the rope cannot be removed except through the discovery of the real rope. But those grievous diseases of the body which do not arise through the original cause can be overcome by *Mantras,* medicine and many means used by the men in the field of medicine.

Rāma wanted to know more about the mental diseases. Vasiṣṭha proceeded: When *Manas* is agitated, then the body also follows in its wake. And when the body is agitated, there is no proper perception of things that are in one's way and the *Prāṇa* flies from its usual path on to a bad road, staggering like an animal wounded by an arrow. Through such agitation, *Prāṇa* vibrates everywhere at an unequal rate, instead of pervading steadily and equally. Consequently, the *Nāḍis* are not steady, and quiver.

The *Prāṇas* fluctuate, and the food settling inside the body amidst such commotion gets transformed into incurable diseases. Purification of mind through *Mantras,* and virtuous action, is the sure cure for all mental diseases. The sage then proceeded to narrate the path of *Yoga* for mastering the *Kuṇḍalinī Śakti,* by which one can achieve the *Siddhis,* like flying in the sky, remaining in water for long periods like fish, or entering other bodies.

Resuming the thread of the story of Cūḍālā, Muni Vasiṣṭha continued: Having developed the *Siddhis* Cūḍālā moved throughout the world. She tried her level best to convince her husband of the infinite peace and bliss pervading her, but without any success. Śikhidhvaja could not in the least understand her, and went on taking her as *his wife!* And since he did not know peace of mind she did not initiate him into the secrets of *Jñāna.* Rāma expressed a doubt : If in spite of the sincere efforts by the enlightened Cūḍālā, Śikhidhvaja failed to obtain *Jñāna,* how can others obtain it.

Vasiṣṭha replied that one should have implicit faith in the words of the *Guru* and the *Śāstras.* The disciple should have pure intelligence. To which Rāma again interrupted asking why the *Guru's* words are necessary, if the disciple's pure intelligence alone is sufficient. In reply to this doubt the sage narrated the following story.

In a forest in the Vindhya Mountains, there lived a hunter of a great lineage. One day he lost a cowry-shell[189] while travelling along a grassy road in the forest. So, he set out for searching it, filled with sadness. Having searched for it in vain for three days, he came across *Cūḍāmaṇi,* the gem with the lustre of the full moon. But the hunter passed by the gem—a gem so valuable as to purchase the seven worlds— in his anxiety to recover the lost cowry! *Jñāna* comes to a man in due time through the initiation of *Guru.* When the mind is concentrated on one thing, there arises in it another kind of knowledge through *Guru's* grace, which is not anticipated.

The part of the story dealt so far, describes in detail the process of *Ātmavicāra* or contemplation on the Self. The method adopted by Cūḍālā has been called as *Upasaṁhāra* or retrieval. This is possible only when the mind as such is at a very low level of activity. If the mind is strongly active, it has to be calmed down through *Tapas.* Śaṅkarācārya in his commentary on the *Taittirīyopaniṣad* explains the word *Tapaḥ* as follows:

> 'That is *Tapaḥ* which quietens senses and *Aṅtaḥkaraṇa* as *Brahman* is achieved through it. Concentration of mind and senses alone is the supreme *Tapaḥ.* This alone is superior to all *Dharmas,* the Supreme *Dharma.* (*Mahābhārata-Śāṅtiparva*-250:4) so says *Smṛti*'.[190]

Vāsiṣṭha Caṅdrikā commenting on the mental posture of Cūḍālā, says:

> 'Withdrawing from all activity implies, with peaceful mind and involving in activity means that appropriate

---

189 Cowrie is a small sea shell used as a currency in olden days, it had minimum value.

190 तच्च तपो बाह्यान्तःकरणसमाधानं तद्द्वारकत्वाद्ब्रह्म प्रतिपत्तेः । "मनसश्चेन्द्रियाणां च ह्यैकाग्र्यं परमं तपः । तज्ज्यायः सर्वधर्मेभ्यः स धर्मः पर उच्यते"।। महाभारत, शान्तिपर्व. 250.4 ।। तैत्तिरीयोपनिषद् शंकरभाष्यः ।। 3.1 ।।

activity helping in ripening the *Buddhiḥ* towards her *Ātman* she performed *Vicāra*'.[191]

There is a great hint for persons with relatively calm minds. Śaṅkarācārya uses the word *Samādhāna,* which means *allowing the mind to calm down,* while not *doing* anything, by remaining *Sākṣī,* an un-involved witness. The *Vāsiṣṭha Caṅdrikā* clarifies it further about *directing* such calm and composed mind towards oneself. If one combines both these hints one gets the methodology of *Vicāra.* One begins with "Am I the body?" and gradually proceeds within. However, one must clearly know this *directing* of the mind is *not* thinking but *being* at these various levels of body, senses, mind, etc. For any thought is always *outgoing* because, all thought is *about* something!

This has been beautifully portrayed through the experiences of Cūḍālā. Just after her exclamation on realising her Self, Cūḍālā *sees* that the grosser facets like mind and body get manifested due to *Cetyonmukhatā,* the tendency for activity in the consciousness. The antidote for this process of manifestation has been suggested by Vasiṣṭha, through the word *Antarmukhatā,* or directing the consciousness *inside.* This *internalisation* of consciousness helps in transcending the grosser facets of one's being. For example, when one is at the level of senses, one clearly sees the grossness of the body; at mind, senses, etc.

As already mentioned elsewhere in this study, one does not have to *do anything* to transcend the grosser facet, one has to only delve deeper into the subtler facet, when one sees consciously that all the grosser activity of the facets, is totally dependent on the Pure Consciousness for their very existence. The process, of being on the subtler plane by

---

191 अव्यापृता तूष्णीमासीना व्यापृता वा समुचितं व्यापारं कुर्वाणापि धिया स्वमात्मानमित्थं वक्ष्यमाणप्रकारेण विचारयामास ।। 6.9.19 ।।

withdrawing the involvement from the grosser plane, has been called as *Upasaṁhāra,* or the withdrawal.

Another aspect of human mind has been clearly mentioned, that unless one has completed the transactions at the grosser level of existence, one cannot possibly appreciate the subtler aspects. This has been shown by the question Rāma asks about the *Siddhis* and diseases *after* the graphic description of the methodology of *Vicāra.* According to Maslow's Hierarchical Theory of Motivation, higher needs cannot be understood by persons whose lower needs are not fulfilled. Maslow hypothesizes the needs in the increasing order as: Physiological (hunger, thirst, etc.), Safety (security), Love (belonging and sharing), Self-esteem (status, or power), and Self Actualization (personal achievement based on higher value system). Vasiṣṭha who had achieved the Self Actualization, understood this well and answered the queries of Rāma patiently and in detail.

The story of *Kirāta* or the hunter illustrates that the Truth is available, whatever be the motivation to seek it. The *Bhagavadgītā* says this in one verse:

> 'Whatsoever be the form any devotee worships in
> faith and desire;
> The same faith is strengthened and made unflinching
> by Me'.[192]

Here the word worship is not to be taken as a ritual, but as the act of desiring and hence continual thinking. Man turns his attention towards the higher needs either when they are fulfilled and there is satiation, or when the resulting anxiety, tension and pain become unbearable. As if to bring home this point this *Sarga* deals with the *Ādhis* and the *Vyādhis.*

---

192 यो यो यां यां तनुं भक्तः श्रद्धयार्चितुमिच्छति ।
तस्य तस्याचलां श्रद्धां तामेव विदधाम्यहम् ॥ 7.21 ॥

The heart of this portion of the story however, is the process of *Ātmavicāra* as adopted by Cūḍālā.

No matter how thick the fog, it has to make way for the light of the sun, and to surrender to the solar warmth. In the like manner, the fog of grosser manifestations and activity have to bow down to their subtler causes till every activity comes to a peaceful rest under the benign poise of *Ātman,* or the Truth or Reality, because all of them are IT's manifestations and have their existence only in and through IT.

10

The Story of Śikhidhvaja-I

Trapped in the hollow of the mountain were the clouds courting with its shoulders. The hollow was like a great cup shaped by Mother Nature over eons of patient work with the help of wind and rain. The wall of the cup was the mountain itself, thick with vegetation of variety of plants including the Bamboo. Myriad of birds made these trees their homes. While the animals—so called *wild* by man! roamed about freely and without fear, following the principle of *live and let live* strictly. A youth sat on the rock apparently catching his breath, after the strenuous climb. The truth however was that he was trying to compose himself. There was a strange anxiety, eating his very vitals. He was on his way to *the cave* in which Bodhidharma, the twenty eighth patriarch after Kaśyapa, the direct disciple of the Buddha, lived for the past nine years. Hui-k'o, for that was the name of the youth, had seen him ten years back when he was only twelve years old.

Emperor Wu Li of the Liang area had made preparations for the grand reception of this venerable man. The whole population—well almost, was there to receive Bodhidharma. And when he finally arrived, there had been peals of laughter from the people : the man had appeared with a shoe on his head, a shoe which is fit only for the feet! The emperor had asked him the reason for his humorous behaviour.[193] Strange

193 This act is symbolic of conveying that the intellect is subservient to

as it may seem, but the saint had refused to answer, instead, he had remarked that he was sad that his long journey from India had gone waste, for it appeared no one was eligible for what he had come to give. Bodhidharma had walked away to this mountain and chosen a cave to sit in seclusion.

Then the stories had started : that he sat with his face to the wall of the cave; that he had refused to talk to anyone who went to seek his audience; and when even the emperor had gone there to seek his pardon and instruction, Bodhidharma had said that his communication with the wall was better, at least it was incapable of misinterpretation; .... Hui-k'o however, had been unable to forget the fire in those eyes, and the expression of determination characterised by the firmness of the chin. He *knew*—and he did not have any logical explanation for his feeling, that Bodhidharma had something invaluable to offer to *mankind,* and he wanted to try to seek it from the patriarch. Almost all who had come here earlier, had failed even to see the face of the saint. He had left his home to try his luck... Nay! not only try he thought, but *must* succeed ... else...

He got up, and if someone who had been there during the reception ten years back—someone who had seen the fire in the eyes, as well as the determination on the chin of Bodhidharma, could not help but see the same spirit in this youth. But this mountain slope and forest covering it, responded only with a strange, receptive and potent silence.

Nothing else but *the cave* remained for Hui-k'o. It was as if everything just vanished out of his mind and consciousness. He did not know how, but he found himself standing, looking at the straight back of the patriarch. Rays of the morning sun entered the cave and fell on that back casting shadow on the wall, covering it completely, appearing to represent the

---

the experience in spirituality, to show that both intellect and shoe are on par!

gigantic *being* of Bodhidharma. Taking a deep breath Hui-k'o declared:

'I have come!'

There was no response, only a deepening silence. With the machete he had brought to clear the path in the jungle, he cut off his hand and tossed it for the patriarch to see. He thundered:

'If you do not turn, you will be seeing my head next!'

Hui-k'o, thus became the torch bearer of *Chan* tradition, which came to be known as the *Zen* on reaching the shores of Japan. Unless one has such preparedness for the Truth, so much so, that even the life becomes insignificant as compared to Truth, one cannot possibly achieve It. An event in the life of Shri Ramakrishna is worth remembering.

Shri Ramakrishna had spent sufficiently long time in devotion of Mother Bhavatāriṇī at Dakshineswar. The *Sādhanā* had almost come to a boiling point. But he failed to have the vision of the Mother. Every evening he would tell himself, that one more day has been wasted in vain, without the vision of the Mother. When the pain became excruciating, he started feeling the uselessness of it all, even his life. One day as he entered the *sanctum sanctorum* with such feeling, his eyes fell on the ceremonial *Kṛpāṇaṃ,* a weapon with a curved blade. He rushed and took it off the hook to cut off his own neck. It is said, immediately Shri Ramakrishna had the experience, and he was lost in it for many days. What really happens with such preparedness is explained through this story of Śhikhidhvaja.

Spirituality in particular and religion in general, has always stressed the need for renunciation. The idea is that unless one gives up the lower, one cannot achieve the higher. And it is very rational. The mind indulges more strongly and is more active and restless at the lower or grosser level than in the higher or subtler. To avoid such indulgence and involvement, renunciation is considered to be *mandatory*. Hence, every religion directly or indirectly advocates renunciation and self-control. For most of us, these two steps are like the two wings needed for flight spiritual. But when one has trodden the path for quite a while, these very steps can become hurdles. This too has been dealt very beautifully in this story.

Another most important aspect is *Cittaśuddhi* or the purity of mind. As it is commonly understood, *Cittaśuddhi* is taken to be a state of mind devoid of impure or violent thoughts and having such thoughts characterised by nobler feelings like compassion, love and devotion either towards a chosen deity or concepts like nation and society or humanity. The impure mind is responsible for all the evils existing in the society. Education tries to inculcate the social responsibilities of the citizens. How far it is effective is an entirely different question! *Vedānta* has an entirely different perspective of *Cittaśuddhi*. This again, has been illustrated through this story.

Returning to the story sage Vasiṣṭha continued: King Śikhidhvaja lost in illusion, gave way to grief due to the enormous wealth he had acquired. He felt as though he was enveloped by a great forest fire. He gave away various rare gifts in charity, undertook pilgrimage to holy places and observed religious practices. And yet, he was not free from the load of grief on his mind. Approaching his dear wife Cūḍālā, he poured out his heart. He said that after experiencing everything he had no love left for his sovereignty and wealth and he desired to proceed to the forest; that in the forest there is neither pleasure nor pain, danger nor wealth, to haunt those living there, leading a noble life; he no longer wished to associate himself with the regality; and that Cūḍālā should not oppose him if he had come to a point of changing his residence from the palace to the forest.

This again is a natural development. When one has indulged too much with the worldly activity characterised by sense gratification, hunger for name, fame or power, one gets satiated to the point of misery, and swings towards the opposite direction of sense restraint or withdrawal. If one is positively involved with the world earlier, one starts getting *negatively involved* through dislike or even hatred. That is how we observe some persons observing celibacy, nurturing hatred towards the opposite sex. Indulgence and involvement cannot possibly bring about any lasting peace. And man cannot rest until he gets peace.

Cūḍālā replied that like the flowers blossoming in spring and fruits in autumn, the *Karma* begins to fructify in due course. If the body becomes old and starts dropping, then the desires also fall at which time forest is a fit place. The king, she said had still not come to that state. She argued that he should not go because it appeared as if he was not yet ready. But the king had already decided and asked the queen not to stop him. And as she was still young, she should not follow him. Instead she should look after the kingdom with the help of able ministers, as a good queen should.

Having retired that evening, he performed his *Saṅdhyāvandanam*[194] and slept quietly by the side of Cūḍālā. When she had gone into the lap of mother slumber, Śikhidhvaja stole out into the dead of the night, unperceived by her. Instructing his attendants that he was going on a round of the city alone, and to be where they were, he departed from the town. Bidding farewell to his enslaving possessions he entered the forest, crossing many rivers and hills in the course of twelve days. At last he reached the inaccessible forest on the slopes of Mandāra hills, and made his abode in a *Parṇaśālā* or a hut of leaves, beside a tank full of scenic beauty. There he performed rigorous *Tapas,* consisting of rituals and *Japa.*

---

194 Literally salutation in the *Sandhyā,* the twilight period between day and night, consisting of the meditation on sacred *Gāyatrī Mantra.*

Cūḍālā, sleeping in the palace, awoke and not finding her husband inferred that he must have retreated to the forest abandoning his kingdom as he had declared. She resolved to find out the whereabouts of her husband. She sprang forth in her subtle body, went up into the sky, journeying through the air. Seeing her husband travelling in the forest with a bright sword in his hand, she meditated as to what course she should pursue, and came to a conclusion that she should see him only after his *desires and hatred* have ceased. Accordingly she returned to the palace. She informed her subjects that the king had gone to a certain place for some private work, and wielded the sceptre alone for eighteen years, with true justice. She ascertained that no one felt the king's absence through her noble deeds.

Śikhidhvaja was leading a hard life devoid of any comfort, subjecting himself to long fasts.

Cūḍālā assuming the subtle body visited him and seeing his emaciated body was filled with compassion. She knew that she could confer on him *Ātmajñāna* at that very moment, but knowing that her husband could never accept it from his young wife should she appear in the present form, she decided to assume another form suitable to accomplish the end. She knew that after prolonged *Tapas* Śikhidhvaja was in a receptive state.

Changing her form through *Dhyāna,* she descended from *Ākāśa* before her husband in the form of a young *Brahmin.* The king rose immediately to pay respects the *Brahmin* with a lustrous form. Showing a seat beside him he saluted. Reciprocating the salutation and taking his seat, the guest commented on the genuine humility of king for abandoning the kingship and all the regality associated with it. This comment from the guest surprised the king who wanted to know his name and the purpose of his visit there.

Cūḍālā in the form of the young *Brahmin* told the story of his birth: Nārada was sitting on the bank of Gaṅgā absorbed in meditation and was in the stage of transition from *Samādhi* and normal state. He heard the sound of gaiety and laughter. Directing his gaze in the direction beheld the heavenly nymphs Rambhā and Tilottamā playing in water. Seeing them thus alone and not ashamed of their nakedness, his mind got agitated and experienced sensual desire showing itself in the mind. Controlling himself totally, he released the seed into an embryo of a crystal pot. The embryo grew and through the grace of Nārada, the son was born, who was taken to Brahmā the Creator. Beholding his own grandson, Brahmā helped him attain the goal of *Brahmajñana,* immediately calling the youth Kuṁbha-muni, as he was born in a *Kuṁbha* or pot. Continuing Kuṁbha-muni said that noble Saraswatī is his mother, and Gāyatrī the aunt, he is always accompanied by the four friends, the *Vedas.*

A doubt creeps into the mind of the reader as to how enlightened Cūḍālā could create a mythical story of her birth. But this is how all egos are born *into the limitations,* just as the limitless space is contained in the pot. Nārada not only refers to the divine sage who is associated with the stories of gossip, devotion and moral and ethical code simultaneously, but it is human hood in general. The expansive Reality, adopts the limitedness through identification of desire. Saraswatī and Gāyatrī represent speech and mind respectively, and the four *Vedas,* wisdom in general both secular and spiritual that are always available to an enlightened person.

Kuṁbha-muni wanted the king to narrate his own background and his present state. Śikhidhvaja told about his own life and renunciation and his subsequent penance. However, he confessed that he was far from enlightenment. On the contrary, he said he had become more miserable converting the elixir of life into poison. To which Kuṁbha-muni said that there cannot be any true bliss unless *Jñāna* is instilled into a disciple by the preceptor. All the *acts* of *Tapas* are only diversions to waste time. For those without true *Jñāna,* action alone is a *security* against the restlessness of the mind. The virtuous action helps only to remove impure *Vāsanās*. If the *Vāsanās* are destroyed, then birth, old age and death will have no effect. The *Vāsanās* arise due to lack of awareness, can be overcome through *Brahmabhāva*, or the conviction that everything is *Brahman*, and *Prajñā* or awareness. One must question 'Who am I?; Whence came the universe and into what it is absorbed?' Guru alone will be able to guide the receptive disciple into *Vicāra*.

Śikhidhvaja was moved by these words of Kuṁbha-muni and said that he was in that solitary forest, having left the company of men of wisdom in his kingdom. He had realised his mistake. But since the Muni was present in the forest with him, could he not be accepted as his disciple? Kuṁbha-muni replied that he can enlighten the king only if he concentrates his mind, which was restless at the moment. The king assured him that he was at that moment in a receptive mind and had implicit faith in the words of the *Guru*. The Muni demanded that he should not be interrupted and started narrating a story.

Once upon a time, there lived a man, well versed in all fields of knowledge and possessing great wealth. But he was without *Ātmajñāna* or Self-realisation. He undertook the search for *Cintāmaṇi*, the precious gem, with much effort and *Tapas*. *Cintāmaṇi* is a gem which is supposed to yield anything that is thought of. When the gem appeared before him, he was doubtful as to whether it was the real gem. For how else could such a lowly person as he, could succeed? In such doubt, he let go of a great opportunity, and the gem vanished from his view. He started the search again by wandering in all directions. Some *Siddhas* hidden from his view dropped an earthenware bracelet, which was eagerly picked up by the victim. Believing to be the real gem, he gave up all his wealth and retired to the forest with an intention of avoiding such persons with depraved tendencies! Thus he subjected himself to all kind of hardships degrading himself to the lowest level.

Continuing the Muni narrated another story: In the heart of a great forest, there lived an elephant, one of the largest and strongest kind. Its tusks were exceedingly strong, long and sharp, taking note of which some *Māhuts* in the forest trapped it and bound it with strong chains.

Becoming infuriated with the painful fetters, it shook itself free with the aid of its powerful tusks. The *Māhut* sitting above, felt giddy and fell to the ground. The tusker, finding the *Māhut* fallen on the ground, passed by without hurting him. But the *Māhut* picking himself up and in an angry mood went again in quest of the elephant. Digging a trench in the area frequented by the elephant, he covered it with dry leaves and grass. The elephant fell into the trench and was instantly bound by the *Māhut.* Thus the poor creature was again subjected to torture. Likewise, those who make no inquiry into good and evil come to grief.

When Śikhidhvaja wanted to know the hidden meaning behind the story Kuṁbha-muni said in all compassion, that Śikhidhvaja was like the rich man who though acquainted with all *Śāstras,* was without the beneficent *Tattvajñāna,* and hence had gone in search of *Cintāmaṇi.* For all though well versed in book learning, Śikhidhvaja had not yet developed equilibrium of mind. In order to attain true renunciation which is the true *Cintāmaṇi,* he had forsaken his regality, wife and other relatives and had come to the forest. While the true renunciation had been developing in him, little by little, even while in the world. And he was misled by the wrong conception of renunciation. The present renunciation was not a true one and he had lost track of it, and he was being misled by the false idea of *Tapas* which had afflicted his body and mind. Kuṁbha-muni added that the wise say that those who reject the happiness available to them in their daily lives, and allow the mind to search for imaginary and strange things are only self-destructive.

The adjective 'elephant' was applied to Śikhidhvaja himself. The two long tusks are *Varāgya* and *Viveka. Ajñāna* or ignorance is the *Māhut* who sits upon the elephant to goad it. It afflicted him in many ways. The iron chains are the bonds of desires which are stronger and longer lasting than iron. The breaking of chains and the fall of *Māhut* represents the act of overcoming the ignorance through *Viveka* and *Vairāgya.* The ignorance continues to hover around, as the delusion of wealth is replaced by asceticism, unless one continues to nurture true renunciation through *Viveka* and *Vairāgya.* Thinking that he had achieved true renunciation by giving up his regality, and making the forest his home, he had become complacent. The Muni asked as to why he had ignored the words of delicate Cūḍālā, and thus rejected true renunciation.

And now begins one of the most dramatic and eye-opening dialogues which gives a great hint in spirituality: True renunciation.

Śikhidhvaja interposed: He had given up his kingdom, his palace, his wealth, and even his dear wife. Did not all these actions constitute perfect renunciation? Kuṁbha-muni replied that though he had given up these things it did not constitute the true renunciation. He still had attraction for objects. Unless one gave up attraction completely, bliss cannot arise. The king in exile said that if giving up worldly things did not comprise of true renunciation, and that still he had attraction for objects, what was left was the forest alone full of hills and trees and so, he was giving up the *liking* for the forest in which he dwelt.

Kuṁbha-muni said again: Even abandoning of the hilly and luxuriant forest was not true renunciation. That still he had some painful desires. Only when the king had succeeded in eliminating them, would he have true renunciation. To which recluse Śikhidhvaja said that he was laying aside his cloth, *Rudrākṣamālā,* deer-skin, earthen vessels, and the water gourd thus confining them to the flames. Rejoicing in his new understanding of renunciation and denuded of all possessions, including the cloth to cover his nakedness, he turned to Kuṁbha-muni in all gratefulness. For he did derive a kind of joy after the action.

Kuṁbha-muni smiled in all compassion, and said that in spite of all the actions Śikhidhvaja had not renounced *anything* and still delusion afflicted him. The seeker Śikhidhvaja reflected that the only thing he could call his own was the body composed of the five elements and the organs. If he gave that up perhaps he would succeed in tasting true renunciation. So thinking, the great renouncer Śikhidhvaja ascended to a tall summit and was about to cast himself down, when Kuṁbha-muni, catching hold of his wrist, stopped him from committing the foolish action. He asked whether the body had been any hindrance in his progress; and how could death possibly be of any help. He added that even if he were to behave like an angry bull on a tender calf and jumped off the cliff, he would not succeed in true renunciation. Compassionately he said that if one gave up that which is the cause of all agitation in the body, and which is the seed of all births and actions, true renunciation would result.

The words had a healing touch on the being of Śikhidhvaja who appealed to the Muni to reveal the means by which one can avoid the cause of agitation. The Muni replied: The wise say that *Cittaṃ,* through its *Saṁkalpa* manifests under the different manifestations of *Prāṇa* and *Jīva* is the real cause of gross as well as the subtle universe and hence the attachment to delusive objects. Therefore, true renunciation lies in giving up this *Cittaṃ*. All other renunciations cause suffering, and with true renunciation the self identifies with *Brahman* bringing about peace and perfect quiescence.

The state of mind of Śikhidhvaja before and after the dramatic event is worth noting. Before, he had taken his renunciation for granted, he had even taken his *eligibility for receiving the Truth* for granted! The enlightened sage's comment and his subsequent reactions to it shattered his notions and his slate was clean again; the field was tilled and devoid of any unwanted weeds. The *Guru* could plant the seed of truth in it now!

When Śikhidhvaja asked the Muni to continue the discourse by telling him the cause of *Cittaṃ,* its true nature and the means of overcoming it the compassionate Kuṁbha-muni replied: True nature of mind is the *Vāsanās,* so much so, both are synonymous. But the idea of 'I' is the source and seed of the tree of mind. The sprout which germinates first from the seed of *Ahaṁkāra,* originates without form and ascertainable only by internal experience. When this sprout becomes determinant it is termed as *Buddhiḥ*. From this the ramifying branches called *Saṁkalpa* take their origin. As a result of such differentiation, *Cittaṃ, Manas* and other functions emanate from *Ahaṁkāra.* These functions in turn give birth to innumerable branches called *Vāsanās.* One can either cut the *Vāsanās* one by one, or destroy the seed itself. The seed can be destroyed by the fire of *Ātmajñāna* which inquires into the true nature of 'I'.

Śikhidhvaja was immediately driven towards *Vicāra.* He inquired into the origin of 'I'. As the world is non-intelligent, it cannot be 'I', nor is the body, nor the organs, nor the contemplating *Manas,* nor the *Buddhiḥ,* nor the injurious *Ahaṁkāra.* Supervising the *Vicāra,* Kuṁbha-muni interposed by asking that if 'I' was not all these, then what else is it? To which Śikhidhvaja replied that he was of the nature of that stainless, absolute consciousness which having evolved everything, preserves, as well as destroys it. He was unable to find the cause of this 'I' and could not thrust it aside, at the same time he must do so.

Kuṁbha-muni of infinite patience and compassion, urged him to move further in to seek the cause of *Ahaṁkāra,* which is ever present. He added that since *Ahaṁkāra* is also an effect, it has to have a cause. The disciple entering further within said that the cause of *Ahaṁkāra* is *Vedanaṃ* or knowledge which arises when there are visible objects, which are the effects of *Cetyōnmukhatā* or the *tendency* for thought, that brings about misery, how can one bring about the quiescence of *Cittaṃ* to overcome misery?

In the gloss on the two *Ślokas, Vāsiṣṭha Caṅdrikā* offers the cause of misery as:

> 'I have understood that, awareness of the limitation called *Ahaṁkāra* is due to *Cetyōnmukhatā*. ... *Cetyōnmukhatā* is the diversion of *Caitanya* or consciousness, towards *Dṛśya* or the seen, due to which *Ahaṁkāra* remains in misery....'[195]

The *Guru* commented that the visible things do not really exist, and asked him to seek the basis of *Bodha*. In reply the disciple said that with the perception of forms like body, etc. arises *Vastusattā*, the awareness of impermanent things, like that of the touch of breeze. But this awareness is due to the *Ahaṁkāra*, how can it be impermanent?

This very doubt shows that even after so much effort, Śikhidhvaja could retrieve his consciousness up to *Ahaṁkāra*, beyond which he was finding it very difficult. *Ahaṁkāra* is like a scale forming on consciousness due to the identification with action. More the identification, more thick will be the scale or covering. Ācārya Śaṅkara in his *Vivekacūḍāmaṇi*, attributes two functional qualities to *Ahaṁkāra*: *Āvaraṇa* or the covering of Truth and *Vikṣiptatā* or scattering of consciousness. Śikhidhvaja had managed to overcome the *Vikṣiptatā*, through *Tapas* and renunciation. But by the very

---

195 अहमिति दोषस्य अहंकारस्य वेदनं चितश्चेत्योन्मुखत्वमेव कारणं वेद्मि ।
चितश्चैतन्यस्य चेत्यान्मुखत्वं दृश्यानुसंधानं तेन हेतुना अयमहंकारो दुःखाय स्थितः ॥
6.9.381, 382 ॥

acts of *Tapas* and *Vairāgya,* his *Ahaṁkāra* had become stronger. The *Ahaṁkāra* as such is always *directed without,* due to which, it is able to be aware of only *its* manifestations like *Buddhiḥ, Manas* and body and *never itself.*

Understanding the state of Śikhidhvaja, Kuṁbha-muni urged him to look further within by saying that all the faculties starting from *Ahaṁkāra* are only superimposed entities like the rope being misunderstood as a snake and are all effects. He must look within for the cause for these. To which the king asked an apparently unconnected question: Is not Brahmā who is the first ancestor, the cause of the world? The preceptor replied the question patiently: In the beginning, only *Brahman* which is *Alone,* Tranquil and Supreme exists. IT is *without the second* due to which, IT just IS, without any cause. Being without the second, how can there be the actor and experiencer? The universe is self-created. The supreme or the *first Saṁkalpa* of that absolute Consciousness is Brahmā.

Mythologically, Brahmā is supposed to have brought about this creation, and has his own time period. But *Vedānta* interprets it differently. Brahmā the Creator, is attributed with four heads, each head represents a faculty: *Ahaṁkāra, Buddhiḥ, Cittaṃ,* and *Manas.* As far as an individual is concerned, there can be no creation *for her or him,* unless these faculties function. He is supposedly manifested from a lotus from the navel of Viṣṇu, the all pervasive Principle. Lotus, as such symbolises consciousness. So the cause of Brahmā is consciousness, which is all pervasive.

Still unable to understand, Śikhidhvaja sought further clarification. *Cit* or Consciousness alone is the cause, from which all effects get manifested in which they survive, and into which the merge. They have their existence only due and in the consciousness and no *separate* existence. To transcend the manifestations one has to be in the mood of '"I" am not the doer, "I" am not the experiencer, Everything is Peaceful and Unmoving.' With such a mood, *Ajñāna, which is the hold of Ahaṁkāra over its manifestations, gets loosened.* That which is named as Brahman is nothing but the quiescent, unmanifest or passive state of this universe.

With these potent suggestions of Kuṁbha-muni, Śikhidhvaja gratefully acknowledged that all his doubts were dissolved, and he had experienced the clarity of vision; he said that he had succeeded in *worshipping his Real Self;* and that he was in a position to *stand aside Ahaṁkāra,* and its other manifestations. Kuṁbha-muni added the final advice to his beloved disciple by saying: All the manifestations including *Ahaṁkāra* and the external universe are the differentiated aspects of that ONE. The ONE is not experienced due to the ancient and stubborn habit of making distinctions, the habit can be overcome by just changing the vision. With these suggestions Śikhidhvaja achieved quiescence. Shri Ramakrishna has said:

> 'The darkness of centuries is disposed as soon as a light is brought into a room. The accumulated sins of countless lives vanish by a single glance of God'.[196]

Sage Vasiṣṭha said that Śikhidhvaja attained the radiating *Jñāna,* at that very instant, releasing himself from the fold of *Māyā.* Through his *Guru's* grace, he got absorbed in the Brāhmic state. Being freed from the activity of mind, senses and speech in an instant became totally free and expansive. After being absorbed in the state of *Nididhyāsana* for quite some time, he came back to normal state of consciousness. Observing that Śikhidhvaja had had a glimpse into That state, Cūḍālā in the form of Kuṁbha-muni inquired whether the king had enjoyed the state beyond all pain, the blissful, immaculate, and beneficent Brāhmic state.

Śikhidhvaja replied in grateful tears of joy, that through his *Guru's* grace, he was able to cognize that state of Brahman

---

196 *The Gospel of Shri Ramakrishna* by M. Shri Ramakrishna Math, Madras.

which remains after all else is over. At the same time he did not know why he was unable to attain the state which is ever available, before. Kuṁbha-muni replied that only when the mind is quiescent, and is indifferent towards all experiences, the mind becomes receptive to the words of *Guru*. Otherwise such words though potent drop down like the fruits of the tree. So saying, he blessed the disciple to be a great *Maunī* and alone that is, totally free of the dependency on involvement for being, in the world.

Śikhidhvaja sought a clarification: Are not the actions of *Jīvana-muktas* performed through the mind? How can things go on without the mind's being active? To which Kuṁbha-muni replied that the mind is only a receptacle of *Vāsanās* which generate rebirths. But if one knows the Real Self, as it is in the case of *Jīvana-muktas,* there is no fear of rebirth. The mind free of *Vāsanās* is called *Sattwa,* but the mind without *Jñāna* is termed *Cittam* which is full of desires. That is *Cittam* is guided by the desires while the *Sattwa* is guided by the *Jñāna.* Having mingled *Spanda* or activity, and *Aspanda* or non-activity, into One, the knowers of the Self merge into the Eternal. *Vāsiṣṭha Caṅdrikā* giving clarification these two words says:

> '*Spanda* is the spreading mental activity directed outside, and *Aspaṅda* is *Samādhi* devoid of any activity. Both these are to be transcended by holding on to the One, which is *aware of both Spanda and Aspanda*, through *Anusaṁdhānam* by directing the attention towards the permanent, beyond the spreading and the non-spreading'.[197]

To the doubt how to transcend activity and non-activity, the sage continued: Like the waves of water in an ocean, all

---

197 स्पन्दः चित्तस्य बहिः प्रसारः अस्पन्दः समाधिः तावेकतां नीत्वा सर्वदा स्वरूपानुसंधानेन विक्षेपाविक्षेपावभेदं नीत्वा शाश्वतं नित्यतैक्यं ब्रह्माद्वैततागत्य यथाकामं तिष्ठ ।। 6.9.426 ।।

the universes are nothing but the Non-dual *Cinmātra* or Absolute Consciousness. On this *Cinmātra* when there is slight activity of *Dhīḥ* or pure mind, the *Spandana* or fluctuation is caused, like the water moving due to waves. The ignorant without *Niṣṭhā* or capacity to look within, regard the Supreme Principle, going by several names of Śiva, the auspicious, *Cinmātra, Satyaṃ* or Truth and Brahman, as the universe characterised by multiplicity. The creation is nothing but a *Spandana* on the Absolute Consciousness which dissolves with *Samyagdṛṣṭi*—Vision characterised by non-involvement; but when there is involvement, the Reality gets superimposed by the multiple universe, as the conception of snake getting superimposed on a piece of rope in the twilight. When one directs one's effort on the import of *Śāstras* with a steady mind seeking the company of the experienced wise and practises diligently, *Jñāna* dawns. Concluding the discourse, Kuṁbha-muni said that he had told Śikhidhvaja whatever is necessary for attaining the Ultimate State. Saying that now he had to proceed to *Swargaloka* for meeting his father and preceptor Nārada, he disappeared from the scene.

Śikhidhvaja marveled at the way in which he had missed the State while IT had always been available to him. Śikhidhvaja who had approached the State, was without any fluctuation entered into IT. While Kuṁbha-muni resumed the gentle form of Cūḍālā and reached her chamber in the palace and resumed the noble cause of ruling the subjects with love and care.

Action has binding effect on the mind. When one is too action oriented, as it was in the case of Śikhidhvaja, there is identification with the action, and naturally, the *Ahaṁkāra* also gets stronger. Such persons find it extremely difficult to achieve *Aṅtarmukhatā*. Śikhidhvaja was identified with his kingship and all the responsibilities, duties as well as the pleasures with it, turned his face away from them, to identify himself with *Tapasvin* or the seeker. He had not been able to get rid of his habit of identification. Because of the habit he constantly *remembered* what all things he had given up! Though he had given them up physically, mentally they were very near to him, if not closer than they were when he was involved with them! That was why, it was necessary to bring him to the level of preparedness for giving up his very life. Actually, what happens at such time is that one feels the total uselessness of all egotic associations. The uselessness of *all* action performed by and through *Ahaṁkāra.* So unless the *Ahaṁkāra* is dissolved, nothing can happen. And paradoxically, it is the *Ahaṁkāra* alone which *wants to achieve something,* be it an object or position of enjoyment, or Enlightenment. *Sannyāsopaniṣad* gives a great hint through the following *Mantra*:

> 'Give up *Dharma* or righteousness as well as *Adharma* or unrighteousness,
> Give up both *Satyaṃ* or truth and *ṛtaṃ* or order;
> Having given up *Satyaṃ* and *ṛtaṃ, give up that with which you give up*'.[198]

We do not know for sure, whether Hui-k'o really cut off his hand and threw it in front of Bodhidharma. But the Zen anecdotes are symbolic rather than Historical facts. Hand symbolises action. When Hui-k'o cut his hand and threw it, it only means that he had stopped being a *Kartā* or doer by dis-identifying with all action, and he was ready to give up his head which symbolises *Ahaṁkāra.* The beauty is, when one has stopped being a *Kartā* one has already cut the head, what remains is, to offer it at the altar of enlightenment. But strange as it may seem, that then there is no altar, but only enlightenment!

---

198 त्यज धर्ममधर्मं च उभे सत्यानृते त्यज ।
उभे सत्यानृते त्यक्त्वा येन त्यजसि तत्त्यज ।। संन्यासोपनिषद् 2.12 ।।

11

The Story of Śikhidhvaja-II

Like a youthful maiden, Dawn shines brightly forth,
Stirring to motion every living creature.
Divine Fire was kindled for the use of men;
Dawn created light, driving away the dark.

Sending out her beams, she rose up facing all,
In brilliant robes, resplendent, radiating—
Golden-coloured and glorious to behold,
Mother of plenty, mistress of the days she shone.

Blessed, bearing the sun, the eye of the Gods,
Leading her white horse, magnificent to see,
Dawn reveals herself, arrayed in beams of light,
And with boundless glory she transforms the world.

O fair one, banish the enemy with light!
And prepare for us broad pastures free from fear!
Ward off hatred, bring us your priceless treasure!
O bountiful, shower your blessings on the singer!

Illumine us with your glorious splendour,
O divine Dawn! Enrich and lengthen our lives,
O Goddess full of grace! Grant us fulfillment
And cows, horses, and chariots in abundance!

O Daughter of Heaven, Dawn of noble birth,
Whom the men of glory celebrate in hymns,

Establish in us wealth sublime and mighty!
O Gods, protect us always with your blessings'![199]

So sings the Vedic bard Sage Vasiṣṭha, in the Seventh *Maṇḍala* of the *Ṛg-Veda.* The hymns to *Uṣā* or Dawn in the *Ṛg-Veda* are among those which best exhibit the ancient poets' fine and deep feeling for nature. The language is simple yet rich, and the imagery, brilliant. But the Divine Daughter of Heaven is not just the poetic personification of the rising sun. She is the kindling of the Divine Fire, of the Divine Will, the dawning of the light of Truth in the hearts and minds of men, bringing in her wake abundance of cows, horses, and chariots—that is, of knowledge, strength, energy and health. Vasiṣṭha, one who is filled with the joy of living, one of the ten patriarchs, sings her blessings in this short hymn.

In Indian tradition, the sacred texts have been called as the *Darśanas,* which are also *Śāstras* or teachings, instructions and directions for living a harmonious life with oneself and the surroundings. One of the greatest contributions of our

---

199 उपो रुरुचे युवतिर्न योषा विश्वं जीवं प्रसुवंती चरायै ।
अभूदग्निः समिधे मानुषाणाम् अकर्ज्योतिर्बाधमाना तमांसि ॥ 7.77.1 ॥
विश्वं प्रतीची सप्रथाः उदस्थाद् रुशद्वासो बिभ्रती शुक्रमश्वैत् ।
हिरण्यवर्णा सुदृशीकसंदृग् गवां माता नेत्र्यह्नामरोचि ॥ 7.77.2 ॥
देवानां चक्षुः सुभगा वहन्ती श्वेतं नयंती सुदृशीकमश्वम् ।
उषा अदर्शि रश्मिभिर्व्यक्ता चित्रामघा विश्वमनु प्रभूता ॥ 7.77.3 ॥
अन्तिवामा दूरे अमित्रमुच्छ उर्वीं गव्यूतिमभयं कृधी नः ।
यवय द्वेषः आभर वसूनि चोदय राधो गृणते मघोनि ॥ 7.77.4 ॥
अस्मेश्रेष्ठेभिर्भानुभिर्वि भाहि उषो देवि प्रतिरंती न आयुः ।
इषं च नो दधती विश्ववारे गोमदश्वावद्रथवच्च राधः ॥ 7.77.5 ॥
यां त्वा दिवो दुहितर्वर्धयंति उषः सुजाते मतिभिर्वसिष्ठाः ।
सास्मासु धा रयिमृष्ठं बृहंतं यूयं पात स्वस्तिभिः सदा नः ॥ 7.77.6 ॥
॥ ऋग्वेदः ॥

Darśana-Śāstras, when compared to the Philosophical thought developed in the West, is its practicality and usefulness in our day-to-day life. Unfortunately, the Philosophy as such remained at the level of arm-chair and intellect or thought in the West. So much so, the philosophers were considered to be absent minded and impractical as depicted from their lives. An episode from the life of Immanuel Kant will illustrate this.

Kant was a man of fastidious habitual routine. It is said, that seeing Kant many people used to set their clocks! Once, he returned home well past his sleeping time. He entered his room, without taking any supper. Next morning, when his attendant entered the room he found the bed unoccupied. Instead of his master, he found the familiar walking stick on the bed. Looking around the servant found him standing in the very place where the stick was supposed to be kept. Instead of keeping the stick in the corner and entering the bed, Kant had *stood in the corner, and put the stick to bed!*

The reason for such behaviour is that Philosophy mostly, is nothing but the *human involvement at the level of thought.* Any involvement can only be the flow of consciousness *outside,* towards the objects of the world. Even if the object is as subtle as the mind it is still *external.* But the Indian *Śāstras* have been called as the *Darśanas,* or Visions. And most of them, if not all, stress on increasing the awareness which necessarily encompasses both internal as well as the external and *not on the improvement of thought* that is, changing the thoughts from bad to good. They do offer very reasonable thought, but aimed *solely at developing the awareness.* Shri Ramakrishna always used to say, that the person who has chosen spirituality is not a fool who can be taken for a ride, but one who is intelligent and *aware.* But yes, they do tend to lose interest in the world of sense objects. And the temptation of being absorbed in the divine beatitude is very strong.

The future Swami Vivekananda, under the guidance of

Shri Ramakrishna, experienced the state of *Nirvikalpa* quite a few times. When he approached the Master for showering the grace on him, so that he could remain absorbed in the *Nirvikalpa Samādhi* permanently, Shri Ramakrishna admonished him for being so selfish. He said that persons like Narendra had been born in this world not to seek their own salvation, but to guide humanity. Shri Ramakrishna told him that he would lock that experience and keep the key with himself, and give it to him only when his mission on earth was over!

Scriptures like the *Bhagavadgītā* or *Yoga Vāsiṣṭha* are examples of such practical spirituality. Both Arjuna in the *Gītā,* and Rāma in this scripture in the beginning, show a tendency to shirk action, and in the end both Arjuna and Rāma are enlightened and actively participate in the drama of life. This is because, there never was any division between the mundane and the spiritual as everything was considered to be part of one whole existence. Everything was based on the solid foundation of spirituality.

The last part of the story of Śikhidhvaja, the topic of the present chapter, is aimed at bringing home this point that one need not discontinue action after the enlightenment. On the contrary, such person becomes a better executor of action as she or he alone is capable of non-involvement, the boon for efficient action. *Bhagavadgītā* defines *Yoga* as the skill in action and how it comes about:

> 'Endowed with the Wisdom of evenness of mind, one casts off in this very life, the identification with the good as well as the evil deeds; therefore, devote yourself to *Yoga* as *Yoga* is the skill in action'.[200]

The evenness of mind and ceasing to be an *actor* can happen only when one has identified with the Whole. The quality of action by such a person is very much different

200 बुद्धियुक्तो जहातीह उभे सुकृतदुष्कृते ।
तस्माद्योगाय युज्यस्व योगः कर्मसु कौशलम् ।। 2.50 ।।

from the ordinary action. However, even after the enlightenment, one has to continue the action, as one cannot help but act till the body remains. Of course, what actions are performed by the enlightened Person is left to her or his aptitude and nature. A Kṛṣṇa or a Rāma may continue with his kingship, a Buddha may choose to be a soothing balm for the suffering humanity, a *Sufi* Master and a *Bhakta* like Kabirdasa may even stick to his trade of weaving!

Continuing the story, Vasiṣṭha said: Having ruled the kingdom for some years, Cūḍālā went to the forest to join her husband in the guise of Kuṁbha-muni. Śikhidhvaja was found in an immovable state of *Nirvikalpa Samādhi*. Kuṁbha-muni tried to see whether it was deep enough by leonine roar, and even physical disturbance. But he found that Śikhidhvaja had really merged into the state of *Brahman*. Then Cūḍālā in the form of Kuṁbha-muni wanted to find out whether there was any residue of *Sattwa* in the being of Śikhidhvaja or the merger was complete. In which case she too could leave the body and opt for a total merger. She thus concentrated her consciousness in the heart of Śikhidhvaja and found a residue of *Sattwa*.

At this stage, Rāma wanted to know how a residue of *Sattwa* could remain in those who had destroyed their mind, for *Nirvikalpa Samādhi* was possible only when the mind was totally destroyed. To which Muni Vasiṣṭha replied, that like flowers and fruits latent in a seed, a residue of *Sattwa* always rests in the heart. Even in the *Jīvanamuktas*, whose mind is destroyed, the body does not perish. At the same time, the *Jīvanamuktas* are unaffected by pleasures and pain in spite of moving among them.

At this juncture, a point of view given by Shri Ramakrishna, one of the greatest men of practical spirituality is worth noting:

> 'When the mind goes into *Samādhi*, the aspirant loses all consciousness of the outer world. He can no longer

retain his physical body. If milk is poured into his mouth, it runs out again. In that state the life breath lingers for twenty-one days and then passes out. Entering the "black-waters" of the ocean, the ship never comes back. But the *Īśvarakoṭis,* such as the Incarnations of God, can come down from this state of *Samādhi.* They can descend from the exalted state because they like to live in the company of devotees and enjoy the love of God. God retains in them the "ego of Knowledge" or the "ego of Devotion" so that, they may teach men'.[201]

In this scripture, the life retaining 'ego' has been referred to as the *Sattwa.* It is something like an anchor, used for keeping the boat in one place. These 'egos' are not the usual *Ahaṁkāras* governed by the *Vāsanās* or desires. But to an onlooker, they may *appear* to be so. For instance, to hold himself from merging into the repeated states of *Samādhi,* Shri Ramakrishna would ask for water or a piece of sweet. Ācārya Śaṅkara retained intellectual activity through debates and discussions, evident from his victories over the advocates of streams of thought other than the *Advaita.* Unless one has a glimpse of the beyond, no one can *judge* anybody else let alone the enlightened Persons. However, we do judge, which only goes to prove that we haven't yet had the glimpse!

Sage Vasiṣṭha said, that giving up the form of Kuṁbhamuni the consciousness of Cūḍālā entered the body of Śikhidhvaja and found a residue of *Sattwa* in it and created a *Spandana* in it. Then once again, coming out and resuming the benign form of the Muni, started chanting the *Sāma.* The *Sattwa* began to manifest itself in the log-like body of Śikhidhvaja. Slowly the manifestations like *Ahaṁkāra, Buddhiḥ, Manas,* and *Indriyas* became steady in regard to the external world of objects.

---

201 *The Gospel of Shri Ramakrishna* by M, Shri Ramakrishna Math, Madras, p. 457.

When he beheld his *Guru,* Śikhidhvaja paid due respects and expressed his gratitude. After mutual pleasantries, as well as exchange of the descriptions of 'That' state, remained happy in each other's company. During this period, Cūḍālā concentrated on the mind of Śikhidhvaja and found it to be free of all stains and also stable. She thought to herself that if persons like Śikhidhvaja left the luxury and the responsibilities of the palace life, to remain in the forest devoid of any temptation and test how can one say, that they have known the *Tattva?* Deciding to test her husband she said, that she must attend a festival in *Devaloka.* Then she left his company as well as Kuṁbha-Muni's body to reach the palace and perform her duties there.

As promised earlier, Cūḍālā appeared before her beloved husband, in the form of Kuṁbha-muni, but this time with the façade of misery on the countenance. Concerned about the state his enlightened preceptor was in, Śikhidhvaja asked about the reason for the misery. Kuṁbha-muni made the following narration. He said that persons with equal vision cannot be considered as *Jñānis* unless they perform actions of the *Indriyas* so long as they possess a body. Instead of exhausting all the existing *Karmas,* if one avoids them, fresh ones are generated. Pain and pleasure are inevitable to the physical body as it is governed by *Jñānendriyas* and *Karmendriyas. Ajñānis* as well as *Jñānis* are exposed to the sense objects of the world. But the difference between them is that the *Jñānis* perform the action that has come to their lot with unruffled mind till the bodies fall off. While the *Ajñānis* are ever agitated by and drowned in pleasure and pain. They continue to take on new bodies birth after birth, to work out the ever generated *Karmas.*

Then Kuṁbha-muni narrated what had passed as to cause him pain. After attending the court of Indra, he was returning and on way, he saw *Ṛṣi* Durvāsas. Paying him due respects, Kuṁbha inadvertently passed an impertinent remark on the clothes worn by the *Ṛṣi* which resembled an ill-famed woman in search of her paramour. The great *Ṛṣi,* famous for his short temper, cursed that Kuṁbha would turn into a woman every night. And that evening, Kuṁbha confided that he could not even beg the pardon of the *Ṛṣi,* as Durvāsas disappeared immediately. This incidence had left him sad and ashamed. Śikhidhvaja, who had already mastered his mind and emotions, consoled Kuṁbha-muni that he was certain that the womanhood or manhood could not possibly touch his inner being.

As the sun went down, Kuṁbha-muni started developing the signs of womanhood and was soon transformed. Kuṁbha-muni went by the name of Madanikā at nights. In that state, both of them spent days and nights together. When Cūḍālā looked into the being of Śikhidhvaja, she found therein no disturbance whatsoever, instead there was only stabilization and ripening of *Jñāna.* One noon Cūḍālā in the guise of Kuṁbha-muni told the king that Madanikā should taste the pleasures incidental to the womanhood, and that was why she should seek a lord as her husband. And only Śikhidhvaja could be the fit husband for her. Like a child, the enlightened king agreed to the proposal. They performed the marriage as enjoined in the *Vedas,* and led a happy married life. Even at this stage Cūḍālā found the king in a quiescent state, neither afflicted with indulgence nor with involvement. Every now and then Cūḍālā would visit the kingdom to administer justice.

Convinced that Śikhidhvaja had no attraction for the worldly pleasures, Cūḍālā wanted to see, whether he had any longing for the pleasures of *Swarga.* With this in mind she created, through the power of *Māyā,* the likeness of heaven, with Indra heading the *Devas,* celestial maidens and all other objects associated with it. When Indra approached him, Śikhidhvaja paid respects due to him, and wanted to know the cause of his visit. Indra said that pleased with his life of *Tapas,* he had come to offer all the heavenly pleasures for a long period. To which Śikhidhvaja replied that he had known all pleasures including those of *Swarga,* and for him space had ceased to have any effect, and so it did not matter whether he was in *Swarga* or on earth. Since he did not have any longing or desire, it would be good if the king of Gods returned to his abode.

The response of her husband left no doubt in Cūḍālā, that the lower mind had been completely annihilated. So she thought of conducting an *acid test* on him! One day when pure Śikhidhvaja was performing his *Japa* on the bank of the Gaṅgā at twilight, Madanikā entered a thick bower nearby and created a lover, seated on a pleasant seat of flowers, making a show of embracing him. After having performed his daily rites, and sought in vain for his wife Madanikā in all places, Śikhidhvaja saw on his return his wife and a male figure in mutual embrace. This sight did not disturb him in the least, but observed only the joy the two were deriving from each other, and he entered the state of eternal bliss! Withdrawing from the cottage so as to avoid any disturbance to the lovers, Śikhidhvaja went and sat near a rock. Nearly forty-eight minutes later he was found unruffled and without any anger whatsoever. Madanikā, just to see his response appeared before the *Rājayogi,* with signs of her love tryst such as dishevelled hair, etc., in an attitude of shame. Śikhidhvaja only asked her not to feel bad about it since love is so difficult to come by. He told her that, she could go back to her lover for further gratification if she wished.

When Madanikā begged his pardon and said that it is only the great and unblemished, who could overlook the faults of the ignorant. Thereupon Śikhidhvaja said that a tree may grow in *Ākāśa,* but the anger could never rise in him. But the code of *Sādhutva* did not permit him to retain her as his wife. When Cūḍālā looked into the consciousness of her beloved and enlightened husband, she found every word uttered by him to be true.

A little discussion at this point will clarify certain doubts. Why is it necessary to conduct such extreme test? Is it right to cause such a great disturbance of an enlightened person? Lust and anger are the two basic emotions which are very difficult, if not impossible, to eliminate. And as far as the lust is concerned, man is an exception. The only creature to indulge in it at *any time,* is man, while rest of the animals and creatures have seasons. Another thing is he is the only creature who indulges in it for sensual pleasure and not just for propagation of his species. Moreover, the mind being predominant in him, he can indulge in it even at the cerebral level, and that makes him more complicated! Over indulgence brings in boredom, and naturally he seeks to experiment with newer ways of sense gratification. And human History—at least a part of it, is the story of his exploits in search for sensual pleasure, and his success or failure to acquire it!

So the test conducted by Cūḍālā is two fold : seeing someone in the act of sexual indulgence can and does provoke lust; secondly, if one of the persons who are seen, happens to be a near and dear one, especially the wife, it provokes anger! Both these did not have any effect on Śikhidhvaja. On the contrary, he went into the state of *Samādhi* looking at the two lovers enjoying the company of each other! This is certainly the toughest test that can ever be conducted on a person, even though he is enlightened! This just points out the ideal of *Cittaśuddhi,* the purity of mind. Nothing can ever disturb it. But is it humanly possible to come out of this test unscathed? Shri Ramakrishna is one such person who has achieved the impossible.

Shri Ramakrishna is perhaps the only person who has dared to travel not one, but many paths and to come to a definite conclusion that all the paths lead to the same Goal. One of the most dangerous paths he tried and succeeded was the *Tantra,* especially the *Vāma-tantra,* the left or wrong hand technique. In one of the fifty-nine *Vidyās,* one is to sit on the lap of a youthful lady and meditate. It is said that when Shri Ramakrishna just touched her, he went into a state of *Samādhi!* For him, anything and everything could be a reason enough for *Samādhi.* A boy standing by the side of a tree in *tri-bhaṅga,* body bent in three places would remind him of Kṛṣṇa; a lion, of Mother Durga; why, even a prostitute would appear to him as the personification of Motherhood. And in all these he would enter into *Samādhi.* When Holy Mother Śaradā, his wife came to Dakshineswar, he kept her in the same room, and they slept on the same bed. When she slept, he would wake up and intentionally try to tempt his own mind. But invariably, it would end with an experience of *Samādhi.*

Having tested her husband Śikhidhvaja, Cūḍālā decided to appear before the king in her original form. When she did so, Śikhidhvaja recognising her, was surprised. Cūḍālā told him that it was she who had initiated him into the mysteries of *Ātma-Jñāna* assuming the bodies of Kuṁbha-muni and Madanikā, who had tested the depth of his *Jñāna.* She then asked him to plunge into *Nirvikalpa-Samādhi,* to see the truth of her statement. When the king did as he was told he understood it clearly. Then Cūḍālā told him that he can take over the responsibility of kingship from her while continuing to enjoy the *Ātma-Jñāna.* Both of them returned to their kingdom and reigned over it till they achieved *Videha Mukti.*

Some of us may feel, like many other stories this too is a symbolic story. The word Cūḍālā has a meaning 'resting on the head'. That which rests on the head, the Pineal Gland is supposed to be the seat of *Buddhiḥ* the higher mind even beyond 'ego' and not just intellect. Śikhidhvaja means one having peacock flag. Higher *Manas* is supposed to have the colour of the peacock according to the occult symbology.

But then, why is it not possible to believe that a lady did initiate her husband into *Ātma Vidyā* which resulted in his enlightenment? From the continuing disparity existing in the society between the sexes, this appears more relevant. Women are walking shoulder to shoulder in all walks of life, why not in spirituality? This story, not only depicts the equal spiritual status, but also illustrates, the acme of womanhood, the limit to which woman is capable of reaching.

In this sense, women have the capacity to be *Uṣa,* the dawn of enlightenment in human life.

12

The Story of Kaca

It was spring, the time when cuckoos fill the atmosphere with their music, when the Mango trees are in bloom and there is joy in the air. It was more so, for a small group of people who considered themselves privileged, as they were the disciples of an enlightened *Guru*. Their *Guru* had come to his *Indian Āśrama* on a short visit, after almost three years, and they could get his *Satsaṅga* or holy company that intensified their aspiration for the life divine. They all had left their mundane duties to be recipient to his nectar like words, which appeased their spiritual hunger. And why not? For it was He, who had tickled their spiritual aspiration. It was He who had taken the message of hope across the seas to the struggling humanity in other countries. He spoke to them directly and simply, in a language comprehensible to even common people involved in their day-to-day problems. The way in which he carried himself, his gait, voice and mood expressed his enlightenment.

He had three *Āśramas* in the United States, one in Australia, one in New Zealand. All their locations had breath-taking natural surroundings, which spoke highly of his sense of beauty and love for nature. He had three in India and was intending to start more, so as to reach more people. It appeared that he had lost all distinctions of country, religion, race and status. It was quite touching that afternoon to observe the devotees reach the *Āśrama,* and meet their Master. There was respect, love, a complaint for he had not come to India in the past three years, and of course genuine happiness in their eyes. In a way, the spring appeared to have manifested externally from their hearts!

After the excitement of the re-union, they all met in the prayer hall where they eagerly awaited their Master to begin his *Satsaṅga.* He entered the hall, in his inimitable graceful and slow gait, and occupied his seat. It was hot and humid, as it usually is at that part of the year. The Master remarked that it was very hot, and the manager should arrange to provide air-conditioners in the prayer hall. Only this remark helped the devotees to become aware of the physical climate, of which they had been totally oblivious! A few of them were surprised, for seldom did he remark on the physical discomfort, and he had always helped them rise above it. Then He talked about his *Āśramas* in the United States, Australia, and New Zealand and of his foreign devotees. May be the devotees were expecting too much from their Master, but some of them had discovered that in these times the Master was involved more in taking care of the *Āśrama* properties than on the devotees or their spiritual welfare!

This is not a stray case when it comes to the men of religion and spirituality. The gullible people, who have *habitual* respect for the ochre clothed monks have been exploited repeatedly. And yet, many, if not most of us have short memories, as we get attracted to those who renounce in the name of God time and again. The reason for this is simple: a man who can give up the comforts and security of his home and who holds aspiration dearer to his heart than mere survival is rare indeed. This thought has been ingrained in the psyche of this country. That was why, Swami Vivekananda said repeatedly that *renunciation and service is the twin ideal of our country. If we channelise Her in that direction, everything will be taken care of.*

Unfortunately, renunciation is taken to be only the physical distancing of oneself from the sense objects or relationships. This very shallow understanding has brought about many a catastrophe in the lives of seekers, like the Swami in the above episode. The reason for the above behaviour of the monk is not only due to the shallow understanding, but a façade of wisdom due to the *intellectual understanding* of *Vedānta*, as well as the proficiency in the art of public speaking and presentation. Just by being an effective speaker on topics of spirituality need not make one really wise! In fact, in many cases it becomes a hindrance due to the pride.

Even if one does not venture into *teaching* spirituality, one still has the risk of stagnation and downfall with the wrong understanding of renunciation. First of all, one faces the risk of insulation from the society as one tends to become an escapist. The second thing is that in *avoiding* the things and choosing seclusion, one may have to tackle the very things one left, later in life! A story told by Shri Ramakrishna illustrates this.

> 'There was a Sannyāsī whose only possession was two pairs of loin-cloths. One day a mouse nibbled at one piece. So the holy man kept a cat to protect his loin-cloths from the mouse. Then he had to keep a cow to supply milk for the cat. Later he had to engage a servant to look after the cow. Gradually the number of his cows multiplied. He acquired pastures and farm land. He had to engage a number of servants. Thus he became, in course of time, a sort of landlord. And, last of all, he had to take a wife to look after his big household. One day, one of his friends, another monk, happened to visit him and was surprised to see his altered circumstances. When asked the reason, the holy man said, "It is all for the sake of a piece of loin-cloth"!'[202]

---

202 *The Gospel of Shri Ramakrishna* by M, Shri Ramakrishna Math, Mylapore, Madras, 1974, p. 388.

The above story may be an extreme example, but many times persons walk at least half way through! Their time is consumed by the maintenance of the *Āśrama* property and accounts! Another thing which is more subtle and hence stronger is the *'holier than thou'* attitude, which perhaps is the most catastrophic event for a seeker. If we just analyse our behaviour we find that invariably it is the 'ego', which is responsible for all the problems that plague the society. The inter-personal relationships, the class wars, begin, continue and even end due to egos! Someone's ego is uncompromising, while another's is quite accommodative; in some other cases both egos are adamant! Why, even the nations have their own egos! One of the greatest problems with this ghost called ego is that it can and does survive on *anything, as well as* ***nothing****!*

For instance, we are aware that the ego gets strengthened by flattery, indulgence and involvement. All these are available to us when we live in society and our so-called down to earth lives. But it also gets strengthened, perhaps to a greater extent, when one leaves everything, either through withdrawal or measured and practised non-involvement! Because, then it says '***I*** do not care for any attention, ***I*** can live on my own!' But all along, the ***'I'*** goes on expanding! If one chases it out of the front door, it comes back through the back door if not the window! All it *demands* is a little attention to itself. It survives and thrives *only on attention.*

The most important aspect of *Sādhanā* or spiritual practice is to become aware of this fact, and to slowly start eliminating this *attention.* The story under discussion, tries to bring home this important point.

Sage Vasiṣṭha said that like Śikhidhvaja, Kaca, the son of Bṛhaspati, the *Ācārya* or the teacher of Gods, too followed the same path to reach the most exalted State. To which Rāma requested the sage to narrate him the story of Kaca. Vasiṣṭha replied: Muni Kaca who had the wisdom of subtle things approached his father to know the means of enlightenment, and the path he should tread. The *Devaguru* said that wide ocean of *Saṁsāra* can be crossed only by the incomparable power of total renunciation, involving great effort and *responsibility*.

At these words of his father Kaca retired to the forest renouncing everything and lived there for eight years. At the end of his period, Bṛhaspati visited him. Kaca approached him with due respect, and poured out his heart, that in spite of a life of renunciation for eight years, his mind was still sorrowful. To this doubt of Kaca, Bṛhaspati said that he should give up everything. When the father left, Kaca left wearing even the bark of the trees and roamed about naked and total abstinence. Again after three years he approached his father and said that in spite of leaving everything, he had not known peace.

This is one of the most common problems that are encountered by seekers during their journey. Because many of us take even spirituality as an *object of achievement* and *Sādhanā* to be an *investment!* This is to be understood carefully. In the world of objects, it is inevitable that one has to invest one's time and effort to achieve something, be it an object or a position of power. In the process, one has to court anxiety and tension. One has to necessarily evoke the 'ego', because it is the ego which is the *achiever*. A creature of habits that man is, he continues this attitude even in the spiritual plane! Earlier he used to seek sense objects, or material fulfillment in lieu of his effort, now he seeks peace of mind and spiritual experiences! Not realising that by this, he is again courting anxiety and tension.

One more reason, and perhaps a very strong reason is when a person renounces the world of objects he is not *convinced,* that there is no relationship between the happiness and the sense objects, though he leaves them in search of *lasting peace and happiness!* This innate doubt remains even when he *invests* his effort with an *expectation*. Then there is disappointment with consequent sorrow. It is also true, that such persons—and that constitutes most of us!—*remember* what they have *left* all along, which proves that what has been left *continues to be important!* Though the objects are renounced physically, they continue to remain in the mind, perhaps a little more strongly! If the renunciation is positive, then there is no place for sorrow, as the objects have fallen off the mind.

Bṛhaspati said: The great opine that the mind is all and that its mastery leads to the renunciation of all. Through such mental renunciation one can free oneself from all pain. So saying, he left the scene, leaving Kaca to himself, who contemplated on his father's words. He thought that he had been inquiring as to what mind is, and had not yet come to any understanding. If the body with its *Indriyas* is different from the mind, the effort to separate them is useless, as they are already separate. When he approached his respected father with this doubt, Bṛhaspati replied, that the wise who have understood what mind is, say that it is nothing other than *Ahaṁkāra.* The idea of 'I' exists in all creatures.

Kaca observed that it is very difficult to avoid the idea of 'I'. How can one destroy this hard rock? Bṛhaspati replied that it is not very difficult to remove this idea. What one has to learn is only to change the vision. If one meditates on the One and only Principle, which is Non-dual, endless and Supreme *Jñāna,* one is instantly freed from the ghost of *Ahaṁkāra.* Just like dust which can never arise out of waters, or waters out of fire, *Ahaṁkāra* cannot arise out of the Eternal. *Tattva Jñāna,* the Non-dual, is not subject to the forms generated by space, time, etc., and hence, beyond suffering. In *Kaivalya* the final liberation, *Ahaṁkāra* is known to be unreal. Therefore, Bṛhaspati added, one *should neither think of giving it up or taking it up,* like no one tries to hold the non-existent horns of the hare!

Rāma asked a doubt: how did the element of *otherness* manifest in the *Brahman?* Vasiṣṭha replied that the emergence of concepts of diversity which are unreal generates rebirth; but the realisation of Non-dual Reality without doubt is the freedom from rebirth.

One may feel after reading this story that it is easier said than done! The *Jñāna* vision, which this story hints at, cannot be explained. Because all doubts and problems exist only at the level of mind and *Ahaṁkāra.* However, the compassionate sages who had such vision, wanted everyone to have it, because it is not only everyone's birth right, but everyone can have it. The only condition they ever put is to wake up from the sleep of *Ahaṁkāra* and its manifestations. Most of us are asleep, some in deep slumber, some others in lighter sleep. Sages like Vasiṣṭha are ringing alarms to wake us up.

A Zen master on waking up from sleep, called his disciple and asked him to analyse a dream he had seen in his sleep. The disciple however, brought him warm water to wash the face, and kept it in front of the master. After the ablutions, the disciple took away the vessel. The master called his second disciple and again repeated what he had told the first disciple. The disciple instead of speaking brought a cup of tea and placed in front of the master. The master laughed joyously, for the disciples were alert and had learnt.

The fact that the master was asking the disciples to analyse the dream, itself showed that the master was still in his sleep! For on waking up from sleep, the dream is irrelevant. So the first disciple brought water. When the master still insisted on the analysis, the second disciple brought him the tea! In Zen tradition, tea stands for awareness. All the descriptions are in a way analyses of dreams in the form of further dreams! They are only means for waking us up like water or tea. Whether to wake up or not is left entirely to us!

13

The Story of Mithyāpuruṣa

The horizon turned amber as the sun made his exit behind a small hillock. The fleecy clouds above were gradually getting transformed from bright gold to reddish brassy hue. An ancient banyan stood in that plain surrounded by rocky hillocks. Hundreds of birds gathered on the banyan, which offered its benign canopy to a record area of the five and a quarter acres. The winged creatures had made this tree, their home for many generations. It was very difficult to make out the original trunk from its offshoots. The banyan is one such tree which goes on spreading by the phenomenon of rooting in its branches, so much so, that many times one feels that it is not one tree but a group of interconnected trees. The banyan has not only been associated with Indian psyche for millennia, but has been used to compare it with the inner world of mind, by our sages in the scriptures. They observed that *Ahaṁkāra* or the 'I-doness' is quite similar to the banyan.

The 'I', call it by any name: the ego, the self, etc., remains a great driving force for all activity and being. All actions are motivated by and are performed for this entity. And yet, most of us hardly know anything of this great enigma. Religious lore in general and Vedāntic literature in particular has tried to throw light on this entity. While religion as such—of the Hindu or of the Judaic origin, has tried to convince the practitioner that it creates a *barrier* between him and the God.

And so, they recommend its annihilation through surrender. This is only right, as the religion in general, caters to the needs of common man involved with the day-to-day existence.

Vedānta however, is more direct, as it goes into the root cause of the problem. It tries initially to analyse intellectually and then to intuitively understand what this entity is, which has been taken for granted all along. During *Nididhyāsana* or the states of meditative contemplation, they discovered the Truth, and in their compassion for the struggling humanity, which was *needlessly* suffering—from their point of view!—they tried to use stories, similes and symbology to help the suffering, alleviate the so-called problems *through their own effort.* They started with very logical questions: 'Who is it that experiences pleasure and pain?'; 'Who is this entity "I" that is behind all experience and knowledge?' An *Upaniṣad* begins with the following *Mantra*:

> 'Willed by whom does the mind fall towards the object? Being directed by whom does the *Prāṇa* that precedes all, proceed towards its duty? By whom is this speech willed that people utter? Who is the effulgent being who directs the eyes and the ears'?[203]

The spirit behind these fundamental questions is, that unless we find out *for ourselves,* who is it that suffers, enjoys, acts or understands, it is useless to solve the problems. Paradoxically, we see this happening with us and around us all the time. A man spends most of his time in acquiring wealth, but in the process does not have any time for enjoying it as he is totally involved with the acquisition! Life appears to be just a mad chase, without the experiential answer to the fundamental question: 'Who am I'?

Trees, especially the *Aświattha* and the Pīpal, have been used as similes in Vedāntic literature. This may be due to the

---

203 केनेषितं पतति प्रेषितं मनः केन प्राणः प्रथम प्रैति युक्तः ।
केनेषितां वाचमिमां वदन्ति चक्षुः श्रोत्रं क उ देवो युनक्ति ॥ 1.1 ॥

fact that our *Ṛṣis* were nature lovers, and had come to many valuable conclusions by observing it carefully. That must be because, they had come to realise that man and nature are parts of the Non-dual Existence, and naturally have many things in common. The *Bhagavadgītā* begins a chapter with the *Śloka*:

> 'There is an indestructible *Aśwattha* tree having its roots upward and its branches below, the leaves are the *Vedas;* he who knows it, is alone a *knower of Veda*'.[204]

If one looks at the above *Śloka* superficially, it appears strange. How can a tree possibly have its roots *upwards?* But when we understand the symbology, we discover a great truth through this verse. In the Vedāntic symbology the upper and the internal directions refer to the subtler aspect, and the lower and the external directions refer to the grosser aspect, of the same Non-dual Existence. The *Aśwattha* tree represents the *Saṁsāra,* which is subject to constant change, characterised by multiplicity. The origin is subtle. Any tree, big or small, has its beginning in the seed and the lone tender sapling. *Yoga Vāsiṣṭha* keeps repeating over and over again that the seed of *Saṁsāra* lies in the *Saṁkalpa* or the *tendency to contract the consciousness.*

Vedas in the above verse refer to knowledge in general or the *faculties for knowing* in particular,[205] which are *Ahaṁkāra, Citta,* or memory, *Buddhiḥ* or intellect, *Indriyas* or senses, and the body. If one knows this truth experientially, one becomes the *knower of the process of knowing.* The *Śloka* suggests the seeker to go back to the *root.* Some common experiences can help us understand the meaning of the verse at *least intellectually.*

---

204 Aśwattha is the Pīpal tree.

ऊर्ध्वमूलमधःशाखमश्वत्थं प्राहुरव्ययम् ।
छन्दांसि यस्य पर्णानि यस्तं वेद स वेदवित् ।। 15.1 ।।

205 *Véda* is derived from *Vid* which means 'to know'.

Richard Bach writes of an episode in his book 'Illusions'.[206] In a small town one night while walking back to their planes, Richard asks Donald Shimoda, the reluctant messiah, as to why at all we choose to come to this world. Instead of replying, Don asks him to enter a movie theatre. Richard settles down and starts enjoying the movie, forgetting why he is there. When the movie advances further, Don asks him, why is he in the theatre! To which Richard replies that it is a good movie! Don again asks as to why the movie is good. Richard replies with annoyance, that he will reply later! Don continues to whisper dramatically, that it is only an illusion. Richard is so *identified* with the movie, that he is unable to understand the import of Don's question! When they come out, a very interesting conversation follows.

The only problem we as human beings face is *identification.* We identify with the body and become miserable. Pain, pleasure, sickness are natural for the elemental body, while the *misery* is due to the identification with it. The misery which is psychological is at *all levels* from body through senses, mind, intellect, or ego. And the funniest part is that all of us know innately that pleasure and pain, are transient. They are never permanent. Childhood comes and goes; youth appears and disappears; and dotage advances and retreats. However, the entity who *witnesses* all the events happening in life remains. It is due to the *witness* that we are able to *remember* them. Besides the gross body, we have worlds of thoughts and feelings, each his or her own!

Tamas or lethargy is the first obstacle we face in life. We tend to remain self-complacent. Our country ails from this illness. What is it that helps us break away from the barrier of lethargy? Having come out of lethargy what goads us towards achievement, excellence, success, anxiety, disappointment, anger and host of emotions? Experiencing the pains and gains

206 Published by Dell 1989. pp. 101-104.

of *Rajas* or activity, what cajoles us towards nobler qualities like compassion, love and harmony? In spite of all these, what inspires us to seek something which transcends even *Sattwa,* say Enlightenment, Fulfillment, or whatever one chooses to call IT?

There is only one entity behind all inspiration and activity: *Ahaṁkāra*. Literally, *Ahaṁkāra* means 'I-do-ness' or *identification with* ***any*** *activity, be it Sphandana or pure vibration or thought or gross actions.* If *Bodha* or Pure Awareness *falls* into any such identification, *Ahaṁkāra* is formed. And with this ghost of *Ahaṁkāra,* the *Saṁsāra* or the worldliness with its multiplicity and complications get created. *Ahaṁkāra* is a ghost, because it is really not an entity but an activity! And this activity, like walking or running can be slowed down or even stopped. This particular point is elaborated by the story under discussion.

Vasiṣṭha said that it is not necessary to afflict oneself with misery like the Mithyāpuruṣa. In a nook of *Cidākāśa,* where there is no universe, a certain male personage arose. He was clothed in *Māyā* and was full of *Ajñāna.* He arose like the imaginary city in the sky or the water in a mirage. He went by the name of Mithyāpuruṣa. Unaware of his own growth, and the *Cit* or consciousness that manifests itself as if distinct from the universe, he *contracted* the *Saṁkalpa* of creating the highest, infinite *Ākāśa* and created it. Then in order to set a limit to it, he constructed an enclosed abode. With the idea that the *Ākāśa* was pent up in that habitation, his desires were bound by and identified with that limited *Ākāśa.* In course of time, it became dilapidated and gave way. Then the Mithyāpuruṣa felt miserable at the disappearance of the *Ākāśa.* Having finished his lamentations over the *Ākāśa* house, he created a well and entered it. He grew attached to it as he did not have any disturbance from outside. As before, he became disappointed when the well too became useless and old. Then he created a new pot. Enamoured by its beautiful structure, was chained to it by affection. This continued with many creations and he worked, got attached, lived and died with them.

When Rāma asked for the esoteric meaning of the story, Vasiṣṭha explained: The Mithyāpuruṣa is the *Ahaṁkāra* arising in the void. The *Ākāśa* is self-existent, all-full and endless. In it the idea of 'I' arises like the sense of touch in *Vāyu* or air; and this void of *Ahaṁkāra* fancies itself as protecting the *Cidākāśa* of the *Ātman*. Then encased in several bodies symbolised by well, etc. which are created by itself, it subjects itself to repeated pain. With the body, it *contracts* itself further to *Bhūtākāśa* thus distancing itself from the *Ātman*. The indestructible *Ākāśa* cannot disappear when the limiting pots and wells get destroyed. The *Ākāśa* continues in their presence, *as well as their absence!* It is only through direct spiritual vision that the transcendental *Brahman, Cinmātra* or pure being, and *Sat* or awareness, shines everywhere. But the *Ahaṁkāra* is destroyed like a pot.

There is really no such thing as the birth or death. Only Brahman ever is, and manifests as the universe. *Ahaṁkāra* is the source of all accidents, non-eternal, dependent and discrimination-less, the seed of all sins, and of *Ajñāna*, of birth and destruction. Destruction of this *Ahaṁkāra* is the *Jīvanamukti* state.

Herein, *Yoga Vāsiṣṭha* gives a great hint on the mechanism of *Ahaṁkāra*. First of all, by calling *Ahaṁkāra* as Mithyāpuruṣa, it is suggesting that *Ahaṁkāra* is not a permanent entity, because, *Mithyā* means that which *appears,* but is really not. Then it says that the Mithyāpuruṣa tries to *limit* the Infinite Space into smaller spaces repeatedly. Putting both these facts together we can safely conclude that *Ahaṁkāra* is the *act of contracting or focusing the Pure Awareness*. As already discussed earlier in the story of Puṇya and Pāvana,[207] when the Pure

---

207 Refer to the second story in *Upaśama Prakaraṇa.*

Consciousness gets contracted 'I' is formed and along with it, duality.

Pure Consciousness is like a light falling on all objects in the room, while the 'I' is the identification with one or two objects. The 'I' is also a ray of the Pure Awareness, but *imagines* that it is the *protector* of the Awareness! It is natural, that the Infinite *appears* threatening, as It does not have any boundaries. It is beyond the mind and senses and hence is unknowable and is awesome and mysterious. While the finite gives a feeling of security, as the finite falls under the purview of 'I', mind and sense or body experience. Because of this reason, it appears convenient. But actually, the act of focusing is just an obstinate habit like any other habit. Spirituality is nothing but being aware and conscious of this habit, it is a change of vision and attitude. Being aware of this, *the Ṛṣis said, that the only thing required is to wake up from this sleep of defective vision in the methods of Jñāna.* And on waking up One finds that everything is only That, the friend, foe, relation, as well as the universe.

In a palace of a king, there was a room full of mirrors. Somehow, a dog got trapped in it one night. Next morning its dead body, full of blood was found in a corner. The whole night, it had fought with its own *reflection!* The human story is not very different from that of the dog! Whatever exists is That Non-dual Reality, but in our ignorance we take the world to be different, the 'I' to be something else, and Reality to be a separate Self! While the fact is, that the difference is only an appearance.

There was a Sufi saint by name Shilbi. He used to say that he had many preceptors, but three were most important.

THE BEACONS THREE

Sitting on the bank of a fast flowing river,
He was enjoying the reflections in the water mirror.
Attracted by moving of steps behind his shoulder,

Beheld a dog restlessly thirsty, approaching the water.

The object of his curiosity was plainly scared, as it saw
Another of its own kind staring at it with anger and awe.
But the thirst was more menacing as it made its throat raw,
Lapping the water, discovered no dog but its own image it saw.
He learnt that the world with all its beings and things is nothing
But one's own reflection and the good or the bad was only a feeling,
Getting brewed in the mind and the world is a means of escaping,
From the torture of one's own desires and fears that need projecting.

In need of a pied-à-terre exhausted from the journey on foot,
He entered a village one night to find it asleep devoid of all moot.
He found a man trying to break the door of a shop to loot,
Approaching the man he asked whether he can allow him to rest his foot.

Looking into his eyes the man said:

'You appear to be a holy-man and I do not want to hide my race,
I am a real thief, a professional thief not knowing any polish or lace.
You can stay with me if you want, till you want, at my place.'
Hearing these words the saint's eyes felt the blood rushing on to face.

Noting hesitation in the man's mood the thief smiled and again said:
'I understand you are one of those who practise religion for bread,
Without really being religious that needs real authenticity in head,
Do not worry I shall take you to a place offering the poor, bread.'

The words awakened the man from his stupor for he insisted to be with,

The thief to stay and observe for over a month and to shatter the myth,
That thieves are fallen men on ground like worms that crawl and writhe,
For in face of failure ever hopeful and joyous he found this man with.

He learnt to be authentic in his thought, word and deed,
Never to lose trust through hope at whatever cost or in need.
For he was on a journey without end his being was the only steed,
It dawned on him that *the way to heaven itself is heaven indeed.*

Seeing his own image in every being and thing he shed his pettiness,
With authenticity and hope he turned his face away from otherness.
And the sun of compassion and love arose bringing in godliness.
With that he roamed around spreading fragrance of happiness.

Reaching a town he heard of Junaid who had led many towards the light,
A wish arose to meet him and share his experience and delight.
Seeing him come Junaid's wife tried to leave the room in flight,
Junaid said that Shilbi was absent, there was no need for any fright.

Hearing Junaid's approval, Shilbi fell from the Oneness due to pride.
The fall made him cry like a small child afflicted by some chide.
Junaid's wife laughed as her husband made her leave his side,
And the laughter made Shilbi learn that his ego still gave him a ride.

The laughter continued to echo in consciousness reminding him,
That unless one has the total awareness one can fall off the rim.
As the ego only needs a reason and can even create out of its whim.

The teachers three made Shilbi a smokeless lamp that could never dim.[208]

There is a wonderful thought from the book 'Illusions' written by Richard Bach:

The
original sin is to
limit the Is.
Don't.[209]

Ahaṁkāra is the mistake that limits the Infinite through identification though, it cannot be and should not be called a *sin!* In the *Bhakti* tradition, the creation and obviously the *Ahaṁkāra,* which is at its root is considered to be *Līlā* or the play of the Lord!

Only on becoming aware of the root can one think of understanding the complex tree called the universe. And most surprising thing that comes out of such awareness is that the root, the branches, the leaves and all, exist not without the vitality of the Reality which is One without the second. And the fact is, IT only IS!

---

208 From *Splendour of Isolation* by the author Published by Ocean Paperbacks.

209 *Illusions* by Richard Bach, Dell, 1989, p. 128.

14

The Story of Bhṛngīṣa

Aged and experienced Margosas stand guard, spreading thick shades in the premises. The architect who had designed the campus had adapted his plan in such a way that no huge tree was touched. Even the roads were not straight. Consequently, the buildings are not visible from the highway that passes by the campus. Deer cross the roads, and graze the grounds fearlessly. In this sense, it not only makes an ideal setting for the prestigious Indian Institute of Technology, but gives *the right milieu* for a research scholar. For a teen-ager in his decisive years IIT is *the* dream, closest to his heart! And why not? When one gets a total opportunity to learn and to exploit one's full potential, who can ever think of complaining? Added to these advantages, one gets openings for bright careers even before completing the course.

But then, human mind is such, that it discovers, and even *creates* reasons to complain and grumble. Everything looks attractive and grand from a distance. Go closer to it, and .... So even those in the IIT-s or in other Institutions have their problems, many of which are self-created! As Professor Ramamurthy sat in his room, in the Department Aeronautical Engineering, he tried analysing his behaviour. He did not know what had been happening to him in the recent past. For over a month, he had been losing temper apparently for no reason, on his students as well as his colleagues. When he realised that they were *avoiding* him, he had started becoming irritable at home. His wife whom he loved with all his heart, wanted to go home for a change, and his son too wanted to accompany her in spite of the fact that he would miss his school. It had been three weeks since the trouble started. Presently, it struck him that during this period, in fact a week before that, he had started facing a peculiar problem.

He could not concentrate on his work. Whenever he took up any work, he got distracted to such an extent that he would come back to it, after the mind roamed around for long intervals of time. He had avoided even giving lectures, which was not only considered mandatory, but was thoroughly enjoyed by him as well. This dawned on him when he tried to read through a newly published paper in an international journal. Consequently, he realised, that nothing seemed to satisfy him : food had become insipid, discussions boring, the evening walks in the campus monotonous. Luckily for him, he met a person who guided him in solving the problem by performance of some simple *Āsanas* and *Prāṇāyāma*.

The problem faced by Ramamurthy is neither peculiar nor singular. It is a most common problem faced by one and all, one time or the other in life. The mind is so restless that even the normal life gets disrupted. At such times, it is difficult, if not impossible to resort to methods of *Vicāra*. When the enemy is invincible, the guerrilla warfare is resorted to. Similarly, when the mind is very strong and acts as an enemy, may be an imagined one (!), *Ṛṣis* have devised indirect methods to bring it under control.

The existing literature on mind quietening methods is literally mind boggling! However, if one understands the principle behind the methods, and remembers their single aim of quietening the mental activity, it becomes clear. Those who have great restlessness find indirect methods useful, and others who have comparatively calmer mind, find the direct methods more useful. In the indirect methods, the mind is *influenced* by tackling other faculties like body, through *Āsanas; Prāṇa* or vital force through *Prāṇāyāma;* emotions through *Bhakti;* and action through *Karma Yoga.* Most of the 'isms' stress on the indirect methods, and only a few advocate the direct methods. In the direct methods, the mental activity is handled directly, through *Dhāraṇā, Dhyāna, Nididhyāsana,* etc. In spite of the fact that *Yoga Vāsiṣṭha* is predominantly a *Jñāna-Śāstra,* it does in many places throw light on the indirect methods as well, which are invaluable to a seeker.

There are two approaches to the spiritual practice. The first is to just begin the practice without going into the theoretical details. In which case, the practitioner may tend towards mechanical-ness, or empty gestures, as it has in many of our so-called religious practices. *Pūjā, Arcanā, Parāyaṇa* or devotional chanting of the sacred literature, *Japa* are some of the examples. If we were to assess religiosity of a person through the time he or she engages in such practices, then India is perhaps the most religious country, and we know it is not! This is due to the fact, that most of us have been blindly following what our elders have been doing for centuries. Of course, added to the blind practices, is the most dangerous justification that the sins committed get washed off through them! Consequently, there is no appreciable change in persons in spite of years of such practice.

The other approach is to *understand* the mechanism of the practice, at the same time, be *aware* of the ways and mechanism of the activities called mind and others which *cause* the disturbance. Even this approach is not foolproof in the sense that one may tend to be a theoretical *Yogi* involving oneself in endless discussions and arguments! A little theory is definitely necessary, but the practice is mandatory! *Yoga Vāsiṣṭha* gives the necessary details of the mechanism of all activity in such lucid manner that one can take advantage of it to plunge deeper and deeper into oneself. In the last *Sarga* it was hinted that *Ahaṁkāra,* the 'I-do-ness' is the cause of ignorance and misery. In the present *Sarga,* how the *Ahaṁkāra* and other activities consequent to it are to be quietened has been discussed.

Sage Vasiṣṭha said that the universe manifests itself through *Ātma Jñāna* or Self-awareness, like the illusion of a serpent arising out of a rope. To those contemplating on the rays of the sun as nothing other than the sun itself, the sun alone exists. But the rays and the sun are considered separate then diversity appears. *Saṁkalpa* or the initial contraction produces restless motion on the tranquil *Brahman.* As soon as the *Saṁkalpa* is born, the restlessness expands and differentiates into the form world, when it becomes *Manas* and begins to see itself through itself. Thus the universe is nothing but the *Saṁkalpa* itself. It is neither real nor unreal; it manifests itself like dream creations. The seer, hearer, speaker, feeler, smeller, walker and doer are not separate creations but one Truth. All activity is in truth the stainless *Jñāna.* As the real nature of *Mahat* or the Cosmic Consciousness, is *Brahman,* there is no such thing as the independent universe.

What is hinted at by Vasiṣṭha is, that *everything* perceived or unperceived have a single cause: Non-dual *Brahman.* It is like electricity, all appliances can operate only through its power. And it remains hidden, while its effects like the heat, sound, light and motion steal the show, to the extent that we tend to become oblivious to it! Two similes are given to explain the mechanism of manifestation. The first is of the illusion of serpent arising from rope. It is due to a wrong interpretation of the sense stimulus. The Non-dual Reality is misinterpreted as duality. The simile is that of a dream. The characters, locale and the reactions are creations of the dreamer. And the dream is real, *during the activity of dreaming,* as evident from the palpitating heart, the excitement, which sometimes continue even *after* the dream. But when the dreamer comes back to the wakeful state, he realises that it was only his or her own mental projection. Ultimately, it is like the waves, foam, and the perpetual motion of the ocean.

At this stage, a concept from the *Sāṅkhya* is being introduced. *Puruṣa* is the static aspect of the Reality, and *Prakṛti,* the dynamic aspect. It is like the ocean and its faculty of waving. Out of *Prakṛti* the first manifestation is, *Mahat. Mahat* is the first *Spandana* or the pure vibration without any attributes. From *Mahat, Ahaṁkāra* is born, and then all other manifestations.

Vasiṣṭha continued: As all are aspects of *Cit* or consciousness, and the universes are nothing but *Cinmātra* or pure consciousness. There is nothing like *Bandha* or bondage and *Mokṣa* or liberation. One has to abandon all differentiations by observing Mauna or silence, without a tinge of *Ahaṁkāra.* Performing actions without *Ahaṁkāra,* one can live as a great actor and enjoyer, yet as a renouncer of all. Rāma requested to the Master to throw more light on who is the great actor, great enjoyer and great renouncer? To explain it Vasiṣṭha started narrating the story of Bhṛngīṣa. Bhṛngīṣa went to the summit of Mahāmeru and having worshipped Parameśvara, sought his help to overcome the worldly delusion and to achieve lasting peace. When the Lord Śiva, blessed him to become *Mahākartā,* the great actor, *Mahābhoktā,* great enjoyer and *Mahātyāgī,* great renouncer. Bhṛngīṣa sought clarification of these terms.

Parameśvara replied: He is the great actor, who is indifferent to the fruits of action, free of pleasure and pain, *Dharma* and *Adharma,* and one who performs actions without any desire. He is the great actor who, being silent is free from 'I' or self-identification with objects and activity, who performs actions without fear or despondency and attachment for the fruits of action, but a *witness to all, with equal vision over all.* Such mind is undisturbed in all situations, birth or death, appearance or disappearance of objects.

He is the great enjoyer who does not, through anger, long for or reject anything, but enjoys fully those things that come to him. He never loses his equilibrium of mind even in the enjoyment of illusory pleasures and pain, productive of fear; he considers in the same light, things or stimuli, which lead one to dotage or death, regality or poverty, the virtuous or the vicious. He is the great and true renouncer who is intelligent to abandon *Dharma* and *Adharma,* pleasure and pain, birth and death. Who does not have even an iota of desire or doubt. He is free of all duality and pairs of opposites, of all thoughts and mental activity. He has eradicated all thoughts of visible things from his consciousness.

Concluding the story, Vasiṣṭha blessed Rāma to develop the vision as told by Parameśvara to Bhṛngīṣa, and protect the subjects. The Reality alone is, and everything else is in the plane of duality and pairs of opposites. The *Ahaṁkāra* can be destroyed entirely with *Niṣṭhā,* the firm conviction that there is nothing foreign to 'That' which is not affected by either *Sat,* the existence, or *ASAT,* the non-existence. One can free oneself of *Ahaṁkāra* by developing *Aṅtarmukhatā* or internalisation, and the harmonisation of the external with the internal to remain unaffected by the pain of past actions.

As usual, this grand scripture presents great truths to the seeker, through apparently simple statements. The words *Mahākartā, Mahābhoktā,* and *Mahātyāgī* appear to suggest three different approaches to the same end: the annihilation of *Ahaṁkāra. Ahaṁkāra* manifests itself at three levels: *Jñātṛtva,* the 'knowership', *Bhoktṛtva,* the 'experiencership', and *Kartṛtva,* the 'doership'. Mostly, we are aware of the *Kartṛtva* and *Bhoktṛtva.* At these two levels of the body and senses, the mental activity is quite intense and hence gross. Unless this activity is quietened it is difficult even to become aware of the subtler activity like thoughts. All the spiritual literature tries to give methods for quietening the activity.

Kartṛtva is charaterised by identification with the external activity through *Karmendriyas,* or the instruments of action, and through the resultant fruits of the actions. In this sense, the motivation for any action is the desire for the fruit, and *normally* action is almost impossible without such motivation. From a common man, who works for the resulting fruit, pleasure, security, or power and name, to a seeker, who is seeking enlightenment, the action is motivated. Thus it is very difficult to give up attachment to the fruits of action. *Bhagavadgītā* has a *Śloka*:

> 'The right is to work only, but never to its fruits; let not the fruit-of-action be your motive, nor let your attachment be to inaction'.[210]

This *Śloka* while being one of the most famous is also perhaps, one of the most misunderstood ones! Because if one gets detached to fruit of action, then the normal tendency is to avoid action altogether! This verse is a message for developing efficiency. It means that *during* the action if one keeps dwelling on the result of action obviously one gets distracted from the work itself and definitely brings down the efficiency. Keeping this in view, the verse warns us against being *attached to inaction.* In the very next verse Lord Kṛṣṇa takes us to a deeper level:

> 'Perform action, O Dhanañjaya! abandoning attachment, being steadfast in *Yoga,* and balanced in success and failure. Evenness of mind is called *Yoga*'.[211]

It is possible to transcend the attachment to fruits and yet perform the action by being steadfast in *Yoga,* which is clarified by *Vāsiṣtha,* as being a *witness to all activity.* The

---

210 कर्मण्येवाधिकारस्ते मा फलेषु कदाचन ।
मा कर्मफलहेतुर्भूर्मा ते सङ्गोऽस्त्वकर्मणि ॥ 2.47 ॥

211 योगस्थः कुरु कर्माणि सङ्गं त्यक्त्वा धनंजय ।
सिद्ध्यसिद्ध्योःसमोभूत्वा समत्वं योग उच्यते ॥ 2.48 ॥

Bhoktṛtva is at the level of experience, through senses and mind. Even this activity is to be *witnessed,* without any involvement whatsoever. When one is deeply involved with either action or experience, it is difficult if not impossible, not to get disturbed, either negatively or even positively, by the outcome of such action or experience. The seekers are suggested to spend some time on the meditation seat, to learn the aspect of non-involved witnessing. Gradually, with continual practice, one is able to *see* objectively one's own action and experience as if the action or experience is happening at a distance, and there is an entity 'I' which is the *witness.* This is the second approach.

The *Jñātṛtva* is the knowership, the 'I-am-ness' is the subtlest, which detaches oneself from all activity, is the *watcher on the hill,* one who is the witness. The term *Tyāgī* used by Parameśvara suggests this. The greatest *Tyāgī* or *Mahātyāgī* is *one who has transcended the memory of Tyāga.* This perhaps is the toughest barrier in the seekers journey. One gives up the attachment for grosser objects and objectives for the sake of the subtle. One gives up family ties, comfort, sense objects, etc. for the sake of life spiritual, but one keeps *remembering* what one has renounced.

By introducing the word *Mahat,* which is the progenitor of *Ahaṁkāra,* the seeker is suggested to transcend this activity called 'I-do-ness' or in other words, 'I-renounce-ness'! *Mahat* is *Spandana* or pure activity without any attribute. A *Mantra* from *Kaṭhopaniṣad* sums up the whole process described in this *Sarga* :

> 'A person filled with *Prajñā,* or awareness, should merge the speech into the *Manas;* the *Manas* into the intelligent self; he should merge the intelligent self into *Mahat;* the *Mahat* into the *Tranquil* Self'.[212]

---

212 यच्छेद्वांमनसि प्राज्ञस्तद्यच्छेज्ज्ञान आत्मनि ।
ज्ञानमात्मनि महति नियच्छेत्तद्यच्छेच्छान्त आत्मनि ॥ 1.3.13 ॥

Speech is the grossest and the *Śānta Ātman,* the Tranquil Self the subtlest. Ādi Śaṅkarācārya in his commentary on the above *Śloka* clarifies the meaning of *speech*:

'Here speech is meant to represent all the senses'.[213]

The two wings required for the flight towards the Reality are *Asaṅga,* the non-involvement and *Aṅtarmukhatā,* while the tail that gives direction to the flight is *Prajñā,* or the awareness. *Asaṅga* in the initial stage is towards the fruits of action, in the next stage to the play of senses and the last is *to the process of Asaṅga itself. Asaṅga* is the companion throughout the pilgrimage. Shri Ramakrishna used to explain it with a very beautiful simile:

> 'First rub your hands with oil and then break open the jack-fruit otherwise they will be smeared with its sticky milk. First secure the oil of divine love, and then set your hands to the duties of the world'.[214]

The oil can be of *Bhakti* or of non-involvement. All our so-called troubles begin with involvement. The moment we learn the art of being non-involved, *Aṅtarmukhatā* ripens. Without *Asaṅga* even the *Aṅtarmukhatā* is reduced to internal dialogue or even brooding! This advice is given by Parameśvara the Lord of *Yogis,* to Bhṛṅgīṣa or the lord of bumblebees! Bee represents senses and *Manas* in the Vedāntic symbology.

Because the senses and *Manas,* the faculty of *Antaḥkaraṇa* behind them, keep changing the objects like the bee changing the flowers. In this sense the *Sarga* describes the journey of the individual from the senses to the Ultimate Reality.

For a child looking at the ocean in turmoil, the mighty waves, the froth and the apparent violence associated with

---

213 वागत्रोपलक्षणार्था सर्वेन्द्रियाणाम् ॥ शंकरभाष्यम् 1.3.13 ॥

214 *The Gospel of Shri Ramakrishna* by M, Shri Ramakrishna Math, Mylapore, Mardas, p. 6.

the activity appear threatening. It is unable to appreciate the beauty as it sees every wave different from the other. But a mature person, sees that the wave is nothing but the ocean waving, and the ocean nothing but a quietened wave! *Sādhanā* consists of growing up to recognise this Oneness of Existence.

15

The Story of Ikṣvāku

The silvery lake mirrored the reflection of the moon, which in turn reflected the borrowed light from the sun. The tall mountain ridge surrounding the lake scattered the moonlight from their rich and bright snow caps. The sky was crystal clear with infinite stars, star systems, and planets vying to exhibit themselves. At the height of nearly six kilometers above the sea, the air was comparatively rarer. But it carried a pleasant smell of the water, vapourised during the vertical fall from the most beautiful of the peaks, *Harmukh.* The name was chosen, perhaps because of its head like shape, with matted locks, through which streams of molten water from the snow cap flows to form the emerald green lake which presently appeared like molten silver. The lake, most appropriately named the *Harmukh Gaṅgā.*

One could hear the sounds of sheep bleating, the shepherds speaking to one another to pass the long cold night. For the once in a life time adventurer who was enjoying all these sense stimuli, the life of shepherds was enviable, because they could *live* near this mountain and enjoy it from every angle! While the shepherds envied the visitors who could go back to the luxurious cities instead of living in this God forsaken place, leading miserable lives! And the truth was in thinking of *the other and the unavailable,* both the adventurer and the shepherd were missing the present and available, which was more than enough for ushering in joy!

The act of dreaming is itself a paradox. Without dreams the mankind would not have been what it is. It is the dreams that have brought in scientific and technological breakthrough and leaps to progress in civilization. It is the dream again that has developed the heart through art and literature. It is due to dreaming that we have the sense of beauty, of goodness and of harmony. When we are troubled by anxiety, worry, or are threatened by challenges, we retreat into our dream world. But then it has become a stubborn habit for us. The perpetual dreaming goes on as a constant and steady undercurrent inside the mind detaching us from the present moment or *'what is'*, and to nurture the attraction for *'the other'*, which takes root in our mind.

One of the greatest problems facing mankind is the attraction for *the other,* other than what is available at hand. So much so, that this habit has become a second nature for mankind. Consequently, it remains perpetually discontent and disillusioned. The habit has gone so deep, that when the desire is fulfilled one does not even wait for the mind to settle back in satisfaction, it is again activated by a new desire, which perhaps requires greater effort, energy and time! And this search for the horizon continues from womb to tomb, life after life. And with every effort involved in the fulfillment of the desire, the habit gets strengthened until it becomes a strong *Saṁskāra* or impression. These *Saṁskāras* do not allow the boat of life, any movement.

A story is told of a group of thieves who burgled a village after crossing a river in a boat. When they had successfully collected the loot, one of them suggested that a celebration was justified after such a successful operation! They drank away to glory, and when the night had well advanced, they returned to the boat and started paddling the oars. In the morning, they were caught by the villagers. For the boat had not moved an inch, as they had remained on the same bank where they were! They had forgotten to weigh the anchor in their intoxication!

The story of most of us is not very different. The *Saṁskāras* act like the heavy anchor, gaining weight with every life, which stops our boat from embarking into the ocean of consciousness and bliss and freedom. One of the most effective means of *lightening* this anchor is by the reduction and ultimately elimination of desires by means of *Asaṅga* or non-attachment. *Asaṅga* has been recommended in every religion in some form or the other. Three approaches have been used for developing *Asaṅga.* They are *Indriya-nigraha* or control of senses, *Karuṇā* or compassion, and *Dāna* or charity to tackle indulgence, anger and cruelty, and greed respectively.[215]

However, these three approaches form only the basic and initial steps to turn in the direction of spirituality. These three: *Indriya-nigraha, Karuṇā* and *Dāna,* bring in the realisation that there is something more than survival, that life has a greater purpose, and that life as it is, is a great dependence and bondage. They help us in calming the restlessness of the mind to an extent, but in no way, should we take them to be ends in themselves. In this sense, *Asaṅga* takes on deeper significance, every time one transcends a level.

But used that we are for living in darkness and dependence and misery, we cannot possibly conceive of a state that is ever free, transcending the pairs of opposites, and light itself. This forces us to keep asking questions like 'what will happen if one overcomes all desires, can such a

---

215 A story from *Bṛhadāraṇyaka Upaniṣad* illustrates this. *Devas,* the divine, *Dānavas,* the demonic and men went to the Creator to ask the meaning of *Dharma,* the way. He said *Da-Da-Da. Devas* or Gods who by nature are sensuously indulgent took it as *Damana,* the control of senses; *Dānavas,* or demons who are cruel by nature, took it as *Dayā,* or compassion; while men who are greedy by nature, took it as *Dāna,* or charity! We have an element of each of the\ three beings in us through sense indulgence, cruelty or and anger, as well as greed.

one continue to live?' or 'will such person have any reason to live?' Or 'what will happen to the world when one attains to the Oneness?' or 'is it not selfish to think of one's own salvation, when there is so much of misery in the world?'.... But we will do well to remember, that all these questions are from the level of mind and intellect, and are raised by them, and used as intravenous injections for their own survival! For the questions are just reflections of the fear arising out of knowledge that enlightenment means, that the mind and intellect and *Ahaṁkāra* lose control over the person and the person will start having control over them; and that all along, the person was *their* instrument and now *they* will be the person's instruments!

There is another trick used by the *Antaḥkaraṇa* or the inner instrument. It starts gathering all the travel details, without really embarking on the journey. Then there is the greater danger of shallow *Pāṇḍitya* or scholarship, which *thinks* that it has known. While the fact is, it is only playing with words! Since the intellect is very articulate, it can *explain* what ought to be and what ought not to be to *others* while fostering and nurturing ignorance within itself! And it has a powerful attraction, because the others will respect such persons who apparently have control over their minds! It is possible that a really ignorant person may succeed in coming out of darkness, but for a scholar, it is very very difficult. Because he is taking his intellectual slumber to be wakefulness!

To avoid such pitfall, the enlightened great have always suggested that the *Śāstras* are meant for *Sādhanā,* and not for intellectual gymnastics. It is for personal guidance of the seeker and not for public debates. Perhaps with this in mind, one is discouraged from discussing religion in some of the organised religions. But they took it too far, reducing religion to some empty gestures. The religion has been—for them—restricted to a particular practice at particular time and place, and the life remains untouched by the practice.

The *Upaniṣads* and other *Śāstras* are mostly the dialogues between the *Guru* and *Śiṣya.* The *Ṛṣis* have accepted the place of intellect in one's being, and have respect for it. So all the questions asked by the disciple are patiently replied initially. But ultimately the disciple is gently guided back to the practice itself, by the *Guru.* And when the seekers continue to remain as seekers of knowledge or information, then the Masters become very strict by not allowing any digression. To make spirituality practical, persons like the Buddha refused to be drawn into *Vāda-Vivāda* or intellectual discussions and arguments.

This *Sarga* begins with a quarry from Rāma as to what happens when the mind is divested of the *Ahaṁkāra* with its illusory form, and what are its distinguishing characteristics. Vasiṣṭha replied:

No desire, illusions and other stains can unsettle a person who is firmly established in his *Ātman,* like water on a lotus leaf. Benevolence and other good qualities start showing themselves, the sins are destroyed; the bond of *Vāsanās* gets loosened; anger and the tendency for desire is eliminated; all impulses of *Kāma* or passion, are dispelled. He will be undisturbed by pleasure and pain; the senses will lose their dominance; there is no *reaction* in the face of adverse pain or sickness afflicting the body.

Continuing Vasiṣṭha told *how* one can attain to this stage: The inquiry 'Who am I?' has the potential of bringing quiescence to mind enabling it to cross the ocean of multiplicity. But even this question can be reached only after seeking replies to questions like 'what is the nature of universe?; what is the use of material enjoyments'?, etc. According to the *Vedas,* such discriminative inquiry is the best means. To illustrate this, Vasiṣṭha narrated the story of Ikṣvāku—the first of the kings from the Solar dynasty, the son of present Manu Vaivasvata.

Ikṣvāku the great king, once asked himself as to what is the stainless cause of the world characterised by dotage, death and decay, pleasure, pain, fancies and misconceptions. In spite of his deep contemplation he was unable to solve the problem. He visited the first Manu Svayaṁbhūva, in *Satyaloka,* the plane of Truth, and sought clarification for his doubts : from where has this universe manifested?; what is its form?; how long will it last?; can one release oneself from the snare of the universe like a bird from its cage?...

Manu was glad to note that they were not ordinary questions meant to appease one's curiosity. So he replied that all the universes which are experienced, really do not exist, but are like the *Gandharva* or imaginary city, or like a mirage in a desert. Only Ātmic Reality is, transcending the mind and senses, unlimited by space and time. All visible objects composed of the five elements are reflections in this great mirror of *Ātman.* The spreading of effulgence of Brahman, gave birth to certain *Śaktis* or potencies, which in turn mingled together to form *Brahmāṇḍa,* the cosmic egg. Some remained unmanifest, while some manifested into the elemental forms. There is nothing like *Bandha* or *Mokṣa,* neither duality nor Oneness, *Brahman* alone is. Like infinite waves, foam emanate from one ocean, everything emanates from the *Cit.* By dispelling the thoughts of bondage and liberation one can be free from all fear and attain the firmness of a rock. Should one associate oneself with *Saṁkalpa Cinmātrajñana* or the Pure-Being gets degraded to the state of *Jīva,* like water transforming into waves, etc. The condition of happiness-sadness-infatuation, etc. is peculiar to mind and not to the *Ātman.*

A discussion can throw more light on the explanation of Svayaṁbhūva Manu. Like the space enclosed by pot, vessel or even house cannot be limited by them and remains unchanged by them during the enclosure, or after the enclosures have fallen, the *Ātman* is never affected by the illusive superimpositions like *Ahaṁkāra, Buddhiḥ, Manas, Indriyas* and body. And these manifestations are nothing but reflections in the mirror which remains unaffected by the object it reflects. Seeing the image of the body, we take It to be the body, as the body is the grossest; image of the mind makes one feel that It is the mind, etc.

A very deep statement is made by the scripture at this juncture:

> 'The invisible *Rahu*[216] is perceived through the eclipsed moon. In the same way, the *Ātman* who is a pure experience is perceived through objects'.[217]

A doubt invariably arises when one understands that if *everything* without exception, exists in and due to the Ultimate Reality, and if one has to ultimately realise that Non-dual state, then why at all these manifestations? One solution to this doubt has been given by realised persons like Shri Aurobindo:

> '...the call of the unknown, the joy of danger and difficulty and adventure, the will to attempt the impossible, to work out the incalculable, the will to create the new and the uncreated with one's own self and life as the material, the fascination of contradictories and their difficult harmonisation... were the temptations that led to the fall'.[218]

Many of the realised persons have observed that the manifestation of the Reality at the grosser levels is actually a fall, and one has to rise to the subtler levels to go nearer the Reality which is the subtlest. Sage Patañjali calls the process

---

216 The earth's shadow is ranked in Hindu astrology as a planet *Rāhu.*

217 अदृश्यो दृश्यते राहुर्गृहीतेन यथेन्दुना ।
तथानुभवमात्रात्मा दृश्येनात्मावलोक्यते ।। 7.13.29 ।।

218 *Letters on Yoga* by Shri Aurobindo, Volume 22, Shri Aurobindo Centenary Library, Deluxe Edition, 1970, p. 29. Refer Story of Ākāśaja The Origin-1'.

of going from manifested stage to the ultimate cause as the act of *Pratiprasava,* re-absorption. But *Yoga Vāsiṣṭha* tries an entirely different approach to explain this, through the above *Śloka.* It more than succeeds in helping a seeker from the level she or he is presently in reaching the ultimate state.

It says that as such, *That State,* transcends all experience of senses, mind and *Ahaṁkāra.* At the same time, the experience is possible only in Its presence, and in Its absence nothing is ever possible! By giving the example of *Rāhu* this scripture illustrates this point. *Kenopaniṣad* clarifies it further:

> 'That which is hearing of our hearing, mind of our mind, speech of our speech, and that too is Life of our life-breath, and sight of our sight. The wise are released as they pass from this world and become immortal.
>
> There sight travels not, nor speech, nor the mind. We know It not, nor can distinguish how one should teach of It; for It is other than the known; It is there above the unknown. This has been declared by the old who brought That to our understanding.
>
> That which is unexpressed by the word, that by which the word is expressed, know That to be the *Brahman* and not this which men follow after here.
>
> That which one thinks not with the mind, That by which the mind is able to think, know That to be the *Brahman* and not this which men follow after here'.[219]

This idea helps a seeker to change his or her attitude towards the so-called disturbance in life. The senses and *Manas* which is connected with their activity mostly cause

---

219 श्रोत्रस्य श्रोत्रं मनसो मनो यद्वाचो ह वाचं स उ प्राणस्य प्राणः ।
चक्षुषश्चक्षुरतिमुच्य धीराः प्रेत्यास्माल्लोकादमृता भवन्ति ॥ 1.2 ॥
न तत्र चक्षुर्गच्छति न वाग्गच्छति नो मनः न विद्मो न विजानीमो यथैतदनुशिष्यात् ।

restlessness. With the idea that they are after all, the ways in which the Reality expresses Itself, the seeker will at least not treat them as the enemies, and stop *fighting!*

Svayaṁbhūva Manu said: that one should look upon the organs in the same indifferent manner in which a wayfarer regards the objects on his way. It is not proper on the seeker's part to either desire or hate the organs, since the body and other objects are the result of past actions and will inevitably come to be. So the best way is to give them up mentally, and making one's mind calm without the feverish thirst. The identification of the 'I' with the body produces the bondage of existence. This does not happen to the aspirant after liberation when the aspirant becomes the nature of *Cinmātra.* The impartial wisdom of such a person becomes all pervading and shines on all forms like sun's rays, and enters the heart of all beings like gold in the golden ornaments. He becomes like an ocean which remains unaffected in spite of all the rivers flowing into it. Like a mother who, forgetful of the child that rests on her bosom becomes afflicted at heart and searches everywhere for it, so people without cognising the *Ātman* within, which transcends birth and death, suffer all sorts of grief, imagining that they have no protector, or that they are destroyed with the destruction of the body nourished by food.

Like water generating waves through agitation in it, through excess of *Saṁkalpa,* delusions of *Citta* increase greatly. But should the *Saṁkalpa* be removed through concentration on the *Ātman* one can maintain the calm and quietude even

---

अन्यदेव तद्विदितादथो अविदितादधि इति शुश्रुम पूर्वेषां ये नस्तद्व्याचचक्षिरे ॥ 1.3 ॥

यद्वाचाऽनभ्युदितं येन वागभ्युद्यते ।
तदेव ब्रह्म त्वं विद्धि नेदं यदिदमुपासते ॥ 1.4 ॥

यन्मनसा न मनुते येनाहुर्मनो मतम् ।
तदेव ब्रह्म त्वं विद्धि नेदं यदिदमुपासते ॥ 1.5 ॥

amidst the tossing waves of the ocean of *Saṁsāra*. The *Ātman* through its *Kriyā-Śakti,* the creative potency, creates diverse objects, and through *Samhāra-Śakti* or destructive potency, brings about the quiescence. Like precious gems displaying lustre with the shining sun, or the fruits and leaves coming out of the tree, or the drops of water in the mountain torrents, the illusory world of *Buddhiḥ,* etc. producing activity, arises out of Brahman. To those who have not cognised *Brahman* this universe appears real and generates pain. The power of *Māyā* is such that though the *Ātman* is ever present and permeates all levels, It deludes men through *Māyā* stopping them from cognising their own *Ātman.*

Manu blessed king Ikṣvāku that he sever the thoughts of differentiation through non-involvement and to attain the State of *Brahman.* Continuing, he suggested that *Prajñā* should be developed through a deep study of the *Jñāna-Śāstras* and association of the wise. This *Śubhecchā,* or aspiration, forms the first *Yoga-Bhūmikā* or stage of *Yoga.* Ceaseless *Ātma-Vicāra* constitutes the second stage, *Asaṅga* or non-attachment is the third stage; the fourth stage destroys *Vāsanās* from their root. In the fifth, one starts being in the bliss within one-self, to attain *Jīvanamukti.* The sixth stage is characterised by total bliss, devoid of any recognition of external stimuli.

The seventh is the stage of *Mokṣa,* whole, immaculate, and quiescent. Of these seven stages, the first three may be included under *Jāgradavasthā,* the wakeful state. The fourth stage, in which all universes appear like a dream, falls under *Swapna,* dream state. The fifth stage, which is filled with bliss alone, comes under the category of *Suṣupti,* the deep sleep. That which is of nature of being filled with bliss alone, the sixth stage comes under *Turya* or the fourth. Then comes *Turīyātīta,* or that which transcends *Turya,* the seventh stage beyond the reach of everything.

If one develops equanimity during the pairs of opposites, one gradually attains the state of *Jīvanamukti,* no matter whether he involves himself in actions or not, whether he is a householder or an ascetic, whether he is conscious of the body or not. Such a one never droops in spirit, since there is conviction that one neither dies nor lives, neither exists nor cease to exist. There is no mind with its *Vāsanās* forcing one to cling to anything. An object enjoyed through *Vāsanās* begets a train of pleasures, but when it perishes it invariably brings in pain. It is a fact that majority of mankind does not seek to liberate themselves from pleasure and pain which are so inter blended that they manifest themselves together, and disappear together.

When the *Vāsanās* decay, the effects of past actions drop off on their own. As long as the *Ātman* rests in the desire, so long will it be termed *Jīva.* Desires arise out of *Aviveka* or non-discrimination and die out with the rise of *Viveka* or discrimination. It is the duty of those who wish to end rebirth to venerate such exalted persons who have attained *Jīvanamukti,* and seek their company which is enough to confer gifts of *Tapas,* and to free themselves through *Jñāna.* Having thus taught king Ikṣvāku, Manu retreated to his abode, so concluded the great sage Vasiṣṭha.

Horizon has been a source of attraction for man from times immemorial. It is the conceptual place where the sky meets the earth. It is but *an idea.* It is appears near, yet it is far away. The more one tries to go near it the more elusive it gets. The nature of sky is such that it cannot possibly meet the earth. In this sense, it is identical to human beings. In human being, consciousness meets matter. An impossible thing has apparently happened in humankind. He is *conscious of his body and mind.* In reality however, it only *appears* to be so, because by its very nature consciousness cannot meet matter. He is only a bridge between them, if he uses the bridge through non-involvement, he can attain to the state of transcendence, but if he misuses it through indulgence, involvement and identification then he continues to be what he is: a restless, discontent and miserable being. But the restlessness is also the sign of the consciousness rebelling to come out of the cage of matter. Ultimately it has to succeed, for it is against its very nature to be caged.

No wonder horizon has always fascinated human kind!

16

The Story of a Muni and a Hunter

Once there lived a very wise and venerable sage. From one end of the land to the other, learned men began to hear of the old sage and soon many sought visage of his wisdom. But silent remained the sage to all who came with questions. Instead, with his bamboo staff he drew upon the ground these words :

'One who has contentment in his heart
finds good everywhere
and at all times'.

Or sometimes he would write:

'Where discontentment exists,
all effort is in vain'.

Or sometimes:

'Be silent, be still and you will know'.

But those who visited seemed not satisfied with these answers. They were cryptic and there was no guidance given —no map delivered. And they would not understand why the sage refused to answer them directly. And why? Surely he knew the answers, but why did he choose to scratch in the sand such babblings? The other sages gave advice and prescribed paths, and talked of austerities to be observed, why not this one? The sermon he gave could not be heard by the ear, or for that matter seen by the eye.

Yet it is written that during the feast of Christ a young man appeared. No staff bore he, nor the scrolls of wisdom, nor were there questions at his tongue. Only in his eyes there was purpose and great passion. Straight on to the sage strode he. Neither sitting, stopping nor prostrating himself as others had done. He gazed upon that ancient and tranquil face without word. And soon, to the amazement of the others he took the staff from the hand of the sage and drew upon the dusty earth these words:

'How does thy brightness
dispel the darkness?'

Patiently the sage took back his staff and stretched beneath the young man's ply:

'What darkness?
Are you lost in darkness?'

To which the young pilgrim countered :

'Is getting lost, losing way?
Is getting lost really getting lost?'

The silent sage contemplated the face of the young pilgrim for some time and then drew upon the ground these words :

'Only forgotten'.

A roar of laughter went up from those who had gathered, and the sage erased what he had written and wrote again:

'What desire brings you here?'

Eager eyes watched the staff change hands:

'Desires...? I have none'.

Observing the pilgrim closely, the sage took his staff, rose to his feet, extended his right foot, tapped it three times, then became still as the breaths of those who watched. Whereupon the young visitor broke his silence and asked 'Why did you do that'?

The sage quickly scratched:
'Curiosity is a form of desire'.

Back and forth the staff continued until the frustrated pilgrim cried back with the point of the staff:

'It has been said
that there is a sacred Mantra one may recite
that will join him to the universe in oneness'.

The sage quickly scratched again:

'Have you ever been
apart from the universe'?

And with that the old sage swiftly raised his staff and tapped it down upon the head of the seeker, sending him into a deeply blissful trance. Days passed. And in those days the young pilgrim truly began to savour the sweetness of the great sage, as he sat surrendered before him. Not once did he question in the presence, and a fathomless love grew between them. But on the third day the sage broke his long years of silence. 'So you have come at last'! the hoarse voice came.

The young man replied not, but looked deeply into the sage's eyes for some time, then taking once again the staff from the old bony hands wrote:

'Only remembered'.[220]

This is our own story. All *Swādhyāya* and *Sādhanā,* is meant to eliminate the forgetfulness caused by the stupor of involvement and identification. Most of us are in a kind of metaphysical sleep characterised by the intoxication of *Saṁkalpa* and *Ahaṁkāra.* We go after the stones and rocks rejecting the precious gems in front of us. We choose temporary, pain-bearing experiences instead of the everlasting and the infinite bliss. The habit of eons has made us forget

220 A story by Ken Reed which appeared in an old magazine, collected from a friend's diary.

our own nature, and seek to go after Its reflection in objects and people. We attempt to understand ourselves through the opinion of other people. Naturally misery has to follow.

Many, if not most of us, are not even aware of the misery hidden behind every act of ours. Like the camel eating thorns, or a dog chewing a bone to savour the taste of its own blood, we have started *enjoying* our misery. Even our so-called humour is based on misery as it has insult for others if not our own selves. We are over eager to put the blame on others for our fate. While most of it is self-created, if not in the present life, definitely in lives earlier.

When a person intends becoming a pilgrim instead of being an aimless wanderer, one has to assume complete responsibility for all actions and their consequences. The mind starts getting *centered,* from the energy dissipating randomness, as it starts coming back to itself. With this begins a journey within, during which one begins to discover the ways of mind, observe the dance of thought and emotions and come to recognise one's own mistakes as being the cause for either happiness or misery in one's life which are obverse and reverse of the same coin.

The most important aspect of *Jñāna-Sādhanā* is to reduce the limiting indulgence and involvement of the consciousness. *Vedānta* tries to give hints to seekers by making them aware of the different approaches to tackle the problem. The main aim of all these methods is to bring about *Aṅtarmukhatā.* This *Sarga* gives one more approach.

The experiencer of the pairs of opposites is *Ahaṁkāra,* the 'I', and it flows into three *Avasthās* or states of *Jāgrat, Swapna* and *Suṣupti,* that is, wakeful, dream and deep sleep respectively. Most of us are conscious of our activity and transactions taking place during the wakeful state. But generally, we tend to discount our existence during the sleep and dream states which constitute nearly a third of our life on earth. And yet, all the three states of wakeful, dream and deep sleep are so closely connected, that they affect one another. For instance, if one is disturbed by anxiety and worry, one has a disturbed sleep, with disturbing dreams. On the contrary, if one has relaxed wakeful state, one experiences a relaxed sleep with perhaps equally pleasant reams! But then the task of a seeker is not just to have a relaxation in the three states, but to transcend *all activity*.

On being questioned by Rāma as to the traits of the *Jīvanamuktas,* or those who have realised the Brahman while living, who do not pay any attention to the psychic powers, Vasiṣṭha said: The wisdom of the *Jñānī* lies in getting absorbed in the delight of Non-dual *Ātman*. Having achieved rest in the *Ātman,* all the psychic powers dissolve into insignificance. The psychic powers are sought by *Siddhas* through expansion and intense effort. The *Atmajñānīs* do not belong to this class *since they have freed themselves from all traces of desire.* Desire, anger, pain, greed, and others dwindle into insignificance.

Like a noble person degrading himself into a lowly one, through the limiting action and behaviour, the Reality *reduces* Itself into a *Jīva.* The cause for such degradation is not there on this plane of mind and intellect. But having reduced or contracted from all expansiveness to a limiting existence, *Jīvas* flourish and subject themselves to rebirth through *Karmas* or actions performed by them. Though there is no cause for the rise of *Jīvas* or beings, their existence and *Karmas* are reciprocally the cause and effect of one another. All *Jīvas* arise without cause, out of Brāhmic State, yet their *Karmas* are the cause of their pleasure and pain. And *Saṁkalpa* arising from the delusion which is ignorance of *Ātman* is the cause of all *Karmas.*

As the cause of bondage is *Saṁkalpa,* it should be uprooted completely. The destruction of *Saṁkalpa* is itself *Mokṣa,* which is to be practised with higher or subtler mind. *Be aware* whenever there is perception of sense objects by slowing down the identification of the experiencer with the experienced. This can bring about the destruction of *Saṁkalpa.* One should not identify oneself with *Grāhya,* the experienced or object, nor should one identify with the *Grāhaka* or the experiencer. Having given up all *sense of becoming,* One merges with What remains. When the sense organs are enslaved by their objects along with the mind, the ensuing desires cause bondage, while non-attraction constitutes *Mokṣa.* If there is *any* attraction in mind it is bondage, the state of complete non-attraction is liberation. That is why one should free from all attractions subtle and gross, from a blade of grass up to gold.

When there is no desire, what can there be to feed upon, to perform or to abandon? One is neither the agent nor enjoyer. The wise can never grieve over the past, nor worry about the future. They are always in present. Pride, illusion and desire are the binding cords of the mind. The lower mind is to be dissolved with the help of higher mind itself. It is the iron which is cold, cleaving iron which is hot, or the dirt which is soap, removing dirt from the cloth, or venom with the help of an antidote which is also a poison.

In the few paragraphs above, many interesting working facts are presented for a seeker, which command a discussion.

The first and the foremost premise which forms the basis of *Vedānta* is that we all are trying to achieve or be *what we already are.* The only problem *Vedānta* claims, is that we all have forgotten our true nature. This state of forgetfulness of one's own nature has been called as the *fall* by this scripture. This fall results in the vicious circle of wrong action of *contraction* or of limiting the limitless. Then it becomes like a person in the marsh, who due to panic gets more entangled in the quicksand. To discourage a seeker from falling for the temptation of asking the question 'why' of this fall, the scripture clearly says that it is causeless. This *fallen state* is called as the *Jīva,* and the *Saṁkalpa* is the activity that brings about further contraction. These form the causes for further identification, involvement, and indulgence.

Indulgence increases the involvement which in turn is the progenitor of desires. *Vāsiṣṭha* gives a technique of thinning the desires through the *awareness* that is to be developed *during* the contact of the senses with their objects and slowly separating the experiencer from the object. At this juncture, *Vāsiṣṭha* gives the most wonderful hint on the origin of all desire as the *sense of becoming*, a wish or an aspiration of becoming something or someone, other than what one is already not. Thus the sage warns Rāma of the subtle and the gross desires.

This happens to be a very valuable point for the seeker at all stages of his journey. The play of desires is very very complex and subtle! A person gives up comforts to achieve a goal which again is a desire, may be *gift-wrapped!* The *expectation* in any form, in lieu to *any* action is a desire. For example, if one *expects* to *achieve* enlightenment, *after* giving up all desires, then one is only playing another subtle hide and seek with desire! In continuation of this very hint, the scripture says that in fact, one is neither the *Kartā,* the doer, nor *Bhoktā,* the experiencer. This understanding frees one from time, in the form of the past and the future.

Vasiṣṭha continued: The *Jīva* has three forms, namely the gross, the subtle, and the Transcendental. Dwelling on the Transcendental, the other two fall off. The gross body with the senses and organs is meant for the *Jīva,* to experience the elemental. The mind with its *Saṁkalpa,* produces the conception of *Saṁsāra* is *Ātivāhika* or the subtle body. While the Transcendental is *Satyam,* or Truth Eternal, *Nirvikalpa,* or without *any* activity, and Pure Consciousness. This is characterised by the *Turya,* the Fourth. Remaining in the Fourth, the first two get rejected.

At these words of Vasiṣṭha, Rāma requested him to describe in detail the *Turya* which transcends the three states of *Jāgrat, Swapna* and *Suṣupti.* Vasiṣṭha replied: The state of consciousness in which the conception of 'I' and 'Not-I' is totally absent and Pure, as It is devoid of even a trace of attachment, is called as *Turya.* That which is stainless, balanced and quiescent state of *Jīvanamukti* is *Turya.* It is neither *Jāgrat* nor *Swapna* which are dominated by *Saṁkalpa,* nor is it *Suṣupti* as there is no knowledge of enjoyment. For those who have attained to this quiescent and beneficent and lofty state, this world itself is *Turya* and for those who have not, it is multiple and diverse. With the idea of 'I' gone, one sees all things equally, and performs actions in such an unattached way, that it is as if they have not performed the actions at all.

For illustrating his statements, Vasiṣṭha narrated a story. In a forest lived a *Tapasvin* or recluse who had achieved the state of *Mahāmouna.* A hunter who was an expert archer approached the *Muni* and asked him whether he had seen a stag escaping his arrows. The *Tapasvin* replied that being recluses living in the forest, they never involve themselves in the activity of *Ahaṁkāra.* It is the mind that associates itself with the organs and the actions. It was long since he had freed himself from *Ahaṁkāra.* And he had not known the difference between waking, dreaming and the deep-sleep states. At that moment he was in the *Turya* state. Without understanding whatever the *Muni* had said, the hunter left the place.

Concluding the story Vasiṣṭha said that there is no state other than *Turya;* the *Jñāna* divested of all its diversity or multiplicity is *Turya.* The *Jāgrat* is associated with terrible or gross actions; the *Swapna* with peaceful or subtle actions while the *Suṣupti* with ignorant actions. When the gross mind is dead, and one is established in the *Sattwic* equipoise, only then does a *Yogi* attains to That State. Only such *Munis* who have transcended all *Saṁkalpa* established in Self and quiescence are in *Turya* and are ever-free.

One of the greatest contributions of modern science, especially in the late nineteenth and the twentieth century's is speed. Whether it is travel or communication or manufacture, speed has affected our life style. It has its advantages, like improvement of the comfort level, elimination of the so-called deadly diseases, etc. As has already been mentioned elsewhere in this study, in the external life, goals and effort to achieve them, dreams and a will to realise them are almost mandatory. Without them, life as such will be synonymous with vegetation. India is a very good example. Centuries of foreign oppression and slavery has robbed us of the capacity to even dream. Most in our country still continue to struggle for survival, so much so that we do not have any idea as to what is happening to our country.

But the speed also has its disadvantages : life has become very fast, tense, and is filled with avoidable worry and misery. This is because, life needs are *not just* external, and there are internal needs as well. Else, there would be no misery in the affluent class of people whose external needs have been more than fulfilled. This is because it is the rule of the nature that when the needs of a grosser level are met, the hungers of the subtler level start afflicting man. And one *cannot* adopt the same approach to fulfill the subtler need. *Saṁkalpa* is mandatory for the gross, while the same *Saṁkalpa* is detrimental to the subtle. But most of us habitually understand and act as we do in the external or the gross world. So for us, *quietening of mind also becomes a goal* and we start *working with the same attitude.* Even our *Sādhanā* is governed by speed, competition, effort and anxiety!

For example, when we begin the quest, our most predominant question is 'what should I *do*'? In the process, we forget that for calming down all one has to do—if the word *do* is to be used, is not to *do* anything, but just wait patiently, to *allow* the activity to calm down. Another thing which shows itself in most seekers is the impatience to *reach* the goal. We invariably connect our practices with time. We constantly ask, 'In spite of practising whatever has been suggested for *six months,* why is it that I do not see any results'? Such attitude makes us restless with expectation, and when we fail—as the expectation is never fulfilled, we experience depression. Because by its very nature, expectation breeds in more restlessness, and what we are trying to do is to reduce this very restlessness!

This *Sarga* offers a general rule for the seeker through the following *Ślokas*:

> 'Become aware of the non-changing Principle, during the meeting of *Grāhya* or object and *Grāhaka* or the subject by *slowly* removing the speed of involvement.
>
> 'Do not identify with the object, and do not identify with the subject; giving up all identification, become That'.[221]

Whether it is during the sense perception, or the internal experiences like the three states of consciousness *Jāgrat, Swapna* and *Suṣupti,* normally we are not aware of the involvement, as it is very sudden. One is suggested to slow down the process so that one becomes aware of the mechanism of awareness. *Meditation is this process of slowing down each and every act.* Consequently, it follows that it is not really connected with any posture of the body. When each action becomes *meditative,* then and only then can one hope to attain *Aṅtarmukhatā.*

One of the persons who gave a very practical way of achieving this slowness, through the technique of observation, was the Buddha. In his path, he suggested one to observe the

---

221 सावधानो भव त्वं च ग्राह्यग्राहकसंगमे ।
अजस्रमेव संकल्पदशाः परिहरञ्शनैः ।। 6.14.13 ।।
मा भव ग्राह्यभावात्मा ग्राहकात्मा च मा भव ।
भावनामखिलां त्यक्त्वा यच्छिष्टं तन्मयो भव ।। 6.14.14 ।।

in-coming and out-going breath, without changing the mode of breathing. This he called as the *Ānāpāna-Sati,* or remembrance of the in-going and out-going breath. After tackling the mind at the gross level, he suggested that the attention be shifted to the different sensations on the body, and then mind, etc. This has been called as *Vipassanā,* the special way of seeing. The most important thing is that the seeker is suggested to remember *all the time and at all stages of his Sādhanā,* is *never to get involved with whatever he is observing.*

The rules that govern the physical world need not be relevant to the inner world. This is a very useful hint that this scripture has to offer to those who are interested to transcend all activity, change and the consequent pairs of opposites.

All spiritual practices are meant to bring the aspirant to the point of *'Āhā'!!,* that is, the stage of recollection of his real nature, that has always been his.

17

The Seven Stages of Yoga-I

The region has been aptly named *Maḷenadu,* the land of rain, as this coastal area opening itself to the Arabian Sea on the western side and guarded by the *Sahyadri* mountains in the east, has the most intense monsoon in the state of Karnataka. One of the most important rivers in the state is the Sharavati. She meanders gracefully down the plateau where the Western Ghats or *Sahyadri* as they are known, merge with the *Nilagiris* or the Blue Mountains. The tropical forests on these immovables are thick with ancient trees, creepers, and bushes. The rich flora and the fauna make it an ideal locale for trekking enthusiasts and other adventurers. The river drops suddenly into a gorge nearly nine hundred feet below by dividing herself into four streams named *Raja,* the king, *Rani,* the queen, *Rocket,* and *Rover.* The sight itself can be so absorbing that, it is quite easy to lose oneself in admiration. The spot is called the Jog Falls.

More than a hundred years back, this beautiful place was popularised by a British surveyor, who had spontaneously exclaimed :

> '*Oh, what a wondrous sight!* I only hope it is protected from man's greed'!

A few years later, M. Vishweshwarayya, the famous Engineer on seeing this great falls uttered:

> '*Oh, what a waste of energy*'*!*

He planned a hydro-electric power station downstream, which became a major source of energy for the state! The Jog falls are still a great tourist attraction. During the monsoon, thousands of people come from all over the world to enjoy the beauty and to carry home with them the pleasant memories. A tourist car with a businessman and his family from Ahmadabad stopped on the road overlooking the great falls. As he got down along with others, he asked the accompanying guide as to why the car was stopped. The guide using his talent at his control, showed dramatically the falls, and described the four streams, the height and other details. The businessman was clearly not impressed for he said in a mood of dejection:

> 'We made this trip all the way only to see some water falling down? *Oh, what a waste of money*'!

It was the same spot. But three different persons responded to it in three different ways. And the funniest part is that *all of them were right in their own points of view!* That is because each one of us lives in one's own self-created world.

To prove the defects in the witness method of judiciary in solving crime, a well known lawyer invited some intellectuals, and enacted a crime sequence in presence of ten chosen persons. These ten persons were asked to go out of the hall and wait outside. One by one the witnesses were called to give their observations. And there were ten different versions! This is because each one of us perceives the world not *as it is,* but as it *appears to each of us* through our individual spectacles, of nature, impressions and training. And yet, there is a common thread as it were, which joins all the different coloured flowers blossoming in the garden of consciousness.

The *Ṛṣis* were highly successful in giving panacea for the ills ailing mankind, as they recognised and accepted the diversity existing in human nature. The methods are suggestions to help the human beings by initiating the change from the level each person is in. Spirituality is the journey of the human being from the gross level, when she or he is identified with the body, to the subtlest, when there is merging with the Universal. And the scriptures give all the details required by the pilgrim.

The milestones or the stations on way, indicate the extent to which one has progressed in one's journey. Similarly, there are different stages one has to pass through while undertaking the journey within. To know *for oneself,* the extent to which one has progressed, the *Ṛṣis* have roughly sketched a map. A sincere seeker has no time to look and judge others, but it is good to remember that this map is to be used for *self-evaluation* and *not for judging others!* This ultimate *Sarga* in a way is an essence of all the details given out by the book.

Sage Vasiṣṭha continued: Certain *Ātma-Jñāna Śāstras* conclude that the whole world should be seen as a dream. The truth is, neither *Avidyā* nor *Māyā* exist, *Brahman* which is quiescence itself, alone Is. Abiding in all, It is the immaculate *Cidākāśa.* Diverse men superimpose attributes upon the Non-dual. Some call it void; some *Parameśvara;* and some others *Mahā-Vijñāna.* Preferably one should avoid all attributes, to rest in silence. The transcendence is devoid of all mental activity, and an abode of tranquility. This state can be achieved only by continual *Antarmukhatā* and total non-involvement with the body-sense-mind activity. Having established in the Self, one can perform actions outside, by remaining unaffected inside.

The mental activity increases the pleasure and pain, and when it is quietened, the pairs of opposites can be transcended. One should remain unaffected during the painful and pleasurable situations through balanced mind. If one wishes to free oneself from endless births and deaths, one should neither seek pleasure, nor avoid pain, *nor seek the middle.* Only by increasing the non-involvement can one hope to transcend misery. One whose being is filled with the cool elixir of the Be-ness of all planes is in *Mokṣa,* though performing all actions is not really performing them.

Once again, *Vāsiṣṭha* gives a *password* or a master-key as it were in these opening verses: non-involvement at all the levels of body, sense, *Manas, Buddhiḥ,* and *Ahaṁkāra.* A paradoxical statement is made by sage Vasiṣṭha when he suggests that one should not seek or put one's effort to achieve *even the middle.* It can be understood, that one should not seek pleasure, as this creates a positive involvement, and avoiding pain causes a negative involvement. But pointing to the *middle* or a state in-between, he does in no way mean transcendence, but an act of *ignoring* them both which has a subtle involvement of *avoiding* them both! Even this has to be shunned by developing the non-involved observation, that is, by becoming a *Draṣṭā.* Like a light bulb which lights up the place without bothering to care about the activity going below it.

Rāma asked about the means by which the seven *Jñāna* stages can be practised, and the characteristics of those *Jñānīs* who have cognised them. Vasiṣṭha replied, that there are two types of people in the world: *Pravṛtta*—those who still have faith in desire, and *Nivṛtta*—those who have started understanding the limitations of desire. A *Pravṛtta* is one who doubts and belittles that which cannot be perceived by the senses, and chooses to gratify the body, senses, mind and *Ahaṁkāra.* Such persons consider the aspiration for Self-realisation as the choice of the lazy people. Like a tortoise thrusting out its neck through a hole in a rock in the ocean, a *Pravṛtta* develops discrimination after several births.

A tortoise dwelling in a hole on the rocky shores of the ocean extends its head and legs and is at once lashed by a wave. It immediately retracts into the hole, withdrawing all the organs. As the wave recedes the tortoise comes out again, and is again hit by the wave. This is the story of man. When he enters life, waves of the *Saṁsāric* Ocean, characterised by involvement in the pairs of opposites and repeated life and death, give him constant blows. The entry is like the act of sticking out its head by the tortoise, and his death is like that of its withdrawal. When this happens repeatedly, gradually man starts thinking of an alternative way of life. This is when *Viveka* dawns on such a person. *Viveka* is a development of consciousness which analyses and helps in assessing life and its purpose. Sage then described the observations of such a person.

The ordinary values governing the life have no substance. They are repetitive bringing about boredom, making life insipid and wasteful. When such thoughts bring about a conviction that one wants the supreme peace which transcends all action, one becomes a *Nivṛtta.* How can one develop non-attachment to cross over the ocean of *Saṁsāra?* With such inquiry, one becomes wise and develops a kind of distaste for the act of desiring itself, and starts deriving joy out of noble acts that are spontaneous and unselfish. Such person avoids base and energy dissipating activity, criticism of others, and opts to perform meritorious action. He is also aware of the binding action and avoids it. He speaks and does only the best things at appropriate time and place; his words and actions are full of love, compassion and sympathy. Such a person is said to have reached *Śubhecchā,* the first stage of *Jñāna.* His thoughts, word and deed reflect the fragrance of goodness and nobility. Such a person tries to study spiritual books even if they are rare. With his effort to bring about a transformation in the quality of his life, he comes to be called as *Ārya.*

Many a time, whenever some problems stare at us or incidents traumatise us, we generally tend to take refuge in the *so-called* religion. A discourse here, a visit to a holy place there, gives us a relief and it also rejuvenates us to *involve* in life with fresh vigour! It is *almost like* the *change* which is sought by many in sense enjoyment or drinking, the basic difference being, in the type of forgetfulness they bring about! This is not to belittle the importance of either discourse or pilgrimage. Many of us have the conviction that changing *a milieu or action is enough to change oneself.* We will do well to remember, that the fundamental change can be effected only when this is eliminated. An illustration can clarify this point further.

The best time for observing this, is when there is unpleasantness in relationships. Instead of trying to find out whether there is any expectation, or jealousy, or selfishness or any other mental attitude which is responsible for the relationship to get sour, if one changes the person, the same thing gets repeated with other persons. For that matter, with a sense experience, when one gets bored, one goes on changing the sense objects instead of finding out what in the first place, caused boredom. If the interest in spirituality is such a change of milieu or objects, then it *cannot* be *Śubhecchā* or aspiration. However, if either the discourse or any other experience brings about a basic change in the behaviour as described above, it is *Śubhecchā.* A person in the stage of *Śubhécchā* has diagnosed his illness as an internal problem almost independent of the external circumstances. Only such person can be called as an *Ārya.* So the *Āryans* need not be really the people who supposedly migrated from Central Asia.

The sage described the characteristics of the second *Bhūmikā* or stage. He enters the second stage in the path of *Jñāna* called *Vicāra.* Such a one approaches the Self-realised Persons who have mastered the *Śāstras* to get the real and essential interpretation of *Śrutis* or *Upaniṣads, Smṛtis* or the code of conduct, *Sadācāra* or imbibing what is given therein, *Dhāraṇā, Dhyāna,* etc. Discriminating between the Real and the unreal, he knows which actions are to be performed and which to be avoided, like the master of the house acquainting himself perfectly with his domestic affairs. Like a serpent discarding its worn skin, he easily casts away arrogance, vanity, quarrelsome disposition, religious hypocrisy, sensuality and dependence on external things for his happiness. Obtaining a new awakening by association of the saintly wise he starts having a perfect and complete grasp of the true significance of the *Śāstras*. A little explanation on the traits and characteristics peculiar to this *Bhūmikā* will be worthwhile.

The foremost eligibility of a person to enter this second stage has been described indirectly here. When a person is convinced that the happiness and sadness are only states of mind that are not dependent on the external objects, such a one *walks out of* vanity and other binding habits, like a snake moulting its skin. This is because all our appendages like vanity, exaggeration, arrogance, etc. are there because of this stubborn conviction. On entering this second stage, the person approaches the Realised Saints. This can also be interpreted as: *on entering into this stage the person is able to recognise such Men,* because many a time, the person may be very much present right in front of us. But our *preoccupation* with other external things may stop us from recognising them. Someone has rightly said that the Realised Persons always inhabit the earth, but recognising and taking their help depends on the priorities we keep!

There is another useful interpretation of the words *Śruti, Smṛti,* and *Sadācāra*: *Śruti* can be taken as the *Śravaṇa* or listening to the lofty truths described by the realised saints or by the sacred lore. *Smṛti* is the constant remembrance of these truths so as to keep the mischief of the activity of the mind at bay. And *Sadācāra* is acting in accordance with these very truths. That is, to keep the thought, word and deed in tune with whatever is given by the sacred lore or wise men.

Sage Vasiṣṭha described the entry into the third *Bhūmikā:* One glides into the third stage called *Asaṁsaṅga,* the unattached state, as a bridegroom falls onto the soft bridal bed. One fixes one's mind on the ultimate essence of the *Śāstras* and goes to the *Āśramas* of realised sages for having dialogues on the technique of Self-realisation. The sages also teach one how to get rid of the binding aspects of *Saṁsāra* and develop *Vairāgya.* Thus one lives without fear, care or worry—whether one is on a rock or a nice bed, as it will be the same. The seeker, who has known the Divine Law and is in harmony with it, spends the time peacefully with the unique joy of *Asaṁsaṅga,* whether in a city or a forest. Study of *Jñāna-Śāstras* and by following their essence in life, the *animal* called man has a wonderful glimpse of the Reality.

The glimpse as it is referred to above should not be taken as the enlightenment. But as an inkling into the state which transcends all activity and involvement. Apparently it appears as though the activity and involvement is mandatory, but it is discovered by such person, that the unchanging principle behind all, is the *Sākṣī,* the uninvolved witness, who has seen the different stages and experiences of life and hence separate from the happenings themselves. But just having a glimpse is not enough, the following verses explain how one can strengthen and stabilise the stage.

The third *Bhūmikā* awakens the seeker. *Asaṁsaṅga* is of two types: ordinary and extraordinary. The ordinary *Asaṁsaṅga* has the constant *Bhāva* or mood, that one is neither the experiencer nor the actor, neither is one conditioned nor does one condition others. One's joys and sorrows are the result of the past *Karma.* Everything is done by the Divine alone. Whether one is having *Sukha* or *Dukkha,* how can their agency be attributed to anyone? Excessive enjoyment is really a source of fatal illnesses. All wealth is a source of great dangers. All unions have innate separation in them. Everything ultimately results in mental agony, physical pain and anxieties. *Kāla* or time is projecting things like a magician. Whatever is there in the world as an entity, will be destroyed and absorbed back by *Kāla.*

The greatest enemy is of a *Sādhaka* is the forgetfulness. It is so very easy to resort back to the old habit of involvement and indulgence as it is an ancient and stubborn habit. In the four preceding verses *Vāsiṣṭha* gives the different methods by which one can develop the *Samyak-Smṛti* or the memory of That. One of the primary nooses that tie us down to the world is the identification with the experience and action. In fact, it is the experience that makes us extroverts and action which binds us to the world. The constant remembrance that 'I am neither the *Bhoktā* nor the *Kartā*' can be a very good method of contemplation. The other suggestions: to attribute all the cause of the present state of affairs to the past actions; to transfer all agency to the Divine; to constantly remember that this world of objects is transient and constantly changing, and there is no exception to it as *Kāla* destroys everything, are the various moods by which one can keep alive the memory of the *Sākṣī,* the uninvolved Witness. When one keeps the memory of the *Sākṣī* alive the *apartness* from all activity gets more prominent. Sage Vasiṣṭha then proceeded to tell about the supreme *Asaṁsaṅga.*

With the association of the wise, the dissociation of the binding and also constant practice of the moods such as 'I am not the doer, nor the experiencer, nor the bound nor even the binding', one takes leave of the limiting tendencies of the mind. By sincere effort and will power one is able to behold the truth as if holding a gooseberry in one's palm. When this happens, even the moods 'I am not the doer or all things happen due to *Karma*' etc., will then be thrown away. The essence of the Supreme Cause, which transcends the ocean of *Saṁsāra,* seat of Great Silence and Quiescence, is called the supreme *Asaṁsaṅga.* It is neither within nor without; neither below nor above; neither in the eight directions, nor in the sky; neither in the material objects nor again in emptiness; neither is it in inert things nor in the conscious mind. That splendid state is called the supreme *Asaṁsaṅga* which is the ultimate refuge of all things, by whose power all things are revealed, but itself cannot be revealed by anything, which cannot be thought of, which has neither an origin nor end and is *Śānta,* supremely peaceful.

The state is sweet, blissful and satisfying; it is the offshoot of all virtues and noble acts. It is riding on the top of the flame of *Citta.* Realising this state brings an end to all trials and tribulations in life and obstacles to peace and bliss. The third *Bhūmikā* will bear fruit of supreme non-attachment when the lotus of *Viveka* blossoms forth with the sunrise of *Vicāra.*

Each of these first three states is very important. As if to reiterate this fact Sage Vasiṣṭha repeated, how one should journey through the first three stages. The first *Bhūmikā* dawns in the heart, through the contact of pure souls, combined with the accumulated effect of the noble deeds, as it happens in the case of a ripe palm fruit falling down when a crow casually sits on it. The small offshoot bearing traces of pure bliss, shooting up with the contact of great souls has to be protected, nourished with effort, using the water of discrimination. By nurturing, with systematic *Vicāra,* this joy, which is an infinitesimal fraction of the bliss of the Self, has to be developed just like the farmer taking care of the young offshoots every day. The third *Bhūmikā* will bring forth the supreme *Asaṁsaṅga,* wherein the seeker relinquishes the mind itself which is so full of thoughts, feelings and imagination.

If one has to cross these stages in the journey towards Self, a natural doubt crosses the mind of a seeker. This doubt was voiced by Rāma, our representative: How can *Mukti* be attained by the unintelligent, born in bad families, who are involved in binding activity, who are of low character and who never come across saints and *Yogis?* Moreover, if a person dies having reached the first, the second or the third *Bhūmikās,* what is the fate of such a person?

Sage Vasiṣṭha replied: The ignorant, who has all evils in him, will have to struggle through hundreds of births until such time when he comes to the first *Bhūmikā.* Or the contact with and compassion of the experienced wise, a critical observation of life in the world starts in him bringing in *Vairāgya.* This can occur sometimes, as easily as the palm-fruit falling down due to the crow's perching on it. When this animal called man starts having *Vairāgya* he enters the first *Bhūmikā*. Then alone the *Saṁsāra* stops influencing him.

Sage Vālmīki appears to be writing this from his own experience! In his earlier life he was Ratnākara, a robber who used to rob the travelers, and kill them if necessary. He met Nārada the *Devarṣi* who asked him why he was involved in such heinous action. Ratnākara replied that he was doing it to take care of his family. When Nārada asked him to go home and find out whether any one was ready to share the fruits of his action, neither the children, nor the mother, nor even the wife was ready. They all said that looking after them was his duty and they did not know how he did it! Moreover, they said that the actions were *his* so he alone was expected to face the consequences! It is said that Ratnākara was shocked into an understanding of the ephemeral relationships in the temporary life and became a great *Tapasvin,* so much so that an ant hill grew over his body, which in turn gave him the name *Vālmīki.*[222]

Vasiṣṭha continued: If a person dies when he is established in the first, second or third *Bhūmikā,* will get the effect the evil deeds exhausted in proportion to the stage one is in. Then one will get into the celestial planes or caves of mount *Meru* and be happy with one's companion. With the exhaustion of the enjoyment such persons will be reborn in much better circumstances such as the families of persons who are wise, wealthy, good and pure, who cherish virtues as precious possession. They will continue the pursuit of the path of *Jñāna* as they had in the previous life. Then visualising or remembering the *Bhūmikā* one left off at the time of death, continue the *Jñāna-Niṣṭhā* again, rising subsequently to the higher stages. The wise say that the first three *Bhūmikās* belong

222 Refer to The Story of Karkaṭī.

to the *Jāgrat* or wakeful state, as the sense of difference between oneself and the things of the world prevails in them.

For those practising *Jñāna-Niṣṭhā* the maximum attainment in the first three stages is *Āryatva* or nobility. *Āryatva* is so sublime and noble state that even idiots, seeing an *Ārya,* would aspire to attain freedom through his inspiration. They would be greatly inspired by his personality and life. *Āryas* are those who do only things to be done and would leave things that ought not to be done as they are established always in a natural state. *Āryas* do their *Vyavahāra,* the worldly duties and actions, according to *Ācarās* or the established norms, *Śāstras,* the changing circumstances, and also as impelled from within. *Āryatva* comes up as a small off-shoot in the first *Bhūmikā;* it blossoms in the second; and bears fruit in the third. By practising the three *Bhūmikās* *Śubhecchā, Vicāraṇā,* and *Asaṁsaṅga,* ignorance gets completely dissipated. The *Jñāna* settles itself firmly in the consciousness like the rising of the full moon.

Different stations or the milestones that the traveller passes by are indications of the extent of his progress of his journey. Similarly, the *Bhūmikās* described in this chapter are the signposts of a seeker's evolution. The first three *Bhūmikās* broadly deal with all the conscious methods to be adopted by the seeker in his wakeful state. The various methods are like the different ways and means one has to resort to wake up from the deep sleep, *after one has convinced oneself that one is asleep, and that one has to wake up at whatever cost!*

18

The Seven Stages of Yoga-II

He had never seen anything like this before. Nature at its very best, and the local people totally in tune with it. The apricots, pears, and apples, only reflected the sweetness of the people. The snow capped peaks depicted their innocence. The Godwin Mount or K2 as it is called, could be seen almost throwing a challenge to scale it. But he was not a mountaineer, nor was he an adventurer in the strictest terms. He was a Doctor, posted at Gilgit by the Government. He was fulfilling his duty. And strangely enough, the duty as such was very pleasant. Because the people belonged to a very healthy stock, whose main diet was the fruits, both seasonal and dried. After his arrival here, he had innately felt that he—a doctor, had many things to learn about health from the people! He had seen the old dying, never of sickness, only of old age! All of them were natural. The middle aged, the youth and the children were exuberant, overflowing with health and energy. The respect he developed for them, and they for him was mutual.

He decided to make a tour around the area. It was one of those mountain villages where the houses are in different levels. His arrival had been known to the people there, who had arranged for his accommodation in a hut on top. It was evening when he felt like a stroll and also drinking from the ample nature. The amber sunlight reflected from the snow caps, the violet vegetation on the lesser hills, the clouds brushing the shoulders of the immovables, the red and winding foot-paths that showed the *bridges* between the people's hearts,... involved him so much that he did not realise the passage of time. By the time he started back to the residence for the night, it was dark. And he had forgotten the way back, and he was alone, and he was new. All that beauty he had felt got transformed itself into fear! He could feel his heart thumping, mouth becoming dry, breathing had taken the style of palpitation... And wherever he turned and walked, he felt convinced that none would help him. There was panic, a chaos.

The situation was so shocking, that it woke him up! But everything he had seen in the dream was so vivid. Of course it had to be. There were many things in the dream that had become part of his memory. He still was a doctor, he had been to Gilgit and spent his first few years there. He had learnt about health from the lovable people there, as they were the personification of health itself, for he had never used his medicine on them! So much so, that he had chosen to become a scientist committed to the research of medicines and their harmful effects, and to devote himself to the science of naturopathy. The sense of beauty of, as well as attraction to the place and the sense of fear and repulsion for the same place were real. And most of all, the palpitation and violent heartbeat continued for some time!

There were some things which were not real in the dream. The Godwin Mount or K2 was not the part of that time. It was fairly recent, the *image* of the mount was from a magazine and was over-imposed in that area in his mind! He had never lost his way while in Gilgit, for he was never alone there. Suddenly, a peculiar question crossed his mind, was the *memory* of his experiences some fifty years back, real? Were they not images of the days gone by in the brain, as much real as the photograph of K2, he had seen in a magazine? And from the point of view of science, perhaps the mount was more real as he could show the magazine to others!

Many a time such sudden awakenings, act as the starting points for the quest. Sometimes the seizure is so violent, that it wakes up a person permanently as it did in the case of Maharshi Ramaṇa,[223] when the fear of death totally internalised his consciousness permanently. But most of the time—as most of us are totally involved with survival, these experiences only act as lullabies to put us back to deeper slumber!

There cannot be however, any general rule for the initiation of the quest. As *anything* can become an impetus for the turning point. Many times the indulgence or involvement with the world itself may give such a shock to a person so as to transform her or his life. Because the very indulgence or involvement become cause for intense pain and misery in life. And all the scriptures start their guidance at this point. That is why many of the *Śāstras* begin with the word *Atha* (and now) or *Athāthā* (and now therefore),[224] which indicate that the person eligible to study the *Śāstra* has to be at the point, when he or she has started experiencing *a sense of bondage to the world, because without it there is misery.* And each one of us gets this inner call some time or the other in life. An irreplaceable loss or a death of a near and dear one invariably turns the sufferer into a philosopher! Perhaps, the most congenial place for discussing philosophy is the cremation ground! But only a very few transform their life after coming back from there! George Gurdgieff used to narrate a parable to describe the condition of man:

There used to be a shepherd who was also a talented magician. He had thousands of sheep. He had a very ingenious way of protecting his stock. He would individually hypnotise them and suggest that it was a tiger while all others

---

223 Refer to The Story of Lavaṇa-I.

224 Refer to the second story in *Vairāgya Prakaraṇa*—'Limitations of the World'.

were sheep. This practice had a great advantage, that the sheep would be totally free from the fear of death. So much so that even when its companions were slaughtered for the feasts in front of its very eyes, it would think, 'one more sheep has been slaughtered'! Each one of us thinks that one is unique, strong, and talented. When someone dies, it never crosses the mind that it happens to everyone without exception! But then, all these belong to the common rung of persons who have to take repeated births to become eligible for spirituality.

The very second *Śloka* of this scripture describes the eligibility as an intense feeling of bondage as well as an aspiration to free oneself from it. The first three *Bhūmikās* are the three *conscious, willful and effortful* steps to be taken by such eligible persons. Necessarily, they are very important and decisive in a seeker's journey. The details of the techniques and attitudes have been given in all the preceding chapters. The gist is given by the scripture while explaining the first three *Bhūmikās: Śubhecchā, Vicāraṇa,* and *Asaṁsaṅga.* At the end of the third *Bhūmikā* one has the glimpse into the Reality. But it is only a glimpse. Sage Vasiṣṭha continued:

By repeated *Samādhi,* when they start seeing the whole manifest phenomena as nothing but the expression of Brahman, which is indivisible and without beginning or end, they will enter the fourth *Bhūmikā.* Established in the fourth *Bhūmikā,* they have perfect *Advaita* or Non-dual, vision. The perception of *Dwaita* or duality, will not be there in them. They then see the world as in the dream. The first three stages can be classified as coming under *Jāgrat* or wakeful consciousness, while the fourth is similar to the dream. In the fourth *Bhūmikā,* the mind perishes like a cloud in the *Sarat* or autumnal days.

At the end of the third *Bhūmikā,* the glimpse leaves one restlessly thirsty for repeated experiences of *Samādhi.* This is a very vital stage in the journey. He starts putting *all* the effort at his disposal, yet there is delay. Sometimes the pang of separation from the experience is so much, that one can even lose one's balance. We find this in the life of many saints, especially Paramahansa Shri Ramakrishna. During such times he would spend sleepless nights, and disturbed days; he would roll on the ground in intense pain, shed tears, cry out aloud, and go without food for days. People were convinced that he had become mad! Of course, he would say later that he had become mad! He would also add that everyone was mad. Someone was mad for money, some other for wife, yet another for name and fame. While he was mad for God!

This particular stage is referred to in the Christian tradition as the *'dark night of the soul'*. If one understands this state, one can cross it over without much difficulty. And this is where the details of the *Bhūmikās* are of immense help to us. The seeker gets a glimpse *only when he is free from all thought and expectation.* This pining for another glimpse or the aspiration of stabilizing it *is also a desire,* though more noble than the desire for a sense pleasure! By repeated *Samādhi,* it means by continual *Asaṁsaṅga*—non-attachment, one gets rid of even the aspiration for *Samādhi.* The fourth *Bhūmikā* which is called as *Sattvapatti* is the state wherein the grip of the mind over sense objects has reduced and the realisation is achieved, where there is ***apartness** with the manifestations like thought, body etc.* Vasiṣṭha then described the fifth *Bhūmikā*:

When only the *Sattā* or the Be-ness remains, the fifth state is reached. The world delusion cannot arise with the dissolution of the mind. Having reached this state which can be called *Suṣupti* or deep sleep, there is no movement and only the establishment of the blissful state of *Advaita,* the Non-dual State. All notions of duality and multiplicity vanish. Totally rid of the duality there will be no recognition of tribulations with no cognition, as in the state of deep sleep. Though dwelling in world like any other men, he remains peacefully in *Antarmukhatā* appearing to be asleep, because there are no reactions for the external turmoil.

If this continues then one steps into the fifth stage called *Asaṁśakti,* which has been stated to be a state of *Advaita* because there is *No-other.* Because the dividing factor, the mind, is totally annihilated. This is the state of *Jīvanamukti.* The actions of such a person are not tainted by the notions, desires, expectations and other spectacles to impair the vision. When such persons walk amidst the so-called normal men, he appears dazed, forgetful and careless about his gross appearance. Shri Ramakrishna would say of such men—he spoke out of his experience as it happened to him, that they are like the fisherman who has put a bait into the pond of fish: absent-minded to other things around while being attentive to the hook, line and sinker. Nothing else matters for him. Similarly, the consciousness is *internalised,* in the fifth *Bhūmikā.* What happens to the consciousness after the fifth stage is only of academic interest, because the practice as such, stops with the fourth and fifth *Bhūmikā.*

Vasiṣṭha, one of the *Yuga-Gurus,* the preceptors of the age, described the next stage: After being in the fifth stage when even the subtle *Vāsanās* are burnt off, one slips into the sixth stage of *Turīya,* also called *Padārthabhāvanī* or absolute non-perception of objects. In this stage, there is neither 'I' nor 'not-I', neither difference nor non-difference, neither being nor non-being. The *Jñānī* cannot fix whether he is embodied or otherwise; he will be without thoughts, beyond the notions of duality and oneness. In this state, unaffected as it is by the knot of *Ahaṁkāra,* he is indeed a *Jīvanamukta,* for the *Jīva Bhāva* has gone. Although he would not have attained the *Nirvāṇa* state—*Videhamukti,* he is all the same having *Nirvāṇa,* for he does not cognise his body anymore. His body will be like that of a lamp in the picture with just the appearance but with none of its other features. He is empty within and empty without, like a pot held in the air; he is also full within and full without, like a pot immersed in the ocean. He possesses nothing, yet he possesses everything. Remaining in the sixth stage for a while, he slips into the seventh *Bhūmikā.*

In that state, the distinction between reality and non-reality ceases; so also that of duality and non-duality. Reality is there only in relation to unreality. When one transcends the mind and comes to a state where there is no thought or movement, it is neither real nor unreal, but *transcendental.* Sometimes, when such a one acts, the onlookers may think that he has the 'I' notion; but there is neither the presence nor the absence of 'I' as there only *Advaita.* The world and the notions of time, space, subject, predicate, object, joy, misery, etc. will not be within him, for there is nothing like 'within' for him. That is, there is no activity called the mind, and because of this, there is no 'without' also. That is why, the simile of a pot held in the air and water is given.

He does not cognise the objects and he does not have any sense of possession. But since he realises himself to be the consciousness, which is in everything, he has everything, which means that he has merged with *Brahman,* the substratum of the universe. Having tried to describe the sixth stage, Vasiṣṭha tried to do the same with the seventh state:

Ṛṣis say that the seventh *Jñāna Bhūmikā* or the stage of wisdom is *Videha Mukti.* It is the last frontier of the realm of *Jñāna.* It is pure peace and sublime quiescence that cannot be explained by the power of speech. That is the Ultimate State, there is nothing beyond that. Some call it *Śiva;* some others *Para Brahman;* yet others *Viṣṇu;* while some others *Śūnya;* some call it Pure Energy; some others unconditioned Time; yet others *Prakṛti* and *Puruṣa.* Although the Ultimate cannot be explained by words, people call It by different names. Different persons try to name It according to their nature and aptitude. Vasiṣṭha inspired Rāma to practise these seven stages.

Continuing Vasiṣṭha said: There is a mad, rutting elephant with great tusks, showering water as it goes, stalking the world with its writhing trunk spotted with white. If this animal, generating never ending pain be slain then the mankind will cross all the various stages of *Jñāna*. So long as this mighty elephant spraying water is not killed through one's might, one cannot become a great warrior in the battlefield of universe full of pain. Rāma sought clarification of the words mighty elephant, the battlefield, and also the method of annihilating it.

Compassionate Vasiṣṭha replied: The wild elephant showering water is no other than pain-generating desire, that always tries to get hold of the 'I', all the things of the universe with great relish and has its residence in the forest of body. It has its young ones, the insatiable *Indriyas,* the senses. It acts by identifying with the mind. The terrible twin *Karmas* of the good and bad, are its two tusks. The *Vāsanās* are the waters shed by it. It moves everywhere and at all times, as in fact, space and time are also its progenies! All the perceivable objects that forms the *Saṁsāra,* is the battlefield. The elephant desire, which becomes a victor repeatedly puts an end to many *Jīvas*. All the *Vāsanās* with their modifications, existence, *Manas, Buddhiḥ, Saṁkalpa* and the rest pertain to the *Antaḥkaraṇa,* the lower mind only. With the weapon of *Dhairya* or the patient courage, one should conquer this rutting elephant of desire.

If the mind longs after things of the world childishly, one should destroy it, for so long as the desire exists, the poisonous disease of *Saṁsāra* creeps in. The mind then takes control of the person, which is *Saṁsāra* itself. Destruction of the mind itself is *Mokṣa.*

If the disciple's mind is cleansed of all its illusions, and is initiated by his preceptor, he obtains quiescence and remains separated in the world like a drop of oil on the water surface. The calamity called the mind full of desires can be overcome by the process of *Asaṁvedana,* or non-reactivity to sensations. Through the weapon called *Asaṁvedana,* the *Vāsanās* which try to overpower the mind in so many ways, can be totally destroyed. When the mind through the practice of *Pratyāhāra* is freed from the *Vāsanās,* it remains still, this effort is called as *Asaṁvedana.*

A little explanation on the technique of *Asaṁvedana,* appears necessary here. The grossest facet of the *Antahkaraṇa, Manas,* is associated with the *Indriyas,* the senses. This facet is also the most restless. Unless this is quietened, one cannot possibly hope to enter the sacred temple of meditation. The effort of the *Ṛṣis* has been to first negotiate with this activity. *Pratyāhāra* is one such technique. *Āhāra,* or the food in Vedāṅtic understanding, is not only that which is eaten, but all the food for the body-mind complex, and necessarily includes whatever is perceived by the senses. So *Pratyāhāra* is that practice where this intake of food through the senses is made less disturbing. Sage Patanjali describes *Pratyāhāra:*

> '*Pratyāhāra* is *as it were,* the imitation by the senses of the mind by withdrawal from their objects'.[225]

Most of us are aware of this phenomenon happening to us. In spite of many sense stimuli bombarding our consciousness, we are not aware of all of them. Because, the capacity of the mind is limited, and it can do only one action at a time. While senses are subservient to *Manas,* we act *as though we are subservient to the senses.* So in this sense, *Pratyāhāra* is the process of remembering the superiority of the *Manas!* There are as many techniques as there are people, but the method of the Buddha appears to be nearest, to the technique of *Asaṁvedana,* mentioned here.

Normally, a seeker tends to *judge* the sense stimuli as pleasant or otherwise, good or bad, etc., and *react* to them. This act of judging as well as reacting, forces not only the *Manas* to indulge, but also *Buddhiḥ, Cittaṃ* and *Ahaṁkāra* to involve with the world outside. Buddha suggests just observing *without either judging, or reacting.* Not only this, but he suggests

---

225 स्वविषयासंप्रयोगे चित्तस्वरूपानुकार इवेन्द्रियाणां प्रत्याहारः ।। 2.54 ।।

further that all activity be observed in the like manner, so that one can *witness all activity, without getting disturbed.* He also added that the world and with it the stimuli it offers to the psyche is *Aniccā* (*Anitya*) or impermanent, and it appears and disappears.

Vasiṣṭha said: The wise say, that the idea of 'mine' is the source of mind, by giving this up one succeeds in giving up the mind. Remembrance is *Saṁkalpa,* while its absence is beatitude, in which state, there is neither the known nor the knower. Forgetting everything, one remains like a log of wood, without any identification with the objects. Then he made a very bold statement:

> 'O Rāma, just by remaining silent he definitely achieves the highest State, compared to which, even the empire appears like straw'.[226]

Turning to those in the assembly the great sage said: This has been the declaration of those who have trodden the path. To put it briefly, *Saṁkalpa* is bondage and its absence is liberation. The world with its multiplicity is actually the manifestation of the Quiescent, Infinite Consciousness. One who sees the Consciousness amidst all elements and objects can remain ever blissful. The wise say, that *Avedanaṃ,* non reaction is the real *Yoga,* being in such *Yoga* one should act, and give up all *involved* activity. *Avedanaṃ* is *Yoga* and is the peaceful *Āsanam,* the posture, remain in this state, declare the wise. By totally eschewing the mood of 'I' and 'mine' one is freed from all misery, as one cuts at the root of desire. By identifying with this state, even if one performs action, one is said to have given up all action.

This was how sage Vasiṣṭha initiated prince Rāma into *Ātma-Jñāna.* The same was repeated by sage Vālmīki for the benefit of his disciple Bharadwāja.

---

226 किल तूष्णीं स्थितेनैव तत्पदं प्राप्यते परम् ।
परमं यत्र साम्राज्यमपि राम तृणायते ।। 6.15.106 ।।

The heaviest anchor which does not allow the ship of being, to leave the port of *Saṁsāra,* is the sense of involvement or identification. When the mind or senses are not directly in contact with their objects, the involvement is nurtured by *the memory* or *remembrance,* as mentioned in these verses. The suggestion to keep *quiet* for attaining the highest is not to be taken in as inactivity. There are two aspects of Reality: one is the movement or activity, the other is non-activity. It is impossible to totally stop the activity even for a short duration of time. However by identifying oneself with *Draṣṭā,* that which *witnesses,* one can and does remain *unaffected* by the activity. This has been hinted very clearly in the verses extolling *Yoga* of *Avedanaṃ.*

The whole story of life as such appears to be the play of *Ahaṁkāra,* the activity of limiting the consciousness. With this *first fall,* the speed increases with *Cittam,* the remembrance and accelerates with *Buddhiḥ, Manas* and *Indriyas,* till one is totally on the *terra-firma* of indulgence and misery! Each indulgence is a potential habit of involvement, as it gets stored in the consciousness as the memory. And this memory or the act of remembrance can continue to pester the seeker.

The trick lies in learning the art of observing *without reaction,* beginning with the grosser manifestations like the body, up to the *Ahaṁkāra* itself, when one realises that all the so called gross are nothing but the expressions of the Divine.

If one aspires to climb the terrace of the house, one has to climb the steps. Each time a step is climbed, one has to leave or give up the lower step. On finally reaching the terrace, one realises that the steps, whether lower or higher, are made of the same stuff: brick, lime and mortar! So also, everything is made of pure consciousness.

The whole story of the [illegible] the [illegible] the activity of limiting [illegible] *that fall* the speed increases [illegible] and accelerates until [illegible] totally on the [illegible] indifference [illegible] the unconscious [illegible] or [illegible] and [illegible].

[illegible]

[illegible]

If one aspires [illegible] stages. [illegible] to rise up the [illegible] that [illegible] state of pure [illegible].

THE CONCLUSION

THE CONCLUSION

The autumnal winds had started blowing to rob away the warmth from the air. The grass had begun losing its green and was turning gold. The harvest season was over, and the granaries were full; so also the farmers, who did not have to sweat it out in the sun; so also were their families who could think of exchanging the hard earned grain with cloth and other things which had not been useful while working in the farms. Li Erh was on his way back from the emperor's court, where he worked as an astrologer and a religious adviser. He was more than happy as the emperor was especially benevolent to him with favours. 'And why not?' asked Li in his own mind. He had been not only useful to the country, but had proved his worth and more than justified his presence in the emperor's court.

As he walked steadily, the sun became harsher, and it reached its zenith. He was pleasantly tired, as one does, when one does something which one likes most. For Li liked walking more than any other occupation, as he experienced, that his thoughts got more and more organised with this activity. Seeing a huge tree spreading its thick and benign shade, he sat under it, stretching his legs. A nightingale sang, using one of the branches for a stage, and its note was so sweet, that even an owl sitting in the tree-hollow was inspired, and joined by supplying a kind of monotone to the song! Nearby, the gurgling sound of water from the water wheel could be heard. Everything was as peaceful as it could be.

Li had always taken pride in his power of observation, and the nature just fascinated him. His eyes fell on the canopy of the tree itself. It had turned flaming red from the usual lively green. How strange the nature is, felt Li. There is beauty at every stage of its life. While life was represented by green, the old age by red, and death was represented by yellow. Suddenly, his eyes fell on a beautiful mustard-yellow leaf, dismembering itself from the mother tree and falling. For Li however, its fall appeared almost eternal. In its journey Li had seen his own life and death. He never went back to the emperor's court; he was never the same again, his whole being got transformed; he had *seen through* what is normally known as life. He became the first Taoist Master and came to be known to the world as Lao Tzu, which means 'the Old Master'.

A leaf falling is not even noticed by most of us. Even if we see, it has hardly any effect on us! But persons like Li are very very rare. They have already woken up from their metaphysical sleep, a slight breeze is necessary, a bird-song perhaps, at the most a word from someone.

A king was in his court, conducting the business for the day. A *Ṛṣi* entered the court. As was the custom at that time, he left his throne and started climbing down the pedestal. The *Ṛṣi* just said: 'Stop'!! And it is said, the king got enlightened. The suggestion went so deep as to help him identify with That which transcends all movement!

There is a story on king Janaka. He made a public announcement throughout his kingdom, that he would give away half of his kingdom, to such a person who would help him to achieve enlightenment between the time *when he would put his foot in the left stirrup and the right, after climbing the horse.* Most of the wise men in the kingdom opined that Janaka had lost his head! How could *anyone* help him to achieve *Jñāna* is such a short time? No one came for a long time. Once again the announcement was repeated. Yājñāvalkya came into his court on the next day. He asked Janaka to get the horse into the court, and asked the king to come near the horse.

Then Yājñāvalkya asked the king to give the kingdom before sitting on the horse, as after enlightenment, there would be no sense of possession left in Janaka! When half the kingdom was given away the *Ṛṣi* asked Janaka to put his left foot in the stirrup, and *to give his mind away while climbing the horse!* It is said, Janaka got enlightened!

Such persons are in microscopic minority who do not need special effort to wake up. Anything can become a reason for them to do so. Obviously, these persons do not need any special help from either the Masters or scriptures. While the majority is so fast asleep, that even an awakened one like the Buddha cannot awaken them! And even if he comes in front of them, their *nature does not allow* them to recognise Him. So neither the enlightened ones nor the *Śāstras* are of any use to them. On the contrary, they get angry on them, for a person in deep sleep hardly likes anyone waking him up!

There is a minority which realises that metaphysical sleep is the cause of all misery, and they are interested in waking up from it. They have a *gut-feeling,* that life as such, is *not just survival* but it must have something else to it. They are like the bird which has realised that it has been imprisoned and is using its wings to fly within the limited space of the cage, without much success. And since they are tied to the ground, with their habitual involvement and indulgence, they may or may not recognise the enlightened persons. If they can recognise, they are saved, no doubt with their own effort and company of the enlightened persons. But not everyone is fortunate enough to recognise such persons, even if they are available. To those who are at such cross road, scripture like the *Yoga Vāsiṣtha* can be of great help.

The boredom due to repetitiveness of life; the realisation that the misery is due to the involvement with the impermanent and the subsequent invasion of desires, anger and the like, which are initiated by the *Ahaṁkāra*; and an intense aspiration to come out of them. How do these dawn on a person have been beautifully analysed in the *Vairāgya Prakaraṇa.* Initially, the behaviour and the observation of such a person appears life negating. It is necessarily so, for the chains become painful and are discovered under the light of involvement and indulgence. And the involvement and its progeny indulgence can be reduced by keeping oneself *physically* away from the objects which cause them at least *in the initial stages.*

The realisation of the impermanence of life, or the innate gift of misery in all the so-called actions, definitely turns the eyes towards such literature giving the details of the journey, goal, illustrated with the lives of the enlightened Masters. But then, one may get stuck with the intellectual gymnastics and theoretical philosophy. It is like going on a trip, by sitting on an arm-chair in front of the fire-place, at the most, watching a television! One has to start the journey, no matter how humbly. *Mumukṣu Prakaraṇa* gives the attitude one has to nurture which prepares the pilgrim for undertaking the long and arduous journey. It gives the reason for the state of misery as the *Aśubha Vāsanās,* the binding tendencies, which can be thinned with the help of *Śubha Vāsanās,* the freeing tendencies. Like using the needle, which is also a thorn, to remove the thorn from the body, the *Śubha Vāsanās* are developed to thin the *Aśubha Vāsanās.* One should have faith in oneself, and should be ready to put utmost effort in this divine adventure.

One should have the sweet patience to persevere in spite of all odds. Even the over eagerness to *reach the goal* can become a great hurdle. The sense of satisfaction at what one has, *not as a consolation,* but *due to the conviction that all the hankering of the mind directed* ***outside,*** is an important companion. Every one of us has the capacity to distinguish the right from the wrong, and to analyse life situations. This capacity is to be made use of in trying to solve the fundamental questions like 'Who am I?'; 'What is the purpose of life?';

'Why do I behave in a particular way?'; 'What happens to me when I become miserable?', etc. When the mind ripens, we start recognising such persons who can guide us and one starts seeking their company to derive immense benefit. These four companions *Śama, Saṁtoṣa, Vicāra* and *Sādhu-Saṅga,* have been called as the four sentinels of the palace of *Mukti,* by this scripture.

With constant *Vicāra* one starts getting convinced that the real culprit for all the life's problems is the 'I', which is behind all experience, action and reaction. How does it originate? How it is intimately connected to either the *Śubha Vāsanās* or the *Aśubha Vāsanās?* How does its thinning or thickening affect our life? These and some more questions are answered in the *Utpatti Prakaraṇa.*

Having a blossomed *Ahaṁkāra,* it is better in most cases to allow the *Ahaṁkāra* to ripen, for if it is suppressed it can rise its head any time. Moreover, such suppression can and many times does result in spiritual stagnation that can last for many lives. The *Ahaṁkāra* gets nourished by the food of attention, leading one into the vicious circle of involvement, indulgence and fear and the like leading one towards increased attention. The dilution of *Ahaṁkāra* takes place by the art of being in *here-now* by dropping all the attention enhancing qualities. This has been amply described in the *Sthiti Prakaraṇa,* with the help of stories therein.

For bringing about quiescence one should understand the mechanism of *Ahaṁkāra.* The constrictive activity of the ever Expansive Consciousness is *Ahaṁkāra.* The word means, 'I-do-ness'. When the Pure Consciousness gets identified with feeling, thought, action, or for that matter *anything,* the *Ahaṁkāra* is born. And with this ghost of *Ahaṁkāra,* the *Saṁsāra* with all its multiplicity and also complications gets created. The *Upaśama Prakaraṇa* illustrates this fact and suggests the methods of tracing the root of this ghost, through stories.

The *Ahaṁkāra* manifests in different forms of activity, *Prāṇa,* or pure activity, thought, feelings and finally gross action. The tracing of *Ahaṁkāra* is effected by different methods like *Prāṇavidyā,* ritualistic worship, and unattached action. These are described through the stories in the last episode entitled *Nirvāṇa Prakaraṇa.* After tracing the root of 'I-do-ness', one reaches the state which can be called as *'the watcher on the hill'*. And this is a very lofty state, compared to the indulgent or involved state. But the *watcher* continues to be like a glass wall in front of the Non-dual Reality stopping one at the penultimate state. Shri Ramana Maharshi used to call this as the policeman posted to stop the mischief of the thieves called thoughts and their children, the actions! Even this policeman is to be withdrawn into the Reality. We should be very careful not to interpret the teachings of this scripture for escapism, because, after the dialogue with Vasiṣṭha, Rāma devoted his entire life for activity characterised by compassion, love and service of the people. He was at such a point to totally separate himself from action non-action, and involvement non-involvement. He had realised the Oneness of Existence. At the same time we should remember, that each one of us exists according to one's own nature.

Some of us may continue to work, like Rāma, and Kṛṣṇa, while others may continue to just *be,* and doing only such actions which are spontaneous, apparently leading an inactive life!

As the climax to this poetic masterpiece called *Yoga Vāsiṣṭha,* the author gives two wonderful facts. The first one is summarized aptly through a Zen poem:

Sitting silently,
Doing nothing,
The spring comes,
and
The grass grows
By itself.

But the one and only problem with most of us is we *cannot keep silent!* Theoretically and intellectually we do understand what is meant by *sitting silently,* but we ask *what should one* **do** *to sit quietly!* As if to cater to the need of such persons—and which constitutes the majority, the scripture gives another equally beautiful suggestion:

Sitting on the bank of
the fast moving river,
Just *witness* whatever flows
in the turbulent water.
Keep sitting, and *seeing*
but do not react,
And soon you will learn,
That you *are silent as you are.*

The fast moving river is our mental activity. The scripture does not tell us to *avoid* or *run away* from activity. It asks us to learn the art of passive, non-involved witnessing. Even if all the chapters are not studied by a seeker—and it is really not necessary to study them, if one remembers *Asaṁvedana:* non-reaction and *Tūṣṇīm sthita:* to sit quietly, one would have understood the essence of this scripture. Once a person reaches the stage of *Sākṣī,* everything merges into a One Single Whole. Then there is *nothing to hold, nor is there anything to avoid! One simply IS!*

It was twilight, when the hectic activity finally succumbs to the silent strength of the night. All animals and birds and people were preparing themselves for the relaxation and rest. Some of the people were entering the places of worship, be it a mosque or a temple or a church. A man entered a village at the time and beheld a young boy of ten carrying a lighted candle to the church, for keeping it on the altar. His hand was protecting the flame from going off, and the soothing golden light lit up the face which was the personification of innocence itself. Charmed by the sense of sublimity, the man asked the child—may be just to build a bridge between him and the child, and not really with any intention of getting a reply:

'My dear Boy, from where did this beautiful flame come?'

Innocently, the boy looked into the eyes of the stranger, then on to the flame. Suddenly, he blew the flame off the candle, and with the ringing laughter he said:

'From the same place, where now it has returned!'

This in short, is *Nirvāṇa, Adwaita, Śūnya,* or whatever be the name we designate to the *Nameless!*

RASHTRAPATI KALAM
Philosopher or Scientist

I was concerned that the most brilliant students, whether in Vidyabharti (which educates about 25 lakh students throughout the country from its network of schools) or in my own school run with the guidance of Ramakrishna Mission, want to go for commerce in the college. It is only after they fail to get admission in commerce they reluctantly take up Science. I wrote to Shri Abdul Kalam, the then Scientific Advisor to the Government of India, about my concern on this trend. In response to my letter, a telephonic talk with Shri Kalam took place some time in 2001. He also shared my concern. I then suggested that if a group of our brilliant students along with a few science teachers visit Indian Space Research Organisation (ISRO) at the time of the next satellite launch, it could be a motivation to them. He immediately agreed. I formed a small team of students and teachers and decided to join the team myself. But, at the last moment, ISRO found it difficult to allow our visit due to security reasons.

Shri Kalam, thereafter, became the President of India in July 2002. In his lecture to the scientists and technologists in the month of April 2004 at the Indian Institute of Technology, *Mahamahim* mentioned that the peacock feather does not lose its original colour for a number of decades. Dr. Kalam got a scientific analysis done and it was revealed that it is due to God's own creation of nano-materials coated in a peacock feather. He mentioned that the global market in 2004 for nano-tools, nano-devices and nano-biotechnology is expected to be over hundred billion dollars.

The next ten years will see nano-technology playing the most dominant role in the global business environment and it is expected to go beyond one trillion dollar. Our research in nano-sciences can lead to a product which will be useful for imparting similar lasting colour to our shirts, sarees, fabrics and apparels.

Being a textile industrialist, I was quite excited and sought a meeting with Rashtrapatiji, giving a reference to my previous unsuccessful effort to visit ISRO. Rashtrapatiji was kind enough to give me an appointment on 21st September, 2004.

I opened the conversation with my meeting in 1956 at Calcutta with the Puri Shankaracharya Jagat Guru Swami Shri Bharati Krishan Tirthaji Maharaj. Rashtrapatiji gave me lot of time and explained to him how vedic mathematics could perform large multiplications, divisions, etc. in minutes. Bharati Krishnaji explained to me integral and differential calculus as well as solid geometry, etc. He Illustrated to me by actual examples on a slate with chalk. I was myself a brilliant student being a gold medalist having stood first in Calcutta University in 1946 in Mathematics. Thereafter, I joined postgraduate classes in mathematics where I had the good fortune of being a student of Shri Satyen Bose.

Dr. Kalam accepting the painting of Jhunjhunwala's daughters-in-law Rita

From left to right : *Shri Sheridon, Dr. Amarnath Maitra, Smt. Vasantha, Shri J. P. Jain, Shri Raghunandan, Dr. Kalam, Swami Gokulanandan Ji Maharaj, Sh. L. N. Jhunjhunwala, Shri Churiwal, Shri Shekhar Aggarwal, Shri Anil Batra, Shri T. N. Chaturvedi, Smt. Rita Jhunjhunwala and Smt. Shashi Aggarwal.*

Shri Satyen Bose was conducting some experiments with Einstein and his Bose-Einstein theory had made him the topmost Indian scientist of his time. I was his very beloved student and had great respect for him. He used to wear white *Dhoti* and *Kurta*; was well-built, fair-coloured, large round face giving the impression of our ancient *rishis.* I was keen to continue my studies and later moved to higher studies in astronomy. The family had made great sacrifices to enable me to continue my studies even to this level and I had a moral obligation to respect their feelings. Still I did continue my classes of Shri Satyen Bose and simultaneously attended to the family business started by my uncle. But the studies suffered. Shri Bose was very disappointed when I had to discontinue my studies after about 10 months. After my exciting meeting with Shri Shankaracharya I rushed to him to tell him all about Vedic mathematics. He did not take this seriously till I gave him illustrations on the blackboard. I had gone to him with a request to preside over a function where Shri Jagatguru Shankaracharya would talk on Vedic mathematics with illustrations and Shri Bose

Dr. Kalam and Sh. L.N. Jhunjhunwala with his fractured leg in Mughal Garden

was to give his reaction thereafter. He reluctantly agreed and a programme was organized in 1956 in Bhartiya Sanskrit Sansad, a cultural forum of Calcutta where I was very active.

Mahamahim expressed great disappointment that I lost an opportunity of continuing my studies in Mathematics inspite of having a good fortune of being a favourite student of a rare scientist like Satyen Bose. I also feel in retrospect now that I could have been a space scientist if I would have continued my studies. Rashtrapatiji was very affectionate after hearing about my interest in mathematics and my respect for Shri Satyen Bose. He immediately agreed that while ISRO would not allow us to attend the missile launching, but *Mahamahim* would see that permission is given for our team to visit the next satellite launching.

—L. N. Jhunjhunwala

AT RASHTRAPATI BHAVAN

A Memory for a Lifetime

Shri Lakshmi Niwasji Jhunjhunwala, Chairman Emeritus, LNJ Bhilwara Group, Chairman Ramarpan Educational Society, who had been instrumental in getting the book published by Motilal Banarsidas, the famous Indological Publishers, had to meet H. E. Dr. A. P. J. Abdul Kalam, the Honourable President of India at the Rashtrapati Bhavan, New Delhi, for some discussion on nano technology in the first week of August, 2004. Shri Lakshmi Niwasji had with him a copy of 'The Wisdom of Vasiṣṭha'. When H. E. saw the book and flipped through some of the pages, he wanted to know about the author. After hearing about him Dr Kalam expressed his wish to meet the author. Shri Lakshmi Niwasji said that it could be arranged without any difficulty. Consulting his Secretary, a date was given in October, when the book would be released while meeting the author.

On October 18, 2004 H. E. A. P. J. Abdul Kalam, Honorable President of India, released the book 'The Wisdom of Vasiṣṭha'. A group of nineteen persons were in Rashtrapati Bhavan between 2:30 and 4:00 pm. They met Dr Kalam in the Study at 3:20 pm.

When we entered the room we did not see him, but heard his voice saying '*Baiṭhiye*'*!* When we turned in the direction we found him at work on his computer. In a minute he was with us with his copy of the book and a computer print-out of his observations on the book. It appeared as though he had given considerable amount of time to go through the contents of the book. After releasing the book by removing the wrapper, he made the staff photographer to click a few photos, inviting all the guests to join. He even joked, that the photographer should click only when everyone is smiling! Then the following conversation took place.

H. E. (Dr A. P. J. Abdul Kalam): How much time did you take to write this book?

Raghunandan: Seven years for writing, but I have been studying this work since 1977.

H. E.: I see. It has come out very well.

Raghunandan: Thank you.

H. E.: I have gone through the contents. I am familiar with *Aṣṭāvakra Gītā*. How is this work different or similar to *Aṣṭāvakra Gītā*?

Raghunandan: Basically all of us are familiar with two dimensions Sir. First is the objective dimension, the material, which we can perceive through our senses; the second is the subjective dimension, which consists of thoughts, feelings, and emotions. For example, meeting you and the book being released by you is a great honour for us, this feeling of elation and joy is of subjective realm. The third is the transcendental that envelops both, but is beyond both these dimensions. It can be called as awareness. Being aware of the objective and the subjective is its characteristic feature.

H. E.: Can we call the third as consciousness?

Raghunandan: Certainly Sir. *Aṣṭāvakra Gītā* takes up this consciousness or awareness directly, whereas, *Yoga Vāsiṣṭha* takes it up through the objective and the subjective, that is why it is quite lengthy. In fact, our *Upaniṣads* and other Vedāntic literature use this technique of 'from the known to the unknown' in their approach.

H. E.: I am impressed by the references you have given. On page 285, you have quoted the *Chain of Conditioned Arising* of Buddha: 'with the base of ignorance, reaction arises...' etc. Now this ignorance, has it got anything to do with ego?

Raghunandan: It is the ego which reacts to the external stimuli or situations. The reactions cause ignorance.

H. E.: It means that when this ego is subdued or eliminated, we get peace. Now how to subdue this ego?

Raghunandan: Actually ego is very much like poison. It acts as a medicine when one is inactive and lazy. But if the same increases through pride, endless desires, anger, etc., it causes misery. If I were to use a simile, I would say that ego is like darkness—which is nothing but the absence of light. When the awareness or consciousness is absent, there is this ego, which is just a shadow. By increasing the awareness the ego gets eliminated on its own.

H. E.: (Jokingly) I was disappointed not to find any reference to *Aṣṭāvakra Gītā* in your book.

Raghunandan: Actually, I was so engrossed in the study of *Vāsiṣṭha,* that I did not have time to study *Aṣṭāvakra Gītā.* But now I shall take it up!

H. E.: All right!

Raghunandan: Sir, we have presented your book 'Ignited Minds' to many of our students. I have a copy here. Would you please autograph it?

Not finding the pen in his pocket Dr Kalam walked to his desk and fetched it himself and returned the book after autographing it. He was given all the five issues of the '*Aspiration*' the magazine of Vivekananda Kendra Vidyalaya,

Hurda, and a copy of '*A Silent Journey*' my first publication. He was also showed the Silver Jubilee Issue of *Aspiration* (2002-2003).

Raghunandan: Sir, we had requested your office for a message for this issue. But perhaps it did not reach you. We took the liberty of including your inspiring thoughts in this issue along with your line sketch.

Looking at it carefully, he observed the address of our Vidyalaya and asked:

H. E.: Where is this Hurda?

Raghunandan: Sir it is nearly seventy kilometers from Ajmer.

H. E.: Ajmer? I have to visit Ajmer. I will visit your school.

Raghunandan: Thank you so much Sir, we will be truly honoured!

Dr. Kalam releasing Shri Raghunandan's book along with Mr. J.P. Jain of the famous publishers of Indology Motilal Banarsidass

We came out of the study at 3:55 pm. This perhaps is one of the proudest and most memorable moments in my life.

—Raghunandan

INDEX

N

O

P

R

S

T